The Media Offensive

STUDIES IN **CMR**
CIVIL-MILITARY RELATIONS

William A. Taylor, Series Editor

The Media Offensive

How the Press and Public Opinion Shaped Allied Strategy during World War II

Alexander G. Lovelace

 University Press of Kansas

Published by the University Press of Kansas (Lawrence, Kansas 66045), which was
organized by the Kansas Board of Regents and is operated and funded by Emporia State
University, Fort Hays State University, Kansas State University, Pittsburg State University,
the University of Kansas, and Wichita State University.

Library of Congress Cataloging-in-Publication Data

Names: Lovelace, Alexander G., author.
Title: The media offensive : how the press and public opinion shaped Allied strategy during
World War II / Alexander G. Lovelace.
Other titles: How the press and public opinion shaped Allied strategy during World War II
Description: Lawrence, Kansas : University Press of Kansas, 2022 Series: Studies in civil-
military relations | Includes bibliographical references and index.
Identifiers: LCCN 2021043894
  ISBN 9780700633289 (paperback)
  ISBN 9780700633296 (ebook)
Subjects: LCSH: World War, 1939–1945—Press coverage. | World War, 1939–1945—Public
opinion. | Politics and war. | Allied Forces—Press coverage.
Classification: LCC D798 .L68 2022 | DDC 070.4/333—dc23/eng/20220121
LC record available at https://lccn.loc.gov/2021043894.

British Library Cataloguing-in-Publication Data is available.

Printed in the United States of America

10 9 8 7 6 5 4 3 2 1

The paper used in this publication is acid free and meets the minimum requirements of
the American National Standard for Permanence of Paper for Printed Library Materials
Z39.48–1992.

To my brilliant and beautiful wife, Kelley Bergsma Lovelace, PhD

Contents

Series Editor's Foreword   *ix*

Acknowledgments   *xi*

Introduction   1

Prologue: The Media and Total War   10

1. "You Shoot Bullets with Your Typewriter"   23

2. "I Shall Return"   57

3. "Pitiless Publicity"   91

4. "War in a Museum"   129

5. The Liberation of France   151

6. The Press of Prestige   186

Conclusion   220

Notes   *239*

Bibliography   *315*

Index   *341*

Series Editor's Foreword

William A. Taylor

In *The Media Offensive: How the Press and Public Opinion Shaped Allied Strategy during World War II*, Alexander G. Lovelace explores the powerful, intricate, and significant links between the media and the military during World War II. Throughout this exceptionally fine book, Lovelace shows how the military employed media within the conflagration of total war and explores why the reasons for doing so varied, at times quite dramatically, ranging from improving resolve to deception operations. Lovelace establishes how once enjoined, the strong combination of the military and the media proved quite formidable but also changed both partners in intriguing ways. Commanders sought to shape public opinion through the media, but military strategies often also morphed in response.

In this innovative and pioneering work, Lovelace contributes to literature on the media during World War II by showing how the media, and by extension public opinion, affected the military in momentous ways, including vital choices on battlefields around the globe. Lovelace covers a striking array of examples, highlighting the essential partnership between the media and the military during World War II, including President Franklin D. Roosevelt's Germany First strategy, Gen. Douglas MacArthur's exploits in the Southwest Pacific Area Theater, Lt. Gen. Dwight D. Eisenhower's and Maj. Gen. George S. Patton Jr.'s campaigns in North Africa and Sicily, Lt. Gen. Mark W. Clark's actions in the Italian campaign, and the media's influence on an operation as large as D-Day as well as throughout the final campaigns of World War II. Lovelace concludes his work by exploring the changing context of subsequent limited wars for the media-military relationship previously evidenced during total war. Along the way, Lovelace uncovers a series of crucial dichotomies in a democracy: media and military, public opinion and battlefield decisions, home front and front line, civilian and military, and national interest and international security.

Lovelace expertly conveys a number of weighty themes that advance understanding of the media, the military, and the complex liaisons between them during World War II. He illustrates the ways in which the media and the military worked together to accomplish national goals during total war. In doing so, Lovelace adds a nuanced perspective on this vital affiliation, exhibiting how the media maintained its independence to be critical at times, revealing by what means the military sought to leverage accurate reporting for positive results, and exposing in what ways both entities recognized the value of even bad news. Among many noteworthy achievements, Lovelace clearly expounds how the United States used the media as one potent weapon in its arsenal during World War II. Lovelace discloses one of the major developments of this total war, emphasizing the media as a key component of military affairs. The media's newfound position and prominence reinforced information as a vital instrument of national power to be leveraged in combination with diplomatic, military, and economic capacity within coherent grand strategy.

Lovelace grounds his cogent analysis in a most impressive plethora of archival research from dozens of manuscript collections located at fifteen repositories across the country. Equally extraordinary, Lovelace integrates his extensive primary source research into the existing literature, displaying an outstanding command of both timeless classics and the newest research. The commendable result is a groundbreaking work that enhances comprehension of the multifaceted and complicated connections between the media and the military during World War II. Readers interested in the subtle yet profound sway of the media on strategic decision-making during World War II will greatly profit from reading this book. In addition, anyone drawn to the media, the military, total war, and many important intersections among them will find immense value in this deeply researched, lucidly written, and convincingly argued book that breaks much new ground on the ways in which the media proved both largely indispensable and highly instrumental during World War II.

Acknowledgments

I once had an idea for a book of quotations entirely comprising awkward expressions of gratitude taken from other books' acknowledgment sections. I still think it is a splendid idea. Nevertheless, attempting to recognize my own debt in writing this book has helped me appreciate the difficulty of expressing deeply felt gratitude.

I must start by thanking Dr. Ingo Trauschweizer for his endless help, careful edits, and unending patience. I could not ask for, nor imagine, a better adviser. Thanks are also due to Dr. Chester Pach and Dr. Michael Sweeney, both of whom gave excellent advice on the manuscript. Particular thanks are due to Dr. John Brobst, whose unswerving generosity with his time, unsurpassed knowledge of his subject, and dedication to graduate studies has greatly enriched my time at Ohio University.

Thanks are likewise due to the faculty and staff of the History Department at Ohio University and the Contemporary History Institute (CHI). These include Drs. Patrick Barr-Melej, T. David Curp, Marvin Fletcher, Steven Miner, and Assan Sarr. Particular thanks are due to Dr. Robert Ingram, whom I worked for as a teaching assistant for six semesters, and Dr. Paul Milazzo, who served on my comprehensive examination committee. I must also thank Connie Hunter for helping make CHI a more enriching experience. Thanks are also due to Sherry Gillogly and Brenda Nelson, who administered the distribution of the grant money that made my research trips possible.

One specific blessing of attending Ohio University was the generosity of research funding that made this book possible. The John Cady Fellowship and the Klinder Dissertation Fellowship allowed me two years free from teaching. The research for this work has also been funded by several Ohio University grants, including the Original Work Grant, the Graduate Student Research Fund, and the Student Enhancement Award. Ohio University's Alden Library bestowed an 1804 Special Library Endowment to purchase microfilm from the Douglas MacArthur Memorial. The US Army Heritage and Education Center (USAHEC) likewise awarded me a General and Mrs. Matthew B. Ridgway Military History Research Grant.

Together, this funding allowed me to visit eight archives. I owe much to the staffs of the Air Force Historical Research Agency, the Manuscript Division at the Library of Congress, the National Archives at College Park, Maryland, the Eisenhower Presidential Library, the George C. Marshall Foundation, the Franklin D. Roosevelt Presidential Library, and the York County History Center. In particular, Valoise Armstrong of the Eisenhower Presidential Library and Patrick Fahy of the Franklin D. Roosevelt Presidential Library were extremely helpful in arranging my visits. James Zobel of the Douglas MacArthur Memorial was equally helpful and later assisted with Alden Library's purchase of some of MacArthur's papers on microfilm. Thomas E. Buffenbarger and the staff at USAHEC assisted in retrieving documents and suggesting other sources. Jessica J. Sheets was particularly helpful in pointing out useful collections. I am especially grateful for being allowed to use the Omar Bradley interviews that were temporarily out of circulation. I thank Suzanne Christoff, Susan Lintelmann, and Elaine B. McConnell, along with the staff of the library at the US Military Academy, for making my stay at West Point very profitable. Finally, it would be wrong not to mention the circulation and interlibrary loan staffs, along with the librarians and archivists at Alden Library, who showed me great patience.

One final blessing of studying at Ohio University was a congenial group of colleagues. For fear of missing anybody, I will start by thanking the cohort I entered the program with, who will always have a special place in my heart. I also thank Adam and Seth Givens along with Luke Griffith, Maj. Jeffrey Mills (USA), and Steven Wills (USN Ret) for much guidance. I would especially like to thank Kyle Balzer, Caitlin Bentley, James Bohland, Fred Coventry, Cameron Dunbar, Harrison Fender, Michael Fitzpatrick, and Matt Johnson, along with Shalon and Tristan van Tine, for many joyful hours spent together. Jeremy and Sally Hatfield provided many kindnesses and much encouragement. Finally, special thanks must go to Robert Venosa for excellent conversation and companionship through many trials.

This book was furthered blessed by finding a home at the University Press of Kansas. My editor, Joyce Harrison, and the series editor, William Taylor, were incredibly helpful and encouraging. I would also like to thank this book's peer reviewers, Steven Casey of the London School of Economics and Nicholas Evan Sarantakes of the US Naval War College. Together they, along with Joyce, William, and the rest of UPK's staff, made this a much better book.

If I have experienced a greater blessing than those mentioned above, it is my friends and family, in particular Matthew Drum, Tim Marks, Nick Schmuck, and Aldrich Veluz. I thank them and their wonderful wives for their support and friendship. I especially thank Jordan and Abigail Souder for opening their home to me during my month-long research trip in Carlisle.

No one who has not been to graduate school can appreciate how much parental support and understanding matter. My parents, Martin and Marie

Lovelace, deserve my everlasting thanks for their constant support, encouragement, and understanding. Not least of their many gifts was my brother, Aaron Lovelace, whom I also thank for his endless patience toward me.

As I began this project, I met Dr. Kelley Bergsma at an InterVarsity Bible study. Three days after I submitted this project to my doctoral committee in March 2020, she became my wife. By the time we returned from our honeymoon a week after our wedding, the United States had entered the COVID-19 lockdown. I thank her and her wonderful parents, Dr. Derk and Cheryl Bergsma, for their endless kindness through these peculiar times. As with my family, friends, and enemies, I am not sure why Kelley loves me so much. But it certainly must count as one of the greatest blessings of my life.

In the book that follows, the mistakes are mine, and the glory is God's.

Introduction

World War II was a media war. A vast number of journalists chronicled the conflict in print, over the radio, or for motion pictures. They worked for small-town newspapers, major news corporations, military publications, or state-operated news outlets. Every military employed large staffs and organizations to facilitate and control news, propaganda, and public opinion. During the war, all major commanders of the US Army had a public relations officer (PRO) on its staff.[1] World War II laid the groundwork for the ways that journalism, television, and social media are deployed as weapons in conflicts today.

What truly made World War II a media war was the importance the military placed on the press and public opinion as weapons for total war. Most commanders thought accurate news reporting—as opposed to propaganda—would boost morale. Some believed the modern media could help them connect with their soldiers. Others hoped that the press could be used to attract public interest to their theater or campaign and force the Allied governments to allocate more resources to their missions. A few even used the press to deceive the enemy.

To accomplish these objectives, military commanders began to allow the media and public opinion to influence their battlefield decisions. This was the case in Tunisia, Sicily, and Rome, during the breakout from Normandy, and on the advance into Germany. The media-fueled disputes and jealousies shaped George S. Patton Jr.'s race to Messina, Bernard Law Montgomery's advance into the Netherlands in the fall of 1944, and Omar Bradley's decisions during the Battle of the Bulge. Generals' media reputations influenced not only the command appointments of Dwight Eisenhower, Montgomery, and Patton, but even the creation of an entire theater for Douglas MacArthur. National prestige was also taken into consideration in inspiring the Doolittle Raid against Japan and its unintended consequences for the Pacific War, Eisenhower's sustained tolerance of Montgomery, and the decision to defend Strasbourg to save French morale. Media publicity is even at the root of why the army and navy now share the Pentagon building.

Today, when most people get their knowledge of war from the mass media, it is generally assumed that news reporting and public opinion can influence military action. The Vietnam War is often cited as an example of a

1

critical media turning public opinion against the war and causing the United States to lose the conflict.[2] A host of books, however, including the US Army's own study on reporting during Vietnam, has found no direct link between negative media coverage and public support for the war. As Daniel C. Hallin notes, historians "have been essentially unanimous in rejecting" the ideas that the media was "decisive" in "turning the public and policymakers against" the Vietnam War.[3] Studies of the influence of cable news on policy and military decisions during the 1990s and 2000s, usually called the "CNN Effect," have produced no consensus on the influence of the media on military decisions.[4] In any case, both Vietnam and the CNN Effect dealt with television coverage and a much different media landscape than that which existed during World War II.

Meanwhile, current scholarship on World War II journalism has largely overlooked the military-media relationship or any connection to the press's influence of military decision-making. Broadly speaking, historiography dealing with the media during World War II falls into three distinct groups. The first group chronicles the adventures of war correspondents.[5] Although some are excellent in relaying what being a war correspondent was like, they seldom explain how reporters fit into the larger war or how their reporting influenced those they covered. The second group comprises studies that focus on propaganda. While this research focuses on the creation of policy and the effect of propaganda on friend and foe, propaganda cannot be classified as news. American reporters during World War II were generally careful to avoid being viewed as propagandists. The Allied militaries likewise maintained a sharp line between news and propaganda. Finally, there are a plethora of books on censorship, yet they tell only part of the story of how armies interact with the media.[6] This book attempts to take scholarship in a different direction, an approach that could be called the "new history of war reporting."[7] Instead of focusing on how the military controlled the press through censorship and propaganda, this book instead demonstrates how the media influenced the military.

A few other books take a similar approach, and thus fall under the category of the new history of war reporting. Colonel Barney Oldfield's memoir *Never A Shot in Anger* relates the author's experience as a PRO in Europe. While the book is a treasure trove of information about the US military–media relationship during World War II, it is still a personal memoir with inherent biases and limitations. Historian Richard W. Steele's *The First Offensive 1942* showed how public opinion shaped the decision to invade North Africa.[8] Yet Steele limited himself to one campaign and did not show that this was a larger trend. Steven Casey's *Cautious Crusade* examines the role of public opinion on President Franklin D. Roosevelt's strategy against Nazi Germany.[9] Though it is an excellent study, Casey limits himself to public opinion and focuses mostly on broad policy decisions of the Roosevelt administration instead of military action. Charles F. Brower examines the role of political influence on the US Joint Chiefs of Staff in creating the strategy for the Pacific War. His book *Defeating Japan* finds the "sensitivity of the joint chiefs to the link between the national will and strategic choice was perhaps the most essential element in their conduct of the war against Japan."[10] Nevertheless, the book focuses solely on one theater of the war and discusses politics in general rather than the role of the media in shaping command decisions. The book that comes closest to answering these questions is Steven Casey's *The War Beat, Europe* which examines the exploits of an array of reporters along with their relationship to Allied generals and the PRO staff.[11] But Casey's focus is still on the exploits of the war correspondents, and not on they influenced command decisions. Likewise, Nicholas Evan Sarantakes's article "Warriors of Word and Sword" shows how the media shaped command decisions during the Battle for Okinawa. P. M. H. Bell similarly wrote an article on how British public opinion on the Darlan Deal (see chapter 3) influenced Allied strategy. Both Sarantakes and Bell, however, focus their analysis on only one episode.[12] Therefore, the broader history of how the media and public opinion shaped Allied military decisions on the battlefield has yet to be published.

Regarding broader themes in military history, this book does not fit into either the "old" military history, with its focus on battles, or the "new" military history's interest in the societal aspects of conflict.[13] As in old military history, generals and battles crowd the pages. However, the focus is only enough to give the barest details of the fighting to support the larger argument. As in the new military history, this project takes seriously the idea that society and the home front can shape warfare, while never pretending that conflicts are decided any other way but through battle. Rather, through the conduit of the media, this book hopes to connect the civilian to the military, the home front to the battlefront, and national interests to international action. It can thus be best described as a middle way between the old and new ways of studying war.

This book traces how the military-media relationship shaped the battlefield decision-making of the US military during World War II. It begins with a prologue briefly outlining how total war and the modern press evolved together and eventually merged during World War II. Chapter 1, which begins right after the attack on Pearl Harbor, shows how Roosevelt skillfully steered the press, public opinion, and his commanders into implementing the Germany First strategy. The second chapter, conversely, demonstrates what limitations public opinion placed on that commitment and how MacArthur successfully used the press to secure resources for the counteroffensive against Japan from the Southwest Pacific. Chapter 3 compares how

Eisenhower and Patton attempted to utilize the press as a weapon, but soon found it shaping their decisions on the battlefield in North Africa and Sicily. Press influence reached a new level in the Italian campaign, during which, as the fourth chapter shows, General Mark Clark's desire to gain media glory dominated his actions in disastrous ways. Chapters 5 and 6 demonstrate how the media shaped D-Day and the final campaigns across Europe. The conclusion not only sums up the findings but demonstrates how the military media relationship from World War II transferred into later limited wars. Likewise, the conclusion highlights several themes that emerge from this research and how they fit into the larger scholarship on World War II.

The first theme is how the military and the media merged to fight a total war. Although both sides kept their distinctive identities, prejudices, and institutions, this fusion can be seen in three areas. First, reporters covering the Allied armies became part of the military. They were inducted into the service, submitted to censorship, accreditation, and military discipline. Second, many former reporters took this a step further and joined the military not as war correspondents but as staff officers. This group tended to be assigned as PROs and became an important conduit between the military and the media. Third, most of the highest-ranking generals in the army had former reporters as staff officers. Their tasks often encompassed not only traditional military staff work, but also dealing with press relations. Given their literary abilities, these staff officers were later often major sources for the history of World War II. Thus, an important reason why the press was such an effective weapon for total war was the absorption of the media into the military.

A closely related second theme is the importance of accreditation of reporters. Despite the amount of scholarship devoted to censorship, accreditation was at least as important for the military to control information and war correspondents. It was also mutually beneficial. Accreditation allowed reporters to be selected for special access, and fear of losing that license could coerce good behavior. At the same time, both American and British leadership felt freer to trust accredited war correspondents.[14] Allied generals routinely brought reporters into their confidence, briefing them on coming battles, offering suggestions of where to find stories, and treating them as part of the military team. "Of course, when you brief a bunch of correspondents, you are running the risk of a breach of security," Bradley recalled, "but very little, because the correspondents accredited to a combat zone are a very high type bunch of people, and patriotic people, and they don't let you down."[15] Accreditation allowed the military more control over war correspondents but provided accredited journalists with a vast amount of information.

Despite accreditation, and popular memories of the military-media relationship during World War II, an additional theme of this project is the recognition that the American press was hardly the unthinking supporter of the military or government. This is a fact overlooked in much of the scholarship on war reporting. One notable exception is historian Steven Casey, who makes challenging this claim a central argument in *The War Beat, Europe.* He concludes that the "idea that the media and military were on the same side, the war reporters effectively acting as cheerleaders for the Allied cause, conceals more than it reveals." He adds that the more time reporters spent in the field, the less willing they became to side with the military and the more willing they became to follow their own opinions.[16] Moreover, throughout World War II, there was a loyal opposition press in the United States, comprised of mostly Republican papers, and usually centered in the Midwest. Indeed, the Democrats lost seats in the 1942 election, and Roosevelt's last presidential bid in 1944 was his closest presidential race.[17] Likewise, the military and its leaders came under harsh press criticism during the war. The press attack on Eisenhower's alliance with former Vichy leaders in North Africa made him fear for his job. Patton was repeatedly criticized in the media to such an extent that several times he was almost relieved of command. The decision to focus on defeating Germany first instead of Japan was also debated freely in the media.

Critical public and press opinion in a democracy during wartime was seen by many as a major weakness. "It's one of the disadvantages of democracy that it can't conduct politics or war according to logic and intelligence," wrote Nazi propaganda minister Joseph Goebbels, "but have to respond to the up-and-down swings of public opinion."[18] Some Allied leaders feared he was right. George C. Marshall worried that "a democracy cannot fight a Seven Years War."[19] Or, more bitterly reflecting on strategy after the war, Marshall noted that "we failed to see that the leader in a democracy has to keep the people entertained."[20] Yet perhaps Marshall had little to worry about given that some scholars conclude that government control over the press during wartime meant a media dominated by censorship. Truth, as Phillip Knightley concluded, quoting Senator Hiram Johnson, in his widely read history of war correspondents, is the first casualty of war.

Despite all this, a recurring theme throughout this book is not only that the media was useful as a weapon, but that its power was intricately connected to the truthfulness of information. Rather than attempt to create good morale by lying to their soldiers and countrymen with unadulterated propaganda, the US military repeatedly discovered that the best effects resulted from accurate news stories. Thus truthful news reporting—defined as news reporting that accurately depicts the events it described—could not be created by the military or even the media, but could only emerge by a free press searching for it.[21] This, of course, is a challenge to the Nietzschean and postmodern ideas of truth as a relative exercise of power created by humans.[22] As is seen throughout this book, the use of *true* information, as opposed to fake news, was viewed as having a power of its own.

Even the Axis—whose leaders habitually lied to their subjects—were forced to be careful how much they exaggerated success or downplayed failure. Reich propaganda minister Joseph Goebbels, a man not usually associated with truth, fretted about the need for frankness in propaganda.[23] The new technology of long-distance radio transmissions was responsible for this increased honesty. The problem was particularly acute for Germany since the German people could easily obtain the BBC. Japan also recognized this reality. After the Japanese government admitted the loss of the midget sub force used during the attack at Pearl Harbor, Admiral Matome Ugaki reasoned that "since the Washington press reported" the story, "Japan could not but announce it."[24] Another example occurred later in the war. "I listened to one of their [Tokyo Radio] broadcasts and it is comparatively conservative," wrote General Robert Eichelberger to his wife in the spring of 1944. "Being directed at white listeners I guess they try not to let it sound foolish, although of course they present an improper picture."[25] Though the Western democracies were much more honest in their news, Axis broadcasts also forced them to loosen censorship. When the American government refused to release casualty figures, Steven Casey observes, the Allied media turned to Axis radio figures with "surprising frequency."[26] As chapter 2 demonstrates, Axis radio stations began broadcasting distorted information, which occasionally made the Allies respond by publishing accurate figures that might otherwise have been censored.

Far from always pushing rosy news stories, commanders skilled in using the press as a weapon understood the usefulness of bad news. In his book on photograph censorship during World War II, George H. Roeder Jr. argues persuasively that to destroy American complacency about victory, the War Department released pictures of dead American soldiers that had been formerly censored.[27] Casey makes a similar point, noting that Eisenhower loosened censorship because he feared the damage caused by overly optimistic war news.[28] This book takes these observations a step further and argues that overly optimistic news was a major concern for commanders after 1943. The War Department also held back bad news to provoke anger at an opportune moment. One example was delaying the news of the execution of the captured Doolittle Flyers. As indicated in chapter 1, when the story was released it sparked one of the largest war bond drives in US history. Conversely, as chapter 2 demonstrates, MacArthur desperately wanted the story of the Bataan Death March released because he believed it would cause additional resources to be sent to his theater.

A critical press, an emphasis on truth when possible, and the understanding of the power of bad news paints a much more complicated picture of the military-media relationship than is often shown. Therefore, this book is a major revision to books, such as Phillip Knightley's *The First Casualty* (probably the most famous book on war correspondents ever published), that view reporters as lackeys of the military and mostly a means of providing distorted propaganda to the masses. Truth may have been scarred, but reports of its death were greatly exaggerated.

Another important theme is the media's ability to connect distant theaters in a global war. The concept of World War II as a global struggle with different theaters influencing each other is an idea highlighted by several historians.[29] It was also well understood by Allied commanders. Asked in the late 1960s about the then-prevailing historical consensus of the Atlantic and Pacific Theaters as separate conflicts, General Bradley disagreed. It was the Germany First concept, Bradley believed, that united the conflict under a single strategy.[30] What is missing from this historiography is the role of the press and public opinion in these international connections. First, as chapter 1 demonstrates, facing pressure to retaliate against Japan after Pearl Harbor, Roosevelt deliberately created a press campaign to link Germany to Japan and build public support for a Germany First strategy. Although this was successful, chapter 2 shows how it was also effectively challenged by Douglas MacArthur's own media campaign to supply the Southwest Pacific Area with resources. Meanwhile, international tensions between the United States and her allies were often played out in the press. By the end of the war, which nation got "credit" for a battle was an important factor in strategy.

How did commanders follow news about their battles? Certainly, most generals did not have easy access to stateside news. George C. Marshall, whose duties as army chief of staff kept him near Washington, remembered that though he was not officially briefed on editorial opinion, he still read nine newspapers a day.[31] More typical was Eisenhower, who repeatedly claimed during the North African campaign that he did not receive American newspapers.[32] But neither were they ignorant of current events. They could and did listen to the radio, particularly the BBC, and intelligence staffs sometimes prepared digests of stateside news coverage. Family members also sent newspaper clippings, as did superiors in the War Department. This lack of regular news highlights a larger finding of this book. Commanders often acted on what they thought news and public opinion *might* be rather than firsthand knowledge. Therefore, the final theme of this book suggests that the lack of the morning paper did not stop generals from speculating what it might contain. What they perceived the news to be was more important than what the press actually said.

The same was true of public opinion. At least one historian has written, correctly, that "one still cannot claim to completely comprehend or define 'public opinion,'" but concluded, incorrectly, that during World War II

"American leaders remained largely removed from the opinions of commentators and citizens."[33] Scientific polling was still new but widely used, with results often appearing in the newspapers. Polls also appeared in intelligence reports prepared for President Roosevelt. Indeed, one important source for this book is the reports concerning news and editorial opinion provided by Archibald MacLeish at the Office of Facts and Figures. At the beginning of February 1942, MacLeish inquired whether the president would be interested in these reports. "I want all of them from the beginning," Roosevelt scribbled at the bottom of the letter.[34] This project uses these scientific polling sources when they are available and appropriate. But, as with newspaper opinion, it should be remembered that generals sometimes confused public opinion with what they thought it should be.

To solve the problem of what news and public opinion commanders had access to, this book looks at what generals recorded seeing or thinking about the news. Thus, it does not attempt to show what public opinion *actually* was during the war, which likely could not be done with any degree of certainty. In any case, such a conclusion would not be known to military commanders and hence would be useless in explaining their actions. Therefore, this analysis relies on the personal papers, memoirs, official documents, cables, letters, interviews, and newspapers of generals and their aides along with the reporters who covered them. These sources, of course, have their limitations. One problem was noted by historian Russell F. Weigley in his classic book *Eisenhower's Lieutenants*. "To aggravate the problems of locating the source of decision and tracing the process whereby decisions took form," Weigley explained, "twentieth-century transportation and communication made it possible for World War II commanders to work out their most critical designs in face-to-face conferences or telephone conversations, neither of which were necessarily recorded in full."[35] This is true. Nevertheless, Allied headquarters during World War II produced vast quantities of records. General Bradley recalled that his Twelfth Army Group Headquarters handled 1,100 bags of communications a day.[36] Richard Sutherland, MacArthur's chief of staff, spent the war reading 500 documents a day.[37] Since Weigley published *Eisenhower's Lieutenants* in 1981, the source base has only grown. To complete this project required sifting through dozens of paper collections spread over fifteen archives and combing through hundreds of newspaper articles.

Because of the vastness of the topic and the resources involved, there are several glaring omissions. First, this project is weighted heavily toward the European war, as opposed to fighting in the Pacific. For reasons that are not entirely clear, the European war provided more examples of the press shaping battlefield decisions than the war in the Pacific. Second, this account does not look at either the US Army Air Force's or the US Marine Corps's public relations in any systematic manner. Both services, however, had well-known public relations operations to ensure their postwar growth. Historian Aaron O'Connell's study of the marine corps notes, "Marines did not just fight wars and rest on the laurels" but recruited journalists and editors to help their public relations campaign.[38] CBS's William J. Dunn recalled being on a transport with the First Marine Division before an invasion and being reminded repeatedly to "tell the folks back home the marines did it."[39] With confidence that future studies of these services would only strengthen this book's argument, the author asks their members' forgiveness for their neglect. The China–Burma–India Theater is also ignored for similar reasons.

Finally, it cannot be emphasized strongly enough that though this book argues that the media was an important element in military decisions, it was hardly the only influence, or even the most important factor. Strategic, operational, and tactical choices are an amalgamation of factors of terrain, logistics, intelligence, training, alliances, weather, intuition, and many other elements. This book's argument dismisses none of these factors. Because of the nature of space and in attempting to prove a point, the book focuses on the media's influence. The author hopes this will be an addition—not a subtraction—when future historians seek to untangle the factors of military decision-making in warfare.

The Media and Total War

Before examining the media's influence on World War II, it is necessary to examine the history of the modern press and its relationship to warfare. This book contends that the military-media relationship during World War II was a product of total war. To assess this claim, however, one needs to understand how the modern press developed and how it intersected with the advance toward total war. Scholars differ over which wars reached the total war stage, and even over a uniform definition of the concept. In this book "total war" will be defined by the shifting emphasis of the center of gravity of military operations from armies and objectives on the map to populations.[1] Beginning with the Napoleonic Wars, the relationship of the military and the media, and the correlating effect of public opinion on warfare, emerged together, driven by changing technologies. As conflict progressed toward total war, the media was a necessary part of the process.

Although an exact definition of total war and its origins is elusive, a case can be made that modern total war had its intellectual roots in the French Revolution and the Napoleonic Wars. Historian David Bell argues, for example, that the "intellectual transformations of the Enlightenment, followed by the political fermentation of 1789–1792, produced new understandings of war that made possible the cataclysmic intensification of the fighting over the next twenty-three years."[2] It was no coincidence that Napoleon Bonaparte—in Bell's words "the world's first 'media general'"—took great care in how his deeds were reported. During his Italian campaigns, Napoleon established two newspapers for his army. The *Courier of the Army of Italy* was meant for the troops and went out of its way to highlight their commander's concern for his men. Napoleon himself even contributed articles. *France Seen from the Army of Italy*, on the other hand, targeted civilian audiences. Likewise, as Bell argues, Napoleon took great care to create a personality cult, both for his soldiers and for Frenchmen at home. Although this often took the form of art and propaganda, the press was also an important component.[3] It did not hurt that Napoleon's name sold well, which encouraged even opposition papers to cover his exploits, and during his early campaigns he was mentioned much more than other generals.[4] This was the beginning of commanders taking a new interest in motivating their soldiers. As Bell notes, "in the eighteenth century, few works of military strategy had given much consideration to what we would call 'psychological issues.' Napoleon's famous statement that in battle, 'moral' factors weigh three times as heavily as 'physical' ones already pointed to a new approach, as did the reflections of German reformers, such as Scharnhorst."[5] In Napoleon's words the "printing press is an arsenal."[6] Nevertheless, his media campaign often backfired. "Napoleon wrote his own bulletins and impressed nearly everyone but his soldiers," observes historian James L. Stokesbury, "to whom the phrase 'to lie like a bulletin' was a commonplace."[7] Nevertheless, Napoleon succeeded in using the media to create an extremely close bond with his subjects.[8]

The first war correspondents also emerged at this time, though they proved no more reliable than Napoleon's bulletins. Henry Crabb Robinson was hired by the *Times* as a foreign correspondent and was dispatched to cover the Napoleonic Wars. "Cover" is perhaps too generous a term since Robinson did not take the trouble to witness any battles.[9] This, however, did not stop him from writing about them—a method that would be followed by other nineteenth-century war correspondents. Yet Robinson demonstrated that public interest was beginning, if only tentatively, to require independent observation of far-off military actions.

Napoleon also proved susceptible to the same spell that he cast. During the yearlong peace with Britain in 1802, he was repeatedly driven to distraction by the mockery of the British press. Although hardly the organ of government that the French media had become, the British press heightened tensions between the two nations as they drifted toward renewed conflict in 1803.[10] This fact demonstrated that even in its early form the media could contribute to policy decisions. British newspaper criticism was hardly limited to the enemy. Though the Duke of Wellington acknowledged the importance of a free press, and claimed to ignore criticism directed at him, he wrote that "much mischief is done in England, not only to me personally, but to the character of the army and of the country, by foolish observations upon what passes here, in all the newspapers." The English were used to ill-informed press criticism, Wellington wrote, "but in Spain, a country unaccustomed to these discussions, in which all, even the best men, are objects of suspicion, and every measure is considered the result of a treasonable conspiracy, it is highly dangerous to expose men in the situation of the Marquis de la Romana to this description of calumny, and unfair statement and sophistical reasoning on his conduct."[11] Thus in the infancy of total war, press criticism was already influencing military operations, or at least causing concern that it might do so.

The importance of sustaining or destroying public morale was not lost on Napoleon's and Wellington's contemporary, the Prussian military theorist Carl von Clausewitz. Modern war was fought for political ends, argued Clausewitz, and politics and popular support were never far apart. Like Napoleon, Clausewitz believed war was never limited to physical force, but also had a psychological dimension. "Military activity," he wrote, "is never directed against material force alone; it is always aimed simultaneously at the moral forces which give it life, and the two cannot be separated."[12] It was only through the "shame and humiliation" of defeat that victory could be achieved, since its "psychological consequences of the transformation of the balance" were "the only element that affect public opinion outside the army; that impresses the people and the governments of the two belligerents and of their allies."[13] Enemy morale, both civilian and military, had to be defeated as much as the enemy army. Sustaining public morale required keeping the population informed of military actions. Clausewitz, ever interested in the practical, observed that the direction of enemy attacks "will usually be announced in the press before a single shot is fired."[14] If war was an extension of politics by other means, and politics the extension of a people's will, it was this will that sustained military operations.

Despite foreseeing the all-consuming nature of people's war, Clausewitz himself did not yet view enemy populations as the main target of military operations. The major objective for victory—what he titled the "center of gravity"—was still the enemy army or capital. Only in popular uprisings did he list public opinion as an objective. "In countries subject to domestic strife," he wrote, "the center of gravity is generally the capital. In small countries that rely on large ones, it is usually the army of their protector. Among alliances, it lies in the community of interest, and in popular uprisings it is the personalities of the leaders and public opinion."[15] Thus, Clausewitz is describing something different from later total war theorists, for whom the population itself became a target.

Clausewitz's ideas were, nevertheless, essential to the development of a theory of total war since he saw popular support as an important new factor in warfare. His understanding that wars were supported by the civilian population, according to historian Michael Howard, was a "factor left out of account by all strategists before Clausewitz and most of them since."[16] Howard concludes that Clausewitz's focus on the population has "lasting relevance" since the "essence of his teaching about popular participation in war is not to be found in the famous chapter 'The People in Arms'—which is almost always misleadingly quoted out of its context—but in what he had to say about the long-term political processes that were making such participation inevitable."[17] Clausewitz's focus on politics, which was growing increasingly democratic—even in totalitarian systems that ruled in the people's name— saw a growing role for civilian populations. As political scientist Eliot Cohen observes, "For Clausewitz there is no field of military action that might not be touched by political considerations. In practice, politics might not determine the stationing of pickets or the dispatch of patrols, he writes, but in theory it could (and, one might add, in the day of CNN often does)."[18] This early focus on popular support was a key insight that chronicled an emerging development in modern war.

Not only was the nineteenth century increasingly democratic, but it also brought revolutionary new technologies for both the military and reporters, setting the conditions for total war. Armies, made more lethal by the invention of breech-loading rifles, had their reach and speed of movement expanded by trains and the telegraph. The media likewise benefited from steam power and the telegraph that allowed information to travel further and faster. By the time of the US Civil War, the world was experiencing the "First Communications Revolution," beginning an era, as Cohen writes, "when it became possible to communicate useful quantities of information almost instantaneously and to move large quantities of men and war materiél [*sic*] at great speed by means of mechanical transportation."[19] Historian Susan Carruthers points out that many of the technologies that created modern journalism, such as the sight mechanism of the camera or the telegraph, were developed for war.[20] As technology increased the scope, speed, and destructive power of war, it also gave war correspondents increased abilities.

The Crimean War (1853–1856) exhibited the power that new technology gave journalists on the battlefield. For example, the press dispatches of war correspondent William Howard Russell and others highlighting major military problems brought outrage in Britain and military changes, and considerably assisted the fall of the Aberdeen cabinet.[21] More importantly, according to correspondent Edwin Godkin, who also covered the conflict, reporters demonstrated to "the War Office the fact that the public had something to say about the conduct of wars and that they are not the concern exclusively of sovereigns and statesmen."[22] It certainly provoked a response, including an irate Prince Albert sending his royal photographer, Roger Fenton, to the battlefield to give public opinion a more positive image.[23] Russell's photographers depicted an abundance of weaponry and food when in fact both were in low quantity or quality. The Crimean War, Barney Oldfield amusingly notes, also saw the creation of the first military public relations officer when a British soldier made a table for Russell to write his dispatches.[24] Not only did reporters' opinion matter after the Crimean War, but they were now part of warfare.

The US Civil War (1861–1865) demonstrated both the increasing speed of the press and the irritation it gave to military commanders. Indeed, the war brought the first communications revolution to the United States. "During the Civil War," writes J. Cutler Andrews, "for the first time in American history, the transmission of war news by telegraph was undertaken on a large scale."[25] After one battle, for example, General George Meade marveled that "with the telegraph and the night train, it is actually a fact that at 11 A.M. to-day I read in the Philadelphia papers of this date an authentic account of the affair."[26] Yet, the military also saw the swarm of correspondents as a security risk. When General William Tecumseh Sherman threatened to execute a number of reporters as spies, he was simply the loudest expression of this general distrust throughout the army.[27] The security concern was also real, with Robert E. Lee admitting he often looked at Northern newspapers for military intelligence.[28] For his part, Meade quickly lost his admiration for the press. By the time of Cold Harbor, he had become so frustrated that he publicly humiliated and expelled a reporter for "libeling" him. In retaliation, the press instituted an almost total blackout of Meade's name in the papers.[29] Despite the hardships, security risks, and the extreme dislike of professional soldiers, the public was desperate for news and newspapers were happy to provide. The *New York Herald* alone spent over half a million dollars and sent sixty-three reporters to cover the conflict.[30] The war, in Knightley's words, had "the effect of making war correspondence a separate section in the practice of journalism."[31]

If the US Civil War made war correspondents an accepted addition to the battlefield, the Russo-Japanese War (1904–1905) added censorship. Though the war attracted some of the greatest war correspondents of the nineteenth century, including Richard Harding Davis, Frederick Palmer, and the writer Jack London, the Japanese kept them away from the front and strictly censored what they wrote.[32] For an emerging nation, the Japanese policies were patently modern. As historians Michael S. Sweeney and Natascha Toft Roelsgaard observe, "What Japan did in 1904 was to integrate news, propaganda, and censorship into a campaign to create favorable pictures in the heads of its soldiers and civilians, as well as readers of newspapers and magazines abroad." This, they add,

> anticipated the twentieth-century phenomenon of postmodernism, which says there is no "Truth." Instead, truth—with a lower-case "t"—is what we make it out to be. The Russo-Japanese War may have been the first truly modern war not only in its huge, conscripted armies of civilians and weapons of mass slaughter, but also in its creation of "truths" intended to mobilize public opinion, both through promotion of positive narratives about the war and censorship erasing conflicting accounts.[33]

The Japanese reason for hindering the press was also very modern. They feared many of the foreign reporters were spies and thus a weapon that had to be parried.[34]

World War I (1914–1918) was a total war, but neither the press nor the military-media relationship had yet developed enough to fully exercise power over conflict. The association, nevertheless, grew closer throughout the conflict. World War I solidified the media's power to shape events for total war. Historian Alexander Watson argues that "popular consent was indispensable in fighting the twentieth century's first 'total war.'"[35] According to Watson:

> [World War I] was not a "people's war" in the old sense, in which civilians rose up under arms, but in a new way, where whole societies contributed less violently yet indispensably to deciding the outcome. Public support and consent were crucial. Pre-war military plans had focused on shifting bodies, on concentrating soldiers at the front; now, however, it was hearts and minds at home that had to be moved. States gave some guidance, but societies proved to an extraordinary extent to be self-mobilizing. Intellectuals, journalists, clergy and politicians, with marginal prompting from governments, interpreted the long war for the public.[36]

Under these conditions, public opinion—often expressed through journalism—began shaping military action. For example, Watson notes that the German chancellor Theobald von Bethmann Hollweg and the chief of the German General Staff, General Helmuth von Moltke, both delayed war mobilization until Russia appeared ready to launch an invasion, since for "public opinion, this was crucial. The leaders of Austria-Hungary and Germany, having failed in their bid for localized war and triggered instead a general conflagration, were beholden to their peoples."[37] Devastatingly costly battles, such as Verdun, became for both the Germans and the French a "prestige objective. To disengage without shaking public morale meant being able to demonstrate some tangible achievement."[38] Thus, total war linked journalism, public opinion, and military decision together.

This blending of war, politics, and public opinion created new opportunities for commanders. General Erich Ludendorff personally oversaw the German army's freshly established press service, the Deutsche Kriegsnachrichtendienst, while Field Marshal Paul von Hindenburg went to great lengths to maintain good relations with the press. "He was undoubtedly vain," Watson writes of Hindenburg, "yet he was also acutely aware of the power conferred by his popular following. . . . The political capital gained from his personality cult gave him a unique chance to impose radical change on how not just Germany's army but the whole society waged war."[39] Though this was hardly limited to Germany, one must be careful not to overstate this point. As World War II veteran and literary critic Paul Fussell notes, "During the Great War names like Haig and Foch and Pershing were well known, but the publicity mechanisms that might trumpet the names and merits of lesser commanders had hardly been developed. By the time of the Second World War they were in vigorous condition, and army, corps, and division, and even lesser-unit commanders could now be celebrated."[40]

The United States was also concerned with the press and public opinion, and its policies began laying the groundwork for the military-media relationship of World War II. The Committee on Public Information (CPI)—usually referred to as the Creel Committee after its most prominent member—oversaw censorship as well as the most successful, and controversial, propaganda campaign in US history. As historian Stephen Vaughn notes, the "CPI proved spectacularly successful in mobilizing public opinion behind the country's participation in World War of 1917–18."[41] However, it also encouraged excesses and left many Americans deeply disillusioned with propaganda and censorship.[42] Creel was among the disillusioned. In the coming war, he declared in 1941, censorship "is not the answer" for military secrecy. The CPI, nevertheless, influenced the Office of War Information (OWI) during World War II.[43]

At the front, the War Department instituted a stringent "accreditation" process for reporters.[44] John J. Pershing, commanding the American Expeditionary Forces (AEF), eased the situation somewhat by appointing the veteran war correspondent and his personal friend Frederick Palmer as head of his press relations. This began the practice, continued into World War II, of assigning former reporters to public relations staffs.[45] One major concern for the army was how casualties were reported. News accounts of gruesome deaths could hurt home-front morale, while reporting accurate casualty figures might provide valuable information to the Germans. Thus, news stories were carefully censored and casualty statistics cautiously released. Historian Steven Casey convincingly argues this policy backfired after the war into mistrust of the military and disillusionment about war.[46] Nevertheless, as historian William M. Hammond writes, "World War I had a profound effect upon the way governments handled the press in future wars. A total war that massed not only armies but entire economies and peoples against one another, it made news a strategic commodity, an all-important means of buttressing civilian morale."[47] Using or controlling the media in total war gave new power to military commanders.

Although it is difficult to argue that World War I was not a total war, the definition came only afterward in Ludendorff's *Der Totale Krieg*. When the book was translated into English, the title became *The Nation at War*, while Ludendorff's "total war" became "totalitarian war."[48] According to Ludendorff, Clausewitz had seen armies as the center of gravity and focused on their annihilation, but he had also envisioned wars growing to involve more of the nation. Ludendorff argued that the World War had brought a new kind of war. "What made this war different from all others was the manner in which the home populations supported and reinforced their armed forces," he claimed. The hostile population had become the center of gravity since "totalitarian war which, far from being the concern of the military forces alone, directly touches the life and soul of every single member of the belligerent nations." After blaming Jews and Catholics for this situation, he added that "totalitarian war is the result also of the introduction of universal conscription, on account of an increasing population, and of the use of new means of warfare, the effects of which have become more destructive." Yet it was not simply new weapons that were part of totalitarian warfare, but propaganda. "Nations are now directly involved in a war through blockades and propaganda, just like the inmates of closed fortresses who as we know from the history of wars, are compelled by warlike pressures and lack of the necessaries of life, to surrender their strongholds," wrote Ludendorff. "Totalitarian warfare is thus directed not only against the fighting forces, but indirectly also against the nations themselves."[49] Total wars were conflicts between peoples where information was another weapon.

The importance of the press in total war was realized not only by the German high command but also by an Austrian corporal named Adolf Hitler. In *Mein Kampf,* Hitler recorded that his first realization of propaganda came in his early days of fighting in Flanders. He and his comrades found that the British soldiers opposing them "did not exactly jibe with the pictures they had seen fit to give us in the comic magazines and press dispatches." It was there, he added, "that I began my first reflections about the importance of the form of propaganda."[50] Hitler was not alone. As historian Robert Edwin Herzstein notes:

> German nationalists after 1918 believed that the collapse of Germany had in large part been caused by the failure of German propaganda and by the success of the Allies' subversion of the German war effort. . . . This belief, so dear to the German right, was closely related to the "stab in the back" legend, according to which Germany had not lost the war in 1918, but had collapsed because of subversion, both domestic and foreign.[51]

Hitler's interest in press and propaganda was central to his success. After the war, he was recruited to the press and propaganda section for the Reichswehr Group in Bavaria, which led him to the Nazi Party, where he soon became head of propaganda.[52] Thus, press relations and propaganda was Hitler's last job in the German army and his first in the Nazi Party.

When the Nazis took power in 1933, radios were still out of the price range for most Germans, causing the Nazis to launch a highly successful program to bring cheap radios, along with Hitler's speeches, to Germany.[53] As a US Army exchange student at the German War College in the 1930s, Albert C. Wedemeyer observed the link between technology, information, and warfare. He remembered after the war, that as "science had been improving our means of killing human beings and destroying their works, it had also sharpened and diversified weapons for the distortion or murder of ideas in the battle for the mind. The Nazi and the Communists had recognized the ever-increasing importance of propaganda—the modern methods of influencing the thinking of people in accomplishing strategic aims both in peace and war."[54] During World War II, Hitler would take time to personally edit—or distort—German news stories.[55] He also perused American magazines, which he insisted on seeing in their original form.[56] Noting how angrily Hitler reacted to press stories, particularly from foreign media, as opposed to intelligence briefs, Albert Speer later reflected that Hitler "considered the reverberations more important than the realities; that the newspaper accounts interested him more than the events themselves."[57] Media and war were thus interlinked for Hitler. "Don't ever doubt," observed the American publisher Henry Luce from Brussels, where he was observing the German 1940 blitzkrieg at close quarters, "Hitler keeps a close eye on American opinion."[58]

Luce was well qualified to make that observation since he had been at the center of the emerging media revolution in the interwar years. In the 1920s, Luce and his partner Briton Hadden founded *Time* magazine as a weekly periodical that offered a condensation of the news, aimed at busy professionals. After Hadden's death, Luce would go on to publish *Fortune*, followed by the hugely popular *Life*, the first picture magazine in the United States, which was partly influenced by the German *Berliner Illustrierte Zeitung*.[59] By 1939, Luce's *Life* and *Time*, along with *Look* and *Newsweek*, reached 45 percent of the American electorate.[60] Like Luce's magazine empire, commercial radio was born in the 1920s and soon delivered news throughout the United States. Newsreels, enhanced by the addition of sound in 1927, brought moving pictures of events coupled with narration. Moreover, public opinion on everything from a president's actions to the impact of news could now also be measured, to a certain degree, by George Gallup's polls.[61] Flights over, and telephone lines under, the oceans along with radio signals sped up the delivery of news.[62] Eighty percent of Americans owned radios and could benefit from this speed of news.[63] This revolution in communications technology drastically increased the speed by which news traveled and provided a major increase of visual images. More importantly, the public was receiving not only more news but also the same news, with magazines, newsreels, radio, and some newspapers having national audiences. These changes in media technology not only made total war possible, but also massively increased the media's ability to cover it.

An example of this new communications revolution was the speed at which Ludendorff's idea of "total war" spread. For Americans, it was popularized by correspondent William Shirer, who covered Nazi Germany for CBS before the United States entered World War II.[64] Many nations accepted not only the idea that conflict was heading toward total war but also, as historian Jochen Hellbeck has shown, Ludendorff's emphasis on the importance of propaganda and information on the enemy's morale.[65] In his 1941 book *America and Total War*, historian Fletcher Pratt dedicated an entire chapter to the role of Nazi propaganda as a weapon.[66] Writing the introduction for Matthew Gordon's *News Is a Weapon*—a chapter of which was titled "The News Arm in Total War"—OWI director Elmer Davis observed that news "is part of the enemy's total attack on the American people."[67] These examples, coupled with the actions of the United States' government and military during World War II, demonstrate that the media were viewed as a component of total war.

Not only did the military benefit from much of this new technology, but also reporters were becoming increasingly influential. Winston S. Churchill had spent the Boer War as a war correspondent creating trouble for himself and others. "Alas," wrote Churchill around that time, "the days of newspaper enterprise in war are over. What can one do with a censor, a 48-hour delay, and a 50-word limit on a wire?"[68] Quite a lot, it turned out. Although never a reporter himself, Franklin D. Roosevelt had remade American politics with his employment of the radio during the Great Depression and later used the press to skillfully guide American public opinion toward support of the Allies. As historian James Sparrow observes, Roosevelt was also surrounded by former newsmen, including "Archibald MacLeish, who had written for Henry Luce's *Fortune*, and the CBS broadcaster Elmer Davis, who would succeed [MacLeish] as head of the OWI. The polling pioneers George Gallup and Elmo Roper were also creatures of the news business; both offered their services to the president on occasion." Sparrow added that "most news veterans shared Gallup's optimism about managing the new public sphere, which he betrayed when he described public opinion as the very 'pulse of democracy.'"[69] In the lead-up to the United States' entry to World War II, Roosevelt's reliance on opinion drew Churchill to despair, grumbling to the House of Commons, "Nothing is more dangerous in wartime than to live in the temperamental atmosphere of Gallup polls."[70] Thus, Allied leaders were well aware of the emerging power of the press.

In no country was the media apparatus closer to the center of power or more integrated with the idea of total war than Nazi Germany. Joseph Goebbels, the Reich propaganda minister, had absorbed Hitler's lessons about propaganda in *Mein Kampf* and, according to historian Robert Herzstein, believed he could have saved Germany during World War I using propaganda.[71] "News policy is a weapon of war," Goebbels believed. "Its purpose is to wage war and not to give out information."[72] Indeed, the Germans were quick to merge battlefield activities with media operations. "I shall give a propaganda reason for starting the war," Hitler told his generals a few days before the invasion of Poland. "The victor will not be asked afterward whether he told the truth." He sent a message to Mussolini "cordially" asking "to support my struggle psychologically with your press or by other means."[73] While Poland was careful not to mobilize for fear of providing Germany with a propaganda excuse, the Germans created their own by faking an incident along the Polish border to build public support for the invasion.[74] As German troops moved into Poland they were accompanied by Propaganda Kompanien (PK), support troops trained in propaganda, who, in historian Phillip Knightley's words, "became a vital part of the German war effort, a combination of straight war correspondent, publicist, and master of what the British later termed 'black propaganda.'"[75] The PKs quickly demonstrated the power of the media to the total war battlefield. Four days before the fall of Warsaw, they established a fake "Radio Warsaw" spreading disinformation and confusion among the Polish defenders.[76] This was the first of many examples of the use of the press as a weapon in World War II. Goebbels, in fact, pressed for the Third Reich to commit to total war well before any of the other Nazi elite. With the clouds darkening over Germany in 1943, Goebbels would get his wish, rhetorically asking the German nation if they wanted total war.[77]

Nor was the power of the media in total war lost on the Japanese government as they began to plan their attack against Britain and the United States. The opinion of the ordinary man on the street did not matter much in Japan. Yet in the weeks before Pearl Harbor, the Japanese press had deluged the populace with anti-American rhetoric, including a blast on December 6 stating that the United States was preparing for war.[78] Japanese military leaders also allowed public opinion to factor into their military planning. Along with clearing the Pacific of US warships, American morale was one of the targets behind the thinking of Admiral Isoroku Yamamoto, who had conceived the idea of the Pearl Harbor operation. As Yamamoto's collaborator Rear Admiral Takijiro Onishi explained to another Japanese officer, "Yamamoto not only intends to cripple the US Pacific Fleet severely at the beginning of hostilities; he counts heavily on smashing the morale of the American people by sinking as many battleships as possible."[79] Yamamoto, who had attended Harvard University, visited the US Naval War College in 1924, and twice served as naval attaché in Washington, had few illusions about the vast resources of the United States. To force the Americans to yield to Japanese dominance in Asia, Japan would need to achieve an early psychological victory against the United States to force them to seek peace.

The Japanese knew they were attacking a country that was bitterly divided. In the lead-up to the Pearl Harbor attacks, the American public had been split over what role, if any, the United States would have in the war. Roosevelt had carefully used the news media to guide America toward a more active role in the war.[80] This had sparked a debate that left a media no less divided and bitter than that of the press in the twenty-first century United States. Arthur Schlesinger Jr. would later describe the discussion of whether the United States should become involved in World War II as "the most savage political debate in my lifetime." Not even the Vietnam War, he added, "so tore apart families and friendships as this fight."[81]

The most prominent and powerful opposition to Roosevelt and intervention was the *Chicago Tribune*, led by Colonel Robert R. McCormick. The *Tribune* had more than one million daily readers and exercised huge influence throughout the Midwest.[82] Closely related by more than opinion was the *New York Daily News*. It was owned by McCormick's cousin Joseph Patterson, whose sister Eleanor "Cissy" Patterson owned the equally isolationist and anti-Roosevelt *Washington Times-Herald*. Roosevelt titled the three "the Mc-Cormick-Patterson Axis," bringing to American politics the distasteful habit of comparing partisan opponents to Nazis.[83] The cousins were joined in their opposition to Roosevelt by the media empires of William Randolph Hearst and Roy Howard.[84] Hearst's had been hit hard by the depression, but in 1941 he could still boast thirteen Sunday papers, seventeen daily papers, with over eleven million subscribers. One in four Americans, one study notes, read a Hearst paper.[85] Howard's Scripps-Howard chain consisted of twenty-four newspapers and a weekday circulation of almost two million readers.[86] Leary of Roosevelt, but also prointerventionist, was another group represented in the media most prominently by the *Time*, *Life*, and *Fortune* magazine empire of Henry Luce.[87]

The vast majority of editorial pages of newspapers generally supported the administration. However, reporters—and their views—were diverse, and could provoke presidential irritation even from friendly papers.[88] Nor did journalists necessarily share the views of their papers' editors. By one scholarly estimate, *Time* magazine, and its conservative editor, had fifty communists secretly employed there during the 1930s and 1940s.[89] The large radio networks of CBS and NBC tended to favor Roosevelt and his policies. This was not so much out of sympathy but fear, since Federal Communications Commission (FCC) intervention, along with antitrust actions, could be brought against the networks if they were too hostile to the administration.[90] Most radio commentators were therefore prointerventionist, including the war correspondent Edward R. Murrow, the liberal commentator Drew Pearson, and Walter Winchell's tabloid broadcasts.[91]

Yamamoto's attack on American morale backfired, since Pearl Harbor ended the rancorous debate over the United States' involvement in World War II. Michigan senator Arthur Vandenberg, for instance, had been arranging newspaper clippings about his leadership of the isolationist movement when he learned of the attack. Abandoning his scrapbooks, he immediately telephoned Roosevelt to pledge his support. Neither were the isolationist newspapers slow in shifting their position. "Japan has asked for it. Now she is going to get it," raged the editors of the *Los Angeles Times*. "Recriminations are useless and we doubt that they will be indulged in," wrote the fiercely isolationists editors of the *Chicago Daily Tribune.* "Certainly not by us. All that matters today is that we are in the war." Nostalgia has often exaggerated the solidarity of the American people during World War II. Yet it is also true that the Japanese attack did what Roosevelt, or any American, could not, by uniting the American people in determination to win the war. An hour after Roosevelt declared December 7 "a date which will live in infamy," Congress had declared war on Japan with but one dissenting vote.[92] Nevertheless, waging total war on the Axis did not mean peace between Roosevelt and his critics.[93]

Speaking to a group of African American newspaper editors a few hours before Congress declared war, army chief of staff George C. Marshall highlighted the media's importance to total war. "Never," Marshall stated, "has the press of our country been called upon to play a greater part in the functioning and the strengthening of democracy than now lies before it. It is more essential than ever before that all our people have prompt and uninterrupted access to the truth, and all the help that wise editorial interpretation can give them."[94] Marshall understood that the armies required for a total war would come from the civilian population. In retirement, he reflected that the prewar volunteer army "had no representation by vote. A citizen army can vote, and it can get the attention of the press and the attention of Congress in a moment. . . . That was great political power. We have seen the manifestations of it in one way or another."[95] Yet, as the United States was plunged into total war, Marshall probably could not have imagined how integral the press and public opinion would be to how World War II was fought.

Chapter One

"You Shoot Bullets with Your Typewriter"

Two days after the Japanese bombed Pearl Harbor, President Franklin D. Roosevelt spoke over the radio to the largest national audience ever assembled to hear a single speaker. Roosevelt had utilized the radio to deliver "fireside chats" during the Depression. Yet never had the topic been so grave. With reports from Pearl Harbor still flowing in, nobody really knew the extent of the disaster. Nevertheless, the president intended to use the address to explain the future of the war to the American people.

It is thus significant that Roosevelt dedicated a large section of the speech to the role of the press in wartime. He promised to release all news not harmful to the war effort and cautioned against rumors. False news did more than damage morale, Roosevelt explained; it could cause military harm. For example, he continued, the Japanese claimed they obtained complete naval superiority of the Pacific, which was "an old trick of propaganda. . . . [The] purposes of such fantastic claims are, of course, to spread fear and confusion among us, and to goad us into revealing military information."[1] The president's message was clear: in total war the press was a weapon. Or, as his adviser Harry Hopkins told a reporter, "You shoot bullets with your typewriter."[2]

"The papers are not running the war," Roosevelt stated at a press conference a few hours before his national address.[3] Yet Historians are divided on this question. Some writers argue that Roosevelt resisted public pressure for an offensive in the Pacific or a hasty invasion of France.[4] Nevertheless, there is a large body of scholarship demonstrating that Roosevelt took media and public opinion extremely seriously and that it even entered strategic decision-making.[5]

Reexamining the strategic problems during 1942 resolves this historiographic tension. To begin with, scholars now view Roosevelt as more involved in directing strategy during World War II than previously believed.[6] Since Germany was the strongest enemy, and because of the dangerous situation of both Britain and the Soviet Union, the president understood the Nazis must be defeated first. Yet US forces were too weak to create a second front by launching a cross-channel landing in France. Domestically, Roosevelt was under considerable pressure to focus on the war in the Pacific.[7] Indeed, though historians often view the Germany First policy as the most important strategic decision of the war, it can be argued that events during America's first year in World War II proved that the strategy existed in name only.[8] The Japanese advance toward Australia by sea was checked at the Battle of the Coral Sea, and their carrier strength was decisively broken a few months later at the battle for Midway. Likewise, the major offensives in the Solomon Islands and New Guinea were begun months before any US offensive against Germany. When that offensive did come it was not directly against the Germans, or even in Europe, but against the Vichy French in North Africa. It would take more than a year and a half before US forces set foot on European soil in Sicily. Even Roosevelt pressed for an immediate strike against Japan, which eventually took the form of the Doolittle Raid. In this light, Roosevelt appears more pragmatist than strategist.

This chapter argues that Roosevelt's overall strategic goal for 1942 was to implement a Germany First strategy. But finite Allied resources and the US public's desire for revenge against Japan limited his strategic choices. Therefore, Roosevelt implemented a media campaign to accomplish his strategic ends. In the days after Pearl Harbor, the White House and its allies in the media successfully linked Germany to Japan's attack on Hawaii. Casting Germany as the main opponent allowed Roosevelt to pursue the Germany First strategy without losing US support. Yet the president also knew that public support would likely be drawn to any place US troops fought, a conclusion confirmed by swings in public opinion surveys. For Roosevelt, as historian Mark A. Stoler writes, "the date was much more important than the actual location of the first American offensive action in the European theater."[9] Therefore, Roosevelt undertook three military actions to solidify public support. First, he ordered Douglas MacArthur from the beleaguered Philippines, which satisfied the large number of Americans who saw both the general as a military genius and the Pacific as the main theater of the war. Second, Roosevelt pushed for at least a symbolic strike against Japan almost from the start of the war. This occurred with the Doolittle Raid in April 1942, which demonstrated that the Pacific Theater would not be forgotten and boosted Roosevelt's popularity. Third, seeing that a cross-channel landing in France was impossible in 1942, Roosevelt, nevertheless, understood that it was essential to have US troops fighting somewhere against the European Axis and approved the invasion of French North Africa.

All three actions also had unintended consequences that shaped the course of World War II. The rescue of MacArthur to satisfy his supporters also required the Pacific Theater to be split between him and the US Navy. The Doolittle Raid made the Japanese consolidate their plans to attack Midway and also to launch a campaign of revenge against China. The invasion of North Africa set the Allies on the road to becoming more involved in the Mediterranean Theater in 1943 and eventually forestalled a landing in France until 1944.

Germany First?

For the advocates of a Germany First strategy, it was unfortunate that Japan, not Germany, attacked the United States. When Roosevelt met with his cabinet on December 7, Henry Stimson, secretary of war, highlighted the "importance of a declaration of war against Germany before the indignation of the people was over." Roosevelt declined, explaining he planned to make a full case against Germany over the radio on December 9.[10] Even Hitler declaring war on the United States a few days later did not change the fact that the Japanese had bombed Pearl Harbor. With the help of the press, Roosevelt spent the next month successfully arguing that Germany was the main enemy and must be defeated first.

During the December 9 fireside chat, Roosevelt began by noting that Japan's surprise attack fit a pattern of Axis aggression. Japan had moved from paralleling Germany's and Italy's conquests to "actual collaboration so well calculated that all continents of the world, and all the oceans, are now considered by Axis Strategists as one gigantic battlefield." Roosevelt added, "Your Government knows that for weeks Germany has been telling Japan that if Japan did not attack the United States Japan would not share in dividing the spoils with Germany when peace came." Japan was conducting their strategy as part of a joint plan with the Nazis. "Remember always," Roosevelt concluded, "that Germany and Italy, regardless of any formal declaration of war, consider themselves at war with the United States at this moment."[11] Attacking Germany, the President implied, was just another way to destroy Japan.

Other members of the administration had already laid the groundwork for connecting Germany to Pearl Harbor. Donald Nelson, chairman of the War Production Board, stated in a radio address on December 7, "We are face to face with attack directed primarily from Berlin."[12] On December 9, the White House press secretary, Steve Early, explained that "obviously Germany did all it could to push Japan into the war. It was the German hope that if the United States and Japan could be pushed into war that such a conflict would put an end to the lend-lease program."[13] Later in January, the Office of the Coordinator of Information encouraged journalists to make a propaganda broadcast telling the Japanese that they were being used by the Germans.[14] These statements, and others like them, were given wide attention in the press.

Such talk fell on fertile media ground. "This was never an 'intra-European war,'" the *Washington Post* editorialized on December 8. "It was intended from the beginning as a world war. . . . It would be fantastic folly to think of the Japanese engaging on their cosmic adventure alone."[15] Columnist Westbrook Pegler took it for granted that Hitler was the "principal enemy."[16] On the same page, Walter Lippmann stated that Hitler was mistaken if he thought the United States would focus only on Japan. "No victory we can win in the Pacific," Lippmann observed, "could give us security if we had then to turn around and face Hitler victorious in Europe and Africa and in the Atlantic."[17] Columnist Dorothy Thompson wrote in the *Daily Boston Globe* that Germany was behind the attack since it wanted Britain and the United States fighting Japan.[18] The next day the *Globe* reported that in "Congressional circles" it was being debated whether German pilots bombed Pearl Harbor.[19] This oft-repeated charge is usually chalked up to American racism toward the Japanese.[20] But it also was part of a larger pattern linking the two Axis powers. The editors at the *Los Angeles Times* believed that the charge that Japan "was inspired by Germany to curtail our lease-lend aid to Britain is probably true."[21] As a December 12 survey of editorial opinion summarized, "Even prior to the formal announcement of hostilities against the United States by Germany and Italy there was general recognition that the Japanese action was part of an Axis plan, that the Pacific constituted only a minor theater of a world-wide conflict. The essential qualities of the war's scope and nature seem to be understood by the great majority of the American press."[22] Much of the press was willing to believe Germany partly responsible for Pearl Harbor.

Roosevelt's address linking Germany and Japan also received press support. "The democratic nations know that there can be no security, no peace, nothing but a poisoned, chaotic and terrorized world," wrote the *New York Times* in an editorial praising Roosevelt's speech, "so long as the madmen of Japan and Germany stand at the head of unbeaten armies."[23] The editors of the *Daily Boston Globe* agreed: "As the President made plain in his radio address to the nation, this country has now recognized openly the unity of plan which ties the three Axis members together."[24] The idea lingered. As late as March 1942, Pierre J. Huss was still writing in *Cosmopolitan* that Hitler "jumped the Japs on us."[25]

How successful was the Roosevelt administration in convincing the American people that Germany was the main enemy? This is difficult to answer since public opinion fluctuated as news from different theaters captured the public's attention. When asked who they believed the main enemy was, 31.7 percent of people polled responded Japan and 58.8 percent said Germany in late December 1941. By the middle of February, after a string of Japanese victories, the number changed to 37.5 percent for Japan, with only 41 percent viewing Germany as the main enemy. A March 2, 1942, report delivered to Harry Hopkins explained, "The concentration of attention on Pacific fighting is reflected by an increased public disposition to regard Japan either as our prime enemy or as equal in importance with Germany."[26] By April, after even more Japanese victories, polls found that 46 percent of Americans saw Germany as the main enemy and 35 percent said Japan. Yet, 62 percent believed the United States should focus on Japan first. This may have been the result, as the following chapter demonstrates, of Douglas MacArthur's press campaign for the Southwest Pacific to be made the main theater of the war. By mid-July, after the massive Japanese defeat at Midway, this would shift to 40 percent believing that the United States should concentrate on Germany and only 21 percent for Japan and another 23 percent saying both.[27]

The successful linkage of the Axis partners set the stage for the editorial support for Roosevelt's Germany First approach. For instance, navy secretary Frank Knox drew criticism along with much editorial praise after stating, "The enemy who, before all others, must be defeated first is not Japan, not Italy, but Hitler." "Japan," Knox added, "like Italy, is just the tool of Hitler."[28] "The average American," the *New York Times* stated in its defense of Knox, "knows that a victory over Japan would bring us no security whatever so long as Hitler remained unconquered, whereas the defeat of Hitler would enormously hasten the defeat of his Eastern ally."[29] The editors at the *Los Angeles Times* also defended Knox, explaining that "when you set out to kill a rattlesnake you do not . . . begin by whacking at its tail. Hitler and Germany are the head of the collective Axis rattlesnake."[30] While noting that Knox's statement was criticized by the right-leaning *Chicago Tribune* and the left-leaning New York daily *PM*, a government survey of editorial opinion concluded that "despite such anxieties, however, the press, as a whole, heartily approved Secretary Knox's definition of the Far East as a secondary theater of the war."[31] In January 1942, at least, most of the editors of America's newspapers continued to support the Germany First strategy.

A few months later a collection of editorials from mid–April 1942 gathered by the Intelligence and Analysis Branch of the War Department's Bureau of Public Relations showed that public opinion realized the importance of military action in Europe. "It is hard to lose Bataan," wrote David Lawrence in the *Evening Star*, "but, psychologically, as the Philippines are for the moment written off, the attention of the Nation can be fixed on the all-important European front in the coming months of decisive warfare." The reasons often reflected the thinking of policy makers, with Raymond Clapper of the *Philadelphia Inquirer* noting that Russia needed assistance in knocking Germany out of the war. His colleague Kirke L. Simpson added that Japan might be a distraction for both the Soviet Union and the Western Allies. Writing in *Newsweek* Ernest Lindley recalled that Knox had been heavily criticized for promoting a Germany First strategy in January. "Knox could make the same speech today without raising a storm," Lindley believed.[32] Thus, the report demonstrates that Roosevelt's campaign to focus on Germany first was at least partially successful.

Like public opinion, editorial opinion also fluctuated with the military situation. As the situation in the Pacific worsened, an administration survey of editorial opinion noted that "American newspapers have found their attention drawn from the West to the East. Most of them retain their intellectual conviction that the war is indivisible. In general, they agree with Secretary Knox that the Pacific is no more than a secondary theater of the war. But their emotions are now mainly concerned with the Far Eastern conflict."[33] A week later, another survey of editorial opinion noted that although Knox's remarks had received general editorial support, "there appears now to be almost complete agreement in the press that the Far East is at least the most urgent, if not the most important, sector of the war today."[34] Another study in March 1942 likewise found that the vast majority of editorials focused on Japan and that the "mass of editorial opinion does not yet regard the war with Germany and Japan as one war, and our strategy as one of global strategy."[35] Yet another survey found that while there was an increasing demand for action, it was directed toward both Japan and Germany.[36] Two conclusions can thus be drawn. First, even though editorial opinion fluctuated with military events, it never reached a point that prevented Roosevelt from pursuing a Germany First strategy. Second, Roosevelt understood that military action would automatically create press and public support for the theater in which it took place. This understanding drove his planning during the first year of the war.

Roosevelt's belief that public opinion could be shaped by military action was highlighted at the Arcadia Conference with US and British leaders that began on December 23, 1941. After a wide-ranging discussion of possible operations around the globe, including sending US troops to replace British soldiers in Ireland (Operation Magnet) and landings in French North Africa (Operation Gymnast), Roosevelt stated that "he considered it very important to morale, to give this country a feeling that they are in the war, to give the Germans the reverse effect, to have American troops somewhere in action fighting across the Atlantic."[37] Churchill agreed and "reiterated the principle that the American Armies must get into this war as soon as possible, and not only get into the war but we must take the offensive against the Germans and against the Japanese to bolster up not only the people of the U.S. but also the other nations fighting on the side of Great Britain and the United States."[38] George C. Marshall agreed. Debating a plan for landing in North Africa with the Combined Chiefs of Staff a few days later, Marshall stated that the "operation might result in the first contact between American and German troops. Success should not be jeopardized by failure to provide adequate means. A failure in this first venture would have an extremely adverse effect on the morale of the American people."[39] For Roosevelt, Churchill, and Marshall, US public opinion was an important factor in debating the first US offensive of World War II.

The First Hero: MacArthur's Escape from the Philippines

Despite Roosevelt's early marshalling of media and public opinion, the Germany First strategy was challenged from the beginning by General Douglas MacArthur and others who saw the Pacific as the main theater of World War II. The unfolding tragedy in the Philippines would lend weight to this view. Since the Spanish-American War, the United States had ruled over the Philippine commonwealth with the goal of granting it eventual independence. With this end in mind, institutions had been established, leaders groomed, an army raised, and a date set in 1946 for independence. But the islands stood directly in the way of the Japanese southwestward advance. To meet the coming invasion was an ill-prepared force of Americans and Filipinos commanded by MacArthur. Not only would the Philippines dominate the headlines in the months after Pearl Harbor, but it was at this time that the press made MacArthur one of the heroes of World War II. Media pressure would cause Roosevelt to order MacArthur to escape from the Philippines and thus reshape the strategy in the Pacific to such an extent that it would challenge the Germany First priority.

It is difficult to imagine Roosevelt making the same decision if the man who fought the first US ground battle of World War II had been anyone other than one of the most remarkable figures in military history. MacArthur was born in 1880 to a Union war hero and an unreconstructed Southern belle. He attended the US Military Academy at West Point, where not only did he graduate first in his class, but his cumulative academic score was the third highest in the academy's history.[40] MacArthur emerged from World War I with a major general's commission, the admiration of his troops, and a reputation for bravery attested to by two Distinguished Service Crosses, seven Silver Stars, and a slew of foreign decorations.[41] Though MacArthur was a devout Christian, there was something about him, historian Stephen Ambrose observed, that "encouraged blasphemy."[42] This came from his gift for the English language that rivaled Churchill's. It was a talent that would both help his press relations and damage his reputation with historians. The eloquence of his memoirs, for example, was overshadowed by self-serving distortion of facts, his need to mention every medal, and the reproduction of a seemingly endless collection of letters of congratulations from world leaders, accompanied by passive-aggressive sniping at old enemies. It was also reflected in his communiqués, which made him famous, but his press relations infamous. To balance his incredible talents with his weaknesses poses a challenge for any assessment of MacArthur.

World War II caught MacArthur in a desperate situation. As Japanese planes returned from Pearl Harbor, Marshall cabled MacArthur to inform

him of the attack and ended by stating that he had "the complete confidence
of the War Department and we assure you of every possible assistance and
support within our power."[43] Marshall's cable reached a country that had an
ill-equipped military and a commander who was paralyzed by the news of
Pearl Harbor. That was also what the Japanese Air Force found a few hours
later when they destroyed nearly half of MacArthur's planes on the ground,
followed soon after by a ground invasion.[44] With the Japanese massive offensive sweeping across the Pacific, with much of the US Pacific Fleet at the
bottom of Pearl Harbor, with British naval power in the East neutralized by
the sinking of *The Prince of Wales* and *Repulse*, with the Filipino and US armies ill-equipped, and with his own air force largely destroyed, MacArthur
was trapped in a military disaster.

From the beginning of the battle, the US media nevertheless showered
MacArthur with incredibly positive publicity. "The situation in Luzon has
developed in favor of the defenders," incorrectly proclaimed the editors of
the *Washington Post* a few days after Pearl Harbor, "thanks to the skill and
courage of the Philippine and American forces under the superb leadership
of Gen. Douglas MacArthur."[45] Such stories continued even as conditions
in the Philippines worsened. A report to Roosevelt on media opinion during
the first week of February noted that "*news stories paid increased attention to
the exploits of General MacArthur and his men*. Each Japanese attack repulsed
was headlined, each individual act of heroism dramatized and the General
himself all but apotheosized."[46] Around this time, the *Chicago Daily Tribune*
and the *Los Angeles Times* printed full-page pictures of "the gallant defender
of the Philippines," more commonly known as MacArthur, while the *Daily
Boston Globe* and the *Washington Post* serialized biographies of MacArthur
titled "A Soldier's Story" and "MacArthur the Magnificent," respectively.[47]

Nor was the media adulation accidental, since MacArthur had extensive
experience in working with the press. America's entry into World War I
found MacArthur handling the press and censorship for the secretary of war.
His tenure was short, but his conduct so outstanding that when the press
heard that MacArthur was leaving, twenty-nine reporters collectively sent
a letter to the secretary of war lavishly praising MacArthur for censoring
them.[48] During World War I, he roamed the battlefields of France with a
silk scarf and riding crop. This attire distinguished him from other officers,
boosting morale by his presence and attracting newsmen. In World War II,
aviator sunglasses and a long-stemmed corncob pipe served the same purpose.[49] "The general always looks as if he has received the best possible news,
and his calm assurance sets an example for his men," the AP gushed. "His
heavily braided hat, worn at a jaunty angle, his long brown cigarette holder,
brown jacket, and silk scarf are well known to troops on the firing lines. At
62 he looks far younger."[50]

MacArthur also employed more forceful methods of ensuring positive publicity. He wrote or edited many of his communiqués and imposed strict censorship, which meant that most of the news coming from the Philippines was reviewed by him. One hundred nine of the 142 grandly worded communiqués that came out of his headquarters during the defense of the Philippines mentioned only MacArthur by name, often attached to phrases such as "MacArthur's right flank." One reporter even began signing his bylines "with General MacArthur on the Bataan Front." Misstatements and rumors also worked themselves into the communiqués. A few days after Pearl Harbor, a false story began circulating that the Twenty-First Philippine Division had repelled a major Japanese landing on Luzon. The story, however, was confirmed by MacArthur's headquarters, and headlines around America trumpeted a major Allied victory. The next day another false account, this one of Captain Colin P. Kelly Jr.'s sinking of the Japanese battleship *Haruna*, became a major news story and was also confirmed by MacArthur's headquarters and believed by military leaders in Washington.[51] The grandiloquence and questionable accuracy of these communiqués hurt the morale of MacArthur's troops.[52] "It seems strange that a man of MacArthur's intelligence," the naval historian E. B. Potter observed, "should not have realized that his famous communiqués . . . would ultimately sully his reputation. They were generally taken at face value by the current reading public, but many contemporary officers and journalists and all future historians, able to compare the general's publicity with the facts, would note the disparity between the two."[53]

If US leaders were taken in by MacArthur's communiqués, however, they had little excuse. One message to Washington, signed "MacArthur" but almost certainly not written or seen by him, read, "I will endeavor from now on to send daily reports for your press release section. This report may at times contain propaganda and where it differs from my operation reports the latter will be accurate. From now on I must rely entirely on your efforts as regards influencing public opinion."[54] Washington was happy to help. "You had the wisdom to appreciate the importance of propaganda warfare as an adjunct to the actual battles you were fighting," gushed Roosevelt's speechwriter Robert Sherwood to MacArthur a few months later, "and you sent us explicit and most valuable instructions as to the type of propaganda you wanted. We attempted to put all these instructions into immediate effect. We obtained from the President statements and proclamations that you asked for."[55] Indeed, as grand as his public utterances could be, they were accompanied by a long string of deeply worrying private cables from MacArthur.[56] On at least one occasion MacArthur even warned Washington not to publicize positive material from one of his dispatches.[57] Nor could the press claim they were misled, since the War Department read some of MacArthur's more troubling secret cables to reporters, even though they would not allow them to be published.[58]

It is also true that MacArthur was receiving plenty of reports from Washington that help was on the way. These assurances were untrue, since as early as December 15, War Department supply officers had determined that while they would try to send assistance from Australia, it likely would not reach the Philippines.[59] Historian Arthur Herman observes that Washington "continued to send messages that would encourage hope of coming relief without actually lying to" MacArthur. This MacArthur passed along in his communiqués. When help did not come, it was MacArthur who took the blame.[60]

Perhaps tacitly admitting that the only help that was coming was moral support, US officials did their best to build up MacArthur and his soldiers in the press. On December 12, Roosevelt made public a statement to MacArthur where he offered "personal and official congratulations on the fine stand you are making."[61] Eight days later, Roosevelt promoted MacArthur, making him the only four-star general in the US Army besides Marshall.[62] On New Year's Day, Stimson noted in his diary, "At the press conference I had quite a large number of questions, mainly about the campaign in the Philippines in which I took occasion to defend General MacArthur and the masterly campaign which he has been carrying on against tremendous odds."[63] The occasion of MacArthur's birthday was marked by flattering speeches in Congress and by a public message from Roosevelt congratulating him on "the magnificent stand that you and your men are making."[64] In his fireside chats on February 23, Roosevelt stated, "General MacArthur has magnificently exceeded the previous estimates of endurance; and he and his men are gaining eternal glory therefor."[65] Dwight D. Eisenhower, who was then working in the War Plans Division and had previously served under MacArthur in the Philippines, wrote after the war that Marshall was also interested in improving the morale in the Philippines by distributing unit citations, awarding promotions, and giving medals to MacArthur.[66] Thus, the press was not acting alone in praising MacArthur and making him the first American hero of the war.

One unintended consequence of this press adulation was to make MacArthur a political liability. On December 25, 1941, Stimson received a visit from Henry "Hap" Arnold, head of the US Army Air Force, Eisenhower, and Marshall. They showed him a paper detailing a meeting between Roosevelt and Churchill the night before where the president reportedly discussed sending US reinforcements meant for MacArthur to Britain. Stimson called Hopkins and threatened to resign but was assured that the paper was untrue. Stimson, his Christmas "pretty well mashed up," dictated to his diary that the paper "would have raised any amount of trouble for the President if it had gotten into the hands of an unfriendly press."[67]

Another potential media crisis came with a desperate message from Manuel Quezon, the president of the Philippines, asking Roosevelt to give the islands self-government. Quezon would then declare the islands neutral and both the Americans and the Japanese would withdraw their troops. The message was accompanied by a letter from MacArthur that could be read as a tacit endorsement. Eisenhower wrote after the war that "such a confession of weakness would have had unfortunate psychological reverberations" if it had become public.[68] Conversely, historian Kenneth S. Davis speculated that refusal to remove doomed US troops "when knowledge of it became public . . . would expose the President to possible devastating fire from those American millions who had been conditioned by the conservative media, aided and abetted by what amounted to 'appeasement' by the administration itself, to regard MacArthur as one of the great captains in all history."[69] Tactfully refusing such an absurd demand cost a huge amount of time for Washington leaders, but reminded them that the loss of the Philippines and MacArthur would be costly politically. In the same message in which he denied Quezon's request, Roosevelt told MacArthur that he should begin making plans for Quezon and his own family to evacuate the Philippines.[70]

Roosevelt first brought up rescuing MacArthur at a December 27 White House meeting.[71] Marshall and Stimson were pushing for unity of Allied command in the Pacific. Roosevelt suggested the British general Archibald Wavell might be a compromise choice to command Allied forces in the Pacific, but the president also suggested MacArthur.[72] That very day, according to the *Chicago Daily Tribune*, the idea of placing MacArthur in charge of Allied armies in the Pacific was being publicly voiced by others in London and Washington.[73] Yet, after being assured by Arnold that MacArthur could be evacuated from the Philippines, Roosevelt settled on Wavell. For their part, the British accepted the suggestion, but worried that US public opinion would turn against them if US forces under Wavell's command met with disaster. Thus, Wavell was appointed the commander of the American, British, Dutch, Australian Command (ABDACOM).[74]

Despite this new command structure, Allied forces in the Pacific were falling back on every front. On January 11, the Japanese advanced into the Dutch East Indies, while on the same day the carrier USS *Saratoga* was attacked off Hawaii by a Japanese sub. On January 15, the Japanese invaded Burma. By January 23, the Japanese were moving south into New Britain, Borneo, New Ireland, and finally the Solomon Islands, threatening Australia. As MacArthur's forces in the Philippines took defeat after defeat, the British in Singapore surrendered on February 15, 1942.[75]

As the situation in the Pacific worsened, the press increasingly began calling for MacArthur's rescue. On February 15, the *Chicago Daily Tribune*'s Walter Trohan wrote about "military experts" who said MacArthur could "still be saved for the American army if his second in command . . . should be made commander of the American defense forces and told to order MacArthur out."[76] At a press conference on February 17, Roosevelt was asked to comment "on the agitation to have General (Douglas) MacArthur ordered out of the Philippines and given overall command." The president evaded the question.[77] On February 26, the *Washington Post* published an editorial advocating MacArthur's rescue, claiming the alternative would "be worse than the disaster of Pearl Harbor many times over."[78]

More ominous was the growing pressure to put MacArthur in overall command of the war. This began on December 17, 1941, when Trohan noted rumors were flying that MacArthur and Admiral William Leahy, then the ambassador to Vichy France, would be made commanders of the Allied armies and navies. "The suggestion was advanced almost simultaneously in the house of commons and in Washington," wrote Trohan, "that the supreme allied military command be given to Gen. MacArthur."[79] On February 13, the *Tribune*'s editorial page put forward the need for an overall commander in chief for the armed forces and suggested MacArthur.[80] "Bring home Gen. MacArthur," former Republican presidential candidate Wendell Willkie had proclaimed the previous day. "Place him at the very top. Keep bureaucratic and political hands off him. Give him the responsibility and the power of coordinating all the armed forces of the nation to their most effective use."[81] Willkie's remarks did not go unchallenged. Though *Time* magazine observed that "the U.S. echoed Willkie in the press, in Congress, [and] on the street," it concluded, "MacArthur seemed to be doing all right where he was."[82] The Democratic House majority leader, John McCormack, took a more direct swing at Willkie, replying that "if the Philippines are lost all of us hope that Gen. MacArthur will leave and that his great military leadership will be used in other fields, but the thought cannot escape my mind that if Gen. MacArthur were ordered to leave the Philippines before it was actually necessary that such orders would be unwise and subject to criticism."[83] Yet Roosevelt could hardly ignore the growing clamor to recall MacArthur and put him in charge of the Pacific war.

Even more concerning, MacArthur was becoming a rallying point for those critical of the Roosevelt administration's conduct of the war.[84] On Corregidor, MacArthur's officers openly told reporters to write dispatches to appeal to the American people for help. The reporters needed little persuasion. One such story was about US soldiers on Bataan who had taken up an ironic collection to buy a bomber for themselves. Since it was well known that MacArthur censored the news from the Philippines, reporters correctly read the story as a sign of disagreement with Washington.[85] This led a White House correspondent to inquire whether "MacArthur is a little at odds with the high command here as to the possibility of reinforcing him." The president's rambling and incoherent reply dodged the question.[86] Yet, as William Strand of the *Chicago Daily Tribune* wrote a few days later, many political leaders in Washington were wondering why more was not being done to help MacArthur when $13 billion had been sent to foreign governments.[87] Even the Japanese press was demanding—facetiously—that Roosevelt send troops to MacArthur instead of Ireland.[88] And while a survey of editorial opinion found that little of the criticism was directed against the president personally, "there is a manifest feeling of frustration, a loss of confidence in leadership."[89]

What the president could not tell the reporters was that he had already ordered MacArthur from the Philippines a week before his press conference. Along with not wanting to lose a public hero, Marshall wanted MacArthur in command of ABDACOM. Not only had the Australians asked for MacArthur, but it would place him in a position for the army to have more control over the navy, whose performance up to this point in the war neither Stimson nor Marshall—nor MacArthur for that matter—found inspiring.[90] "Message to MacArthur was approved by president and dispatched," Eisenhower grumbled to his diary on February 23. "I'm dubious about the thing. I cannot help believing that we are disturbed by editorials and reacting to 'public opinion' rather than to military logic. 'Pa' Watson [Roosevelt's military adviser] is certain we must get MacArthur out, as being worth 'five army corps.'" After observing that MacArthur was "doing a good job where he is," Eisenhower shrewdly observed, "but I'm doubtful that he'd do so well in more complicated situations. Bataan is made to order for him. It's in the public eye; it has made him a public hero; it has all the essentials of drama; and he is the acknowledged king on the spot. If brought out, public opinion will force him into a position where his love of the limelight may ruin him."[91]

MacArthur still had to be persuaded to leave. Fleeing his doomed garrison would hardly make him look heroic. Likewise, if the story got out that MacArthur had refused to leave, it could hurt Roosevelt politically while adding to MacArthur's legend.[92] In reply to Roosevelt's suggestion that his family should leave with Quezon, MacArthur had replied that he was "deeply appreciative of the inclusion of my own family in this list but they and I have decided that they will share the fate of the garrison."[93] On February 22, 1942, a direct order from Roosevelt arrived ordering MacArthur to Australia to assume the command of the Southwest Pacific Area (SWPA).[94] At first, MacArthur refused and began planning to resign and join the defense as a volunteer. But his staff convinced him that forces must be waiting for him in Australia to rescue the garrison. Finally, MacArthur agreed, but requested that he be allowed to pick the moment of his departure for the right "psychological time" to prevent a collapse. "MacArthur says, in effect, 'Not now,'" wrote Eisenhower in his diary. "I think he is right. This psychological warfare business is going to fall right into the lap of WPD [War Plans Division]."[95] One factor in MacArthur's planning may have been the media, since on March 9, a summary of his portrayal in the press over the last six days was prepared and presented to his chief of staff. With only these news summaries as a guide, one could be forgiven for thinking MacArthur was winning the battle for Bataan. One paper even suggested that MacArthur's face should be added to Mount Rushmore. However, it was an entry from the *Army and Navy Journal* on March 9 suggesting that MacArthur was about to be made commander of the Allied forces in the Southwest Pacific that likely caught the general's eye. The paper editorialized that such a move "would inspire all United Nations to greater resistance [and] that [the] Filipino people would feel that he had not abandoned them."[96] It is unknown whether the document had any bearing on his decision, but two days later MacArthur decided it was time to leave.

At dusk on March 11, MacArthur, his wife Jean, and their son Arthur were driven in silence to South Dock, where PT-41 was waiting along with three other PT boats and the small group of officers MacArthur had chosen to accompany him to Australia. The growing night was illuminated from time to time by the flash of the big guns of Corregidor as the MacArthurs boarded the rickety little craft that was to carry the group through the Japanese blockade. By 8:00 p.m., the small flotilla had gone through the minefields, and as they began the journey, enemy signal flashes showed that the Japanese knew their blockade would be tested that night. Silhouettes of enemy ships appeared on the horizon, but the choppy sea hid the boats. Dawn brought new dangers when one of the PT boats mistook PT-41 for a Japanese destroyer and, despairing of flight, broke off its attack only at the last moment. Stopping to rest and hide during the day, the PT boats embarked again at dark only to run straight into a Japanese warship, which somehow missed them. Early in the morning of March 13, the small convoy reached Cagayan, where a B-17 transported MacArthur to Australia.[97]

MacArthur's escape presented its own public relations problems. Roosevelt knew from opinion polls that about half of the US public would resent MacArthur abandoning his garrison in the Philippines. Japanese and Nazi propaganda would also be sure to paint the escape as cowardly. The pollster Gerald B. Lambert suggested that Roosevelt hold a press conference to highlight the fact that MacArthur left only after a direct presidential order.[98] At his press conference on March 17, however, Roosevelt declined to take direct credit and instead delivered a warning about Nazi propaganda before reading a statement saying:

> I know that every man and woman in the United States admires with me General MacArthur's determination to fight to the finish with his men in the Philippines. But I also know that every man and woman is in agreement that all important decisions must be made with a view toward the successful termination of the war. Knowing this, I am sure that every

American, if faced individually with the question as to where General MacArthur could best serve his country, could come to only one answer.

The president added, "In other words, he will be more useful in Supreme Command of the whole Southwest Pacific then [*sic*] if he had stayed in Bataan Peninsula."[99] It was also to avoid public criticism that Marshall successfully pressed for MacArthur to be awarded the Congressional Medal of Honor. As Marshall remembered later, "I wanted to do anything I could to prevent them from saying anything about his [MacArthur's] leaving Corregidor with his troops all out there in this perilous position."[100] In a letter to Stimson, the chief of staff explained that "I am certain that this action will meet with popular approval, both within and without the armed forces, and will have a constructive morale value."[101] MacArthur would be the only former public relations officer to receive the Medal of Honor.[102]

The administration need not have worried. "It was too much good news at once;" exalted a survey of editorial opinion, "the type fonts were inadequate to the occasion. Reporters on the scene were unabashedly exultant. . . . The deep spell of depression which had been cast upon the press by the news of the battle of Java was completely swept aside." The survey could not find a single comment against MacArthur's transfer to Australia. "President Roosevelt did it," proclaimed the highly anti-Roosevelt New York Daily News Syndicate. "The entire credit goes to the President, and there can be no room for anything but the highest, most unstinted praise."[103] The equally anti-Roosevelt *Washington Times-Herald* gushed that rescuing MacArthur from the Philippines was possibly the "only intelligent and universally approved move that the Administration has made." The move was due to "popular demand," the editorial continued. "And the enthusiastic reception of the general's promotion to a more important, although not more patriotic, duty must reveal to Mr. Roosevelt the advisability of heeding the public judgment rather than that of Secretaries Knox and Stimson, or the other courtiers of his Cabinet."[104] Stocks rose to signal Wall Street's approval.[105] Boosting American morale, therefore, had the welcome side benefit of increasing the public's confidence in Roosevelt.

Marshall and Roosevelt used the positive publicity from MacArthur's escape for diplomatic and command purposes. With Wavell's departure and ABDACOM's disintegration, there was a need for a new Allied commander in the Pacific. The *Sydney Telegraph* suggested in early March that MacArthur be named supreme commander.[106] Years later, Marshall recalled that Australia and New Zealand wanted Wavell's deputy, US general George H. Brett, to become the new commander of the Southwest Pacific command. Marshall made no reply, for MacArthur was already leaving the Philippines and the chief of staff was reluctant to suggest him as the commander until it was known that he had reached Australia. When on March 17 Marshall was informed that MacArthur had arrived safely, he immediately informed the prime ministers of Australia and New Zealand and said that he wanted MacArthur to be the commander in the SWPA and that they should "agree in order to protect MacArthur against Japanese propaganda that he had run out."[107] Roosevelt sent a similar message to Churchill. After noting that Australia and New Zealand had requested an American supreme commander, the president stated that he had recommended MacArthur. Both countries, Roosevelt added, "urge immediate joint press release to avoid [a] leak. This I think highly important if Axis propaganda attacking MacArthur's departure from Philippines is to be forestalled."[108] Not only had media pressure been a driving force behind MacArthur's evacuation from the Philippines, but the need to shield the decision from negative Allied public opinion and Axis propaganda allowed Roosevelt and Marshall to enact their long-term goal of putting MacArthur in command of Allied forces in the South Pacific.

The decision to order MacArthur to Australia thus shaped the command arrangements for the rest of the Pacific War. But MacArthur was only in command of the Southwest Pacific.[109] Nor was the navy about to let an army general control the Pacific, where they saw themselves playing a dominant role. What emerged, as will be explored in more detail in following chapter, was a two-pronged offensive against Japan, with MacArthur advancing army forces from the south and Admiral Chester Nimitz commanding naval forces advancing through the central Pacific. MacArthur would have naval forces assigned to him, and Nimitz would use a greatly expanded marine corps as a naval army. Rather than unite Allied forces in the Pacific, MacArthur's arrival in Australia served to split US resources and jettisoned the age-old principle of unity of command. It also placed one of the most informed and articulate spokesmen for the "Asia First" lobby in a position of considerable influence. Eisenhower saw the danger, worrying "that we will move too heavily in the Southwest. Urging us in that direction now will be: Australians, New Zealanders, our public (wanting support for the hero), and MacArthur. If we tie up our shipping for the SW Pacific, we'll lose this war."[110] Stimson agreed, writing in his diary, "It may mean some difficulties to us in the strategic control of events. MacArthur will make great demands upon us and he will not always be easy to manage in respect to other theatres of action which may become more important than his." But, Stimson added two days later after a press conference, "I think the MacArthur arrival has done a great deal to give the press of this country confidence in the government."[111]

The Second Hero: The Doolittle Raid

As events in the Philippines moved toward their dismal conclusion, a raid occurred that would have profound repercussions both for US public opinion and for the strategic direction of the war. The first bombing of Japanese cities on April 18, 1942, by Lieutenant Colonel James H. Doolittle had the limited objective of improving US morale. Roosevelt pushed for the attack , believing that Americans desperately needed a victory. The president was likewise influenced by media pressure that urgently wanted the United States to begin striking back against Japan. But the raid had strategic results that would profoundly change the Pacific War. It also allowed Roosevelt to demonstrate that the United States was striking back at Japan while focusing on continuing the Germany First strategy.

"From the start of the war," recalled Henry Arnold, "Franklin Roosevelt wanted a bombing raid on Japan proper."[112] This began at a White House meeting on December 21, when Roosevelt inquired "when we would deem it possible to occupy and operate from [air] fields in East China against the Japs."[113] Arnold recalled that Roosevelt hoped the psychological effect of the strike would improve US morale at home coupled with causing the Japanese to worry, and thus forcing them to devote more resources to air defense.[114] Arnold disagreed, arguing that no bombing of Japan should take place unless substantial and sustained damage could be inflicted, which, he believed, would require at least fifty planes.[115] The president, however, continued to press the military for ideas on hitting Japan, stating in a meeting on January 10 and again on January 28 that such action was needed for public morale.[116] As the final proposal for what eventually became the Doolittle Raid stated, "An action of this kind is most desirable now due to the psychological effect on the American public, our allies, and our enemies."[117] It was thus for morale and public opinion that Roosevelt demanded the bombing of Japan.

Media pressure likewise played a role in Roosevelt's eagerness to bomb Japan. An intelligence analysis of editorial opinion delivered to the White House on December 15 stated that there was "almost unanimous endorsement of forceful action against Japan."[118] On December 16, for example, the *Washington Post* ran a story helpfully noting that Tokyo was only seven hundred miles from major air bases in the Soviet Union.[119] Columnist Al Williams of the *Washington News* suggested a month later that the United States bomb Japan by simply "grab[bing] the Soviet air bases in Kamchatka and argue about it afterwards."[120] A summary of newspaper opinions given to the president after the fall of Manila found "numerous newspaper comments demanding aggressive prosecution of the war in general and punishment by bombing of the Japanese in particular."[121] Roosevelt was facing increased political pressure with the disaster at Pearl Harbor and the subsequent investigations often dominating the news, with the Roberts Report on the disaster causing great excitement in the press.[122] After a long discussion over how to handle the Pearl Harbor investigation on the day the Roberts Report was presented to Congress, the president returned to the need to bomb Japan to improve American spirits and hurt Japanese morale.[123] Around this time, Doolittle learned later, Roosevelt was becoming increasingly "impatient about the prospect of operating heavy bombers against Japan from Mongolia." He added, "The President had let it be generally known that he would like to have something sensational happen, because it was politically expedient to get some good news."[124] Media pressure was thus a major contributing factor to Roosevelt's desire to bomb Japan, but it was still unclear how it could be done.

On the evening of January 10, Admiral Ernest King was finishing dinner aboard his flagship, *Vixen*, moored near Washington, DC, when Captain Francis S. Low, one of King's operations officers, asked to speak to him. Low had just returned from Norfolk and, after seeing the new carrier *Hornet*, believed that army two-engine bombers could take off from it, increasing the carrier's striking power.[125] King was aware of the president's desire to bomb Tokyo. In fact, Roosevelt had brought up the subject again earlier that day. King's cold eyes regarded Low for a minute as the submariner prepared to be chewed out by the carrier admiral. "You may have something there," King finally replied, and he ordered Low to contact Captain Donald B. "Wu" Duncan. The two captains set to work and discovered that the army's B-25 bomber could theoretically take off from a carrier, but could not land. Therefore, the bombers would have to be launched from the *Hornet*, fly five hundred miles to Japan, and then land somewhere in China. Impressed, King took the plan to Arnold, who suggested his old friend Jimmy Doolittle be put in charge of the mission.[126]

Arnold had first met Doolittle after the close of World War I when his adjutant had approached him saying, "Colonel, there is a man down at Ream Field whose conduct has been so bad it requires your personal attention." The man was Lieutenant Doolittle, who had gotten bored and bet a buddy that he could sit on the crossbar of the wheels of a biplane as it landed. Doolittle won five dollars and a month on the ground from Arnold, along with his lifelong friendship.[127] As Arnold knew, the daredevil stunts and cocky smirk hid another side of Doolittle. In the interwar years, he was one of the pioneers of aviation, setting records in flight time and studying aeronautics, which eventually culminated in a doctorate from MIT in aeronautic engineering. Doolittle had been the first to perform the supposedly impossible outside loop, the first to fly across the United States in twelve hours, and the first to land a plane using only instruments.[128] "The selection of Doolittle to lead this nearly suicidal mission," wrote Arnold after the war, "was a natural one."[129]

Despite Arnold's postwar recollection, Doolittle hardly appeared the officer to lead such a dangerous and publicly sensitive mission. The last thing the United States needed was a failed attempt to bomb Japan and the loss of a famous aviator. Doolittle realized this, but desperately hoped to go.[130] About a month before the mission, Doolittle was in Arnold's office and broached the subject. Arnold said no. Doolittle argued. Finally, Arnold said that Doolittle could lead the mission if he could get General Millard F. Harmon Jr., Arnold's chief of staff, to agree. Doolittle saluted, dashed down the hall to Harmon's office, and repeated what Arnold had said. "Well, whatever is all right with Hap is certainly all right with me," a surprised Harmon replied. Doolittle thanked him and departed as the telephone rang. But he lingered just long enough to hear Harmon say, "But Hap, I told him he could go."[131]

On the gray morning of April 18, 1942, the first B-25, with Doolittle at the controls, lumbered off USS *Hornet*'s deck and over thirty-foot waves toward Japan. Each of the sixteen planes carried four five-hundred-pound bombs, some with Japanese medals awarded to US sailors during happier days lashed to them.[132] The mission was beginning further away from Japan than planned, because the task force, under the command of Admiral William F. Halsey Jr., had been sighted by a Japanese picket ship.[133] Doolittle sighted Japan eighty miles north of Tokyo and turned his B-25 south.[134] Earlier the US carrier taskforce, now scurrying back toward Pearl Harbor, had picked up another Tokyo broadcast: "Reuters, British news agency, has announced that three American bombers have dropped bombs on Tokyo. This is a most laughable story. They know it is absolutely impossible for enemy bombers to get within five hundred miles of Tokyo."[135] As Doolittle's bombers sped closer to their targets, the Americans could see planes circling over the Japanese mainland, including one carrying the Japanese prime minister Hideki Tojo, who was about to land at the Mito Aviation School when a US bomber streaked past. Doolittle was now coming in low enough that he could see Japanese civilians waving at him.[136] At 12:30, Tokyo time, the US bombers were over their targets.

April 18, 1942, had begun like a typical day for Admiral Matome Ugaki, chief of staff for the Japanese Combined Fleet, and its commander Admiral Yamamoto. Ugaki was a stern man and, as historian Evan Thomas notes, "in a culture that revered the military, [was] a kind of war god."[137] After breakfast, a report had come in from patrol boat *Nitto Maru*. Like other Japanese officers, Ugaki had anticipated that the United States would try to strike Tokyo.[138] Thus, the outer perimeter of the Japanese Empire in the Pacific was screened by a fleet of picket ships. *Nitto Maru* had radioed it had sighted three enemy carriers, then fallen ominously silent. Combined Fleet quickly issued orders to hunt down the task force, to no avail. At 1:30 p.m. Combined Fleet received word that Tokyo had been bombed. "This is more than regrettable," Ugaki confided to his diary, "because this shattered my firm determination never to let the enemy attack Tokyo or the mainland."[139] Ugaki was hardly the only Japanese officer "shattered" by the attack. Pale and depressed, Yamamoto left Ugaki to organize the pursuit and disappeared into his cabin.[140]

The Doolittle Raid succeeded in dealing a psychological blow to Japan. Japanese news reports were at best confused and at worst hysterical. One Japanese broadcast, heard by Halsey's retreating taskforce, postulated:

> There has been no damage at all to military objectives, but several schools, hospitals, and shrines have been destroyed. Thirty primary-school children on their way home from morning classes were machine-gunned in the street. . . . Our patrol planes were already in the air when this armada of Chinese, American, and Russian planes came in from the sea. . . . Nine of the enemy bombers were shot down.[141]

Doolittle's planes had machine-gunned no children, the Japanese had shot down no bombers, and the Soviet Union was not even at war with Japan, but the Japanese media were in no mood to draw distinctions. "The enemy, already withdrawn far to the east," observed Ugaki angrily in his diary, "through radio must have observed our confusion with contempt."[142] That was precisely what Stimson was doing. "The news has come wholly from the Tokio [*sic*] broadcastes [*sic*]," he wrote in his own diary, "but evidently the Japanese have been taken wholly by surprise and were very much agitated by it. . . . It has not been at all well self-controlled."[143] Robert Guillain, a French journalist who witnessed the Japanese reaction, observed new heavy machine guns, barrage balloons, and air-raid drills becoming part of life in Tokyo.[144] As the increased defenses showed, the Japanese were set on edge by the raid. A Japanese schoolgirl wrote at the time, "The bombing of Tokyo and several other cities has brought about a tremendous change in the attitude of our people toward the war. Now things are different; the bombs have dropped here on our homes."[145] Two years would past before US bombers would again return to Tokyo.[146] Psychologically, however, the Doolittle Raid had already shaken Japan.

In the months before the Doolittle Raid, media pressure had increased on the Roosevelt administration to be more aggressive in prosecuting the war. A summary of editorial opinion dispatched to Hopkins on March 9, 1942, by the Office of Facts and Figures stated, "The superficial unity following Pearl Harbor is not only gone but the sentiment favoring acceptance or consideration of a peace offer from Germany, even by Hitler, is by no means insignificant."[147] On March 16, Stimson met with Gifford Pinchot, a Progressive icon from Theodore Roosevelt's days, who warned his old friend that "hostile public opinion to our war effort . . . seems to be growing up throughout the country and said that drastic efforts must be taken to create public unity."[148] The Office of Facts and Figures March 27 report observed, "It seems no overstatement to declare at this juncture that the President is in danger of losing an essential part of the warm confidence with which most American newspapers have supported his conduct of the war. For there is an uneasy belief that he is fumbling."[149] All this was set against continuing Allied defeats in the Far East.

As Roosevelt had hoped, the Doolittle Raid proved a boon to US public opinion. "Tokyo bombed! Yokohama bombed! Kobe bombed!" gleefully noted the editorial page of the *Washington Post*. "After four months of defeats in the Pacific War these words have abruptly electrified the pulse of America and started a chain of repercussions throughout the world."[150] The raid was, according to the headline of the *Baltimore Sun*, the "First Test of Jap Morale on Receiving-End of Total War."[151] Hanson Baldwin, the military columnist for the *New York Times*, wrote that the raid "expressed the will of the American people; morally and psychologically it has uplifted our hearts; morally and psychologically it has unquestionably aided the Navy and set a pattern of offensive action that should be—and probably will be—oft repeated."[152] The *Salt Lake Tribune* followed that theme by declaring that the "Raid Proves Grim Omen for Japanese."[153] The *Tampa Tribune's* headline happily noted that "Bombs Bring Japan Reminder War Can Strike Both Ways."[154] This good news was sorely needed. Nine days before the raid Bataan had surrendered.

The origin of the attack caused a good deal of newspaper speculation.[155] With the Allied nations silent, it was left to the Japanese to state that the planes were B-25 bombers launched from carriers.[156] Baldwin, for one, was unconvinced. "The islands of Metropolitan Japan lie on the fringe of a vast and mysterious continent, never fully explored," Baldwin speculated. "There is room in China and even in Japanese-held Manchukuo for many secret advanced fields . . . fully as well-hidden as those described in James Hilton's 'Lost Horizon.'"[157] Unbeknownst to Baldwin, Roosevelt also had Hilton's novel and his secret valley of Shangri-La on his mind. The president ordered John McCrea, his naval aide, to "ask Ernie King if he doesn't think it would be a good idea to say the raid came from Shangri-La." That way, "every Japanese will be busy looking at his or her equivalent of the *Rand-McNally Atlas*."[158] King consented, and the president got a laugh from the reporters when he announced that the bombers had come "from our new secret base at Shangri-La!"[159]

Doolittle, whose past fame had almost prevented him from going on the raid, now proved to be a huge asset for publicity. Gazing at his crashed bomber and wondering if the rest of his flyers had reached China, Doolittle believed he would be court-martialed, disagreeing with one of his crewmen who insisted he would be made a general and awarded the Medal of Honor. On May 19 Doolittle, a newly minted brigadier general, found himself, without warning, on the way to the White House trying to explain to Arnold and Marshall that he did not deserve the Medal of Honor. "I happen to think you do," snapped Marshall. A delighted Roosevelt agreed and told Doolittle that the raid "had the precise favorable effect on American morale that he had hoped for."[160] This was the first time the identity of the raid's commander had been revealed, a fact that apparently pleased Roosevelt.[161] Many papers put the picture of a beaming president decorating Doolittle on the front page. Thus, the raid's positive publicity redounded to Roosevelt's benefit.

Japanese propaganda focused on vengeance. Guillain recalled that a few days after the raid the Japanese "press, radio and the official propaganda machine launched an extraordinary campaign of racial hatred of a virulence not to be equaled at any other time during the war."[162] The Japanese had managed to capture eight of Doolittle's men who had bailed out over Japanese-controlled territory, and on August 20, 1942, they were put on trial for war crimes. As the flyers were paraded blindfolded before the cameras, the Japanese press unleashed a diatribe of abuse and accusations against them. Convicted ex post facto under a law that made bombing civilians punishable by death, all were convicted, and on October 10, 1942, three were executed. The trial and execution received huge publicity in Japan.[163] *Chubu Nippon*, a Tokyo newspaper, defended the executions since it was "as natural as night follows day for this country to repeat these measures should any enemy airmen again raid it with the same objectives and intentions."[164] "And by the way," stated a Japanese English-language broadcast after the executions, "don't forget, American—make sure that every flier that comes here has a special pass to hell, and rest assured it's strictly a one-way ticket."[165] The executions, therefore, were done not simply as an act of vengeance or to satisfy Japanese public opinion, but also as a warning against future US raids.

The Japanese media onslaught did manage to embarrass the Roosevelt administration. All details of the Doolittle Raid were kept secret, including the fact that some of the flyers had been captured. Japanese radio news—which Allied news agencies monitored—broadcasted that though the State Department denied that any US flyers had been captured, they were also making inquiries of the International Red Cross to locate several airmen. "The American public," explained the Japanese broadcaster, "has a right to know." Japanese radio eventually forced the War Department to admit that eight of Doolittle's fliers had been captured.[166] But there was no mention of any executions. This ended in April 1943 when the UP managed to publish details on the raid for the first time. Facing the angry media, the White House released the news.[167] But not before again being scooped by the Japanese Imperial Headquarters, who took "pleasure in telling the people of the United States the full story." This forced the US government to give a detailed account of the raid, soon followed by Roosevelt's announcement that the Japanese had executed US fliers.[168] This episode is another example of an enemy press keeping its foe honest.

The news of the execution of Doolittle's men happened to coincide with the Second War Loan Drive in the United States.[169] Bond sales soared, reported the *New York Times*, motivated by "a nation-wide wave of anger at the revelation that the Japanese had executed some of the American fliers who bombed Tokyo."[170] The District of Columbia reported the largest bond sale since Pearl Harbor, with an overnight jump of over $4 million. The *Washington Post* relayed stories of angry Americans calling their banks to increase their war bonds.[171] Meanwhile in Chicago bond sales also doubled overnight.[172] Mayor Fiorello La Guardia, speaking at a war bond rally of five thousand angry New Yorkers, bellowed that the United States "will not take it out on innocent soldiers or sailors of Japan that we have captured or may capture. But by the living God, we will take it out on the dirty, contemptible, brutal and bestial gentlemen of Japan at the proper time."[173] "Soon our bombers will be there again," Doolittle stated, "not last year's limited effort, but a devastating attack that will continue until the Japanese Empire crumbles and they beg for mercy."[174] On the floor of the Senate, meanwhile, Tom Steward, a Tennessee Democrat, suggested that all people of Japanese descent living in the United States be arrested in retaliation for the executions.[175] Other senators demanded the Pacific War be taken more seriously.[176] This was echoed in a *Chicago Tribune* editorial that demanded the Roosevelt administration give more attention to MacArthur and the Pacific Theater.[177]

Although the Doolittle Raid had been planned because of media pressure and to boost US morale, the most important consequences were strategic. The bombers had done little material damage, but to Yamamoto, Ugaki, and the others charged with defending Japan and her sacred emperor, the bombing was a mark of shame. As Mitsuo Fuchida and Masatake Okumiya explained, the Japanese military's "sharp sensitivity to the enemy air threat was largely a spontaneous and unreasoned expression of the almost religious devotion to the Emperor which has long characterized the Japanese national psychology."[178] Shaken, the Japanese took three specific strategic responses.

The first strategic action was to punish China. As the Japanese quickly discovered, most of Doolittle's men had made it to the Chinese mainland. Thus, the Japanese Eleventh and Thirteenth Armies began an offensive in Chekiang and Kiangsi (Zhejiang and Jiangxi) to take airfields held by the Chinese. One hundred thousand Japanese soldiers spent the next three months in a campaign that covered twenty thousand miles. General Claire Lee Chennault, adviser to Chiang Kai-shek, described the Japanese advance, recalling that "entire villages through which the raiders had passed were slaughtered to the last child and burned to the ground." Chennault estimated that "a quarter-million Chinese soldiers and civilians were killed in the three-month campaign."[179] When the killing, raping, and burning of villages was not enough, the Japanese unleashed weaponized anthrax, cholera, and plague on the Chinese population.[180]

The second strategic step taken by Japan was to expand the strategic defense perimeter southward to protect the Japanese home islands and secure the base at Rabaul by invading New Guinea and the Solomon Islands.[181] Because the Midway operation required the main Japanese naval force to be refitted, only two carriers were available for the South Pacific and the operation was moved up to early May. At 9:15 a.m. on May 7, 1942, planes from a US carrier group found the Japanese fleet. In the Battle of the Coral Sea that followed, each side lost a carrier, but the Japanese landing was turned back at Port Moresby.[182]

The third, and most important, strategic result was that the raid codified the Japanese decision to attack Midway. After their string of conquests in the months following Pearl Harbor, the Japanese Navy was left divided about what to do next. Roughly, the Japanese had three ideas for their next possible strike at the United States. The first idea was the Marshall Islands in the Central Pacific. Second was toward Australia, with the Japanese Naval General Staff arguing for the conquest of Samoa and the Fiji Islands to entice the US Navy into battle. Finally, the Aleutians presented a tempting target. Admiral Yamamoto, however, favored a strike at Midway for three reasons. First, the US Navy was still strong. Second, the Japanese Navy was designed for speed as opposed to distance, and Midway was closer to the home bases. Finally, as he had done with Pearl Harbor, Yamamoto took US public opinion into consideration. Exotic island chains in the South Pacific were less threatening to the American psyche than were islands off Alaska and Hawaii. Much of the navy was opposed, and Yamamoto had to hint he might resign before the Japanese Navy accepted the plan with the Aleutians thrown in. Even then, not all of the navy was convinced, and the army was still opposed. The Doolittle Raid forced a consensus.[183] Kameto Kuroshima, an officer on Yamamoto's staff, remembered that "it was just as if a shiver had passed over Japan" after the raid.[184] When it was discovered that planes flown from carriers had executed the attack, the need to expand the Japanese defense perimeter to Midway and destroy the US carriers was vindicated. The army was also finally onboard for the Midway operation. In the battle that began on June 4 and lasted for three days, the Japanese lost four aircraft carriers and one heavy cruiser along with 332 planes.[185] The Japanese Navy would never recover.

The Doolittle Raid was also used to explain Allied intelligence successes at Midway. The US victory was largely due to a dedicated group of brilliant codebreakers who managed to decipher the Japanese messages. The fact that Japanese codes were compromised was secret, yet before the guns had fallen silent, the information had been published in the press.

On June 7, 1942, the *Chicago Sunday Tribune* carried a front page story headlined "Navy Had Word of Jap Plan To Strike at Sea." The unsigned article gave detailed information on how the US Navy knew the Japanese attack at the Aleutian Islands to be a diversion while the main striking force would be directed at Midway. "The navy learned of the gathering of the powerful Japanese units soon after they put forth from their bases," the article explained. "Guesses were even made that Dutch Harbor and Midway Island might be targets." This knowledge, the *Tribune* continued a bit self-importantly, "enabled the American navy to make full use of air attacks on the approaching Japanese ships, turning the struggle into an air battle along the modern lines of naval warfare so often predicted in Tribune editorials." The article also gave the number and names of the Japanese ships, in what order they approached, and the fact that Midway was known to be the first step to an invasion of Hawaii.[186]

The intelligence source involved made the *Chicago Sunday Tribune*'s article one of the most dangerous leaks of the war. In Washington, DC, where the story had been picked up by the *Washington Times-Herald*, it caused consternation in the White House and War Department. Roosevelt proposed that treason charges be brought against the offending papers—who also happened to be his most zealous political opponents—and debated with Stimson whether to remove all civilian reporters from the military and replace them with public relations officers.[187] A very concerned Marshall asked King to give a press conference to repair the damage. "The purpose of the conference would be to give you an opportunity," he explained, "in a seemingly casual impromptu fashion, to offset the possibility of the Japanese suspicioning that we had broken their code."[188] It was thus that Admiral King, who hated reporters and disliked publicity, came to give his first press conference of the war.

King used Doolittle to explain away how the United States knew the Japanese would attack Midway. Marshall had suggested this, advising King to say "that after the surprise raid on Japan proper we would be subjected to some sort of reprisal operations."[189] King agreed, telling the correspondents that "after General Doolittle's raid on Japan, General Marshall and I both felt, knowing the Japanese psychology, that some reprisal in kind was inevitable in order that they might 'save face.'" The Battle of the Coral Sea, King continued, had only added to this worry, and Dutch Harbor and Midway Island seemed a likely choice. King stated that the Allies did not know exactly where and when the attack would come, but took a "calculated risk." The admiral waited till the end of his remarks to issue an off-the-record warning concerning the leaked information. Stating that the leak came with serious consequences and "compromises a vital and secret source of information, which will henceforth be closed to us," King asked the reporters to guard against any information that could help the enemy. For the same reason, the origin of the Doolittle fliers was still secret since, King explained, "we have every reason to believe that the Japanese do not yet know how it was done."[190] In the case of Midway, however, the United States was lucky, and Japan overlooked the *Tribune*'s story.[191]

Second Front Now

During his June 7 press conference on the victory at Midway, Admiral Ernest King brought up the topic of a second front in Europe. Speaking off the record, King said, "You gentlemen have cause to know how public opinion is reported in Britain pressing for a second front, but that is one of those things much easier said than done, and take [*sic*] a long time."[192] The press and public were indeed pushing hard for a second front. Likewise, many Allied military leaders also believed a cross-channel landing should be the next move in the war. Yet in the end, Churchill and Roosevelt would open a second front not in France but in French North Africa. Although they went against the opinion of the media and military professionals, Churchill and Roosevelt also had the press and public opinion in mind. As with the Germany First debate, Roosevelt believed the public had to see the military in combat in 1942 if he wanted to keep public support.

Operation Gymnast, the invasion of French North Africa, had been considered earlier in Allied war councils. In fact, an invasion of France appears nowhere in the transcripts of the Arcadia Conference.[193] At a meeting of British and US military leaders on December 24, 1941, Field Marshal John Dill reflected British thinking that Africa was a main priority, while General Marshall acknowledged that US planners were working on a possible invasion of North Africa.[194] Yet the deteriorating situation in the Pacific made plans for Gymnast unworkable, and even before Arcadia ended, Gymnast was canceled.[195] When it quickly became clear that neither the Philippines nor Singapore could be held, Allied planners began focusing again on Europe. "We've got to go to Europe and fight," Eisenhower confided to his diary on January 22, "and we've got to quit wasting resources all over the world, and still worse, wasting time. If we're to keep Russia in, save the Middle East, India, and Burma, we've got to begin slugging with air at West Europe, to be followed by a land attack as soon as possible." This was the origin, according to Eisenhower, of Operation Bolero, which proposed landing Allied troops in Western Europe in 1942 or 1943.[196] By the end of February, Stimson was also convinced that it was time to limit resources sent to the Southwest Pacific and instead that it would be a "good thing psychologically if we could press hard enough on the expeditionary force through Great

Britain to make the Germans keep looking over their shoulder in their fight with Russia."[197]

A second front via a cross-channel invasion took a big step forward at a White House meeting on March 5, 1942. Stimson had visited Roosevelt and found him pondering a depressing cable from Churchill summarizing the disasters of the previous few months and wondering where the war would go next. Stimson saw a chance to propose an offensive. He proposed two alternative plans, followed by outlining why they would not work. Then, the secretary of war proposed sending an overwhelming force to the British Isles and threatening an attack on the Germans in France. He argued that this was the proper and orthodox line of our help in the war as it had always been recognized and that it would now have the effect of giving Hitler two fronts to fight on if it could be done in time while the Russians were still in. It would also heavily stimulate British sagging morale. Roosevelt was interested, as was Arnold and Marshall, the latter of whom informed Stimson that Eisenhower was already working on such a project in the War Plans Division.[198] Thus a cross-channel assault became the military objective for 1942.

The British still had to be convinced, and in early April 1942, Hopkins, Marshall, and a few aides—traveling in mufti and under assumed names— were dispatched to London to sell Bolero. On April 1, Roosevelt wrote to Churchill that a cross-channel landing would be acceptable to the Soviets, and "I think it will work out in full accord with [the] trend of public opinion here and in Britain."[199] The Americans were in effect pushing two plans. The first was Bolero, which envisioned a buildup of Allied forces in Britain for a cross-channel invasion during 1943. The second was Sledgehammer, which would be an emergency landing in 1942 if the Soviets appeared ready to collapse. Finally, Marshall hoped, if possible, to establish a beachhead in France in September 1942.[200] The British were skeptical. In an ironic reversal, they worried that such a massive buildup would take forces desperately needed in the Pacific, leaving India defenseless. They also worried about the logistical limitations and pointed out that most of the troops would be British.[201] Worse, Brooke made the disturbing discovery that the Americans had given no thought to what would happen after the landings.[202] Yet Churchill was delighted, at least, that the United States was still committed to the Germany First offensive.[203] The Americans departed wrongly believing that the British had agreed to a cross-channel invasion as soon as possible.

Lurking behind the practical military issues was concern for public opinion. When selling Roosevelt on a cross-channel invasion, Stimson had suggested it would boost British morale.[204] Bolero would also be a psychological weapon against Germany since building up US forces in Britain would prevent a Nazi invasion. It would likewise add to the "psychological pressure" that was already causing unrest in Germany's occupied populations.[205] This was supported by an intelligence report by William Donovan on March 10 saying that the British public wanted "an offensive attitude on the part of the fighting forces instead of continual retreat and defense."[206] During his April visit to England, Hopkins had raised the issue of US public opinion. While acknowledging that opinion favored a Japan First approach, he said the American people likewise wanted the United States to do its part in Europe. Churchill was also thinking of public morale and, likely seeing this as an opportunity to cement the United States into the Germany First strategy once and for all, suggested that "the English-speaking peoples were resolved on a great campaign for the liberation of Europe, and it was for consideration whether a public announcement to this effect should in due course be made."[207] Though Roosevelt hesitated before making any announcement, Marshall's trip alone created a boost to US morale. Historian Richard W. Steele notes that "statements by various Allied leaders, including General Marshall and Lord Beaverbrook, were interpreted by the press in the light of the mission to London to indicate that offensive operations were being planned and that a second front would be opened before the year was out." Steele adds that a survey made by the Office of Facts and Figures demonstrated that most editorials saw Marshall's trip to London as the prelude to a second front.[208] A cross-channel landing was viewed as necessary for press and public opinion.

A worried Brooke also observed that public opinion was influencing strategy during the London meetings. Talking to Marshall the following day, Brooke discovered that both King and MacArthur were trying to transfer forces to the Pacific. "To counter these moves," Brooke wrote, "Marshall has started the European offensive plan and is going 100% all out on it! It is a clever move which fits in well with present political opinion and the desire to help Russia." Reflecting on the US plan the next day, he added, "Public opinion is shouting for the formation of a new western front to assist the Russians. But they have no conception of the difficulties and dangers entailed!"[209]

The Soviets were indeed attempting to persuade Western public opinion that a second front was needed. In February, Maxim Litvinov, Soviet ambassador to Washington, speaking at the Overseas Press Club, said material aid was not enough to defeat Germany since it would take "simultaneous offensive operations on two or more fronts" to defeat Germany.[210] From then on, Stalin's government never hesitated to remind the Western Allies publicly that the Soviet Union was bearing the brunt of the fighting.[211]

Soviet demands for a second front were echoed in the press of the Western Allies. At the end of March, the Office of Facts and Figures survey of editorial opinion found that "with growing vigor commentators suggest the opening of a new front in Europe as the one effective means of supporting Russia and perhaps crushing Hitler now."[212] By late June, Eisenhower recalled after the war, "the press of the United States and Great Britain was echoing the Russian cry for a 'second front.' To the professional soldier this was disturbing, not because of any quarrel with the soundness of the idea but because the impatience of the public clearly demonstrated a complete lack of appreciation of the problems involved, particularly of the time that must elapse before any such operation could be launched."[213]

Such pressure did not go unnoticed by the Nazis. "The man in the street screams for a Second Front, and it remains an open question whether Churchill and Roosevelt might, in certain circumstances, together with the deteriorating military situation for the Russians, have to give in to such pressure," wrote Joseph Goebbels in his diary. "It's one of the disadvantages of democracy that it can't conduct politics or war according to logic and intelligence, but has to respond to the up-and-down swings of public opinion."[214]

The likelihood of a cross-channel landing in 1942 quickly faded. The basic problem was one of supplies. There were not enough troops or equipment in Britain to make anything more than a suicidal landing in France. Likewise, shipping was extremely limited.[215] On June 17, Roosevelt stunned his military advisers when he suddenly announced that he wanted to consider Gymnast again since it would bring additional relief for the Soviet Union. "The only hope I have about it at all," an enraged Stimson scribbled in his diary, "is that I think he may be doing it in his foxy way to forestall trouble that is now on the ocean coming toward us in the shape of a new British visitor."[216] That "British visitor" was Churchill, who had decided that it was finally time to make a definite decision on strategy for 1942. The trip had apparently been prompted when Roosevelt told the British admiral Lord Louis Mountbatten that helping the Soviets was so imperative that the Allies must take any opportunity offered by deteriorating German morale to land in France in 1942, even if it was a "sacrifice" landing.[217] Roosevelt also told Mountbatten, according to Brooke, that he was "worried because US troops would not be engaged with the enemy on any scale this year. He feared a continental operation next spring would be too late and was turning toward North-West Africa as a possible let-out this year."[218]

Churchill and Roosevelt met privately at Hyde Park, while Brooke and the other members of the Combined Chiefs of Staff gathered in Washington. Both the US and British military leaders found themselves in agreement that Bolero should be launched in 1943, that Gymnast should be abandoned, and that operations should take place in 1942 only "in case of necessity or if an exceptionally favorable opportunity presented itself."[219] Brooke was glad at the consensus, "but am a little doubtful as to what PM and President may be brewing up together."[220] Stimson was also "a little bit uneasy" about leaving Roosevelt and Churchill unsupervised since both "are too much alike in their strong points and in their weak points."[221]

Brooke and Stimson were right to be worried, for although Bolero was not yet off the table, neither was Gymnast. When Churchill and Roosevelt returned to Washington, the prime minister was very displeased at the combined chiefs' conclusion. Events provided more weight to an operation in North Africa. During a White House meeting on June 21, news arrived of another mass British surrender at Tobruk, Libya.[222] Thus, the conclusion emerged that Bolero was still on for 1943 but that it was "essential" for the Western Allies to "prepare to act offensively in 1942." Though a cross-channel landing would yield the greatest political benefit if the political conditions were right, "the best alternative in 1942 is Operation GYMNAST."[223] Though Marshall and Stimson still backed Bolero and Sledgehammer, by the time Churchill departed, both plans were on life support.

What ultimately saved the invasion of North Africa was Roosevelt's overriding need to have US troops on the offensive in 1942. "The Churchill-Roosevelt reasoning was political rather than military and not totally unexpected," summarizes historian Mark Stoler. "Because of recent promises to Stalin as well as the state of public opinion, both leaders believed that offensive action in the European theater was mandatory in 1942."[224] The crisis came to a conclusion in July when Churchill decided that the "moment had come to bury 'Sledgehammer'" and informed Roosevelt that "no responsible British General, Admiral or Air Marshal is prepared to recommend SLEDGE-HAMMER as a practicable operation in 1942." The prime minister concluded Gymnast was "by far the best chance for effective relief to the Russian front in 1942. This has all along been in harmony with your ideas. In fact it is your commanding idea. Here is the true second front of 1942."[225] A desperate Marshall suggested that perhaps the Allies should focus on Japan instead of Germany first. A furious president ended that idea.[226] Again, Roosevelt dispatched Hopkins, King, and Marshall to Britain, with instructions that it "is of the highest importance that US ground troops be brought into action against the enemy in 1942."[227] Roosevelt emphasized that it was vital to support the Soviet Union, and thus Sledgehammer had to be launched in 1942 if at all possible. "If SLEDGEHAMMER is finally and definitely out of the picture," the President instructed, "I want you to consider the world situation as it exists at that time, and determine upon another place for U.S. Troops to fight in 1942."[228] The meeting ended with Churchill flatly stating that the British could not agree to Sledgehammer. On July 25, Roosevelt cabled Hopkins to begin planning for an invasion of North Africa—an operation renamed Torch the previous day—no later than October 30, 1942.[229]

A bitter Marshall would conclude that Torch was simply an attempt to gratify public and press opinion. After the war, he told the historian Samuel Eliot Morison "that the great lesson he learned in 1942" was that "in wartime the politicians have to do *something* important every year. They could not simply use 1942 to build up for 1943 or 1944; they could not face the obloquy of fighting another 'phony war.'"[230] In another interview with his biographer Forest Pogue, Marshall repeated several times that "we failed to see that the leader in a democracy has to keep the people entertained. . . . People demand action. We couldn't wait to be completely ready. Churchill [was] always getting into side shows. . . . But I could see why he had to have something."[231] Albert Wedemeyer, who was working for Marshall on war planning, wrote that the chief of staff "realized that, for political reasons, a democratic nation at war must fight at least one major campaign a year."[232] Marshall deemed Roosevelt's decision on Gymnast to be something that favored press and public opinion over the advice of his military leaders.

Marshall's conclusions about the linkage between public and press opinion to Roosevelt's decision in Torch has not gone unchallenged. "The 'people' of America and the free world certainly demanded action," concludes historian Nigel Hamilton, "as newspapers in the United States and Britain trumpeted in 1942—but in terms of political pressure, the action they wanted, by an overwhelming majority, was Marshall's Second Front." Roosevelt was doing the opposite of public opinion, Hamilton writes, "patiently preferring, as U.S. commander in chief, a military operation that had a reasonable chance of success."[233] Though he does not dismiss Marshall's statement, historian Steven Casey likewise writes that "Roosevelt's desire for action in 1942, then, was neither a product of intense popular pressure for a second front nor principally the result of electoral politics." Instead, it was based on the fear that leaving large numbers of young men in training camps would cause political criticism as had happened in 1941. Even more importantly, Roosevelt knew how significant events could alter public opinion. "In particular," Casey wrote, "if GIs were fighting the Wehrmacht, this would undoubtedly dominate media coverage and the minds of the mass public, thereby leading to a relative decline in interest in the Asia conflict. As a result, popular support for 'Germany first,' which had previously depended on the intensity of fighting in the respective theatres, might well become more firmly ingrained."[234]

What both explanations miss, however, was the pattern in Roosevelt's thinking that was clearly evident to Marshall. The president was less concerned with the place of the second front than the timing. As Roosevelt had reiterated since the Arcadia Conference, it was vitally important for public morale to get US soldiers fighting somewhere in 1942. The US government must be seen to be doing something, both to help the Soviet Union, prosecute the Pacific war, and, as Casey notes, get US troops out of training camps and into combat. That had been the logic behind saving MacArthur and the Doolittle Raid. The publicity brought by both incidents had given the American people a much-needed boost in morale and the administration an equivalent boost in popular support. Yet public opinion for action was also increasing. The Office of War Information reported at the end of July that there were growing demands for a second front and that if these were not met, it could lead to major problems in public opinion.[235] Since a cross-channel invasion was impossible in 1942, Roosevelt settled for the next best option that would deploy US soldiers in the shortest possible time. The United States had substantial forces in the Pacific and had already won a major victory. Timing for Torch mattered for another reason as well. Roosevelt's cable to Hopkins accepting Torch stated that the operation should take place no later than October 30, 1942, placing it a few days before the midterm election.[236] Roosevelt would later publicly deny that anyone was "thinking about [the] election" when the Torch date was decided.[237] Yet at one meeting on Torch, Roosevelt, placing his hands together in an attitude of prayer, asked Marshall to "please make it [the invasion] before Election Day." When that proved to be impossible for military reasons, the White House press secretary, Steve Early, was furious. But Roosevelt never mentioned it, which Marshall respected.[238]

For his part, Stimson still hoped public opinion could save Sledgehammer. He wrote in his diary on July 27:

> Though Sledgehammer was beaten by the British War Council, it is so strongly supported by the people and soldiers of Great Britain that there is likely to be a revolution in sentiment against such a decision. Marshall did succeed in insisting that preparations for Sledgehammer and Bolero should go on until it became absolutely clear that the Russian Army was beaten. That leaves quite a loophole in which public sentiment may restore some of the British leaders' morale.[239]

The next day, Stimson even believed that he had convinced Roosevelt. "The more I see of Marshall the more I think he feels that the British leaders' hands may be forced by the pressure of public opinion in regard to Sledgehammer and, when I spoke to the President over the telephone this evening, he said the same thing. That would be the best way out."[240] Accustomed to dealing with politicians, Stimson vainly hoped that simply marshaling more public opinion to one side of an issue would be enough to sway Roosevelt.

Conclusion

Night had fallen on America's capital on November 7, 1942, when a mob of newsmen descended upon the office of Major General A. D. Surles, head of public relations for the War Department. When questioning failed, the reporters progressed to pleading and then to threats. Finally, a reporter said, "Come on, boys, let's go to the White House; they're always good to us there."

On their arrival, Steve Early greeted the reporters, then disappeared. A journalist tried the door and discovered they were locked in. Suddenly, Early reappeared. "It's all over boys! Our troops have landed."[241] After reading Roosevelt's statement, Early refused to comment whether the landing constituted a second front and directed the reporters back to Surles for more information.[242] Thus, the announcement of Torch came from Roosevelt, not the War Department. This was fitting, for with Torch and many other strategic calculations during the months after Pearl Harbor Roosevelt was the driving force. "I am happy today," Roosevelt wrote the newspaper editor and former secretary of the navy Josephus Daniels, "in the fact that for three months I have been taking it on the chin in regard to the Second Front and that this is now over."[243]

Roosevelt understood that the press and public opinion formed a vital weapon in the battle against the Axis. Faced with defeat after defeat, the president had as his overriding priority to have Americans fighting in both theaters by the end of 1942. Yet focusing on public opinion did not mean military factors were unimportant, but rather that they were also influenced by concern for public opinion. To accomplish this Roosevelt set the stage for the militarily sensible Germany First precept by actively linking Germany to Pearl Harbor. Forced by events to send reinforcements to the Pacific, the president also pressed for the bombing of Japan to show the public that his administration was hitting back. Convinced of the need for a second front, Roosevelt backed Bolero and Sledgehammer until it was clear both plans were not militarily feasible in 1942. He then backed Gymnast. Historian Richard W. Steele concluded that Roosevelt's "expectation that his manipulation of military activities could significantly affect national attitudes without interfering with the proper prosecution of the war appears vain."[244] Yet Roosevelt believed that he could not exercise freedom in military choices without taking into account and pacifying public and press opinion.

His commanders agreed. Stimson, Marshall, and MacArthur understood public opinion mattered and tried to harness it through the press. As he had done in December 1941, Marshall still believed that no matter where the first offensive occurred, it must be a success for the sake of public opinion. Writing to Eisenhower in August about Torch, Marshall noted "the extreme seriousness of the effect on the peoples of occupied Europe, India and China if the United States should fail in its first major operation."[245]

Even limited military decisions made for the sake of positive publicity had unintended strategic consequences. MacArthur's evacuation from the Philippines not only ensured the Pacific First lobby would gain a powerful spokesman, but also resulted in the Pacific War being fought under a divided command. Likewise, the Japanese reacted to the Doolittle Raid by launching an offensive in China and toward Midway that proved disastrous for Japan.

Another unintended result was the creation of military heroes by a public that was starved for good news. The press lionized MacArthur and Doolittle, while the military quickly made use of their public relations value. The unintended result was that both officers also had to be given important commands to fulfill their public role. And, as the next chapter shows, MacArthur would use the press to successfully challenge Roosevelt's Germany First strategy.

Chapter Two

"I Shall Return"

The old black locomotive lugging two passenger cars lumbered out of the red dust of the Australian desert and into the city of Adelaide. It was met by a small group of reporters. A door opened and out stepped a haggard Douglas MacArthur. To the months of strain from Corregidor were added the grueling journey by PT boat, bomber, and finally slow train. Worse yet, MacArthur had just been informed that instead of an army awaiting him, there were only twenty-five thousand American soldiers in Australia, none of them combat troops. "God have mercy on us," he mumbled as the color drained from his face. Composing himself, MacArthur stepped from the train, unfolded a rumpled piece of paper, and read: "The President of the United States ordered me to break through the Japanese lines and proceed from Corregidor to Australia for the purpose, as I understand it, of organizing the American offensive against Japan, a primary object of which is the relief of the Philippines." MacArthur's voice was subdued, and he reached the end of the statement without emotion. "I came through, and I shall return."[1]

The last three words opened not only MacArthur's campaign to retake the Philippines but also his media offensive to make it a reality. In the coming years "I shall return" would be stamped on everything from matchbooks to soap.[2] But in 1942 it was still uncertain whether MacArthur could fulfill his promise. Washington and London were struggling to put the Germany First strategy into action. The US Navy wanted vengeance against Japan but intended to extract it in the Central Pacific. Meanwhile, Australia was facing invasion. The only hope to reverse the Japanese offensive would be to obtain resources from the United States. This fact was captured by MacArthur's less remembered remarks to the throngs that greeted his arrival in Melbourne. "No general can make something from nothing," he told the crowd. "My success or failure will depend primarily upon the resources which our respective governments place at my disposal."[3]

In the end, MacArthur used the press to successfully challenge the Germany First strategy that Roosevelt's own press campaign had so carefully sold to the American people.[4] This was unique in American history. From half a world away, an American general would engage the president of the United States in a press battle to alter military strategy. Scholars have highlighted the global connectedness of the war and shown how military events in one theater influenced others.[5] This chapter demonstrates the media's role in connecting the theaters of the war through competition for resources and strategy.

It helped that MacArthur's escape from the Philippines only added to his popularity with the American home front. Babies were named in his honor—thirteen between March 1 and April 8 according to the *New York Times*—and so were streets, parks, and at least one dance and a flower. The general was showered with awards and memberships, including becoming an honorary tribesman of the Blackfeet Indians of Montana with the name of Chief Wise Eagle.[6] MacArthur's "heroic defense of the Philippines" inspired the city fathers of Syracuse, New York, to rename their baseball stadium.[7] A 1942 song, "Most respectfully dedicated to, Gen. Douglas MacArthur" contained this refrain:

> From the fox holes of Bataan,
> Safely came our miracle man,
> With scores of wings and planes to fly,
> He'll place a rainbow in the sky.

The song carried the ring of a political jingle.[8]

Powerful media figures also expressed their support for MacArthur. Robert R. McCormick, publisher of the fiercely anti-Roosevelt *Chicago Tribune*, telegrammed, "Congratulations on your wonderful defense of Bataan and on your appointment as commander in chief."[9] Henry Luce—ruler of the *Time*, *Life*, and *Fortune* magazine empire—delayed a few months before also telegraphing, but explained, "It is only because our feelings are completely merged into the daily thoughts of admiration and affection which go out to him from all America."[10] After a junket around the United States, H. V. Evatt, Australia's minister of external affairs, was struck by the amount of publicity for MacArthur in American newspapers where he "is very nearly a national idol."[11] Meanwhile, a summary of Australian newspapers by the US consular general showed wide editorial support for MacArthur as commander of the Southwest Pacific Area (SWPA), a fact confirmed when the Australians inaugurated "MacArthur Day."[12] Australian mothers, apparently, were even using MacArthur's name to coerce their children to eat spinach.[13] Such exuberant hero worship appears today at best excessive. Yet one cannot understand MacArthur's use of the press without appreciating the devotion the general commanded even in defeat.

Some scholars have praised MacArthur as a master of public relations.[14] Others have viewed him as a scam artist. Phillip Knightley, for example, argues that MacArthur implemented a "policy of shielding the nation from reality, maintaining morale by avoiding the truth, and convincing the public that the war was being conducted by a command of geniuses."[15] Still, other historians have dismissed MacArthur's military accomplishments as a creation of propaganda. What did the "thespian general" contribute to victory in World War II, asked Eric Larrabee? "Not much, really" was his, and other historians', answer.[16]

Certainly, MacArthur's public relations policy was less successful when it came to those he commanded. Some of his generals begrudged his monopolization of press attention.[17] GIs were even more resentful.[18] In the end, MacArthur would never be liked in the way Eisenhower was by his soldiers or create the pride often mentioned by Patton's veterans, nor has anyone ever called MacArthur "the GI General" as Bradley was labeled by the press. His biographer William Manchester, himself a veteran of the Pacific War, suggests MacArthur's aloof Victorian reserve—which had worked so well with the doughboys of World War I—was anathema to the egalitarianism of World War II GIs. Master Sergeant Paul P. Rogers, who took dictation for MacArthur throughout the war, concluded that the general's focus on his destiny was a result of his intellectual development beginning in the late nineteenth century, since "men thought differently in those days." Former Wisconsin governor Philip La Follette, also on MacArthur's staff, discovered an unexpected similarity between the reactionary general and his Progressive father in the "way they both spelled 'honor' with a capital 'H.'" This generational divide spilled over into MacArthur's handling of the press. "He yearned for public adulation," Manchester observes. "His treatment of the press guaranteed that he wouldn't get it."[19] Yet MacArthur's press strategy was not shaped so much by a desire for personal glory, but by the need to attract resources to the SWPA to enable his return to the Philippines. Generals in Europe could afford to use the media to glorify their subordinates and soldiers to build morale. MacArthur had to use the press simply to obtain troops to command. Indeed, MacArthur's contribution to victory in the Pacific was substantial, and his use of the media was an essential part of his success.

Forging the Weapon

The reporters who met MacArthur at the Adelaide train station were the vanguard of the thousands of correspondents who would cover World War II for the 7,000 magazines, 11,000 weekly papers, 2,700 daily newspapers, along with radio stations and newsreels, where Americans received their news during World War II. In the prewar newsroom a college degree was not required, and since it was a profession open to talent approximately a hundred women would serve as war correspondents. The US War Department would accredit 1,828 news personnel to have access to its press conferences and to receive material support and transportation. In exchange, the war correspondents were mustered into the military, given officer rank, and agreed to abide by censorship.[20] The task of informing, providing, and controlling the war correspondents fell on the theater public relations officers (PROs). The World War II manual, The Officer's Guide, devoted more than six pages to the duties of PROs and emphasized honesty with reporters and the selection of officers who had both a military and a journalistic background for public relations duties. Thus, many PROs were former reporters themselves. Eventually, more than seventy-six officers and men would serve in the SWPA Public Relations Division (PRD), mostly working as censors.[21] It is a testament to the brutality of the Pacific War that of the fifty-four reporters who died covering US forces during World War II, twenty-three were killed in the Pacific.[22]

MacArthur wasted little time outlining his press strategy. "There has been nothing more astonishing in the progress of war . . . than the place that public opinion occupies," he explained to a gathering of reporters. "One cannot wage war under present conditions without the support of public opinion, which is tremendously moulded by the press and other forces of propaganda." Nor, he added, would soldiers fight "unless they know what they are fighting for." This brought him to censorship, which was needed to block dangerous information. Indeed, public opinion would demand censorship to protect soldiers. Yet, if the public did not know the truth, "their confidence is reduced. . . . It is therefore of the most prime importance that the public be instructed so that they can summon all their confidence, all their determination and all their purpose in the support of the war effort." Thus, MacArthur explained, the press was "one of the most valuable components that I have. . . . I want your help. Without it we cannot get the maximum out of the situation. . . . To that end my main purpose is not to suppress news from you but to get news for you." MacArthur added that the reporters were not obligated to use the news released by his headquarters or to "limit yourselves to 'canned' news." Nor should they abstain from criticism. But, he warned, "when you start to tear down, you destroy public confidence in all the leaders of a military movement." The general added he would always be happy to give reporters his full knowledge for background material.[23] Throughout the war, MacArthur would return to the theme of the importance of accurate and free reporting for the war effort.[24]

There was still censorship, of course, and it is fair to ask if MacArthur's actions lived up to his rhetoric. Journalism professor Jeffery Smith thinks not, dismissing MacArthur's remarks about the press as "bluster."[25] Historian William Manchester observes that SWPA censorship was heavy and got worse as the war progressed.[26] Phillip Knightley claims that MacArthur "established almost the tightest censorship of any theatre of the war." Dispatches were controlled, and any correspondent who interviewed a member of the armed forces without permission would be banned from the combat zone. This policy, Knightley adds, was to keep morale and MacArthur's image high.[27] The general may have talked in public of the importance of truth, journalism historian Michael S. Sweeney concludes, but "MacArthur's definition of truth required journalists to slant their dispatches."[28]

There is likewise evidence that MacArthur's censorship policy was much heavier than he would have preferred. Although each theater commander could create his own rules of censorship, MacArthur was under pressure from several powerful factors, beginning with the Australian government.[29] Censorship in wartime Australia is an underresearched topic. But as historian Robert W. Desmond notes, "official Australian censorship . . . was one of the most severe in any country."[30] At the beginning of the war, Prime Minister John Curtin established the Department of Information with a censorship office that contained representatives of the different armed services, to which the censorship office usually deferred.[31] Australian censorship was particularly sensitive when it came to Americans.[32] Soon after MacArthur's arrival in Australia, there was an important loosening of press restrictions. The fact that US soldiers were in Australia at all was censored until MacArthur's arrival, which, as the *Chicago Tribune* happily noted, lifted the lid of secrecy at the "direction of Gen. MacArthur, who is known not only as a brilliant military leader but also as a master of psychology."[33] Originally, both US and Australian air forces were off-limits to reporters, but soon after MacArthur's arrival, restrictions were lifted for American flyers.[34] Radio broadcasts to the United States were likewise initially forbidden, but this also soon ended.[35] Even a journalist critic of SWPA censorship admitted that "from a military standpoint, MacArthur's censorship was notably more liberal than that in most other theatres; units in combat could be named and other morale-building information published."[36] MacArthur knew the power of accurate news reporting, and this relaxation of censorship was driven by the need to issue corrections to Japanese broadcasts on American losses.

This easing of censorship ended when naval forces around Australia began complaining to Washington that press releases were providing useful information to the enemy.[37] A few weeks later, the navy was further irritated when MacArthur issued a flurry of communiqués about the Battle of the Coral Sea to counter Japanese propaganda and reassure Australians. The navy fretted about leaked information, while Roosevelt privately accused MacArthur and Prime Minister Curtin of attempting to steal credit for the battle.[38] Marshall raised the problem with MacArthur, who shot back that he could not control publicity and that Australians had a right to news of war happening on their doorstep.[39] Henry Stimson then drafted a letter expressing his disappointment with MacArthur's response and ordered that in the future all naval publicity would be controlled by Admiral Chester Nimitz.[40] Stimson followed up in a memorandum to Roosevelt, suggesting he get involved.[41] The president had already done so. "The only difficulty I am having here is a good deal of loose newspaper talk coming out of Australia," Roosevelt wrote the general, "and I suggest you do all possible to get a censorship on all outgoing messages from Australia and possibly New Zealand."[42] Yet even before the navy complained, Marshall had been pushing MacArthur to tighten censorship. MacArthur replied that he did not have the authority to order Curtin around.[43] He also defended his communiqués by arguing they were more heavily censored than the Australian "liberal" censorship policy.[44] Nevertheless, MacArthur met with the prime minister, who agreed that censorship could be tightened for military reasons and received partial control over news releases.[45]

There was at least one story MacArthur desperately wanted released. Several months after US forces at Bataan capitulated, three escaped American prisoners arrived in Australia. They told a story of a forced march of American and Filipino soldiers where hundreds died of Japanese brutality. MacArthur ordered the story of the Bataan Death March released immediately. But Washington, fearing retaliation against other POWs, censored all stories of the atrocities.[46] "Perhaps the Administration," MacArthur fumed in his memoirs, "which was committed to a European-first effort, feared American public opinion would demand a greater reaction against Japan, but whatever the cause, here was the sinister beginning of the 'managed news.'" He added, "It was the introduction, under a disarming slogan, of a type of censorship which can easily become a menace to a free press and a threat to the liberties of a free people."[47] If released, the story would have been a useful contribution to getting more resources to the SWPA.

Along with the censorship imposed by Canberra, Washington, and the US Navy, MacArthur's Public Relations Division added an additional layer of review. It was headed by LeGrande A. Diller, who had escaped from the Philippines with MacArthur, and like many of the "Bataan Gang" was suspicious of Washington because of the many failed promises of help. Correspondent Clark Lee later described a state of mind on MacArthur's staff "that took shape during the Bataan days when MacArthur's men were left alone to face an overwhelming foe. A persecution complex was born, and with it the determination that no word should be written or broadcast from MacArthur's area that would in any way injure the general." After having seen censorship in all theaters of the war, Lee concluded, "I feel competent to pronounce his [Diller's] censorship the worst that existed anywhere." Lee's critique is made all the more devastating since he genuinely admired MacArthur, who he believed was not to blame for Diller's excesses.[48] CBS's William Dunn wrote a far less harsh assessment of his "amigo" Diller, but lamented that he occupied two contradictory jobs: press chief and censor. Like Lee, Dunn believed Diller insisted on occupying both positions because of his intense loyalty to MacArthur.[49] George Kenney, head of MacArthur's air force, re-membered that Diller and his staff's attitude toward MacArthur bordered on "idolatry" and that "unless a news release painted the General with a halo and seated him on the highest pedestal in the universe, it should be killed." He added, "They didn't trust the newspapermen to interpret MacArthur properly."[50] Because Diller's papers are not available, it is difficult to weigh his conduct against the charges of a correspondent who clearly despised him. It seems clear, however, that Diller did not take any chances with MacArthur's reputation.

Yet as Rogers, the stenographer, would later explain, the "imposition of censorship was pressed by Roosevelt and George Marshall."[51] Washington also forbade MacArthur, and other commanders, from giving one-on-one interviews.[52] Later in the war, MacArthur lamented to a small group of re-porters that there were no outstanding war correspondents anymore and no reporters came to get his opinion of the battles. "You men are not to blame," he told the correspondents. "The trouble is censorship. I am strongly op-posed to all censorship, but the War Department insists on it." Clark Lee was at a loss to reconcile this with MacArthur's staff implementing the "most rigid and dangerous censorship in American history."[53] As he wrote later, "no reporter believed" that Washington was to blame for SWPA censorship.[54] Nevertheless, it should also be remembered that of the almost two hundred reporters who served in the SWPA, not one was ever disciplined for evading censorship.[55] No other theater of the war could make that claim. It did not help MacArthur's media reputation that he continued censorship in occupied Japan. But during the Korean War, MacArthur instituted "self-censorship" and resisted formal censorship—in historian Steven Casey's words—with "a tenacity that suggested he was a true believer." Casey argues that censorship was impractical in Korea. Considering the above information, the answer might also be, as MacArthur's PRO explained during the Korean War, that "censorship is abhorrent to General MacArthur."[56]

MacArthur did not hold many press conferences during the war, but those few he did hold were major performances.[57] One press conference in late 1943 was described in detail in the Australian Air Force's official history. The correspondents

rose as the general made an impressive entry. . . . His phrasing was perfect, his speech clear and unhalting, except for pauses for dramatic emphasis; the correspondents took notes but there was no interruption of any kind. The conference room had become a stage, MacArthur the virtuoso, the other officers the "extras" in the cast, and the correspondents the audi-ence. . . . The statement ended, the general again raised his right arm in salute and strode from the room. . . . The conference was over. One man alone had spoken—the Supreme Commander. There was no questioning, no opportunity to clarify the meaning of the statement. It had come direct from the lips of General Douglas MacArthur, and as such it was, evidently, beyond question.[58]

This oft-quoted and vivid description has been used by some historians as an example of the SWPA commander's imperious attitude that alienated reporters.[59] Yet the picture is misleading. An Australian reporter told MacArthur he had traveled 2,500 miles to attend the press conference and it had been worth it.[60] Other accounts recorded war correspondents held spellbound as MacArthur paced, orated, and captivated. He also took questions from correspondents and would entrust reporters with his plans for coming battles. The Australian correspondent George H. Johnston recalled that when asked a question during press conferences, MacArthur "never hesitated in giving an answer that was not only utterly complete but was in itself, taken down verbatim, a polished essay on military lore."[61] Historian Patricia Beard has even presented credible evidence that MacArthur told Roy Howard, president of the Scripps-Howard newspapers, about the secret work to develop an atomic bomb.[62]

Certainly, MacArthur went out of his way to court the press. He was the first commander to decorate war correspondents. To evade War Department regulations forbidding one-on-one interviews, MacArthur offered to review Roy Howard's articles on the Pacific war. When the reporter Noel Monk tired of SWPA censorship and decided to head for Europe, MacArthur invited him to his office and said, "You're going away from the big front, the big war, son."[63] Stick with me, MacArthur told CBS radio correspondent William J. Dunn, and I will "take you back to Manila."[64]

Nevertheless, MacArthur remained a target of derision for some journalists. The BBC broadcaster Chester Wilmot was unimpressed with MacArthur's first press conference along with his focus on beating Japan instead of Germany and did not stick around to change his opinion.[65] Frank C. Kunz, who worked as a stenographer for the Public Relations Division, overheard correspondents complaining that MacArthur did not take visitors to his Brisbane headquarters because he did not want reporters to see him in comfortable accommodations.[66] Rogers remembered a new group of correspondents who "had not seen MacArthur on Corregidor and were tainted with the 'Dugout Doug' syndrome and an anti-MacArthur attitude."[67] War correspondent Gavin Long would later accuse MacArthur's staff of contriving "to create a picture of a commander of more than human stature."[68] "That wasn't necessary," one PRO explained, "he took care of that himself."[69]

Was this image of a man of destiny that excited reverence in some and derision in others a true reflection of the man beneath? It is a question that has filled multivolume biographies on MacArthur. Rogers, his stenographer throughout World War II, was in as good a position as any to observe his boss, and admits his depiction might "surprise many who have seen only the MacArthur of press and screen." He describes a man both "gentle," "fair," and emotional yet coldly logical. But, he confesses, "MacArthur never revealed himself completely to anyone" and those "who thought they understood MacArthur were lacking in wisdom."[70] There is also evidence that MacArthur fully understood he was playing a part. During the landings at Los Negros in early 1944, MacArthur said to Roger Olaf Egeberg, his physician, "I wear this cap with all the braid. I feel in a way that I have to. It's my trademark . . . a trademark that many of our soldiers know by now, so I'll keep on wearing it."[71] As historian Arthur Herman notes, the exchange was the "closest anyone ever came to hearing MacArthur talk about the visuals of leadership, the idea he had embraced during . . . World War One. The cap and corncob pipe had become in effect his heraldic crest, like that of a knight of the Middle Ages, the sight of which told his men that their commander was with them."[72] Like Patton, MacArthur was a complicated man who was also an actor. Like Eisenhower, he understood the media and its place in modern war. But unlike Patton, MacArthur's acting was enhanced by a steely detachment, and unlike Eisenhower, he did not have any of the jocular, small-town-USA friendliness.

Part of the act were MacArthur's communiqués, which had lost nothing of their grandiloquence and controversial effect. Admiral William Halsey ordered that messages not be sent through MacArthur's headquarters because he believed it would leak through the communiqués.[73] Marines sang, "Mine eyes have seen MacArthur with a Bible on his knee, He is pounding out communiqués for guys like you and me."[74] And soon after MacArthur arrived in Melbourne, a committee from the Australian Parliament was demanding to know why there were differences between figures given in intelligence reports and those in the communiqués.[75]

This drew a lengthy response from MacArthur, arguing that the differences in casualties between the communiqués and intelligence estimates could be easily explained: only casualties known to the enemy were released, while others, such as those that had happened in training, were hidden. He added that Washington was complaining that he put far too much information into his messages. Further, it was

not the purpose or desire of military authorities to use the official communique [*sic*] for propaganda or to affect in any way the free flow of public opinion. Under no circumstances should the communiques be regarded as a substitute for energetic and thorough reportorial effort. They are historical records with the emphasis which animates a local press. They are designed to influence the policy of the press and to control it just as little as possible.[76]

When the complaints reemerged two months later, the SWPA commander added that his communiqués were "not intended in any way to be what might be termed 'news copy'—it is a historical report of the events which have occurred in the past twenty-four hours." His communiqués were not news, MacArthur was arguing, they were notes for history. Reporter Clark Lee realized this when he grumbled that MacArthur's problems with the press "were caused by the fact that he [MacArthur] was operating in terms of history to be written 2,000 years hence, and the reporters were working against tomorrow morning's deadline."[77]

Others have disputed MacArthur's explanation. Historian D. Clayton James asserts that after Australia granted SWPA control over censorship and publicity, "Australian newspapers would have to rely almost solely on his GHQ communiqués for news of the war in the Southwest Pacific."[78] This is a conclusion Lee shared, noting that reporters were discouraged from the independent gathering of information.[79] Other reporters disagreed. "All pertinent information from the entire Pacific gravitated to that [MacArthur's] headquarters," recalled CBS's William J. Dunn, "and the enterprising reporter could learn a lot more than was handed him routinely in the official communiqué. Daily press conferences were structured around the communiqués, but we usually gleaned more from the questions it prompted."[80]

MacArthur's communiqués also contained serious errors that hurt military morale. One mistake, repeated throughout the Pacific War, was the announcement that fighting had ended before it had actually ceased. General Robert Eichelberger, whose public and private writings recorded many mistakes in the communiqués, wrote in his memoir that "public-relations officers on General MacArthur's staff chose to call this last phase of the Papuan campaign a 'mopping-up operation.' Instead, it was a completely savage and expensive battle."[81] Another oft-quoted statement by Eichelberger on this incident, written months after the battle to his wife, claimed, "General MacArthur announced his return to Australia by saying that there was nothing left in Papua but some 'mopping up' at Sanananda. This was just an excuse to get home as at that time there was no indication of any crackup of the Japs at Sanananda."[82] Yet the general had forgotten—as have several subsequent historians—that it was Eichelberger's own letters that likely gave MacArthur the impression that fighting had ended. Nor did the communiqué use "mopping up" but instead said the Sanananda position had been encircled and the destruction of the Japanese forces in Papua could be "now regarded as accomplished." Nevertheless, taking Sanananda cost more Allied lives than taking Buna.[83] The same thing happened again during the liberation of Manila in early 1945 when MacArthur prematurely announced it had fallen.[84] MacArthur's communiqués are all the more surprising since he understood that American troops were "quick to detect propaganda and inclined to resent it."[85]

Criticism of MacArthur's communiqués, on the whole, misses their purpose. Despite what the marine ditty claimed, Rogers explained, the general was not writing "for the benefit of his troops, the press, or the politicians in Canberra, London, and Washington. He wrote it for the American public, whose opinion could influence political forces in decisions of strategic planning and control." He added that the purpose was to "focus the attention of the American people on SWPA and its needs."[86] In the process, perhaps unavoidably, the communiqués hurt the morale of MacArthur's soldiers along with his legacy.

The Battle for Washington

With Japanese forces just over the Australian horizon, MacArthur's press campaign began as soon as he stepped off the train in Melbourne. He informed the crowd—and through the press, Washington and London—that his military success would depend on their allocation of resources.[87] After another press conference, where MacArthur again stressed the need for resources, correspondents asked one of the PRO staff if MacArthur wanted them "to write stories on his need for troops and supplies[,] thus aiding him in his quest."[88] That was exactly what MacArthur desired. As on Corregidor, MacArthur's PRO staff worked on creating a media campaign for resources. "From MacArthur's area you were not able to admit that there were two sides to the question," grumbled Clark Lee. "Stories either stressed the Pacific war, or they were killed. Thus, Diller's censorship became one of propaganda and special pleading for one area of the global war."[89] George Weller of the *Chicago Daily News* remembered, "MacArthur perceived that publicity was the lever of American power and he used it openly." He added that MacArthur's "ruthless censorship was a means not to deceive the Japanese enemy but to keep his material supplies increasing in an uncritical atmosphere."[90] Other reporters eagerly embraced the part. "When Prime Minister John Curtin of Australia voiced his appeal for a more urgent view of the Pacific war by those who formulate global strategy," intoned William Dunn of CBS over the radio, "it can't be denied that he struck a sympathetic note for those of us who have watched the preliminaries . . . and the progress of that war."[91]

MacArthur even had a public relations officer touring America in the person of Carlos P. Romulo. A Filipino newspaper editor, Romulo had fled to Corregidor and worked as a press aide broadcasting propaganda. He had been the last man to escape, flying out on an old plane under fire on the day Bataan fell. Reaching Australia, he was assigned to MacArthur's Public Relations Office, where he began dictating his book on the fall of the Philippines and repeatedly referred to MacArthur's actions during the battle as miraculous.[92] It was to become a best seller.

With the approval of MacArthur, Quezon, and Stimson, Romulo traveled across the United States, telling of the heroics of the Filipinos, but also representing MacArthur. In books, articles, interviews, and lectures, Romulo set about his work, visiting 466 Americans cities along the way. On a visit to Cooperstown, New York, he addressed a crowd of ten thousand who came to their feet to cheer when MacArthur's name was spoken, a response repeated in Philadelphia and New York. Romulo informed MacArthur that American public opinion wanted a second front opened in the Southwest Pacific Area and MacArthur in Washington as the supreme commander of the United States' armed forces: "This is the consensus of opinion among newspapermen and among leaders of thought I have talked to." So well did Romulo perform his task that Quezon added him to his cabinet in exile as secretary of information and public relations.[93]

MacArthur first began using news stories to spur Washington to make military changes soon after his arrival in Australia. On arrival, he discovered that his command had not yet been officially established. Nor would Washington define it for another month as the army and navy bickered over who would control the Pacific war. Though the reporters were kept apprised of the situation, MacArthur refused to allow any publicity. After four weeks, the reporters—and apparently MacArthur, too—had enough. An "unofficial" spokesman from MacArthur's headquarters met with a group of correspondents who, as William Dunn recalled, "made it plain we thought the time had come for the media to raise its voice." Nevertheless, the spokesman would only release a brief statement saying that MacArthur was still waiting for his command to be organized in Washington and told the reporters not to take a side on the story. Dunn, for one, found a way around the restriction by broadcasting that "despite President Roosevelt's announcement at his weekly press conference in Washington yesterday, the official status of General MacArthur is still a source of puzzlement to correspondents in Australia this evening." After relaying the brief statement, Dunn quoted the lead editorial from the *Melbourne Herald* that MacArthur's command needed to be formalized and "there is a fairly widespread idea that there has been some nibbling attempt at encroachment, by politicians or Generals, or both, in America and perhaps even here, upon the supreme commander's authority." Dunn later remembered that "other correspondents filed similar reports, which were given good play in the American press," and MacArthur's official command of the SWPA was soon established.[94]

It did not take long for Allied leaders in Washington to discover what MacArthur was up to. Supreme Court Justice Felix Frankfurter repeated a rumor to Stimson that "MacArthur is talking very disloyally to the Australians about the plans of his superiors here. In short, he is arguing very strongly and really egging the Australians on to try to make the Australian theatre the main theatre of the war and to postpone what we are trying to do in regard to fighting Hitler first."[95] At a private meeting with Stimson and Major General Alexander D. Surles, head of the War Department's PRD, correspondent Clark Lee said many in MacArthur's command believed they were not getting the supplies needed because their chief was a "political threat." Surles responded cryptically that "the worst day in MacArthur's life was the day the Patterson-McCormick press named him as a presidential possibility."[96] Surles had other ways to handle columnists who promoted the Pacific war too aggressively, delivering a harsh lecture to the influential military columnist George Fielding Eliot when Eliot began advocating for an offensive in the Pacific.[97] After Major General Charles Willoughby—MacArthur's G-2— visited Marshall in Washington, he reported to Eichelberger that he felt that "something may and will be done to hurt the Japs but that everything possible will be done to see that the Jap is hurt and MacArthur not helped in doing it."[98] Nevertheless, neither statement proves a conspiracy against MacArthur.

Certainly, as his biographer D. Clayton James observes, MacArthur became "extremely sensitive about any suggestions in print that his theater faced further subordination in global strategy and logistical planning."[99] A prime example of this came when MacArthur complained to Marshall that the *New York World-Telegram* had editorialized that Australians could not be faulted for complaining they were not getting enough supplies since Allied commitments showed "Australia no longer can count on priority." MacArthur explained that the editorial was "featured in all Australian papers and has caused a tremendous upheaval of bitter resentment throughout this country." Marshall agreed that such editorials were damaging to morale and altogether untrue. He added that MacArthur could "do much to counteract the ill effects of this editorial through the medium of press releases emanating from your headquarters."[100]

Marshall then attempted to curb MacArthur's press offensive. A few days earlier the *Washington Post* had written about "a veiled suggestion that the American public has been misinformed on the number and strength of United States forces ready to meet the Japanese in the Australian sector." Marshall assumed the source was MacArthur. "This press release originating from your headquarters can only serve to fan the indignation and resentment that has resulted from such editorial of which you complain," Marshall admonished. He added that the "article mentioned above creates the impression that you are objecting to our strategy by indirection. I assume this to be an erroneous impression." MacArthur denied having anything to do with the article, except in attempting "to protect government and military leaders by showing that sufficient resources were not available to do what was believed possible by the public and demanded by the [Australian] opposition." [101] Such statements could not have fooled Marshall.

In his campaign for resources, MacArthur was battling not only the War Department but commands in Europe and the Mediterranean whom he viewed as the beneficiaries of Germany First favoritism. He certainly was watching events in Europe carefully. MacArthur wore every decoration ever awarded to him but stopped when he saw a photo of Eisenhower wearing none of his medals.[102] After talking with MacArthur in late 1943, General Eichelberger noted that George Patton was viewed as "a great fellow until he began to get a lot of publicity, and then I haven't heard anything more about what a great soldier he is."[103]

In January 1944, General T. J. Davis—one of Supreme Headquarters Allied Expeditionary Force's (SHAEF's) PROs—wrote MacArthur saying Eisenhower and company watched the SWPA as closely as he did the European Theater of Operations.[104] He might have added it was with the same amount of jealousy. As the North African campaign drew to a close in the spring of 1943, Harry Butcher—a close aide to Eisenhower—visited the United States and was dismayed to find the "American public seems more interested in activities in the Pacific, perhaps because hardships have been dramatized and victories, no matter how small or large, thoroughly exploited in newspapers, magazines, and radio, and not only through normal news coverage, but by public relations men who returned from the Pacific to broadcast and to lecture." Butcher reported to Eisenhower that unless his theater began publicizing their accomplishments, "public opinion is likely to succumb to the wooing of the salesmanship of the Pacific."[105] These and other reports coming from America caused Eisenhower to worry that the Germany First strategy might be abandoned.[106] A few months later correspondent John Gunther reported to Butcher that

> the "Beat Japan First" slogan affords convenient refuge for a number of dissident groups—those who hate the British, those who fear the Russians, the Australians, the New Zealanders, the Hearst press, the Chicago Tribune, and those who are simply against anything the present administration wants to do. Thus, and with the others should be included those Republicans who want MacArthur for a presidential candidate, the "beat Japan First" group has developed into a first class cabal.[107]

A concerned Eisenhower began telling reporters that Germany must be defeated before Japan.[108] By the spring of 1944, Butcher complained to Eisenhower that Roosevelt might feel pressure during an election year to send more supplies to MacArthur.[109] Another officer recorded that Eisenhower kept up with the press on MacArthur. "Ike had just read [war correspondent] Frazier Hunt's book deifying MacArthur," recorded Everett Hughes in his diary on September 16, 1944. "Ike certainly hates McA—was with him 9 years."[110] Likewise, during the Battle of the Bulge, Omar Bradley's staff blamed their supply shortages on the SWPA and the breakdown of the Germany First strategy.[111]

Despite the rivalry, Butcher could not help being professionally impressed by the skill of MacArthur's public relations. Shortly after Kenney's planes virtually annihilated a Japanese convoy at the Battle of the Bismarck Sea in March 1943, he, along with a group of MacArthur's staff, including a member of the PRO, arrived in Washington to lobby for more aircraft. "The papers were full of the Bismarck Sea story," Kenney remembered, "as it was the best news to come out of the Pacific for some time."[112] Butcher heard the story from George Marshall and "was impressed especially by the showmanship ability of the MacArthur people. MacArthur's delegates had arrived at the 'Home Office' just after a good victory and succeeded in exciting a wide spread [sic] interest. Not that they weren't entitled to all credit and perhaps even to more credit because of their ability to cash in!"[113] Roosevelt, who had carefully laid the media foundation for the Germany First strategy, was thus challenged by MacArthur at every turn in the press.

Naval Engagements

The United States' military was divided on how to fight the war in the Pacific. The US Navy hoped to implement a version of their prewar strategy known as War Plan Orange. It held that the navy would advance across the Central Pacific, destroy the Japanese fleet, and secure strategic island bases on a direct route to Tokyo.[114] The fly in the ointment was MacArthur. Like the navy, he also had a defeat to avenge and wanted to advance up the islands of the Southwest Pacific toward the Philippines. For their part, the Joint Chiefs of Staff (JCS) saw the Pacific Ocean Area (POA) under Admiral Nimitz as the main theater of the Pacific War and planned to allot supplies accordingly.[115]

The result was a division of resources between Nimitz's advance across the Central Pacific and MacArthur's advance from the South Pacific. As historian Ronald Spector writes, the "adoption of this course of action was due less to strategic wisdom than to the army and navy's reluctance to entrust their forces to the command of an officer of the rival service, together with the almost insolvable problem of what to do with a popular hero like MacArthur." Yet as Spector and other historians have noted, the two-pronged advance under a divided command could, and almost did, lead to disaster. As with other theaters, it was only America's massive material output that made the strategy work.[116] Yet no future critic was more cutting than MacArthur himself, writing after the war that the split command "resulted in divided effort, the waste, diffusion, and duplication of force, and the consequent extension of the war, with added casualties and cost."[117]

MacArthur made attacking the Central Pacific advance a central part of his media campaign. "As a consequence," historian William Manchester notes, "dispatch [*sic*] from 'Somewhere in Australia' repeatedly quoted 'authoritative military and civilian circles' as saying that the war against Japan would be won much more quickly if men and equipment were diverted from Nimitz and sent to Australia."[118] When the marine corps took heavy losses at Tarawa in November 1943, MacArthur pounced on the opportunity to make the case for his own advance.[119] He likewise received assistance from the War Department. Marshall, for example, quietly got Admiral Ernest King to agree to put the Philippines in MacArthur's theater for "psychological reasons."[120]

Despite Marshall's intervention, MacArthur lost the first round of debates in 1942 to the navy. Admiral King decided that the large Japanese base at Rabaul, even though it seemed to be in SWPA's area, should be the navy's initial objective and devised a plan that would send naval forces straight through MacArthur's command. Marshall—who had a furious MacArthur on his hands—managed to reach a compromise where the army would move toward Rabaul through New Guinea and the western Solomon Islands, while the navy would advance along the eastern Solomons. Both services agreed to support each other as needed, and the SWPA theater was redrawn slightly to give the navy control over Guadalcanal.[121] At the beginning of July 1942 the Allies learned the Japanese were building an airfield on Guadalcanal, and the US Navy began to draw up hasty plans to land the First Marine Division.[122]

Thus, it came to pass on August 7, 1942, that the First Marine Division landed on Guadalcanal and began a brutal six-month struggle in the shadowy jungle. After the Japanese inflicted a stinging defeat on Allied naval forces at the Battle of Savo Island, the navy departed. "With the exception of Pearl Harbor," writes historian Craig L. Symonds, "it was the worst defeat in the history of the United States Navy." The navy concealed their losses for as long as censorship could be justified. In fact, they did not bother telling the army until two months later.[123] MacArthur's headquarters knew, of course, and so did the war correspondents. "Story going around that during the battle of SAVO ISLAND during night [*sic*] of Aug 9–10, our own ships fired on each other in the confusion," George Kenney wrote in his diary. "The newspaper crowd seem to know about it and hint that they got the information from some

Navy personnel . . . hard to understand why the Navy on the 10th pulled away from GUADALCANAL all combat ships and also the supply vessels with cargos still on board that were badly needed by the Marines."[124] Nor were army leaders in Washington fooled. "The Navy is trying to temper the news to the outside world," Stimson reflected after learning of the defeat. "I think that is a mistaken doctrine. The public can stand it better when bad news comes in a single lump and it does not beget distrust of the service authorities."[125]

Around the same time, the naval leadership in Washington chose to pick another fight with MacArthur over censorship. Marshall wrote explaining that the navy was concerned that an American broadcaster in Melbourne had given the naval strength in the Solomon Islands.[126] MacArthur replied that the offending news items had come from New Zealand, which was under Nimitz's jurisdiction. But, he added, there was increasing "resentment here on lack of authoritative info from our own people." Marshall replied the next day inquiring why the offending stories carried the byline "Gen. MacArthur HQ." MacArthur pointed out the stories had come from other Allied nations that had reporters stationed in Australia. He promised to remove his headquarters as a dateline, but again warned of "growing resentment by Austns [Australia] against lack of news on an opn [operation] in their immediate neighborhood, affecting their security, in which their navy actively engaged." He then took a renewed shot at the navy's censorship demands:

> Austn Govt cooperates fully within scope of its laws but latter do not authorize complete rigidity evidently desired by Navy. I can attempt to suppress by arbitrary action the foreign transmission of all references to Solomons engagement but it is contrary to Austn law with no justification in Amer or Brit law. Rules of censorship issued from Wash (completely understood and followed) carry no authority for arbitrary decisions for special purposes and when exceeded a dangerous situation involving legal action is risked.[127]

The next day MacArthur reiterated this point by passing along a message from Curtin asking when news of the sinking of the Australian cruiser *Canberra* could be released.[128] King balked, and news of the sinking was concealed for another two months.[129] Meanwhile, MacArthur told Marshall that Curtin complained that the only news he received of the Solomons campaign was from the navy's official dispatches.[130] In other words, almost nothing.

When *New York Times* journalist Hansen Baldwin arrived on Guadalcanal, he found confusion, supply shortages, despair, and heavy censorship. Only 1,500 words had been released about the battle, mostly by MacArthur. On his return to Washington, Baldwin's account of the battle soon leaked to columnist Drew Pearson, who quickly published it. Working with the Office of

War Information (OWI)—whose staff were sick of naval reticence—Baldwin published an eight-part series castigating the navy and the Germany First strategy along with lamenting that MacArthur was more a figurehead than a supreme commander. This irritated Stimson and Marshall, who read it as another salvo from MacArthur's supporters in the press against the evils of the divided command. Stimson recorded the press had "gathered together in full cry like hounds on a hot trail." There were geographic reasons for two commands in the Pacific, he added, but the "press will not . . . understand these hard outstanding facts and insists that the division has been made at the behest of the Navy for the purpose of belittling MacArthur." Nevertheless, Baldwin's story inspired Frank Knox, secretary of the navy, to take public relations out of King's hands.[131] Baldwin's articles, and the subsequent press storm, also had a more enduring effect on command in Washington. King, who according to Stimson was "in a very humble frame of mind on account of the pounding he is getting from the press," suggested that he move his offices into the newly built Pentagon beside Marshall to create better interservice communication. Marshall happily agreed. The days when top army and navy leadership occupied separate buildings were gone forever.[132]

There was a notable exception among the admirals' suspicion of the press, and he arrived to take command of naval forces in the South Pacific just as Baldwin was writing his articles about Guadalcanal. Despite having an active war career, William "Bull" Halsey had not yet attracted much publicity. The Solomons campaign would make him a household name. Halsey's skill with the press was evident on his first visit to Guadalcanal. He was pleased to see reporters, gave as much information as possible, posed for photographs, and offered a few colorful opinions about the Japanese. By the end of the month, Halsey's face was on the cover of *Time* magazine.[133] The coauthor of his memoir would later write that Halsey was "merely a victim of the press's conviction that the American public requires its military heroes to be picturesque."[134] A member of his staff would get closer to the truth when he observed that Halsey was "a seagoing Hamlet."[135]

The admiral understood the power of public opinion and its ability to shape military decisions. This trait was most vividly revealed on January 2, 1943, when Halsey visited New Zealand. The Japanese drive southward had been checked, but it was unclear whether the halt was permanent. That at least was the view of the New Zealand public, who also noted their island's lack of adequate defenses. Facing calls to bring home the New Zealand divisions then serving under Bernard Law Montgomery in North Africa, Prime Minister Peter Fraser knew he had to do something. He met Halsey at the airport and on the way to the hotel told him of his problem. Halsey offered to help, which was fortunate since Fraser already had the reporters waiting. In the typically colorful interview that followed, Halsey stated emphatically that "Japan's next move will be to retreat. . . . They will not be able to stop going back." New Zealand's divisions remained in North Africa to play an important part in the Mediterranean theater.[136]

Halsey's focus on press attention had its detractors, who raised serious concerns about some of Halsey's actions. Samuel Eliot Morison, official historian for the US Navy, concluded that in the admiral's "efforts to build public morale in America and Australia, Halsey did what Spruance refused to do—build up an image of himself as an exponent of Danton's famous principle, 'Audacity, more audacity, always audacity.' That was the real reason for his fumble in the Battle for Leyte Gulf."[137] Another damaging mistake came during the New Zealand press conference when Halsey stated the war would be over before the end of 1943. Widely quoted in the media, the remark caused an uproar in Washington. Industrialists worried that workers would slacken production. War Department bureaucrats worried industrialists would believe the prophecy and begin retooling for peace. To his credit, Halsey realized his mistake. After the war, he admitted that "I knew we wouldn't be in Tokyo that soon! . . . I may be tactless, but I am not a damned fool! What the civilian bigwigs didn't consider is this: my forces were tired; their morale was low; they were beginning to think that they were abused and forgotten, that they had been fighting too much and too long. Moreover, the new myth of Japanese invincibility had not yet been entirely discredited." But as E. B. Potter, Halsey's most important biographer, argues, "few officers were more careful about the image they projected. It seems unlikely that he would willingly have made a fool of himself in the international press." Potter contends

that the admiral began making such predictions during the dark days of October and November as a means of encouraging the embattled troops on Guadalcanal, a sort of coach's pep talk to hearten his apparently losing team, and that he continued to exude optimism through habit when better times arrived. According to this explanation, the newsmen who saw him regularly understood that such talk was for local consumption and did not report it. But when Halsey repeated it at general press conferences, the story reached the worldwide media with embarrassing repercussions.

Whatever the reason, Halsey became much more circumscribed in his dealings with the press.[138]

The Press of Battle

As MacArthur began his own counterattack in the jungles of Papua New Guinea, his press campaign led to grumbling among some of his commanders because all units and personnel were censored in the early part of the campaign.[139] A few subordinates, and several subsequent historians, have argued that MacArthur purposely denied his commanders media attention. Historian William Leary, for example, argues that "MacArthur's subordinates were the forgotten men of World War II. While European battlefield commanders such as Bradley and Patton became familiar names to the American people, Krueger and Eichelberger were relatively unknown."[140] Other historians have seconded this conclusion.[141]

The man most responsible for propagating the idea of MacArthur's forgotten generals was Robert Eichelberger. With the situation in New Guinea deteriorating rapidly, MacArthur summoned Eichelberger and ordered him to take over American forces there. Eichelberger described the interview: "'If you capture Buna,' the Allied commander said, 'I'll give you a Distinguished Service Cross and recommend you for a high British decoration. Also,' he continued, referring to the complete anonymity under which all American commanders in that theater functioned, 'I'll release your name for newspaper publication.'"[142] MacArthur knew how to motivate Eichelberger, for he was a man obsessed with publicity—mostly his own. Leaving the command of the Seventy-Seventh Division before coming to the SWPA, he asked an aide to send him the news stories of his departure.[143] While Eichelberger was commanding I Corps in Australia, his headquarters found soldiers were singing less-than-patriotic ditties about army life and issued a memorandum suggesting these tunes be rewritten to celebrate the corps and its commander. One suggested lyric went:

> Oh we'll fight this war to the finish
> And we're sure we will conquer the foe
> For we've vowed not to halt our advances
> Until "Eich" reigns within Tokyo[144]

Such an attitude was bound to cause trouble, particularly in MacArthur's publicity-sensitive command.

It was Eichelberger's fate to never get the recognition he craved and deserved. He was brave, cared about his soldiers, and led from the front. When Buna fell, MacArthur kept his promise, and Eichelberger was decorated and his name released to the press.[145] Yet he was angered when MacArthur blocked an attempt to award him the Medal of Honor, denied a request for him to be transferred to Europe for an army command, and gave a new field army command to Walter Krueger instead of Eichelberger.[146] Later, he wrote that after Buna "when . . . articles began to come back from the States in such magazines as *Life* and *Saturday Evening Post*, General MacArthur sent for me. . . . He said, 'Do you realize I could reduce you to the grade of colonel tomorrow and send you home?" There is only Eichelberger's recollection of this encounter, and he did not provide context. It did, however, make him suspicious of publicity, telling a friend in the Bureau of Public Relations he would "rather have you slip a rattlesnake in my pocket . . . than to have you give me any publicity."[147] These comments have been used by many historians as examples of MacArthur's egotism and unwillingness to share press attention with subordinates.[148] Perhaps MacArthur was simply aping John J. Pershing from World War I. As he knew from bitter experience, only the AEF's commander had been allowed any media glory from that conflict.[149]

There is also evidence that Eichelberger's complaints represented resentment more than reality. If one tracks Eichelberger's name in the *New York Times*, his publicity dipped when he was not in the fighting. But it did not disappear. In late 1944 and 1945 when he had sworn off publicity, he was mentioned more frequently than after Buna.[150] MacArthur also saddled Eichelberger with the job of escorting Eleanor Roosevelt when she visited the SWPA. It was a stressful chore for Eichelberger, a Republican, but hardly one designed to deny him media attention. Nor did MacArthur hide Eichelberger in his memoirs, praising him as "fearless in battle" and "a commander of the first order."[151]

Likewise, some of Eichelberger's colleagues rose to fame without feeling the jealous rage of the SWPA commander. Kenney, for example, was under censorship for four months before his name was released to the press. But he also received plenty of headlines after the Battle of the Bismarck Sea, remembering, "I almost began to believe I was as big a shot as the papers said."[152] This included the cover of *Life* magazine.[153] In fact, MacArthur praised the airman extravagantly at press conferences.[154] Walter Krueger would appear on the cover of *Time* in January 1945 and later in MacArthur's memoirs as an army commander unmatched in the "annals of American history."[155] As the war moved out of New Guinea and thus out from under Australian censorship, even Eichelberger had to admit MacArthur's subordinates received more publicity. "You have doubtless noticed from out here a release of information about people which would have been unthinkable a year ago," he wrote to his wife in January 1944. "I have always thought we should build up more publicity on our men and their achievements and incidentally on our officers."[156]

There were other reasons MacArthur's commanders did not always get the publicity they deserved. One day Eichelberger was going over a report with his aide, Captain Robert M. White, when General Walter Krueger, commander of the Sixth Army, appeared. Eichelberger introduced White as a former journalist. Krueger silently assessed White for a moment then said, "I wouldn't have a newspaper man on my staff." White, who came from two generations of reporters, stormed back to his desk, where a couple of current newspapermen were lounging. "I think you will find if you check the records of the Southwest Pacific theater," White wrote years later, "it was 18 months before General Krueger's name was filed out of the theater by any correspondent. And only then after he got on his staff an acknowledged newspaperman."[157] It is true that despite having his picture on the cover of *Time* magazine near the end of the war, Kruger received so little publicity that a few months later a reporter could title his article "General Walter Krueger: Mystery Man of the Pacific." Yet the four thick folders of carefully arranged newspaper clippings from Krueger's time commanding Third Army in the Louisiana Maneuvers during 1941 do not suggest unusual modesty.[158] Historian William M. Leary has noted that Krueger tried to deflect publicity, both because he feared the jealousy of rivals such as Eichelberger and because he was generally disinterested in it.[159] The White incident also shows that the press still had the power to control publicity.

It is true, as Eichelberger understood, that censorship also hid the gallant fighting of the Australians and American soldiers in New Guinea. "Watching the communiqués that come out from Colonel Knox and the Marines following every little fight," wrote Eichelberger, "I feel a mistake was made when our hard fighting [on Buna] was played down over here."[160] This is evident in that battles such as Guadalcanal are today remembered much more than the numerous landings along the New Guinea coast. Clark Lee wrote after the war, "Buna was nearly as bad as Tarawa or Guadalcanal . . . but Buna is already a nearly forgotten name in the American public mind. It is my conviction that Diller's censorship is partially to blame."[161] Over a half century later, little has changed.[162] Indeed, though MacArthur downplayed the casualties, many more Americans had died for Papua than for Guadalcanal.[163]

Meanwhile, the Pacific war was changing. At the Casablanca Conference in January 1943, Ernest King had argued that 30 percent of Allied resources be devoted to fighting Japan. This proposal went nowhere, although by this point 15 percent of resources were already reaching the Pacific, and many more US soldiers were fighting the Japanese than the Germans.[164] At Casablanca, American and British staff officers agreed that Rabaul, the main Japanese base in the South Pacific, should be taken. Richard Sutherland, MacArthur's chief of staff, explained, however, that MacArthur would need six additional divisions plus air support and supplies. He got two. But MacArthur was already working on an operation codenamed Cartwheel that put the lessons of Guadalcanal and Buna into use. Rabaul was cut off by landings made against weak spots in the Japanese-controlled islands, while other Japanese garrisons were left to wither on the vine.[165] How they fought was also changing. Despite MacArthur's battle with the navy, he and Halsey had forged an effective relationship. Meanwhile, Kenney had rebuilt MacArthur's air force to a great level of proficiency. In historian Mark Perry's words, this interservice cooperation was the "most successful air, land, and sea campaign in the history of warfare."[166]

Evidence that the tide had turned came in early March 1943, when a Japanese convoy sailing from Rabaul with reinforcements for New Guinea was discovered by Kenney's pilots. In the following battle, the Allies sank most of the ships, including all the transports using new "skip-bombing" tactics and slow-fused bombs. The Allies lost only six aircraft. The battle forced Japan to abandon using large convoys in supplying New Guinea, creating major supply shortages.[167]

Kenney awoke MacArthur at 3:00 a.m. on March 4 to tell him the news. The airman had never seen his boss so delighted, and after making "some wonderful remarks about what a great guy I was . . . [he] started outlining his communiqué."[168] Using Kenney's figures, MacArthur wrote that 22 Japanese ships consisting of 12 transports and 10 warships had been "sunk or are sinking" and 55 enemy planes were destroyed. Of the troops transported, MacArthur stated that almost fifteen thousand have been killed. Diller warned MacArthur that early pilot reports were often exaggerated. MacArthur snapped that he trusted Kenney. Eichelberger would claim later that the Australians also had their doubts. On March 7, MacArthur issued another communiqué raising enemy losses to 102 planes.[169] Unlike what later historians would claim, the figures were given to MacArthur by Kenney and he did not enlarge them for the communiqués.[170] By March 5, Kenney was on his way to Washington, DC, to lobby for more planes and for MacArthur's coming offensive against Rabaul. By the time he reached Hawaii, the Battle of the Bismarck Sea was big news.[171]

MacArthur took the victory as a chance to remind the US Navy of the ascendancy of air power. Frank Knox had recently reassured the Australians that Japan would need a huge naval force to invade the continent. MacArthur released a communiqué that noted Japan had naval control of the seas around Australia, adding that "control of such sea lanes no longer depends solely or even perhaps primarily upon naval power, but upon air power operating from land bases held by ground troops." An enraged King stalked the Pentagon looking for Marshall, who had the good sense to stay out of this latest MacArthur-Navy fuss.[172]

Only praise was heard for the Battle of the Bismarck Sea for five months until suddenly Kenney received a letter from the intelligence division of the army air force saying a "detailed study" of the battle "based on information forwarded here from the Southwest Pacific and on other data" showed the Japanese casualties cited in MacArthur's communiqué were grossly exaggerated. Only sixteen ships were present, of which three likely escaped. Kenney apparently ignored the letter until a month later when Marshall asked MacArthur if he had seen it.[173] MacArthur responded immediately and forcefully. He admitted that minor changes were made to the initial re-port but claimed they only upped the actual figures. He defended the com-muniqués as "factual and definite" and provided twenty-one names of the sunken ships, nineteen of which came from "captured documents and 2 addi-tional through air photographs." MacArthur concluded, "Official reports as well as the communiqué issued in this area are meticulously based upon offi-cial reports of operating commanders concerned and I am prepared to defend both of them officially and publicly."[174] However, most historians—including MacArthur's loyal chief of intelligence Charles A. Willoughby—have agreed with the lower figures.[175]

A more difficult question is why the investigation was begun at all. Even with the reduced numbers, the Battle of the Bismarck Sea was still a great victory. Naval resentment could be understood, but it was the normally pub-licity-obsessed army air force that began the wartime investigation. Two days before the letter was sent to Kenney, for example, Henry H. Arnold had written lamenting the lack of publicity for his airmen and hoping to find a "way of increasing the flow of material suitable for public announcement."[176] Naturally, MacArthur and his staff suspected a naval plot. MacArthur told Kenney that the navy was trying to belittle the battle since "it's against the rules for land-based airplanes to sink ships."[177] Fifty years later, Rogers de-scribed the incident as "one of the most insipid exercises in ingenuity and petulance ever organized by a general staff to discredit two of the nation's senior commanders."[178] If this is indeed the case, concludes historian D. Clay-ton James, it "cannot be decided for want of evidence."[179] Whoever did begin the investigation, however, could be sure that the controversy would come out during the war.[180]

Why did MacArthur defend his communiqués so strongly? He could have easily and credibly claimed that his fliers—unlike the investigators—were too busy fighting to count accurately.[181] Instead, his stubborn defense laid him open to historians' charges that the whole incident was characteristic of MacArthur's hunger for press glory and typical of his public relations policy and his communiqués.[182] Kenney's biographer has even suggested the airman was simply being loyal to an egotistical MacArthur in going along with the story.[183] Yet, as Rogers notes, "it was not MacArthur's duty to verify Kenney's operations reports. He was required by common sense, in the absence of proof to the contrary, to accept them as valid. If they were in error, Kenney's head was on the block, not MacArthur's."[184] MacArthur's motives are likely simple: he trusted Kenney's reports and defended his communiqué against what he believed was an attempt by the navy to discredit him. In this, the battle of publicity with the navy also played a role. "Halsey claimed to have killed 40,000 [enemy] in one convoy," MacArthur mused to Eichelberger, "so I guess I can claim to have killed 15,000."[185]

MacArthur for President

As Operation Cartwheel rolled forward, another battle was brewing in the United States. It had begun during the battle for Bataan when Senator Arthur Vandenberg of Michigan noticed that the praise MacArthur was receiving might be translated into a presidential campaign. Ever since, MacArthur had been inundated with requests that he challenge Roosevelt in 1944.[186] At least some newspapers were determined to help. "From the Republican point of view, the most available and satisfactory candidate is you," wrote the publisher of the *Army Navy Journal*, John O'Laughlin, to MacArthur. "You have enormous popularity throughout the country. There is public understanding that you have not been supplied with the means to inaugurate a real offensive against Japan, and the public belief is that in this failure to reinforce you, the President is actuated by a desire to make you the forgotten man."[187] Powerful Republican newspaper barons such as the Hearsts and the Pattersons set their media empires to begin campaigning for MacArthur.[188] Publisher Frank Gannett worked to draft MacArthur.[189] Robert McCormick, as usual, went a step further and was part of a small group that placed MacArthur's name on the ballot.[190] "The home front is on the 'ball,'" wrote Julius Klein to MacArthur, "the Chicago Sun published by my old friend Marshall Field and the Tribune of good old Bertie McCormick at least agree on one thing—MCARTHUR [*sic*]."[191] For these supporters the MacArthur for president campaign was the natural extension of Pacific First advocacy.

MacArthur's own intentions have caused considerable debate among his biographers.[192] His staff likewise had mixed opinions. After MacArthur's death, Diller could not recall hearing MacArthur ever say he wanted to be president, but believed he "would have liked" the job.[193] One reporter remembered that Diller wanted to be MacArthur's White House press secretary.[194] Diller's subordinate Philip La Follette actively attempted to get MacArthur the nomination.[195] Lloyd Lehrbas, another officer on Diller's staff, was violently opposed to the idea and told MacArthur so.[196] Meanwhile, Willoughby was in contact with Vandenberg about MacArthur's candidacy, but later claimed his boss was not interested in being president.[197] Kenney was opposed, and said MacArthur agreed with him.[198] Rogers, for his part, remembered MacArthur jokingly making plans for his presidency.[199] Eichelberger wrote his wife that MacArthur had spoken of the Republican nomination and that Eichelberger believed that the general expected it would be his.[200] Meanwhile, columnist Raymond Clapper visited MacArthur and reported back that he believed the general would take the nomination if it was offered to him. As another reporter later observed, MacArthur did not issue a denial, while the *New York Times* published a similar report from its own correspondent.[201]

Why then did MacArthur allow—and at times tacitly encourage—such talk? At least part of the answer lies in the fact that a presidential challenge was another way to put pressure on Roosevelt for more resources for the liberation of the Philippines. Eichelberger understood this, writing to his wife that the "one interview I saw repeated over here intimated . . . [MacArthur] did not want to be President but wanted to capture the Philippine Islands. I can see why it would not be desired to let it be known that the Presidency is *not* wanted since it would discourage certain supporters. . . . He doesn't want to say he wants to be President and he doesn't want to say he doesn't."[202] Many of his newspaper backers were accusing Roosevelt of not sending more support to the SWPA.[203] Likewise, letters of his supporters make clear that the lack of resources for the SWPA would be a major issue in a MacArthur presidential campaign. Publisher Roy Howard privately explained that his papers' lack of openly pressing for a MacArthur presidential run was to focus "public attention on the importance of the task entrusted to you and the urgent necessity of your being given adequate support in the attainment of your military objectives."[204] MacArthur certainly saw running the war as the main perk of the presidency. As he joked with Sutherland, "Dick when I get elected we will go back to Washington. . . . We will move into the War Building and we will run the war. I will let Congress run the country." Later, Rogers recalled typing an unsigned memorandum offering political support in exchange for being placed in command of all US military forces. Sutherland secretly visited the likely Republican nominee, Thomas Dewey, soon afterwards, though nothing else is known of the meeting.[205]

Fueling this possible presidential run was the suspicion that Roosevelt was purposely attempting to deprive SWPA of resources. This was a favorite accusation of Roosevelt's opposition.[206] McCormick told an interviewer in the summer of 1943 that "Roosevelt is in a hell of a position. If MacArthur wins a great victory, he will be President. If he doesn't win one, it will be because Roosevelt has not given him sufficient support."[207] After one of MacArthur's denials of interest in a presidential run—which he made occasionally—the supportive *San Francisco Examiner* proclaimed that "politicians, having nothing further to fear from him politically, should now be willing to send him sufficient men and equipment."[208] Historian Mark Perry notes that MacArthur's "command retained its reputation as a hotbed of paranoid anti-Roosevelt military operatives, a view that he fed."[209] Likewise, when Roosevelt's former speechwriter Robert E. Sherwood visited MacArthur's headquarters near the end of the war, he found "an acute persecution complex at work."[210]

If MacArthur and his aides were worried about Roosevelt, it was understandable. According to Rogers, MacArthur kept up with his fan mail, and from America poured in letters warning that he was despised by the New Dealers and their leader. "Among the higher councils of the New Dealers your name is tabu and you are a marked man," reported Carlos P. Romulo. "I don't know where they got the idea that you are a candidate for President and because of this there seems to be an effort—underhanded of course—to sidetrack you." Of course, Romulo did know, since he added that the Republican papers continued to praise the general and it "seems to infuriate the New Dealers more."[211] All this played into MacArthur's resentment of Roosevelt and the others in Washington for abandoning his army on Bataan.

The very suggestion of a MacArthur candidacy was already threatening to tarnish the general's image. Allowing praise to be heaped on a distant soldier was one thing, but if he entered the presidential race, MacArthur would be fair political game. In January 1944, John McCarten published the first critical article of MacArthur since Pearl Harbor in the *American Mercury*. MacArthur reacted with rage. He told Eichelberger, "They are afraid of me because they know I will fight them in the newspapers." Meanwhile, the article caused embarrassment to the War Department when it was added to the suggested reading list at the Army War College, a fact that drew condemnation from the floor of the United States Senate. The next month, the War Department suppressed another article critical of MacArthur in *Harper's Magazine* on security concerns. This in turn drew an angry editorial from *Harper's* that castigated the War Department and asked if "a man who stands protected by censorship should permit his name to be considered for the Presidency." Other news outlets agreed.[212]

Meanwhile Roosevelt, the political genius of his age, quietly watched. If MacArthur challenged the president for starving the SWPA of supplies and abandoning the Philippines, historian James MacGregor Burns writes, Roosevelt was ready with pre–Pearl Harbor messages from MacArthur promising the Philippines could be defended.[213] But the president was content to wait for the inevitable to happen. It came when a pro-MacArthur congressman gave the press an exchange of letters between himself and the general. MacArthur had agreed with the congressman's worries that left-wingers and New Dealers were establishing a monarchy in America and the congressman's desire to prevent this with a MacArthur presidency. True to his strategic goal, MacArthur added, "Out here we are doing what we can with what we have. I will be glad, however, when more substantial forces are placed at my disposition."[214] Reporter Allen Drury summed up the letters as showing the "general to be more than a little interested in the Republican nomination and in all probability reduces even further the remote likelihood of his getting it."[215] As his enemies pounced, MacArthur issued another statement denying any interest in running for office.[216] At the Republican Convention, he received one vote. MacArthur's romance with a 1944 presidential run never passed flirtation. That was enough, however, to create agonized longing from Republicans, jealous suspicion from Democrats, exasperation from the War

Department, and eventual embarrassment for the SWPA commander. It also brought plenty of condemnation from historians who used it as evidence for MacArthur's megalomania. Likewise, there is no way to know if it made anyone in Washington more eager to allocate additional resources to the SWPA.

Roosevelt and MacArthur's Hawaii Tête-à-Tête

As Cartwheel encircled Rabaul, Nimitz's forces had begun the drive through the Central Pacific. It began on November 20, 1943, when US Marines landed on the small atolls of Makin and Tarawa in the Gilbert Islands. Besides the loss of an escort carrier sunk by a submarine, American losses on Makin were light. Not so on Tarawa. By the time the island was secured after three days of fighting, more than one thousand Americans were dead and an additional two thousand wounded. Newspapers showed pictures of dead marines to a stunned American public. Next up were the Marshall Islands, where the marines landed on January 31, 1944, on the small islands of northern and southern Kwajalein Atoll. Because of lessons learned at Tarawa, American losses were lighter. The Mariana Islands of Guam, Saipan, and Tinian were attacked at the end of July 1944. Tinian fell easily. Guam was a bloodier fight, with the Americans losing over one thousand killed and more than six thousand wounded. But it was Saipan that was bought at the highest price: fourteen thousand dead Americans, thirty thousand dead Japanese soldiers, and twelve thousand noncombatant Japanese who added the new horror of mass civilian suicide to the Pacific War. It was a grim reminder of the power of Japanese propaganda.[217]

The high casualties on Saipan reopened public debate on strategy in the Pacific. It began when the marine commander on Saipan, Lieutenant General Holland M. "Howlin' Mad" Smith, fired the commander of the US Army's Twenty-Seventh Division, Major General Ralph Smith, for alleged lack of aggressiveness. William Randolph Hearst's *San Francisco Examiner* saw a chance to promote MacArthur for overall command of the Pacific. The *Examiner*'s headline of the story read, "Army General Relieved in Row over Marine Losses" and argued that the US Navy's Central Pacific strategy was causing heavy casualties. Other newspapers echoed these charges and argued for MacArthur to be put in overall command. *Time* and *Life* came to the Marine Corps's defense by castigating the fighting ability of the Twenty-Seventh Division. Though many in the army were concerned about the damage done to the morale of the division, Marshall decided not to correct the story, instead hoping—in vain—the Smith vs. Smith controversy would die.[218]

The heavy losses of the Central Pacific offensive occurred at a time when MacArthur's casualties were decreasing. After the long and bloody battles in

Papua and eastern New Guinea, Operation Cartwheel was paying off. Strong Japanese defenses were bypassed, and strategic points were occupied. After Rabaul had been isolated, MacArthur's forces leapfrogged along the equator, cutting off Japanese garrisons. Between April 22 and July 30, six landings were made with a total of 1,583 Americans killed in action.[219]

By the midsummer of 1944, it was clear a major decision would have to be made on the next objective of the Pacific War. MacArthur, of course, thought the next goal should be the Philippines. Led by Ernest King, the navy began arguing for bypassing the Philippines and landing on Formosa. As King explained after the war, the Formosa plan would have cut Japanese communications to their forces and natural resources in the south. It would also have provided a supply line to China.[220] In June, the JCS informed MacArthur, Nimitz, and the Combined Chiefs of Staff that Formosa would be the main objective rather than the Philippines. MacArthur responded with a long message arguing for the strategic importance of the Philippines but also for their psychological importance. Bypassing the archipelago "would admit the truth of Japanese propaganda to the effect that we had abandoned the Filipinos and would not shed American blood to redeem them . . . we would probably suffer such loss of prestige among all the peoples of the Far East that it would adversely affect the United States for many years." He then brought up public opinion: "I feel also that a decision to eliminate the campaign for the relief of the Philippines, even under appreciable military considerations, would cause extremely adverse reactions among the citizens of the United States." Marshall dismissed MacArthur's arguments, reminding the SWPA commander not to let "our personal feelings and Philippine political considerations to override our great objective."[221] MacArthur offered to return home to make his case. As one member of his staff later observed, the general likely believed Roosevelt would prefer to keep the politically dangerous MacArthur out of Washington in an election year.[222]

If this was MacArthur's reasoning, Roosevelt outsmarted him, and on July 6, the general was ordered to Hawaii. MacArthur was irritated. As he flew toward Honolulu, he grumpily paced up and down on the plane. Weldon E. "Dusty" Rhoades, his pilot, recalled MacArthur did not know what the meeting was about but suspected he would have to make the case for the liberation of the Philippines. MacArthur assumed that if, as he suspected, Roosevelt was to be present, the whole event was an election-year ploy.[223]

The election would indeed overshadow the entire visit. Along with a few political aides, the president was accompanied only by Admiral Leahy.[224] The stated rationale for the trip was to decide on future operations in the Pacific. But Roosevelt also realized that being seen with his commanders could not hurt him in the election. His staff certainly thought so. Steve Early, Roosevelt's press secretary, wrote as the president's ship approached Hawaii that

Early "urgently hope news photographs can be arranged showing President in action and [in] conference with members [of] his staff and those he will meet at [the] first stop. . . . Present importance greater than at time of Casablanca, Tehran, Cairo."[225] On Hawaii, Seabees would temporarily remove palm trees and construct a hidden ramp so Roosevelt could exit his car without being seen in a wheelchair.[226]

Yet if the trip was for propaganda purposes, it was a game MacArthur knew two could play. The general was late for the first meeting aboard the USS *Baltimore*, and his absence was growing embarrassing. Suddenly, Roosevelt's speechwriter Samuel I. Rosenman remembered, "a terrific automobile siren was heard, and there raced onto the dock and screeched to a stop a motorcycle escort and the longest open car I have ever seen." It was MacArthur, complete with stars, field marshal's hat, and a leather bomber jacket. "When the applause of the crowd died down, the General . . . dashed up the gangplank, stopped halfway up to acknowledge another ovation, and soon was on deck greeting the President." Rosenman was impressed.[227] "Douglas, why don't you wear the right kind of clothes?" inquired Leahy facetiously. MacArthur had eaten little and had not slept for twenty-eight hours. But Leahy saw "no strain other than looking a little tired."[228] He might have been hot in the leather jacket, but the first photographs showed MacArthur looking young and vigorous next to a haggard Roosevelt draped in an oversized white suit. Later Leahy, MacArthur, Nimitz, and Roosevelt were all photographed in front of a wall map with Nimitz and MacArthur taking turns holding a bamboo pointer. Nimitz pointed at Japan, MacArthur the Philippines. MacArthur had won the first round of the publicity bout.

For two days, MacArthur and Nimitz calmly and factually presented their respective cases.[229] MacArthur argued that the Philippines would isolate Japanese troops and resources in the south in the same way the Formosa operation promised to do. But Formosa contained a hostile population, while the Philippines held seventeen million friends. Roosevelt asked at one point about the heavy losses that could be expected from a landing on Luzon. MacArthur answered that his "losses would not be heavy, anymore than they have been in the past. The days of the frontal attack should be over. Modern infantry weapons are too deadly, and frontal assault is only for mediocre commanders."[230] This was a swipe at the navy's Central Pacific drive and a reminder of the bad press it had gathered.[231]

MacArthur also explained that he disagreed with the Formosa plan "not only on strategic but psychological grounds" and argued that morale and public opinion must be taken into consideration. The liberation of the Philippines would show the world that Japan was doomed. Bypassing the islands would mean thousands of American men, women, and children would die in concentration camps. He also brought up the still-open wounds of Corregidor and told the president that reinforcements could have been sent to the "Bataan and Corregidor garrisons, and probably not only saved the Philippines, but thereby stopped the enemy's advance." MacArthur said, "that to sacrifice the Philippines a second time could not be condoned or forgiven."[232] Likewise, "American public opinion will condemn you, Mr. President. And it will be justified."[233] He added that this resentment would be registered "against you at the polls this fall."[234]

By the time the conference ended, MacArthur had convinced the president and the two admirals.[235] Even the navy's official historian would later admit that "General MacArthur's strategic plan was sound, even if stripped of its political overtones" and add that postwar studies showed that Formosa was heavily defended and Japan would soon control most of China's coast.[236] MacArthur had won the second round of the publicity bout.

Roosevelt profited politically from both the meeting and the decision to invade the Philippines. His speechwriter, Robert E. Sherwood, later noted that "some cynics . . . remarked in undertones that perhaps the President's choice had been influenced by the thought that the Philippines would provide a more popular victory in an election year."[237] Certainly, Roosevelt wasted no time in telling reporters, holding a press conference right after MacArthur departed. A correspondent asked if MacArthur was going to "return" to the Philippines. "The only thing I could say in answer to that question . . . would be such as to possibly give the enemy an inkling as to which way we are going," the president fumbled. "We are going to get the Philippines back, and without question General MacArthur will take a part in it. Whether he goes direct or not, I can't say." Another reporter asked if they could write MacArthur was going to return to the Philippines. Yes, Roosevelt replied, and added, "He was correct the day he left Corregidor, and I told him he was correct. Remember, I came out and said it then?"[238] As troops landed on Leyte, Roosevelt issued a statement about the landing right after his opponent Thomas Dewey had charged that he had starved MacArthur of material. "It was clear," smirked Rosenman, "that the Republican candidate did not know what he was talking about." Roosevelt was more direct a few days later: "Speaking of the glorious operations in the Philippines—I wonder whatever became of the suggestion made a few weeks ago, that I had failed for political reasons to send enough forces or supplies to General MacArthur."[239]

Historian D. Clayton James claimed that Roosevelt and MacArthur made a deal to keep positive news coming from the Philippines. MacArthur issued communiqués greatly exaggerating the progress of Allied forces in Leyte, and when reporters complained, they were told by the PRO that "the elections in the United States are coming up in a few days and the Philippines *must* be kept on the front pages." Though James admits there is only circumstantial

evidence for a deal, other historians have taken the idea seriously.[240] Roosevelt
had won the third round of publicity.

Several historians have pointed out that the decision to invade the Philippines was not decided at the Honolulu Conference.[241] This is incorrect.
While the JSC did not end the debate until October 3, the evidence provided
by the participants clearly show all four men decided on the Philippines.[242]
MacArthur, of course, believed this, and his later autobiography as well as
the books by his aides provide confirmation.[243] Better evidence comes from
Admiral Leahy, who wrote in his diary that MacArthur and Nimitz's "agreement on the fundamental strategy" had made the "entire journey . . . fully
justified."[244] Not only did Roosevelt strongly suggest at his press conference
that MacArthur would soon return to the Philippines, but he also described
the meeting as "very useful" and "one of the most important we have held
in some time."[245] This may have been Roosevelt justifying his junket to the
Pacific. However, he told the same thing to John W. McCormack, the House
majority leader, who later wrote MacArthur, "Of the meeting at Hawaii—in
a most important conference—he gave the entire credit to you for selling
the Philippine campaign. He told us that you sold it to the other Naval and
Military leaders who were present at that conference in twenty-four hours,
that the plans were flown back to Washington for final action and approval."[246]

Conclusion

In early October 1944, word reached the SWPA Public Relations Division
that they would land in the Philippines on the first day of the invasion. Field
equipment and carbines were issued, and the PRO staff were squeezed onto
LST 452.[247] Since the landing in Normandy had been made famous with the
name D-Day, MacArthur christened the October 20 invasion of the Philippines "A-Day."[248] Diller instructed reporters, "On this great day nothing
shall be said or done that will detract in any way from the personal publicity or glorification of the commander-in-chief."[249] MacArthur, his staff, the
Philippine president, Sergio Osmeña (successor to the late Manuel Quezon),
and a small group of reporters came ashore on a landing barge that grounded
some thirty yards from the beach. The party waded ashore while a military
photographer snapped one of the most iconic pictures of MacArthur during
the war. Unlike later rumors suggested, the general's walk ashore was not
planned, rehearsed, or repeated that day.[250]

With wet sand clinging to his shoes, MacArthur had finally accomplished
his objective. When he had arrived in Australia, he knew that Allied military
and political leaders had settled on the Germany First strategy. If the cries
of a dying American army in Bataan had not brought help from America, no

amount of reasoning in secret cables and conferences would make the Pacific a priority. But MacArthur also knew that public opinion could be used to obtain troops and supplies. He therefore set about a press campaign to put as much pressure on Roosevelt and the War Department as possible. The result was an unprecedented challenge to Roosevelt's own press campaign to build public support for a war against Germany, demonstrating how the media influenced different theaters.

By the landings on Leyte, MacArthur's media campaign had produced tremendous results. Though the Allies always maintained that they were continuing the Germany First strategy, the army forces sent to the Pacific had more than doubled from December 1942 to December 1943. This, according to the official army history, was one hundred thousand more than what Washington planners had expected. By the end of 1943, total US military forces in the Pacific, China, Burma, India (CBI), and Alaska were slightly more than those in the other theaters of the war.[251] Because of preparations for the cross-channel invasion, by October 1944 roughly twice as many US military personnel were in Europe as in the Pacific.[252] Nevertheless, it was a major shift away from the Germany First strategy. The Pacific war had grown into what historian Ronald Spector described as "a unique and unprecedented conflict—the first, and probably the last, to be waged on such a scale and upon such a stage."[253] As MacArthur waded ashore, off the coast of Leyte Gulf the US Navy was engaged in the largest naval battle in history.[254] MacArthur could also take pride in the fact that the counteroffensives in the Solomon Islands and New Guinea had begun months before the landings in the Mediterranean and a year before American troops touched European soil. The SWPA commander and his media campaign could not claim sole credit. Admiral King, Prime Minister Curtin, and pressing events also made the case for resources to be sent to the Pacific. But King had no intention of these resources going to the SWPA, nor was it inevitable that the Philippines would be a major objective. MacArthur had used every resource at his disposal, including a highly successful media campaign, to set him once again on Philippine soil.

Yet, his media campaign had come at a tremendous personal cost. MacArthur has been severely criticized for the heavy censorship in the SWPA, which was largely forced on him by the Australians, the US Navy, and the War Department. But MacArthur and his staff were also to blame. Historian Steven Casey has correctly noted that MacArthur's press policy changed as the war progressed and underwent a major overhaul after even reporters from friendly papers began a mass exodus of the SWPA in disgust.[255] His communiqués, which would have likely not raised an eyebrow in a nineteenth-century context, were ridiculed and mistaken as a product of a massive ego rather than an attempt to create a case for a higher priority for the SWPA.

This was made worse by a public relations staff who believed they must defend their leader. MacArthur and his staff may have exaggerated the perfidy of the general's foes. But enemies he had, and the US Navy, the New Dealers, and irritated reporters fought back. They were provoked by MacArthur's demands for supplies, annoyed by the pomposity of the communiqués, and enraged that MacArthur could even think of being president. In this last regard, the general's friends in the United States were as damaging as his enemies, allowing him to maneuver into an embarrassing political position.

MacArthur's press campaign likewise did nothing to endear him to his subordinates. The general was not the egomaniac and military fraud that some historians have described. Indeed, Kenney, Halsey, and to a lesser extent Krueger made reputations with the public and for posterity. But the resentment still existed. American GIs also found little to love about MacArthur, and false rumors metastasized about the general's cowardice and conceit. These stories even reached the enemy. Yamashita, the Japanese general commanding in the Philippines, apparently also believing the "Dugout Doug" myth, was convinced MacArthur was still in Australia, and even refused to believe the photos of the general wading ashore. If he had known that MacArthur was on the beach, he lamented after the war, he would have sent a suicide mission to kill him.[256] There was ample opportunity since it took more than an hour for the signal corps to get the radio transmitter ready. With the sound of rain and gunfire in the background, MacArthur took the microphone. "People of the Philippines," he intoned, "I have returned."[257]

Chapter Three

"Pitiless Publicity"

Major General George S. Patton Jr. gazed from the deck of the USS *Augusta* toward the flickering lights of the twin Moroccan cities of Fedala and Casablanca. It was 2:00 a.m. on November 8, 1942, and stretching across the placid sea illuminated by a few stars was the largest American invasion fleet yet assembled during World War II. An offshore wind mingled the scent of the sea with the smell of coal fires and grass ashore. The historian Samuel Eliot Morison, observing the same scene from the deck of the USS *Brooklyn*, remembered later that "Africa was never so dark and mysterious to ancient sea-rovers as she seemed that night, veiled in clouds and hushed in slumber."[1] After months of raucous debate on where to strike, the US Army was finally in the war against Hitler.

The coming campaign in North Africa and Sicily would showcase the respective fighting philosophies of Patton and his commanding general Dwight D. Eisenhower. In his book *The Echo of Battle*, historian Brian Linn argues that the US Army's understanding of warfare has been shaped by "three distinct intellectual traditions." The first were the Guardians, who saw warfare as a science and focused on fortifications and military expertise. The second were the Heroes, who "emphasized the human element, and defined warfare by personal intangibles such as military genius, experience, courage, morale, and discipline." Finally, the Managers argued that "modern warfare" was the "logical outgrowth of political and economic rivalry" and focused on mobilizing the nation for mass armies led by "educated professionals." Although such categories risk oversimplifying complex actors, it is no coincidence that Linn uses Patton and Eisenhower as examples of Hero and Manager, respectively.[2] Indeed, the different philosophies of war embraced by the two officers has been the central characteristic highlighted by historians.[3] Nevertheless, no scholar has yet shown how these different philosophies of war shaped each general's approach to the press.

As the invasion fleet cruised toward Casablanca, Patton wrote a long letter to Major General A. D. Surles, head of the Public Relations Division for the War Department, laying out his philosophy of warfare and how it shaped his view of the media. Arguing that the main job of a commander was to inspire his soldiers, Patton believed the modern media was important to achieving this connection. "It is my opinion that in spite of our large conversation about

the psychology of war, we utterly fail to utilize the simplest means of stimu-
lating pride and valor in the troops," he wrote to Surles. Observing that the
names of units and commanders were not mentioned in the Pacific, Patton
presumed that "this is done with the erroneous belief" that it would "aid
the enemy." Dismissing this as "foolishness," Patton argued the military was
missing an opportunity to give soldiers publicity. "If the people at home know
that the boys from Lensville [sic], Illinois or Junction City Kansas are fighting and doing well, they will get a great kick out of it and will write to the
soldiers with the result that the soldiers will fight harder than ever." Patton
was "so convinced of this that it seems to me a national tragedy not to utilize
man's innate love of fame and fear of censure to develop a fighting spirit." He
concluded, "I believe that you could not possibly do a greater service to the
country than by persuading the powers that be to permit pitiless publicity,
giving names and units, with regards to the good and bad actions of troops in
combat."[4] As for his own place in the media, it was but another tool to inspire
his soldiers. "I feel that my claim to greatness," Patton scribbled in his diary
a few days before the invasion, "hangs on an ability to lead and inspire."[5]

This "ability to lead and inspire" was central to Patton's philosophy of
warfare. In his study of the American soldier, *Wartime*, Paul Fussell noted
that World War II differed from past conflicts by the combatants' "uniform
and anonymous" characteristics. The methods of turning human beings into
"quasi-mechanical interchangeable parts," Fussell argued, "reflect the success of human mass-production between the two world wars, a process fueled
by dramatic increases in population and assisted by the rapid rise of 'media
culture,' with its power to impose national uniformities."[6] Though Fussell
was writing more of ordinary soldiers than of the war's leaders, historians
have highlighted that American soldiers during World War II rarely saw their
generals or even knew their names.[7] The mass armies required by total war
and the often extremely limited knowledge of an individual soldier made it
difficult for commanders to make any personal impressions on their soldiers
and invited leadership by Managers.

One exception to this was Patton. "Staff systems and mechanical communications are valuable," Patton wrote in the 1920s, "but above and beyond
them must be the commander. Not as a disembodied brain linked to his men
by lines of wire and radio waves, but as a living presence, an all pervading
visible personality."[8] In a 1926 article, "The Secret of Victory," he laid out
his philosophy on inspirational leadership. "The history of war is the history of warriors; few in number, mighty in influence," he wrote. "Alexander,
not Macedonia, conquered the world. Scipio, not Rome, destroyed Carthage.
Marlborough, not the Allies, defeated France. Cromwell, not the Round-
heads, dethroned Charles." These leaders, Patton argued, had the ability to
inspire their soldiers, which was the decisive element to victory. "Nor is it

even in the speed of the operations that the secret lays [*sic*]," explained the general who would make speed his trademark in World War II, "but in the inspiring spirit with which they so inoculated their soldiers as to lift weary footsore men out of themselves and to make them march." Turning Fussell's future observation of the lack of individuality upside down, Patton concluded, "Truly in war; 'Men are nothing, a man is everything.'" The commander must embody the military virtues of courage and have a keen knowledge of his profession, Patton believed, but "[a] cold reserve cannot beget enthusiasm, and so with the others, there must be an outward and visible sign of the inward and spiritual grace." "It then appears," Patton added, "that the leader must be an actor and such is the fact. But with him, as with his bewigged compeer, he is unconvincing unless he lives his part."[9]

Patton would spend much of his career living "his part" by creating an image of a warrior to inspire his soldiers. It is an image that has survived time: a steely-faced general, ivory-handled revolvers on his hips, riding crop in his gloved hand, and a scowl on his face. The press would give it a name, "old blood and guts." "Generals must never show doubt, discouragement, or fatigue" he advised future officers in his postwar memoirs. "Generals should adhere to one type of dress so that soldiers will recognize them."[10] To support his claim of the destruction of individuality during World War II, Fussell quoted nurse-turned-writer Vera Brittain's assertion that the change came from the interwar years with its new forms of communication, such as radio, which propagandized industrial mass production to obscure the human individuality of soldiers.[11] Yet, as historian Joseph J. Mathews observes, "one of the paradoxes of war-news development [was] that as the progressive mechanization of warfare reduced the relative importance of the individual soldier, the news became centered increasingly on him."[12] It was the same media that made Patton's "blood and guts" image famous.

Those closest to Patton knew the tough-guy image was an act. His friend Harry H. Semmes noted the general was an actor and "much of what Patton did seemed outrageous by ordinary standards, but often was a studied attempt to work on the youthful imagination and curiosity of soldiers."[13] Eisenhower, likewise, recalled that Patton had a "flair for the dramatic" but that all "the mannerisms and idiosyncrasies he developed were of his own deliberate adoption."[14] Historians agree. "The mask of command was a tool," wrote historian James Kelly Morningstar in his study of Patton's ideas of war, "not a goal."[15] But the "blood and guts" image came with a price. Patton explained to his nephew near the end of World War II:

People ask why I swagger and swear, wear flashy uniforms and sometimes two pistols. Well, I'm not sure whether some of it isn't my own damned fault, but, however that may be, the press and others have built a picture of me. So now, no matter how tired, or discouraged, or even really ill I may be, if I don't live up to that picture my men are going to say, 'The old man's sick, the old son-of-a-bitch has had it.' Then their own confidence, their own morale, will take a big drop.[16]

Forgotten in this moment of self-pity, however, was that Patton spent his life working to create the "blood and guts" image propagated by the media that no more reflected his true character than the ghostly shadows inside Plato's metaphorical cave represented true forms.

Although he would often be accused of searching for publicity, considerable evidence exists that Patton distrusted much of the attention he received from the press. In his letter to Surles before Torch, Patton asked his help in squashing another *Time-Life* story about him that contained "several very objectionable features," including an offer to challenge Erwin Rommel to personal combat, exaggerated accounts of his athletic abilities, and "the usual line about my swearing." For his present assignment, Patton worried, such a story was "highly detrimental."[17] Well before his media scandals added to his fame, Patton was aware of the damage the press could do.

Many miles to the northeast, deep within the Rock of Gibraltar, Eisenhower also viewed the media as a key part of combat, but in a way that embodied his own managerial philosophy of warfare. Eisenhower believed that modern wars were won by logistics and Allied cooperation, and less by "warrior spirit" from inspired leadership. Like Patton, Eisenhower agreed that leadership was important and that "no thing . . . so improves the morale of the soldier as to see his unit or his own name in print—just once."[18] But in "a modern army, navy, and air force, rich organizational experience and an orderly, logical mind are absolutely essential to success. The flashy, publicity-seeking type of adventurer can grab the headlines and be a hero in the eyes of the public, but he simply can't deliver the goods in high command."[19] Or, as Eisenhower told a press conference, he did not want GIs thinking they are "fighting to make Ike Eisenhower look like a hot shot."[20] For Eisenhower, the media was a tool of communication rather than inspiration.

In keeping with his managerial outlook of warfare, Eisenhower treated journalists as part of his military team. The war correspondents, Eisenhower insisted, "occupy positions as quasi-staff officers on my staff."[21] He ordered that "public relations in this theater shall be conducted in a liberal and sympathetic manner, that representatives of the press, radio, and picture services shall be treated with courtesy and consideration."[22] Effectively using new technology such as radio and newsreels, Eisenhower minimized his military image and came across as human and unassuming.[23] "When I search my mind for Dwight Eisenhower's outstanding characteristics both as a man and a general," wrote *New York Times* correspondent Drew Middleton, "I always return to the same answer—his reasonableness."[24] Correspondent Virgil Pinkley remembered that Eisenhower's "aura of warmth and friendliness lit up the office better than the electric lights." The big grin, the coming around the desk to sit with the reporters, and the insistence to "please call me Ike" was charming, as was "his understanding of our requirements for news, our obligation to our bureaus, newspapers and readers, and his obligation to supply us with all the facts, within limits of security, so that fighting men, their relatives and friends and every taxpayer funding the war could be properly informed."[25] His ease with reporters would go a long way toward helping Eisenhower accomplish his goals.

Despite claims to the contrary, Eisenhower not only was skilled at handling the press, but also carefully worked to gain press attention early in the war. As historian Craig Allen suggests, "Eisenhower's instincts as a communicator thus help explain his rapid rise in the military."[26] Not only did he spend many years in Washington observing high-level interactions between civilian and military leaders, but his youngest brother, Milton, was also there as the director of public information for the Department of Agriculture and brought Eisenhower into contact with many of his reporter friends. The most significant newsman that Eisenhower met in Washington was Harry C. Butcher, who would serve as his naval aide during World War II.[27] The title was misleading since Butcher—who referred to hatches as "holes," could not remember the difference between latitude and longitude, and confessed in the middle of the war that he had never been on a battleship—was not a sailor but an unofficial public relations officer for Eisenhower. Before he departed for Britain, Eisenhower asked Butcher to come and help him with press relations. His many contacts with journalists made Butcher the most important link between Eisenhower and the media during World War II.[28] Finally, the War Department was attempting to give Eisenhower publicity long before he was ordered to England. "Surles trying to give Ike foreign publicity and perhaps he will command the new AEF through France," recorded Eisenhower's friend Everett S. Hughes in his diary at the end of April 1942.[29] Originally when he arrived in Britain, Eisenhower—like MacArthur—was one of the few American generals who could be mentioned in the press.[30] This quickly changed, and Eisenhower made other overtures to journalists. For example, Edward R. Murrow received a call of thanks after airing a positive story on the new commander of American forces.[31] "When we talk of Public Relations I have a feeling that I will gain a reputation as an expert in this lousy field," Butcher wrote in his diary. "I'll be getting the credit for Ike's good sense as he is the keenest in dealing with the press I have ever seen, and I have met a lot of them, many of which are phonies."[32]

The relationship between Eisenhower and the press was not perfect. By August, Eisenhower was worried that newspaper stories on him might make it seem as if he was publicity hungry, and he tried to limit them to little avail. "It's a hard life in this war for any general who wants to avoid publicity," Butcher commented.[33] When British intelligence intercepted a reporter's message to the United Press saying that he had learned Casablanca would be invaded, Eisenhower was concerned that the operation's cover had been blown. "Ike's first reaction to that was to have Morris [the offending reporter] shot as a traitor," Butcher recorded, "but on second thought he realized that any undue action or curiosity on our part would simply validate the story."[34]

The United Press incident underscored the tension between the press and military. Eisenhower confined his response to lecturing reporters a few days later at a luncheon hosted by the Association of American Correspondents in London. The supreme commander warned the journalist not to speculate on coming operations. Ray Daniell, the association's president, assured their guest that the press "would do anything necessary within the bounds of truth and accuracy to help win the war." Eisenhower could not agree and said so. He told the group that "he would lie, cheat, steal and even give orders for assassination . . . to beat the Huns." Though he again promised to the press "fair play and good sportsmanship," he did not believe they were in a war that could tolerate the same values. For reporters, the military was news stories of the home team. For generals, the press was another weapon. Nevertheless, according to Butcher, the speech went over well.[35] A few days later, Eisenhower began ratcheting up publicity for soldiers arriving in England as part of the deception operation for Torch.[36]

Part of managing modern warfare, Eisenhower believed, was working closely with allies. Long before the start of World War II, his friend and mentor General Fox Conner had impressed on Eisenhower that the next war would be fought by coalitions.[37] On his arrival in Britain, it was only natural for Eisenhower to view the press as a tool to build the Anglo-American alliance. Concerned that the American troops entering Britain in 1942 would cause social tensions, Eisenhower foresaw the need to keep both the British and the Americans well informed, and he "began the practice of holding short, informal conferences with the press, for the purpose of discussing our mutual problems and finding common solutions for them."[38] Early on, Eisenhower warned journalists of "fifth columnists" spreading rumors about anti-Allied feelings and asked the reporters to look for stories about British and Americans getting along.[39] Along with military secrets, inter-Allied criticism was one of the two reasons a story could be censored.[40]

Finally, Eisenhower understood the power of public opinion in modern war. "There is no doubt in my mind of the place of public opinion in winning the war," Eisenhower told a group of reporters before Torch.

I think you can simplify it to this—that it's only public opinion that does win wars. It's only public opinion that translates into the soldiers' mind the things to win wars with and makes them want to fight. So I have no doubt in my mind of the place of the American newspaper and particularly en masse over here and the service they've got to do toward winning this war.[41]

Or, as he told Butcher, "an Army fights just as hard as the pressure of public opinion behind it."[42] The idea that "public opinion wins wars" would be Eisenhower's constant refrain throughout the conflict.[43] He had had a ringside seat in the War Department during the Germany First debate.[44] Throughout the North Africa and Sicilian campaigns, he would be aware that failure or dissatisfaction could lead to renewed calls to focus on the Pacific. This not only mandated military success, but also required that the press be managed correctly.

Not only would Eisenhower's managerial and Patton's heroic philosophies shape the campaigns across North Africa and Sicily, but these philosophies also influenced how they viewed the role of the media. Both agreed that news about ordinary soldiers improved morale and unit effectiveness. Indeed, at least one major study highlights how important it was for soldiers to see their name or unit in the media from home.[45] Yet each general's use of the media was different and came with a price. By the close of the Sicily campaign, both generals had learned just how pitiless press publicity could be.

Clark, Darlan, and Other Media Problems

As US troops stormed ashore in North Africa, back in Washington George C. Marshall was concerned with how to continue the positive press that the Torch landings generated. On November 8, he cabled Eisenhower, "From time to time we will give to the American press newsworthy items which do not pertain to future operations. On what date can we release story of Clark's submarine rendezvous."[46] Marshall was referring to a secret mission to North Africa by Eisenhower's deputy commander, Major General Mark Clark, a few weeks before Torch. Smuggled in by submarine, Clark met Robert Murphy, the US State Department representative in North Africa, and a group of pro-Allied Frenchmen. When the Vichy police raided the hideout, Clark and his companions fled, only managing to return to the submarine after the loss of much of the party's equipment, including Clark's pants and seven hundred dollars in gold.[47] When Eisenhower hesitated, citing the "many delicate aspects of this operation," Marshall elaborated that not only did he wish to fill a "dry spot" of news coverage, but he also wanted the creation of press heroes.[48] Though Eisenhower complied with Marshall's request, he was still worried that the Clark story made the French contacts look like greedy traders.[49]

The real publicity problem came, nevertheless, from Eisenhower's handling of the delicate political situation in North Africa. With the fall of France in 1940, the country had been divided between the German-occupied north and a collaborationist government under Marshal Philippe Pétain with its capital at Vichy. Vichy France retained the French colonies, including those in North Africa, and its fleet.[50] At the time of Torch, Admiral Jean François Darlan, commander in chief of Vichy's armed forces and high commissioner in North Africa, happened to be in Algiers. One of Pétain's key lieutenants, Darlan had twice met with Hitler to negotiate closer cooperation with Nazi Germany, and he outranked those French officials who the Allies hoped would help them in North Africa.[51] Nevertheless, Darlan also had the power to make the French military cease resisting and perhaps turn Dakar and the French fleet over to the Allies. As US troops were preparing to land, Murphy tracked down Darlan, informed him of the invasion, and asked him to order his soldiers not to resist. The little admiral's pale face turned purple and he began striding up and down, drawing heavily on his pipe. "I have known for a long time that the British are stupid," he snarled, "but I always believed Americans were more intelligent."[52] It was not till three in the afternoon that Darlan was persuaded to order a cease-fire.[53]

The Allies understood that they would need French assistance in North Africa. Since much of the Vichy leadership saw Charles de Gaulle as a traitor, and General Henri Giraud, who the Allies hoped would be acceptable to the French military, failed to rally any support, this left Darlan. Clark arrived in Algiers and began negotiating what became known as the Darlan Deal. It took a while, and Clark pounded the table repeatedly during the conference, but the result was that Darlan issued a general cease-fire. Yet which Frenchman would be running North Africa was still uncertain when Eisenhower arrived on Friday, November 13.[54] Soon after, however, an agreement was reached. The French would help the Allies in Tunisia, recognize Giraud, fight the Axis, and attempt to get the French fleet to go over to the Allies. In exchange Darlan would be supported in controlling the French colonies in North Africa.[55] After the war, Eisenhower would justify the Darlan Deal by explaining that the "Arab population was then sympathetic to the Vichy French regime, which had effectively eliminated Jewish rights in the region, and an Arab uprising against us, which the Germans were definitely trying to foment, would have been disastrous."[56] Thus, the Darlan Deal saved lives and allowed the Allies to focus on fighting the Germans instead of the French.

The trouble began when Edward R. Murrow blasted the Darlan Deal on his CBS radio broadcast from London, accusing Eisenhower's command of being "consistently sympathetic with the Vichy regime."[57] Murrow's broadcast was echoed by many in the media. Journalist Virgil Pinkley recalled that reporters in North Africa were particularly harsh on the Darlan Deal and were "revolted by Vichy-appointed officials who cared less about ridding *La Belle France* of Nazis than about their daily graft, by openly persecuted Jews, [and] by Arabs beaten with little or no provocation."[58] As Murrow's CBS colleague Charles Collingwood wrote his parents from North Africa, "I wonder whether we will enter Germany and say that we must not interfere with German politics."[59] On the request of the Allied leaders, Eisenhower was forced to write a long message explaining his actions.[60]

What made Murrow's broadcast even more devastating was the dearth of news coming from the war zone. Though preparations had been made for American broadcasters to land with the troops, they did not arrive until five days after the fighting had ended. Equipment failures and lack of assistance from public relations officers resulted, as an army report noted later, in the only "impact of broadcasting from North Africa upon the listener at home" being "in the initial stages slight."[61] This was compounded when the cable connecting North Africa to Britain was severed during the invasion, leaving Radio Moroc the main source of news. But Radio Moroc was operated by Frenchmen loyal to de Gaulle, who spread anti-Darlan propaganda. Eventually, the Frenchmen were removed and Office of War Information personnel installed. Many of the OWI staff, however, were former reporters who, one observer remembered, "were indifferent to the distinction between their previous roles as private newsmen and their responsibilities as representatives of the United States Government."[62] They thus saw nothing wrong with publicly and privately attacking Darlan. "Last night Percy Winner and Jay Allen, OWI . . . came to dinner, and directly and indirectly lambasted the Darlan deal to Ike," wrote Butcher.[63] This storm of criticism from correspondents supports historian Steven Casey's observation that the media during World War II was hardly the lapdog of the military.[64]

Back in Washington, Murrow's broadcast shook the Roosevelt administration. Samuel Rosenman remembered that the president was "criticized most sharply by many of his own liberal adherents" and that he "showed more resentment and more impatience with his critics throughout this period than at any other time I know about."[65] The fact that the criticism had begun with Murrow, whom the president considered an ally, was also infuriating. On his return from London, Secretary of State Cordell Hull dressed down Murrow with words that "cut and stung."[66] There were also political implications and worries of weakening Roosevelt's recently shaken political base. As historian Thomas Fleming noted, the recent midterm elections "had revealed that his [Roosevelt] traditional allies in the Democratic Party, the Irish and other ethnic groups, were staying home in droves. With the South hostile, the liberals were the only bloc of support he had left."[67] Thus the political danger was real, and historians have speculated that it must have crossed Roosevelt's mind to sacrifice Eisenhower's career on the altar of public opinion.[68] As Harry Hopkins told the journalist John Gunther, "No matter what victories he wins, Ike . . . will never live that one down."[69] However, there is no evidence Roosevelt, Stimson, or Marshall ever seriously considered relieving Eisenhower. Instead, all three sprang to his defense.

Stimson focused on Eisenhower's New Deal critics. He had a few of the more disturbed "cherubs"—as he derisively called the New Dealers—to tea at his mansion, Woodley.[70] The guests included Supreme Court Justice Felix Frankfurter, director of the Office of Facts and Figures Archibald MacLeish, and Secretary of the Treasury Henry Morgenthau, the latter of whom appeared to Stimson to be "almost for giving up the war which he said had lost all interest for him." Stimson explained that the Darlan Deal had saved Allied lives and read Eisenhower's cable. Morgenthau was unconvinced and launched into a long rant on the evils of Darlan. Tempers cooled when someone said the president had issued orders to overturn many of the oppressive Vichy laws. Stimson even agreed to read Murrow's broadcast that Morgenthau had brought.[71] Though Stimson believed he had made his case, Morgenthau would not be satisfied until Roosevelt personally assured him that no permanent deal would be made with Darlan.[72] After the "cherubs" departed, Stimson moved on to the former Republican presidential candidate Wendell Willkie, who was about to attack Eisenhower and the Darlan Deal on the radio. After listening to Eisenhower's cable, Willkie made no promises, but later removed all reference to the Darlan Deal from his speech except for asking rhetorically, "Shall we in America be quiet . . . when our State Department continues its appeasement of Vichy?"[73] Willkie's temporary silence on the matter satisfied Roosevelt and Stimson, but fooled few and did not last long.[74]

Meanwhile, Marshall read Eisenhower's cable to a carefully selected group of congressional leaders, who agreed to defend the deal on the floor of Congress and to keep Marshall's actions quiet.[75] Marshall did the same thing with a group of journalists, which included Walter Lippmann, Ray Clapper, and Ernest Lindley, as well as representatives of *Time* and the *Herald Tribune*. One reporter noted that Marshall never seemed "so concerned" as he did reading Eisenhower's cable and asking for the journalists help to defend his commander. All complied with articles defending Eisenhower. Alexander F. Jones of the *Washington Post* went a step further and persuaded the directors of the American Society of Newspaper Editors to form a committee to work with the military and investigate controversial stories to avoid future media storms.[76] This committee, in Marshall's words, acted "as a contact with me in case of any matter such as the Darlan incident so that the editorials throughout the country might be properly influenced."[77]

At first, Roosevelt was silent about the Darlan Deal, but the storm of criticism had reached such a height that his advisers pressed him to issue a statement.[78] At a press conference on November 17, Roosevelt answered a question on North Africa by reading a statement that emphasized that the agreement was temporary and accomplished the military objectives of saving Allied lives and saving time in mopping up resistance.[79] The statement was a relief to Eisenhower. Though press criticism continued, Stimson's, Marshall's, and most of all Roosevelt's actions reassured much of the media. "Indeed, for all of FDR's constant complaints that editors, columnists, and journalists were biased hacks with little influence," historian Steven Casey concluded, "most were perfectly willing to echo his description of the Darlan deal as a 'temporary expedient.'"[80]

As he was handling the press in Washington, Marshall wrote Eisenhower expressing concern over how military leaders were being portrayed in the press. Though he said Eisenhower had handled the publicity well, Marshall also warned him not to allow his staff to "cheapen you or your leaders. They have quoted you several times to bad effect considering your high position. . . . Have them play up your leading subordinates on sound lines and I think it best to avoid quotations from them." Marshall was likewise annoyed at how the Clark story had been portrayed and that the subsequent publicity focused—as Eisenhower had feared—on the loss of Clark's money and pants. He quoted from a letter that journalist Walter Lippmann had written to Stimson in which Lippmann worried that enemy propaganda would claim that Clark was using the money as a bribe, could not see why the censors had passed the story, and suggested that an experienced public relations expert be sent to Eisenhower's headquarters.[81]

Combined with the backlash of the Darlan Deal, Marshall's cable shook Eisenhower and forced him to tighten his press policy.[82] He explained that he had only allowed himself to be quoted for three reasons:

> The first was to express regret that we had to fight [the] French. This was deliberately done for obvious reasons in advancing this campaign. The second was [for] a morale purpose involving praise of principal subordinates and general satisfaction with way all ranks performed arduous duties. The third was to express satisfaction with results achieved by our superiors and all other ranks in unifying an Allied force of all services.[83]

This quote succinctly expresses how Eisenhower not only managed the media as a weapon in military operations, but also used it to strengthen the Anglo-American alliance. Eisenhower added that he would try to direct more media attention to the lower ranks. "In accordance with your desire," he explained, "I have had my people seek out material of human interest type particularly involving enlisted men and junior officers." By contrast, "Quotes from senior officers of United States Army will not, repeat not, hereafter be authorized for publication, except for strictly local and important military reasons."[84] For weeks after Marshall's cable, Eisenhower stopped giving press conferences.[85] Thus, the first change brought by the Darlan and Clark stories was that Eisenhower restricted the flow of information to the media.

Another major change to his handling of the press was spurred by the arrival in North Africa a few weeks later of Eisenhower's youngest brother, Milton. Now an associate director of the OWI, Milton Eisenhower had been dispatched by Roosevelt to investigate the Darlan Deal.[86] Milton Eisenhower made numerous suggestions, such as linking the different organizations that dealt with the press to coordinate "information, propaganda, censorship, and political warfare activities," having a committee to devise press policy, and locating the various organizations that interacted with the press in one building. Other ideas dealt with fixing the current crisis by making it possible for reporters to send messages directly to America (bypassing London) and using Darlan's name as little as possible. But most of Milton's suggestions focused on how Eisenhower could control the news. This included tightening official censorship, encouraging voluntary censorship, making Eisenhower the only source of news, and limiting the number of press conferences in London held by American officers. Milton also suggested Eisenhower begin holding regular press conferences again "and be as generous as possible with off-the-record background stuff."[87] For the first time since Marshall's cable, Eisenhower held a press conference, writing to Surles, "Unquestionably, my brother's visit to this sector has accomplished a lot of good. . . . He was able to uncover for us many weaknesses here."[88] Eisenhower would control the news more tightly than ever. But this also allowed him to give more information as "background" to journalists.

Unbeknownst to Eisenhower, a coordinated effort was also underway to repair his reputation. Acting on "Milton's sagacious suggestions" and a secret message from Marshall to "put General Eisenhower as Allied Commander on a 'pedestal' and to keep him there," Butcher began working on repairing Eisenhower's image. He started by trying to "figure out some compromise between letting this hdq. be slugged 'Eisenhower's Headquarters,' a la Mac-Arthur, and relative inattention as to who is really the boss."[89] More directly, Butcher began helping journalists write about Eisenhower, even helping stories delayed by the War Department get through faster.[90] This extended to film, which Butcher had reviewed to make sure Eisenhower was not captured in "any undignified or non-soldierly poses."[91] All this was necessary, Butcher reasoned, since Eisenhower was much too modest.[92]

One of the biggest consequences of the media storm over the Darlan Deal was that it took Eisenhower away from the battlefield and into politics. As one historian of the campaign has estimated, Eisenhower "spent at least three-quarters of his time worrying about political issues, and that preoccupation poorly served the Allied cause."[93] After he suggested Eisenhower visit the front, Patton recorded that Eisenhower "feels that he cannot, due to politics."[94] With Eisenhower distracted, British officers began to fill the vacuum in command, to the anger of many Americans. Admiral Andrew Cunningham wrote after the war that "the American papers said it looked as if Eisenhower was to be the stooge and that the Tunisian campaign was to be run by Alexander, Tedder and Cunningham—which was what happened."[95] Thus, the media storm weakened Eisenhower's command of the battlefield and allowed the British to fill the void.

On Christmas Eve, 1942, Darlan was assassinated by an "act of Providence"—Clark's description—enacted by a young pro–de Gaulle Frenchman.[96] Giraud replaced him, and the oppressive Vichy laws were gradually removed.[97] To the end of his days, Eisenhower defended the Darlan Deal. He told reporters that the Allies had estimated that Torch would cost 8,000 casualties, but the agreement had limited the fighting to 1,800.[98] Privately, Patton estimated that it would take 60,000 Allied troops to police Morocco alone if the local French had refused to help.[99] Indeed, Allied leaders who worked with Darlan—Eisenhower, Clark, and Murphy—all later acknowledged that the French admiral kept his word and created a stable rear for the Allied armies.[100] No such consensus exists among historians.[101] Certainly, the Darlan Deal continued to cause trouble. At the end of the Casablanca Conference, Roosevelt made one of the most controversial of his wartime decisions when he announced that the Allies would accept only unconditional surrender. Steven Casey and other historians have argued that Roosevelt was motivated by the negative press on the Darlan Deal and the need to reassure the Allied nations that no compromise with the Axis would be accepted.[102] Even after his death, Darlan continued to haunt the Allies.

The Battle for Tunisia

During the Casablanca Conference, Butcher reflected on the absence of any public praise for Eisenhower from Churchill or Roosevelt. He surmised that neither politician wanted to be "caught holding the bag for a General who had made an unpopular decision, and hadn't yet got Tunisia." Eisenhower's neck was "in a noose," Butcher concluded, "and he knows it."[103] Yet, victory in North Africa would not only be a major military achievement for the Allies, but also secure Eisenhower's position. His philosophy of command rested on Anglo-American cooperation. History, personalities, pride, and prejudice nevertheless seemed bent on separating the Western allies. Eisenhower's attempt to merge the American and British into a unified force caused tensions that played out in the media and had repercussions that would lead Allied commanders to make battlefield decisions to satisfy public opinion.

The Axis response to Torch was plagued by their own military and propaganda problems. November 1942 was a disaster for the Third Reich. On November 4, Rommel began his retreat from El Alamein with General Bernard Law Montgomery's Eighth Army in pursuit. On November 8, the Torch landings began. Two weeks later the Soviets started their massive offensive to surround Axis forces at Stalingrad.[104] As historian Douglas Porch has written, "Hitler and Mussolini might have extricated Rommel's beaten but valiant force, gained a Dunkirk-like propaganda victory, preserved their dwindling resources, and consolidated their defenses on Europe's southern shore. But neither Axis leader was psychologically prepared to confront the reality of impending defeat in the Mediterranean."[105] Joseph Goebbels hoped through "firmness and assurance" to conceal weakness and "as Churchill did after Dunkirk, to whip up every ounce of energy." But the Reich's propaganda minister conceded that "things are not easy for German propaganda in the present circumstances."[106] Meanwhile Hitler was attempting to find a solution to Torch, but it was not until Darlan's radio address on November 9 that he contacted Albert (Albrecht) Kesselring, the overall commander in the Mediterranean, and set in motion the German invasion of Tunisia. Yet the Germans still waited until Pétain agreed to the occupation. When he did so, German parachutists started landing in Tunisia and began receiving assistance from the local Vichy French. This stopped abruptly when an Italian fighter squadron, acting—according to Kesselring—"for reasons of prestige," joined the Germans in Tunisia and infuriated the French.[107] The following day German troops occupied Vichy France. By the end of the month, there were twenty-five thousand Axis troops in Tunisia.[108]

As the Germans were dropping into Tunisia, the Allies were advancing at a much slower pace. Between the coastal supply bases and the front stretched a huge wasteland where people, water, and shade were rare. This was compounded in the winter months by heavy rain that turned the dry earth into a sea of mud. To cover this vast wilderness was but one dilapidated railway and a few primitive roads. "Resupply," as one historian of the campaign noted, "was to become the single most difficult problem facing the Allies during the Tunisian campaign." The result was that the Allied armies were understrength, were undersupplied, and existed in poor living conditions.[109] The British First Army commanded by Kenneth Anderson moved slowly toward Tunisia accompanied by the US II Corps, commanded by Lloyd Fredendall.[110] Both Anderson and Fredendall were chauvinistic, incompetent, and disliked the other.[111] More broadly, many US officers were beginning to be dissatisfied with the British dominance in operational command. For their part, the British resented having an inexperienced American general in over-all command, and, as Porch notes: "Eisenhower was too far from the front and too distracted by *l'affaire Darlan* and its aftermath to exercise effective control."[112] Thus problems of supply, leadership, and Allied cooperation marred the campaign.

Even before Torch, Eisenhower believed the main role of the press was to unite the Anglo-American alliance. In a cable to Marshall a few days after the landing, Eisenhower explained that he planned to emphasize the "excellence of American troops" and the "efficiency of all senior subordinates" to the press. He also "wanted to conduct these matters so as to preserve and even improve the admirable Allied relationships that exist throughout this command." Thus, it would be better for local stories to be released to the press in North Africa, since "almost every incident that comes to light involves some kind of cooperation between British and Americans." With both Allies equipped with wire services at his headquarters, Eisenhower reasoned, news stories would simultaneously reach each nation.[113]

The system of Anglo-American media cooperation Eisenhower described also spread antagonism. This was highlighted by the experience of correspondent Walter Cronkite of the United Press (UP), who had witnessed the landing at Casablanca. Bursting into the UP's newsroom after being flown home by the US Navy, Cronkite learned that UP had not received any of his dispatches since he left Norfolk. In fact, American reporters were having problems getting their stories sent home from North Africa. Following instructions, Cronkite had given his stories to the USS *Texas*'s radio operator to wire them to the British naval communications center at Gibraltar. The British, apparently giving their own country's newsmen priority, failed to pass the dispatches of American reporters along in a timely manner.[114] This, of course, did not delay the press from complaining. On December 7, Marshall wrote Surles that the *New York Times* had run a long story in which the paper reported all the news from North Africa coming from England and accused the British of delaying American dispatches. Marshall could not believe that Eisenhower would allow the British to control all the press communication and assumed there was a simple explanation.[115] It is true, as Casey explained, that the British had a more efficient system of handling reporters, allowing their stories to be processed faster. Whatever the cause, it was fodder for the American isolationist press, and Robert McCormick's anti-British *Chicago Tribune* picked up the story. So too did Joseph Goebbels, who began focusing on the Allied news dispute in German propaganda, forcing Eisenhower's press officer to publicly deny any favoritism.[116] Yet even Butcher was privately suspicious that the British censor "doesn't want anything good, at least too good, to go out on Ike."[117]

Other issues, often reflected in the press, were causing trouble in the

Anglo-American alliance. Frank Kluckhohn of the *New York Times* reported to Butcher that there was "much bitter feeling between Americans and British at the front."[118] In the rear, American generals believed the British were attempting to control the command. Marshall apparently agreed, warning the journalists at his off-the-record press conference defending the Darlan Deal that any criticism of Eisenhower would play into British demands to replace him and that the United States would probably not get another top command position.[119] Nor were the British short on grievances. These were summarized by Alan Brooke, chief of the Imperial General Staff, who sniffed after the war: "It must be remembered that Eisenhower had never even commanded a battalion in action when he found himself commanding a group of armies in North Africa! . . . I had little confidence in his having the ability to handle the military situation confronting him."[120] The arrangement that left Eisenhower as the overall commander, but with the British general Harold Alexander as his deputy commanding the campaign, satisfied the partisans of neither nation.[121] American isolationist papers reflected these concerns and charged that Eisenhower was simply a figurehead, which was exactly what Brooke intended. When Joe Phillips, one of Eisenhower's PR officers, returned from Britain in early February he reported "a surprising amount of bitterness between Americans and British in London. The news and radio men reflect it."[122] Butcher blamed CBS's Murrow and Collingwood for "contributing heavily to the growing Anti-British feeling in American [*sic*] and that their one-sided reporting and pointed editorializing against Giraud, Murphy and Eisenhower have had the effect of sabotaging the good will of the two countries, and of playing into the German's hands for propaganda." Butcher, a former executive for CBS, considered complaining to his old employers. He confined himself, instead, to lecturing Collingwood on what it meant to broadcast an unbiased story.[123] Collingwood agreed, and then told Walter Winchell, who wrote a story that Butcher had tried to "pressure" Collingwood.[124] For his part, Eisenhower cabled Marshall that "such publicity as is given in the U.S. should stress the American grip on the whole affair."[125] Nor was press favoritism limited to nationality—many in Anderson's British First Army were jealous of the attention lavished on Montgomery's Eighth Army.[126] Given these tensions, it was therefore inevitable that Allied, and even unit, rivalries would be reflected in the media.

Montgomery was not the only press hero in North Africa. Erwin Rommel had skillfully built a media persona, which had garnered him respect even with the Allies.[127] So skillful was Rommel's use of the press that Goebbels had admiringly referred to him as the first "modern general."[128] Lacking connections that came with birth in the Prussian military elite, historian Douglas Porch observes, "the Swabian Rommel was continually forced to play for broke, snuggling up to Hitler, chancing life and career in risky exhibitions calculated to attract publicity."[129] At the end of the long retreat from El Alamein, Rommel saw just such an opportunity. "The Americans had as yet no practical battle experience," Rommel wrote later, "and it was now up to us to instil [*sic*] in them from the outset an inferiority complex of no mean order."[130] On February 14, 1943, Rommel struck, smashing the American forces at Sidi Bouzid and driving them back toward Kasserine Pass. Though Rommel's attack soon ran out of steam, II Corps lost 6,000 casualties, 183 tanks, and 200 guns.[131] The Battle of Kasserine Pass had several important consequences. First, Patton replaced Fredendall. Second, the US II Corps was detached from Anderson's First Army and placed directly under Alexander's Eighteenth Army Group.[132] The result was that II Corps would be a symbol of American prestige, which Patton and later his successor, Omar Bradley fully appreciated.

More importantly, Rommel confirmed British opinion of the inferiority of US troops. The Americans "simply do not know their jobs as soldiers," Alexander informed Brooke.[133] "BBC says American forces etc. etc.," complained one of Eisenhower's generals in his diary. "It used to be *First* Army."[134] Nor were the negative feelings confined to the British. Frank L. Kluckhohn published a story on March 2 highlighting how irritating many GIs found the British.[135] A day later, Drew Middleton, also of the *New York Times*, informed Butcher of the "existence of bitter feeling[s] of Americans against [the] British because of the recent American defeat." He added, "Certain members of the newspaper corps are taking up the criticism and the feeling generally is bad." When Butcher observed that the news dispatches he saw did not show anti-British feeling, Middleton stated that the correspondents knew that overly critical stories would not be passed by the censor.[136]

To some commanders, the press appeared to be deliberately trying to encourage disagreement between the Allies. At a press conference on March 8, Eisenhower "noticed an apparent effort on the part of one of the American correspondents to use the Kasserine Battle as a means of starting a newspaper argument regarding the placing of blame and credit as between British and Americans." Eisenhower responded by lecturing the reporters against such talk, ending by warning that harmful stories would be censored and that if he "found any reporter persisting in any such attempt, I would remove him from the theater." He also informed Alexander about the incident, since "it is more or less typical of a certain type of reporter we have" and it called for "positive leadership" to prevent small differences hurting the alliance.[137] The British had similar experiences. A few weeks later, Hansen Baldwin of the *New York Times* "accosted" Montgomery and suggested that American soldiers were of poor quality and not fighting well. Montgomery had the good sense to reply that he had "not seen the American soldiers but that I definitely could not believe him; I then changed the subject & got rid of him. He struck me as a dangerous chap."[138] With these decaying Allied relations in mind, Eisenhower ordered Patton to repair not only the II Corps but also the "spirit of partnership between ourselves and the British forces."[139]

Patton's revitalization of II Corps has been well documented by his contemporaries, historians, and Hollywood. It was reporters, however, who first brought Patton to the American public. "He hit Tunisia like a whirlwind, amazing men who had never served under him not to mention the Axis army he attacked," wrote correspondent Frank L Kluckhohn.

> Officers and "dogfaces" from one end of our lines to another learned what was meant by the expression, "You have never lived until you have been cussed out by General Patton." He rages through his command like an indignant lion, insisting that the troops be washed and clean, that trucks travel fifty yards apart, and that officers wear their rank insignia on their battle helmets and have their unit arm "flashed" as well. He enforced a new order that officers should be fined $25 if encountered without helmets throughout the United States forces; $35 if without sidearms.[140]

A radio broadcaster observed that Patton "has enough dash and dynamite to make a Hollywood adventure-hero look like a drugstore cowboy." In factories across the United States, posters of Patton appeared with quotes urging his soldiers forward.[141] "The flamboyant, gun-toting Patton, one of the most aggressive and hell-for-leather generals in the American Army, is out to settle the Tunisian affair and to do it in a hurry" was how another article described him.[142] "George Patton at 57 Can Outshoot, Outfight, Outcuss and Outsmart Any Man in His Tank Outfit," stated the *Morning Call*, "So Look Out, Rommel, Here He Is."[143] "These are picturesque attributes," editorialized the *New York Times* approvingly, "and Americans love them."[144] In other words, as the *Bismarck Tribune*'s headline put it, "Gen. Patton Is Colorful Leader."[145] It helped, as Casey notes, that the name of II Corps's new commander was censored until Gafsa had been taken, giving Patton an immediate victory. Eisenhower had counseled Patton that modern battles were fought from the command post.[146] Patton ignored him. Instead, his actions embodied his heroic philosophy of warfare, where a commander needed to make his presence felt on the battlefield. Such media stories were simply another way to accomplish this goal.

Contrary to popular and some historical opinion, Patton attempted to divert publicity from himself to his soldiers.[147] "The private who is out there getting shot at does most of the work in this war," he told the *United Press*. "He gets damned little credit out of it, too."[148] Patton wrote Surles, "I cannot too strongly express my admiration for the unwavering and cheerful fortitude of the American soldier. . . . I do not deserve or desire publicity, but I do believe that everything that can be handed to the American soldiers . . . should be handed to them." He wrote his wife on March 25, "I fear the papers are making an unnecessary hero out of me. I never felt less deserving in my life. The only way I influence things is by providing drive and keeping my temper with the B's [British]." A few days later, he wrote again that he was getting "a lot of cheap publicity and fear that I shall get a lot more. There are 49 correspondents and photographers here sniping at me." As the campaign entered its final stage in April, Patton confided to his diary that "things look pretty good but I fear the papers will make too much of a play about me."[149]

Despite the transformation of II Corps, the British could still point to the failure of the US Thirty-Fourth Division as proof of American military incompetence. The Thirty-Fourth Division had been assigned to British IX Corps, commanded by Lieutenant General John Crocker, for an attack on Fondouk. Crocker had little use for the US Army. For their part, the Americans were unimpressed with Crocker and his plan for taking Fondouk. Patton had complained to Eisenhower about the Thirty-Fourth Division being placed under the British. Eisenhower had promised to change the arrangement but failed to convince Alexander. There were also tactical objections. The Americans were to make a frontal assault over open ground toward Axis troops defending a steep ridgeline. Given the division's previous experience at Fondouk, morale plummeted and life insurance purchases increased along with church attendance. The attack went badly, with heavy American casualties. As historian Rick Atkinson notes, "A great opportunity had been lost, but there was always time for recriminations." And that was just what Crocker did, castigating the Thirty-Fourth Division in front of four war correspondents and suggesting it be withdrawn from combat and the junior officers retrained by the British.[150]

To the horror of the Americans, Alexander's staff took Crocker's suggestions seriously. Nor did this incident improve II Corps leadership's opinion of Eisenhower. Bradley groused that Eisenhower had threatened to send any American who criticized the British home, but "it didn't work both ways, as General Eisenhower saw fit not to apply it . . . [to] Crocker."[151] Expecting no help from Eisenhower, whom Patton castigated as "more British than the British," he and Bradley instead focused on Alexander. Patton wrote a letter of protest noting that the Thirty-Fourth Division needed experience and should be part of the II Corps attack. "Further," Patton explained, "consideration should be given to the fact, that since the 34th is a National Guard Division, its activities assume local interest of great political significance."[152] Bradley was dispatched to Eighteenth Army Group Headquarters to deliver the message and drive home the point. This appeal to national sensitivities apparently convinced Alexander, who overruled his staff.[153]

The Thirty-Fourth Division's failure was already headline news in the United States. "Rommel Escapes Trap: Yanks Fail to Take Objective on Schedule" blared the headline of the *Boston Globe*.[154] "Americans Late in Taking Fondouk Objective," echoed the *Chicago Daily Tribune*.[155] On April 19, *Time* magazine characterized the American performance at Fondouk as "downright embarrassing" and said the battle "afforded a sharp [and unfavorable] comparison between British and U.S. troops."[156] Marshall was concerned. "Press report cleared from your headquarters indicates that failure of 34th Division to cooperate successfully with corresponding British force wrecked opportunity to intercept Rommel," Marshall wrote. "Other minor items from Algerian press reports have been played up by columnists here to disadvantage of American part in recent actions." Marshall worried that Eisenhower might be giving "way too much to logistical reasons with unfortunate results as to national prestige. . . . General Surles reports marked fall in prestige of American troops in minds of pressmen and in reaction of public."[157] Marshall's message was clear: prestige of US forces mattered, sometimes even more than banal military reasoning.

Not only was Eisenhower dealing with the fallout from Crocker's comments, but Patton and Bradley were now arguing that Americans must have a more important role in the campaign for the sake of public opinion. Alexander's final plan called for the British First and Eighth Armies to squeeze out II Corps as it approached Tunis. This meant US forces would not be part of the final victory. Bradley had argued with Alexander about the plan but was informed that it was logistically impossible to support II Corps. Bradley was unconvinced, believing that the move was tactically unsound because it wasted a corps, broke up US forces under different commands, and removed the opportunity of American soldiers to share in the victory.[158] But that was not the argument Bradley made to Eisenhower. "The people in the United States want a victory," Bradley explained, "and they deserve one." He suggested that II Corps be assigned to take Bizerte, at the northern tip of Tunisia.[159] Though he left it out of the published version of his memoirs, Bradley also warned Eisenhower that "although he was trying to emphasize the fact that he was an *allied* commander, eventually he would have to answer to the American people."[160] Contrary to Patton's private accusations, Eisenhower had in fact written Alexander in March asking that II Corps be allowed in the final act of the Tunisia campaign because of "reactions at home" and the morale of the US military.[161] Coming as it did with the bad publicity around the Thirty-Fourth Division, Bradley's suggestion made sense.

Eisenhower still had to persuade the British that it was worth jettisoning sound logistics so the American public could enjoy part of the victory. Just to get II Corps into position meant crossing British supply lines, adding to the confusion.[162] Nor would it be easy to supply II Corps or to take Bizerte. Eisenhower visited Alexander to explain the situation. According to Butcher:

Ike emphasized the danger to Britain and America if Americans were given to feel that they had not taken an effective part in the Tunisian campaign. Much of our choice equipment, Sherman tanks, as well as ammunition and food had gone to the British. . . . If the Americans feel we have not played a substantial part they will be even more intent upon prosecution of the war against the Japs.[163]

Patton made a similar argument to Alexander, warning him not to place II Corps under First Army again since it was a question of "prestige."[164] Alexander consented to Eisenhower's request, and all American divisions were placed under II Corps for the attack toward Bizerte. For Bradley, it was a moment of personal triumph. "It gave the people back home a concrete accomplishment," Bradley wrote in an unpublished draft of his book, "not alone of their sons and friends, but of their own war effort back home."[165] American soldiers had another chance to prove themselves in battle.

Eisenhower returned from his meeting with Alexander to find another "disconcerting message" from Marshall that, according to Butcher, "laid Ike low."[166] To Marshall's suggestion to worry less about logistics if there was a chance to produce some glory for the United States, Eisenhower replied that he was doing exactly that with II Corps. Instead of blaming Crocker, however, Eisenhower blamed the censor at his headquarters and assured Marshall that "every senior British officer sees this problem exactly as you have described it and is anxious to do his part in preserving and increasing the prestige of American troops." Eisenhower promised to improve censorship and hold a press conference highlighting GI contributions in the North African campaign.[167] He wrote Marshall again the following day explaining the "fool censor" had excused his actions by stating that since Eisenhower had forbidden criticism of himself being censored that also applied to allowing criticism of American units. "I do not often get even temporarily discouraged," Eisenhower wrote, "but I must say that last night was a bad one."[168]

"We are masters of the North African shores," Alexander cabled Churchill on May 13, 1943.[169] The Allies captured 238,000 Axis prisoners.[170] As had been hoped, the victory not only boosted Eisenhower's reputation as a commander, but also vindicated Roosevelt for his insistence on Torch and the Germany First strategy. According to the polls, Steven Casey observes, "Americans had certainly lost their fixation with the Pacific war."[171] The campaign had also bloodied American troops and commanders. Indeed, the most famous commanders of the war in Europe—including Eisenhower, Alexander, Montgomery, Patton, Bradley, and Clark—were all brought to the public's attention. By comparison, generals who had missed the North African battles, such as Jacob Devers, who commanded an army group in France, would never attract as much public attention.[172] Marshall was also concerned how publicity had been handled through the Tunisia campaign. He had made sure that Fredendall, and other relieved American officers, were shown in the best possible light in the press.[173] Marshall was also worried that Eisenhower did not receive enough credit for the Tunisia victory, writing Surles to see that Eisenhower got some praise in the press for the "magnificent job" he had done.[174] Despite Marshall's concern, Eisenhower's reputation with the theater war correspondents had largely recovered by the end of the Tunisia campaign. The same could not be said for Anglo-American press relations, as the Allies next campaign in Sicily would show.

The Road to Messina

The three American newsmen strode into the lavish palace of the kings of Sicily, now home to George Patton. It was July 1943 and Demaree Bess of the *Saturday Evening Post* and Quentin Reynolds of *Collier's* had just arrived at the newly captured city of Palermo on the northern coast of Sicily. The third man was *International News* photographer Sammy Schulman, who had offered to introduce them to the Seventh Army's commander. Schulman explained that his companions were new to Sicily and needed transportation, and he suggested that Patton brief them on the battle so far. "Of course, Sammy," Patton said, grabbing a pointer and heading toward a wall map of Sicily. Patton explained the Allies had invaded Sicily, codenamed Operation Husky, on July 10. Montgomery's Eighth Army had landed in the east with the objective of driving up the coast and cutting off the Axis retreat into Italy at the city of Messina. Patton's Seventh Army had landed on the west coast, largely in a supporting role. Nevertheless, the British had made slow progress toward Messina and Patton had taken the opportunity to move north and capture the city of Palermo. The briefing continued until Schulman, whom Reynolds had caught yawning, stood up and announced that it was time to get his companions back to their hotel. Outside Reynolds, shocked by Schulman's casual interaction with the general known as "old blood and guts," inquired where the bodies were buried. "You boys don't understand," replied the cameraman. "He just loves to have his picture taken."[175]

Though Patton undoubtedly enjoyed publicity, his view of the media in Sicily was influenced by his philosophy of war. This included giving recognition to his soldiers in the belief that they would fight better. Before the invasion of Sicily, Patton had campaigned for the Allies to publicly name units in the press down to the company level.[176] But by the time Allied troops landed in Sicily, as historian Rick Atkinson observed, "a new front had opened between the British and the Americans."[177] Inter-Allied conflicts over the quality of US soldiers and the role of the Seventh Army in the campaign accompanied the Allies from North Africa. This would drive Patton to make battlefield decisions in the hope of gaining prestige for his army.

Eisenhower likewise still saw the press as a key part of modern warfare. First, despite all the setbacks over the Darlan Deal, Eisenhower's relationship with the media had improved to one of mutual respect, trust, and teamwork.[178] With Husky just under a month away, Eisenhower shocked his public relations officers by revealing at an off-the-record news conference that the next operation would be Sicily.[179] Two days after the landing, Eisenhower had been convinced by journalists to go ashore in Sicily since it was of "great historic significance" (Butcher's words) and also a great news scoop.[180] Eisenhower, however, still saw the main usefulness of the press as building up the Anglo-American alliance. As Husky approached, he moved his advanced headquarters to Malta, which was closer to Sicily but also had a better cable for news stories to Britain. Though he was concerned that the London dateline on news stories would increase anti-English sentiment among some American newspapers, Butcher was pleased that an American reporter and a British reporter had been pooled to cover the advanced headquarters. Eisenhower impressed upon the two correspondents that they should try to give both nations equal credit and coverage. "Ike's thesis," Butcher recorded, "was that Americans like to feel they are doing something important, and are making a substantial contribution to the war effort. If they feel Americans are doing well over here—hoping we do—then they will be less inclined to want to sack the grand strategy of beating Germany first." The reporters left "determined to help in every way."[181] Nevertheless, Eisenhower's focus on Allied cooperation backfired as biased news coverage turned the Sicilian campaign into a competition between the two nations.

Allied tensions were often exacerbated by the media. When Bradley's II Corps took Enna after a hard fight, the BBC announced that the Canadian division under Montgomery had captured the city. "This was no isolated journalistic misstatement," Bradley grumbled. "Throughout the Sicily campaign, BBC and other British media credited Monty with all the hard fighting while we were depicted as 'eating grapes' and 'swimming.'"[182] Not only was the BBC the main source of news in Sicily, but it also reflected the British opinion of their American ally. "Alexander was powerfully influenced by the conviction that American fighting ability was still inferior to that of the British army," writes historian Carlo D'Este. "He refused to acknowledge that the U.S. Army now fighting in Sicily bore scant resemblance to the army that had been humiliated at Kasserine."[183] In the middle of the campaign, Major General Clarence Huebner, recently fired as the US liaison officer at Alexander's Fifteenth Army Group, informed the Seventh Army's chief of staff that Alexander was determined to have Patton "in a secondary role."[184] Montgomery shared Alexander's condescension, and was just as good at hiding it.

Months before the invasion, he had lobbied for the American forces to be placed under his command.[185] This suggestion went nowhere since George Marshall was convinced American morale would be helped by the establishment of the US Seventh Army.[186] Right after the landing, Montgomery issued a statement that Butcher noticed mentioned the Americans only once.[187] This was made all the more galling by the slow speed of the British Eighth Army. Patton contemptuously noted that the Seventh Army's "system of continued attack is better than the British system of attack, build up, and attack; because everytime [*sic*] they halt to build up, the enemy build up in front of them, whereas in our system he does not have time to do this."[188] Near the middle of the campaign, Montgomery successfully lobbied Alexander to move the boundaries between the two armies, taking a road that supplied Bradley's II Corps and three of the four roads to Messina. The Seventh Army would not even get to take Palermo.[189] In effect, Montgomery was asking the Seventh Army to protect his army's rear.

The repeated slights and the continual subordination of the Seventh Army for Montgomery's advance drove Patton and the other American officers to distraction. On July 17, Patton flew to Fifteenth Army Group. "I shall explain the situation to General Alexander on the basis that it would be inexpedient politically for the Seventh Army not to have equal glory in the final stage of the campaign," he wrote in his diary.[190] General Albert Wedemeyer, on a special mission for Marshall, accompanied Patton and chimed in that the "American people" would not stand for such a secondary role.[191] Alexander relented, allowing Seventh Army to drive to the northern coast of Sicily and also advance northwest to the city of Palermo. As with the final campaign in Tunisia, Alexander had let his battlefield decisions be swayed by American arguments about public opinion.

The decision to advance north to Palermo has drawn much criticism. "The Seventh U.S. Army . . . was allowed to wheel west towards Palermo," complained Montgomery after the war. "It thereby missed the opportunity to direct its main thrustline [*sic*] northwards in order to cut the island in two."[192] Bradley later argued that the drive toward Palermo was simply a publicity stunt since "the city had no real strategic significance—it lay in the opposite direction from the German defense line around Mount Etna—but it had a legendary and a glamorous history and its capture was sure to make headlines."[193] General Lucian K. Truscott later also told an interviewer that the "glamor" of Palermo attracted Patton.[194] Unbeknownst to the Allies, Kesselring had decided that western Sicily had no further military value and began moving troops toward the east.[195] Many historians have likewise agreed that Palermo had no importance except for creating headlines for Patton.[196] Nigel Hamilton points out that the harbor at Porto Empedocle provided all the support Patton would need to supply his army. "No serious historian," he added, "can deny that Patton's 'obsession' with Palermo was a wild and unmilitary distraction from the main campaign in Sicily."[197]

Bradley's, Montgomery's, and Hamilton's observations, however, conceal much more than they reveal. To begin with, Palermo was not lacking in strategic value. Though it was about to fall, the port at Porto Empedocle had not yet been taken when Patton received his new orders from Alexander. More importantly, Porto Empedocle was located on the southwest coast while Palermo was on the northern coast. The city was a major port and would be an excellent supply base for a drive east on the main coastal road to Messina. As the authors of the official US Army history of the campaign note, Palermo would be the center of logistics for the Seventh Army, which was still relying on supply from over the beaches more than one hundred miles away. "With the build-up of supplies through Palermo," they add, "General Patton could now turn his full attention to getting the Seventh Army moving to the east on Messina."[198] Even more importantly, the city was perfectly located to support amphibious operations along the northern coastal road. When Patton met with Alexander, he made sure to reserve landing craft for amphibious operations about the northern Sicilian coast.[199] As Carlo D'Este has observed, "the drive to the north coast was a clever ploy by Patton to maneuver Seventh Army into a position to capture Messina."[200] Rather than an attack in the wrong direction, the advance toward Palermo was the first step in Patton's plan to take Messina.

It is true that Patton hoped to gain media attention by taking Palermo, but historians have missed that it was publicity intended specifically for his old command, the Second Armored Division. The diary of Bradley's aide, Chester Hansen, illuminates his commander's later criticism. To take Palermo, Patton would have Bradley's II Corps continue to support Montgomery, while a Provisional Corps commanded by Major General Geoffrey Keyes and supported by the armored division would move toward Palermo.[201] "This [realignment] deprives us of our objective in Palermo and robs us of the opportunity of chalking up another apparent victory," Hansen bitterly recorded. "Efforts of the [II] Corps seem to go unnoticed and unappreciated unless we succeed in taking objectives well known to the general public. If Armored takes Palermo . . . the show given that force will again deprive the doughboy the rewards that comes in public recognition of the job he is doing so masterfully."[202] This was exactly what Patton and Keyes intended. When Truscott said that there seemed little for the Second Armored to do, "Keyes admitted as much, but thought that even so it would be a good [press] buildup for American armor."[203] Before the city fell, Patton would hold two regiments of infantry back so the armor could enter the city at the same time.[204] Correspondent Don Whitehead, who accompanied the Second Armored Division into Palermo, recalled that "Patton was irked by the fact the doughboys of the Third Infantry Division had outsprinted his tanks to reach Palermo first. Patton wanted the glory reserved for his tankmen." He added that Patton's boasting of his tank drive "wasn't quite convincing in trying to sell that story to the correspondents."[205] Thus, Bradley's later criticism was likely motivated by not simply his disagreement with the advance north, but annoyance that he was left protecting Montgomery's rear while armor units were given credit for taking the Sicilian capital.

Palermo fell on July 22, 1943, with the help of a war correspondent. The photographer Robert Capa had attached himself to Second Armored Division and was one of the first correspondents to enter the city. At the city's gates, however, the unit was ordered to halt to wait for Keyes, who soon arrived and enlisted Capa as an interpreter. When the Italian commander was finally located, he explained that he had already surrendered four hours before to the American infantry. Keyes demanded another surrender, and Capa explained in Italian "that surrendering the second time ought to be much easier than the first."[206] The fall of the Sicilian capital brought Patton press adulation, with the July 26 issue of *Time* magazine putting him on the cover.[207] Beatrice Patton wrote her husband four days later that Montgomery hardly figured in the press coverage. "The N.Y. Times tonight calls you the brilliant and mobile soldier, pretty good from them," she wrote. "But take my advice and have the c[orrespondent]'s put out that the resistance was bitter or people may think otherwise." For his part, Patton praised his troops to Eisenhower and asked that Keyes's name be released to the press. Keyes "realy [*sic*] deserves most of the credit," Patton wrote Beatrice, "and I have handed it out to him via the press."[208] Despite this publicity, the fall of Palermo did not create the praise that Patton hoped would inspire his soldiers. "Nor," as Porch notes, "did Palermo's capture advance the American cause in inter-Allied relations—to the annoyance of an enraged Patton, the BBC continued to emphasize that the Eighth Army carried the brunt of the fighting."[209] Indeed, since Patton had not seen any American papers for almost two weeks after Palermo's surrendered, the main source of news was the BBC, which continued to ignore or belittle the Seventh Army's accomplishments.[210] The knowledge that his troops were still being disparaged by the American and British press only added to his determination to make a spectacular drive to Messina.

Unbeknown to Patton, the source for much of the one-sided news coverage was Eisenhower. Following his philosophy of Allied unity and not wishing for one of the Allies to steal all the glory, Eisenhower made sure to praise the British in the press at the expense of Seventh Army. On July 17, he held a press conference where, as Butcher recorded, Eisenhower "stated on-the-record that Montgomery was having tough going because of German opposition and difficult terrain, whereas Patton's opposition was less and he was primarily fighting Italians."[211] This was true, and as Montgomery continued to move slowly, the British became increasingly appreciative of Eisenhower. When Henry Stimson visited Algiers—after a trip from London—he reported that Churchill was grateful for Eisenhower's attempt "publicly to balance the progress between the stalled British 8th Army and the rapidly advancing American 7th Army." But Butcher added that "the 8th Army has been getting a great deal of publicity for any kind of movement and the 7th Army, which has been going great guns, is still somewhat under the cloud of the great reputation of the 8th."[212] By the beginning of August, however, Eisenhower started to be increasingly annoyed that Alexander's Fifteenth Army Group's messages were reaching London before his own cables. Churchill, according to Butcher, enjoyed "scooping" his generals and gave military information to the public, and Eisenhower sometimes heard it on the BBC before he heard it from Alexander. It turned out that not only was Alexander sending private messages to the British government, but Fifteenth Army Group had a high-speed radio transmitter connected directly with London.[213] An investigation by AFHQ discovered that Montgomery also was communicating directly with Churchill.[214]

As he was attempting to discover why his British commanders were communicating with London instead of him, Eisenhower was also becoming concerned about the BBC coverage of Seventh Army. Lucas had lunch with Major General Everett S. Hughes, who informed him that "the British had overstepped a bit. It seemed the B.B.C. broadcast that the American Seventh Army in Sicily was doing nothing except sit under the trees and eat dates (or nuts, or something). This was the straw that broke Ike's back and he went into action in a loud tone of voice and got a retraction."[215] Such coverage not only threatened Eisenhower's effort to build Allied unity, but also violated his idea of the press's role in warfare. On August 4, he wrote Churchill that "the one thing for which I have struggled during the past year is a complete unification of Allied military efforts. . . . I carry this idea into all my press conferences, communiques and into every contact with the public." Such an effort was needed, Eisenhower claimed, "if we are to develop full-out enthusiasm for the policy of whipping Germany first." It was thus disturbing that a "recent broadcast by the B.B.C. stated in effect that the Seventh Army was lucky to be in the unoccupied western portion of Sicily eating grapes." After noting that he was still attempting to be balanced in his press conferences, Eisenhower suggested that the BBC scripts be inspected by representatives of the British Chiefs of Staff Committee.[216] Eisenhower also made sure Alexander saw the cable.[217] Butcher noted in his diary on August 14 that the news from the BBC had "notably improved" since Eisenhower sent the letter.[218]

Back in Sicily, the working relationship between Montgomery and Patton had notably improved. On July 25, the two generals had met and found they were in agreement on how the final phase of the campaign should proceed.

Montgomery would continue to push north toward Messina. The Seventh Army would now also push along Highway 113, often called the coastal road, to Messina.[219] Patton was unnerved since Montgomery had "agreed so readily that I felt something was wrong."[220] Why was he suddenly so open to change? His biographer argues that Montgomery simply realized his original plan had failed, saw a chance for Patton to take Messina, and wanted to begin preparing for the invasion of Italy.[221] D'Este agrees that Montgomery simply wanted a new plan to end the campaign quickly and adds that even if they wanted to strike first, Eighth Army was in a poor position to race the Americans to Messina.[222]

Both explanations are plausible, but the "race" to Messina was also characterized by how Montgomery and Patton's philosophies of warfare intersected with the press. The two generals had much in common. Both had been wounded in World War I, they were both religious and eccentric, and both were serious students of war. Likewise, they valued the lives of their men, but where Patton saw speed as the best way to spare his soldiers' lives, Montgomery believed in careful set-piece battles with overwhelming strength. The two officers were again alike in that they used the media to connect with their soldiers. El Alamein had thrust Montgomery into the national spotlight, giving him fame and media attention.[223] Unlike what some contemporaries have claimed, Montgomery's fame was not the product of media buildup or an inflated ego.[224] Indeed, he used his fame to boost morale, which his chief of staff Francis de Guingand claimed Montgomery held to be "the most important single factor in war."[225] As the Sicilian campaign came to a close, Montgomery wrote out his thoughts on morale. First, he believed morale was simply soldiers' confidence in their commander. To gain it, Montgomery was careful never to lose a battle. Likewise, he ensured by frequent visits and his unique black turtleneck and beret that he was known to his troops. He concluded that "hero-worship" was "inherent in the British public, and because I have never failed to give them success my troops regard me as the sort of General they like."[226] Montgomery was certainly as successful as Patton in connecting to his soldiers. As a Canadian officer recalled, "The most remarkable thing about General B. L. Montgomery . . . was his lack of remoteness. Six distinct levels of command existed between the man with the rifle and 'Monty.' . . . Yet, to the private soldier the Army Commander seemed to be his own personal commander, with no one else really in between."[227] If moving slowly would win the battle, save the lives of his soldiers, and improve their morale, Montgomery was ready to pay that price.

Like Montgomery, Patton believed that being with a winning general was important for morale, but so was speed. "Death in battle is a function of time," he wrote as the Tunisia campaign ended. "The longer troops remain under fire, the more men get killed. Therefore, everything must be done to speed up movement."[228] Daring advances also made for good newspaper headlines, which Patton saw as bringing credit to his soldiers and himself. Therefore, though the race to Messina was driven by media and national rivalries, it was also in keeping with Patton and Montgomery's philosophies of war.

Speed, coupled with a desire to demonstrate to the press and the British the fighting power of Seventh Army, characterized Patton's drive to Messina. Even before Husky, Patton had seen speed and press coverage as interlinked. Right before the invasion, Lucas documented a conversation with Eisenhower and Patton about a *Life* magazine article "which was highly critical of the North African campaign, particularly for its slowness."[229] Now remembering weeks of British and press insults and facing difficult terrain, Patton merged the two elements. "The northern coastline of Sicily is the kind of country described in tourist literature as picturesque," wrote the war correspondent Don Whitehead. But the steep mountains running down to the sea with roads cut into them were "a soldier's hell."[230] The Germans took full advantage of the terrain. "The destruction of the bridges and mountain roads by the Germans in their retreat is the most expert and successful demolition operation I have ever dreamed of," Lucas observed.[231] The topography increased Patton's need for speed. "The mountains are the worst I have ever seen," he wrote. "It is a miracle that our men can get through them but we must keep up our steady pressure. The enemy simply can't stand it, besides we must beat the Eighth Army to Messina."[232] As Carlo D'Este observed, Patton was joined in these views by many of his commanders.[233] Thus, terrain, military philosophy, and desire to beat the British drove Patton toward Messina.

Patton clearly saw his drive to Messina as a race, but it is doubtful Montgomery shared this impression. In fact, both Montgomery's and Patton's most prominent biographers agree that Montgomery was happy to let the Americans take Messina.[234] Montgomery's private writings from the time support the idea of seeing Seventh Army's drive along the coast as a vital part of the campaign, and those were further confirmed by his staff officers.[235] He even took the unheard-of step of praising Seventh Army on the BBC.[236] For Montgomery the best publicity was to win a battle with as few casualties as possible, and he viewed Patton's drive as the best way to accomplish this objective. Not all British officers agreed. "At the time a number of us were rather worried by the comparison of achievement," remembered Francis de Guingand about the drive to Messina, "and on occasions I had to swallow hard when this was pointed out to me."[237] But Montgomery, unlike Patton, did not feel that he had anything to prove.

His desire to beat the British to Messina, his philosophy of speedy attacks, and his lust for publicity set the stage for one of Patton's most controversial actions of the war. On August 8, Patton launched an amphibious landing behind German lines. "It had been the toughest fight we had had so far," Truscott remembered, but German casualties were also high. Patton was pleased and ordered II Corps to prepare for another "end run" for the early hours of August 11.[238] Truscott's Third Division would attack along the coastal road while the Second Battalion of the Thirtieth Infantry, reinforced by tanks and artillery, would land twelve miles down the road at Brolo Beach, near Mount Cipolla, and attempt to cut off the Twenty-Ninth Panzergrenadier Division.[239] Both Bradley and Truscott believed that the operation was too risky, wanted it postponed, and later agreed that Patton refused to halt the landing because it would cause unfavorable media attention. Before Patton's visit, Truscott had spoken to Keyes, who said Patton wanted "the operation to go on. Arrangements had already been made for a large number of correspondents to accompany it, and there would be criticism if the operation were postponed."[240] The US Army's official history of the campaign agreed that Patton did not "relish having to tell the writers that the end run had again been delayed."[241] In fairness to Patton, neither his diary nor that of his chief of staff Hobart Gay mentions any media motivation for the landings.[242] Yet it is also true that at least three reporters, representing major publications, landed with the Second Battalion at Brolo.[243]

If Patton intended to impress the reporters, the end run at Brolo had the opposite result. Soon after the landing, the Second Battalion found itself in a dreadful fix, cut off from any supporting units and enduring heavy German counterattacks. By early evening, the battalion had withdrawn from the beach and fallen back to Mount Cipolla and lost communication with Truscott. As darkness fell, the Germans began retreating down the newly cleared highway.[244] By morning they were gone, and the Second Battalion was reunited with the rest of Third Infantry Division. The American official account tallied German losses at 100 killed and a gain of fifteen miles at a price of 41 dead GIs and 136 other casualties.[245] As war correspondent Don Whitehead observed the destruction along the highway, Patton's jeep pulled up with the general and Senator Henry Cabot Lodge Jr. Patton stood "tall and straight in his command car" as he made a brief speech praising the American soldiers. "All at once the whole little tableau sickened me," Whitehead remembered. "I wanted to get away from the voices of the general and the senator. The dead scattered on the hillside and in the lemon grove spoke eloquently enough."[246]

Later, there would be debate over what exactly the end run at Brolo was supposed to accomplish. The Thirtieth Infantry's after-action report stated that the main objective was to trap "the withdrawal of the enemy rear guard force."[247] Both Bradley and Truscott agreed. "Had we delayed a day," Truscott believed, "we might have captured most of the German force. Nevertheless, we had gained important time."[248] But Patton valued time more than prisoners and refused to waste a day in the race to Messina. Though his diary for August 11 noted that the Germans were about to pull out "if they *can* pull out," indicating that he hoped to trap the enemy, the next day he added, "The hazards of the landing were more than justified, as it pushed the enemy so fast that he had no time to make demolitions."[249] A few days later, he ordered another end run landing, again over Bradley and Truscott's protest. Once again Patton overruled them, Bradley believed, "mainly for publicity reasons."[250] Truscott, who correctly predicted that the advance on land would overrun the beach before the amphibious force could land, likewise recorded that "Patton was not averse to profiting from such a spectacular operation."[251] By the time the soldiers landed, the campaign was almost over.

"By 10 a.m. this morning, August 17, 1943," Alexander cabled Churchill, "the last German soldier was flung out of Sicily and the whole island is now in our hands."[252] That morning Patton, Truscott, and a few staff officers appeared on top of a hill looking down at what was left of Messina, captured by Seventh Army the previous evening. They paused as Patton made a brief statement into a BBC Dictaphone, complimenting the "work of the 3rd Division most highly, and particularly the effects of the enlisted men involved."[253] Then, serenaded by the sound of artillery, the group descended upon Messina. Later, however, Patton confessed to his diary that he felt let down.[254] Likewise, when he saw the press coverage a few days later, Patton sadly noted that "the fall of Messina received scant notice."[255] This was compounded by the escape of 125,000 Axis troops.[256] Patton's conduct also came under criticism. Bradley, for one, believed Patton "was trying to get headlines instead of a victory. It's all right to get both but you want the victory first with minimum losses."[257] Nevertheless, the advance of Seventh Army had been remarkable. At the start of August, Alexander had stated that Sicily would not fall for another month, and Montgomery believed even that was optimistic.[258] Throughout the campaign, Patton had melded his philosophy of warfare and his press policy to direct major battlefield decisions. As his official biographer, Martin Blumenson, observes, "Still smarting from what he considered to be the condescending attitude of Alexander and Montgomery and other British officers toward American troops . . . Patton became obsessed with reaching Messina ahead of the British—not so much for his personal glory, although that was important, but rather to prove to the world that American soldiers were every bit as good as—indeed, better than—British troops."[259] Patton's operations in Sicily were a turning point for the US Army in World War II. After Sicily, American troops could no longer be dismissed as novices.

The Slapping Incidents

Unfortunately for Patton his spectacular drive across Sicily was soon overshadowed by two incidents that took place along the road to Messina. It all began at 12:15 p.m. on August 3 when Patton arrived at the Fifteenth Evacuation Hospital and found "the only arrant coward I have ever seen in this army. I asked him what was the matter, and he said he just couldn't take it. I gave him the devil, slapped his face with my gloves and kicked him out of the hospital."[260] On August 10, Patton did it again. In the middle of preparing for the landing at Brolo, Patton stopped at the Ninety-Third Evacuation Hospital and found "another alleged nervous patient—really a coward."[261] Patton cursed out the GI, slapped him across the face twice, and shouted at the hospital staff to return the soldier to his unit.[262] Word of the slapping incidents quickly reached Eisenhower. A few days before, Butcher had recorded "Patton's great progress gives Ike a warm glow as there are many army officers who could not see through Patton's showmanship and boisterousness to discern his fine qualities of leadership on which Ike banked so strongly. In addition the success of the 7th Army lets Americans hold their heads high amongst the British and other allies who had been a bit skeptical."[263] Yet the report that reached Eisenhower on the day Messina fell brought Patton's leadership into question and threatened to undo his positive publicity.[264] The "slapping incidents" would damage Patton's relationship with the press, but also show Eisenhower's success in gaining the respect and trust of war correspondents.

On the evening of the second slapping incident, a Seventh Army PR officer visited one of the nurses at the hospital and heard the story. Feeling that something must be done, but fearing regular army channels would be useless, the officer leaked the story to the press.[265] The next day Demaree Bess of the *Saturday Evening Post* visited the hospital along with Merrill Mueller of NBC, John Daly of CBS, and Al Newman of *Newsweek*.[266] There they met doctor Donald E. Currier, who, after extracting a promise to keep his name out of any publicity, told the reporters the story.[267] The correspondents left with signed statements from the medical personnel and a carefully written report by Bess. While debating what to do next, they ran into Quentin Reynolds, who suggested that Bess and Mueller accompany him to visit Eisenhower. On arrival in Algiers, Reynolds called Harry Butcher to arrange a meeting. "I know what you're coming to see him about," said Butcher.[268]

Eisenhower met with the correspondents and received Bess's report. It concluded by reminding Eisenhower of "what the effect on the army would be if this material were published. If I am correctly informed, General Patton has subjected himself to a general court martial by striking an enlisted man. I am making this report," Bess continued, "in the hope of getting conditions corrected before more damage has been done."[269] Now Bess repeated this to a miserable Eisenhower while Reynolds—never one to forgo drama—chimed in that "at least 50,000 American soldiers . . . gladly would shoot Patton if they had the slightest chance."[270] Finally, Eisenhower smiled weakly, told the reporters that they had a good story, and said that he could not justify censoring it since no secret information was involved. "Quent and Mueller and I have been discussing what would happen if we reported this," Bess said quietly, "and our conclusion is that we're Americans first and correspondents second." Mueller then added that they would kill the story and deny it if any others reported it.[271] Eisenhower relaxed and informed the reporters that he had already reprimanded Patton. Next, Eisenhower assembled the other reporters and repeated that Patton had been reprimanded and ordered to apologize. He then explained that Patton was important to the war effort and would save many American lives if he continued in command. "You all know that there is something more important in this war than a single story," Eisenhower added. "If you want to write about these incidents, you may do so, and there will be no censorship. There will be no recriminations on my part. I leave each of you to use your conscience and do what you feel is best."[272] Reynolds left with new respect for Eisenhower. Apparently, other correspondents shared it, since not one of the sixty reporters in Algiers and Sicily reported the story.[273]

Even before meeting with the correspondents, Eisenhower had taken steps to correct the incident. He wrote Patton a harsh, though unofficial, reprimand and ordered him to apologize to the slapped soldiers, the medical personnel, and his troops. Next, he dispatched John P. Lucas, Everett S. Hughes, and Herbert S. Clarkson, the theater inspector general, to collect the facts about the incidents and see whether Patton still had the respect of his men.[274] Lucas, who had witnessed the first slapping incident and was sympathetic to Patton, delivered Eisenhower's reprimand and told him to stop wearing his ivory-handled pistols and acting like a madman or he would lose his command. Hughes, also an old friend of Patton, helped him draft a suitably penitent reply to Eisenhower and "insisted" that he "quit saying that he had done no wrong." The inspector general was hardly as accommodating, but Hughes managed to convince him not to recommend Patton's relief.[275] Patton apologized to all involved and returned to Algiers with Hughes, where Eisenhower lectured him for an hour and forty-five minutes, which Patton tried to accept "in the spirit intended. I feel that he likes me. Of course he should."[276] Though he was left in limbo as to his next command, it appeared that the slapping incident was closed.

This illusion was shattered three months later at a meeting between the columnist Drew Pearson and his lawyer Ernest Cuneo. Pearson, an influential commentator with a large audience, was in trouble—again—after claiming on his radio broadcast that Secretary of State Cordell Hull was trying "to bleed Russia white" by opposing a second front in Europe. This caused Roosevelt to hold a press conference where he categorized Pearson's remarks as "detrimental" to the war effort and called the commentator "a chronic liar." Though the incident was almost three months old, Pearson's biographers agree that he was still shaken by the charge and open to advice when Cuneo suggested breaking a sensational story. As it happened Cuneo, who worked for the Office of Strategic Services (OSS), had just such a story about a famous American general striking a hospitalized soldier.[277] Pearson liked the idea and "decided it was time to let loose on [Patton]."[278]

Pearson submitted the story to the OWI, which checked with the War Department. Though they believed it would hurt morale, the War Department staff admitted that Pearson's story presented no risk to security, and the OWI cleared it.[279] In justifying the decision to publish the story, Byron Price, director of censorship, explained that no part of the censorship regulations "requests the withholding of information about the conduct or shortcomings of military officers," adding that there was no way "the enemy could make use of the Patton incident except for propaganda purposes."[280] Even before Pearson received approval, two Chicago newspapers were inquiring if the story had been cleared.[281] Pearson had his story cleared for November 14, but delayed broadcasting until November 21, when he delivered a garbled account of the slapping incidents.[282]

Not since Eisenhower's Darlan Deal had the press reacted so strongly to the actions of an American general. In his radio broadcast, Walter Winchell predicted Patton would be shot by one of his own soldiers.[283] The *Washington Post* editorialized that Patton was still in command from a "perverted sense of values. He is supposed to be an able general. As to this, we have no knowledge, and for some time have felt that no judgement can be formed about our field generalship because of the prevailing censorship." This did not stop the *Post* from declaring that Patton had lost the confidence of the country and that "he is no longer an asset, if he ever was, but a decided liability."[284] To underline their point, the next day the paper published a collection of editorials from around the country summarizing that *"representative American newspapers . . . express concern both with the general's lack of control, casting doubt on his capacity to command."* The *San Francisco Chronicle* editorial stated that "General Patton should be relieved of his command." The *Herald Tribune* worried that Patton's "usefulness as a field commander is at an end."[285] Pearson continued to pass on rumors "that when the General lectures either a man or an officer he whips out his pearl-handled revolver and fires it into the air—giving the impression at first that he is going to fire at the man he is talking to."[286]

Eisenhower heard of the Pearson story when he returned to AFHQ late on November 22, 1943, and found that the theater correspondents were furious with him. Mueller phoned Butcher and told him that Colonel Frank McChrystal, the new information director, had read a statement that not only was Patton still in command of the Seventh Army, but that he had never been reprimanded. "Red [Mueller] took violent exception to the latter," Butcher wrote, "saying the reaction would be hostile in the home press and that it left Ike in the position of 'covering' his own effective action." In the meantime, Eisenhower had received his own phone call from a reporter decrying his "shabby treatment of the press." Eisenhower found that while he had written a press release for McChrystal, his cantankerous chief of staff, Walter Bedell "Beetle" Smith, had added that Patton had not been reprimanded. This was technically true, since Patton's reprimand was unofficial, but missed the spirit of Eisenhower's actions. "Beetle is an efficient Chief of Staff," reflected Butcher in his diary, "but he is also a bit bumbling when dealing with the press." Butcher suggested an off-the-record press conference to clear up matters, but Eisenhower demurred. Suffering from a head cold and trying to recover his strength, he simply had a correction issued. But to Eisenhower's surprise, the story had reached the United States a mere ten minutes after McChrystal's press conference. It was a lesson for Eisenhower and the rest of his staff on the speed with which news now traveled and a warning that "we plainly had to be right the first time."[287]

Some newspapers, and a few historians, incorrectly claimed that Eisenhower had imposed censorship.[288] But as Eisenhower explained to General Surley "not only did I refuse to place any censorship on the case, but I have inquired among my staff and I am certain that no repeat no one in this headquarters ever attempted to do so." He added that Bess and Reynolds had at once returned to the United States after the story broke and had kept silent even when censorship would not apply.[289] There were, in fact, only two instances of censorship with the slapping incidents. The first came after the story broke when the censor for the Seventh Army, acting on his own fear, refused to allow the *Stars and Stripes* to publish the AP's article on the scandal.[290] The second came before Pearson's broadcast when the Eighth Army's newspaper was prepared to print a rumor that Patton was under investigation. Montgomery, who usually gave his paper editorial freedom, angrily killed the story because "Patton was a good man."[291] The false censorship story may have been an attempt to deflect criticism from the journalists. Virgil Pinkley recalled that newspapers harshly criticized their war correspondents, including Pinkley himself, whose editor demanded to hear his "lousy excuse" for not reporting the story.[292]

The botched response of Eisenhower's headquarters drew heavy press criticism. The *Cleveland News* editorialized that "army censorship is exposed as an instrument which kept the truth from the people for no other reason than that it was unpleasant and reflected unfavorably upon a member of the military hierarchy." The editorial lamented that "good news, and bad has been hushed and manipulated, depending on whether someone in high places considered that the people ought to be stimulated by confidence or spurred on by fear. The Army and Navy have shown their inevitable instinct to make this a professional men's war rather than a people's war."[293] The *St. Louis Post Dispatch* opined that the "facts of the case are bad enough, but the effort to cover them up is inexcusable."[294] "The Patton incident loomed large as an Army scandal chiefly because of extremely poor public-relations work," wrote *Newsweek*, adding, "General Smith's evasion and the subsequent proof of the truth only served to magnify the affair."[295] As his biographer notes, it was Smith, not Eisenhower, who "ended up in hot water."[296]

As he had done during the Darlan Deal, Henry Stimson began repairing the damage. He had been friends with Patton for decades and was, in fact, entertaining Beatrice and one of the Pattons' daughters the night before Pearson's "nasty" broadcast. Stimson "decided that it would be best not to notice the items today but Surles will watch carefully to see whether the matter is growing or fading in the press." He also wrote out a statement saying that the War Department had no knowledge of the incident, that it was Eisenhower's responsibility, and that Stimson did know that at least parts of the story were false.[297] Stimson was not able to give his press conference for another few days, by which time Surles was tired and depressed from handling the media and informed Stimson the "case was bad." Stimson, who was more optimistic, focused the press conference on importance of giving commanders such as Eisenhower the freedom to handle matters in their theater as they saw fit. Later that day, Eisenhower's report of the slapping incident arrived. A carefully paraphrased version was sent to the Senate's Military Affairs Committee.[298] Stimson wrote to Senator Robert R. Reynolds, the chair of the committee, asking him to drop the matter, which Reynolds did.[299] "General Eisenhower's straightforward account of the Patton case will alleviate much of the indignation which the incident has aroused," noted the *Washington Post*.[300]

"I think the squall is about over," wrote Stimson to Beatrice Patton on November 26.[301] And so it was. Despite the criticism from the press and politicians, support for Patton among the American public and servicemen remained remarkably high. Gallup reported that 70 percent of respondents thought Patton should be left in command, with only 22 percent saying he should be returned home.[302] Meanwhile, Patton's aide-de-camp recorded that the general's mail was running 11 percent protest and 89 percent in support of Patton.[303] Likewise, the editor of the left-leaning New York City newspaper *PM* admitted that for every letter he received agreeing with his publication's call for a court-martial, five letters were received against it.[304] Though "no columnists ever came right out and defended you [or] your actions," Beatrice wrote her husband, she did list thirteen columnists who supported him. Beatrice also noted that none of the war correspondents had come out in full support, but a number had written fair-minded stories, including Wes Gallagher,

Hal Boyle, and Ernie Pyle, who "never mentioned it [the slapping incident], but spoke well od [*sic*] you." She listed six correspondents who were against Patton, including the three reporters who had brought the story to Eisenhower. Overall, seventeen papers supported Patton and thirteen were against him, though there was also overlap as papers changed their positions.[305]

Patton survived a media assault, but the scandal shaped his military actions. The first result was a tenser relationship with reporters. Gone was the easy association, now replaced by mutual suspicion. It is untrue, as some historians have suggested, that because of the slapping incident Patton was passed over for the command of US troops for D-Day that Bradley received.[306] It was Marshall, not Eisenhower, who made the decision, and Marshall as yet knew nothing about the slapping incidents. On August 24, 1943, Eisenhower wrote Marshall praising Patton lavishly, and only alluded indirectly to the slapping incidents.[307] Yet even as Eisenhower sent this cable, one from Marshall arrived requesting Bradley to be sent to England.[308] Eisenhower stood up for Patton during the slapping incidents, but Patton failed to see it and began to fear upsetting his boss again. "I was told that I was too impetuous to do what Omar has to do," Patton wrote his wife after visiting Eisenhower. "Apparently I am a man of deeds not words. Except when I talk too much."[309] The scandal and the long period of uncertainty that followed only made Patton more determined to redeem himself in battle.

Conclusion

"In the last analysis," wrote Eisenhower before Husky, "no battles are won with headlines, although I appreciate that wars are conducted by public opinion."[310] The campaigns across North Africa and Sicily certainly bore that out, with Alexander, Bradley, Eisenhower, and Patton all allowing media and public opinion considerations to influence their battlefield decisions. Bradley successfully convinced Eisenhower, who in turn persuaded Alexander, that American soldiers needed a significant part in the Tunisia campaign. Eisenhower knew the United States had to have media attention for the Germany First strategy to be continued. In Sicily, Patton twice convinced Alexander that American public opinion demanded that his Seventh Army be given a meaningful role in the campaign. Believing that the British were monopolizing press interest, Patton tried to gain attention for his armored forces by making sure they entered Palermo first. He, likewise, craved the publicity Messina's capture would give his army. To accomplish this, he made controversial end runs along the Sicilian coast, believing the risk was outweighed by the positive publicity and speed.

Were Heroes or Managers better at press relations? The answer is complicated—both Eisenhower and Patton got what they wanted from the press, as well as much that they did not want. Eisenhower was swept up by the controversy surrounding the Darlan Deal, which drew heavy press criticism. The result was that he spent much of his time on political matters and ceded control of the front lines to British commanders. This angered many American officers, who were more sensitive to comparisons of the Allies by the press. One of the most critical press scandals concerned Patton, who was in a so-called race with the British to Messina when he slapped two soldiers. During such scandals, both generals received significant support from Stimson and Marshall, who successfully worked behind the scenes with media and political contacts. Yet in the long term, Eisenhower's ability to befriend and manage reporters proved much less controversial than Patton's focus on creating a warrior image. As a beleaguered Patton watched Clark start the Italian campaign and Eisenhower and Bradley depart to begin planning the landings in Normandy, he might well have reflected on just what "pitiless publicity" really meant.

Chapter Four

"War in a Museum"

Fame and promotion did not prevent Jimmy Doolittle from bombing Axis capitals. On July 19, 1943, he led five hundred heavy bombers in a raid on Rome. The attack, according to Doolittle, was "the largest aggregation of bombing planes ever assembled up to that time."[1] The target was a massive marshaling yard crucial for moving forces to southern Italy, where Allied troops would soon land.[2] Likewise, as Doolittle claimed later, the Allies knew that the Italian government was wavering and that an attack on its capital might help undermine popular support.[3]

Doolittle's raid was the first bombing of Rome during the war. Politically, the raid was as sensitive as his previous attack on Tokyo, but came with a much greater publicity risk for the Allies. Rome was not only an Axis capital but home to much of the cultural heritage of Western civilization along with being the political center of Catholicism.[4] In Washington, Henry "Hap" Arnold remembered, Roosevelt and Stimson were being pressed "from all sides" to avoid bombing the Eternal City.[5] Eisenhower's aide Harry Butcher was also opposed. The vibrations from the bombing might cause Vatican buildings to collapse, he told Eisenhower. Was it worth the risk of angering the world's Catholics? What if such an attack rejuvenated faltering Italian morale? It was all well for Churchill and the British to advocate the bombing, but the blame, of course, would fall on Eisenhower.[6] Eventually, the raid was ordered directly by the Combined Chiefs of Staff, with Roosevelt drafting a public letter of explanation to the pope.[7] As Doolittle remembered later, it had been expected that the Axis press would use the raid for propaganda, but much of the harshest criticism came from the Allied media.[8] Butcher observed that for once the BBC was giving the Americans "liberal credit" for the bombing.[9]

In Feltre near Venice, Benito Mussolini, the once-powerful dictator of Italy, was enduring a harangue by Hitler, who was attempting to rekindle Italian morale from the top down. In the middle of the tirade, word came of the bombing. As Mussolini's plane approached the Italian capital a few hours later, the city was covered in black smoke.[10] The invasion of Sicily and the realization that the fighting would soon reach the Italian mainland had already weakened the Fascist government's resolve.[11] Soon after his return to Rome, the Fascist Grand Council voted to remove Mussolini from the control of the war, and on July 26, 1943, the Italian monarch, Victor Emmanuel III, first dismissed and then arrested the duce. Marshal Pietro Badoglio took his place and began planning to take Italy out of the war.[12] Thus, Doolittle was correct in claiming "as with the raid on Tokyo, the raid on Rome had a significant psychological effect on the Italian people," or at least on the Fascist elite.[13] This was fitting enough since the coming campaign for Italy would be heavily influenced by public opinion.

Historians have viewed the campaign in Italy as either a strategic necessity or a costly diversion. Its defenders point out that the Germans were forced to divert to Italy and the Balkans various divisions that were needed on other fronts. They also point to the fact that Italy provided bases for the Fifteenth Air Force to extend the range of the strategic bombers to the oilfields of Romania.[14] Critics, however, point to the price of these strategic gains. "To Allied strategists," conclude historians Williamson Murray and Allan Millett, "the Italian theater had been a major disappointment; but to the troops who fought there it had been a horror, and for the Italian people it was nothing short of a catastrophe."[15]

Both arguments contain truth, but it should also be noted that public opinion made the campaign in Italy almost inevitable. This was due in part to the global military situation in the middle of 1943 and the cultural heritage of Italy. The Soviets were continuing to drive the Axis out of Russia, while the second front in France had been delayed once again.[16] Public opinion, reasoned Allied leaders, would hardly allow the Allies to stand still while the Soviets bled the German armies. Field Marshal J. C. Smuts reminded Churchill of this reality while he was at the Quebec Conference. He worried "public morale" was being hurt by the long delays between Allied offensives and the Soviets' bearing the brunt of the war. "If by the end of 1944 we have done no better than merely nibble at the enemy's main position," he added, "we may experience a dangerous revulsion of opinion, and rightly so." The prime minister reassured Smuts that Allied troops would soon be in Italy.[17] Roosevelt, for his part, allowed American politics to shape his view of the campaign. Catholics and Italian Americans were part of the Democratic Party's electoral base. It was therefore natural for the president to declare the invasion of Italy a "crusade to save the Pope."[18] Likewise, the promise of knocking one of the Axis countries out of the war and liberating its capital was hard to pass up. Once troops were in Italy, public opinion would hardly let the campaign falter. "While there is no denying the lack of strategic focus and wishful thinking that informed Operation Avalanche," writes historian Douglas Porch on the invasion of Italy, "it is difficult to imagine that the Western Allies, having driven to the doorstep of the peninsula, could simply forsake its alluring promise in September 1943."[19] With these considerations, it is unsurprising that the press and public opinion would prove important factors in waging the Italian campaign.

The focus of the Italian campaign was Rome. For Churchill, the city's capture would cap a successful campaign in the Mediterranean and symbolize Allied victory.[20] The Allies saw the propaganda value of taking an Axis capital. The Germans were equally determined to hold it for the same reason. As Eisenhower wrote after the war, "the constant threat against Rome and the Italian industrial centers to the northward would cause unrest through the Balkans and other portions of Europe, which would depress German morale and raise our own."[21] A century before, the Prussian military theorist Carl von Clausewitz had written: "Of all the possible aims in war, the destruction of the enemy's armed forces always appears as the highest."[22] Although the Allies talked at considerable length about holding down German divisions in Italy, the real objective was always Rome.

Marcus Aurelius Clark

The man most responsible for allowing the press to influence the Italian campaign was Mark W. Clark. The general was an army brat who had graduated from West Point in 1917 in time to be wounded in World War I. He was one of the youngest lieutenant generals in the history of the US Army and the only high-ranking US general in World War II to leave a large collection of letters to his mother. A likable man with an excellent mind, Clark spent much of his time at the front.[23] At the beginning of the Italian campaign, Eisenhower viewed Clark as "not so good as Bradley in winning . . . the complete confidence of everybody around him, including his British associates. He is not the equal of Patton in his refusal to see anything but victory . . . but he is carrying his full weight and, so far, has fully justified his selection for his present important post."[24] That "important post" was as the commander of the Fifth US Army, in which Clark was destined to play an important role in the Italian campaign.

The weakness of this bright young general, historians agree, was his intense ambition and obsession with press attention.[25] The stories of Clark's press arrangements are legion. Only the left side of the general's face was to be photographed so his three stars could be shown.[26] Nearly fifty men would work on his public relations staff, along with ample stateside help from his wife and mother. Some PRO instructions included mentioning the general's name three times on the first page of press releases and using "Lieutenant General Mark W. Clark's Fifth Army" in communiqués.[27] He encouraged the presence of reporters. Once, after C. L. Sulzberger complained of a censor's injustice, Clark threw his arm around his shoulder and said, "Cy, when we make our breakthrough I want you to ride in a jeep with me. I'll see to it when we get there that you can tell the world just how Mark Clark took Rome."[28]

That was not the answer Sulzberger wanted. As historian Martin Blumenson wrote, "Clark was ambitious and frankly so, for he looked on ambition as the goad that spurred a man to considerable exertion and eventual success."[29] It would indeed spur Clark to extraordinary lengths in the Italian campaign.

It is one of the arguments of this book that modern total war impelled or even compelled military commanders to consider media factors as an important part of their operations. Clark understood this as well as anybody. But unlike other American generals, publicity became an objective for Clark rather than a weapon. MacArthur used the press to get resources for the SWPA, but it was for the military objective of liberating the Philippines and destroying the Japanese Empire. Bradley had insisted that US troops had to be part of the surrender of Axis forces in North Africa, but it did not delay the surrender. Patton had raced to Palermo and then Messina for press glory, but he knew he would also be blocking the Axis escape route. Clark's actions near Rome, by contrast, would forsake the destruction of the enemy army for personal glory and prestige objectives. In Italy, Clark was driven by the greatest publicity siren of all—the city of Rome. Even before the Fifth Army landed in Italy, General Lucian Truscott remembered, Rome "was already looming large as an objective with General Clark and others."[30]

Reporters had mixed feelings about Clark. Eric Sevareid believed Clark "spoke exclusively in terms of his own Fifth Army" and made his soldiers sing songs glorifying their commander. Any support given to reporters—and Sevareid admitted it was a lot—was so that journalists could give generals "personal publicity without which war-making is a dull job."[31] For his part, Clark was unimpressed with Sevareid's ignorance about the campaign.[32] Sulzberger was less critical than Sevareid, but admitted Clark was "fearless but he never impressed me by his brilliance and he was certainly obsessed with vanity."[33] Ernie Pyle, on the other hand, liked Clark and saw him as "straightforward" and "a thoroughly honest man." Nor did he blame him for the slow progress of the Italian campaign.[34]

Long before he arrived in Italy, Clark's lust for publicity was already causing concern in Allied headquarters. To Bradley, Clark "seemed false somehow, too eager to impress, too hungry for the limelight, promotions and personal publicity."[35] Patton, who spent much of 1942 jealous of Clark's rapid rise, observed that during President Roosevelt's visit to North Africa, "millions of pictures were taken and none for the glory of the troops, all for the glory of F.D.R., and for Clark when he could get a chance. It was very disgusting."[36] Clark's subordinates agreed. Fred Walker, commander of the Thirty-Sixth Division in Italy, bitterly told reporter Blair Moody that his name was censored because "Clark does not tolerate any competition in the news. News items must refer to 'general Clark's soldiers' or to 'General Clark's Fifth Army.'" Nor were divisions serving under Clark usually named in the press.[37]

Both Marshall and Eisenhower repeatedly warned Clark of the dangers of publicity. The story of Clark's secret landing by submarine to meet anti-Vichy French leaders before Torch had captured public imagination, as had the fact that Clark had lost his pants in the process. Eisenhower disliked the story since it appeared that the Allies were willing to buy supporters among the French. Butcher recorded that "when the 'lost his pants' story broke, Marshall was greatly upset. Clark still thinks Marshall is wrong in believing the story 'done him wrong.'" Marshall argued that the story made Clark look like a "buffoon" to the parents of the men he commanded. Likewise, Marshall worried that "other generals who may have lurking ambitions for the head-lines may follow . . . [Clark's] example. With an Army of publicity-minded generals the little news-interest points about them, some of which would be silly or at least un-officer-like, would spread a feeling of lack of respect." The chief of staff ordered Clark to stay away from reporters.[38]

Unfortunately for Clark, his family also enjoyed giving him publicity. Like the wives of other high-ranking American generals, Maurine Doran "Renie" Clark worked hard raising money for the war. By the close of the conflict, she had helped sell $25 million worth of war bonds. But Renie also spent much time promoting her husband, publicly reading his letters and even displaying the recovered pants he had lost in the secret visit to North Africa before Torch.[39] In an article titled "Pants for Posterity," the *New York Times* reported that the Smithsonian Institute kept receiving in-quiries whether it had yet obtained Clark's trousers.[40] The attention quickly drew the War Department's irritation. "General Marshall complained to Ike that General Clark was being victimized by his wife, Renie, who indulged in release to the press of his personal letters to her," Butcher recorded in his diary. "She also displays his much publicized pants, now shrunk by salt water [*sic*], when she lectures for the war bond drive. The Chief of Staff said General Clark should be cautioned that the publicity is harmful and that he frequently has been held up to sarcasm and ridicule because of it."[41] Eisenhower wrote Clark the next day explaining that the chief of staff was concerned "that nothing occur that can damage the dignity of your present position or your future prospects."[42]

Clark immediately wrote Renie and ordered her to keep his name out of her talks, but added that he disliked to "write to you about this publicity business, for I feel your work is superior." Clark also instructed his mother—she and Renie were not friends—to watch her publicity activities. "I note what you say about magazines writing to ask you for a boyhood story of me," he wrote his mother a few days before the Anzio landings. "I sincerely hope that you will not give it. I well understand what the public wants, but there are many people in the Army who resent those things and there is no use antagonizing them, so please do as you have done and refrain from giving any publicity on me.''[43] A couple of months later, Clark lamented, "I find so many of my letters being published that I am getting a little shy of writing.''[44]

The situation was not helped by Clark's superior Sir Harold Alexander, who commanded the Fifteenth Army Group. A pleasant personality without much desire for excessive publicity, Alexander was a favorite of Churchill and Eisenhower.[45] But his friendliness and grace made him the type of general to prefer suggestions to orders. And though he still harbored less-than-admiring opinions of the US Army from the Tunisia campaign, he understood the delicacies of the Grand Alliance.[46] No matter the nationality, Alexander received little respect from his subordinates. During a planning meeting in Sicily involving Montgomery, Patton, and Walter Bedell Smith, Alexander had arrived after the decision was reached. As Montgomery and Patton's commander, he asked to have the plan explained. Montgomery said it was already decided and there was no need to go over the plan again. Alexander insisted. A photo captured the four generals with Alexander clearly on the edge of the group. As historian D. K. R. Crosswell observes, "Montgomery's actions stripped away any pretense of Alexander exercising any real authority.''[47] Montgomery confirmed this when he told Patton, "If you get an order from [Alexander's] Army Group that you don't like, why just ignore it. That's what I do.''[48] Now in Italy, Montgomery gave Clark similar advice. "From time to time you will get instructions from Alex that you won't understand," Montgomery explained. "When you do, just tell him to go to hell.''[49] It was a lesson Clark would remember.

Surrender and Invasion

The fall of Mussolini signaled to the Allies that Italy would likely try to seek peace. To help them along, Eisenhower prepared a broadcast saying that the Italians could "have peace immediately.''[50] His British and American political advisers, nevertheless, reminded him that London and Washington needed to be informed. This set off a round of tedious cables between Allied leaders.[51] Roosevelt endeavored to help by stating at a press conference that the Allies would work with anyone in Italy who would disarm the country and keep order.[52] One of the first requests the Italians made was that Rome be declared an open city. Believing British public opinion would react negatively, Churchill strongly opposed the request.[53] Then, to Churchill's fury, Eisenhower's headquarters announced it would halt bombing raids in northern Italy. "I hope you will realise that I am liable to be cross-examined in the HOUSE on the exact wording of every declaration to the Italian people that carries or purports to carry your high authority," Churchill wrote Eisenhower in an unusually testy cable. "I cannot therefore disinterest myself in communiques which, at moments when public opinion is so sensitive, profess to explain the attitude of our joint government in ITALY."[54] Behind this fuss, as Roosevelt admitted, lay the ghost of Darlan and the dangers of hostile public opinion in making peace with Axis countries.[55]

By this point, Eisenhower was becoming irritated with the negotiations. He wrote after the war that the whole incident was a reminder that a "modern commander in the field is never more than an hour away from home capitals and public opinion."[56] He had been in Malta when the British Political Warfare Executive (PWE) issued the statement on halting the bombing of Rome. The Allied air forces in the Mediterranean had requested a rest for the bomber crews, which the PWE had decided to use for propaganda. But Eisenhower approved both decisions. As he explained to Marshall, the PWE statement had two purposes. "The first was a continuation of the effort to induce the Italian people to increase peace pressure on the new government. The second was the continuation of the threat that persons in or near war industries and military stations were likely to be killed by our bombs." He added that the "Combined Chiefs of Staff have provided me with personnel who are presumably expert in the business of using propaganda in a particular theater as a new but effective weapon of war."[57] And, according to Butcher, the proclamation had been effective, because the Italians were emptying their cities.[58] Meanwhile, the Italian envoys were claiming that if Rome was bombed again there would be an open revolt that would lead to brutal German suppression.[59] Harold Macmillan, Eisenhower's British political adviser, argued that was a fine idea.[60] The supreme commander demurred, but during the official surrender negotiations a month later, the renewal of the bombing of Rome would be a major threat used in obtaining Italian capitulation.[61]

Field Marshal Albert Kesselring, commanding German forces in Italy, met King Victor Emmanuel III on the day after Mussolini's arrest. During the friendly meeting, the king explained that Mussolini had been deposed since he "had lost the goodwill of public opinion."[62] Nevertheless, Kesselring and the Nazi high command smelled trouble, and German reinforcements began moving south. Meanwhile, the Italians had approached Eisenhower to open armistice negotiations. The talks were long and complicated. As historian Gerhard L. Weinberg summarizes, the "Italians did almost everything as stupidly and slowly as possible."[63] The Allies attempted to get a quick surrender, while the Italians begged for Allied troops to protect them against German vengeance.[64] As more German forces poured into Italy, the plotters panicked. On September 8, Badoglio cabled Eisenhower that he was backing out of the surrender plans. Among other things, this forced the last-minute cancellation of the landing of the Eighty-Second Airborne Division in Rome.[65]

As Badoglio wavered, Eisenhower showed just how powerful a weapon he wielded in the press. "I intend to broadcast the existence of the armistice at the hour originally planned," he wrote Badoglio. "If you or any part of your armed forces fail to co-operate as previously agreed I will publish to the world full record of this affair. Today is X-day and I expect you to do your part."[66] Eisenhower also wrote the Combined Chiefs of Staff that he intended "to proceed in accordance with [the] plan for the announcement of the armistice and with subsequent propaganda."[67] The move showed a new sophistication in Eisenhower's understanding of the press as a weapon. Even before the Italians offered an armistice, according to Admiral Leahy, Eisenhower's headquarters suggested using "a 'black radio' false proclamation of an armistice in our projected offensive."[68] The surrender went off that evening as scheduled.[69]

By that point, the fighting had already reached the Italian mainland. On September 3, Montgomery's Eighth Army crossed from Sicily to Italy. They were opposed only by a monkey and a puma who attacked a few Canadians after being inadvertently freed from a zoo by Allied gunfire.[70] But from news of German reinforcements flowing south, it was becoming clear that opposition would soon increase. Meanwhile, Clark's Fifth Army was not yet in Italy. The plan called for his American VI Corps and British X Corps to land at Salerno on the west coast of Italy, link up with the Eighth Army coming up from the south, and advance toward Naples.

The media played a role in the campaign from the start. Fred Walker, commanding the Thirty-Sixth Division, wondered about the "stupidity of some of the higher staff officers" who insisted combat vehicles be unloaded "to make room aboard ship for cameramen and newspapermen with their vehicles." The media played another unfortunate role in the landings when the news of the surrender was broadcast as Allied troops were about to land at Salerno, yielding to the inevitable false hopes of an easy victory. Less encouraging news also came over the radio, saying that the Germans expected a landing around Naples and Salerno.[71] Certainly, German defenders opposed the landing with ferocity. Clark, in fact, contemplated withdrawing Allied troops. This was prevented by reinforcements rushed to the beachhead and by close naval gun support, as well as by lack of German reinforcements.[72]

Like many American commanders, Clark had developed an acute Anglophobia from his experiences in the North African campaign. It was an unfortunate attitude for an Allied commander in a theater that included not only Americans and Brits, but also Algerians, Australians, Brazilians, Canadians, French, Indians, Italians, Moroccans, Nepalese, Poles, and South Africans. Clark had listened in anger as the BBC, first in Africa and then Sicily, had largely ignored American contributions to the victory in favor of highlighting British exploits.[73] This impression had been reinforced when, during the planning for the Italian campaign, the British protested that Clark's plan had the Americans closer to Naples than the British. As Montgomery's Eighth Army fought slowly toward Salerno, Clark was further annoyed by the BBC "suggestion" that Montgomery was dashing to his rescue. "This," Clark wrote after the war, "eventually proved pretty irritating at times."[74]

Clark was further annoyed when the British entered Naples ahead of the Americans, even though, as historian Martin Blumenson notes, it was part of the original plan.[75] Nor were British press and censorship regulations to his liking. As the Germans withdrew from Naples, the first censorship instructions came down from Alexander's headquarters. Clark's communiqués had to conform to political considerations of the many nationalities making up the Fifteenth Army Group. One guideline stated, "First, play up the Eighth Army progress henceforth. Second, the Fifth Army is pushing the enemy back on his right flank. Americans may be mentioned."[76] These media slights combined with his Anglophobia would shape Clark's actions in Italy. He surrounded himself with newsmen to promote himself, his soldiers, and his Fifth Army. In the strategic realm, the greatest prize of all was Rome, and Clark decided it would be his objective. As Blumenson writes, the unfair treatment by the British press made Clark determined that his "crowning achievement and one that he desired ever more ardently to give his army— and incidentally himself—was the glory of liberating Rome."[77]

Anzio

Despite the Allies' determination to capture Rome, the Italian campaign quickly slowed to a crawl. Rugged mountains favored the defenders, while a front confined by the eighty miles' width of southern Italy made maneuver difficult.[78] *Life* magazine photographer Robert Capa captured the mood at the front in words as well as pictures. "The rains started," he wrote years later. "The mud got deeper and deeper. Our shoes, designed for walking in garrison towns, thirstily drank in the water, and we slid two steps backward for each step forward. Our light shorts and trousers gave us no protection against the wind and rain. . . . With every costly five-hundred-yard advance, Rome seemed farther and farther away."[79] By December, Eisenhower's headquarters was reporting to Washington that when it came to propaganda they were emphasizing "conservative frontline reporting."[80] Despite the hardships, the Allies continued to inch forward.

By early January, the Allies had broken through the German Winter Line only to discover that the much more formable Gustav Line lay behind it. Stretching across southern Italy and centered on towering mountains looking down at the Rapido River, the Gustav Line brought the Allied advance to a halt. By order of Hitler, Monte Cassino was the linchpin of the Gustav Line, and from its peak more than four hundred pieces of artillery looked down to the valley below. Nevertheless, the most direct road to Rome was Route 6, which snaked through the town of Cassino and across the Gustav Line near Monte Cassino. The combination ensured one bloody battle after another that brought Rome no closer.[81]

As the stalemate deepened, the Allies began looking for a way to outflank the Gustav Line by sea and capture Rome. Churchill pushed for the plan, which called for the Fifth and Eighth armies to strike the Gustav Line across the Garigliano and Rapido Rivers and draw in German reserves. Once the line had been penetrated, the Allies would drive up the Liri Valley. As the Germans were busy defending the Gustav Line, the Allies would land part of the Fifth Army behind German lines at the towns of Anzio and Nettuno, just south of Rome. The landings were codenamed Operation Shingle. It would, the planners hoped, force the Germans to withdraw, leaving the advance clear to take Rome.[82] It was not only the stalemate at the Gustav Line that spurred on Shingle but also the desire to hasten the fall of Rome. Clark wrote that "it was essential for various reasons—mostly political and psychological—that the Fifth Army capture Rome prior to the invasion of France. From where I stood, it was apparent that this was a large order for the Fifth, and I was busy trying to work out methods for speeding up our advance."[83] "There was nothing wrong with the basic conception of Shingle," concludes historian Carlo D'Este. "In fact, if the operation had been carried out with a sufficiently large force, Kesselring might well have been forced to abandon the Cassino front in favor of a stand along the Gothic Line [well north of Rome]."[84]

The offensive quickly ran into trouble. At the Gustav Line, the Allies launched a bloody attack that failed to cross the Rapido River. In fact, if the German commander is to be believed, the enemy was unaware that the Americans had even made a major attack until a postwar congressional inquiry belatedly brought it to their attention.[85] The battle, as Martin Blumenson describes it, was "one of the most shocking defeats of World War II."[86] It was also one of the most controversial. Clark would later defend the attack—and himself—by noting that "we were under strong political pressure to capture Rome. The Germans, at the same time, were under pressure just as great. We later found an order to the German troops that said, 'The Fuehrer demands from each and every man to hold the Gustav Line to the very last. A complete success may have political repercussions.'"[87] The Gustav Line held.

Meanwhile, the Allies had landed at Anzio on January 22, 1944. Operation Shingle initially appeared to be proceeding as planned. As Butcher ruefully observed, the British press was doing some "sly crowing" about the ingenuity of Alexander's generalship. But as Anzio quickly turned into a bloody stalemate and the Germans contained the Allies in the beachhead far short of Rome, the media coverage also changed. Watching from England, where he was planning the invasion of France, Eisenhower became so worried about the negative press that he privately told reporters of his confidence in Alexander and Clark. Butcher heard reports that Alexander's staff believed he had been slighted by not being theater commander and that they had concocted a scheme "by which all news of fighting in Italy had to be written in Italy and sent from headquarters of 15th Army Group." Clark had become aware of this when "the Associated Press and the United Press said the success of the end run was due to the brilliant strategy of General Alexander." The correspondents were also growing suspicious.[88] "One was accustomed to being told what one could not write," remembered Eric Sevareid. "It was a surprise to go with the other reporters to Field Marshal Alexander's headquarters at Caserta and to be told by his staff officers what one *ought* to write."[89] Almost a month after the landing, Alexander visited Anzio and talked to the press. "This morning's papers carried stories of Alexander's press conference . . . in which he upbraided the correspondents for irresponsible reporting," Butcher recorded. "He said he had received a cable from 'home' indicating the press had reported over-optimistically at the outset and over-pessimistically more recently. . . . The stories also carried news that radio transmission of stories from Anzio had been stopped and that in addition to censorship for military security, that for policy had been added." The London papers printed the story of Alexander's press conference along with editorials denouncing his censorship policy. As Butcher concluded, "Alexander's honeymoon is over."[90]

Axis propaganda quickly took advantage of the Anzio stalemate. German radio broadcasts were often recalled by veterans of the beachhead. For a long while, it was the only thing to listen to, which caused Clark and General Lucian Truscott—who would soon take over the command of Anzio—to fret. When much of the Fourth Ranger Battalion advanced too far, was cut off, and captured, the Germans paraded the POWs through Rome and in front of the movie cameras, while Clark, fearful of publicity according to Truscott, opened an investigation.[91]

As the landing at Anzio stalled, the Allies continued to press against the Gustav Line with little success. Towering over the battlefield was the massive Benedictine abbey atop Monte Cassino. In ancient times, the Romans had recognized the area's strategic importance and put up a fort and a temple to Apollo. The wild area was still pagan when in AD 529 Saint Benedict established a monastery. From there, he had changed history by establishing the Rules of Saint Benedict for monastic life that spread across Europe. Later, a five-year-old Thomas Aquinas began his cloistered life at the abbey, and eventually his wealthy mother successfully lobbied the pope for him to be made abbot. Aquinas turned down the offer. Nevertheless, the abbey had produced popes and saints, and as its power grew, art, wealth, and power flowed into it. There was no better example of what Kesselring meant when he referred to the Italian campaign as a "war in a museum."[92]

The abbey also had seen plenty of violence. It had been destroyed by Lombards in the sixth century, Saracens in the ninth century, an earthquake in the fourteenth century, and the French in the final year of the eighteenth century. After the last sacking, the monastery had been rebuilt as a fortress, with high walls ten feet thick, loopholes, and the endorsement of the modern Italian Army, who believed the abbey was invincible.[93] The Germans were not so sure. A few months before the Allies arrived in the valley below, the Hermann Göring Division appeared and with the blessing of Abbot Dom Gregorio Diamare began removing the abbey's treasures. Given the looting hobby of the division's patron, it is unsurprising that fifteen crates of art treasures found their way to Germany. As one of the Hermann Göring Division officers joked, "If we're supposed to do all that, there'll have to be something in it for us too. Just a couple of paintings." In the long run, the division also expected credit for saving the abbey's art treasures.[94]

As the battle to break the Gustav Line raged around it, the abbey's neutrality had been strictly observed. After removing the art, the Germans had stayed clear of the abbey. General Fridolin von Senger und Etterlin, commanding the XIV Panzer Corps at Cassino, was the only German soldier to enter the abbey, and then only for Christmas Mass, where he carefully avoided looking out of the window.[95] But as the stalemate progressed, the abbey's presence increasingly began to vex those who fought in its shadow. Lynn Heinzerling wrote in the *Daily Boston Globe* that Allied soldiers at Cassino "have complained for weeks about the immunity enjoyed by the monastery. Its use by the Germans undoubtedly has resulted in Allied deaths."[96] "I hate to se [*sic*] an old relic like that knocked down;" a soldier told reporter George Tucker, "but it sure looks domn god [*sic*] to me."[97] Allied soldiers, officers, and even generals began seeing Germans in or around the monastery. One intelligence summary claimed that the abbey had cost two thousand Allied lives.[98] There was little evidence for any of this, but an idea was growing that something had to be done about the monastery.

To the soldiers' mumbling was added newspaper grumbling. As historians David Hapgood and David Richardson write, "Correspondents covering the Cassino front were reporting the opinions of the soldiers. . . . concerning the immunity of the abbey. The generals were extremely sensitive to this reporting: it was on the basis of these news stories that they were being judged."[99] There were plenty of examples. "Sooner or later," said *Collier's* correspondent Frank Gervasi as he looked up at the abbey, "somebody's going to have to blow that place all to hell."[100] The *Times* reported that though the Allies would not shell the abbey, the "Germans trade on this discrimination and our men can see wireless aerials established on the roofs and telescopes at the windows." Meanwhile, Lynn Heinzerling complained that Allied artillery still avoided the abbey, to the anger of the soldiers.[101] Under the headline "Clark Order Prohibits 5th Army from Attacking Church Property: Courtesy to Vatican Handicaps Advance as Enemy Is Said To Use Religious Sites for Artillery Observation," C. L. Sulzberger wrote in the *New York Times* that Clark would not allow religious sites to be attacked even though the Nazis were using them. Sulzberger said there were three examples of this fact, with the Monte Cassino Abbey being the first. The monastery was a "definite handicap in our progress over exceedingly difficult territory, especially since the Germans are believed to be utilizing some clerical possessions for military purposes." He ended by reminding his readers that "many lives may be lost by the caution necessarily involved affecting the tactics of certain operations."[102] Sulzberger wrote again a few days later, noting that German artillery at Cassino seemed more accurate than before and repeated that the Germans were using the abbey for observation.[103] Anne O'Hare McCormick, after reciting the monastery's contribution to civilization, added, "The Americans have strict orders not to shell the monastery, which is Vatican territory, but the Germans are established on the hill and apparently they pay no more attention to the signs warning that it is neutral ground than to the Red Cross signs marking the hospital tents they bombed yesterday at Anzio." She added, "This is the kind of war it is. What the Dark Ages saved, this fire consumes and there can be no sanctuary, no island of peace or safety for anyone until it is put out."[104] Such stories brought angry letters to the War Department claiming American lives were being traded for old stones. As Hapgood and Richardson conclude, it was against this background of press stories that the decision to destroy the abbey was made.[105]

In early February, the provisional New Zealand Corps commanded by General Bernard C. Freyberg moved into position. Contemporaries came to widely different assessments of the New Zealand general. Churchill called him "the salamander of the British empire," apparently a reference to Freyberg's ability to pass through danger unharmed. Montgomery, on the other hand, saw him as "a nice old boy, but a bit stupid." Clark believed he was simply "a bull in a china closet." Whatever the case, Freyberg held power far beyond his rank. First, he was a friend of Churchill. More importantly, he had the political backing of one of the dominions of the British Empire, whose people were far from uncritical of how the metropole was employing their soldiers.[106] The Americans understood this. In December, a report from Algiers explained that the press section was emphasizing news of Allied soldiers—other than the British or Americans—fighting in Italy for their respective countries.[107] This delicate political situation caused Freyberg's superiors to tread carefully in their dealings with him.

As he prepared for the assault on Monte Cassino, Freyberg telephoned

Alfred Gruenther, Clark's chief of staff, and requested air support. Gruenther asked what targets he had in mind. "I want the Convent attacked," Freyberg responded. Gruenther clarified that Freyberg had meant the monastery and explained that it was not on Clark's target list. "I am quite sure it was on my list of targets," Freyberg replied, "but in any case I want it bombed." In fact, Clark had already said no twice to the attack. Gruenther spoke to Clark and Keyes, whose II Corps had just been relieved by Freyberg's troops. Both opposed the request. But Alexander backed Freyberg. Clark replied that if Freyberg was certain the bombing was necessary he would authorize it. Freyberg was certain. He said the Fourth Indian Division commander had requested the raid. If they failed to receive support, Freyberg added, higher command would be responsible if the attack failed. The next morning Alexander phoned Clark and repeated that he supported Freyberg's request. Clark replied that they did not need "to destroy one of the art treasures of the world. Besides, we have indications that many civilian women and children are taking shelter therein. The extent of our air effort which we can put on it will not destroy the building but will merely give the Germans an excuse to use it." Keyes's intelligence officer had reported that the abbey housed two thousand civilians and that there were no reports of fire coming from the building. Nevertheless, Alexander insisted on backing Freyberg. "Remember, Wayne, he is a very important cog in the Commonwealth effort. I would be most reluctant to take responsibility for his failing and for his telling his people 'I lost 5,000 New Zealanders because they wouldn't let me use air as I wanted.'" Clark said that if an American had brought the request, it would be denied. But, understanding Freyberg's "position in the British Empire" and that the "situation was a delicate one," he finally consented.[108]

Alexander would later defend the destruction of the abbey as a necessary morale booster. He claimed that he had no idea whether the Germans had been in the abbey, that its destruction likely did not hurt German morale, and that the bombing made the structure easier to defend. But the abbey's annihilation was "necessary more for the effect it would have on the morale of the attackers than for purely material reasons." He added, "Every good commander must consider the morale and feelings of his fighting men. . . . Thus the commanding general must make it absolutely clear to his troops that they go into action under the most favourable conditions he has the power to order."[109] Alexander was famous for being walked over by his subordinate commanders. It had happened in Sicily with Montgomery, who later suggested it to an attentive Clark. The above passage suggests Alexander would also easily yield to the opinions of his ordinary soldiers.

As movie cameras rolled and soldiers and war correspondents cheered ecstatically, 250 heavy bombers blasted the ancient monastery with almost six hundred tons of bombs. Hundreds of refugees—the numbers are uncertain—died in the attack.[110] One of the great monuments of Christendom—what historian Robert M. Edsel calls "a fortress of art"—disappeared in a pillar of dark smoke as if a volcano had erupted under it.[111] The Germans immediately occupied and fortified the ruined abbey. Freyberg proved incapable of taking advantage of the destruction he had campaigned for so hard. The Fourth Indian Division, which was to spearhead the attack, was not told that the plan had been moved up until fifteen minutes before the bombing began. The attack was repulsed with the Indians and New Zealanders taking around eight hundred casualties. It would not be until May 18, 1944, after long and bloody assaults, that what was left of the abbey was captured by the Poles.[112]

The destruction of the abbey was likewise ill-advised from the angle of the media war. Oddly enough, though worries about German propaganda were in Clark's and Keyes's minds, they do not seem to have entered the debate with Freyberg and Alexander except for vague comments of dominion troops' special "position" in the Allied forces and concern over future New Zealand public opinion.[113] Yet as Clark wrote after the war, the destruction of the abbey was "an unnecessary psychological mistake in the propaganda field."[114]

Unlike the Allies, the Germans had missed the chance to film the destruction of the abbey, but they improvised brilliantly. As the dust cleared over the wreckage, a pitiful band of monks emerged, and, in a procession led by Abbot Diamare and a large wooden crucifix, made their way out of their ruined home. Reciting the rosary and carrying wounded civilians from the abbey, the wretched party worked its way down the steep mountain paths. Suddenly a German staff car appeared and whisked Diamare to the headquarters of the XIV Panzer Corps.[115] General von Senger was waiting with the cameras, and Diamare consented to sit for an interview. "Everything was done on the part of the German Armed Forces . . . in order to give the opponent no military ground for attacking the monastery," Senger explained. "General," the Abbot answered, "I . . . can only confirm this." Senger explained he heard too late that the Allies had dropped leaflets warning of their intentions. "I have the feeling that the leaflets were intentionally dropped so late in order to give us no possibility to notify the German commanders, or, on the other hand to bring the some 800 guests of the monastery out of the danger zone," Diamare replied. He added, "We simply did not believe that the English and Americans would attack the abbey. . . . They have destroyed the monastery and killed hundreds of innocent people." "Can I do anything more?" Senger inquired sympathetically. "No, General, you have done everything—even today the German Armed Forces provided for us and for the refugees in model fashion."[116] The news cameras captured Senger carefully helping the seventy-eight-year-old abbot into a staff car to be driven to Rome.

Meanwhile, on orders from Berlin, German news crews were photographing the destroyed abbey.[117] As they had hoped, the Hermann Göring Division's project of removing the abbey's treasures was prominently featured in German newsreels.[118] A German radio broadcast carried a statement from the pope that if the Allies "had wanted, Monte Cassino could have been saved. It would have needed good-will only and consideration not of my person but of the Catholic world."[119] The newsreels and radio did not, of course, tell that after he had left Senger, the SS had kidnaped Diamare on his way to Rome and forced him to sign a statement of events in much harsher language than he wished. Once Diamare was in Rome, Goebbels's office also badgered the abbot for an even stronger statement. Diamare angrily refused.[120] Nevertheless, the Germans had again fended off the Allied attack and had a propaganda bonanza to boost.

Allied propaganda tried to defend the bombing. A British newsreel crew interviewed the abbot of a group of Anglican Benedictine monks in Kent, England, who defended the destruction of the abbey at Monte Cassino. Alexander's headquarters and British newsreels asserted Germans were seen fleeing the monastery, a claim historian Rick Atkinson rightly dismisses as "ludicrous."[121] Roosevelt made a statement that he regretted the necessary destruction of the abbey and suggested the Germans be made to rebuild it.[122]

As they had done before the attack, the Allied media largely supported the bombing of the abbey. When Gervasi returned to the United States, he told the *New York Times* that sparing the abbey had cost the Americans 776 lives. "Because of politics and the Vatican's request to respect Vatican property, we did not move until the Huns had had time to completely fortify it," he added.[123] The *Los Angeles Times* reported that the bombing ended "German immunity behind holy walls at a cost of Allied lives." The article added, without explanation, that the attack "was a decisive step to save American lives taken only after every effort had been made to force the Germans to respect the religious neutrality of the monastery."[124] In an editorial titled "Bombing of Monte Cassio Unfortunate Necessity" the paper added, "Many lives of Allied soldiers were sacrificed to keep the monastery intact. No one could reasonably expect that such sacrifice could be continued indefinitely."[125] George Tucker of the *Washington Post* wrote that the destruction of the abbey sent "gray-uniformed German soldiers racing like rats from the lofty stronghold they had employed to obstruct an Allied drive to the relief of the Anzio beachhead."[126] Drew Middleton did reflect on the propaganda aspect of the bombing, but concluded that the "destruction of a priceless painting here or a venerable building there in the march up Italy will fail to stir Britons to any great degree."[127] Nor did it, apparently, stir many Americans. A Gallup poll found that 74 percent of Americans approved of the destruction of historic or religious sites if military commanders believed it was necessary.[128]

The Glory of Rome

The stalemate at Cassino and Anzio dragged on for the rest of the winter and became increasingly embarrassing for the Allies. Clark remembered that by March the "continued delay in our offensive operations to link the Fifth Army on the Cassino front with the Anzio bridgehead was confusing to the public and resulted in criticism of our beachhead forces for failure to push further inland toward Rome."[129] But as the Italian spring neared, so did the end of the stalemate.

On May 11, the Allies opened a new offensive toward Rome. For Alexander, the main objective was not to liberate Rome itself but to create a trap for the German armies. The British Eighth Army was to advance from the Liri Valley toward Valmontone. There it would meet Truscott's VI Corps that was to move up from Anzio through the Valmontone Gap. This would cut Highways 6 and 7 and encircle the German Tenth Army. The road to Rome would thus be open.[130] Alexander titled the attack Operation Buffalo.

That at least was Alexander's plan, but Clark had his own. On May 6, before Buffalo began, Clark visited Truscott to complain about Alexander and the British and stated that capturing "Rome is the only important objective." He feared that the British intended to get there first. He told Truscott to prepare for Buffalo but also to have other plans ready if the situation changed. As Truscott's VI Corps fought its way toward the Valmontone Gap, he received another visit from Clark. "He wanted to know whether or not I had considered changing the direction of the attack to the northwest, toward Rome," Truscott remembered. He had. Truscott explained that such a move might alert the Germans to the danger on their flanks and make them more determined to resist long enough for all their forces to withdraw from a potential trap. At that point Clark still agreed. Nevertheless, on May 25, he ordered the VI Corps to change the direction of the attack to the northwest and open Highway 7 toward Rome. Truscott protested that this would mean he would be attacking enemy strongpoints instead of the weak forces in the Valmontone Gap. "Considering the congested area and restricted road net available for these preparations," Truscott reflected, "a more complicated plan would be difficult to conceive." Clark was out of phone contact, preventing any debate. "Such was the order," Truscott summarized after the war, "that turned the main effort of the beachhead forces from the Valmontone Gap and prevented the destruction of the German X Army."[131] The plan was appropriately titled Operation Turtle.

The move was disastrous. VI Corps failed repeatedly to open Highway 7 for the Allies or close Highway 6 to German forces in the Valmontone Gap. The German Tenth Army slowly retreated through Valmontone for more than a week.[132] "If ever there was vindication for having continued Operation Buffalo on May 26," concludes historian Carlo D'Este, "it was Clark's tardy decision that the way to Rome indeed led through Valmontone."[133] "Ironically," Martin Blumenson observes, "had the VI Corps made its main effort toward Valmontone, Clark would have undoubtedly reached Rome more quickly."[134] Thus, Clark allowed the Tenth Army to escape in good order to fight north of Rome.

Clark's decision has been roundly condemned by historians. "Mark Clark would spend the rest of his long life defending an indefensible impertinence that for more than sixty years has remained among the most controversial episodes in World War II," writes Rick Atkinson.[135] Jon B. Mikolashek, Clark's biographer, concludes that "Clark's decision was a grave mistake and the worst decision of his career."[136] Carlo D'Este notes that "there is every reason to believe that Truscott's Buffalo force would at least have taken a heavier toll on the retreating German army than it did. Nor could the Germans have prevented VI Corps from seizing the Valmontone Gap."[137]

Surprisingly, there is little debate about Clark's motives. He wanted Rome and he wanted it for publicity reasons. As early as February he knew the invasion of France was imminent and began to worry that the "capture of Rome prior to that invasion would be of tremendous psychological importance to the Allied cause."[138] Indeed, Churchill and Marshall had both pressed Clark to capture Rome before the Allies invaded France.[139] What was more, Operation Anvil was scheduled to take troops away from Italy for the invasion of southern France.[140] Unlike Alexander, Clark believed that the Germans were "too smart" to allow themselves to be trapped. He also believed that the lack of roads around Valmontone would slow his advance.[141]

Most importantly, Clark was openly pining for press glory for himself and his army. In his postwar memoirs, he wrote:

> We not only wanted the honor of capturing Rome, but we felt that we more than deserved it; that it would to a certain extend [*sic*] make up for the buffeting and the frustration we had undergone in keeping up the winter pressure against the Germans. My own feeling was that nothing was going to stop us on our push toward the Italian capital. Not only did we intend to become the first army in fifteen centuries to seize Rome from the south, but we intended to see that the people back home knew that it was the Fifth Army that did the job and knew the price that had been paid for it. I think that these considerations are important to an understanding of the behind-scenes differences of opinion that occurred in this period.[142]

This statement—so honest in its hunger for glory and oblivious that other Allied armies had also suffered in the Italian winter—is likely the most unvarnished public statement by an American general on how media and public opinion shaped his military action on the battlefield.

Clark's Anglophobia had grown over the course of the Italian campaign to the point where he now believed the British planned to steal the glory of Rome. Referring to the above quote, Clark's biographer observes that the "trouble with this statement is that it is not true" since Clark knew Alexander did not intend the attack to take Rome.[143] Nevertheless, he doubtless believed it. During the battle for Anzio, Clark had been irritated when Alexander's headquarters passed along a message from Churchill saying that the American and British troops in the beachhead should be called the "Allied Bridgehead Force" instead of the "Fifth Army" in news releases. "This didn't seem right to me," Clark wrote after the war, "since all the troops at Anzio were in the Fifth Army, so I sent a message to Alexander protesting that the change would not help the morale of either British or American troops at Anzio."[144] Though Alexander had assured Clark that the Fifth Army would take Rome, Clark was still suspicious.[145] He wrote in his diary that the "British have their eye on Rome, notwithstanding Alexander's constant assurance to me that Rome is in the sector of the Fifth Army."[146] After Churchill's renewed plea that both nations would share in the glory, Alexander proposed that the announcement of Rome's fall would read "Rome is now in Allied hands." Clark exploded that the British always "carefully avoid the use of 'Fifth Army'" and denied the request. He remembered later that "this was more important to the men of the Fifth Army—and to me—than it might seem." He also ignored Alexander's suggestion that a Polish unit be included as recognition for their heroism at Monte Cassino. When five Yugoslavian officers visited the Fifth Army, Clark snapped angrily, "The first thing you know the claim will be that the Yugoslavs were the first to enter Rome." And though Alexander later denied the story, Clark claimed the British general ordered that the Eighth Army be fired on if they approached the city. In his postwar memoirs, Clark admitted, "I was determined that the Fifth Army was going to capture Rome and I probably was overly sensitive to indications that practically everybody else was trying to get into the act."[147] Early in the campaign, Montgomery had warned Clark to disregard Alexander's orders when necessary. Clark now did exactly that at Valmontone. "But," as Williamson Murray and Allan R. Millett have written, "the difference was that Montgomery's disobedience reflected the field marshal's operational analysis of the situation, while Clark's disobedience reflected a vainglorious pursuit of publicity and prestige."[148]

Alexander was far from pleased with his orders being disobeyed. He later stated that Clark had lied to him by claiming the attack toward Valmontone had been halted by the Germans, forcing Clark to change directions.[149] "If he had succeeded in carrying out my plan the disaster to the enemy would have been much greater;" Alexander wrote after the war, "indeed, most of the German forces south of Rome would have been destroyed." He concluded,

"I can only assume that the immediate lure of Rome for its publicity value persuaded him to switch the direction of his advance."[150]

Clark carefully prepared for the media attention that would accompany the battle. He began by ordering that there would be no restriction on his location for the press so reporters could find him more easily. On May 22, he held a press conference at Anzio and explained the operation to the correspondents. Though he stated that Rome was not the operational objective, he quickly added that they would get it anyway in the process. Reporters were informed as they departed that Clark was "in personal command."[151] He requested that Alexander give him permission to issue a communiqué as soon as the Fifth Army's corps advancing from Cassino linked up with the forces in Anzio.[152] When the linkup did happen, Clark arrived with two dozen reporters and had the meeting reenacted for the cameras.[153] As Jon Mikolashek observes, "war correspondents and historians alike became disgusted with how Clark handled the situation." He added that even Clark was "mildly embarrassed by the way journalists and the public viewed the link-up" and wrote his wife, "It may have sounded dramatic in the papers the way I rushed to witness the joining of the two forces. . . . The way some of the correspondents expressed it may have sounded as though I was looking for publicity. Did you get that impression?"[154]

In Clark's defense, Mikolashek writes, the media attention he attracted "was not just for him, but for his soldiers. He wanted the parents and loved ones of his soldiers to know what they were doing."[155] Yet this did not extend to his field commanders. As with Douglas MacArthur, historians and journalists have noted that only Clark's name was mentioned in press communiqués of Fifth Army. Yet unlike the SWPA chief, Clark deliberately suppressed his subordinates' publicity on the road to Rome. When his chief of staff suggested that Truscott's role be publicized, Clark confided in his diary, "I do not feel that his exploits have been sufficiently outstanding yet."[156] As the Thirty-Sixth Division approached Rome, Clark told its commander, Fred L. Walker, "I am going to see to it that you and the 36th Division get credit for this in the newspapers back home." Walker, who believed he and his division had been systematically denied publicity by Clark, quickly got hold of a reporter, had him write a story, and put him on his plane to the main army headquarters so his article could be quickly censored. The reporter soon returned, and when Walker asked if the story was off, the reporter replied that "Clark had changed his mind, and my story did not get by the Army Censor."[157]

Despite Clark's blunder, the fate of Rome had been decided. For the Germans, holding Rome had much to do with denying the Allies a prestige objective. Yet the city had to be treated carefully. If destroyed, the Germans would receive a propaganda defeat. Hitler ordered Rome to be declared an open city.[158] As Carlo D'Este writes, even Hitler "recognized the extremely negative propaganda value that would ensue if Rome were destroyed."[159] Perhaps the führer even speculated that after the destruction of Monte Cassino he could pose as a protector of Western civilization against Allied barbarism. On June 4, Rome fell to American forces with very little destruction.

Conclusion

As in a Roman triumph of old, General Mark Clark entered the Eternal City on June 5, 1945, and headed for Capitoline Hill. But unlike the Roman heroes of yore, he got lost. Eventually, with the help of a priest and a boy on a bicycle who insisted on bellowing "Clark!," the Fifth Army commander reached his destination. Also, unlike previous conquerors, Clark's first inclination was to hold a press conference. At Capitoline Hill, he was soon joined by his generals and the ever-present reporters. "Well, gentlemen, I didn't really expect to have a press conference here—I just called a little meeting with my corps commanders to discuss the situation," Clark began disingenuously. "However, I'll be glad to answer your questions. This is a great day for the Fifth Army." Clark's generals blushed with embarrassment. "That was the immortal remark of Rome's modern-day conqueror," fumed Eric Sevareid. "It was not, apparently, a great day for the world, for the Allies, for all the suffering people who had desperately looked toward the time of peace. . . . (Men of the Eighth Army, whose sector did not happen to include Rome but without whose efforts this day could not have occurred, did not soon forget the remark.)"[160] It was in keeping with Clark's other actions in the campaign toward Rome.

Like in a Greek tragedy, Clark's lust for publicity had almost killed him on the very steps of Rome. The general had hoped to enter the city on June 4. As his small party, accompanied by the habitual group of correspondents, moved toward the eternal city, Clark spied a road sign saying "Roma." Someone suggested that it would be a great photograph for Clark and his generals to stand next to the sign. As they made their way up, a German sniper put a bullet through the sign, which persuaded the group of generals to remove themselves to a ditch. Clark decided his entrance would have to be postponed until the next day.[161]

From its inception, the Italian campaign had been influenced by public opinion and shaped by media considerations. Not only was Italy the first Axis partner to be defeated, but it was also the cultural center of Europe. These two facts along with continual pressure for a second front made Allied leaders realize that public opinion would not let them bypass Italy. Once Italy had been invaded, Rome became the natural symbol of victory. The city had little military value. But as a propaganda sign of Allied victory or German endurance, the city was priceless. The cultural significance of Rome and the rest of Italy also presented propaganda challenges. The Allies not only fretted about bombing Rome but also succumbed to bombing the abbey at Monte Cassino from pressure from reporters and commonwealth troops. However, the move was a propaganda disaster of which the Germans took full advantage. Nevertheless, Axis propaganda about the destroyed abbey hardly hurt the Allied cause at the time, though it did weigh on the verdict of history. Yet the symbolism of the ancient surroundings and the public attention they attracted explained why Kesselring would describe the fighting for Italy as a war in a museum.

The influence of propaganda and the media likely could not have been avoided, but the personalities involved accentuated the role of the press. At the beginning of the campaign, Eisenhower demonstrated in his negotiations with the Italian government how skillfully he had learned to use the media as a weapon. Later, Clark's obsession with press attention gave the media a role in making military decisions that would have otherwise been absent. This was tolerated by Alexander, who allowed himself to be pushed around by his subordinates. Clark's dash to Rome shows both points. The general claimed after the war that he saw the capture of both Rome and the German army of "equal importance."[162] His actions showed that this was not the case.

The briefness of Clark's triumph was another irony the ancients would have appreciated. The next morning, June 6, 1944, Clark was awakened to the news of the Allied landings in France. "They didn't even let us have the newspaper headlines for the fall of Rome for one day," the general lamented.[163] As Eric Sevareid watched his fellow correspondents discard their stories about Rome's capture, he realized, "The 'play' had suddenly been taken away from the Italian campaign, and after weeks of worldwide attention we had in a trice become performers without an audience."[164] But, as historian Thomas R. Brooks writes, though "correspondents would soon pack up and leave for more newsworthy fronts, the soldiers would remain to fight on for another eleven months."[165] These soldiers as well as their commander would from then on comprise a forgotten front of World War II.

Chapter Five

The Liberation of France

Henry Stimson spent the evening of June 5, 1944, contemplating the thousands of Allied soldiers preparing to land in Normandy. The war was "one of the great crises of the world," he reflected in his diary that night, "perhaps the greatest and sharpest crisis that the world has ever had, and it all has focused together on tonight." Before retiring, Stimson placed a small portable radio by his bed. The Stimsons awoke to hear the first reports from correspondents who had flown with the paratroopers over France. Throughout that day, as Stimson recorded, the nation was "swamped with the greatest volume of reporters' reports and commentators' reports on the radio that we have ever had. Never has any great operation been reported in the detailed way from people right on the ground . . . as this one. Never has the radio shown up so fully as it has this time."[1]

Others were less impressed. A *New Yorker* columnist complained that the "idiot babble of the radio followed us wherever we went," while historian Stephen Ambrose observes some commentators' "military analysis ranged from misleading to silly." Nevertheless, the news deeply connected the American people to events thousands of miles away. The president of Lord & Taylor ordered his three thousand employees to stay home to pray. In New York City, Macy's closed as well but used a speaker to broadcast news updates to people walking outside. Led by President Roosevelt over the radio, most of America appeared to be praying.[2] Never before had the news so connected the American people to such a distant battle.

The use of the press for Operation Overlord was the culmination of the Allies' mobilization of the media for war. Indeed, the transformation of the press from hostile outsiders—as the British often viewed them—to members of the military team—as Eisenhower saw them—was completed in the battle for Normandy. "When I first met Generals Alexander and Montgomery in Africa," Eisenhower wrote after the war, "they favored the imposition upon press representatives of strict rules and regulations, and their list of censorable items was long." But such an attitude treated "the press as a necessary evil rather than as a valuable link with the homeland and as an agency that could be of great assistance in the waging of a campaign."[3] With that in mind, press problems were carefully studied by the Public Relations Division (PRD) of the Supreme Headquarters Allied Expeditionary Force (SHAEF). Though historians of the Normandy battle have largely neglected the role of the media, by the liberation of Paris the press had influenced the campaign in three overarching ways.[4]

First, the press was still an important factor in maintaining the Anglo-American alliance. As in the Mediterranean, Eisenhower worked to ensure harmony between the Americans and the British in the media. Even Telek, Eisenhower's Scottish terrier, got involved in the public relations campaign. After learning that it would be frowned upon by the British press if the mandatory dog quarantine laws were waived, Eisenhower allowed Telek to be confined. The need for positive publicity, however, did not extend to Eisenhower agreeing to be photographed with Telek, forcing photographers to engineer a crude form of photoshop to get pictures of the general visiting his dog.[5] For his part, Montgomery used the BBC to broadcast that he was also looking for canine companionship.[6] "If *Dog News* didn't get a man over pretty quickly to cover the dog angle of the invasion," joked Ernie Pyle about the large variety of news outlets covering D-Day, "I personally would never buy another copy."[7] Despite the mutual affinity for pets, building Allied harmony in the media was made more difficult since much of the British military leadership was more suspicious of the press than the Americans were. The Normandy campaign would painfully demonstrate to the British just how influential the media was in total war and again test the foundations of the Grand Alliance.

This was the result of the press being an important weapon for total war. In a fiery speech in February 1943, Reich propaganda minister Joseph Goebbels had rhetorically demanded whether the German people wanted total war and was met by thunderous "Ja!"[8] Soon after D-Day, Goebbels would be made "Reichs Plenipotentiary for Total War."[9] It is telling that the man who controlled the media in the Nazi empire was also the one to proclaim World War II a total war. Nor was the war's nature lost on those planning the Overlord landings. After observing that war correspondents would encounter "limitless political problems inter-meshed inseparably with the military problems" after the invasion, a report from the SHAEF PRD added:

> It is perhaps pertinent, in this war, to judge the above in terms of the statement by Von Clausewitz when he says: "The war of a community—of whole nations, and particularly of civilized nations—always starts from a political condition, and is called forth by a political motive. It is, therefore, a political act. . . . Now, if we reflect that war has its root in a political objective, then naturally this original motive which called it into existence should also continue the first and highest consideration in its conduct.[10]

The media knew it, too. As Robert Bunnelle, the London bureau chief of the AP, reminded the PRD in the final stage of the Normandy campaign, the US

Army was "the people's army" fighting "the people's war."[11] The reaction of the American people to the news of D-Day underscored this connection. Finally, in the Normandy campaign and beyond, the press continued to influence the battlefield decisions of Allied commanders. His earlier media scandals caused General Patton to be overly cautious in challenging his superiors, and postinvasion comments by Montgomery created a firestorm of controversy. The fear of popular discontent caused by Hitler's "vengeance weapons" even forced the air forces to shift from focusing on industrial targets to attempting to destroy V-1 launch sites instead. Eisenhower would likewise use discontent in the press to motivate Montgomery to greater efforts. The press was a weapon of war, but dangerous even to those who wielded it.

Preparing the Press for D-Day

The extensive media preparations for Overlord were based on experience from the Mediterranean. "Public Relations has become a highly important factor in the waging of the present war," stated a report by the Information and Censorship Office. But the report also noted that lack of communication facilities and issues with censorship in North Africa had caused major problems.[12] A few months later, Thor Smith, chief of the US Press Policy Section of the SHAEF PRD, observed that British reporters had consistently gotten their stories out of the Mediterranean much more quickly than American correspondents. "Every effort should be made to have available every possible type of facility so that the transmission of news can be expedited," Smith concluded. He suggested teletype and said that a "combination of motorcycles, car, and airplane should always be available to get the copy back to a transmission point."[13] Although beachhead broadcasting was forbidden for security reasons, three large radios for transmitting messages were included in the landings on the beaches on D-Day.[14] To the annoyance of military intelligence, carrier pigeons were also procured. New innovations were adopted. The PRD attached movie cameras to tanks to capture the first moments of the landings.[15] An Invasion Reference Library was created to fill any gaps in the news during D-Day.[16] Correspondents were part of the planning as well. Working as a liaison between the military and media, CBS's Edward R. Murrow, historian Lynne Olson observes, "was deeply involved in virtually every aspect of the D-Day preparations."[17] Yet how the media would influence military decisions could not be planned, and before the first Allied soldier set foot on Normandy's soil, the press and concern for public opinion were already shaping decisions for the coming campaign.

Public opinion influenced the selection of Overlord's leaders. President Roosevelt selected Eisenhower in late 1943 to serve as supreme commander.

Churchill had originally wanted Alan Brooke for the job, but Roosevelt successfully lobbied that American public opinion demanded an American supreme commander. Marshall, who was the natural second choice after Brooke, later marveled how Churchill had braved British public opinion to agree to an American commander.[18] When Roosevelt decided he could not spare Marshall in Washington, Eisenhower was selected. Though there is no evidence that the general's fame influenced Roosevelt's choice, Eisenhower's Mediterranean victories and adroit handling of the press had made him a media sensation. By the end of the Normandy campaign, editors were telling their correspondents to cover Eisenhower as if he was an American president.[19] Montgomery was selected as ground force commander since, as Churchill explained to Roosevelt "the War Cabinet desires that Montgomery should command the first expeditionary Group of Armies. Eisenhower would have chosen Alexander, but I feel the Cabinet are right, as Montgomery is a public hero and will give confidence among our people."[20] Bradley was to command the First Army and, after more armies were brought to the continent, Twelfth Army Group. Courtney Hodges would succeed Bradley at the First Army, while Patton would command the Third Army.

Even before Allied commanders arrived in Britain, the press was being used as a weapon of deception. Eisenhower's brief visit home was kept secret since German propaganda was predicting a cross-channel winter invasion and Marshall hoped to keep the Germans on edge. When Eisenhower arrived in London, this deception operation was continued in a carefully worded press statement that implied Eisenhower had been in England for several days.[21] Montgomery's arrival from the Mediterranean had been delayed since—according to Francis de Guingand, his chief of staff—"Churchill's intense desire to capture Rome before the changes occurred, and also it was thought that the Russians might think we intended to 'pipe down' in Italy if Montgomery and others left the theater too early."[22] Arriving before Eisenhower on January 2, 1944, the British general took up his new command with a great deal of press attention.[23] Despite this, British intelligence decided to attempt to keep the Germans confused as to his whereabouts. Though his headquarters was located at Portsmouth, German intelligence was successfully convinced it was just south of London and nearer to the Pas-de-Calais.[24]

This was all part of a larger operation code-named Fortitude. Although Fortitude mobilized many resources—including double agents, phony equipment, fictitious units, and artificial radio traffic—the role of the press was important. In a memorandum to his commanders, Eisenhower wrote that the press could assist the invasion by keeping "the enemy in a state of nervous tension as to whether or not the landings . . . are but a foretaste of something which may be repeated anywhere anytime will be of the greatest possible help. A high state of nervousness and tension may be expected among the inactive flanking troops who at the beginning will be awaiting attack on themselves."[25] In April, the Allies released the names of major units in Britain to the press, but not before first giving them to German double agents so as to strengthen their credibility with enemy intelligence.[26] Press assistance with Fortitude North, the plan to make it appear that the invasion was coming in Scandinavia, was another example. Fake news stories along with Royal Navy attacks on Narvik, Norway, and Royal Air Force (RAF) violations of Sweden's air space were used to create headlines and convince the Germans that media hype about the cross-channel invasion was a diversion.[27] Correspondent Don Whitehead heard first about Norway and then the Pas-de-Calais as the invasion's location.[28] Though the Germans were not fooled, thirty-six years after D-Day, US officers who were stationed in Ireland at the time still believed that their original destination had been Norway.[29]

Despite bitter experience with the press in the Mediterranean, Eisenhower was more determined than ever to have a relationship with the media that maximized both press freedom and its usefulness to the war. At a meeting at Norfolk House near the end of January 1944, Eisenhower took umbrage when some of his officers suggested denying accreditation and any secret information to reporters. Instead, he wished to "play ball" with the media so they would not attempt to ferret out secret information.[30] When a few days later Churchill suggested a very strict policy of keeping information from the press, Eisenhower responded that his headquarters was working with the British to ensure "the best means of keeping the Press securely in the dark, while at the same time not appearing to treat them as complete outsiders." But, he added, "I should feel disturbed if I thought that I or my Public Relations Staff were held as anything but the friends of the Press."[31]

There was, of course, censorship to maintain secrecy, and naturally reporters resented it. "At times we felt that the censorship was not related to security," recalled correspondent Don Whitehead after the war, "but on the whole the censors were liberal in their handling of our stories."[32] In a letter to his commanders, Eisenhower reiterated that he considered accredited war correspondents as "quasi-staff officers" and that commanders should give them "the greatest possible latitude in the gathering of legitimate news" and should provide reporters "all reasonable assistance" in performing their job.[33] This was stated even more explicitly in a pamphlet prepared by the SHAEF PRD for Allied generals, entitled *Know Your War Correspondent*. "It is possible to prevent misunderstandings," the pamphlet's authors counseled, "if we in the Army understand the war correspondent and his purposes better and try to make him a 'part of the team' by going half-way to meet him." After a few pages on the importance of the First Amendment and the free press, the pamphlet continued that commanders should also do "everything possible . . . to help the war correspondent get his news out."[34] As Whitehead recalled, Eisenhower's "attitude became the attitude of his subordinates, and it filtered through the command."[35] "Journalists were frustrated but cooperative," one PRD officer recalled. "They knew that they were an important part of the war effort and whatever they wrote or put on the airwaves could have a far-reaching effect."[36] It is thus worth highlighting the fact that though much of the scholarship on war reporting focuses on the military's desire to hoodwink the media through censorship and secrecy, SHAEF hoped to work with, and not against, reporters.[37]

Military cooperation with the press was even more important since accredited correspondents were an important weapon in modern war. As *Know Your War Correspondent* explained, "we are all aware that the power of the printed and spoken word have proved to be a vital weapon of war to the enemy," in the struggle for Allied morale. Accurate battle reporting had to help protect the morale on the home front—an "important factor in a successful war"—from Nazi disinformation. Correspondents, likewise, helped with soldiers' morale since the soldiers knew people at home would read about their exploits.[38] On May 31, 1944, Eisenhower shared secret guidelines with the Combined Chiefs of Staff for what was expected from the press. He explained that the coming invasion would likely release great public stress and emotion and that these energies "should be directed where they will do [the] most good for the Allied War Effort. Such direction will not be easy but it is encumbent [*sic*] on all concerned with the press and radio to ensure that these moulders [*sic*] of public opinion are given such guidance as will cause the emotional forces liberated by the breaking of the news of the invasion to be kept within defined channels."[39] This could be done in several ways. Reporters should remind the public that after the landings there would still be hard fighting. Gloating over perceived German weakness or speculation on Allied decision-making was to be avoided. When correspondents were "describing the preparations which have gone before to make a landing possible at all, stress should be laid on the integration of effort between all the Allied Forces engaged."[40] Praising the logistical magnitude of the operation was also encouraged, while journalists were discouraged from making comparisons to World War I. Eisenhower concluded by stating that the Allies should encourage the press to "present a correct and sober representation of events as they occur, and to leave the future to unfold itself."[41] After reading his May 11 memorandum at an off-the-record press conference, Eisenhower reiterated his belief that he was leading the "People's Armies" and that "without public opinion back of us we would be nothing more than mercenaries." Both he and the reporters had a common goal, he continued, and that was "to defeat the Axis as soon and as thoroughly as possible."[42] In other words, Eisenhower saw the press as a weapon of war because World War II was a people's war and therefore a total war.

Closely connected to both deception operations and to keeping civilians and soldiers informed were speeches made by generals. They also created controversies that would come to shape the battle for Normandy. This began with Montgomery, who, despite the grumbling from officers and politicians, attempted to speak both to large civilian audiences and to every soldier who was to participate in Overlord.[43] As he explained, "the soldier wants to know what's going on. . . . If you do that with the British soldier, he will do anything for you."[44] Montgomery used these speeches to hammer home his philosophy of warfare, including the civilians' part in total war. He pleaded "for the help of the whole nation in the task of inspiring the soldiers of our land at this momentous time." Since troops were influenced by civilians, how the populace felt about the war directly shaped military morale. Thus, he added that the "fighting services cannot pull *their* full weight on the battle front without the full co-operation of the home front." Likewise, soldiers needed to have faith in their leader, which was a "pearl of very great price" earned by success in battle. This speaking tour also gave Montgomery a chance to observe British civilian morale. From these talks, he wrote long after the war, "I gained the impression that the mass of the people were jaded and war weary. . . . It seemed to me more than ever necessary to end the war in Europe in 1944. The people needed it and I made a vow to do all I could to finish the German war by Christmas; I was sure it could be done if we made no mistakes."[45] Montgomery's concern about civilian morale, plus his philosophy of carefully planned battles fought without mistakes, shaped some of his most controversial actions in France.

George Patton's preinvasion fame became an important part of Fortitude, but also influence his actions in Normandy. Still under a cloud from the slapping incidents, Patton's involvement in the Overlord operations was hardly inevitable, with some of Eisenhower's aides worrying that the announcement would generate considerable negative publicity.[46] Indeed, one of Eisenhower's PROs from the Mediterranean argued against Patton commanding anything at all.[47] At the last moment, Eisenhower suggested that give Patton's "prestige" it might be better to leave him in the Mediterranean to command an army in the invasion of southern France.[48] Yet it was this very "prestige" that made Patton invaluable to Fortitude. As historian Michael Howard wrote, "Patton was not of a retiring disposition. He could be relied upon to figure, controversially and often, in newspaper headlines, and in consequence in German intelligence reports." Patton took command of the phony First United States Army Group (FUSAG), which was apparently preparing to invade northern France.[49] As correspondent Andy Rooney wrote later, "Patton was very good playing his part" with even the *Stars and Stripes*—Rooney's paper—being "suckered" into the deception with the headline "Patton in UK to Lead Invasion Force!"[50] In case their subscriptions to Allied newspapers had lapsed, the British made sure that German double agents in London informed the Nazis that sources in the Ministry of Information were supplying details of troop formations.[51]

Patton proved far too good at attracting attention. Eisenhower wanted no press release that Patton was in Britain. His aides successfully argued, however, "that if Pattons [*sic*] name was not released, it would provide ammunition for some unscrupulous columnist to write that General Eisenhower and the War Department were keeping Pattons [*sic*] presence here concealed because of unwillingness to let the American people know that he was to exercise a command in the invasion forces."[52] Yielding to this reasoning, Eisenhower, nevertheless, told "George to avoid press conferences and public statements. . . . A speech he made to an American division shortly after his arrival in the United Kingdom caused more than a ripple of astonishment and press comment, and I well knew that it would be far easier to keep him for a significant role in the war if he shut off his public utterances."[53] Nor was Eisenhower's mind relieved by two soldiers accused of shooting prisoners in Sicily who claimed that Patton had ordered them to do it during one of his fiery speeches.[54] "You talk too much," he told Patton. "If you order me not to I will stop," the Third Army commander replied. "Otherwise I will continue to influence troops the only way I know." "Go ahead," Eisenhower relented, "but watch yourself."[55]

A few weeks later Patton was at a welcoming club in Knutsford when he was asked to make an impromptu speech. He rose to the occasion in typical fashion:

> Until today, my only experiencing in welcoming has been to welcome Germans and Italians to the "Infernal Regions." . . .
>
> I feel that such clubs as this are a very real value, because I believe with Mr. Bernard Shaw . . . that the British and Americans are two people separated by a common language, and since it is the evident destiny of the British and Americans, and, of course, the Russians, to rule the world, the better we know each other, the better job we will do.[56]

Patton had been told that no reporters were present, but the next day a garbled and more colorful version of his remarks, which did not mention Russia, appeared in British newspapers.

Outrage followed. Most of the criticism centered on Patton's supposed omission of the Soviet Union as one of the postwar world's future rulers. "In England, Lieut. General George S. Patton Jr. again put both feet in his mouth, where there was obviously room for his cavalry boots as well" observed *Time* magazine.[57] "We do not mean to be prissy," the *Washington Post* prissily editorialized, ". . . but we think that Lieutenant Generals, even temporary ones ought to talk with rather more dignity than this. When they do not they run the danger of losing the respect of the men they command and the confidence of the public they serve. . . . Whatever his merits as a strategist or tactician he has revealed glaring defects as a leader of men."[58] The *New York Times* observed that comments from Congress "ranged from 'unfortunate' to 'balmy' and 'another face slapping.'"[59] Representative Jesse Summer of Illinois compared Patton's statement to something Hitler would say.[60] The Knutsford Incident was also used to attack Roosevelt. Republican senator Kenneth S. Wherry of Nebraska stated, "If this is a new foreign policy of the New Deal they have sent up as a trial balloon they had better call their general off the stump."[61] As one editorial angrily observed, "If General Patton deliberately tried, he could hardly have produced . . . a bigger batch of propaganda for the Nazis, the Japanese, and the Chicago Tribune."[62] Despite these comments from politicians and journalists, Henry Stimson noted that "the papers here, while they criticize his indiscretion, have not gone so far as to seek his relief—that is, all except this one editorial in the Post."[63] Nevertheless, Patton was closer to losing his command than he had been after the slapping incident.

Once again Major General Everett Hughes stepped in to save Patton. "Why can't he shut up?" he scribbled in his diary before heading off to visit Eisenhower.[64] He found the supreme commander writing to Marshall to relieve Patton.[65] Earlier that day, Eisenhower had cabled Marshall that Patton was "unable to use reasonably good sense in all those matters where senior commanders must appreciate the effect of their own actions upon public opinion." He then inquired if Patton's remarks would "tend to destroy or diminish public and government confidence in the War Department?"[66] Patton had sent Hughes his comments along with sworn statements from witnesses, which Hughes presented to Eisenhower, who read them and finally said, "Oh hell," and began rewriting the cable.[67] Patton was not yet safe. Marshall replied quoting the *Washington Post* editorial at length, but left the decision to fire Patton to Eisenhower.[68] Eisenhower decided to relieve Patton and so informed Marshall.[69] This prompted another cable from Marshall concerned that "my quotation from one editorial may have resulted in over-emphasis in your mind of the necessity for drastic action." Marshall added "that you should not weaken your hand for OVERLORD."[70] Eisenhower met with Patton on May 1 and reminded him, among other things, that it was an election year, and left him with the impression that he would be relieved. "It is sad and shocking to think that victory and the lives of thousands of men are pawns to the 'fear of They,'" Patton fumed in his diary, "and the writing of a group of unprincipled reporters, and weak kneed congressmen."[71] Two days later, however, Eisenhower decided he could not spare Patton's talents in the coming battle.[72] Patton would repay Eisenhower's confidence with victories, but the memories of negative press coverage would also shape his actions in Normandy.

The Knutsford scandal was not the only incident involving commanders' public statements before D-Day. Soon after he arrived in Britain, Montgomery spoke to the US Twenty-Ninth Division and informed them, in no uncertain terms, that they and the rest of the First US Army were under his command. Montgomery admitted in his memoirs that he was never sure how to gauge the reaction of American soldiers. General Robert McClure, head of censorship at SHAEF, did know and censored Montgomery's address.[73] Around the end of March, Montgomery caused another small ruckus when he gave an exclusive private interview with a few American correspondents. Joining the chorus of complaining reporters was the SHAEF PRD, which restated that Eisenhower wanted "commanders to refrain from press conferences or remarks for direct press quotation unless his prior approval had been obtained."[74] At the beginning of April, Bradley also addressed the Twenty-Ninth Division. "Patton had talked to them . . . and he'd emphasized the losses and did a lot of his cursing and so forth," Bradley remembered. "I had to sort of correct that."[75] To Bradley's annoyance his remarks were reprinted in the *Stars and Stripes* and later in other US outlets, complete with his statement that Overlord was the "greatest show on earth."[76] Bradley believed his speeches would be censored and angrily informed the SHAEF PRD that "I have had to take particular pains to bar all correspondents from being present when I made my inspections and, of course, this puts me in the wrong light with our correspondents."[77] Eisenhower understood the problem. As he explained to Marshall, he had "issued flat orders that nothing I say is ever to be quoted directly or indirectly and in fact I have gotten to the point where I will not even allow a newspaper man to be in the same locality when I am talking. Yet on three different occasions I have found my words quoted almost exactly in the papers."[78]

Although the Knutsford Incident and other media leaks added restrictions on commanders and reporters, they did not stop generals from addressing their troops. In fact, Eisenhower encouraged such talk. Two weeks after deciding to keep Patton, he issued a statement to all commanders that it was necessary to "make absolutely clear to our men the stark and elemental facts as to the character of our Nazi enemy" and the creation of a "fighting spirit."[79] The famous speech opening the 1970 movie *Patton* was in fact taken from an address the Third Army commander gave to the XII Corps after the Knutsford Incident.[80] Eisenhower himself continued to address troops, since it fit his managerial philosophy of war. After giving a speech, he would speak to individual soldiers, whose photos and names could then be sent to their hometown newspapers.[81] In a total war, commanders could not ignore the most basic way to communicate with soldiers.

In the leadup to D-Day, PRD dealt with numerous press issues designed to keep the Germans guessing. When in May 1944, two LSTs were sunk by German E-boats off Slapton Sands in a landing exercise, the navy convinced the PRD to hide the number of ships sunk to prevent other attacks.[82] As D-Day approached, the PRD worried that the disappearance from London of famous war correspondents for the landings could tip off Axis spies that the invasion was imminent. As with the commanders of Overlord, elaborate precautions were taken to hide the movements of correspondents.[83] Eisenhower ordered censorship on the artificial harbors that would be towed to Normandy to continue after D-Day so the Germans would believe another invasion force was coming to seize a port.[84]

Much thought also went into the wording for the initial press release of the invasion. To keep the Germans guessing exactly what troops they were facing, but to avoid giving offense as had happened in the invasion of Sicily, Eisenhower obtained permission from the prime minister of Canada to delay the announcement that Canadian troops were fighting in Normandy. Only "Allied" would be used in the first announcement.[85] Indeed, the wording of the initial communiqué had been debated for months before the invasion. One major goal was to continue Fortitude by not revealing that this was the main landing.[86] The final version of Communiqué #1 read, "Under the command of General Eisenhower, Allied naval forces, supported by strong air forces, began landing allied armies this morning on the northern coast of France."[87] That sounded closer to Belgium than Normandy. As historian Steven Casey notes, in an attempt to confuse the Germans, in early reports Eisenhower hid the "crucial fact that the attack had been launched on the Normandy beaches, emphasizing instead the massive air assault taking place farther north, in the Pas de Calais region."[88] After Eisenhower's messages, recordings from the king of Norway and the Belgian prime minister followed, with veiled hints of landings in their respective countries. Churchill's and Roosevelt's own D-Day messages also suggested more landings to come.[89]

The Allied ships off Normandy received Communiqué #1 at exactly 0930 on June 6, 1944.[90] Yet this was not the first announcement of D-Day that they heard. Despite the elaborate security precautions, the carefully worded statements, and months of detailed planning, the lid came off briefly late on the evening of June 3. An AP bureau typist was practicing for the big announcement when she accidentally broadcast the D-Day message to the world. Though a correction was in the air seconds after the false announcement, it still took twenty-three minutes for the AP to cancel the story. Berlin, Moscow, and other capitals around the world picked up the announcement. At SHAEF Butcher informed an exhausted Eisenhower, who the night before had taken the agonizing decision to postpone the invasion because of bad weather, about the broadcast. "He sort of grunted," recorded Butcher.[91]

Eisenhower spent the day before the invasion with the press. The PRD had detailed six newsmen to cover Eisenhower during the invasion, and the day before the landing, Butcher showed them around the advance command post and then turned them over to the supreme commander, who talked to them for more than an hour. "The nonchalance with which he announced that we were attacking in the morning and the feigned nonchalance with which the reporters absorbed it was a study in suppressed emotions," recorded Butcher that evening. Yet as he talked with the journalists, the clouds, which had been thick all day, parted and a ray of sunlight shot through the tent door. "By George, there IS some sun!" Eisenhower exclaimed.[92] He then invited the correspondents to accompany him to visit the 101st Airborne Division before their departure for Normandy. As he chatted with the paratroopers, a reporter snapped one of the most iconic photographs of Eisenhower taken during the war. It had taken months of debate for his staff to write the D-Day announcement, but on his return to headquarters Eisenhower handwrote the most famous press announcement that was never given. "Our landings in the Cherbourg-Havre Area have failed to gain a satisfactory foothold and I have withdrawn the troops. My decision to attack at this time and place was based upon the best information available. . . . If any blame or fault attaches to the attempt it is mine alone." He signed and dated the note July 5.[93]

The next morning, Eisenhower delayed Communiqué #1 until word was received that Allied soldiers were landing. This allowed the Germans to scoop the Allied press by two and a half hours reporting the invasion near Le Havre.[94] Yet the Germans not only fell for Operation Fortitude but also determined from Communiqué #1 that D-Day was upon them. "That this was the long expected D-Day was evidenced by the fact that Eisenhower's orders were published, followed by speeches by the enemy's prime ministers," noted the OKW War Diary on June 6, 1944.

> It was not as yet clear, however, if this was only the first push designed to tie down our forces or if it was already the major assault. It was surprising that sabotage did not increase noticeably. It was therefore assumed that the enemy at first would attempt to pinch off the Contentin peninsula with the intent to capture Cherbourg, in order to simultaneously or subsequently attack Fifteenth Army with the forces held in readiness in southeastern England.[95]

Through most of the battle for Normandy, the Germans would keep powerful formations waiting for an army group that never came.

The elaborate arrangement devised by the SHAEF PRD to carry news from the battlefield did not work perfectly. Hanson Baldwin, for example, was dismayed to learn that most of his many D-Day dispatches never reached

England, much less the *New York Times*.[96] Nevertheless, the system worked. Before the first Allied soldier touched the shores of France, the media had shown themselves to be a powerful weapon of war.

V Was for Vengeance

Back in London, Walter Cronkite and Ed Beattie of the United Press were searching for a cab on the evening of June 13, 1944, when suddenly out of the darkness, Cronkite remembered, "we heard this lone aircraft, its engine clearly malfunctioning, just clearing the housetops with flames pouring from its tail area. It crashed with a terrible explosion a few blocks away."[97] Earlier that night across the English Channel, twenty-seven V-1 pilotless aircraft— usually called buzz bombs, robot bombs, doodlebugs, and other colorful names—had been launched into the air.[98] The coming of the robot bombs was not a surprise, with Eisenhower having been briefed on them in January, including the concern that they might be loaded with radioactive elements.[99] By the end of May, however, the bombing of V-1 launch sites in an operation code-named Crossbow had diminished the worry about the robot bombs, yet also made Hitler more determined to deploy them.[100]

For the Nazis, the vengeance weapons were as much a propaganda tool as a military weapon. With Germany's fortunes diminishing, Nazi propaganda had come to rely increasingly on "secret weapons."[101] Now, the V-1 gave a visible example that wonder weapons were arriving.[102] Perhaps this is why Hitler categorically rejected the idea that the robot bombs be concentrated on the Allied supply ports of Southampton and Portsmouth, which in any case were difficult to hit, and insisted that London be the main target.[103] It was Goebbels who had thought of putting "vengeance" in the name. Nevertheless, Goebbels was, according to historian Robert Edwin Herzstein, wary of utilizing the word "retaliation" for the V weapons since he could not know the effectiveness of the attacks. "The OKW communiqué was modest and did not mention retaliation," writes Herzstein.[104] A week after the attacks began, Allied intelligence noticed that German propaganda was becoming more guarded about the effectiveness of the V-1 attacks.[105]

It was propaganda and the Allied media's coverage of the robot bombs that, nevertheless, decisively influenced the decision to continue the attacks. In Hitler's headquarters, disappointment was evident with the initial results of the V-1 attacks. As his commanders filled his presence with recriminations, the führer considered calling off the attacks and redirecting the resources elsewhere. "Then," Albert Speer remembered, "the press chief handed him some exaggerated, sensationalized reports from the London press on the effects of the V-1. Hitler's mood promptly changed. Now he demanded increased production."[106] The morale of the British public would be the main target.[107] The V-1 strategy, continued because of Allied media reports, was meant to provide a victory for the Nazi press.

Despite their limited military impact, the V-1s were psychologically devastating. It did not help that the press began—then quickly stopped—calling the V-1s "robot bombs," giving a creepy science-fiction feel to the attacks.[108] Guided by an automatic gyropilot and powered by the first jet engine, the V-1s moved at a high speed and delivered their two tons of high explosives at random.[109] Churchill would write after the war that the "blind impersonal nature of the missile made the individual on the ground feel helpless."[110] Playing off the British slang of referring to the V-1s as "doodlebugs," Butcher speculated that "jitterbugs" would be more appropriate.[111] For their part, reporters were as spooked as anyone else in London. A story circulated around Normandy that during a V-1 attack a correspondent was caught packing his bags at the Savoy. "What's wrong," he was supposedly asked, "are you going to Normandy, you coward?"[112] One such journalist denizen of the Savoy heading to Normandy was Drew Middleton, who recalled that he felt that he was leaving his wife "in far more danger . . . than I was likely to face on the Continent."[113] During June and July, the V-1 campaign killed five thousand people, injured thirty-five thousand more, and destroyed thirty thousand buildings.[114]

The Allied high command quickly realized that the robot bombs could create a public panic that might force a change to their strategy. As historian Richard Havers observes, "The need to maintain domestic morale was an overriding consideration for the [British] government. It was one of those situations where the news needed to be managed." The V-1 story was not released until Friday, June 16, at 1:00 p.m. Following the announcement Herbert Morrison, the British home secretary, spoke on the BBC explaining that the "damage it [the V-1] has caused has been relatively small, and the new weapon will not interfere with our war effort. . . . The enemy's aim is clearly, in view of the difficulty of his military situation, to try to upset our morale and interfere with our work."[115] British press reaction to the V-1s was mixed. The *Evening News*, which broke the story, ran a headline for June 16 that said, "Pilotless Warplanes Raided Britain," followed on the first column by a still more ominous "Attacks May Continue." The *Times*, however, was much more restrained, running an article titled "New Weapon Not a Surprise" and attempting to play down the attacks.[116] On the same day, Churchill informed air chief marshal Sir Arthur W. Tedder that operations in Normandy would not be changed due to the robot bombs.[117]

As the attacks increased in number and lethality the danger grew that Allied leaders would allow the robot bombs to shift the Normandy strategy, thanks to real or imagined media pressures. At a conference on June 16,

Churchill agreed to ask Eisenhower to use the strategic bombers to attack the launch sites as long as it caused "no interference with the essential requirements for the battle in France."[118] In a later meeting, Churchill emphasized that the V-1s could not be allowed to "upset our concentration on the battle in Normandy."[119] On June 18, a V-1 landed a direct hit on the Guards Chapel as the bishop of Maidstone was preparing to give communion, killing 121 soldiers and civilians, with 141 others seriously injured.[120] As the rescue workers pulled bodies from the Guards Chapel, Tedder, Eisenhower, and Churchill met and agreed the robot bombs were a much more serious threat than had first been imagined. Though, as Butcher noted, the "over-all damage is infinitesimal," Eisenhower ordered that V-1 launch sites were now the main priority of the strategic bombers.[121]

Even so, the V-1 launch sites were not easy targets for the heavy bombers. Before the invasion, Eisenhower had fought hard to have the strategic bombers placed under his authority. The commanders of the strategic air forces, Sir Arthur Harris and Carl Spaatz, had protested that instead of heavy bombers being used in Normandy they should instead be employed against strategic targets deep inside the Reich. Now Harris and Spaatz renewed their arguments for returning the focus of the heavy bombers to industrial targets instead of diverting them to the V-1 launch sites. Instead, Eisenhower ordered that the V-1s must remain the focus of bomber command.[122] As Stephen E. Ambrose observes, "There was great pressure on the politicians to 'do something' about the V-1s. . . . If nothing else, the public had to have a sense that somehow the Allies were hitting back."[123] By August, Crossbow had consumed 15 percent of all bomb tonnage from the US Eighth Air Force and British Bomber Command.[124] The bombers, nevertheless, were finding it difficult to hit the small targets because of bad weather and heavy defenses. Butcher recorded that the Germans had located the V-1 sites inside Belgian and French villages and that "to bomb a new site we have to destroy the surrounding village which further impairs our deteriorating relationship with the French, at least as expressed by De Gaulle through his group of ever-active press agents."[125] Bradley's aide, Chester Hansen, described a captured V-1 launch site in Normandy as a "huge concete [*sic*] structure with battery of mixers [antiaircraft guns] on top. Walls and ceiling 16–20 feet high. . . . Square in center of a dirty famyard [*sic*] rform [*sic*] which the [French] apparently have been evacuated. Mark of a bomb hit on the concrete but it did virtually no damage whatsoever."[126] Successful or not, bombing the V-1 launch sites was meant to show the public that the Allies were doing something about the attacks. Thus, the raids received significant attention in the British press.[127] Indeed, as historian Stephen Alan Bourque concludes, it was only after "intense political pressure and against their will, [that] Spaatz and Harris went after the" V-1 launch sites.[128] The incident demonstrates how an important military asset was diverted to a target of little military importance for morale and public opinion.

Allied leaders were growing more concerned about the robot bombs' influence on public opinion, leading to increasingly desperate ideas. The attacks were making the British public angrier. John Gordon editorialized in the *Sunday Express* that the Allies should be bombing German cities and villages and not bother with the launch sites. A fortnight later, the Reverend D. R. Davies titled his commentary "It Is Time for Reprisals!" noting that "by using this weapon, Nazi Germany has hoisted the flag of hell, and by her own deliberate act places herself outside all law."[129] The British home secretary, Herbert Morrison, had stated publicly on June 24 that "if the enemy's intention was to upset the morale of our people he has signally failed."[130] Privately, however, Morrison feared that the morale of the British public was crumbling and pressed for the V-1 launch sites to be bombed.[131] At a cabinet meeting on June 27, 1944, Morrison worried that the British people could no longer tolerate any more attacks. He summed up his views after the war by stating "that the noisy transit of these flying bombs, the awe of a pilotless aeroplane, and the quantity of them had all contributed to a fear among the people possibly, if temporarily, greater than in the conventional raids of a couple of years before."[132] Brooke, who categorized Morrison's remarks as "a pathetic wail," recalled that "Morrison's performance was a poor one, he kept on repeating that the population of London could not be asked to stand this strain after 5 years of war. He suggested that our strategy in France should be altered and that our one and only objective should be to clear the north coast of France." Churchill disagreed.[133] Yet Morrison was back at a War Cabinet meeting on July 3 with a report that 2,000 people had been killed by the V-1s in the last two weeks, along with another 7,403 injured, which he compared to the worst times during the 1940 Blitz. Churchill again reiterated that resources could not be diverted from the battle of Normandy. He nevertheless suggested that new methods be used and proposed that a list be published in the media of previously unattacked German towns that would be destroyed "one by one" if the V-1s were not stopped.[134] Tedder and other Allied commanders strongly objected to the idea, but Churchill had others.[135] Two days later, he suggested that the V-1 launch sites be bombed with poison gas. The next day he explained that "in the last war the bombing of open cities was regarded as forbidden. Now everybody does it as a matter of course. It is simply a question of fashion changing as she does between long and short skirts for women."[136] The rest of the Allied leadership remained unconvinced. "Let's, for God's sake," grumbled an exasperated Eisenhower, "keep our eyes on the ball and use some sense."[137]

The Allied media was also employed to counter the robot bombs. This began with the total news blackout of where the terror weapons landed since it was hoped that this would lessen German accuracy.[138] The Nazi press charged that the British were simply attempting to hide the huge amount of damage the robot bombs were causing, though, by that point, censorship of casualties had been lifted.[139] On July 20, the British paymaster general, Lord Cherwell, began worrying that the Germans were using London obituaries to plot their aim with the V-1s. "It seems unfortunate that the papers have been allowed to print obituaries of those killed by enemy action which quotes the borough or district," he wrote. "One of my people has plotted 70 from *The Times* and 80 from the *Daily Telegraph*, a definitely significant sample." He suggested writing fake obituaries to confuse German intelligence analysts reading British newspapers. John Drew, home defense executive, wrote the British chief censor, Admiral George Thomson, about Lord Cherwell's ideas, suggested that they be implemented, and he added that if the newspapers gave trouble, the admiral could suggest that he would correct the Germans' aim toward Fleet Street.[140]

When asked at a July 10 press conference what effect the robot bombs were having on the military situation, Eisenhower claimed the armed forces were ignoring them. "Quite the contrary," Butcher more truthfully observed.[141] In fact, despite the unwillingness of Allied leaders, the robot bombs were causing serious discussion in Normandy over whether to change the ground strategy. On June 28, Hansen recorded in his diary that Bradley was worried that "political decision[s] [would] compel us to abandon present plan for early seizure of Brittany . . . and push instead toward the Pas de Calais and the german [*sic*] rocket sites." In other words, Bradley worried that instead of directing the Allied efforts east, the Allies would be forced to move north toward Belgium. He added that the Germans were "now believed to be holding large forces for the protection of this area and the rocket guns it contains. Surely they are causing great deal of trouble in Britain and administration there would be very pleased to end the menace quickly."[142] Indeed, part of the German motivation for the use of the robot bombs against England was to lure the Allies into attacking the strong positions along the Pas de Calais.[143] Such a switch in focus would change the main direction of the attack and lead to major supply shortages, while also directing Allied armies against the place where the Germans were most prepared to meet them.

Bradley's fears were quickly vindicated. In his postwar memoir, Eisenhower wrote that "it must be said to the credit of the British leaders that never once did one of them urge me to vary any detail of my planned operations merely for the purpose of eliminating this scourge."[144] Yet, Bradley and his aide tell a different story. On June 29, Hansen recorded in his diary that "it is apparent that Montgomery now favors securing control of the British Second and American First Armies as well as his Canadian buco [*sic*] to lead an assault east to the Pas de Calais area in an effort to crack the defenses surrounding the pilotless aircraft sites." He saw Montgomery as motivated by political considerations of the suffering of British civilians, which was "wearing down on civilian morale, [and] distracting the efficiency of the wartime worker who is bothered by the devices while trying to sleep." Bradley was against any change of plans since it would bypass the capture of channel ports vital to the supply of the Allied advance.[145] Years later, Bradley's official biographer would write that Bradley believed that this change in strategy was a plot by Montgomery to gain permanent command of Allied ground forces. "If the thrust at Pas de Calais were successful and the V-1s were wiped out," Bradley and Blair wrote, "Monty would probably have been canonized."[146]

Much of the pressure for this change to strategy came from the media. Hansen recorded that the British reporter Hal Dilling had talked to Bradley's staff about clearing out the V-1 launching sites to "give the civilians a rest."[147] On July 1, Butcher paid a visit to Normandy and had Hansen show him the captured V-1 launch sites. Butcher reported back to a restless Eisenhower, who "was concerned about the effect of the flying bombs on morale, not so much personally as their cumulative damage. The PM [Churchill] had expressed grave concern and had said there had been 1600 [attacks] to date."[148] That day, Eisenhower flew to France, where Bradley met him at the beach. Over highballs and C rations, the robot bombs and their effect on London was discussed, with Hansen noting that "Judging by his conversation the civilians are alarmed by them [V-1s]. . . . Will not win the war for the Germans but it will cause great political pressure to be brought upon the govt to clean them out."[149] At approximately the same time, across the English Channel, a robot bomb hit yards from Eisenhower's office.[150] The next day, Bradley and Eisenhower visited Montgomery, who, according to Bradley and his official biographer, "made an offhand proposal—I assume it was offhand—that we, in effect, abandon the Overlord plan and concentrate all our efforts on a drive on Pas de Calais to destroy the [V-1] launching sites. He would lead the offensive. . . . Ike and I were astonished. Did Monty mean for us to take him seriously?"[151] Whatever Montgomery's intent, Eisenhower was not about to change the strategy for the Normandy campaign. The pressure of the media and the robot bombs did not alter the direction of the land attack in Normandy. But in coming months overrunning launch sites in Holland would help lead to the Allied disaster in Operation Market-Garden.[152]

The strategy for the Normandy campaign remained the same, but the price for unsuccessfully countering the V-1s and V-2s was costly for the Allies. Historian Phillips Payson O'Brien estimates that Crossbow "represented a far greater economic exertion on both sides than did land battles such as Stalingrad or the invasions of Sicily and Italy." The Germans poured huge resources into their terror weapon's construction, while the Allied air forces "dropped more ordnance on Crossbow targets in the summer of 1944 than they dropped in support of Allied armies in Normandy—in the end it represented 3 percent of the Anglo-American air effort in all theaters throughout the entire war."[153] This was a vast price to pay for an operation of questionable military value but of vast importance to public opinion.

The Master, the Master Plan, and the Unmastered Press

On June 12, Eisenhower, accompanied by Henry Arnold, Ernest King, and George Marshall, landed in Normandy. They were met by Bradley and a gaggle of reporters. King angrily turned to Eisenhower and demanded to know why the correspondents were present.[154] At least one of the photographers was also nonplused and recalled being told what was each general's "good side" to photograph.[155] It must have worked since Butcher received a request at 2:00 a.m. the next morning to release the photos, and reported that the "correspondents are delighted with their stories, although the London papers played the contemporary visit of the P.M. to Monty and mostly overlooked that of General Ike and party."[156] The day before, Ernie Pyle and other American correspondents had complained to Bradley about the BBC bias toward the British forces. Bradley promised to speak to Eisenhower or Churchill about the problem.[157] This alleged British press favoritism can be considered the opening shot of a press battled waged between the Allied correspondents. Since the real battle of Normandy quickly devolved into a stalemate, the media would deploy plenty of criticism. This, in turn, filtered back into commanders' actions in Normandy.

Since Bradley was at the center of both conflicts, his relationship with the media merits some attention. Like Eisenhower, Bradley fits well into Brian Linn's "Manager" category, and historians have generally viewed the homely and modest Bradley as the antithesis to the showy and publicity-hungry Patton. One recent biographer has even gone so far as to claim that Bradley "did not seek out publicity as others had done" and that "his life has been neglected largely because most media outlets dubbed him unexciting or mundane."[158] Yet, if the reminiscences of reporters are any guide, Bradley was extremely well regarded by the press.[159] The cynical Joe Liebling of the staid *New Yorker* allegedly claimed, "Bradley was the greatest man after Christ to hit this world."[160] "The outstanding figure on this western front is Lt. Gen. Omar Nelson Bradley," Ernie Pyle wrote in September 1944. "He is so modest and sincere that he probably will not get his proper credit, except in military textbooks."[161] Indeed, fear that Bradley's apparent disinterest in publicity would damage his place in posterity was as much a part of the Bradley legend as the "GI General." But the legend conceals one of the most adroit handlers of the press in World War II. As veteran-turned-scholar Paul

Fussell observes, "Bradley . . . seemed entirely homespun and guileless, but he equipped himself with a public-relations staff as able as any."[162] The most important of these was Chester B. Hansen, a former reporter himself, whose wife worked at *Time* magazine.[163] Bradley's own wife was close friends with Mary Margaret McBride of NBC.[164] After the war, Bradley admitted that Hansen was useful as a "public relations officer, and he soon became acquainted with all the correspondents that were with our headquarters. He found out what they were thinking, what they wanted to know."[165] Hansen was able to enhance Bradley's image with the press, going so far as to ensure that none of the reporters took Bradley's picture on D-Day, to conceal an untimely nose boil.[166] Though he insisted for the remainder of his days that he was not interested in publicity, Bradley certainly understood how to handle reporters.[167] Eventually, he would even make one his second wife.[168]

Initial attempts to make Bradley famous nonetheless fell flat. During the final battle for Tunisia—the snubs of the British for US soldiers likely still dancing in his mind—Bradley visited the press camp and explained the coming attack so the reporters could find the best place to cover the offensive.[169] Yet at the end of the campaign, George C. Marshall wrote Bradley that his name had "not yet been mentioned in The American Press."[170] Even after his name was finally released, Bradley and his coauthor later concluded that "it is fair to say that none of this publicity turned me into a household name at home."[171] Eisenhower attempted to help. It was around this time that Harry Butcher, Eisenhower's own expert in press relations, told the war correspondent Ernie Pyle to "go and discover Bradley."[172] Pyle caught up with Bradley in an olive grove northeast of Nicosia, Sicily. When Hansen explained that Pyle wanted to profile Bradley, he protested, but finally relented when Hansen said that families of his soldiers had a right to know something about him. Pyle was also reluctant since he had become famous by writing about ordinary GIs.[173] To remain consistent, Pyle wrote that Bradley was the "GI General," soft-spoken and dedicated to the lives of his soldiers, whom he closely resembled. Several scholars have contested this image. "If truth is the first casualty of war," writes historian Carlo D'Este dismissively, "so was the pretense that Omar Bradley was a general of the masses."[174] The image, nevertheless, stuck. By D-Day, *Life* and *Newsweek* had done major stories on Bradley, while *Time* placed his picture on the cover and, mimicking Pyle, called him "The Doughboy's General."[175]

Now in Normandy, Bradley was becoming increasingly sensitive to press issues. Despite the extensive preinvasion preparations for handling the correspondence, the Public Relations Division (PRD) was also having problems. Hobnobbing with a group of correspondents under a tree while sipping Pyle's gin one evening, Hansen received an earful of complaints about the failure of the PRD to provide lodging, food, transport, maps, and better communication with London. Bradley held his first press conference a few days later and apologized for the problems with the PRD. Though Bradley managed to charm the reporters, his aides still worried about his lack of publicity.[176] This press conference also resulted in the first and only time that Bradley and Montgomery openly clashed in Normandy. Hoping to reassure the Allied public that the preinvasion stories of massive losses had been unfounded, Bradley released Allied casualty figures. Montgomery angrily argued that this was helping the enemy and complained to SHAEF, setting off a flurry of cables attempting to discover how censorship had not killed the story. Bradley replied that the Axis would discredit the figures, which German radio obligingly did.[177] A few days later, the First Army commander was incensed when the press reported an ultimatum to the German commander of Cherbourg made by General J. Lawton Collins, which Bradley blamed on a "publicity minded" intelligence officer. As Hansen observed, Bradley was "getting sensitive to what is said in the [newspapers]."[178]

Another press disagreement between the Allies was publicity for units and their commanding officers. Like Bradley and Patton, Eisenhower's philosophy of war held that a unit whose accomplishments were featured in the press would fight better. "The combat soldier wants to be recognized," Eisenhower wrote after the war. "Nothing seems to please him more than to find his own battalion, regiment, or division mentioned favorably in the press."[179] Marshall agreed and wrote Eisenhower suggesting that American formations fighting in Normandy be given press attention. Eisenhower concurred, but responded that the "American practice in this regard has always been much more liberal than the British and I have taken a few days to determine whether or not I could establish a policy that would keep a desired balance."[180] In the middle of July, Marshall wrote that the "release of the names of corps and division commanders has had a happy effect in the home press." He continued that there would be "great advantage in the progress of your battle" by releasing the names of regimental and battalion commanders who had "displayed very aggressive leadership." In this way "everyone in your forces [would] realize that the publicity was not confined only to generals and that if you did a fine stunt you and your unit . . . [would be] mentioned."[181] Eisenhower agreed and suggested that Bradley's PRD should release the stories since, as he explained to Bradley, it "will give your PRD some prestige."[182] This still left the British to be convinced. Two days later, Butcher wrote that Eisenhower was in "negotiation with the British to get them to agree to release of names and identifications of units and commanders, particularly those who have been cited for effective action in the field. The British always are loath to give out this information but General Marshall has been insisting the publicity of our armed forces be spread as widely as possible."[183] That same day, Eisenhower explained to Montgomery that the US military had "always insisted on doing this because . . . this produces a personality in the news that brings the war closer to the people." He closed by expressing hope that the British policy would change to keep things level between the two Allies "even including the intricate problems of public relations and of censorship."[184] For the Americans, at least, publicity for units and commanders improved their fighting quality.

Cherbourg fell by the end of June, but that did not lift an air of pessimism settling over the Allies and the press. This was partly due to the sluggish advance. In the American sector, Bradley's forces were making slow progress against stiff German resistance aided by difficult terrain. The thousands of high hedges (*bocage*) surrounding small fields nurtured by Norman farmers for centuries and connected by sunken roads stymied the American advance for weeks. Meanwhile on the left flank, the British made glacial progress against the city of Caen. There were two reasons for this: German resistance and Montgomery's trademark caution. Called "the Master" by his admiring staff, Montgomery had developed a method of war that, he believed, gained victory at the least cost. "My military doctrine," Montgomery explained after the war, "was based on unbalancing the enemy while keeping well-balanced myself. I planned always to make the enemy commit his reserves on a wide front in order to plug holes in his defences. . . . I then committed my own reserves on a narrow front in a hard blow." Undoubtedly recalling the war weariness he had sensed in Britain, he added that his method "helped to save men's lives."[185] By the end of June, Bradley's staff was beginning to complain about Montgomery's slow advance, while Butcher blamed it for Eisenhower's high blood pressure.[186]

Montgomery's "master plan" called for Caen to be taken on D-Day and an offensive to push past the city while the Americans cleared Cherbourg, took Saint-Lô, and neutralized Brittany.[187] This did not happen. In fact, the British were as much stuck in front of Caen as the Americans were in the hedgerows. To Eisenhower's fury, Montgomery suddenly, and publicly, announced that his primary mission was to hold the main German forces around Caen.[188] He repeated this in his memoir, claiming that he had always planned to hold the German armor so the Americans could launch a breakout on the right and that there had never been a plan to break out from Caen. "I never once had cause or reason to alter my master plan," Montgomery wrote. "Eisenhower failed to comprehend the basic plan to which he had himself cheerfully agreed," he concluded.[189] "First of all he's a psychopath," was Eisenhower's response. "The plan said we must—the British on the left [—] must get all of the high ground or the open ground south of Falaise right about because that's the only land we had to put in our landing fields." When this did not happen, Montgomery changed the plan and then claimed the battle developed "exactly as he had planned it from the beginning."[190] This was the start of one of the most rancorous historical controversies of World War II.[191]

On July 18, the British launched Operation Goodwood, which finally took what was left of Caen before grinding to a stop. To Eisenhower, Montgomery had promised that Goodwood would have "far reaching results," which the supreme commander understood—as he told Montgomery—meant a breakout.[192] The press was also given this impression when Montgomery issued a brief statement to the BBC on July 18 explaining that he was "well satisfied with the progress" before blocking all other press communication.[193] "Second Army Breaks Through" read the *Times* headline, while the *Daily Mail* reported, "Armor Now Swarming into Open Country."[194] The July 19 headline of the *Daily Express* stated, "Our Tanks Fanning Out across the Caen Plain."[195] Montgomery added to his difficulties by holding a press conference on July 19 where he again implied that a breakout had been made and Goodwood had accomplished its objectives.[196] Across the channel, Montgomery's press conference went down flat. Butcher accused Montgomery of covering his failure by highlighting German casualties since D-Day, while Eisenhower glumly wondered how far the Allies could advance on one ton of bombs per mile.[197] In his memoir, Montgomery admitted, "I was too exultant at the Press conference I gave during the GOODWOOD battle. I realize that now—in fact, I realized it pretty quickly afterward."[198] In the end, Montgomery's use of the press during Goodwood only added to the mistrust between the Allies.

Why did the press conference go so badly? After the war, Montgomery explained that he could not possibly tell the correspondents the truth about holding the Germans in front of Caen. Both de Guingand and Bradley made similar statements.[199] Yet, as D'Este concludes, "there was nothing to stop him from telling the press 'off the record' of his intentions" as routinely done by Allied commanders.[200] Likewise, if silence was necessary, it did not call for outright distortion. Bradley and his coauthor later suggested Montgomery had two goals for Goodwood. The first purpose was to support the American breakout, the second "and here I admit to some speculation—might be called public relations or image building. If he were to achieve his goal of remaining ground commander, Monty badly needed a 'victory' to reverse the growing official and public criticism of him."[201] A number of Twenty-First Army Group officers supported Bradley's observation. One later said that Montgomery "felt he had to give the interview because there was a view in Britain and the United States that the British and Canadians were doing nothing while the U.S. were doing everything."[202] Field Marshal Brooke visited Montgomery on the day of the press conference and impressed upon him that "certain circles" were beginning to whisper that the Americans were taking all the casualties because the British were not doing their part in the fighting. "This is amazing," Montgomery wrote in his diary. Obviously furious, he added that Goodwood should "dispel that nonsense." He then headed to the press conference, where he "talked to them on the great need to avoid speculation about the future."[203] De Guingand watched the press conference in dismay and believed that press criticism had gotten to his boss. He "realized the danger of a lack of confidence springing up between the press and the Commander-in-Chief. . . . It is well that the press should realise how even the most dogged and determined characters are influenced by what they say."[204] Montgomery seemed to understand the danger. As he told a group of soldiers a few days after, "I have to spend one third of my time making sure I'm not sacked, talking to the Press, and the Politicians."[205] Along with holding down the stronger part of the German army, it is likely Montgomery hoped Goodwood would repair his image in the press that had suffered from failing to break out.

Instead, Montgomery's press conference only heightened the media's criticism of him. Earlier in the campaign, Allied correspondents had complained that Twenty-First Army Group was delaying their stories.[206] This was compounded by the fact that American correspondents had an advanced teleprinter and powerful wireless that allowed much faster transmission of stories.[207] Montgomery added to this discontent by imposing another censorship ban on Goodwood. "Unanimous protest has been received from press and radio correspondents." wrote R. Ernest Dupuy, the acting chief of SHAEF PRD. "Some correspondents have expressed opinion that Supreme Headquarters fears the outcome of the battle; others intimate that General MONTGOMERY, rather than the Supreme Commander, is dictating press policy." Dupuy added that such types of censorship were "rarely justifiable" and "not good public relations." He suggested Eisenhower end the embargo on stories and hold a press conference, which Eisenhower did two days later.[208] When the news did get out, there was plenty of criticism. "Allies in France Bogged Down on Entire Front" read the headline of the *New York Herald-Tribune*.[209] In London, the *Times* questioned the amount of airpower used for such limited gains and noted acidly that it was "unfortunate that the enemy had the resilience and speed to close the gap—and a gap probably did exist for a brief period—before our leading armour could get through."[210]

De Guingand, for one, worried about the negative publicity. "My Chief undoubtedly suffered a lot from the criticism that appeared in the press and elsewhere about the slowness of progress in the bridgehead," he wrote after the war. He worried that "there were considerable dangers that these outspoken comments might have had an effect upon the fighting qualities of the troops. . . . If they continually read articles criticizing Montgomery . . . they might lose faith in their Commander-in-Chief."[211] Montgomery agreed, writing Brooke, "It is not good for the morale of British troops in Normandy to see headlines in the English Newspapers: Set-back in Normandy etc. etc." He wondered if Sir James Grigg, secretary of state for war, "could have lunch with some leading editors and get this across to them."[212] Montgomery also wrote Grigg, who responded that he would speak to the editors and then accused Eisenhower of existing only "to give the journalists what they think they want and to support them against the soldiers at all costs."[213] Nevertheless, Eisenhower was concerned that the press criticism of Montgomery would hurt the Anglo-American alliance. Earlier, Butcher had summarized British civilian resentment of the media's coverage of the US capture of Cherbourg, along with American accusations of bias in the British press.[214] On the last day of July, Eisenhower wrote General Surles that from "a few recent articles from the United States I am told there has been some sharp criticism of Montgomery." He added that his only concern with the "articles is that criticism directed against anyone of my principal subordinates . . . is certain to disturb the spirit of teamwork that I have so laboriously worked for during the past two years." He requested Surles to inform the reporters that he should be blamed rather than his subordinates.[215]

Yet not all of Eisenhower's subordinates were convinced Montgomery should remain in command. On July 19, Air Marshal Arthur Tedder—a long-time foe of Montgomery—informed Eisenhower that the British Chiefs of Staff would back him if he fired Montgomery. Butcher calculated that the chances of this happening were sixty-to-forty in Montgomery's favor. Montgomery had successfully covered his failure in Goodwood. If he was sacked, Butcher speculated, his removal would cause a firestorm in the press. And even if that problem could be solved, who was there with enough prestige to take over the Twenty-First Army Group? Butcher blamed the "dearth of publicly acceptable British officers to replace Chief Big Wind is the British system of limiting the number of names of British generals who may be written about in the public prints or publicized on the BBC. This limits the number of well-known generals and certainly we can't replace someone with just anything." While Butcher "yearned for Patton," even replacing Montgomery with Bradley would seriously damage Allied relations.[216]

All of this must have been clear to Eisenhower, who instead attempted to motivate Montgomery toward greater aggressiveness by reminding him of the importance of public opinion. He sent a letter to Montgomery on July 21 listing the many military reasons for a continued offensive and saying that while Allied forces were of equal size "we must go forward . . . with honors and sacrifices equally shared."[217] Or, as Butcher interpreted this in his diary, the "home fronts of both countries are naturally becoming impatient and querulous."[218] On July 25, Montgomery noted that Eisenhower had "talked a good deal about public opinion in America and he hinted that there was a feeling that the US troops were doing more than the British troops."[219] The next day Eisenhower expressed his concerns to Churchill, who immediately wrote Montgomery praising Bradley's progress and hoping the British would do the same. Brooke recorded that Eisenhower had "run down Montgomery and described his stickiness and the reaction in the American papers! The old story again. . . . However Winston was in a good mood and receptive to arguments."[220] Brooke rushed a long personal letter to Montgomery explaining that Eisenhower was worried about the press and pushed for the quickest and biggest attack Montgomery could make "or we shall give more cause than ever for criticism."[221] Montgomery promised Brooke a large-scale attack.[222] By this point, Montgomery was paying attention. As he wrote to Brooke the day after Eisenhower's visit, "I have got to fight very hard on the eastern flank while the Americans are battling on the western flank. From one or two things Ike said yesterday when he was here, there is no doubt that public opinion in America is asking why the American casualties are higher than the British."[223]

Despite a concerted effort by Churchill and Brooke to assuage Eisenhower's worries, media pressure continued to mount. Across the Atlantic, meanwhile, the US War Department was fending off inquiries from reporters about the slow progress in Normandy. Robert A. Lovett, the assistant secretary of war for air, wrote of a War Department press conference where "it became apparent that both the press and the people over here [are] beginning to wonder why the heck the Ground armies didn't get rolling. . . . My evasive tactics shook them off my trail but left me convinced that this subject was a burning one." He added that this was confirmed by critical stories in the *Washington Post* and the *New York Herald Tribune*.[224] "In a few days' time we were to gain a victory which was to be acclaimed as the greatest achievement in military history," Montgomery wrote after the war.[225] Yet such comments obscure the great frustration that the slow progress in Normandy caused. Not only did the press become drawn into inter-Allied tensions, but they were also a way for Eisenhower to successfully put pressure on Montgomery.

The Breakout

Things were hardly better in the American sector of the front or in the press. "The Germans have not been able to prevent some Allied gains," wrote Drew Middleton, "but in the opinion of this correspondent the Germans have frustrated thus far the achievement of what must be the principle objective."[226] "There is growing comment in the British papers on the fact that we bomb, and shell and never get far," General Everett Hughes wrote his wife. "Do US papers make some comment?"[227] Of course they did. Hanson Baldwin echoed the worst fears of the British when he wrote that Normandy was not only a "magnified Anzio" but worse than World War I. "In that war," Baldwin explained, "we marched forward over shell-torn ground to death and destruction, but the units actually engaged in the 'hedgerow' campaigns of

Normandy have been locked in some of the grimmest fighting of this or any war."[228] Fletcher Pratt of the *Washington Post* also compared Normandy to World War I and believed the "stalemate" showed no signs of the war ending anytime soon.[229] All this was symbolized for Bradley when Baldwin told him he was returning to New York, explaining he was disappointed at the slow progress and expressing doubt about a breakout. Baldwin did not heed Bradley's advice to wait two weeks, when he would have a great story to report.[230]

Bradley was much more candid a few days later when he visited the correspondents' camp and delivered a briefing about a plan code-named Cobra. He explained that the heavy bombers would lay down a massive bombardment to blow a hole through the hedgerows. Through this gap, Patton's Third Army would exploit a breakout into Brittany. After the war, Bradley acknowledged that many would "question the advisability of my 'briefing' the correspondents on this operation." His intelligence officer certainly did. But, Bradley explained, "I always felt that the people back home were entitled to hear as accurate and prompt a story of what we were doing as possible."[231] The home front was on Eisenhower's mind as well. A few days before Cobra, he sent Bradley a message stating that "the eyes of our whole country will be following your progress."[232] The message was clear. The Allies were running out of time if they wished to sustain popular morale required for total war. After a slow start, and the accidental bombing of American troops, Cobra finally propelled the US Army out of the hedgerows of Normandy toward the open country of France.[233]

Patton had arrived in Normandy exactly a month after D-Day and was immediately accosted by photographers—professional and otherwise—whom he shooed off with the warning that he "was still a secret."[234] This was because Operation Fortitude was still in effect. Patton had come to take charge of the US Third Army, which was assembling on the Normandy beachhead. He was also in no mood to take chances with reporters. When Baldwin paid Patton a visit, one of his aides handed him a list of regulations for correspondents and explained that "due to the past unfortunate newspaper incidents certain precautions had to be taken which were somewhat distasteful to the Third Army, but were necessary."[235] Patton knew his job depended on not making trouble for his superiors. It was an attitude that both helped and hindered the final act in the Normandy campaign.

Unfortunately, Patton quickly ran into more trouble with the press. A few days before Cobra's launch, Bradley learned from the First Army's war correspondents that Patton's press officer had briefed reporters attached to Third Army about Cobra. A furious Bradley phoned Patton, who apologized profusely and explained the briefing was unauthorized.[236] After putting down the phone, he chewed out the war correspondents.[237] Bradley accepted Patton's explanation. But as the Third Army began streaming through the gap opened by Cobra, on July 27, Patton must have reflected on just how close he had again come to losing his command because of the media.[238]

Despite now having open roads before him, Patton's objective was to clear the Brittany peninsula of German forces. Yet this meant the Third Army would be moving west instead of northeast toward the Seine River and Germany. As resistance crumbled, Patton and his commanders began to realize they were bypassing the main German army. As historian Stephen Ambrose writes, "Patton lusted to seize that opportunity. . . . Straight east to Paris, then northwest along the Seine to seize the crossings, and the Allies would complete an encirclement that would lead to a bag of prisoners bigger than North Africa or Stalingrad."[239] Still, Bradley wanted Brittany cleared, and Patton was uncharacteristically unwilling to argue with him. When General John Shirley Wood, the aggressive commander of the 4th Armored Division, quietly began repositioning his forces to bypass, rather than capture, Rennes so as to be in a position to drive east, Patton instructed him to comply with Bradley's orders.[240]

Given the strategic opportunity, it must be asked why Patton did not press Bradley to change his plans. On July 3, Hughes had visited Patton and wrote his wife that the Third Army commander "has learned to keep quiet in several languages. I only hope that the enforced silence has not gotten him into bad habits. I hope he will speak up on matters of tactics. He may not. People form habits and play safe."[241] Several historians, without the benefit of Hughes's letter, have independently concluded that Patton was afraid to challenge Bradley because he was still under a cloud from negative media attention. Martin Blumenson, who not only penned the official US Army history of the Allied breakout but also edited Patton's private papers, agreed with historian Max Hastings's observation that Patton was "desperately anxious not to become entangled in a wrangle with Bradley when his own position" was tenuous.[242] Carlo D'Este, who wrote Patton's main biography, notes that "Patton himself saw the opportunities, but his shaky status in the Allied hierarchy after Sicily and Knutsford left him unwilling to stick his neck out."[243] To this can be added Patton's more recent run-in with Bradley over the press leak of Cobra. Scars from past media scandals made Patton reluctant to challenge Bradley and risk his role in the campaign.

For his part, Bradley was not pleased with Patton's reckless advance into Brittany. As the Third Army was moving through a narrow gap between Avranches and Mortain, Patton's flanks were left dangerously exposed to a counterattack. "Some people are more concerned with the headlines and the news they'll make that [*sic*] the soundness of their tactics," fumed Bradley. "I don't care if we get Brest tomorrow or ten days later. If we cut the peninsula, we'll get it anyhow. But we can't risk a loose hinge." Bradley moved one of Patton's divisions to strengthen his flank. According to Bradley, Patton "sheepishly" acquiesced, though he confided to his diary that Bradley was "naturally super-conservative." As he drove away, Bradley mused that Patton was probably cursing him out, but speculated that "if George were hit by three divisions, he might lose two of his own and that'd be terrible [*sic*] embarrasing [*sic*]. It'd cost him his job."[244]

Bradley had good reason to believe that Patton's fast advance was motivated by headlines. Eisenhower had informed Bradley in early July that Patton had offered him one thousand dollars for each week he agreed to bring him to France ahead of schedule.[245] "George was stimulated by headlines," Bradley wrote after the war, "the blacker the headlines the more recklessly he fought." When Patton first arrived in France, he had pleaded with Bradley, "For God's sake, you've got to get me into this fight before the war is over. I'm in the doghouse now and I'm apt to die there unless I pull something spectacular to get me out."[246] If Patton needed any further motivation, the June 5 edition of *Time* magazine quoted a member of the Senate Military Affairs Committee, which had just dropped his name from the promotion list, saying that if Patton "does something gallant in the field," he would likely be promoted. "But he'll have to keep his mouth shut and control his temper."[247] Bradley speculated after the war, "I've often wondered how much this nothing-to-lose attitude prodded Patton in his spectacular race across the face of France."[248]

Yet, as Bradley knew, Patton was not appearing in any headlines because of censorship. Bradley also received the credit as victory emerged. "Bradley Calm As He Sees His Plan Work Out," read a headline for the New York *Daily News* on August 15.[249] "Big Battle Won," read the subheadline of the *Kansas City Star*, and below "The Credit to Bradley."[250] As historian Steven Casey observes, "it was Bradley, not Patton, who received all the public's plaudits." In fact, it made him a "media star."[251] In part, this secrecy was a tactical decision since it cloaked the strength of the Allied force on the German flank.[252] Not releasing Patton's name was also a form of punishment for past indiscretions. More generally, all statements by generals were censored. Indeed, Bradley personally censored every quotation from officers of the Twelfth Army Group, except for Patton, "whose remarks thoughts, opinions and casual statements shall be stricken from all copy without further reference."[253] On August 12, Bradley suggested that Patton and Hodges's names be released to the press. Eisenhower agreed to Hodges but refused to release Patton's name since he claimed to have only a few "gray hairs left on this poor head of mine after the hard time I had when he [Patton] started and I mean to get him for it."[254] Eisenhower added, "Let George work a while longer for his headlines." Hodges's and Patton's names were finally released a few days later.[255]

Patton's reluctance to risk his position appeared again in the last great act of the Normandy campaign. Any amateur glancing at a map could see that Patton's flanks made a tempting target. The amateur commanding Nazi Germany did just that, and on the night of August 6–7, Hitler ordered a counterattack on the narrow gap of Patton's flank at Mortain. By this point, the Third Army had turned east, while Montgomery pressed south beginning to form a pocket around the German forces. On August 11, Hitler finally broke off the attack at Mortain as Allied pincers closed on the town of Falaise, threatening to encircle two German armies.[256] Patton wanted to advance to Falaise and seal the gap. The SHAEF plan, however, called for the "Third Army to seize Argentan while the Second Army and First Canadian Army driving southward seize Falaise, close the gap, trap and decisively defeat the German forces."[257] Bradley ordered Patton to halt at Argentan and wait for Montgomery's forces. Concerned that Patton's troops would clash with the British advancing from the south, worried that the Third Army flanks would be stretched too thin, and convinced that Montgomery would never let the Americans cross the boundary line to cut off the escape route, Bradley "much preferred a solid shoulder at Argentan to the possibility of a broken neck at Falaise."[258] Patton confided to his diary and posterity: "This halt is a great mistake, as I am certain that the British will not close on Falaise."[259] But again, as in Brittany, Patton was reluctant to press his case. His position in the Allied command was too weak because of his past indiscretions with the media.

As historian Rick Atkinson observes, Bradley's decision at Falaise was "the most controversial order of his long career."[260] Some scholars have followed Bradley's public explanation that he did not wish to collide with the British and wanted to create a "solid shoulder." It is also worth noting that, publicly at least, Bradley took responsibility for not closing the gap, explaining that "Monty had never prohibited and I never proposed that U.S. forces close the gap."[261] Nevertheless, this was not Bradley's original story when he told a press conference after the campaign that it was Twenty-First Army Group that had "prescribed that our advance be stopped at Argentan [*sic*]."[262] In an early draft of his memoirs, he blamed Montgomery directly for not closing the gap.[263] Blumenson notes that Bradley also offered solutions for avoiding friendly fire and did not doubt the ability of the XV Corps to hold the gap closed.[264] He concludes Bradley decided to halt because Montgomery had not moved the boundaries; there was increased German resistance; the XV Corps was overly exposed; faulty intelligence claimed most Germans had already escaped; and finally, the Canadians were about to close the gap themselves.[265] In 1993, Blumenson, by now the undisputed expert on both Falaise and Patton, argued that the "undue weight of the invasion plan, the tensions within the coalition, and the less than adequate abilities of the leaders at the top" created the Falaise Gap. If Patton had been in Bradley's position,

Blumenson speculates, he would have had a better relationship with both Eisenhower and Montgomery. He concludes, "It is easy enough to imagine the Eisenhower-Montgomery-Patton relationship as producing a less discordant Normandy campaign, a happier resolution of Overlord, a firm entrapment of the Germans west of the Seine, and a much earlier end of the war in Europe."[266] D'Este agrees, writing, "One of the gravest mistakes of the war was the reversal of roles between Patton and Bradley."[267]

For their part, Bradley's staff believed Patton had been stopped to save Montgomery's media reputation. On August 12, as Patton was pleading to move toward Falaise, Bradley and his staff were again irritated with Montgomery, not only for overcaution, but for the excuses made for him in the British press. The BBC, for example, had just incorrectly claimed Montgomery was holding off most of the German army.[268] Bradley's operations staff, according to Hansen, claimed "that we were ordered to hold at Argentan rather than to continue the drive to Falaise since our capture of this objective would infringe on the prestige of forces driving south and prevent them from securing prestige value in closing the trap." Believing Montgomery was behind Bradley's order to halt, Hansen added, "Accordingly, our forces were held at the Argentan line and subsequently refueled while the British were still short of their objective permitted [*sic*] much of the strength in the pocket to escape eastward toward the Seine."[269] The next day, Hansen fumed that Montgomery had let the Germans escape because of overcaution. "However," he noted, "it would be folly to criticize Montgomery due to his great prestige position among the British."[270] Bradley was away most of the day and never commented on whether media prestige influenced him or Montgomery. Later, historians would criticize Hansen's remarks as gossip.[271] Yet Hansen never corrected the diary even after he spoke to Bradley. Indeed, the next day he added to the argument, noting that Montgomery was putting prestige ahead of tactics.[272]

This, nevertheless, fed worries of both Allies that the British were not receiving their due in the press. For example, in the fifteen issues of Britain's *Daily Herald* published between July 28 and August 14, US forces were mentioned in the headlines ten times compared to the British and Canadians being only mentioned four times. Bradley's name appeared in the headlines twice, but Montgomery was not mentioned at all.[273] T. J. Davis noted the irritation many British civilians showed when the Americans were mentioned too often on the BBC.[274] In the first week of August, Churchill had asked Eisenhower, "rather plaintively" according to Butcher, to release General Frederick Morgan's name as the main planner of D-Day. Churchill explained "that although the British were contributing quite a bit to the battle in Normandy, their efforts were being blanketed in the press by headlines of Americans' swift advances, particularly in Brittany. He needed something to raise the level of news of British contributions. Ike had readily agreed."[275] As Patton was begging to close the pocket, back in England the acting chief of the PRD wrote Eisenhower's chief of staff, worrying that the "brilliant" American military success should be "summarized and depicted as part of an integrated assault, the importance of the British-Canadian offensive in its relations, as well as distortion of the over-all picture."[276] After the failure to close the Falaise Gap, Barney Oldfield, now working as Bradley's PRO, recalled that the failure was highly criticized in the press, with comparisons made between the American and British armies. Churchill, Oldfield remembered, "abhorred this trend especially, and asked Monty for an accounting. He also asked for some information about future plans for British arms, in case he had to stand up before his public with a defense."[277] A few weeks later, another press scuffle took place when the normally mild-mannered General Miles Dempsey told the London *Daily Telegraph* and *Morning Post* that American troops had delayed his Second Army's crossing of the Seine River. Bradley was furious and let Montgomery and Eisenhower know it.[278] Two weeks earlier, Eisenhower had had to beg Montgomery to give individual units and commanders publicity. Now the British were taking publicity much more seriously.

It is doubtful that Montgomery halted Patton for prestige reasons. Hansen wrote on August 14, "It is possible that Montgomery has subscribed to the vice of extreme over-caution and has made the error of many commanders in denying sound tactics for the prestige value of objective [*sic*]."[279] Patton was also suspicious of Montgomery's motives. "I believe that the order to halt and consolidate emanated from the 21st Army Group, and was either due to jealousy of the Americans or to utter ignorance of the situation, or to a combination of the two," he wrote in his diary.[280] RAF flier-turned-historian Richard Rohmer argues Montgomery had to act to save his face, his job, "and in order to deprive the Americans of the underserved [*sic*] ultimate credit and glory they would receive if it was they who completed the encirclement by driving north to Falaise."[281] To this claim, Carlo D'Este has, quite rightly, responded that the idea that Montgomery "would needlessly sacrifice lives or deliberately allow his enemy to escape in order to enhance his own self-glorification is a preposterous claim and Rohmer fails to offer a single shred of evidence to substantiate his absurd conclusion."[282] Indeed, Montgomery's two main obsessions before and during the Normandy campaign were to end the war as quickly as possible to spare his soldiers' lives. Most importantly, it was Bradley and not Montgomery who stopped Patton's advance.

In the realm of speculation, there is another possibility. Hansen may have accurately recorded the thinking of Bradley from his staff, but applied it to Montgomery instead. Bradley may well have believed that the British needed the prestige of closing the encirclement because of the difficult time in Normandy. Though it certainly was not his only reason, it could still have been in the back of Bradley's mind. If true, it would explain not only Hansen's comments, but also the reason Bradley did not pressure Montgomery to change the boundaries.

"I think I see the end of Germany from here," wrote correspondent Alan Moorehead as he surveyed the destruction at Falaise. Instead of closing the pocket, Allied artillery and air had pounded the retreating German forces. It would not be till November that the last of the slain men, horses, and cattle were buried.[283] Two days after the linkup finally occurred on August 19, Eisenhower inspected the battlefield and observed "scenes that could be described only by Dante. It was literally possible to walk for hundreds of yards at a time, stepping on nothing but dead and decaying flesh."[284] Nevertheless, between twenty thousand and forty thousand Germans escaped, fleeing back to the German frontier, where the fortifications of the "West Wall" were desperately being prepared.[285] German historian Joachim Ludewig notes that this included most of the headquarters units that would be vital for reorganizing the defenses.[286] Thus, the end of the Normandy campaign spurred controversy for years to come.[287] For historian William B. Breuer, the greatest missed opportunity at Falaise was "psychological." If both German armies had "surrender[ed], the impact on the Reich home front . . . would have been devastating. Instead, Propaganda Minister Josef Goebbels bolstered sagging spirits somewhat by lauding the 'fighting breakout from encirclement' and portraying it in the media as 'one of the great feats of German arms in the war.'"[288] Because of command politics, poor communications, misunderstanding, temerity, and Bradley's concern about humiliating Montgomery in the public's imagination, this opportunity slipped away with the German army.

Conclusion

On the Seine River lay Paris, arguably the biggest prestige objective of the war. Bradley believed that as a "symbol," Paris "would be intolerably us[eful] to us" but did not think that the supply problems made it worth a major effort.[289] The correspondents disagreed. At a press conference, they begged Bradley not to destroy the city. After Bradley promised, the reporters started arguing which division should be given the honor of liberating the city. Bradley dodged that thorny issue by suggesting there were enough correspondents to take the city themselves. By that point, the French resistance had taken matters in their own hands and had begun an uprising that motivated the French Second Armored Division to head toward Paris without waiting for orders. This forced Eisenhower and Bradley to agree on the "necessity for taking [the] city immediately to prevent hard feelings, etc."[290] Likewise, it appeared tactful to allow the French to liberate their capital. When the French were delayed by celebrating crowds, Bradley finally had enough, said "to hell with prestige," and ordered the US Fourth Division to support the French. German forces in Paris surrendered on August 25, 1944.[291] In the first weeks of the Normandy campaign, SHAEF had fretted over news accounts of the French population's antipathy to the invasion. It was feared that such news stories "would cause a development of cynicism and disillusionment among troops and civilians alike."[292] Parisian cheers drowned such fears.

Public relations still caused problems for the Allies. Soon after Paris's liberation, Eisenhower visited the city. According to Butcher, the supreme commander wanted not only to check up on Charles de Gaulle's activities but to dispel a BBC report that de Gaulle had liberated the city himself.[293] In Paris, de Gaulle asked Eisenhower for two American divisions to keep order. Eisenhower's mind flashed back to the Darlan Deal, and he began to worry about the dangers of entering French politics. Despite this, he ordered US divisions to parade through Paris on their way to the front. Though Montgomery had been invited to accompany Eisenhower, he declined. By this point, the British press was complaining that the Americans were hogging the prestige of liberating Paris. For Eisenhower, the campaign ended with "merely another instance of the necessity, in modern war, for a commander to concern himself always with the appearance of things in the public eye as well as with actual accomplishment. It is idle to say that the public may be ignored in the certainty that temporary misunderstandings will be forgotten in later victory."[294]

The battle for Normandy saw the use of the media as a weapon for total war come of age. This began before D-Day with extensive preparations going into making sure reporters had adequate facilities to do their job. Part of this was spreading Eisenhower's belief to his subordinates that reporters could help by improving morale, avoiding misunderstandings, and strengthening the Anglo-American alliance. The press could also be used for deception, though they were never to be the target of it. Fortitude was the greatest example, but the press also assisted with redirecting the robot bombs and concealing the Slapton Sands disaster and the presence of the Third Army in Normandy. Not least of the press's duties was keeping the home front informed and motivated. By the end of the campaign, the British were beginning to accept the American belief that publicity for units and commanders would improve their fighting quality. In Overlord the press as a weapon for total war became fully operational.

The media also influenced the Normandy campaign. Allied generals were selected for Overlord because of their media reputations, which also made them difficult to replace. This did not stop Eisenhower from almost firing Patton over his preinvasion comments. Patton was saved from the press mob only by George C. Marshall's intervention. Hysterical British press stories convinced Hitler to continue to waste valuable resources on the V-1 attacks on London. Yet for the same reason, the Allies diverted the strategic air forces away from industrial targets to attempt to stop the V-1 attacks, while ground commanders debated changing the direction of the attack away from Germany and toward Holland. After the breakout from Normandy, Patton was reluctant to imperil his newly restored command that he had endangered through past interactions with the press by arguing with his superiors. This led him to take less aggressive actions in Brittany and at Falaise. As the next chapter will show, media issues, begun during the battle for Normandy, continued through the remainder of the war in Europe.

Chapter Six

The Press of Prestige

As the Allied armies swept across France in the late summer of 1944, Eisenhower finally released the names of his army commanders to the press. On August 15, reporters were told Courtney Hodges was commanding the US First Army and George Patton the US Third Army. Years later Bradley claimed he and SHAEF encouraged the media to focus on Patton's advance to remove the stigma of his past media scandals.[1] In another interview, Bradley explained that he and Hodges were fine with the lopsided publicity because they "didn't care about headlines" and Patton did.[2] Nothing could be further from the truth. Nor were Bradley's and Hodges's staffs as good at hiding their irritation. Even before Patton's name was released, Chester Hansen recorded, "We aides live in Mortal [*sic*] fear that Patton may unjustly crab [*sic*] credit for the breakthrough," and later blamed Patton's headlines for Bradley's decreased fan mail.[3] Hodges's aides likewise expressed frustration after a newsreel mistakenly gave Patton credit for liberating Paris. For his part, Patton considered this "poetic justice" since he claimed he could have taken the French capital if "I had not been told not to."[4] Patton was even being extravagantly praised by the British press.[5]

Eisenhower saw the danger of lopsided publicity. If Patton received too much attention, it might hurt the morale of First Army's soldiers. He ordered a *Stars and Stripes* reporter to interview Hodges to give him a "'build-up' for the troops."[6] At a press briefing, Eisenhower's chief of staff, Walter Bedell Smith, highlighted First Army's prisoner count and tried to improve the "balance" in the press coverage.[7] Smith also directed SHAEF to try to "attract a little more attention to HODGES and BRADLEY as against PATTON's colorful appeal to the press. This without detriment to PATTON."[8]

The problem was that Hodges did not view public relations as an important part of his job. After assuming command from Bradley, Hodges waited twelve days before holding his first press conference. Though correspondents made many requests for interviews, he brushed them aside with the comment "Winning the war's the thing right now."[9] SHAEF suggested to First Army that although they did "*not* know how closely correspondents are permitted to deal with HODGES, think likely he could speak to them on background of operations without quotations and thus tend to bring splendid work of First Army into better play."[10] Soon afterward reporters began making regular appearances at Hodges's evening mess.[11] Correspondents still complained, however, that Hodges's PRO was worn out and would frequently give part of First Army press conferences in German to distract them.[12]

Despite his professed disinterest in publicity, Bradley also complained about the lopsided press coverage. This prompted Eisenhower to assign Colonel Justus Lawrence of the PRD to increase the press coverage for the other commanders. After visiting several American generals and their PROs, Lawrence concluded that they were all "guided by the same philosophy— give all the credit to the units they were commanding." After determining that none wanted to change, Lawrence decided to go to the root of the problem, and over fine French wine and dinner he discussed the issue with an amused Patton. "Quite frankly, I don't actually seek publicity for myself," Patton explained. "What I am deliberately trying to do is to inspire my 3rd Army to believe themselves to be the best fighters in the world! Anything publicly that, as a result may accrue to me, seems to make them very proud of themselves. I don't know why. But I hardly propose to quit what I have been doing." Lawrence departed with an increased appreciation of Patton, but no closer to solving the publicity problem.[13]

More broadly, Eisenhower worried that lopsided publicity could also threaten the Anglo-American alliance. War correspondents were not only playing up the unit or commander that they were accredited too, but also stirring up public competition among units, commanders, and nationalities in the press. Worse, Eisenhower later reflected, this trend for reporters to become "advocates and supporters of a particular unit or a particular commander" could also be dangerous "in an allied command, when the bias has also a nationalistic tinge."[14] Normandy provided plenty of such examples, including Montgomery's staff trying to prevent Third Army's correspondents from even landing in France.[15] The problem was how to encourage reporters to cover a commander and his units without becoming their champion in the press.

The final campaigns in Europe more than justified Eisenhower's concerns about publicity. Many of the battles in fall 1944 and the early months of 1945 would see press and prestige considerations influence military decisions. Often this was tied to issues of command and supply. Montgomery, backed by the British press, struggled to become theater ground commander, to the point of almost destroying his career and permanently souring his relationships with American generals. Many historians have highlighted Bradley's eventual bitterness about the attention Montgomery received.[16] Less known is that this bitterness would come to extend to Americans and even lead to a quiet war with the army newspaper, the *Stars and Stripes*. Though Eisenhower maintained a steady balance throughout these controversies, by the end of the war he had departed from an emphasis on "Allied" coverage and instead was encouraging "American" press coverage.

Issues of Command

The August 15 press announcement sparked one of the greatest Allied command crises of the war in European. At a Third Army press conference, correspondent Wes Gallagher of the AP heard the SHAEF statement that both First and Third Armies were under Bradley's Twelfth Army Group, with the implication that Eisenhower would soon take over the ground command from Montgomery.[17] Knowing news when he heard it, Gallagher wrote that the "United States has in France the greatest fighting force ever massed . . . and General Bradley has the greatest field command." He admitted it was unclear how the command situation worked, and Montgomery's Twenty-First Army Group was the only Allied army group then in France. "However, the British-Canadian components of that Army Group had no announced parallel in a commander, such as General Bradley's new position, except for General Montgomery," Gallagher continued.[18] And for many who read Gallagher's short article it appeared that Bradley was now Montgomery's equal.

The British press reacted with indignation to the news. After the war, Alan Brooke disingenuously claimed that it had been media pressure that forced Eisenhower to become the overall ground commander.[19] Yet long before D-Day, it had been decided that Eisenhower would take over the land battle when sufficient forces had landed.[20] With two army groups activated and a third advancing from southern France, September 1 was chosen for Eisenhower's assumption of ground command. Gallagher's scoop was copied by other news outlets, including, as Butcher recorded, Britain's *Daily Mirror*, which accompanied an outraged editorial with "a rather scathing cartoon."[21] At first, the SHAEF PRD hoped the negative publicity would be limited to the *Daily Mirror*'s demand for an apology.[22] Yet SHAEF's hasty correction infuriated American news outlets. Hanson Baldwin characterized the command situation as "unfortunate," while the *Chicago Tribune* headlined its commentary "British Control of Allied Staff Shown in Press."[23]

Bradley wondered why Montgomery did not put a stop to the rumors.[24] The answer was that the Twenty-First Army Group commander saw himself as the aggrieved party. He first heard the story from the BBC and believed it sounded like he was being demoted. "The Daily Mirror of 17 August had a leading article demanding that an apology be made to me!!" Montgomery noted in his diary. "It also had an amusing cartoon." Originally, Montgomery thought it had been a mistake, but then grew suspicious that "it may have been done on purpose by someone at SHAEF."[25]

The publicity, nonetheless, redounded to Montgomery's benefit. When Eisenhower assumed command of the land battle for Western Europe, Churchill promoted Montgomery to field marshal. As he explained to Eisenhower, "I considered this step necessary from the point of view of the British nation with whom Montgomery's name is a household word."[26] Eisenhower responded that he had finally seen a press summary of the incident and was "quite sure that reports you have had to the effect that British Empire participation in this campaign is not appreciated in the U.S., are greatly exaggerated."[27] But the press clamor had been sufficient to make Montgomery a field marshal.

The reaction of the British press also strengthened the decision to have Eisenhower take over the land battle. Marshall cabled Eisenhower:

> Tremendous publicity was given throughout the U.S. . . . to the creation of an American Army Group under Bradley, your movement to France and your assumption of direct command of the American Group. The recent statement . . . that Montgomery continues in command of all ground forces has produced a severe reaction in the New York Times and many other papers and I feel is to be deplored.[28]

He added, "the Secretary [of War] and I and apparently all America are strongly of the opinion that the time has come for you to assume direct exercise of command of the American contingent."[29] One particularly damaging example of this "poison" news—as Surles called it—was the *Washington Times-Herald*'s response to the *Daily Mirror*'s demand for an apology by noting, "It is generally recognized in Congressional circles and common gossip in Military circles that General EISENHOWER is merely [a] figure-head and that actual command of invasion is in hands of British General Staff and British dominate American War Department and Army."[30] After discussing Marshall's cable with Bradley, Eisenhower replied that though he did not wish for Bradley's public reputation to suffer, he was not ready to take overall command before the scheduled September 1 changeover date. He added that Marshall should inform Surles that Eisenhower approved all major decisions and would take over ground command when the "physical conditions" were right.[31]

The immediate result of the Gallagher story was a shakeup at the SHAEF Public Relations Division. Eisenhower was furious over the media storm and threatened to put the newsmen "under wraps if they can't get more detail and accuracy."[32] An investigation found Gallagher had circumvented the local censor by bringing the story to the London PRD, who assumed it had been cleared in France. This enabled Gallagher to obtain a minor scoop since the original story from Eisenhower's press conference had a time delay.[33] The supreme commander decided it was time to fix the PRD. General Hughes on a visit to Washington met Alexander Surles, who as head of public relations for the War Department PRO had sold Eisenhower to the media since 1942. "Called on Surles," Hughes noted in his diary. "Says Ike must get good PRO and trust him!" He added, "Surles says he has to keep generals built up so that papas and mamas will be happy that their boys are in good hands. Says Ike gets kudos for keeping Patton."[34] Meanwhile Smith, perhaps hoping to remove a rival from the headquarters, successfully suggested that Butcher be sent to London to overhaul the PRD.[35] Surles pushed for Frank Allen to become chief of public relations for Eisenhower, who accepted the suggestion.[36]

The press debate over the ground commander was closely connected to future strategy. Across the Seine River lay two possible objectives: a drive toward Germany by Patton heading east, or clearing of the northern coast of France and Belgium by Montgomery moving north. Montgomery naturally favored the latter option. He envisioned forty divisions under his command, with Bradley's army group protecting his flank, liberating the channel ports and sweeping into Holland. After crossing the Rhine River, the Allies would quickly take the Ruhr, followed by the entire Reich. Writing Brooke on August 18, Montgomery explained that "the initial objects of the movement would be to destroy the German forces on the coast and . . . a further object would be to get the enemy out of VI or V2 range of ENGLAND(.) [*sic*] BRADLEY agrees entirely with above conception."[37] That, however, was not Bradley's opinion, since he favored backing Patton's drive through Metz. Like Eisenhower, he believed crossing the German border would create a terrible psychological blow for the German people.[38] Learning that Eisenhower was leaning away from his northern thrust, Montgomery argued that a broad front strategy could not be sustained and that Eisenhower "should not descend into the land battle and become a ground C-in-C [commander in chief]." If American public opinion was an issue, Montgomery continued, he "would gladly serve under" Bradley. British public opinion, of course, would never allow such an arrangement.[39]

In effect, Eisenhower and Montgomery had exchanged their respective philosophies of war. Eisenhower now wanted a well-balanced advance while Montgomery argued for a daring thrust. In May, Eisenhower had approved a plan for Allied armies to move simultaneously into the Reich by encircling and destroying the Ruhr. This, according to historian Carlo D'Este, was the only known plan for the conquest of Germany. But there is no evidence that either Bradley or Montgomery knew of its existence. Logistics were also worrying the Allied command. Each division required an average of seven hundred tons of supplies a day, all of which was still coming from the Normandy beaches. Without a major port such as Antwerp, Montgomery's narrow front would require enough supplies to incapacitate the rest of the Allied armies.[40] Then there were political realities. With Jacob Devers's forces advancing from the invasion of southern France, the Allies had three army groups controlling eight armies comprising Americans, Brits, Canadians, Frenchmen, and Poles. Eisenhower could hardly allow one nation, army, or commander to sweep up all the glory. Politicians, reporters, the public, and his commanders would never allow it.[41]

Eisenhower never abandoned the broad front strategy, but he was forced to compromise somewhat. He decided that priority would be given to Montgomery's limited advance into Belgium. Bradley agreed. The French and Belgium ports and channel coast were objectives that could not be ignored since they contained the V-1 launch sites that British political leadership had been frantic about since June. The destruction of the V-1s, Bradley believed, would also remove a major Nazi propaganda resource and would be a blow to German morale.[42] He believed that the Germans could not retreat to more defensible positions and had to save the V-1 and V-2 launching sites for propaganda purposes.[43] Political considerations, according to Hansen, were also on Eisenhower's mind. The debate was taking place in the middle of the uproar over Montgomery not accompanying Eisenhower to liberated Paris and Bradley being given his own army group. Hansen recalled talking to Harold Bull, assistant chief of staff at SHAEF, who said: "Let Monty take Brussels, we have one capital on our hands."[44] By September 9, Butcher could report that the "Pas de Calais with its enormous propaganda value is all but lost" to Germany.[45] On that same day, Eisenhower wrote the Combined Chiefs of Staff, "The advance of the ground forces have largely removed the flying bomb and rocket threats and necessity for substantial air effort against CROSSBOW."[46] Therefore, the direction of the Allied effort in late August and early September was driven in large part by removing the pressure of the V-1s from British public opinion and denying a propaganda weapon to the Germans.

The press uproar made the Americans reluctant to be seen giving in to Montgomery. Though agreeing that the British advance would need American support, Eisenhower refused to give Montgomery the First Army since Bradley's Twelfth Army Group would then "only [have] one Army in it, and public opinion in the States would object." Montgomery wanted to know why public opinion should be allowed to create what he believed to be an unsound military decision.[47] For his part, Bradley was furious with Montgomery over the press storm and more eager than ever to be out from under his command. His PRO wrote later that while Bradley was reluctant to comment publicly on the story, he "never forgave Monty for not silencing his adherents at home."[48] When Montgomery attempted to interfere with First Army's support of his offensive, Bradley balked, explaining to his staff that "we've got to make it clear to the American public that we are no longer under any control of Monty's." "People back home are needling Marshall on this issue now," Hansen wrote in his diary. "Ike tends to lean towards Britishers in effort to bring an amicable agreement between the two."[49] In early September Hughes returned from Washington and brought word that Surles was still upset with the publicity situation. "Ike promised to write Surles about public relations," Hughes wrote in his diary. "Says he can't play up Americans [*sic*] side. He had better—he is not going to live in Europe all of his life."[50] Montgomery was not pleased with Eisenhower's decision, but agreed nonetheless. After visiting Twenty-First Army Group, Brooke confided to his diary that "it remains to be seen what political pressure is put on Eisenhower to move Americans on separate axis from the British."[51]

Montgomery continued to stew over Eisenhower's rejection of his northern strategy. The British people, economy, and manpower were stretched to the limit, he wrote after the war. Why should his plan—that he argued could end the war by Christmas—be thrown "away for reasons of American public opinion?" The day Antwerp fell, Montgomery wrote Eisenhower saying it was time for a "full-blooded thrust towards Berlin." That thrust could come from only two possible directions, Montgomery concluded, by going north through the Ruhr valley or by taking Metz and the Saar River basin, but there were not enough supplies for both. Eisenhower countered that there were hardly enough supplies for a drive to Berlin. Montgomery continued to disagree.[52]

The V-2 and fear of collapsing public opinion ended this debate in Montgomery's favor. The V-2 carried one ton of explosives and traveled faster than the speed of sound, making it almost impossible to intercept. Churchill had just publicly declared victory over the V-1s when the V-2s began falling on London.[53] On September 9—the day after the first V-2 hit London—Montgomery received a message from the British government saying the missiles likely came from Rotterdam or Amsterdam and asked if he could overrun the launch sites. "So far as I was concerned," Montgomery wrote after the war, "that settled the direction of the thrust line of my operation." The next day he began laying out plans to cross the Rhine at the Dutch city of Arnhem. That same day, in a stormy meeting with Eisenhower Montgomery warned that the broad front advance would never work and proposed his own operations. Eisenhower departed unconvinced. But the next day he informed the field marshal that Patton's advance would be halted and the majority of resources directed toward the new operation code-named Market Garden.[54] As Eisenhower explained to Bradley, there were two reasons to back Montgomery's drive north. The first was "the necessity for clearing up the Channel ports to get adequate deepwater harbors (Antwerp or Rotterdam or both), and to clean out the V-2 sites, presumably in Holland."[55] Likewise, Eisenhower had expressed an interest in using the airborne army in a large offensive. As with piercing the German border, he believed this would be devastating to German morale.[56] Bradley's aide suggested another explanation. "Monty hopes to control all of [the] effort," wrote Hansen. "Ike apparently unable to say 'go to hell' for diplomatic reasons which are involved. Monty is the darling of the British public, irascible and difficult to work with."[57]

Market Garden was a gamble that failed. Montgomery intended to drive through Belgium and into Holland over a narrow corridor. The airborne divisions would be dropped to secure bridges over the canals and rivers.[58] "Surprisingly," as correspondent Cornelius Ryan later wrote, "Market-Garden, a combined airborne and ground offensive, was authored by one of the most cautious of all the Allied commanders."[59] If it worked, the Allies would be across the Rhine and ready to threaten the industrial heartland of Germany. But it failed. Though the American airborne divisions took their assigned bridges, the British 1st Airborne was cut off at Arnhem by a strong counterattack by a Waffen SS division that was refitting in the area. The ground advance was unable to push through in time.[60] As one historian of the campaign summarized, "Market Garden defied military logic because it made no allowance for anything to go wrong, nor for the enemy's likely reactions."[61]

The cost of Market Garden was more than a lost battle. All other Allied formations not directly engaged in the operation were stripped of supplies, forcing them to a virtual halt. Worse, even though Montgomery had liberated Antwerp and its vital port facilities intact, the waterways connecting it to the North Sea were still in German hands. To launch Market Garden, Montgomery put off clearing the estuary, rationalizing that a quick victory would relieve the supply problems.[62] But that victory did not materialize, and in October Montgomery abandoned any plans of crossing the Rhine soon and began focusing on opening the approaches to Antwerp. It was not until the end of November—twelve weeks after the port had been liberated—that the first Allied supply ship entered Antwerp.[63] Though Twenty-First Army Group was now in a supporting role, that did not stop the British press from exaggerating Montgomery's contribution.[64] Nor did Montgomery cease his campaign to become ground commander. Eisenhower frostily replied that he should open Antwerp and that if Montgomery could not accept the command arrangements he could complain to "higher authority." Montgomery promised, "You will hear no more on the subject of command from me."[65] But Eisenhower would hear plenty from the British press throughout the fall. As historian Neil McDonald writes, around reporters "Monty was quite open about his contempt for Eisenhower's broad front strategy."[66] Three days before the Battle of the Bulge began, Butcher noted that what had begun as a "trickle has now grown practically to a campaign in at least one London paper to put Montgomery in command of the ground battle."[67]

Good Prestige and Bad Publicity

Crippled by supply shortages, slowed by abysmal weather, and opposed by fierce German resistance, the American armies on Montgomery's right sloshed to a virtual standstill during the fall of 1944. Montgomery's burn rate of supplies and failure at Market Garden caused recriminations among the Allies. The war correspondents, often wedded to the unit and commander they covered, reflected these opinions. Butcher informed Eisenhower of the increasing anger in American and British press camps against each other.[68] It made commanders progressively more aware of the prestige of certain objectives and in several significant cases shaped their battlefield decisions.

The Americans' eagerness to report captured objectives had been subordinated to military necessity in the drive across France. On August 10, SHAEF explained that "there is grave danger that the commutative effect of the premature public announcement of the capture of localities will disclose to the enemy the moving of our strength and the broad outline of our strategic plans."[69] Nevertheless, four days later a group of angry American correspondents complained to Bradley that the British were reporting the names of liberated towns that the US military was censoring. Bradley explained they had proof of Axis troops being ordered to towns already held by the Allies and added that he had requested similar censorship for the British.[70] SHAEF reiterated its previous warning on September 11 and added that it would take "necessary action to restrain the British Broadcasting Corporation from making premature announcements."[71] Three days later, a captured German general explained that his best source of intelligence had been the BBC.[72]

Montgomery's battle for supplies and ground command, along with his extensive buildup in the British press, made American commanders more interested in capturing prestige objectives. The port city of Brest near the trip of the Brittany peninsula was an example of this new focus. During the breakout from Normandy, Bradley had rebuked Patton for his advance toward Brest with exposed flanks. "George seems more interested in making headlines with the capture of Brest than in using his head on tactics. I don't care if we get Brest tomorrow—or ten days later."[73] The city, he added, would be "ours sooner or later."[74] By September 9, an emotional Bradley confided to Patton that "I would not say this to anyone but you, but we must take Brest in order to maintain the illusion of the fact that the U.S. Army cannot be beaten."[75] Brest finally fell on September 19, 1944, but the port was heavily damaged and did not contribute to the supply of the Allied armies during World War II.[76]

Patton was also concerned with the prestige of military objectives. The city of Metz sits at the Moselle River, and its strategic location, as well as its forty-three forts, made it a key position in the German line.[77] The toughest fortress was Fort Driant. Patton, angry that the supply shortage had not allowed him to bypass Metz, ordered a massive air and land bombardment followed by an infantry attack. Driant held fast.[78] On October 4, Patton directed his "XX Corps to complete the occupation of this fort if it took every man in the XX Corps, but he could not allow an attack by this Army to fail."[79] It failed. The Third Army prepared for a siege and tried to keep the news of its first "bloody nose"—Patton's description—out of the news.[80]

On Patton's left, Hodges's First Army was having its own battle for prestige. On October 2, the First Army began attacking the city of Aachen, the first major target inside Germany. It was a battle that American commanders had hoped to avoid by encircling and strangling the city. Though the former was done, Hitler had noticed the prestige value of Aachen and rushed in troops. As J. Lawton Collins, the commander of the VII Corps, wrote later, Aachen had "little military significance to either the Americans or Germans now that the XIX Corps, as well as our VII Corps, could bypass it on the way to the Rhine, but it did have great political and psychological importance to Hitler and the Nazi party."[81] All this gave the brutal battle that followed little military importance but great symbolic value.[82] Like Metz did to Third Army, Aachen ended the First Army's drive into Germany as the Allies became entangled in brutal fighting in the Hürtgen Forest.[83]

The Battle for Aachen also marked the beginning of Bradley's quiet skirmish with the *Stars and Stripes*. As Aachen was destroyed block by block, American soldiers began escorting German civilians out of the dying city. This, however, drew the ire of the *Stars and Stripes*. In an editorial, the paper warned against being too nice to Germans since that would only inspire them to begin another world war. General Clarence R. Huebner, the commander of the First Division, was unused to being accused of excessive kindness toward Germans and complained that such editorials undermined the confidence of soldiers in their officers. Bradley agreed and passed Huebner's letter to Eisenhower along with his own, saying, "Any deserved criticism of the action of subordinate commanders is a function of command and not of a paper. Since this is a military publication, I suggest that some steps be taken to prevent occurrence of such articles."[84] When Butcher brought up the subject and tried to defend the editorial, Bradley angrily reiterated his position.[85] Eisenhower took no action, but this was not the last time Bradley and his generals clashed with the *Stars and Stripes*.

The high command's increased irritability with the media reflected the stagnation of progress at the front. In the late summer of 1944 optimism had pervaded Allied leadership. Eisenhower was not alone when he told his commanders that German "resistance on the entire front shows signs of collapse."[86] It was impossible for the press not to be infected. In early September, Harry Butcher suggested to the SHAEF G-2 that he tell the press that there might yet be stiff resistance along the German border. The general agreed, but when the topic surfaced at a press conference, he immediately stated that the Allies would go "right through" the German border defenses. Butcher returned "dejectedly" to his office, to discover that Smith had just cleared for publication an interview of himself saying, "Militarily the war is won."[87]

Now, as their armies battled the Germans and worsening weather, Allied leaders became worried that the press they had received was too optimistic. On October 4, General Surles at the War Department's PRD sent Eisenhower an informal assessment of public and press opinion. Public optimism, according to Surles, had spiked with the liberation of France and peaked with Operation Market Garden. "Now, of course, the pendulum has swung back but surprisingly not as far as might be expected," he added. Surles had been warning the press that Germany was not yet defeated, but since "there is always a build-up starting with the correspondent who is slightly optimistic thence to the rewrite man, who further emphasizes the favorable aspect of a story, up to the headline writer who is aiming solely at circulation, the public invariably gets overplay on the actual happening."[88] A week later, the War Department noted the press had "created the impression of much greater success on the Western Front than are borne out by operational reports. Is this the impression desired?"[89] It certainly was not desired. "One thing that puzzles me is where anyone finds factual ground upon which to base a conviction that this battle is over, or nearly over," Eisenhower wrote a friend. "There could be no greater tragedy now than to witness a let-down at home that would stint us in supplies and ammunition, or which would re-act adversely on the psychology of the fighting man; he is keyed up to do a dirty job but he needs, and is deserving of, both moral and material support."[90] With supply shortages crippling the Allied armies, public optimism was dangerously misplaced.

Many in Bradley's headquarters believed optimism about the war was directly related to supply shortages. Industrial production was shaped by the priorities of the government, which reflected public opinion. If the public and government officials thought the war was about to end, industry would be reluctant to put too many resources into making ammunition. It was thus vital that public optimism be contained so as to keep production high. This overoptimism, Bradley's staff believed, was the result of poor public relations.[91] By mid-December, Bradley would go so far as to tell reporters that overoptimism had prolonged the war.[92]

In his history of American propaganda, *The Censored War*, George H. Roeder Jr. described how American censorship used imagery to control support for the war effort. In 1943, Roeder explained, the United States government began worrying that public opinion was growing complacent and allowed pictures of American dead to be published so as to counter that trend. By the spring of 1945, the censors were allowing blood to appear in press photographs.[93] Allied commanders in Europe also actively attempted to curb overoptimism in the press. The SHAEF PRD issued a new policy directive cautioning "that no impression is given to correspondents and to the out-side world that major developments or a rapid break-through to the heart of Germany may be expected in the immediate future."[94] In contrast to writers who believed that the military strove only to present a rosy picture of the war to the press, the actions of Eisenhower and the PRD present a much more nuanced picture.[95]

As the high command fretted about overoptimism, many generals were using the press as a weapon to keep up their soldiers' spirits. Patton, a major example of this, was eager to have the home front informed about his soldiers. By the end of September, he had persuaded Eisenhower to release the names of regimental commanders to the press.[96] When George C. Marshall visited his army, Patton informed him that one of his generals was about to be divorced. A startled Marshall offered to intercede, to which Patton explained that all he needed to do was release the officer's name to the press since his wife thought he was a slacker. Patton got his point across but later wrote his own wife that he had forgotten that the chief of staff had no sense of humor.[97] Before his November offensive began, Patton told the press to give the corps, division, and regimental commanders all the credit: "I want everybody named. It is very helpful to me and very helpful to the American soldier." As the press conference ended, he asked them to report on the junior officers as well. "Those are the things we should get to the people at home and they would have a tremendous uplifting influence on the people and on the soldiers, and after all, the soldiers are uplifted by the people at home. They don't even read the Stars & Stripes much less than the famous things you represent."[98] Likewise, as Patton reminded a departing reporter, by the "knowledge of the actions of their men in the combat zone, those on the home front are spurred on to greater effort in production and distribution of the sinews of war."[99] At another press conference, Patton made sure to thank the correspondents since "the intimate stories of the front-line troops are the inspirational things which make other troops go forward."[100] As he had done since the Casablanca landing, Patton used the press to praise his soldiers to the home front, believing that such tributes would then be returned to the soldiers by their family and friends and improve their fighting ability.

The US Army institutionalized Patton's idea of highlighting individual soldiers in the press. Groups of roving correspondents were formed whose purpose was to interview ordinary GIs, collect their addresses, and mail the story to their hometown papers.[101] As Tom Curley and John Maxwell Hamilton observe, "Editors and generals liked these stories because they resonated with readers at home." They gave an idea of what war was like, and being close to the front "was a way to support the troops."[102] Not only did this improve the spirit of the home front, but, as one correspondent assigned to this duty remembered, it also gave a "morale boost" to the soldiers since they frequently "received the story clippings from home. I've met soldiers who'd show me well-worn clippings about some story I'd written about them months before."[103] At its height, nearly twenty thousand stories about the exploits of GIs were being sent to hometown papers each week.[104] The United States was not alone in focusing on individual soldiers in the news coverage. War news may have been finally democratized, writes historian Joseph Matthews, but the "totalitarian news mills ground out reams of material on the individual soldier too."[105]

Meanwhile, Bradley discovered that the press could also be used to support certain tactics. Long before the war began, Allied air forces had been dominated by the idea of strategic bombing of enemy cities. The tactical use of planes for ground forces was given considerably less attention.[106] Hoping to influence the debates over air warfare doctrine taking place in the United States, Bradley decided to use the press to draw attention to the tactical air forces supporting his armies.[107] Bradley requested Patton to hold a press conference praising "air-ground support used in this Army in order to defeat the advocation [*sic*] of other methods being used in other theaters."[108] Patton and the commander of the XIX Tactical Air Force, General Otto Paul Weyland, quickly complied, dedicating an entire press conference to praising Patton's air support for domestic consumption.[109] A few days later Bradley assembled more than forty correspondents and had his own press conference praising air-ground cooperation.[110]

In early November, Patton found an even more direct way to weaponize the press. As he prepared for a new offensive to surround Metz and push toward the Rhine, he assembled the Third Army war correspondents and gave a detailed briefing of the coming operation including the reporters' role. He asked the BBC correspondent to perform a "very great favor by lying for me when we attack by saying we are straightening our lines for a winter position. . . . That may gain us 24 hours." Not wanting to be left out, another reporter reminded the general that many of their stories were also sent out to radio stations.[111] "Obviously the purpose of this statement is to mislead the enemy and not the public," Patton's chief of staff, Hobart Gay, explained.[112] When the Third Army attacked two days later it achieved tactical surprise, though, as one historian of the campaign notes, this came primarily from the dismal weather that accompanied the attack.[113]

The Battle of the Bulge

In his letter to General Surles concerning overoptimism in the Allied press, Eisenhower confided that "from the very beginning I have always said that we faced at least one great major battle, with all forces engaged, after we had cleared the French area." He had informed the correspondents of this and told them to expect "a bitter battle of major proportions which may take a very considerable time to decide."[114] Unbeknownst to Eisenhower, planning for this offensive was already under way. Since September 16, the German High Command had been working on an offensive that would slash through the Ardennes, split the American and British armies, capture Antwerp, and force the British into a second Dunkirk. Germany would then deliver a massive blow to the Soviets as American morale on the home front collapsed and forced the Western Allies into a separate peace with Germany.[115] As Hitler explained to his division commanders a few days before the Ardennes Offensive, the operation was psychological since the Allies must be shown that the German people would never surrender. The alliance of the capitalists, communists, and imperialists was an unnatural one, Hitler believed, and with "a few heavy strikes . . . this artificially maintained united front could collapse at any moment with a huge clap of thunder."[116] Thus, in the frigid predawn hours of December 16, the Germans opened a massive offensive by smashing into weak American divisions blocking the Ardennes and creating a large bulge in the line.[117]

Caught by surprise, Eisenhower nevertheless reacted quickly, ordering delaying actions at St. Vith and Bastogne. By December 19, a counterattack was already being planned, with Third Army swinging into the southern flank of the Bulge and driving for Bastogne, and Montgomery attacking the northern flank. With Twelfth Army Group split, Eisenhower decided to place the First and Ninth US Armies under Montgomery's command, leaving Bradley with just Third Army. Or as one of Patton's officers sneered to his diary, an army group "made up of General Patton and Third Army."[118] Tactically, the move made sense, since Montgomery could communicate better with all forces on the north side of the pocket. Bradley understood this but worried it could be interpreted as an acknowledgment of failure on his part.[119] Nevertheless, as historian Jerry D. Morelock observes, Bradley was unable to provide any tactical argument against the move, except that it would negatively "affect his own image and career."[120] Thus, as Eisenhower explained to his troubleshooter, Major General Everett Hughes, over an oyster lunch, he "couldn't do otherwise than to give two American armies to Monty."[121] Despite this, Hughes agreed with many American generals that Eisenhower's decision was a "slap at Brad" for failing to prevent the German Ardennes Offensive.[122]

The Bulge certainly did not cause Bradley to forget about prestige. By December 17, he was receiving reports that German forces were breaking through at the front, and an aide suggested he should prepare the Twelfth Army Group Headquarters to fall back. "I will never move backwards with a headquarters," Bradley replied. "There is too much prestige at s[t]ake."[123] If the transfer of two of his armies to Montgomery was not explained publicly by SHAEF, Bradley worried, "it could be interpreted as a loss of confidence by Eisenhower in me—or more significantly in the American command." Bradley knew he could be relieved, "but if his action were taken to mean repudiation of the American command . . . the damage could be irreparable to our future role in the war."[124] Then and later, rumors would persist that Bradley had been temporarily relieved during the Battle of the Bulge.[125] For his part, Bradley speculated that the panic in the press was allowed by the War Department "to make the people back home realize the war was not over." Whatever the case, Bradley concluded bitterly, "I think the publicity was handled very poorly."[126]

Nor did Patton forget prestige. As his army prepared to attack toward Bastogne, he ordered his staff to prepare situation reports for Bradley since the "future of this Army depends on the impression we make regarding it." When Montgomery stated he could not attack for months from the northern side of the Bulge, he suggested that the Americans to the south would launch the main attack and could get more troops into the fight by giving up the Colmar pocket on the far right of the Allied line and by pulling back from the Saar or Moselle, which Third Army had spent the fall capturing. Third Army did not respond well to this suggestion. Robert Allen, an intelligence officer on Patton's staff, who formerly cowrote the influential "Washington Merry-Go-Round" syndicated newspaper column with Drew Pearson, reflected the mood of others by calling Montgomery every name in the book and concluded that the "public reaction in the U.S.—and perhaps even England—would drive him into the oblivion he deserves. Really, he ought to be shot—and I mean that seriously."[127] Patton also considered the public relations angle. "The American (soldier and public) psychology must be considered," a Third Army memorandum concluded. "Although it cannot be evaluated, it would probably be seriously affected by a voluntary withdrawal. . . . Third Army troops know and understand the attack. They do not know or understand the retreat or general withdrawal."[128] Montgomery's suggestion was abandoned.

How the news was managed during the Battle of the Bulge certainly did the Allied PRD little credit. Early in the battle, the First Army placed a news blackout on the entire front. Correspondents, who risked their lives in the bitter cold during the largest battle the US Army ever fought, watched in fury as the censors kill their stories.[129] Even after First Army began the counterattack—which it was desperate to have reported—SHAEF blocked First Army correspondents from reporting the story and then released it to the newsmen in Paris.[130] In frontline dispatches, journalists began speculating on the scale of the disaster, causing increasing worry on the home front. Reporters also became more combative. In Washington, Ed Lockett of *Time* began suggesting that the military was using censorship to block unfavorable news.[131]

Meanwhile, correspondents in Third Army began a successful campaign to have the chief PRO fired.[132] But Bradley suffered the most. Believing reporters could get better information from SHAEF, he had dissolved the Twelfth Army Group's press camp. Well before the Bulge, Hansen was complaining that Bradley had "slumped into greater obscurity than ever before as a result of his remote command in [Twelfth Army] [G]roup." Now Bradley had no way to explain why he had lost two-thirds of his army group to Montgomery. The correspondents quickly reappeared at Twelfth Army Group and so did special briefings by Bradley.[133]

Montgomery managed to make this awkward situation worse. When he had assumed command of Bradley's two armies, Alan Brooke had warned him that though it was a more "satisfactory system of command," the field marshal must be careful not to "appear to rub this undoubted fact in to anyone at SHAEF or elsewhere."[134] But Montgomery could not resist gloating, and reiterated his case to be made ground commander at a one-on-one meeting with the supreme commander, which Eisenhower summarized with a resigned "Monty, as usual."[135] Nor did it help that Montgomery said he would not be able to attack with First Army for possibly three months.[136] Resignation turned to anger the next day when Montgomery sent a cable stating that the past command structure had failed and the Twelfth and Twenty-First Army Groups needed to be under one ground commander. After explaining that Eisenhower could not "possibly do it," Montgomery made a few suggestions about how the supreme commander should word the order.[137] Eisenhower read it as insubordination.[138]

A chorus of support from the British press forced Eisenhower's hand. On December 30, for example, the *Daily Express* noted on its front page that "Allied Generals May Be Moved" and said that the situation might "again require a regrouping of Allied forces. It is therefore likely that to meet all these contingencies a radical revision of all Allied commands on the Western Front is imminent."[139] That same day, Marshall wrote Eisenhower, "Articles in certain London papers proposing a British Deputy Commander for all your ground forces and implying that you have undertaken too much of a task yourself . . . under no circumstances make any concessions of any kind whatsoever. You not only have our complete confidence but there would be a terrific resentment in this country following such action."[140] In other words, Marshall was stating that British media opinion could not dictate the SHAEF command structure since American press opinion was opposed. "You need have no fear as to my contemplating the establishment of a ground deputy," Eisenhower reassured Marshall.[141] With the British press baying in the background, the supreme commander also concluded he could no longer tolerate Montgomery's insubordination.

It did not take long for Francis de Guingand, Montgomery's long-suffering chief of staff, to hear that his boss was in trouble. He met Walter Bedell Smith, who explained that between Montgomery's letter and the British press's comments, it appeared impossible that the command situation could remain the same. De Guingand accompanied Smith through the winter darkness to a small house where Eisenhower explained that "Bradley's position had become intolerable, and that there was every chance that he would lose the confidence of his troops." He inquired whether Montgomery "fully realized the effects of the line taken up by the British Press, and how Monty himself had helped to create this crisis by his campaign for a Land Force Commander and by the indiscreet remarks he had passed." Eisenhower ended by explaining that he was writing to the Combined Chiefs of Staff to say he could no longer work with Montgomery. A stunned de Guingand explained Montgomery had not meant to cause such offense and successfully pleaded for a day's delay.[142]

Braving terrible weather, de Guingand reached Twenty-First Army Group Headquarters the next day and found the field marshal having tea, surrounded by his staff amid a display of Christmas cards. De Guingand's news ended the festive atmosphere. The field marshal was stunned and "found it extremely hard to believe it possible that he might be relieved of his command after his successes and the tremendous prestige he had gained, particularly in the eyes of the troops and the British public." A cable was quickly drafted in which Montgomery pledged his full support to Eisenhower. He also sped up the timetable for the counterattack.[143] De Guingand's work was not done. Fortified with a whiskey and soda, he immediately set off over icy roads to meet with the War Correspondents Committee in Brussels. He knew the reporters—who represented the major British newspapers—well since they "had met together many a time to find a solution to some knotty problems." Now the general explained the crisis and noted that the press was making things much worse. If the situation continued to fester, "public opinion in the States might demand that in future no American troops should be placed under British Command." He ended by asking the correspondents to pass on the message to their editors.[144] De Guingand had saved Montgomery's job.

Unfortunately, Montgomery still could not control himself. According to his official biographer, "Monty was filled perhaps with an almost childlike desire to atone for his own misbehavior." When Churchill visited, Montgomery suggested the prime minister stop the anti-Eisenhower press in Britain.[145] Churchill reported to Roosevelt that Eisenhower and Montgomery were "very closely knit" and assured him that "in case any troubles should arise in the Press, His Majesty's Government have complete confidence in General Eisenhower and feel acutely any attacks made on him."[146] Montgomery also asked Churchill's permission to hold a press conference, explaining he intended to highlight Allied unity and try to stop the press bickering over command. Churchill, Brooke, and Eisenhower all agreed.[147] Not everyone was convinced that this was a good idea. Brigadier General Edgar Williams, an intelligence officer on Montgomery's staff, recalled suggesting "The Master" not talk to the press. Montgomery responded that Brooke thought it was a good idea, and Williams was left with the realization that "this was going to be awful."[148]

Montgomery's January 7 press conference justified Williams's fears. The following offensive highlights are taken from Montgomery's published notes of the conference. The field marshal began by explaining that the Germans took the US First Army by surprise and "split" the American army group. "As soon as I saw what was happening I took certain steps myself to ensure that *if* the Germans got to the Meuse they would certainly not get over that river," he continued. "Then the situation began to deteriorate. But the whole allied team rallied to meet the danger; national considerations were thrown overboard; General Eisenhower placed me in command of the whole Northern front." The entire "battle has been most interesting," he mused, "I think possibly one of the most interesting and tricky battles I have ever handled." True to his intention, he also added a few words of praise to the American GI and added, "I have tried to feel that I am almost an American soldier myself." After reporting that his fingerprints were on file at the US War Department—"which is far preferable to having them registered at Scotland Yard!"—the field marshal spoke of Allied solidarity. "I am absolutely devoted to Ike; we are the greatest of friends. It grieves me when I see uncomplimentary articles about him in the British Press." Though "constructive criticism" is fine, Montgomery concluded, destructive criticism should end.[149] "Oh God, why didn't you stop him?" moaned correspondent Alan Moorehead to one of Montgomery's officers as they departed the conference.[150]

The American press reacted with fury. Borrowing General Tony Mc-Auliffe's language when he refused to surrender Bastogne, Hugh Schuck wrote, "Nuts to you, Monty" in the *New York Daily News*.[151] Seeing a chance to spread Allied disunity with "black propaganda," the Germans changed a few words of Chester Wilmot's BBC broadcast and rebroadcast Montgomery's statement. One of Bradley's staff officers stated after the war, "You will find American officers who still believe that this famous broadcast actually originated in the BBC studios."[152] Wilmot would claim in later years that it was the twisted German broadcast that started the uproar, an explanation Montgomery supported.[153] Yet the Americans did not need the German version of Montgomery's statement to be angry. As Bradley wrote later, Montgomery had "paid a high tribute to the American soldier as a fighter, but said not a word about the leaders or staffs who so ably and efficiently shifted divisions around to meet every thrust. In my opinion, he tried to create doubt as to General Eisenhower's ability when he said, 'It grieves me when I see uncomplimentary articles about him in the British press.' I never saw any such articles and General Eisenhower told me he never saw such articles."[154]

Even before Montgomery's press conference, Bradley and his staff had been angry about the release of the news that Twelfth Army Group had been split. Because of the media blackout, the news had not been reported. But when *Time* magazine threatened to publish the account of the command shakeup, Eisenhower decided it was time to release the story on January 5.[155] "When the Germans broke through in the first week-end of their offensive," Chester Wilmot intoned on the BBC, "Field-Marshal Montgomery at once brought British divisions south in case the Americans needed them and, as the German threat developed, the roads leading back into Belgium were packed with British convoys day and night."[156] Bradley informed his staff that he was getting "goddam sick and tired of this business. I don't listen to the BBC any more; it makes me madd [*sic*]." His staff agreed. Eisenhower's announcement "has precipitated a crisis in our allied relationship," or so Hansen opened a six-page commentary on press relations. After a detailed recounting of Montgomery's sins and Bradley's long-suffering, he noted that the gist of the stories was to have Montgomery named field commander to "greatly increase the British position in this campaign" and that it was undoubtedly "officially inspired."[157]

The United States' press was part of the problem. Bradley's opinion of the *Stars and Stripes* sank to a new low when the paper referred to First Army GIs as "Monty's troops" and noted "that Bradley continued to command the Twelfth Army Group which now consists of only the Third Army." Patton suggested that the editorials in that paper were lengthening the war by six months, while Bradley told his staff that "you can be sure that if I become the Theater Commander, t[h]e Stars and Stripes will undergo a major readjustment in its policy." "The [press] reaction is amusing," wrote an unamused Hansen, "but intensely irritating." When battles were going poorly, the unit was always identified as the "First American Army" and usually linked to Hodges's name. "Now the First Army of Hodges has suddenly lost its identity and Monty emerges as the commander," Hansen observed. "In all press releases the troops are referred to as "Monty's troops in a palavering gibberish that indicates a slavish hero devotion on the part of the British press."[158] Meanwhile, AP correspondent Wes Gallagher published a long story blaming Hodges, along with Eisenhower and Bradley, for the weak disposition of American troops.[159]

When Twelfth Army Group started receiving news accounts of Montgomery's assumption of command, Bradley began to bombard Eisenhower with angry phone calls. Bradley was concerned for two reasons. First, such news stories threatened to undermine the confidence and morale of the officers and men of the Twelfth Army Group. Second, the American people might also lose confidence in his command and nurture the belief that the British always needed to rescue the Americans. He added that neither he nor Patton would serve under Montgomery. Eisenhower assured Bradley he would not agree to their serving under Montgomery and awarded Bradley the Bronze Star for his part in the Bulge, which Bedell Smith hoped would get some publicity. Eisenhower also promised to take up the matter with Churchill.[160]

Meanwhile, Bradley's staff was pushing for a more drastic solution. Hansen as well as Ralph Ingersoll, another former reporter on Bradley's staff, believed that the British were trying to make Montgomery the figurehead of the campaign to salvage the prestige of the British Empire. This was not necessarily a bad thing, the two aides agreed, nor was it evidently Montgomery's fault. But the damage to American prestige was real, and Ingersoll suggested that Bradley issue a rebuttal to the British. The two staff officers brought their proposal to Bradley along with a copy of a *Washington Post* article lamenting the lack of a formal statement from the US military. They explained that with Eisenhower in an "Allied" position there was no one to advocate for American views. Bradley agreed and wrote a statement. Then, guided by attempting to answer charges in the British newspapers, his aides spent much of the night reworking it. At 3:30 the next afternoon, a group of nervous-looking journalists were ushered into Bradley's office to hear his account of the Bulge. More than simply highlighting the fact that Montgomery's command was temporary, the press conference was a sea change in how the American high command viewed publicity. After the last reporter departed, Bradley's aides pushed for a change of press policy. Hansen explained that for American prestige it was "necessary that the General be paraded down the main streets of public opinion." From that point on, Bradley was the spokesman for the American forces in Europe. This came out of the military necessity, as Bradley put it, "that the American people as well as our American troops retain complete confidence in our command."[161]

Did GIs even care who commanded them, or were they as sensitive to national prestige as Bradley—the "GI General"—claimed? Bulge veteran turned historian Charles B. MacDonald posed the same question. The freezing American soldier fighting for his life would probably ask, "Who was this Montgomery? Who was Bradley? Who, even, was Hodges or Gerow, Collins, or Ridgway? (Patton was another matter.) A frontline soldier was immensely well informed if he knew the name of his company commander." MacDonald concludes that Bradley was "overrating the importance of the issue," since no GI had a radio in his foxhole and the only newspaper was the *Stars and Stripes*.[162] Considered from the vantage point of the GI, Bradley's concern for prestige was either irrelevant or a fig leaf for an argument in a wider battle for influence.

Bradley's concern for the morale of the American soldier may have been groundless, but the controversy was important in souring Allied relations. "In my opinion," Bradley wrote, "the campaign to set up Monty and, in general, to increase British prestige in this campaign . . . is definitely harmful to relations between the British and ourselves; and, more particularly, the campaign carried on recently by those papers backing Monty has caused great resentment among those American officers and men who have seen them."[163] Hansen also worried that the British media's behavior would "exert a dangerous attitude on future Anglo-American relationships. Although the press build-up was designed to distort the importance of Monty's command, its long-term effect will undoubtedly build an American resentment of such tactics that will be carried home with our troops."[164] This appeared to be borne out when General William Simpson, commander of the US Ninth Army, and a man who usually managed to get along with Montgomery, allowed his official diary to gripe:

> Any future moves of the Ninth, therefore, in the light of present British publicity policy, will be to the greater glory of the FM [Field Marshal] himself, since he sees fit to assume all the glory and scarcely permits the mention of an Army Commander's name. Bitterness and real resentment is creeping in because of both the FM's and the British press's attitude in presenting British Military accomplishments won with American blood, broadcast throughout Europe by the BBC.[165]

To fully grasp the damage the press was causing to the Grand Alliance, it must be remembered that Hansen, Ingersoll, and many other American officers had once been Anglophiles. Nor was this confined to Bradley's staff. One of Patton's intelligence officers, Robert S. Allen, another former reporter who had pushed for the United States to aid Britain before Pearl Harbor, was as disillusioned about the British as Hansen and Ingersoll. Montgomery and the British press had gone a long way in squandering their goodwill.[166] Eisenhower wrote after the war that Montgomery's press conference "caused me more distress and worry than did any similar one of the war." Though he believed that the field marshal meant well, he added, "I doubt that Montgomery ever came to realize how deeply resentful some American commanders were."[167]

Bradley allowed his fury about the British media to shape his military judgment. As the Bulge receded, the First Army was returned to Twelfth Army Group with plenty of carefully orchestrated publicity.[168] But Simpson's Ninth Army was kept under Montgomery's command. Bradley protested to Eisenhower that not returning all American troops to Twelfth Army Group "might be interpreted as a lack of confidence in the American command." He added that Ninth Army might be needed for the Twelfth Army Group's coming campaign. Eisenhower resignedly replied "that he had fought the propaganda to put Marshal Montgomery in command so long it was wearing him out . . . and that by putting it under the 21 Army Group at the present time, he might be able to shut up the element that was trying to put everything under Marshal Montgomery." Bradley furiously wrote a memorandum stating that the command setup was tactically wrong, hurtful to efficiency, and done only "to satisfy the British propaganda."[169] When Eisenhower decided to break off the attack in what remained of the Bulge to focus on the push to the Rhine, Bradley again objected. "I am certain I am right," Eisenhower wrote Marshall, "and it turned out that based on *purely military* considerations, Bradley agreed with me. The unfortunate burst of publicity that came out in the British papers in late December . . . is still rankling in Bradley's mind, and I must say that I cannot blame him much."[170] It was a frank admission of how much newspaper and public opinion could influence military decisions.

Another sign of Eisenhower's weariness of the British press was his willingness to yield on the ground commander issue. At the beginning of January, Churchill finally abandoned trying to make Italy a major theater of the war and suggested Harold Alexander replace Tedder as Eisenhower's deputy. Brooke quickly realized that replacing an RAF officer with an army general would be a way to get a de facto British ground commander and keep "Ike on the rails in [the] future."[171] It is clear that Alexander also believed he would be the de facto ground commander. As Harold Macmillan—his political adviser—wrote, Alexander "ought (on professional grounds) to have the [supreme] command."[172] Surprisingly, Eisenhower agreed to the change, but it was not mentioned again until Churchill brought it up to the American Joint Chiefs of Staff at the beginning of February. They also felt compelled to agree, but insisted that six weeks' delay was necessary to prevent the transfer from appearing as a censure of Eisenhower for the setback in the Battle of the Bulge.[173]

Ironically, it was Montgomery who squashed Alexander's transfer. Though he had no love for Tedder and welcomed Alexander's appointment, Montgomery considered that the command issue was now closed and would cause a stink in the press if reopened. He so informed Eisenhower and added he was, at last, happy with the command structure.[174] Eisenhower informed Brooke of Montgomery's views, emphasizing he personally would be happy to have Alexander. But, he added, Alexander should realize he would not be ground commander and if anyone suggested otherwise, Eisenhower would have to make a public statement denying it. This clarification was necessary, Eisenhower explained, because of the uproar in the British press during the Battle of the Bulge and the fuss over Montgomery assuming command of the First and Ninth Armies.[175] Or as Eisenhower explained to Marshall, "The matter is unimportant, except from its Public Relations aspect, but since Public Relations often cause me my biggest headaches, I wanted to make sure that the C.I.G.S. [Brooke] clearly understood."[176] When Churchill protested that the supreme commander would be wasting Alexander's talents, Eisenhower replied that press relations could not allow even the appearance of a ground commander.[177] Churchill finally dropped the idea.[178] The British media's push for Montgomery to lead the land battle, along with the field marshal's own press problems, made any suggestion of a British ground commander impossible.

Problems with the French

In the middle of the dustup surrounding Montgomery's press conference, Eisenhower was dealing with another controversy involving public opinion and military decisions that would "plague me throughout the duration of the Ardennes battle."[179] On the far right of the Allied lines was Jacob Devers's Sixth Army Group, stretched from Alsace to the Swiss border. It consisted of Alexander Patch's US Seventh Army and the French First Army of Jean de Lattre de Tassigny. Together these two armies occupied a significant portion of the front, including around a large bulge in the line called the Colmar Pocket. On December 19, Eisenhower had ordered Patch's army to take over the area of the front evacuated by Patton's forces moving north to relieve Bastogne, forcing Devers to halt his own offensive.[180] Soon afterward, Ultra intelligence informed Eisenhower that the Germans were preparing another offensive, code-named Nordwind, to take advantage of the Allies' weakened right flank. The day after Christmas, Eisenhower ordered the Seventh Army to fall back and abandon the French city of Strasbourg.[181] As he wrote after the war, the "northern Alsatian plain was of no immediate value to us."[182] He also hoped to create a "strategic reserve" by removing two divisions and to prevent any part of the Sixth Army Group from being cut off.[183]

The French could not have disagreed more with Eisenhower's plan. The territories of Alsace and Lorraine had been contested between France and Germany for centuries and since 1870 had featured in three wars. Strasbourg itself had great symbolic and historic significance and was home to six hundred thousand Frenchmen.[184] Charles de Gaulle had in fact recently given a speech at Strasbourg, asserting that it would never again be occupied by Germany.[185] What was more, French morale at the time of the Ardennes Offensive was still poor, both at home and at the front. Recognizing the importance of public opinion, de Gaulle had tried to encourage the French media to pay more attention to the fighting, only to be informed that there was little public interest.[186] Finally, there was fear that German troops would inflict atrocities on recaptured cities. De Gaulle summed up all this in his war memoirs, explaining that if the "French Army should abandon one of our provinces . . . without even engaging in a battle to defend it . . . would be a terrible wound inflicted on the honor of our country and its soldiers, a terrible cause for the

Alsatians to despair of France, [and] a profound blow to the nation's confidence in De Gaulle."[187]

Devers agreed with de Gaulle. He wrote in his diary that Patch had protested giving "up a strong position when you feel confident you can hold it. Also, there is no question that giving up the town of Strasbourg is a political disaster to France."[188] Eisenhower, nevertheless, refused to reconsider. When the Germans rang in the New Year with Nordwind, Eisenhower expected Devers to withdraw. When he delayed, Eisenhower was furious and demanded to know why the Sixth Army Group commander—whom he personally disliked—was disobeying orders.[189]

This delay gave time for the French to intervene. De Gaulle decreed that French forces should ignore the evacuation order.[190] This caused SHAEF to hesitate. On January 2, 1945, Devers was ordered to continue withdrawing his army but to hold his present line with a light force until the situation with de Gaulle was settled.[191] In another letter to Eisenhower, de Gaulle argued that "such an evacuation and under such conditions would be an error from the point of view of the general conduct of the war."[192] De Gaulle ensured that Devers and his French commanders saw his letter and its statement that French forces would not leave Strasbourg even if the Americans abandoned their flank.[193] Though there is some debate on when he changed his mind, it appears clear that Eisenhower would not risk jeopardizing his relationship with the French.[194] Eisenhower's office diary notes that de Gaulle's letter came right before his meeting with Churchill and Brooke and implies that the decision was made at that time.[195] Brooke recorded that "De Gaulle stated that such an abandonment of Strasbourg and of the Alsatians and Lorrainians would lead to an outcry throughout France, which could . . . bring his government crashing to the ground!"[196] In his memoirs, Churchill also states he pressed Eisenhower to change his mind before the meeting with de Gaulle.[197] Both statements fit into Eisenhower's later account to Marshall that the decision was taken before meeting de Gaulle and was due to fears of destabilizing the Free French government.[198]

This did not prevent Eisenhower from having a heated argument when de Gaulle arrived. De Gaulle explained that if they were at a staff college war game he would agree with the decision to pull back, but leaving the "sacred ground" of Alsace would be a national disaster for France and a tragedy for the French population. When Eisenhower pointed out that de Gaulle was offering only political reasons for changing military plans, the French leader responded that "no one knows better than yourself that strategy should include not only . . . military technique, but also the moral elements." For the French soldiers and people, he added, the "fate of Strasbourg is of an extreme moral importance." De Gaulle claimed, or so Eisenhower remembered, that the loss of Strasbourg would shake his administration and might cause "anarchy in the whole country." The supreme commander stated that if the French Army refused to follow orders he could cut off its supplies. If that happened, De Gaulle replied, his countrymen might force him to close off French railways and communications.[199] Yet this "contest of dumb threats," as historian James Scott Wheeler titled it, appears to have ended the debate. Eisenhower wrote to Marshall that he "originally looked at the matter merely as a conflict between military and political considerations. . . . However, when I found that execution of the original plan would have such grave consequences in France that all my lines of communication and my vast rear areas might become badly involved through loss of service troops and through unrest, it was clearly a military necessity to prevent this."[200] In other words, Eisenhower had discarded a sound military plan out of fear of damaging French public opinion if a prestige position was lost.

Holding the line did not solve the problem of the Colmar Pocket, and Devers continued to pester SHAEF for more divisions. On January 24, 1945, Bradley, Hodges, and Patton met to arrange boundary lines for the coming drive toward the Rhine. Just as the arrangements had been settled, British general John Whiteley, SHAEF G-3, called and told Bradley to transfer several divisions from Twelfth Army Group to Devers. For the first—and last—time Patton witnessed Bradley lose control. "I want you to understand," he shouted into the phone, "that there is more at stake than the mere moving of divisions and corps, and of a certain tactical plan. The reputation and the good will of the American soldier and the American Army and its commanders are at stake." Before Bradley had finished, the rest of the generals were applauding, and Patton—suspecting the whole thing was a plot by Montgomery to prevent him and Hodges from attacking and stealing the glory—loudly shouted: "Tell them to go to hell and all three of us will resign."[201] Bradley was no longer sensitive just about losing troops to the British, but also about losing them to other Americans. To prevent what he saw as further harm to his image, he had no hesitation about using the perceived damage of American prestige as an argument.

The incident was also the last straw for Patton. After the meeting of Bradley, Hodges, and Patton ended, the Third Army held its own staff conference, where the chief of staff rose and announced, "A new offensive operation [is] being planned" and in front of Patton warned that total secrecy was needed since "*There are other enemies besides the Germans.*" The other staff officers knew the "other enemies" were Montgomery and SHAEF. If, as one of Patton's aides explained, it was a "matter of national prestige that we should take the chance to get to the Rhine first," stealth would be required.[202] On the advance to the Rhine, Patton would shun publicity in the hopes of presenting his superiors with a fait accompli. Saying sorry was easier than asking permission.

Stars and Stripes for Morale

As Allied armies began pressing toward the Rhine River, the conduct of the *Stars and Stripes* raised issues of how far the military should go to improve GI morale. Bradley had been extremely irritated with the paper's coverage of the Bulge and in particular its failure to publish promptly his rebuttal press conference to Montgomery. Hansen, Ingersoll, and Bradley all agreed that the paper should be "incorporated as a media of command and used honestly and judiciously not only to report the news, but to establish morale and confidence in our troops."[203] Bradley went so far as to complain to the paper and had discussed the matter with Eisenhower, who argued instead that leaving the *Stars and Stripes* alone would improve soldiers' morale and that he was willing to tolerate the paper's editorial freedom.[204]

There is no evidence Bradley encouraged Patton to go after the *Stars and Stripes*, but knowing of Bradley's complaints may have emboldened the Third Army commander. "Wrote the Editor of the Stars and Stripes protesting against his paper as subversive of discipline," he recorded on January 13, 1945. He added that he sent a copy to General John C. H. Lee along with a warning "that unless there is an improvement, I will not permit the paper to be issued in this Army, nor permit his reporters or photographers in the Army area."[205] In the letter, Patton singled out Bill Mauldin's cartoons.[206] Mauldin had served in the Seventh Army in Sicily and had become a sergeant and a cartoonist drawing for the *Stars and Stripes* in Italy. His cartoons showed the common GI in the form of "Willie and Joe" as unshaven, unkempt, and cynical. Mauldin also enjoyed taking shots at officers and often highlighted disparities in privileges.

When word of Patton's fury reached Mauldin, Will Lang of *Time* and Bill Estoff of the *Stars and Stripes* introduced him to Harry Butcher, who proposed that the cartoonist meet Patton. Talking over their differences, Butcher suggested, might clear up the problem. Mauldin was terrified. "He's not half as bad as he sounds," Butcher explained. "Pretty nice guy in some ways when you get to know him." As he reached for the telephone Butcher added, "Don't think Patton won't see the logic and humor in this, too." If he did, Patton disguised it well. "If that little son of a bitch sets foot in the Third Army I'll throw his ass in jail," he bellowed into the telephone. After some cajoling, combined with the tacit implication that Eisenhower was behind the idea, Patton agreed to meet Mauldin.[207]

The cartoonist arrived at Patton's palace headquarters and was suitably impressed. He seems also to have made an impression on Patton's staff. One of his aides recorded, "Undoubtedly Sgt. Mauldin is a great cartoonist, and much to the surprise of the Author, he is merely a boy."[208] Ushered into Patton's office, which he assumed had once been a throne room, Mauldin was awestruck by the Third Army's commander. "There he sat, big as life. . . . His hair was silver, his face was pink, his collar and shoulders glittered with more stars than I could count, his fingers sparkled with rings, and an incredible mass of ribbons started around desktop level and spread upward in a flood over his chest to the very top of his shoulder." Patton began to speak. For a time, Mauldin listened fascinated. "Patton was a real master of his subject. . . . As I sat there listening to the general talk war, I felt truly privileged, as if I were hearing Michelangelo on painting." After a time, Patton concluded, "I don't know what *you* think you're trying to do but the krauts ought to pin a medal on you for helping them mess up discipline for us." Mauldin defended his cartoons by claiming it helped the ordinary soldier blow off steam and reminded him that he was not alone in his feelings. After forty-five minutes the meeting ended, and Mauldin departed on cool terms. Will Lang was waiting outside and Mauldin told him, "Patton had received me courteously, had expressed his feelings about my work, and had given me the opportunity to say a few words." He did not believe that he had changed the general's mind.[209] This was correct, and the arrest threats continued.[210]

Mauldin returned to Italy to continue the adventures of Willie and Joe as disheveled as ever. The meeting was not secret, and word spread around the European Theater of Operations (ETO) that Mauldin had run afoul of Patton. Many GIs who loved his cartoons seem to have taken Mauldin's side. In a survey of GIs, 58 percent stated that they liked Mauldin's cartoons the best out of those published in *Stars and Stripes*.[211] PFC Keith Winston of the 100th Infantry Division wrote his wife, "General Patton is strongly against some of his [Mauldin's] stuff. You might think he'd be above it. Tonight I notice Mauldin didn't appear and our group really miss him. . . . He certainly has captured the true inner feeling of the G.I."[212]

To view the Mauldin-Patton episode—as some have done—as a struggle of military authority versus free press misses a broader point of the encounter.[213] Both the general and the cartoonist instinctively understood that Mauldin's cartoons could help or hurt morale and, by extension, the war effort. As Butcher understood, both Patton and Mauldin "were trying to win the war and, with this common denominator, they ought to be able to settle their differences."[214] This was impossible, of course, since the two men had fundamentally different ideas on what improved morale. In many ways, the incident speaks to the generational changes that World War II veteran and historian William Manchester observed when explaining Douglas MacArthur's decline in popularity among his troops between the two world wars. "Egalitarianism did not become the triumphant passion of Western society until about the middle of this century," explained Manchester. "Veterans of World War I and World War II saw MacArthur very differently. Doughboys were proud to have fought under the General. GIs weren't; by the

1940s antiauthoritarianism had become dominant." Comparing MacArthur to Eisenhower, Manchester adds, "Ike asked to be liked, and he was; MacArthur demanded that he be revered, and he wasn't."[215] Patton, of the same generation as MacArthur, had similar Victorian ideas on inspiring soldiers. Mauldin, instead, argued that his cartoons helped the GIs deal with the inequalities of military life. "I always admired Patton," Mauldin wrote later. "Oh sure, the stupid bastard was crazy. . . . He thought he was living in the Dark Ages. Soldiers were peasants to him. I don't like that attitude, but I certainly respected his theories and the techniques he used to get his men out of their foxholes."[216]

In the end, it was a clash of philosophies Patton could not win. Eisenhower quickly came to the aid of the *Stars and Stripes* and ordered that "no officer or official in this Theater is authorized to issue instructions" to that paper.[217] Though he acknowledged that a "great deal of pressure has been brought on me in the past to abolish such things as Mauldin's cartoons, the 'B' Bag, etc.," he refused to interfere.[218] According to correspondent Virgil Pinkley, Eisenhower ordered Patton in person to leave both *Stars and Stripes* and Bill Mauldin alone.[219] In Italy, Mauldin had much more success with the brass. Both Geoffrey Keyes and Mark Clark gave him profuse congratulations when Mauldin received the Pulitzer Prize. "You are always welcome," Clark added, "at 15th Army Group."[220]

The Final Press Battle

As the press storm over command began to fade, SHAEF renewed its quest to more equally distribute media attention. Eisenhower was unsettled by the "nationalistic feelings aroused in the original change of command in the Ardennes," and on February 3, 1945, some of his officers recommended that "too much personal publicity is being created in regard to the higher commanders" and that "certain commanders themselves appear to be at fault in this." They recommended attention be focused away from army group commanders and onto the army, corps, and division to create better esprit de corps. Likewise, all units should be referred to by their numerical designation and not by the commander's name and quotations by "spokesmen" should be eliminated.[221] This may have been due to Bradley's establishing a press camp for Twelfth Army Group, which some at SHAEF opposed, fearing— correctly—its purpose was to promote Bradley and degrade Montgomery.[222] On February 7, an order was issued that eliminated quotations of "spokesmen," confined press conferences to discussion of that unit's zone of operations, removed mention of army group commanders, and emphasized that all units must be referred to by number and not the name of their commander.[223]

The order had little effect. A month later, the head of the PRD was reporting that correspondents were once again using commanders' names to identify units since "'names make news' and irrespective of briefings terminology colorful commanders have in the past and will continue to receive full attention in the press." Thus, the unbalanced publicity still existed for commanders and "national friction" was not reduced.[224]

Though he grumbled that reporters were the "greatest menace of the war," by March Eisenhower had changed his mind about publicity for American units.[225] He informed the SHAEF PRD that "a good standard practice would be to refer to each Army by both the name of the commander and the numerical designation."[226] Two days later, Eisenhower complained to Marshall that it was easier for the US Marine Corps to get publicity because of its small size.[227] That same day he wrote Bradley and Devers that the feats of individual units should be publicized more and that using a commander's name instead of just the unit's number designator could help. The problem had to be handled carefully so as not to unsettle Allied relations, but careful briefing of skilled reporters could create an interest in profiling exceptional units. "I do not want to be interpreted as saying that we are fighting this war for headlines," Eisenhower wrote, "but proper publicity does have an effect on our troop efficiency. A personalized presentation of the achievements of units of this great force would result in a greater appreciation at home and this, in turn, would have a beneficial result on the morale of every organization."[228]

On March 17, a stunned Patton—who had a perennial complaint that Eisenhower did not praise him enough—recorded that the supreme commander had paid him the "first compliment" of the war and stated "that we of the Third Army were such veterans that we did not appreciate our own greatness and should be more cocky and boastful, because otherwise people would not realize how good the American soldiers are." Eisenhower added "specifically that the newspapers reported the fighting in front of the 4th Armored Division very weak, but did not mention the fact that it was weak on account of the phenomenal speed wich [*sic*] which the 4th Armored had advanced."[229] The supreme commander also told the equally amazed Third Army staff the same thing and emphasized that they should summon "reporters and feed the right kind of stories to them. They'll use them and the folks back home will eat it up. We need the right kind of publicity right now." As soon as Eisenhower left, Patton held a press conference and highlighted two points Eisenhower wanted him to make. First, the Third Army was not getting enough attention. Second, the Marine Corps was getting too much, with publicity for high casualties in the Pacific out of a much smaller force. "Eisenhower didn't know what he is starting when he urged Patton to boast more," a staff member wrote in his diary.[230]

What brought about this change in Eisenhower's thinking is difficult to know for sure. But it almost certainly emanated from George C. Marshall. Allen, one of Patton's staff officers, wrote a few days after Eisenhower's visit to Third Army that Bradley was also demanding more publicity on orders from Marshall. "Wonder what that is all about. Overshadow MacArthur to put someone else in command over there, or what?" It certainly stemmed from the realization that the war was ending and that the postwar army would be dominated by generals who had gained media fame in the war. The more publicity his good officers received, Eisenhower reasoned, the better chance they would control the postwar military.[231] Likewise, interservice rivalries were also major issues for the future. If the marine corps received too much publicity, the American public and their representatives would wonder why they also needed an army.

The crossing of the Rhine River provided ample opportunity to exploit Eisenhower's newfound interest in national publicity. Montgomery was making plans for a major crossing of the Rhine in an operation code-named Plunder. For the crossing, he had marshaled 250,000 soldiers, 700 tanks, and a vast amount of landing craft. Though Simpson's Ninth Army was involved, it was generally understood that no publicity was to be given to the Americans, and the British PROs had been ordered not to mention any American leaders. According to his official biographer, Bradley was furious that at least ten divisions from the First Army and all the Ninth Army would be part of an operation that he viewed as a sop to British prestige. This became less pressing on March 7 when Hodges phoned Bradley that the First Army had captured the Ludendorff Bridge at Remagen intact. Two weeks before Plunder, the US Army had crossed the last major natural obstacle into the Reich.[232]

SHAEF immediately asked to release the news of the capture of the Ludendorff Bridge. Irritated, First Army instead put the story under censorship to allow time to rush troops across.[233] Eisenhower told Bradley to hold a press conference and passed along a cable from Marshall praising Bradley's campaign. Marshall concluded, "If you think it wise . . . as a possible antidote for an overdose of Montgomery which is now coming into the country, you have my permission to release this [statement] in Paris."[234]

By that point, Bradley had another American accomplishment to boast. On the night of March 22–23, Third Army slipped across the Rhine. In contrast to Montgomery, who had carefully planned a massive operation to be covered by fifty reporters, Patton's force had moved with no fanfare and only one correspondent, Edward D. Ball of the AP. When the blackout that Patton had put on news of the crossing was finally lifted, Ball's story explained that Third Army had made the crossing "without the loss of a single man and without drawing a single shot from the Germans for a good twenty minutes after the crossing."[235] At around the same time, Patton phoned Bradley to "tell the world so they will know that I am across before Monty."[236] Bradley did just that in a radio address that evening, stating the "RHINE could be crossed at practically any point now by American forces, without aerial bombardment and without the dropping of paratroops in front of them." Patton, Bradley added, did not even need artillery preparation.[237] "Bradley 'tidied up' scores with Monty tonight," Robert Allen gleefully wrote in his diary. Musing how the Third Army's announcement had coincided with Bradley's statement, Allen added, "Don't know details of what transpired, but has all appearances on basis of what happened of being something that Bradley arranged."[238]

The Rhine crossing showed considerable skill in public relations by both Bradley and Patton. Butcher noted in his diary that the war correspondents were chuckling that Patton had been able to steal a march on Montgomery, who was still making elaborate preparations for Plunder.[239] In his contest with Montgomery, historian Steven Casey observes, "Patton had emerged as the clear victor; his army's exploits across the Rhine grabbed the headlines even as Montgomery seized most of the supplies."[240] General Hughes recorded that the press was upset that censorship had forbidden them to report the crossing. "War correspondents still say that Americans entitled to same information Germans have," he scribbled in his diary.[241] Yet the use of news blackouts to deceive the Germans also had the bonus of creating headlines that surprised readers. Montgomery crossed the Rhine, too, on March 23–24, but it was against tough opposition, and the news was overshadowed by Patton's exploits.

Although press and public opinion influenced numerous battlefield decisions, it certainly was not the only, or even the decisive factor, in every decision. This was illustrated by Eisenhower's choice not to race the Soviets to Berlin. He understood that Berlin "was politically and psychologically important as the symbol of remaining German power."[242] Most of Eisenhower's lieutenants also wanted Berlin.[243] And none of these were more eager than the war correspondents, who each dreamed of a Berlin dateline under their name. Barney Oldfield, now the PRO for the Ninth Army, which appeared to be headed to Berlin, recorded the journalists desperately urging the press camp to be moved east as fast as possible.[244] The exception was Bradley. Even if the Western Allies made it to Berlin ahead of the Soviets, the terms of the Yalta Agreement signed earlier that year meant that the captured territory would be given to Stalin. Bradley estimated that it would cost one hundred thousand casualties to take Berlin. Eisenhower agreed that it was a "stiff price to pay for a prestige objective."[245] In this case, Eisenhower and Bradley put the pressures of the press, public, and even their brother officers aside in making their decision.

As the Cold War emerged, Eisenhower's decision on Berlin would become one of his most debated.[246] This obscures, however, the masterful way

SHAEF diverted the issue in the press. Walter Bedell Smith held a press conference on the afternoon of April 21, and after giving a summary of the encirclement of the Ruhr, he turned his attention to Berlin. After warning that his part of the conference was off the record, Smith explained that though Berlin had "psychological value," it was "nothing like the importance that it had when it was the center of German communications and . . . Government." Instead, Smith explained, the Western Allies would focus toward the Sudetenland where intelligence suggested the Nazis would build a "National Redoubt" and continue the war indefinitely with the help of underground factories, fanaticism, and broadcasts to encourage resistance.[247] Frank Allen, director of the PRD, reported that by the number of words brought to the censors, Smith's press conference had been well received.[248] The National Redoubt turned out to be largely mythical. But Smith had successfully diverted the correspondents' attention away from Berlin. As Wes Gallagher wrote at the time, the ordinary GI "almost to a man . . . felt they could do without the final 'glory' of getting to Berlin and the resulting expense in casualties."[249] After spending thirty years interviewing veterans, historian Stephen Ambrose reached the same conclusion.[250]

Conclusion

At his April 21 press conference, Smith warned there would likely be four more months of fighting, much of it wiping out Nazi guerrillas.[251] Eisenhower had, in fact, warned Washington not to expect a formal surrender and said that the war would likely end by proclamation.[252] Nevertheless, the PRD began preparing for what its director called the "greatest news flash of history."[253] With the fall of Berlin to the Red Army fast approaching, Hitler killed himself on April 30, and his successor, Grand Admiral Karl Dönitz, began seeking surrender terms. SHAEF's staff entered a tense, last-minute debate on how much media should be present at the signing. Eisenhower ended it saying he did not care much in either case "but really desired that the public, through press, radio, and movies, should be given as much information as possible, since, after all, it was their war."[254] The result was inevitable. A war fought with the media as a major weapon and public opinion of both the allies and enemies as a major objective guaranteed that the press would be present at its termination.

The surrender ceremony itself was characterized by one PRO as the "war's greatest press spectacle, and debacle."[255] Seventeen reporters were flown in from Paris and given instructions not to release the story until commanded to do so. The Combined Chiefs of Staff had ordered that the news of the surrender had to be released at the exact same time in each of the major Allied capitals.[256] This was not simply about diplomatic niceties. The Germans desperately wanted a separate peace with the Western Allies so they could continue to fight the Soviets. Field Marshal Alfred Jodl, who negotiated the surrender, openly stated that the Western Allies would soon be at war with the Soviet Union and that it was in their interest to let as many German forces escape to the West as possible. The Soviets were, therefore, sensitive about how the surrender was handled.[257]

The chosen journalists were hustled into a room in Eisenhower's headquarters. General Allen, head of the PRD, refused to allow any more journalists to view the surrender. Outside the window, MPs held a crowd of uninvited and angry reporters at bay. The German generals finally arrived, and the war in Europe was ended. As an exhausted Eisenhower posed for photographers and made a radio recording, Edward Kennedy of the AP wrote his account of the surrender. When Allen summoned the correspondents at 4:00 a.m., Kennedy's story had already passed censorship but was being held for the final release. But Allen informed the correspondents that no story would be released until the middle of the afternoon. Kennedy flew back to Paris and spent the next hours stewing. The final blow came when the Germans broadcast news of the surrender. Kennedy reasoned the story had broken, avoided censorship by phoning London on a private line with his account, and single-handedly sparked one of history's biggest parties until the story was quickly blocked. Allen was furious, suspended the entire Associated Press, expelled Kennedy from the theater, and opened an investigation. Kennedy's fellow war correspondents denounced him and the AP apologized.[258] After the military's years of using the press as an instrument of war, Kennedy had once again demonstrated that the military never had total control over its media weapon.

The last several months of the war in Europe, nonetheless, had seen the media successfully deployed as an instrument of war. Patton had used the press to attempt to deceive the Germans at the opening of his final attack on Metz. Bradley arranged for press conferences to highlight air-ground cooperation and attempt to influence air doctrine with public opinion. Eisenhower, believing publicity was good for soldiers and their commanders, spent considerable energy attempting to make sure media coverage was balanced between individual generals and nations. Generally, all commanders tried to give ordinary soldiers publicity for morale purposes.

Yet the media also strained the Anglo–American alliance. Originally, Eisenhower had viewed the media as a way to minimize national differences. The opposite happened. Issues of credit, supply, and command were made public and magnified by the partisan press of generals, armies, and nationalities. It almost led to Montgomery's sacking and seriously clouded Bradley's military judgment. It is too much to argue that the Grand Alliance almost broke because of the media. But it did squander the goodwill of many

Americans who were originally sympathetic toward Britain. In the end, even Eisenhower began urging his American generals to seek publicity to enhance their prestige.

It was the battle for prestige that allowed media considerations to slip into battlefield decisions. The operations on the German border during the fall of 1944 were conducted with reputations, prestige, and public opinion in mind. Bradley became obsessed with the capture of Brest and Patton with Metz. Hodges fought for the strategically insignificant city of Aachen. Montgomery's drive into Holland, instead of clearing the channel to Antwerp, was done in hopes of regaining ground command. De Gaulle went even further, claiming if the Allies withdrew from Strasbourg, it would destroy French public opinion, quickly followed by his government. It would be simplistic to claim that prestige was the only reason these battles were fought. But the public reputation of a commander and his unit along with the desire to capture headline-making objectives factored into military calculations.

Did this lust for prestige really matter to the ordinary GI? Probably not. Studies of soldiers during World War II emphasized the extreme isolation of the battlefield. Few soldiers knew who commanded their company, much less their army or army group.[259] As for national prestige, most American soldiers were probably content to have another nation take an objective if it meant they did not have to die doing it. Yet the Allied leaders still believed prestige, press opinion, and public relations were significant and took these factors into account in their military decisions. It would be easy to dismiss this focus as out of touch. But it also represented the realities of modern total war. People's wars required that the public be informed, the sacrifice of their soldiers recorded and given importance. Thus, the media, and things that led to more press coverage, could not be ignored.

Conclusion

Douglas MacArthur stood on the deck of the USS *Missouri* and watched as the Japanese delegation signed the unconditional surrender of Japan. The final months of the Pacific War had seen the media continue to play a remarkable role in the war. During the long and bloody battle for Okinawa, press criticism of the fighting disturbed policy makers to such an extent that they considered deploying poison gas.[1] "The publicity side of the war is getting so large, it almost overshadows the fighting side," grumbled Admiral Chester Nimitz.[2] In the end, Japan had agreed to surrender only after the dropping of two atomic bombs and the Soviet Union's belated entry into the Pacific War. Even then, public opinion continued to be inserted into military decisions, with Stalin arguing—unsuccessfully—that Soviet public opinion demanded Red Army troops occupy some of the Japanese home islands.[3]

The final maneuvering for peace had been heavily influenced by public opinion and the media. As the invasion of Kyushu and Honshu islands approached, some American policy makers suggested that unconditional surrender be modified to allow the emperor to remain as a figurehead in Japan. This, they argued, would make the Japanese more willing to surrender. President Harry Truman and other advisers, nevertheless, believed American public opinion would not tolerate retaining the emperor. Polls showed a majority of Americans wanted a harsh peace for Japan. Thus, the final version of the Potsdam Declaration, which urged Japan to surrender, made no mention of the emperor. When Japan ignored the declaration, Truman ordered the attacks with atomic bombs.[4] After much wrangling, the collective shock of a second atomic attack, the declaration of war by the Soviet Union, and the personal intervention of the emperor, Japan capitulated.[5] But the Japanese stipulated that the Imperial House would have to be preserved. The Americans were reluctant to guarantee this, with Truman noting during the discussion that 153 out of 170 telegrams the White House had received in the past day had called for a harsh peace. The Allies attempted to sidestep the question by declaring the Japanese people would choose their future government.[6] Yet the surrender was still uncertain. As the Japanese debated this latest demand, American B-29s began bombarding Tokyo with leaflets of the text of the Japanese surrender. Fearing popular revolt, the emperor again assembled his war cabinet and reiterated that Japan would surrender.[7]

World War II ended with a unique media event for Japan when Emperor Hirohito spoke over the radio for the first time to announce Japan's capitulation. A few hours before, a military coup had attempted to kidnap the emperor. The plotters, however, failed to discover the recording of the surrender announcement, and the coup fizzled.[8] Once the broadcast had been aired, there was no stopping the surrender. The media thus helped bring one of the final acts of World War II to an end.

The United States had deployed the media as a weapon during World War II. In the months after Pearl Harbor, Roosevelt used the press not only to rebuild American morale but also to implement the Germany First strategy. Conversely, MacArthur used the press to successfully lobby for more resources for the SWPA Theater and his return to the Philippines. In North Africa and Sicily, George Patton encouraged press coverage to connect with his soldiers, give them more publicity, and make them more motivated fighters. The media were used for deception in the run-up to the landings in France and the campaigns into Germany.

As the war progressed, the media also came to influence commanders' decisions on the battlefield. Rescuing MacArthur from the Philippines in deference to public opinion forced the Allies to divide the Pacific War between two competing theaters. As historian Edward Miller notes, "The South Pacific offensive was a product of the persuasiveness of Douglas MacArthur. (Imagine the course of events . . . if he had been ordered to Hawaii instead of Australia)."[9] Bradley's concern over American public opinion convinced Eisenhower to change the plan for the final assault against Axis forces in Tunisia so as to include Americans. Patton "raced" across Sicily to gain media attention and British respect. Mark Clark's hunger for publicity and the glory of capturing Rome allowed an entire German army to escape destruction. Negative media pressure and fear of the V-1s damaging British morale provided the impetus for the breakout of Normandy and the unsuccessful attempt to liberate the Netherlands in fall 1944. Montgomery's remarks to the press during the Battle of the Bulge almost caused him to lose his command and created tremendous ill feelings among the Allies. Soon afterward, Eisenhower was forced to hold the dangerously exposed city of Strasbourg because of French public opinion. By V-E Day, even Eisenhower was attempting to get more publicity for American, as opposed to Allied, units.

What were the characteristics of the military-media relationship that caused the press to play such an extensive role in command decisions? First, it was a product of total war. Beginning with the French Revolution, the modern military and the press grew up together. Since wars of nations required a motivated population, the press was a necessary contingent to warfare. Though World War I saw this development continue, it was not until World War II that the media became a fully integrated part of warfare.

The relationship that emerged was necessarily symbiotic. The press needed the military's assistance in providing resources for communication and support for reporters. Journalists had to cooperate not only to receive this support but also to avoid having their stories blocked by censorship. By the time of the attack on Pearl Harbor, the US military understood that total war meant keeping the populace informed, soldiers' morale high, the enemy's spirits low, and policy makers in the know. For those purposes, the media were essential. Nor was mere propaganda sufficient, given the unfavorable memories from World War I. Truth was thus an important means to achieving this end.

One reason the relationship worked was the integration of the media and the military. Accredited war correspondents were nominally part of the military and often overseen by former reporters. This relationship was far from perfect. Eric Sevareid recorded that the

> correspondents' most violent dislike was reserved for a certain type of ex-journalist turned officer—frequently because he didn't like his job or his wife and was poor at getting on with either. These men had never been quite happy as journalists. . . . They suffered a fundamental contempt of their profession. To become an army officer, was to become a real, living, important person. Naturally, as officers, they regarded the war correspondents with contempt.[10]

Though Sevareid's description likely describes some PR officers, it is hardly a fitting verdict for Butcher, Oldfield, and the many other former reporters who worked hard making the war correspondents' lives easier. More significantly, many former newsmen were important staff officers for high-ranking generals. MacArthur had Carlos Romulo and Lloyd Lehrbas. Eisenhower had Harry Butcher. Bradley had Chester Hansen and Ralph Ingersoll. Patton had Robert Allen. Science reporter William Laurence was even borrowed from the *New York Times* to write press releases about the atomic bomb.[11] These relationships were forged between the military and the media by the expansion of the US military for total war.

Despite this integration of the media and military, this book supports the conclusion of historian Steven Casey that reporters were hardly the hapless cheerleaders of the military in World War II.[12] Despite layers of censorship, hardship, and patriotism, the American press remained free and a voice of debate and criticism. Roosevelt's 1944 election, for example, was the closest of his presidency, and his opponents in the press did not go silent.[13] In fact, SHAEF's censors cut only 1 percent of the 163 million words of news they reviewed between Overlord and the surrender of Nazi Germany.[14] The military also found itself under criticism. Eisenhower was vilified for the Darlan

Deal. Patton was lambasted for—among other scandals—slapping hospitalized soldiers, and the military in general was chastised for their handling of the story. During the battle of Normandy, the press used words such as "stalemate" and comparisons to World War I to describe the situation before the breakout.[15] Even the US Army's newspaper, the *Stars and Stripes*, published editorials critical of American officers.[16] To these examples can be added hundreds of smaller news stories that exposed waste or incompetence in the military.

Unlike the negative and dishonest military-media relationship portrayed by some historians, American military commanders generally tried to be as honest and forthright with reporters as secrecy allowed. Sir Francis de Guingand spoke for many when he wrote that he always tried to be "frank" with reporters since it was "no use being anything else with intelligent War Correspondents."[17] Fred Walker, commander of the Thirty-Sixth Division, lamented that censorship—though necessary—often hurt morale, and he observed that when censors "overemphasize the importance of the top command, to the exclusion of subordinate units, they are missing an opportunity to build both morale and loyalty of the civilian population to support the war."[18] Or, as Bradley explained, "The first object is to win the battle at the least cost of lives. But a close second, or third . . . was to let the people back home know what their kids were doing, and so that's why I think you owe a duty to the press, through them to the people back home, to keep them informed."[19] Ernie Pyle is usually seen as the voice of the ordinary soldier. But this overlooks how much support Pyle received from the high command to spread that view. The day before the Battle of the Bulge, Eisenhower wrote Pyle a long, supportive letter explaining that "I get so eternally tired of the general lack of understanding of what the infantry soldier endures that I have come to the conclusion that education along this one simple line might do a lot toward promoting future reluctance to engage in war. The difference between you and me in regard to the infantry problem is that you can express yourself eloquently upon it."[20] Pyle also was not against praising the brass. "Surely America made its two perfect choices in General Eisenhower and General Bradley," he wrote in one of his books.[21] These positive remarks stand in stark contrast to much past writing on the media-military relationship that suggests that militaries were put on earth to lie to reporters.[22]

There were, of course, always exceptions. Walter Bedell Smith once groused that he wanted to "shoot a lot" of reporters. But Smith liked few people and, as Butcher once noted, never understood press relations.[23] Reflecting on the trouble reporters had caused his boss, Patton's chief of staff, Hobart Gay, wrote that "it is a crime that newspaper people, particularly men whose standards are not high, can take it upon themselves, not only to try to ruin an individual, but also to react very adversely towards the success of the Armed effort of a great Nation."[24] Problems with the press even made Eisenhower claim the media were the "greatest menace of the war."[25] But such statements were usually said in anger and should not be mistaken for describing the overall military-media relationship. By the end of the war, even Admiral King had improved his relationship with the press.[26]

How does this media–military relationship fit into the larger scholarship on America's contribution to victory during World War II? Likewise, what role did the media have in creating the history of the war? These are two closely related questions and must be answered together. Journalists, either as former war correspondents or as former officers on a general's staff, were crucial for constructing the history of America's contribution to World War II. One significant example of this was Hansen's work as a ghostwriter for Omar Bradley's *A Soldier's Story*, while former war correspondent A. J. Liebling wrote the book's introduction.[27] Likewise, the diaries of Butcher, Hansen, and other former reporters would later be recognized as some of the best sources of the war. Yet the role of journalists in shaping the historiographical debates would be much more foundational. Ironically, these debates often left out the press's role in shaping America's contribution to final victory.

One of the first examples of journalists crafting the history of World War II paradoxically began with the last event of the war. "In the postwar period," writes historian Michael J. Yavenditti, "Americans not only approved the atomic bombings, they also became increasingly apathetic about the controversy regarding the bomb's use."[28] All this changed on August 31, 1946, when former war correspondent John Hersey wrote a story that filled the entire *New Yorker*, titled simply "Hiroshima." Recounting the horrific experience of six ordinary people in Hiroshima, the article was a huge success and was soon published as a book. For the first time, many Americans began questioning the use of the bomb, to such an extent that it goaded those involved in making the decision to respond. The most important of these defenses was by Henry Stimson, who wrote an article in *Harpers* titled: "The Decision To Use the Atomic Bomb." Though not making a direct response to Hersey, Stimson deftly justified the use of the bomb, and his explanation was generally accepted until the 1960s, when a new generation of historians arose to challenge his claims.[29] "But," as Yavenditti notes, "Hersey laid the groundwork for later assessments by posing the issue of atomic bombing from the standpoint of the human victims. . . . Hersey heightened American sensitivities and contributed to a continuing dialogue over the justification for atomic warfare."[30] Therefore, Hersey's article was the opening shot in one of the longest-lasting historical battles to emerge from World War II.[31]

Those former journalists who had been staff officers at Allied headquarters had the knowledge, literary talent, and inclination to write early histories of World War II. As Hersey was writing on the atomic bomb, Ralph Ingersoll, a former newsman who had been instrumental in the creation of *Life* magazine and New York's adless *PM* newspaper, published a book titled *Top Secret*. Ingersoll had been extremely pro-British and an interventionist before the United States entered the war. But his experience of working as an American staff officer in Britain increasingly soured him on the English. By the fall of 1944, he was already planning a book on British malfeasance.[32] Ingersoll extracted part of his revenge early by helping to construct Bradley's media counterattack against the notion that Montgomery had saved the Americans during the Battle of the Bulge.[33] *Top Secret* lambastes the British who "sought to destroy the armed forces of the Axis—but only by the employment of such strategy as would best further the highly complex economic and political interests of the British Empire." To do this, the British manipulated the Americans, with even George C. Marshall being "pushed around." Ingersoll also revealed shocking facts, such as Bradley's threat to resign instead of serving under Montgomery.[34] As historian Carlo D'Este wrote, *Top Secret* "created more public and private reaction than any other single account of the war: numerous documents in Britain and American archives attest to the anger felt on both sides of the Atlantic."[35] The book spurred other participants to write their memoirs.

Harry Butcher's *My Three Years with Eisenhower* followed closely after *Top Secret*. The book, based on Butcher's heavily edited wartime diary, was hardly hostile to Eisenhower or the British. But it certainly had embarrassing material for all involved. "Since the PM [Churchill] is short and blockily built, his chin isn't very much above the soup plate. He crouched over the plate, almost had his nose in the soup, wielded the spoon rapidly. The soup disappeared to the accompaniment of loud gurglings [*sic*]."[36] "My god!" wrote Eisenhower, next to this passage in the original transcript of Butcher's diary. Perhaps Butcher noticed and had the taste not to include the final line, which had Eisenhower demonstrating Churchill's soup consumption to his staff.[37] More significantly, Butcher related that during the dispute over the invasion of southern France, "Ike said that at his last meeting on Friday the PM [Churchill] had practically wept and, in fact, actually had rolled tears down his cheeks in arguing that the Americans were adopting a 'bullying' attitude against the British in failing to accept their, meaning primarily his, ideas as to grand strategy."[38] There was also plenty on Churchill's reluctance to consent to Operation Overlord. Even before it appeared in book form in 1946, *My Three Years with Eisenhower* had already been serialized in the *Saturday Evening Post* and had caused plenty of excitement.[39]

Both books provoked Eisenhower and Churchill to respond by not only defending the Grand Alliance but also arguing that it was the main contribution of the Western Allies to victory in World War II. Historian David Reynolds quotes Churchill's assertion that both books were "quite untrue and in some cases malicious."[40] Eisenhower was also embarrassed. "I have been much upset by the publication in the United States of a number of so-called 'war histories,' which have in some instances put me in a false light with respect to the relationships I had with my British associates of the war," he wrote Alan Brooke. He added, "Because Captain Butcher was my aide, there is a natural implication that I have had something to do either with the publication of his book."[41] In 1949, Eisenhower published *Crusade in Europe*, which argued that the war was won by the "near perfection in allied conduct of war operations" coupled with American might. "The true history of the war, and more especially the history of the operations Torch and Overlord, in the Mediterranean and northwest Europe, is the story of a unity produced on the basis of this voluntary co-operation," Eisenhower explained. There were differences, he admitted, "but these paled into insignificance alongside the miracle of achievement represented in the shoulder-to-shoulder march of the Allies to complete victory in the West."[42] The following year Churchill published *The Grand Alliance*, the third volume of his *Second World War*. Like Eisenhower, Churchill was clearly writing against Ingersoll's attacks on the British and Butcher's often less than tactful comments. In his study of Churchill's war memoirs, Reynolds traces Churchill's decision to start the project, in part, to the annoyance both books caused. Both *Crusade in Europe* and *The Second World War* would be enormously influential in guiding the later history of the war.[43]

Certainly, the Grand Alliance was an important part of the Western Allies' achievements in World War II. But as later scholarship would demonstrate, particularly after the declassification of documents, Ingersoll and Butcher had not invented Anglo-American tensions. Indeed, numerous books would question just how strong the alliance was.[44] Yet one perspective on this turbulent but essential partnership can be grasped by the media's paradoxical role in the relationship. For example, Eisenhower attempted to incorporate the media into his focus on building the Grand Alliance. His emphasis on giving each ally equal credit certainly helped. But it also infuriated many American officers and did not prevent national differences and public remarks critical of the other nation from appearing in the press. By the Battle of the Bulge, the media war between the Allies had reached crisis proportions. Nevertheless, it is doubtful that firing Montgomery, or Bradley resigning, would have disrupted the alliance enough to forestall Nazi Germany's defeat.

There were other reactions to the Ingersoll-Butcher dustup, and they came to be embodied in Australian war correspondent Chester Wilmot's *The Struggle for Europe*, a book shaped by Wilmot's friendship with the military writer and journalist B. H. Liddell Hart. Among other things, Liddell Hart was famous for advocating the "indirect approach" as opposed to frontal assaults in battle and for his interviews with captured German generals.[45] Facing an uncertain future, the former members of the German high command were busily distancing themselves from Hitler, and Liddell Hart's book reflected their defense. The General Staff "were essentially technicians, intent on their professional job," Liddell Hart wrote, "and with little idea of things outside it. It is easy to see how Hitler hoodwinked and handled them." Nevertheless, he concluded, the "German generals of this war were the best-finished product of their profession—anywhere."[46] By implication, they should have won. *The Struggle for Europe* was also influenced by Montgomery, who was angered by Ingersoll's criticism and the charge that he had failed to take Caen in a timely fashion. Since Montgomery was still a serving member of the British Army, he could not defend himself openly. Wilmot provided ammunition to argue that the Americans had never understood his Normandy plan.[47]

With these sources, *The Struggle for Europe* became the British defense of their actions during World War II. Wilmot wondered "how and why the Western Allies, while gaining military victory, suffered political defeat" and now confronted the Soviet Union. He concluded that the two biggest mistakes during the war were Hitler's invasion of the Soviet Union, which doomed the German Reich, and Roosevelt's miscalculation of Stalin's aggressive tendencies. American strategy, or lack thereof, made Roosevelt's mistake worse. George C. Marshall reflected American military tradition by fighting the war only for military victory and not for political advantage. Channeling Liddell Hart, Wilmot argued that this caused the Americans to insist on a direct invasion of Europe instead of the more careful strategy of the indirect approach favored by Churchill and the British. Failure to exploit the Balkans for an invasion of southern France allowed the Soviets to reach Berlin first. This was further ensured by the Western Allies' mistakes in the fall of 1944 to exploit the breakout from Normandy. The liberation of France, Wilmot argued, would have failed if not for the Soviets holding off the Germans in the east. Roosevelt's demand for unconditional surrender also lengthened the war because it hindered the resistance movement among the German high command.[48] Years later, Liddell Hart and Montgomery would make similar charges, the latter so vehemently that he enraged many of his former American colleagues.[49]

The Struggle for Europe laid the groundwork for future historical debates on Allied strategy during World War II. As this book argues, it was a debate that often left out the media's role in shaping strategy. For example, even if American military chiefs had believed continuing the Mediterranean strategy was a good idea, the media and public opinion would have hardly allowed them to continue an approach seen as hurtful for the Soviet Union and beneficial for the British Empire. The breakout from Normandy and the advance into Germany were also shaped, in part, by media considerations, as chapters 5 and 6 demonstrate. Likewise, as Steven Casey has shown, unconditional surrender was driven by public opinion and the reaction to the Darlan Deal.[50]

Wilmot, Liddell Hart, and Liddell Hart's new German friends likewise laid the groundwork for one of the most popular explanations of the United States' contribution to victory in World War II. If the war was decided in the Soviet Union and the German generals were much better professionals than the hapless American strategists, did the United States really contribute greatly to the victory? The assumption that American combat units were of low quality compared with their German equivalents also drove this question. It was an assumption further supported in the 1970s by S. L. A. Marshall, a former reporter turned official military historian for the US Army, who claimed that most American soldiers had rarely fired their rifles during the war.[51] The conclusion reached by many historians was that the US military's contribution had been of minor significance and the most important service performed by the United States was supplying the Allies.[52] What success the US Army had achieved came not from skill but from firepower and over-whelming material advantage. Or, as Russell F. Weigley argued, the United States "rumbled to victory because it had enough material resources to spare that it could exhaust the enemy's resources even without adequately focusing its own power for a decisive, head-on battle of annihilation, or exploiting its mobility in behalf of a consistent strategy of indirect approach."[53] The same was true at sea. As Craig L. Symonds recently explained, American production created a huge navy that won the war.[54] "Bravery did not win or lose World War II," explains historian Phillips Payson O'Brien. "Air and sea power did" because the Allies had more and better weapons.[55] In this view, the United States contributed to total war in the factory, not the battlefield.

Such an explanation obviously has much truth to it. American production had placed a heavy thumb on the Allies' side of the scales of victory. But was it the only contribution? The same materialist explanation could be used to explain the victory of the United States in the Vietnam War in the 1960s and the Soviet Union's successful occupation of Afghanistan in the 1980s—except that both nations lost these wars to materially weaker foes. "We sometimes forget, I think, that you can manufacture weapons, and you can purchase ammunition," mused a World War II sergeant years after the war, "but you can't buy valor and you can't pull heroes off an assembly line."[56] Matériel is easier for historians to calculate than spiritual factors. But man does not live on bread alone during war any more than he does in peace.

Nor should superiority in resources be confused with an abundance of supplies. No Allied theater of the war was ever without complaints about a lack of resources. As chapter 2 shows, MacArthur and Nimitz campaigned for supplies in the Pacific. The Italian campaign was hampered by a lack of material support.[57] Stillwell's China-Burma-India Theater perhaps suffered the worst shortages of all. Even the European Theater of Operations, which had priority particularly around Overlord, endured major supply shortages. "American commanders in Europe rarely possessed the numerical superiority the revisionists claim overwhelmed the Wehrmacht in 1944 and 1945," concludes historian Peter Mansoor. "Indeed, American commanders, strapped to maintain their divisions at something [not] even approaching full strength, would have resisted the notion that they overwhelmed their adversaries with sheer number or material superiority."[58] There were many reasons for these shortages. First, supplies went to Britain and the United States but also to the Soviet Union, China, and the other allies. Second, American production had to be shipped across an ocean to be deployed against the enemy. Unlike the Axis, the Allies were waging a coordinated global war. The media contributed to the worldwide connectivity of the war by allowing commanders to campaign for resources in the press. As chapter 2 demonstrates, none did this more effectively than Douglas MacArthur.

By the 1990s, a new explanation of America's contribution to World War II was being advocated, which rehabilitated the US Army's fighting power and challenged the materialist explanation of Allied victory. Anchorman Tom Brokaw—born in 1940—gave it a name in his book *The Greatest Generation*, and historian Stephen Ambrose supplied its clearest articulation in *Citizen Soldiers*. Ambrose argued that though the traditional answer of why GIs fought in battle was unit cohesion, in World War II GIs were much less interested in cause and country than what historian James McPherson found of their predecessors in the American Civil War. "And yet there is something more," Ambrose concluded. "Although the GIs were and are embarrassed to talk or write about the cause they fought for . . . they were the children of democracy." He added, "American citizen soldiers knew the difference between right and wrong, and they didn't want to live in a world in which wrong prevailed." In other words, America's "Greatest Generation" achieved victory because democracy bred better soldiers than dictatorship.[59] At the same time, Ambrose could make this argument since *Citizen Soldiers* was one of several books, including those of John Sloan Brown, Peter Mansoor, and John C. McManus, that were challenging the misconception of the quality of American fighting efficiency during World War II.[60]

Studying the military-media relationship during World War II adds clarity to the "Greatest Generation" argument. First, as chapter 3 shows, American commanders were greatly concerned with both motivating and connecting with their soldiers. The media offered a way for commanders to inspire bravery and improve morale. Second, because it was a citizen army, public opinion had a bearing on commanders' decisions. As George C. Marshall noted, "A citizen army can vote, and it can get the attention of the press and the attention of Congress in a moment. . . . That was great political power."[61] Since the US Army was filled with citizen-soldiers produced by a democracy, Eisenhower, Bradley, Patton, and other American commanders were obsessed with their soldiers' getting press credit. They knew it helped the war effort at the front and at home. It was another important necessity for a democracy fighting a total war.

Historian Max Hastings once observed that a person's actions during World War II could shape the rest of their lives.[62] So it was for the generals who commanded US armies in World War II and for the reporters who covered them. But it was also true for the US military as an institution. In the years following World War II, the ability and freedom of reporters to cover conflict drastically increased. This was largely enabled by the military, which took as one of the lessons of World War II that the media were an essential element in modern warfare. Despite this, the relationship grew much more contentious. The reason for this was simple: neither side saw the other fulfilling the role they had played during World War II. Usually, this is explained by pointing to the fact that World War II was popular and later wars were not. Yet this ignores the harsh debate in the United States in the lead-up to Pearl Harbor, the fact that the opposition was still active, and the fact that the United States was not as united as is often remembered. In fatalities, World War II was vastly more deadly than the Korean and Vietnam wars combined. In many ways, the war proved an exception. A total war with straightforward objectives and cartoonish evil opponents was easy to sell, easy to cover, and easy to explain. The limited wars that followed were none of these things. In the end, the media–military relationship built for the total war of World War II did not transfer well to limited wars.

Some commanders adjusted to the postwar media better than others. Patton did not last a month after Japan's surrender. His reputation fell victim to his opposition to denazification, hostile reporters, and loosening of censorship rules.[63] He died in December 1945 of injuries from a car crash. MacArthur prospered until the Korean War, when his opposition to Truman was made public in the press and—in an eerie repetition of the 1944 electoral campaign—his private letters were read in Congress.[64] Others fared better. Bradley skillfully used the press as the head of the Veterans Administration and later as chairman of the Joint Chiefs of Staff. Eisenhower's press experience helped him become the first "TV President."[65] Clark signed the armistice in Korea, retired from the army to run the Citadel, and spent a lot of time sending out signed photographs of himself. Alexander tried and failed in politics. Montgomery became chief of the Imperial General Staff, then NATO's deputy chief Allied commander Europe, and continued to use the media to irritate others.[66] In the long run, it thus appears that Brian Linn's "Managers" handled the media more successfully than those officers in the "Warrior" category.

This mixed record is not to say that the military had not absorbed the lessons of public relations from World War II. Writing directly after the war, de Guingand warned, "It is more important than ever to ensure that we have first-rate men leading our Services, and if possible men with a public reputation. This is because political pressure and public clamour are so liable in the early stages of a war to force us into unsound military ventures." To counter this tendency, he suggested "maximum frankness compatible with security and by well informed press comment, to prevent the public pressing for action that is not in our best interests."[67] Eisenhower wrote after the war, "Among all the contemporary skills with which a soldier these days must concern himself, not the least important is public relations—a phrase almost unknown to the Army and a profession little practiced by it until World War II. That ignorance or negligence may be one reason why at the end of every war the Army was a budgetary stepchild."[68] Indeed, the battles for the budget drove all the services of the US military to actively create postwar public relations operations as the American armed forces were restructured to fight the Cold War.[69]

It was World War II, however, that made the media an important part of the US military. General Albert C. Wedemeyer, one of the chief American planners during the war, argued that strategy needed to take account of the four weapons of the "political, economic, psychological, and military resources." By "psychological" Wedemeyer meant both "overt and covert propaganda."[70] During the war, General Surles had successfully maneuvered the War Department's Bureau of Public Relations into an independent organization. It was later renamed the Public Information Division. In late 1945, the Board of Officers on Reorganization of the War Department advocated that the Public Information Division, the Congressional Division, and the Army Information and Education Division be placed under a single "Director of Information" to "translate public opinion into legislative action."[71] In 1946, Theodore F. Koop, who worked as a special assistant to the director in the US Office of Censorship during the war, advocated that press relations be taught at the service academies.[72] At the War College, meanwhile, diplomat George Kennan was explaining that psychological factors were never "separate from the rest of diplomacy. They consist not only of direct informational activity like propaganda, or radio broadcast, or distribution of magazines. They consist also of the study and understanding of the psychological effects of anything which the modern state does in the war, both internal and external."[73] Unlike Kennan, many in the State Department were unconvinced of the value of information as a weapon. The military proved more helpful, with the assistant secretary of state for public affairs, William Benton, writing that "I have run into no one in the State Department with an understanding of this problem comparable to that already shown by General [George] Marshall, as well as by

Generals [Dwight] Eisenhower and [Walter] Bedell Smith." All three would later support the 1948 US Information and Education Exchange Act allowing American propaganda to be distributed in foreign nations.[74] When Bradley became chief of staff of the army, he made sure to put his ideas of public relations into practice. In particular, he understood that American soldiers had to be kept informed to make them efficient fighters.[75] Though the OWI was disbanded at the close of World War II, Voice of America broadcasting, begun in 1942, continued. It was joined a few years later by the Central Intelligence Agency's broadcasting networks aimed at communist countries.[76] Therefore, the idea that press relations during World War II were a weapon for waging war was important for the postwar US military as well.[77]

The press also drew conclusions from the war. For decades, the American media were led by journalists who had World War II as a formative experience. By the 1960s, former war correspondent Hal Boyle's column was printed in eight hundred newspapers. Bill Mauldin would continue drawing—sometimes well—after the war, but both his personal and professional lives were messy and never as successful as during World War II. Walter Cronkite became an anchorman for CBS and helped Andy Rooney become a broadcaster on *60 Minutes*.[78] Eric Sevareid also had a long career at CBS.[79] Most telling of all was Edward R. Murrow. After retiring from anchoring the CBS news, he served as the equivalent of a Cold War PRO and became the director of the US Information Agency. "I have never worked harder in my life and never been happier," he wrote on leaving the USIA. "I haven't had such satisfaction since the days of covering the London blitz."[80] Many of these reporters had pushed for the United States to enter World War II or at least believed in the cause deeply. Though not the lapdogs of generals or PRO colonels, they identified closely with the military. It was a view that would be severely challenged in the coming decades.

Thus, it came to pass that both journalists and generals entered the era of limited war with views of a military-media relationship created by total war. The Korean War quickly showed how difficult covering a limited war could be. The Truman administration failed to sell the war effectively. The reasons for American involvement were difficult to explain, the objectives shifted, and it was harder to paint the enemy as cartoon villains.[81] At the front, Douglas MacArthur, now the commander of United Nations forces, at first refused to impose censorship and instead provided guidelines for war correspondents. Unfortunately, reporters were often confused about what information could be published, while public information officers (PIOs) were so worried about secrecy that they refused to give much useful information.[82] Nevertheless, the military still complained that much classified information was appearing in the press. The situation became so bad that eventually the war correspondents demanded some form of censorship.[83] When censorship was finally enacted it worsened press relations since the new rules were imposed quickly and without much warning. Nor did it help that MacArthur and his staff began to see reporters as hostile to the war effort. The PIOs spent much of the war trying to repair the shattered press relations.[84] Before that happened, Truman did what Roosevelt never dared and fired MacArthur because of statements made in the press and read in Congress. Self-censorship was reinstated by General Matthew Ridgway after MacArthur's dismissal.[85] MacArthur was not the only press casualty of the Korean War. By 1952 the war was stalemated and increasingly unpopular, and was destroying the Truman Administration.[86] The war in Korea was a bad omen for the media-military relationship in limited wars.

It was the Vietnam War that brought the breakdown of the relationship between reporters and soldiers. As the war progressed with no sight of victory, members of the media repeatedly felt that the military was lying to them by presenting an optimistic picture of the war.[87] The military, for their part, saw negative or incorrect reporting as sapping the national will to achieve victory.

The 1968 Tet Offensive highlighted both these points. Before Tet, President Lyndon B. Johnson and General William Westmoreland, the commander of the ground war in Vietnam, had predicted very publicly that the war was being won. The massive attack shattered what trust many journalists had in the military or Lyndon Johnson's administration.[88] For many in the military, the negative press reports, which ignored that Tet was a massive military defeat for the communists, destroyed the national will to win in Vietnam. Some journalists have also joined this view.[89] But scholars have cast considerable doubt on this accusation, noting that public support for the war actually increased during and after Tet.[90] What both sides often overlook is that public opinion mattered less than what policy makers *believed* public opinion to be. As William M. Hammond writes, the "pessimism appearing in the press [after Tet] had more of an effect on Washington officials than it did on the American public opinion."[91] David F. Schmitz disagrees with this view, arguing Johnson was not persuaded to change course because of the news coverage of Tet, but because of his advisers—the Wise Men—who lost faith in the war after the battle because of their own information.[92] But Johnson's account of the meeting shows how the press shaped the Wise Men's impression. Johnson wrote:

I knew this group had not been reading the detailed reports on Vietnam each day, as I and my advisers had, but they were intelligent, experienced men. . . . If they had been so deeply influenced by the [news] reports of the Tet offensive, what must the average citizen in the country be thinking? . . .

I remained convinced that the blow to morale was more of our own doing than anything the enemy had accomplished with its army.[93]

The media coverage of Tet had damaged elite confidence, not public opinion.

The nature of conflict and the military-media setup had changed from World War II. The United States saw Vietnam as a limited war. As such, its strategic objectives and the way to attain victory were much harder to explain to reporters and a public who had World War II as their major reference point. Nor was the process for transmitting such information conducive to victory. There was no censorship by the US military during the Vietnam War. Instead, reporters were expected to exercise voluntary censorship of secret information.[94] But this made military officers more guarded on what they told reporters and much more eager to place a positive spin on even clearly bad news. This is a point highlighted by Phillip Knightley, who quotes World War II correspondent Drew Middleton's observation that "as long as all copy was submitted to censors before transmission, people in the field from generals down, felt free to discuss top secret material with reporters. On three trips to Vietnam I found generals and everyone else far more wary of talking to reporters precisely because there was no censorship."[95] The contrast was highlighted by Bradley when he was asked what accounted for the good relationship that he had with correspondents during World War II as opposed to the military-media's experience during the Vietnam War. He responded that he had been able to be "perfectly frank with the press" and had confidence that they would not divulge any secrets.[96] Bradley and other generals were free to confide in reporters because they knew layers of accreditation and censorship protected military secrets.

This was not the case in Vietnam, and it fed the natural skepticism of the media. It was also reflected in reporting. Daniel C. Hallin notes Vietnam was not only the first war without censorship, it was also the first war where "journalists clearly did not think of themselves simply as 'soldiers of the typewriter' whose mission was to serve the war effort." He adds that this manifested itself in the reporting, noting that when college "students [were] asked to compare typical news reporting from Vietnam and World War II [they] often observe that the reporting from Vietnam seems, as one put it, like they 'aren't really sure what they're talking about.'" Hallin argues this came from World War II coming "without sourcing" while journalists covering Vietnam used unnamed sources.[97] An alternative explanation is that the sources for covering Vietnam were now afraid to confide to reporters in an environment without censorship.

Certainly, many in the military felt betrayed by the American press. A survey found 89 percent of American generals had a negative feeling about the press, while 91 percent had a negative view of television. Likewise, they generally believed that the media had turned American support from the war.[98] "The camera, the typewriter, the tape recorder are very effective weapons in this war—weapons too often directed not against the enemy, but against the American people," stated marine general Lewis W. Walt.[99] During World War II, Patton argued that positive news stories about soldiers would improve morale since family and friends on the home front would write and tell them about it. Historian Peter S. Kindsvatter's study of American soldiers showed that in the later years of Vietnam the inverse was also true. He writes that antiwar news from the states denouncing American soldiers appeared in "letters from friends and family reflecting little pride in the soldier and his accomplishments, simply urging instead that he avoid the vices and dangers of Vietnam."[100]

Likewise, Omar Bradley spoke for many in the military in a 1970s interview when he made the comparison between how the two wars were covered, wherein he recalled that the World War II reporters were "a great bunch, and in my opinion much better than the correspondents that we had in Vietnam, and I saw both groups."[101] What Bradley overlooked was that in many cases they were the same correspondents. Hal Boyle and Homer Bigart, who both won Pulitzer Prizes for their reporting of World War II, covered the early years of the United States' commitment to Vietnam and quickly became disenchanted with the war. It is true that there were far more younger reporters covering the conflict than World War II news veterans. But they were still influenced by the older newsmen. Bigart, for example, helped mentor Peter Arnett, Neil Sheehan, David Halberstam, and others who became famous for their reporting during Vietnam. The best example of this influence was the former World War II correspondent Walter Cronkite. After a brief visit to Vietnam in February 1968—during the Tet Offensive—Cronkite famously questioned the United States' policy in Vietnam. After hearing Cronkite's remarks, Johnson is supposed to have said, "If I've lost Cronkite, I've lost America."[102]

What had changed by 1968 was the ethos and structure of the media. If *Time*'s Theodore White attacked Chiang Kai-shek during World War II, the pro-Chiang editor Whittaker Chambers was there to revise White's articles, backed up by the magazine's owner, Henry Luce.[103] By the 1960s, the give and take of reporter—often liberal—and editor—likely conservative—had vanished. Television instead made journalists like Murrow and Cronkite powerful opinion leaders. In print media, figures like Hearst, Luce, or the "McCormick-Patterson Axis" that Roosevelt so despised no longer dominated the editorial positions of their publications. Their power was assumed by the reporters, often liberal in politics, progressive in opinion, and—before the last shot was fired in Vietnam—distrustful of the United States' government.[104] An important tension in the crafting of news was gone.

Despite being known as the "TV war," the Vietnam War was not broadcast live from the battlefield. Live reporting of combat began not in the Gulf War, but with the destruction of a leftwing terrorist group inside the United States. The Symbionese Liberation Army (SLA) was a small organization and did little damage. It's "accomplishments" by the time most of the group was cornered in an SLA slum were to rob a bank, shoot up an outdoors sporting goods store, assassinate the first African American school board superintendent of Oakland, California, and kidnap Patricia Hearst. As the latter crime demonstrates, the SLA was obsessed with publicity and the world was watching—literally—when the LAPD and the FBI began a brutal firefight that ended with the incineration of several SLA members. KNXT, a local news channel, was utilizing a new technology that used a microwave transmitter on a truck to broadcast live from the firefight.[105] When the nation watched as the house fortress was consumed in flames, KNXT had made a revolutionary step in live combat news coverage.

The ability to broadcast in real time did not make the military any happier about having war correspondents covering the first Gulf War. To improve public relations, the military studied media policy for World War II, Korea, and Vietnam but concluded that the conflict was much different and needed a different press policy. To the media's collective fury, war correspondents were kept well chaperoned. Saddam Hussein's decision to allow CNN and American journalists to stay in Bagdad, nevertheless, provided live reporting of the bombing.[106] This provided not only excellent visual coverage of the conflict but opportunities for Iraqi propaganda. There were concerns, too, about whether the visual images of the Gulf War would hurt support for the conflict or influence policy makers. One example of this came as Iraqi army divisions fled Kuwait and were caught in the open by the US Air Force. Labeled the "Highway of Death" by the press, the televised devastation provoked a call from Washington to the coalition commander, H. Norman Schwarzkopf, informing him that the White House was getting nervous that public opinion might find the destruction excessive and suggesting that they start thinking about an armistice. This "irritated" Schwarzkopf, who concluded that "Washington was ready to overreact, as usual, to the slightest ripple in public opinion. I thought, but didn't say, that the best thing the White House could do would be to turn off the damned TV in the situation room."[107] In the years after the war, there was much scholarship on whether the "CNN Effect" influenced policy decisions during both the Gulf War and the peacekeeping operations in the 1990s. No consensus was reached among scholars.[108] The CEOs of the defense industries came to their own conclusions. Lockheed's Advanced Development Projects—more commonly known as Skunk Works—began researching unmanned weapons systems such as drones, foreseeing that public opinion would demand low casualties in future wars.[109]

The War on Terror demonstrated that the media is still a potent weapon for limited war. By its nature terrorism thrives on media attention, since its only hope of achieving its political end is to persuade policy makers that the terrorists' demands are worth the cessation of violence. The changes brought by social media and phone cameras have magnified the power of media. No longer need a reporter and a cameraman be present for news to be filmed and broadcast to the world. Now every soldier is his or her own reporter. As Emile Simpson notes in his study of the changing nature of twenty-first-century conflict, "War today is in the process of undergoing another evolution in response to social and political conditions, namely the speed and interconnectivity associated with contemporary globalization and the information revolution."[110] The effect of this new media is only heightened if terrorism is part of an insurgency campaign since it places counter-insurgent forces in a difficult position. Attempting to win the "hearts and minds" of local populations when every misstep is destined for YouTube causes traditional military forces to tread carefully. An example of this was General Stanley McChrystal's reluctance to use effective airpower because he believed it could do more political damage to the United States than to the Afghani insurgence.[111] A full assessment of the media deployment in modern war is worthy of another book. Nevertheless, these few observations suggest that the media's role in future conflicts will only grow.

The United States military appears to be aware of this and devotes many resources to public relations. There have been significant improvements. Harkening back to World War II, journalists were "embedded" in coalition units before Operation Iraqi Freedom was launched. Living and working closely with units made reporters focus on soldiers, and they generally reported positively on the military.[112] The result was that the military still had high public approval in an unpopular war. The relationship is not perfect, with plenty of distrust on both sides. But the success of embedding suggests that the total-war model of the media-military relationship begun during World War II still contains lessons and relevance for limited—and not so limited—wars of the twenty-first century.

Abbreviations Used in the Notes

CHP	Chester Hansen Papers, US Army Heritage and Education Center, Carlisle, Pennsylvania
CSP	Carl Spaatz Papers, Manuscript Division, Library of Congress, Washington, DC
DDEL	Eisenhower Presidential Library, Abilene, Kansas
DEC	Donald E. Currier Papers, US Army Heritage and Education Center, Carlisle, Pennsylvania
FDRL	Franklin D. Roosevelt Presidential Library, Hyde Park, New York
EJK	Ernest J. King Papers, Manuscript Division, Library of Congress, Washington, DC
ESHP	Everett Strait Hughes Papers, Manuscript Division, Library of Congress, Washington, DC
GCK	Diaries of General George C. Kenney, USAAC, 1941–1945, MacArthur Memorial Library and Archives, Norfolk, Virginia
GFE	George Fielding Eliot Papers, Manuscript Division, Library of Congress, Washington, DC
GSPP	George S. Patton Jr. Papers, Manuscript Division, Library of Congress, Washington, DC
HCB	Harry C. Butcher Papers, Eisenhower Presidential Library, Abilene, Kansas
HHAPAF	Henry Harley "Hap" Arnold Papers, Archives Branch, Air Force Historical Research Agency, Maxwell AFB, Alabama
HHAPLC	Henry Harley Arnold Papers, Manuscript Division, Library of Congress, Washington, DC
HLSD	Henry Lewis Stimson Diary (microfilm), Sterling Library, Yale University, New Haven, Connecticut
HP	Harry L. Hopkins Papers, Franklin D. Roosevelt Presidential Library, Hyde Park, New York
HRG	Hobart R. Gay Papers, US Army Heritage and Education Center, Carlisle, Pennsylvania
HVP	History Vault, ProQuest
Index	General Headquarters, Southwest Pacific Area, 1941-1945 Chronological Index and Summary of Communications
JBL	Justus Baldwin Lawrence Papers, Eisenhower Presidential Library, Abilene, Kansas

JHDP	James H. Doolittle Papers, Manuscript Division, Library of Congress, Washington, DC
JLDP	Jacob L. Devers Papers, US Army Heritage and Education Center, Carlisle, Pennsylvania
JPL	John P. Lucas Papers, US Army Heritage and Education Center, Carlisle, Pennsylvania
LOC	Library of Congress, Manuscript Division, Washington, DC
MML	MacArthur Memorial Library and Archives, Norfolk, Virginia
MRP	Franklin D. Roosevelt Papers as President: FDR Map Room Papers, 1941–1945, (online) http://www.fdrlibrary.marist.edu/archives/collections/franklin/?p=collections/findingaid&id=511
NARA	US National Archives, College Park, Maryland
ONBC	Omar N. Bradley Collection, at both USMA and USAHEC. (When I consulted the Omar Bradley papers at USAHEC during 2018 they were in the process of being reorganized, so cited box numbers may have been changed.)
PPPF	Pre-Presidential Papers, Principal File (Eisenhower), Eisenhower Presidential Library, Abilene, Kansas
PSF	The President's Secretary's File, 1933–1945, Franklin D. Roosevelt Presidential Library, Hyde Park, New York
RG	Record Group
SHN	Sidney H. Negrotto Papers, US Army Heritage and Education Center, Carlisle, Pennsylvania
STE	Stephen T. Early Papers, Franklin D. Roosevelt Presidential Library, Hyde Park, New York
TMSP	Thor M. Smith Papers, Eisenhower Presidential Library, Abilene, Kansas
TNA	National Archives, UK, Kew Gardens, London
USAHEC	US Army Heritage and Education Center, Carlisle, Pennsylvania
USMA	US Military Academy at West Point, New York
WDL	William D. Leahy Papers, Manuscript Division, Library of Congress, Washington, DC

Introduction

1. US Army, "Maj. Gen. Alexander Day Surles," *U.S. Army Public Affairs Hall of Fame Inductees*, accessed January 25, 2020, https://www.army.mil/publicAffairs/halloffame/?from=pa_ad.

2. Chester J. Pach Jr., "'Our Worst Enemy Seems to be the Press': TV News, the Nixon Administration, and U.S. Troop Withdrawal from Vietnam, 1969–1973," *Diplomatic History* 34, no. 3 (June 2010): 555–565; Daniel C. Hallin, "The 'Living-Room War' Media and Public Opinion in a Limited War," in *Rolling Thunder in a Gentle Land*, ed. Andrew Wiest (Oxford: Osprey Publishing, 2006), 276–278. Both Pach and Hallin give examples of this reasoning and show the extent to which officials in government, and Americans more generally, propelled or believed the argument.

3. Hallin, "The 'Living-Room War,'" 278; William M. Hammond, *Public Affairs: The Military and the Media, 1962–1969* (Washington, DC: Center of Military History United States Army, 1988), 389; William M. Hammond, *Public Affairs: The Military and the Media, 1968–1973* (Washington, DC: Center of Military History United States Army, 1996), 626–627. See also Pach, "'Our Worst Enemy Seems to be the Press,'" 565; Michael S. Sweeney, *The Military and the Press: An Uneasy Truce* (Evanston, IL: Northwestern University Press, 2006), 149; Alan Hooper, *The Military and the Media* (Hant, England: Gower Publishing, 1982), 219; Chester J. Pach Jr., "The War on Television: TV News, the Johnson Administration, and Vietnam," in *A Companion to the Vietnam War*, ed. Marilyn B. Young and Robert Buzzanco (Oxford: Blackwell Publishing, 2002), 464.

4. See, for example, Piers Robinson, *The CNN Effect: The Myth of News, Foreign Policy and Intervention* (New York: Routledge, 2002); Warren P. Strobel, *Late-Breaking Foreign Policy: The News Media's Influence on Peace Operations* (Washington, DC: United States Institute of Peace Press, 1997), 5.

5. Three of the most useful broad histories of war reporting are found in Phillip Knightley, *The First Casualty: From the Crimea to Vietnam: The War Correspondent as Hero, Propagandist, and Myth Maker* (New York: Harcourt Brace Jovanovich, 1975); John Hohenberg, *Foreign Correspondence: The Great Reporters and Their Times* (Syracuse, NY: Syracuse University Press, 1995); and Sweeney, *The Military and the Press*. Selected studies that examine war reporting during World War II are Robert W. Desmond, *Tides of War: World News Reporting 1931–1945* (Iowa City: University of Iowa Press, 1982); Richard Collier, *The Warcos: The War Correspondents of World War Two* (London: Weidenfeld and Nicolson, 1989), published in the United States as *Fighting Words;* Stanley Cloud and Lynne Olson, *The Murrow Boys: Pioneers on the Front Lines of Broadcast Journalism* (Boston: Houghton Mifflin, 1996); Philip Seib, *Broadcasts from the Blitz: How Edward R. Murrow Helped Lead America into War* (Washington, DC: Potomac Books, 2006); Timothy M. Gay, *Assignment to Hell: The War against Nazi Germany with Correspondents Walter Cronkite, Andy Rooney, A. J. Liebling, Homer Bigart, and Hal Boyle* (New York: Penguin Group, 2012); Ray Moseley, *Reporting War: How Foreign Correspondents Risked Capture, Torture and Death to Cover World War II* (New Haven, CT: Yale University Press, 2017); Steven Casey, *The War Beat, Europe: The American Media at War against Nazi Germany* (Oxford: Oxford University Press, 2017).

6. See for example, George H. Roeder Jr., *The Censored War: American Visual Experience during World War Two* (New Haven, CT: Yale University Press, 1993); Jeffery A. Smith, *War and Press Freedom: The Problem of Prerogative Power* (Oxford: Oxford University Press, 1999); Michael S. Sweeney, *Secrets of Victory: The Office of Censorship and the American Press and Radio in World War II* (Chapel Hill: University of North Carolina Press, 2001). For an excellent article on this subject see John McCallum, "U.S. Censorship, Violence, and Moral Judgement in a Wartime Democracy, 1941–1945," *Diplomatic History* 41, no. 3 (2017): 543–566.

7. For more on the new history of war reporting see my article "Meade and the Media: Civil War Journalism and the New History of War Reporting," *Journal of Military History* 85, no. 4 (October 2021): 907–929.

8. Richard W. Steele, *The First Offensive 1942: Roosevelt, Marshall and the Making of American Strategy* (Bloomington: Indiana University Press, 1973).

9. Steven Casey, *Cautious Crusade: Franklin D. Roosevelt, American Public Opinion, and the War against Nazi Germany* (Oxford: Oxford University Press, 2001).

10. Charles F. Brower, *Defeating Japan: The Joint Chiefs of Staff and Strategy in the Pacific War, 1943–1945* (New York: Palgrave Macmillan, 2012), 151.

11. Casey, *The War Beat, Europe*. As *The Media Offensive* was going to press, Casey published an excellent companion volume titled *The War Beat, Pacific: The American Media at War Against Japan* (Oxford: Oxford University Press, 2021).

12. Nicholas Evan Sarantakes, "Warriors of Word and Sword: The Battle of Okinawa, Media Coverage, and Truman's Reevaluation of Strategy in the Pacific," *Journal of American–East Asian Relations* 23, no. 4 (2016): 334–367; P. M. H. Bell, "War, Foreign Policy and Public Opinion: Britain and the Darlan Affair, November–December 1942," *Journal of Strategic Studies* 5, no. 3 (1982): 393–415, reproduced in *The Second World War*, vol. 7, *Alliance Politics and Grand Strategy*, ed. Jeremy Black (Hampshire, UK: Ashgate Publishing, 2007), 139–415.

13. Robert M. Citino, "Military Histories Old and New: A Reintroduction," *American Historical Review* 112, no. 4 (October 2007): 1071.

14. Cyril Radcliffe to R. A. McClure, February 7, 1944, letter, and R. A. McClure to Cyril Radcliffe, February 9, 1944, letter, Box 1, Folder 0007-1, SHAEF, Special Staff, Public Relations Division, Executive Branch, Decimal File 1943–45, Record Group 331, NARA.

15. Omar N. Bradley, interview by Chester B. Hansen and Kitty Buhler Bradley, Box 1, Folder 11, ONBC, USAHEC.

16. Casey, *The War Beat*, 3, 347, and 352. Richard A. Fine has made a similar point in two recent articles. See Richard A. Fine, "'Snakes in Our Midst': The Media, the Military and American Policy toward Vichy North Africa," *American Journalism* 27 no. 4 (2010): 59–82; Richard A. Fine, "Edward Kennedy's Long Road to Reims: The Media and the Military in World War II," *American Journalism* 33, no. 3 (2016): 317–339.

17. David M. Jordan, *FDR, Dewey, and the Election of 1944* (Bloomington: Indiana University Press, 2011), 321.

18. Entry 21.7.1942, Joseph Goebbels, *Die Tagebücher von Joseph Goebbels*, ed. Elke Fröhlich (Munich: K. G. Saur, 1995), Teil II, Brand, 160, quoted in Nigel Hamilton, *The Mantle of Command: FDR at War 1941–1942* (Boston: Houghton Mifflin Harcourt, 2014), 317–318.

19. George C. Marshall, quoted in Maurice Matloff, "Allied Strategy in Europe, 1939–1945," in *Makers of Modern Strategy from Machiavelli to the Nuclear Age*, ed. Peter Paret (Princeton, NJ: Princeton University Press, 1986), 681.

20. George C. Marshall, *George C. Marshall Interviews and Reminiscences for Forrest C. Pogue*, ed. Larry I. Bland and Joellen K. Bland (Lexington, VA: George C. Marshall Research Foundation, 1991), 622.

21. I am indebted to the University of Southern California philosophy professor the Reverend Dallas Willard (PhD) for directing me to Tarski's theory of truth, on which the above sentence is based. Dallas Willard, "Truth: Can We Do

without It?," Dallas Willard, accessed April 2, 2020, http://www.dwillard.org/articles/individual/truth-can-we-do-without-it.

22. Christopher Butler, *Postmodernism: A Very Short Introduction* (Oxford: Oxford University Press, 2002), 110–112; Norman J. Wilson, *History in Crisis? Recent Directions in Historiography*, 2nd ed. (Upper Saddle River, NJ: Pearson, 2005), 126.

23. Joseph Goebbels, *The Goebbels Diaries: 1942–1943*, trans. Louis P. Lochner (Garden City, NY: 1948), 239, 457, and 458.

24. Matome Ugaki, *Fading Victory: The Diary of Admiral Matome Ugaki 1941–1945*, ed. Donald M. Goldstein and Katherine V. Dillon, trans. Masataka Chihaya (Annapolis, MD: Naval Institute Press, 1991), 57–58.

25. Robert Eichelberger, *Dear Miss Em: General Eichelberger's War in the Pacific, 1942–1945*, ed. Jay Luvaas (Westport, CT: Greenwood Press, 1972), 96. This view should not be overstated. As one study of Japanese propaganda against Australia notes, most of it was untrue. See L. D. Meo, *Japan's Radio War on Australia 1941–1945* (London: Melbourne University Press, 1968), 1.

26. Steven Casey, *When Soldiers Fall: How Americans Have Confronted Combat Losses from World War I to Afghanistan* (Oxford: Oxford University Press, 2014), 48.

27. Roeder, *The Censored War*, 10–11.

28. Casey, *The War Beat*, 85 and 163.

29. See Gerhard L. Weinberg, *A World at Arms: A Global History of World War II* (Cambridge: Cambridge University Press, 1994); Mark A. Stoler, *Allies and Adversaries: The Joint Chiefs of Staff, the Grand Alliance, and U.S. Strategy in World War II* (Chapel Hill: University of North Carolina Press, 2000); Jeremy Black, "Midway and the Indian Ocean," *Naval War College Review* 62, no. 4 (2009): 131–140; Craig L. Symonds, *World War II at Sea: A Global History* (Oxford: Oxford University Press, 2018).

30. Omar Bradley, interview by George S. Pappas, August 14, 1969, Box 1, Folder 8, ONBC, USAHEC.

31. Marshall, *Marshall Interviews and Reminiscences*, 486.

32. Eisenhower to Charles Kenon Gailey Jr., January 1, 1943, letter, in Dwight Eisenhower, *The Papers of Dwight David Eisenhower*, vol. 2, *The War Years*, ed. Alfred D. Chandler Jr. (Baltimore, MD: Johns Hopkins Press, 1970), 883; Dwight Eisenhower to Edgar Eisenhower, February 18, 1943, letter, in Dwight D. Eisenhower, *The Papers of Dwight David Eisenhower*, vol. 1, *The War Years*, ed. Alfred D. Chandler Jr. (Baltimore, Johns Hopkins Press, 1970), 962; Eisenhower to Alexander Day Surles, April 6, 1943, letter, in Dwight D. Eisenhower, *The Papers of Dwight David Eisenhower*, vol. 2, *The War Years*, ed. Alfred D. Chandler Jr. (Baltimore: Johns Hopkins Press, 1970), 1081.

33. John D. Chappell, *Before the Bomb: How America Approached the End of the Pacific War* (Lexington: University Press of Kentucky, 1997), 5 and 151.

34. Archibald MacLeish to Grace Tully, February 2, 1942, letter, Box 145, Folder Office of Facts and Figures, PSF.

35. Russell F. Weigley, *Eisenhower's Lieutenants: The Campaign of France and Germany 1944–1945* (Bloomington: Indiana University Press, 1981), xvii.

36. Omar N. Bradley, interview by C. K. Hanson, February 24, 1975, Box 2, Folder 14, ONBC, USAHEC.

37. Paul P. Rogers, *The Good Years: MacArthur and Sutherland* (New York: Praeger, 1990), 290.

38. Aaron B. O'Connell, *Underdogs: The Making of the Modern Marine Corps* (Cambridge, MA: Harvard University Press, 2012), 3.

39. William J. Dunn, *Pacific Microphone* (College Station: Texas A&M University Press, 1988), 200.

Prologue: The Media and Total War

1. See Jeremy Black, *The Age of Total War, 1860–1945* (London: Praeger Security International, 2006), 1–11; Michael Broers, "The Concept of 'Total War' in the Revolutionary—Napoleonic Period," *War in History* 15, no. 3 (2008): 247–268.

2. David Bell, *The First Total War: Napoleon's Europe and the Birth of Warfare as We Know It* (Boston: Houghton Mifflin Harcourt, 2007), 9. Daniel C. Hallin also connects the beginning of total war with the French Revolution. Daniel C. Hallin, "The Media and War," in *International Media Research*, ed. John Corner, Philip Schlesinger, and Roger Silverstone (New York: Routledge, 1997), 208.

3. Bell, *The First Total War*, 198–199.

4. Andrew Roberts, *Napoleon: A Life* (New York: Viking, 2014), 130.

5. Bell, *The First Total War*, 312–313.

6. Roberts, *Napoleon*, 243.

7. Martin Blumenson and James L. Stokesburg, *Masters of the Art of Command* (Boston: Houghton Mifflin, 1975), 5.

8. Bell, *The First Total War*, 198.

9. Barney Oldfield, *Never a Shot in Anger* (New York: Duell, Sloan and Pearce, 1956), xi. The exact time of the emergence of war correspondence is a matter of debate. See Knightley, *The First Casualty*, 4; Sweeney, *The Military and the Press*, 5.

10. Roberts, *Napoleon*, 316.

11. "Selected Historical Combat Retorts to Directives from Non-Combatants (Civil and Otherwise)," Box 12, Folder November 1943 (Personal), CSP.

12. Carl von Clausewitz, *On War*, ed. and trans. by Michael Howard and Peter Paret (New York: Alfred A. Knopf, 1993), 157.

13. Clausewitz, 277.

14. Clausewitz, 248.

15. Clausewitz, 720.

16. Michael Howard, *Clausewitz* (Oxford: Oxford University Press, 1983), 56.

17. Howard, 72.

18. Eliot A. Cohen, *Supreme Command: Soldiers, Statesmen, and Leadership in Wartime* (New York: Free Press, 2002), 8.

19. Cohen, *Supreme Command*, 6; Cherie Steele and Arthur A. Stein, "Communications Revolutions and International Relations," in *Technology, Development, and Democracy: International Conflict and Cooperation in the Information Age*, ed. Juliann Emmons Allison (Albany: State University of New York Press, 2002), 29.

20. Susan L. Carruthers, *The Media at War* (New York: Palgrave Macmillan, 2000), 3.

21. Kevin Williams, "Something More Important than Truth: Ethical Issues in War Reporting," in *Ethical Issues in Journalism and the Media*, ed. Andrew Belsey and Ruth Chadwick (New York: Routledge, 1992), 155; Alan Hankinson, *Man of Wars: William Howard Russell of The Times* (London: Heinemann, 1982), 83–84; Nathan A. Haverstock, *Fifty Years at the Front: The Life of War Correspondent Frederick Palmer* (London: Brassey's, 1996), 27; Andrew Lambert and Stephen Badsey, *The War Correspondents: The Crimean War* (Gloucestershire, England: Alan Sutton Publishing, 1994), 1.

22. Williams, "Something More Important than Truth," 167.

23. Lambert and Badsey, *The War Correspondents*, 14.

24. Oldfield, *Never a Shot in Anger*, xii.

25. J. Cutler Andrews, *The North Reports the Civil War* (Pittsburgh: University of Pittsburgh Press, 1955), 6. For a good, though slightly dated, list of books on journalism during the Civil War see James M. McPherson, *Crossroads of Freedom Antietam: The Battle That Changed the Course of the Civil War* (Oxford: Oxford University Press, 2002), 188.

26. George Meade to Margaretta Meade, December 21, 1861, in *The Life and Letters of George Gordon Meade*, vol. 1, ed. George Gordon Meade (New York: Charles Scribner's Sons, 1913), 236–237.

27. James M. Perry, *A Bohemian Brigade: The Civil War Correspondents—Mostly Rough, Sometimes Ready* (New York: John Wiley & Sons, 2000), 176; John F. Marszalek, *Sherman's Other War: The General and the Civil War Press* (Memphis, TN: Memphis State University Press, 1981), 3.

28. Sweeney, *The Military and the Press*, 20.

29. Andrews, *The North Reports the Civil War*, 546–548.

30. Andrews, 20–21.

31. Knightley, *The First Casualty*, 39.

32. Knightley, 61.

33. Michael S. Sweeney and Natascha Toft Roelsgaard, *Journalism and the Russo-Japanese War: The End of the Golden Age of Combat Correspondence* (Lanham, MD: Lexington Books, 2020), 200–201.

34. Knightley, *The First Casualty*, 61.

35. Alexander Watson, *Ring of Steel: Germany and Austria-Hungary in World War I* (New York: Basic Books, 2014), 3–4.

36. Watson, 210.

37. Watson, 52.

38. Watson, 299.

39. Carruthers, *The Media at War*, 60; Watson, *Ring of Steel*, 376.

40. Paul Fussell, *Wartime: Understanding and Behavior in the Second World War* (Oxford: Oxford University Press, 1989), 159–160.

41. Stephen Vaughn, *Holding Fast the Inner Lines: Democracy, Nationalism, and the Committee of Public Information* (Chapel Hill: University of North Carolina Press, 1980), xi.

42. Michael G. Carew, *The Power to Persuade: FDR, The Newsmagazines, and Going to War, 1939–1941* (New York: University Press of America, 2005), 8; Christopher Capozzola, *Uncle Sam Wants You: World War I and the Making of the Modern American Citizen* (Oxford: Oxford University Press, 2008), 171. Capozzola's book explains how the CPI fit into larger wartime activities of coercion and state building.

43. Sweeney, *The Military and the Press*, 63; Sweeney, *Secrets of Victory*, 18.

44. Knightley, *The First Casualty*, 124.

45. Haverstock, *Fifty Years at the Front*, 194–197.

46. Casey, *When Soldiers Fall*, 19, 22, 23, and 37.

47. Hammond, *Public Affairs*, 5.

48. Jan Willem Honig, "The Idea of Total War: From Clausewitz to Ludendorff," in *The Pacific War as Total War*, International Forum on War History, Tokyo, National Institute for Defense Studies, 2011, 38, accessed December 8, 2018, http://www.nids.mod.go.jp/english/event/forum/e2011.html.

49. Erich Ludendorff, *The Nation at War*, trans. A. S. Rappoport (London: Hutchinson, 1936), 12–16. Historian Jan Willem Honig warns against conflating Clausewitz's "absolute war" and Ludendorff's "total war." Honig, "The Idea of Total War," 30.

50. Adolf Hitler, *Mein Kampf*, trans. Ralph Manheim (Boston: Houghton Mifflin, 1925), 145. As with everything else he wrote, Hitler's passage here must be used cautiously. Historian Thomas Weber has cast doubt whether Hitler had any political formation at all during World War I. Thomas Weber, *Hitler's First War: Adolf Hitler, the Men of the List Regiment, and the First World War* (Oxford: Oxford University Press, 2010), 345; Thomas Weber, *Becoming Hitler: The Making of A Nazi* (New York: Basic Books, 2017), xiv–xv. However, this particular passage has been persuasively cited by one recent biographer as being important to Hitler's thinking. Brendan Simms, *Hitler: A Global Biography* (New York: Basic Books, 2019), 89.

51. Robert Edwin Herzstein, *The War That Hitler Won: The Most Infamous Propaganda Campaign in History* (New York: G. P. Putnam's Sons, 1978), 73.

52. Heinz Höhne, *The Order of the Death's Head: The Story of Hitler's SS* (New York: Penguin Books, 1969), 14–15; Simms, *Hitler*, 89.

53. Adam Tooze, *The Wages of Destruction: The Making and Breaking of the Nazi Economy* (New York: Viking, 2006), 147–149.

54. Albert C. Wedemeyer, *Wedemeyer Reports!* (New York: Henry Holt, 1958), 79.

55. Carruthers, *The Media at War*, 85.

56. Simms, *Hitler*, 366.

57. Albert Speer, *Inside the Third Reich*, trans. Richard and Clara Winston (New York: Macmillan, 1969), 298–299.

58. Alan Brinkley, *The Publisher: Henry Luce and His American Century* (New York: Alfred A. Knopf, 2010), 252.

59. Brinkley, *The Publisher*, 102 and 209.

60. Carew, *The Power to Persuade*, 8–9.

61. Brinkley, *The Publisher*, 137 and 223; Adam J. Berinsky, *In Time of War: Understanding American Public Opinion from World War II to Iraq* (Chicago: University of Chicago Press, 2009), 34.

62. Oldfield, *Never A Shot In Anger*, xv.

63. Berinsky, *In Time of War*, 39.

64. Honig, "The Idea of Total War," 38.

65. Jochen Hellbeck, "Battles for Morale: An Entangled History of Total War in Europe, 1939–1945," in *The Cambridge History of The Second World War*, vol. 3, *Total War: Economy, Society and Culture*, ed. Michael Geyer and Adam Tooze (Cambridge: Cambridge University Press, 2015), 329.

66. Fletcher Pratt, *America and Total War* (New York: Smith & Durrell, 1941), 63–87.

67. Matthew Gordon, *News Is a Weapon* (New York: Alfred A. Knopf, 1942), viii.

68. Oldfield, *Never A Shot In Anger*, xiii.

69. James T. Sparrow, *The Warfare State: World War II Americans and the Age of Big Government* (Oxford: Oxford University Press, 2011), 35.

70. Lynne Olson, *Citizens of London: The Americans Who Stood with Britain in Its Darkest, Finest Hour* (New York: Random House, 2010), 140.

71. Herzstein, *The War That Hitler Won*, 72 and 74.

72. Goebbels, *The Goebbels Diaries, 1942–1943*, 210.

73. Eric Metaxas, *Bonhoeffer: Pastor, Martyr, Prophet, Spy* (Nashville, TN: Thomas Nelson, 2010), 347; William L. Shirer, *The Rise and Fall of the Third Reich: A History of Nazi Germany* (New York: Simon and Schuster, 1960), 567.

74. Weinberg, *A World At Arms*, 49–50.

75. Knightley, *The First Casualty*, 221. "Black propaganda" is damaging false news created by an enemy and disguised to appear that it is coming from a friendly source. "White propaganda" is propaganda that clearly comes from an enemy.

76. Knightley, 221.

77. Herzstein, *The War That Hitler Won*, 80–84.

78. John Toland, *The Rising Sun: The Decline and Fall of the Japanese Empire 1936–1945* (New York: Random House, 1970), 189.

79. Gordon W. Prange, *At Dawn We Slept* (New York: Viking, 1981), 16–17; interview with Captain Minoru Genda, March 25, 1947, quoted at 21.

80. Two good books on the topic are Carew's *The Power to Persuade*, which looks at how Roosevelt used the magazine industry to achieve his objective, and Casey's *Cautious Crusade*, which explores the public opinion and media influence on Roosevelt. For seeing the impact of the media in the context of larger events, see Lynne Olson's two excellent histories *Citizens of London* and *Those Angry Days: Roosevelt, Lindbergh, and America's Fight over World War II* (New York: Random House, 2013).

81. Olson, *Those Angry Days*, xviii.

82. David M. Kennedy, *Freedom from Fear: The American People in Depression and War, 1929–1945* (Oxford: Oxford University Press, 1999), 404.

83. Kennedy, *Freedom from Fear*, 472.

84. James MacGregor Burns, *Roosevelt: The Soldier of Freedom* (New York: Smithmark, 1970), 212.

85. Ben Procter, *William Randolph Hearst: Final Edition, 1911–1951* (Oxford: Oxford University Press, 2007), 226.

86. National Education Association, "News," in *Building America: Illustrated Studies on Modern Problems*, vol. 3 (New York: Americana Corporation, 1942), 18.

87. Brinkley, *The Publisher*, 457 and 247.

88. Richard W. Steele, "The Great Debate: Roosevelt, the Media, and the Coming of the War, 1940–1941," *Journal of American History* 71, no. 1 (1984): 87–88.

89. Edward Alwood, *Dark Days in the Newsroom: McCarthyism Aimed at the Press* (Philadelphia: Temple University Press, 2007), 82.

90. Steele, "The Great Debate," 75–76 and 82.

91. Steele, 85.

92. Editors, "We All Have Only One Task," *Chicago Daily Tribune*, December 8, 1941; Editors, "Death Sentence of a Mad Dog," *Los Angeles Times*, December 8, 1941; Walter Lord, *Day of Infamy* (New York: Holt, Rinehart and Winston, 1957), 217–218.

93. Burns, *Roosevelt*, 211–212.

94. George C. Marshall, "Address to the Conference of Negro Newspaper Editors," December 8, 1941, George C. Marshall Foundation, Library Website, accessed October 16, 2017, http://marshallfoundation.org/library/digital-archive/41-12-08 -address-to-the-conference-of-negro-newspaper-editors/.

95. Marshall, *George C. Marshall Interviews and Reminiscences for Forrest C. Pogue*, 147.

Chapter 1. "You Shoot Bullets with Your Typewriter"

1. Franklin D. Roosevelt, "We Are Going to Win the War," December 9, 1941, in *The Public Papers and Addresses of Franklin D. Roosevelt*, vol. 10: *The Call to Battle Stations*, ed. Samuel I. Rosenman (New York: Harper & Brothers, 1950), 524–526; Alan Barth to R. Keith Kane, December 15, 1941, Intelligence Report no. 1, Box 145, Folder Office of Facts and Figures, PSF.

2. Quentin Reynolds, *By Quentin Reynolds* (New York: McGraw-Hill Book, 1963), 265.

3. Roosevelt, "The Seven Hundred and Ninetieth Press Conference—the First Wartime Press Conference (Excerpts)," December 9, 1941, in *The Public Papers and Addresses of Franklin D. Roosevelt*, vol. 10, 520.

4. Winston S. Churchill, *The Second World War*, vol. 4, *The Hinge of Fate* (Boston: Houghton Mifflin Company, 1950), 324; Samuel Eliot Morison, *Strategy and Compromise* (Boston: Little, Brown, 1958), 22; Hamilton, *The Mantle of Command*, 345. Steven Casey notes that Roosevelt was "sensitive" to public opinion but warns that "this did not mean that there was a simple correlation between public opinion and policy outcomes. It was not merely the case of the president bowing to a popular clamor for an immediate second front. . . . In fact, when it came to grand strategy, public opinion only entered Franklin Roosevelt's calculations in a highly subtle and complicated manner." Casey, *Cautious Crusade*, 81.

5. For evidence that Roosevelt took public opinion seriously see John L. McCrea, *Captain McCrea's War: The World War II Memoir of Franklin D. Roosevelt's Naval Aide and USS Iowa's First Commanding Officer*, ed. Julia C. Tobey (New York:

Shyhorse Publishing, 2016), 14; Casey, *Cautious Crusade*, 215; Berinsky, *In Time of War*, 2. For arguments on public opinion and strategy see Steele, *The First Offensive 1942*, viii; Stoler, *Allies and Adversaries*, 78.

6. Eric Larrabee, *Commander in Chief: Franklin Delano Roosevelt, His Lieutenants, and Their War* (New York: Harper & Row, 1987), 1; Doris Kearns Goodwin, *No Ordinary Time: Franklin and Eleanor Roosevelt: The Home Front in World War II* (New York: Simon & Schuster, 1994), 609; Joseph E. Persico, *Roosevelt's Centurions: FDR and the Commanders He Led to Victory in World War II* (New York: Random House, 2013), xiv; Hamilton, *The Mantle of Command*, x.

7. Stoler, *Allies and Adversaries*, 72, 74, 76, and 70.

8. Louis Morton, "Germany First: The Basic Concept of Allied Strategy in World War II," in *Command Decisions*, ed. Kent Roberts Greenfield (Washington, DC: Office of the Chief of Military History, United States Army, 1959), 11.

9. Stoler, *Allies and Adversaries*, 78.

10. Henry Lewis Stimson, Diary, December 7, 1941, Reel 7, HLSD.

11. Roosevelt, "We Are Going to Win the War," 523 and 529–530.

12. "Nelson Says Nazis Caused the Attack," *New York Times*, December 8, 1941.

13. "Aid to Allies Won't Falter, U.S. Pledges," *Washington Post*, December 9, 1941.

14. George Eliot Eliot, Diary, January 22, 1942, Box 23, Folder Diary JAN–APR 1942, GFE.

15. "The Hour Has Struck," *Washington Post*, December 8, 1941.

16. Westbrook Pegler, "A Fighter Lead [*sic*] Us," *Washington Post*, December 9, 1941.

17. Walter Lippmann, "Today and Tomorrow," *Washington Post*, December 9, 1941.

18. Dorothy Thompson, "Declare War on All of Axis Partners Now," *Daily Boston Globe*, December 8, 1941.

19. "Nazi Airmen Bombed Honolulu, Rumor at Capital," *Daily Boston Globe*, December 9, 1941.

20. John W. Dower, *War without Mercy: Race and Power in the Pacific War* (New York: Pantheon Books, 1986), 105; Thomas Fleming, *The New Dealers' War: Franklin D. Roosevelt and The War within World War II* (New York: Basic Books, 2001), 45.

21. "'We Will Triumph—So Help Us God!' Unity at Last," *Los Angeles Times*, December 9, 1941.

22. Ferdinand Kuhn Jr. to Alan Barth, "Editorial Opinion on Foreign Affairs: The Nation Rallies," December 12, 1941, Box 80, Folder November 28, 1941–Feb. 27, 1942, PSF.

23. "A Call to Duty," *New York Times*, December 10, 1941.

24. "Germany's Game," *Daily Boston Globe*, December 11, 1941.

25. Pierre J. Huss, untitled, *Cosmopolitan*, March 1943, found in "A Survey of War Strategy as Proposed by Columnists and Writers," Prepared by Intelligence and Analysis Branch Bureau of Public Relations, USAHEC.

26. "Survey of Intelligence Materials no. 12," Office of Facts and Figures, Bureau of Intelligence, March 2, 1942, 14, Box 324A, Folder Book 7, Sherwood Collections, HP.

27. Casey, *Cautious Crusade*, 77.

28. "Knox on Strategy," *Washington Post*, January 18, 1942.

29. "The Navy in Two Seas," *New York Times*, January 13, 1942.

30. "A Recipe for Killing Rattlesnakes," *Los Angeles Times*, January 14, 1942.

31. Archibald MacLeish to Alan Barth, "Editorial Opinion on the War: The Indivisible War," January 23, 1942, Box 80, Folder November 28, 1941–Feb. 27, 1942, PSF.

32. David Lawrence, "Japs Failed in Ruse to Divert U.S.," *Evening Star*, April 10, 1942; Raymond Clapper, "Marshall's Appearance in London Stirs Hopes of Direct Attacks on Axis," *Philadelphia Inquirer*, April 20, 1942; Kirke L. Simpson, "Beaverbrook Calls Russian Victory Quickest Way for Allies to Beat Axis," *Philadelphia Inquirer*, April 25, 1942; Ernest Lindley, "The Layman vs. the Military Strategist," *Newsweek*, April 20, 1942, found in "A Survey of War Strategy," USAHEC.

33. "Survey of Intelligence Materials no. 7," January 24, 1942, Box 145, Folder Office of Facts and Figures, PSF.

34. Archibald MacLeish to Alan Barth, "Editorial Opinion on the War: Response to Candor," January 30, 1942, Box 80, Folder November 28, 1941–Feb. 27, 1942, PSF.

35. "Survey of Editorial Opinion," Statistical Services, No. 96, March 11, 1942, Box 139, Folder Editorial Opinion, HP.

36. Archibald MacLeish to Alan Barth, "Editorial Opinion on the War: The Demand for Action," March 13, 1942, Box 81, Folder Editorial Opinion Rpt., Mar. 6–May 1, 1942, PSF.

37. George Catlett Marshall, "Notes of Meeting at the White House with the President and the British Minister Presiding," December 23, 1941, memorandum, *The Papers of George Catlett Marshall*, vol. 3, *"The Right Man for the Job," December 7, 1941–May 31, 1943*, ed. Larry I. Bland (Baltimore, MD: Johns Hopkins University Press, 1991), 34.

38. "Conference in White House," December 23, 1941, Reel 205, HHAP.

39. "Conference in White House," December 23, 1941; "The Chiefs of Staff Conference," December 27, 1941, Reel 205, HHAP.

40. William Manchester, *American Caesar: Douglas MacArthur, 1880–1964* (New York: Dell Publishing, 1978), 30, 38, and 68.

41. Larrabee, *Commander in Chief*, 309.

42. Stephen E. Ambrose, *Americans at War* (Jackson: University Press of Mississippi, 1997), 108.

43. Marshall to MacArthur, December 7, 1941, radio no. 736, *Marshall Papers*, vol. 3, 8.

44. Ronald H. Spector, *Eagle against the Sun: The American War with Japan* (New York: Free Press, 1985), 73, 107, and 108; Manchester, *American Caesar*, 230–231.

45. "Japanese Strategy," *Washington Post*, December 16, 1941.

46. "Survey of Intelligence Materials no. 8," February 2, 1942, Box 145, Folder Office of Facts and Figures, PSF. [Underlined in original.]

47. "General MacArthur of the Philippines," *Chicago Daily Tribune*, February 6, 1942; "Gen. Douglas MacArthur," *Los Angeles Times*, February 8, 1942; "M'Athur

Portrait in the Tribune today Done by Oskar Gross," *Chicago Daily Tribune*, February 6, 1942; "MacArthur," *Daily Boston Globe*, March 1, 1942; "MacArthur: Life Story of Philippine Defender," *Washington Post*, February 25, 1942.

48. Douglas MacArthur, *Reminiscences* (New York: McGraw-Hill Book company, 1964), 44 and n44. As Michael S. Sweeney observes, MacArthur was less impressed with the press and advocated stronger censorship. Sweeney, *The Military and the Press*, 44.

49. Arthur Herman, *Douglas MacArthur: American Warrior* (New York: Random House, 2016), 92 and 153.

50. "Gen. MacArthur Spends Birthday Working on War," *Chicago Daily Tribune*, January 27, 1942.

51. Toland, *The Rising Sun*, 245–246; December 11, 1941, "#41 Situation Reports-1-December 9, 1941 to March 2, 1942," MRP,1942–1945, Box 38, NARA, online, National Archives Identifier: 27577827, accessed January 8, 2018, https://catalog.archives.gov/id/578215.

52. Clark Lee, "Filipinos Cheer As Flyers Down 3 Jap Bombers," *Chicago Daily Tribune*, February 2, 1942; D. Clayton James, *The Years of MacArthur*, vol. 2, *1941–1945* (Boston: Houghton Mifflin, 1975), 89–90.

53. E. B. Potter, *Bull Halsey* (Annapolis, MD: Naval Institute Press, 1985), 212.

54. Rogers, *The Good Years*, 263. Rogers, a stenographer on MacArthur's staff, claims that neither MacArthur nor his chief of staff wrote this message and that it has been wrongly construed as a confession of distortion of the communiqués.

55. Robert E. Sherwood to MacArthur, July 21, 1942, letter, RG-10, 334, MML.

56. See Stimson's diary for a few examples showing that MacArthur was not overly optimistic about the situation. Stimson, Diaries for December 14, 21, 22, and 25, 1941, Reel 7, HLSD.

57. Harry L. Hopkins, *The White House Papers of Harry L. Hopkins*, vol. 2, ed. Robert E. Sherwood (London: Eyre & Spottiswoode, 1949), 510.

58. Eliot, Diary, January 23, 1942, Box 23, Folder Diary JAN–APR 1942, GFE.

59. Everett S. Hughes, Diary, December 15, 1941, BoxI 1, ESHP.

60. Herman, *Douglas MacArthur*, 354, 370–371; MacArthur's most comprehensive biographer, D. Clayton James, makes the same point. James, *The Years of MacArthur*, vol 2, 52.

61. "Roosevelt Sends MacArthur, Quezon Commendatory Wires," *Washington Post*, December 12, 1941.

62. "MacArthur, Far East Head, Made 4 Star General," *Chicago Daily Tribune*, December 20, 1941.

63. Stimson, Diary January 1, 1942, Reel 7, HLSD.

64. "Roosevelt Leads in Tributes for MacArthur, 62," *Chicago Daily Tribune*, January 27, 1942.

65. Franklin D. Roosevelt, "We Must Keep on Striking Our Enemies Wherever and Whenever We Can Meet Them"—Fireside Chat on Progress of the War, February 23, 1942, *The Public Papers and Addresses of Franklin D. Roosevelt*, vol. 11, *Humanity on the Defensive*, ed. Samuel I. Rosenman (New York: Harper & Brothers Publishers, 1950), 110.

66. Dwight D. Eisenhower, *Crusade in Europe* (Garden City, NY: Doubleday, 1948), 22.

67. Stimson, Diary, December 25, 1941, Reel 7, HLSD.

68. Quezon to Roosevelt by Marshall, February 8, 1942, Radiogram, Reel 7, HLSD; Dwight David Eisenhower, *Crusade in Europe*, 26.

69. Kenneth S. Davis, *FDR: The War President 1940–1943* (New York: Random House, 2000), 431.

70. Dwight D. Eisenhower, *The Eisenhower Diaries*, ed. Robert H. Ferrell (New York: W. W. Norton, 1981), 47; Roosevelt to MacArthur, February 9, 1942, Radiogram, Reel 7, HLSD.

71. Perry argues that the idea of rescuing MacArthur originated with the Australian prime minister John Curtin. Perry, unfortunately, gives no citations, and it is unclear when or if Curtin suggested MacArthur. I have thus gone with Arnold's recollection of Roosevelt. Mark Perry, *The Most Dangerous Man in America: The Making of Douglas MacArthur* (New York: Basic Books, 2014), 140.

72. "Conference in White House," December 27, 1941, Reel 205, HHAP.

73. "A Fighting General," *Chicago Daily Tribune*, December 21, 1941.

74. "Conference in White House," December 27, 1941, Reel 205, HHAP; Spector, *Eagle against the Sun*, 128; H. P. Willmott, *Empires in the Balance: Japanese and Allied Pacific Strategies to April 1942* (Annapolis, MD: Naval Institute Press, 1982), 259.

75. Edward Davidson and Dale Manning, *Chronology of World War Two* (London: Cassell, 1999), 98, 99, 100, and 102.

76. Walter Trohan, "Allies Confer amid Uproar over Reverses," *Chicago Daily Tribune*, February 15, 1942.

77. "Press Conference #806," February 17, 1942, in Franklin D. Roosevelt, *Complete Presidential Press Conferences of Franklin D. Roosevelt*, vol. 19 (New York: Da Capo Press, 1972), 151–152.

78. Ernie Santos, "Wasting Talents," *Washington Post*, February 26, 1942.

79. Walter Trohan, "MacArthur and Leahy May Lead Allied Forces," *Chicago Daily Tribune*, December 17, 1941.

80. "A Commander in Chief Is Needed," *Chicago Daily Tribune*, February 13, 1942.

81. John G. Harris, "Willkie Urges MacArthur Be Made U.S. Army Chief," *Daily Boston Globe*, February 13, 1942.

82. "Bring Home MacArthur," *Time* 39, no. 8 (February 23, 1942): 16.

83. John G. Harris, "McCormack Hits Cry to Recall MacArthur," *Daily Boston Globe*, February 23, 1942.

84. Chesly Manly, "Roosevelt Aims to Calm Critics in Talk Tonight," *Chicago Daily Tribune*, February 23, 1942.

85. William Strand, "Capital Puzzled by Refusal to Aid MacArthur," *Chicago Daily Tribune*, March 1, 1942; Clark Lee, *One Last Look Around* (New York: Duell, Sloan and Pearce, 1947), 141–142.

86. "Press Conference #807," February 24, 1942, in *Complete Roosevelt Presidential Press*, vol. 19, 155–156.

87. Strand, "Capital Puzzled by Refusal to Aid MacArthur."

88. "Survey of Intelligence Materials no. 10," February 16, 1942, Box 145, Folder Office of Facts and Figures, PSF.

89. Archibald MacLeish to Alan Barth, "Editorial Opinion on the War: Discouragement," March 6, 1942, Box 81, Folder Editorial Opinion Rpt. Mar. 6–May 1, 1942, PSF.

90. MacArthur, *Reminiscences*, 140; Stimson, Diary, February 23, 1942, Reel 7, HLSD.

91. Dwight D. Eisenhower, *The Eisenhower Diaries*, 49.

92. Perry, *The Most Dangerous Man in America*, 146.

93. MacArthur to the Adj. Gen., February 11, 1942, Radiogram, Reel 7, HLSD.

94. James, *The Years of MacArthur*, vol. 2, 98.

95. MacArthur, *Reminiscences*, 140; James, *The Years of MacArthur*, vol. 2, 98; Stimson, Diary, January 25, 1942, Reel 7, HLSD; Dwight D. Eisenhower, *The Eisenhower Diaries*, 49.

96. Carlos P. Romulo to Chief of Staff and Press Relations, March 9, 1942, memorandum, RG-10, Reel 333, MML.

97. MacArthur, *Reminiscences*, 142–145.

98. Betty Houchin Winfield, *FDR and the News Media* (Chicago: University of Illinois Press, 1990), 223.

99. "Press Conference #812," March 17, 1942, in Roosevelt, *Complete Roosevelt Presidential Press Conferences*, vol. 19, 208–210.

100. Marshall, *Marshall Interviews and Reminiscences*, 244.

101. Marshall, *Marshall Papers*, vol. 3, n148.

102. Oldfield, *Never A Shot In Anger*, 3.

103. Archibald MacLeish to Alan Barth, "Editorial Opinion on the War: Blood Transfusion," March 20, 1942, Box 81, Folder Editorial Opinion Rpt. Mar. 6–May 1, 1942, PSF.

104. "In the News," *Washington Times-Herald*, March 20, 1942, found in "A Survey of War Strategy," USAHEC.

105. Hughes, Diary, March 17, 1942, BoxI 1, ESHP.

106. "Suggests MacArthur as Chief," *New York Times*, March 2, 1942.

107. Marshall, *Marshall Interviews and Reminiscences*, 244 and 609.

108. Roosevelt to Churchill, March 17, 1942, in Winston S. Churchill and Franklin D. Roosevelt, *Churchill and Roosevelt: The Complete Correspondence*, vol. 1, *Alliance Emerging October 1933–November 1942*, ed. Warren F. Kimball (Princeton, NJ: Princeton University Press, 1984), 409.

109. "The Eight Hundred and Nineteenth Press Conference (Excerpts)," April 14, 1942, in Roosevelt, *The Public Papers and Addresses of Franklin D. Roosevelt*, vol. 11, 198.

110. Dwight D. Eisenhower, *The Eisenhower Diaries*, 52.

111. Stimson, Diary, March 17, 1942, and March 19, 1942, Reel 7, HLSD.

112. H. H. Arnold to Samuel I. Rosenman, April 25, 1949, letter, reproduced in Roosevelt, *The Public Papers and Addresses of Franklin D. Roosevelt*, vol. 11, 214.

113. "Conference in White House," December 21, 1941, Reel 205, HHAP.

114. Interview with H. H. Arnold, "Envelope Columbia University Oral History Notes," Reel 43835, HHAPAF.

115. "The Chiefs of Staff Conference," December 24, 1941, in *Proceedings of the American-British Joint Chiefs of Staff Conferences Held in Washington, D.C. on Twelve Occasions Between December 24, 1941 and January 14, 1942*, USAHEC.

116. Carroll V. Glines, *Doolittle's Tokyo Raiders* (Princeton, NJ: D. Van Nostrand, 1964), 13; H. H. Arnold, *Global Mission* (New York: Harper & Brothers, 1949), 289.

117. James H. "Jimmy" Doolittle with Carroll V. Glines, *I Could Never Be So Lucky Again* (New York: Bantam Books, 1991), 503.

118. Alan Barth to R. Keith Kane, December 15, 1941, Intelligence Report no. 1, Box 145, Folder Office of Facts and Figures, PSF.

119. "Only 700 Miles from Tokyo and Big Ports," *Washington Post*, December 16, 1941.

120. Al Williams, "How to Bomb Japan," *Washington News*, January 30, 1942, found in "A Survey of War Strategy," USAHEC.

121. Alan Barth to R. Keith Kane, January 5, 1942, Survey of Intelligence Material no. 4, Box 145, Folder Office of Facts and Figures, PSF.

122. Stimson, Diary, January 25, and January 28, 1942, Reel 7, HLSD.

123. "FRD and Arnold-Bombing of Japan Jan 1942," Reel 43812, HHAPAF; Stimson, Diary, January 28, 1942, Reel 7, HLSD. Arnold recounts this meeting in his memoirs but claims that he mentioned the need to strike Japan for morale reasons. Arnold, *Global Mission*, 289. The Roberts Commission was appointed to investigate the attack on Pearl Harbor. It was chaired by Supreme Court Justice Owen Roberts.

124. James Doolittle, interview by "Mac" Laddon, August 14, 1970, Reel 43812, HHAPAF. Later, the origins of what became known to history as the "Doolittle Raid" would be debated. In his memoirs Admiral Ernest King claimed credit for the operation for himself and his staff, stating Roosevelt was only brought in later. Ernest J. King and Walter Muir Whitehill, *Fleet Admiral King: A Naval Record* (New York: W. W. Norton & Company, 1952), 376. A few early historians followed King's lead including Quentin Reynolds, *The Amazing Mr. Doolittle: A Biography of Lieutenant General James H. Doolittle* (New York: Appleton-Century-Crofts, 1953), 170, and Samuel Eliot Morison, *History of United States Naval Operations in World War II*, vol. 3, *The Rising Sun in the Pacific 1931–April 1942* (Boston: Little, Brown and Company, 1965), 389. Other historians would give Arnold the credit. Carroll V. Glines, *Jimmy Doolittle: Daredevil Aviator and Scientist* (New York: The Macmillan Company, 1972), 128. However, the evidence is overwhelming that while the basic idea was developed by the Navy and War Departments, the driving force behind the operation was Roosevelt. "From the start of the war," wrote Arnold later, "Franklin Roosevelt wanted a bombing raid on Japan proper." H. H. Arnold to Samuel I. Rosenman, April 25, 1949, letter, reproduced in Roosevelt, *The Public Papers and Addresses of Franklin D. Roosevelt*, vol. 11, 214. Other eyewitness and historians agree. "Conference in White House," December 21, 1941, Reel 205, HHAPLC; James M. Scott, *Target Tokyo: Jimmy Doolittle and the Raid That Avenged Pearl Harbor* (New York: W. W. Norton, 2015), 34; Brig. Gen. Marian C. Cooper, April, 9, 1970, letter, Reel 43812, HHAPAF; Alan Barth to R. Keith Kane, Dec. 15, 1941, Intelligence Report no. 1, quoted in Scott, *Target Tokyo*, 27.

125. Doolittle, *I Could Never Be So Lucky Again*, 216.

126. Scott, *Target Tokyo*, 216–218.

127. Arnold, *Global Mission*, 91. Much later Doolittle claimed that it was not Arnold but another officer who grounded him, though he did remember meeting Arnold around that time. Doolittle, *I Could Never Be So Lucky Again*, 55.

128. Arnold, *Global Mission*, 129; Toland, *The Rising Sun*, 305.

129. Arnold, *Global Mission*, 299.

130. James H. Doolittle, "Unfinished Autobiography," 196, Box 44, JHDP.

131. Doolittle, *I Could Never Be So Lucky Again*, 230.

132. Scott, *Target Tokyo*, 2–3; William F. Halsey and J. Bryan III, *Admiral Halsey's Story* (New York: Whittlesey House, 1947), 12.

133. Halsey and Bryan, *Admiral Halsey's Story*, 102.

134. Scott, *Target Tokyo*, 7.

135. Potter, *Bull Halsey*, 59.

136. Scott, *Target Tokyo*, 7–8; Toland, *The Rising Sun*, 308.

137. Evan Thomas, *Sea of Thunder: Four Commanders and the Last Great Naval Campaign 1941–1945* (New York: Simon & Schuster, 2006), 8.

138. Ugaki, *Fading Victory*, 111; Gordon W. Prange with Donald M. Goldstein and Katherine V. Dillon, *Miracle at Midway* (New York: Penguin, 1982), 24.

139. Ugaki, 111–113.

140. Toland, *The Rising Sun*, 309.

141. Potter, *Bull Halsey*, 63–64.

142. Ugaki, *Fading Victory*, 115.

143. Stimson, Diary, April 18, 1942, Reel 7, HLSD.

144. Robert Guillain, *I Saw Tokyo Burning: An Eyewitness Narrative from Pearl Harbor to Hiroshima*, trans. William Byron (Garden City, NY: Doubleday, 1981), 63.

145. Saburo Sakai with Martin Caidin and Fred Saito, *Samurai!* (New York: E. P. Dutton, 1957), 148.

146. Glines, *Doolittle's Tokyo Raiders*, vii.

147. "Survey of Intelligence Materials no. 12," a–b, Box 324A, Folder Book 7, Sherwood Collections, HP.

148. Stimson, Diary, March 16, 1942, Reel 7, HLSD.

149. Archibald MacLeish to Alan Barth, "Editorial Opinion on the War: Lull before the Storm," March 27, 1942, Box 81, Folder Editorial Opinion Rpt. Mar. 6–May 1, 1942, PSF.

150. "At Our Enemy's Heart," *Washington Post*, April 19, 1942.

151. "Bombs Bring First Test of Jap Morale on Receiving-End of Total War," *Baltimore Sun*, April 19, 1942.

152. Hanson W. Baldwin, "Moral Effect of Raids," *New York Times*, April 20, 1942.

153. Devon Francis, "Raid Proves Grim Omen for Japanese," *Salt Lake Tribune*, April 19, 1942.

154. Glenn Babb, "Bombs Bring Japan Reminder War Can Strike Both Ways," *Tampa Tribune*, April 19, 1942.

155. "Doolittle Led Air Raid on Japan, FDR Reveals," *Miami Daily News*,

May 19, 1942, Box OV 83, JHDP; Polyzoides, "Blasting of Jap Cities Adds Mystery to War," *Los Angeles Times*, April 19, 1942.

156. "Days Pass; Tokio Bombing Still a Mystery To Japs," *Chicago Daily Tribune*, April 21, 1942.

157. Hanson W. Baldwin, "Mystery in Tokyo Raid," *New York Times*, April 21, 1942.

158. "Written by Vadm John L. Mccrea . . . ," Box 11, Folder 4, Papers of John L. McCrea, LOC.

159. Press Conference #820, April 21, 1942, in Roosevelt, *Complete Roosevelt Presidential Press Conferences*, vol. 19–20, 291–293.

160. Doolittle, *I Could Never Be So Lucky Again*, 12 and 265–266.

161. "Doolittle Led Air Raid on Japan, FDR Reveals," *Miami Daily News*, May 19, 1942, Box OV 83, JHDP.

162. Guillain, *I Saw Tokyo Burning*, 60–61.

163. Dower, *War without Mercy*, 49.

164. "Tokyo Press Defends Act," *New York Times*, April 24, 1943.

165. "Threat To Fliers," *New York Times*, April 23, 1943.

166. Scott, *Target Tokyo*, 409 and 410.

167. Casey, *The War Beat, Pacific*, 123.

168. Scott, *Target Tokyo*, 414–416.

169. Dower, *War without Mercy*, 49.

170. "Bond Sales Soar after Executions; City over Quota," *New York Times*, April 23, 1943.

171. "Execution of Fliers Brings Record Bond Sale in D.C.," *Washington Post*, April 23, 1943.

172. "Bond Sales Double Here; Seek More Public Support," *Chicago Daily Tribune*, April 23, 1943.

173. "Bond Sales Soar after Executions; City over Quota."

174. "Doolittle Pledges New Blows To Make Japan Beg Mercy," *New York Times*, April 23, 1943.

175. "Seizure of All Japs in U.S. Demanded," *Washington Post*, April 23, 1943.

176. "Hit Japs, Senators Demand," *Chicago Daily Tribune*, April 23, 1943.

177. "Vengeance with What?," *Chicago Daily Tribune*, April 23, 1943.

178. Mitsuo Fuchida and Masatake Okumiya, *Midway: The Battle That Doomed Japan*, ed. Clarke H. Kawakami and Roger Pineau (New York: Ballantine Books, 1955), 67.

179. Chin-tung Liang, *General Stilwell in China 1942–1944: The Full Story* (New York: St. John's University Press, 1972), 52; Claire Lee Chennault, *Way of a Fighter: The Memoirs of Claire Lee Chennault*, ed. by Robert Holt (New York: G. P. Putnam's Sons, 1949), 169; Rana Mitter, *Forgotten Ally: China's World War II, 1937–1945* (New York: Houghton Mifflin Harcourt, 2013), 261.

180. Scott, *Target Tokyo*, xiv.

181. Richard W. Bates, "The Battle of the Coral Sea, May 1 To May 11 Inclusive, 1942. Strategical and Tactical Analysis," Bureau of Naval Personnel, Naval War College, 1947, 114, online at Defense Technical Information Center, accessed November 11, 2021, https://apps.dtic.mil/sti/citations/ADA003053.

182. Spector, *Eagle against the Sun*, 155, 160 and 162.

183. Prange, *Miracle at Midway*, 21, 22, 23, and 26.

184. Kameto Kuroshima interview, November 28, 1964, Box 2, Series 7, Gordon W. Prange Papers, LOC, quoted in Scott, *Target Tokyo*, 316.

185. Fuchida and Okumiya, *Midway*, 72, 73, and 213–214.

186. "Navy Had Word of Jap Plan To Strike at Sea," *Chicago Daily Tribune*, June 7, 1942. As of 2016 the editors of the *Chicago Tribune* remain unrepentant. The story "did no harm," the paper maintains, and "fighting unwarranted government secrecy is a big part of what news organizations like the Tribune do, in wartime and peacetime." "Breaking the code on a Chicago mystery from World War II," *Chicago Tribune*, September 23, 2016.

187. Sweeney, *Secrets of Victory*, 80. Charges were brought against the correspondent Stanley Johnston, who had written the story, and other members of the *Chicago Tribune*'s staff for violation of the Espionage Act. He was the only reporter for a mainstream news outlet to be so charged during the war. A grand jury dismissed the charges. Elliot Carlson, *Stanley Johnston's Blunder: The Reporter Who Spilled the Secret behind the U.S. Navy's Victory at Midway* (Annapolis, MD: Naval Institute Press, 2017) ix, 5, and 6. For more on this case see also Michael S. Sweeney and Patrick S. Washburn, "The *Chicago Tribune*'s Battle of Midway Story and the Government's Attempt at an Espionage Act Indictment in 1942," *Journalism and Communication Monographs* 16, no. 1 (March 2014): 7–97; Patrick S. Washburn and Michael S. Sweeney, "It Ain't Over 'Til It's Over: Ending (?) the Narrative about the *Chicago Tribune* and the Battle of Midway," *American Journalism* 35, no. 3 (2018): 357–369.

188. Marshall to King, June 7, 1942, memorandum, Marshall, *Marshall Papers*, vol. 3, 227.

189. Marshall to King, June 7, 1942, memorandum.

190. "Press Conference," June 7, 1942, Box 23, Folder Press and Press Releases 1942, EJK.

191. During and after the war there was substantial debate over whether the Japanese saw the story or later heard of the legal action against the *Tribune*. "Quite simply" the most recent scholarship has concluded, "there is no compelling evidence that the Imperial Navy ever took any action as a result of Johnston's story." For this and an excellent summery of the debate see Carlson, *Stanley Johnston's Blunder*, 241 and "CODA."

192. "Press Conference," June 7, 1942, Box 23, Folder Press and Press Releases 1942, EJK.

193. After the war, Arnold would write that he had a "distinct recollection" of advocating a cross-channel landing in December 1941 and was supported by Stimson. Arnold, *Global Mission*, 303. However, there is no mention of this in any of the transcripts or Stimson's diary.

194. "The Chief of Staff Conference" December 24, 1941, Reel 205, HHAPAF.

195. Alan Brooke, *War Diaries 1939–1945: Field Marshal Lord Alanbrooke*, ed. Alex Danchev and Daniel Todman (London: Weidenfeld & Nicolson, 2001), 220.

196. Dwight D. Eisenhower, *The Eisenhower Diaries*, 44.

197. Stimson, Diary, February 24, 1942, Reel 7, HLSD.

198. Churchill to Roosevelt, March 5, 1942, in *Churchill & Roosevelt*, vol. 1, 381–184; Stimson, Diary, March 5, 1942, Reel 7, HLSD.

199. Wedemeyer, *Wedemeyer Reports!*, 98; Roosevelt to Churchill April 1, 1942, in *Churchill and Roosevelt*, vol. 1, 437.

200. Brooke, *War Diaries 1939–1945*, 248.

201. Churchill, *The Hinge of Fate*, 318, 322, and 323.

202. Brooke, *War Diaries 1939–1945*, 249.

203. Churchill, *The Hinge of Fate*, 319–320.

204. Stimson, Diary, March 5, 1943, Reel 7, HLSD.

205. Henry L. Stimson and McGeorge Bundy, *On Active Service in Peace and War* (New York: Harper & Brothers, 1947), 421–422.

206. Donovan Reports, March 10, 1942, FDRL, quoted in Steele, *The First Offensive*, 215n16.

207. Churchill, *The Hinge of Fate*, 318–319 and 320.

208. Steele, *The First Offensive*, 122–123.

209. Brooke, *War Diaries 1939–1945*, 249 and 250.

210. *New York Times*, February 27, 1942, 10:2, quoted in Steele, *The First Offensive*, 86–87.

211. Felix Chuev, *Molotov Remembers: Inside Kremlin Politics*, ed. Albert Resis (Chicago: Ivan R. Dee, 1993), 45.

212. Archibald MacLeish to Alan Barth, "Editorial Opinion on the War: Lull before the Storm," March 27, 1942, Box 81, Folder Editorial Opinion Rpt. Mar. 6–May 1, 1942, PSF. For example, see "War, Not Defense," *Washington Post*, February 28, 1942; "Offensive in Europe by Allies Expected," *New York Times*, March 10, 1942.

213. Dwight D. Eisenhower, *Crusade in Europe*, 52.

214. Hamilton, *The Mantle of Command*, 317–318.

215. Russell F. Weigley, *The American Way of War* (Bloomington: Indiana University Press, 1973), 319.

216. Stimson, Diary, June 17, 1942, Reel 7, HLSD.

217. King and Whitehill, *A Naval Record*, 394.

218. Alex Danchev, *Establishing the Anglo-American Alliance: The Second World War Diaries of Brigadier Vivian Dykes* (London: Brassey's, 1990), 158.

219. Combined Chiefs of Staff Minutes, June 20, 1942, in US Department of State, *Foreign Relations of the United States: The Conferences at Washington, 1941–1942, and Casablanca, 1943*, eds. Fredrick Aandahl, William M. Franklin, and William Slany (Washington, DC: U.S. Government Printing Office, 1968) [hereafter FRUS], 429–431; C.C.S. 83, Report by the Combined Chief of Staff, June 21, 1942, in FRUS, 467.

220. Brooke, *War Diaries 1939–1945*, 267.

221. Stimson, Diary, June 20, 1942, Reel 7, HLSD.

222. Brooke, *War Diaries 1939–1945*, 268.

223. Memorandum, June 21, 1942, *FRUS*, 435.

224. Stoler, *Allies and Adversaries*, 78.

225. Churchill, *The Hinge of Fate*, 433; Churchill to Roosevelt, in *Churchill and Roosevelt*, vol. 1, 520.

226. Stoler, *Allies and Adversaries*, 84.

227. Roosevelt to Hopkins, Marshall, and King, memorandum, July 16, 1942, Box 308, Folder Book 5, Sherwood Collections, HP.

228. Roosevelt to Hopkins, Marshall, and King, memorandum, July 16, 1942.

229. Churchill, *The Hinge of Fate*, 447.

230. Morison, *Strategy and Compromise*, 38–39. [Italics in the original].

231. Marshall, *Marshall Interviews and Reminiscences*, 622.

232. Wedemeyer, *Wedemeyer Reports*, 161.

233. Hamilton, *The Mantle of Command*, 345.

234. Casey, *Cautious Crusade*, 90–91.

235. Steele, *The First Offensive*, 143.

236. Churchill, *The Hinge of Fate*, 447.

237. "The Eight Hundred and Fifty-Ninth Press Conference (Excerpts)," November 10, 1942, in Roosevelt, *The Public Papers and Addresses of Franklin D. Roosevelt*, vol. 11, 465.

238. *Marshall Interviews and Reminiscences*, 593.

239. Stimson, Diary, July 27, 1942, Reel 7, HLSD.

240. Stimson, Diary, July 28, 1942, Reel 7, HLSD.

241. George S. Patton Jr., *War As I Knew It* (New York: Bantam Books, 1947), 3n.

242. Press Conferences, November 7, 1942, Box 41, Folder Press Conferences July–December 1942, Papers of Stephen T. Early, STE.

243. Roosevelt to Josephus Daniels, November 10, 1942, in Franklin D. Roosevelt, *F.D.R. His Personal Letters 1928–1945*, vol. 2, ed. Elliott Roosevelt (New York: Duell, Sloan and Pearce, 1950), 1363.

244. Steele, *The First Offensive*, 181.

245. Mark Clark, *Calculated Risk* (New York: Harper & Brothers, 1950), 46.

Chapter 2. "I Shall Return"

1. Quoted from MacArthur, *Reminiscences*, 145. See also Herman, *Douglas MacArthur*, 418–419; James, *The Years of MacArthur*, vol. 2, 108–109; Rogers, *The Good Years*, 201–202.

2. Knightley, *The First Casualty*, 280.

3. "General Vows To Do His Best; Throng Cheers," *Chicago Daily Tribune*, March 21, 1942.

4. As this book went to press, Steven Casey's *The War Beat, Pacific* was published, which makes the same point regarding MacArthur's goals. See Casey, *The War Beat, Pacific: The American Media at War against Japan* (Oxford: Oxford University Press, 2021), 2 and 297.

5. See Weinberg, *A World At Arms;* Stoler, *Allies and Adversaries;* Black, "Midway and the Indian Ocean," 131–140.

6. James, *The Years of MacArthur*, vol. 2, 133 and 134.

7. Thomas E. Kennedy to MacArthur, March 21, 1942, letter, RG-10, Reel 332, MML.

8. Hugh J. Wolfe and William D. Sabin, *Our Miracle Man* (Binghamton, NY: Hugh J. Wolfe, 1942). I am indebted to my colleague Matt Johnson for this observation.

9. Robert R. McCormick to MacArthur, March 22, 1942, telegram, RG-10, 332, MML.

10. Henry Luce to Melville Jacoby, telegram date and recipient unclear though it appears to be in August 1942 and ended up in MacArthur's papers, RG-3, Reel 411, MML.

11. "Dr. Evatt," Kenney Diary, vol. 1, Box 1, RG-54: Diaries of General George C. Kenney, USAAC, 1941–1945, GCK.

12. Erle R. Dickover to Nelson T. Johnson, April 27, 1942, letter, RG-3: Records of Headquarters, Southwest Pacific Area (SWPA), 1942–1945, 411, MML; Frazier Hunt, *The Untold Story of Douglas MacArthur* (New York: Devin-Adair, 1954), 282.

13. James, *The Years of MacArthur*, vol. 2, 135.

14. Stanley L. Falk, "Douglas MacArthur and the War against Japan," in *We Shall Return! MacArthur's Commanders and the Defeat of Japan 1942–1945*, ed. William M. Leary (Lexington: University Press of Kentucky, 1988), 2; Herman, *Douglas MacArthur*, 92.

15. Knightley, *The First Casualty*, 279.

16. Larrabee, *Commander in Chief*, 350; Richard H. Rovere and Arthur Schlesinger Jr., *General MacArthur and President Truman: The Struggle for Control of American Foreign Policy* (New Brunswick, NJ: Transaction Publishers, 1951), 80; Fussell, *Wartime*, 161; Williamson Murray and Allan R. Millett, *A War To Be Won: Fighting the Second World War* (Cambridge, MA: Belknap Press of Harvard University Press, 2000), 205–206; Davis, *FDR*, 409 and 431; Robert B. Davies, *Baldwin of the Times: Hanson W. Baldwin, A Military Journalist's Life, 1903–1991* (Annapolis, MD: Naval Institute Press, 2011), 143; Moseley, *Reporting War*, 156.

17. John F. Shortal, *Forged by Fire: General Robert L. Eichelberger and the Pacific War* (Columbia: University of South Carolina, 1987), 129.

18. Arthur Vandenberg, *The Private Papers of Senator Vandenberg*, ed. by Arthur H. Vandenberg, Jr., with Joe Alex Morris (Westport, CT: Greenwood Press, 1952), 82.

19. John E. Miller, *Governor Philip F. La Follette: The Wisconsin Progressives, and the New Deal* (Columbia: University of Missouri Press, 1982), 176; Rogers, *The Good Years*, 200; Manchester, *American Caesar*, 20, 352, and 16.

20. Sweeney, *Secrets of Victory*, 4; Walter Cronkite, *A Reporter's Life* (New York: Alfred A. Knopf, 1996), 77; Nancy Caldwell Sorel, *The Women Who Wrote the War: The Riveting Saga of World War II's Daredevil Women Correspondents* (New York: Arcade Publishing, 1999), xiii; Oldfield, *Never A Shot In Anger*, xvi; Dunn, *Pacific Microphone*, 151.

21. "General Headquarters Southwest Pacific Area Public Relations Office," found in RG-15, Box 59, Folder 7, MML; *The Officer's Guide* (Harrisburg, PA: Military Service Publishing, 1943), 334–335.

22. Casey, *The War Beat, Pacific*, 3.

23. George C. Marshall, "General MacArthur's 'Press Creed,'" March 24, 1942, reproduced in Frank C. Kunz, *Decisions That Counted*, 88–89, unpublished memoir, RG-15, Box 59, Folder 7, MML.

24. Douglas MacArthur, *A Soldier Speaks: Public Papers and Speeches of General*

of the Army Douglas MacArthur, ed. Vorin E. Whan Jr. (New York: Frederick A. Praeger, 1965), 127.

25. Smith, *War and Press Freedom*, 158.
26. Manchester, *American Caesar*, 415.
27. Knightley, *The First Casualty*, 281.
28. Sweeney, *The Military and the Press*, 108.
29. Sweeney, *Secrets of Victory*, 51.
30. Desmond, *Tides of War*, 240.
31. Douglas Gillison, *Royal Australian Air Force 1939–1942* (Adelaide: Griffin Press, 1962), 102–103.
32. Anthony J. Barker and Lisa Jackson, *Fleeting Attraction: A Social History of American Servicemen in Western Australia during the Second World War* (Nedlands, Australia: University of Western Australia Press, 1996), 65 and 189.
33. "General Vows To Do His Best," *Chicago Daily Tribune*, March 21, 1942. In fact, MacArthur had nothing to do with releasing this news. The presence of US troops was a secret to hide the fact that convoys were bringing them to Australia. Curtin "badgered" Stimson for the release, to which the secretary of war reluctantly consented. Stimson, Diary, March 16, 1942, Reel 7, HLSD.
34. Neil McDonald with Peter Brune, *Valiant for Truth: The Life of Chester Wilmot, War Correspondent* (Sydney, Australia: NewSouth Publishing, 2016), 233.
35. Dunn, *Pacific Microphone*, 147.
36. Lee, *One Last Look Around*, 139.
37. From COMANZAC to OPNAV, April 17, 1942, cable, Box 39, Folder #50—ANZAC (Australia–New Zealand) Area -1, January 30-April 21, 1942, MRP.
38. James, *The Years of MacArthur*, vol. 2, 164–165.
39. Rogers, *The Good Years*, 256.
40. Stimson to MacArthur, May 11, 1942, cable, Box 163, Naval Aide's Files A7–1 Publicity, Propaganda, Press Releases, Correspondents, Etc., May 11, 1942–October 24, 1944, MRP.
41. Stimson to Roosevelt, May 11, 1942, memorandum, Box 163, Naval Aide's Files A7–1 Publicity, Propaganda, Press Releases, Correspondents, Etc., May 11, 1942–October 24, 1944, MRP.
42. Marshall to FDR, May 15, 1942, memorandum, Box 163, Naval Aide's Files A7–1 Publicity, Propaganda, Press Releases, Correspondents, Etc., May 11, 1942–October 24, 1944, MRP.
43. Rogers, *The Good Years*, 255.
44. James, *The Years of MacArthur*, vol. 2, 167.
45. MacArthur to Marshall, May 15, 1942, message, Box 163, Naval Aide's Files A7–1 Publicity, Propaganda, Press Releases, Correspondents, Etc., May 11, 1942–October 24, 1944, MRP.
46. Spector, *Eagle against the Sun*, 398.
47. MacArthur, *Reminiscences*, 146.
48. Lee, *One Last Look Around*, 139–140 and 145.
49. Dunn, *Pacific Microphone*, 152–154.
50. Manchester, *American Caesar*, 416–417.

51. Rogers, *The Good Years*, 255.

52. Patricia Beard, *Newsmaker: Roy W. Howard: The Mastermind behind the Scripps-Howard News Empire from the Gilded Age to the Atomic Age* (Guilford, CT: Rowman & Littlefield, 2016), 238 and 246–247.

53. Lee, *One Last Look Around*, 144.

54. Clark Lee and Richard Henschel, *Douglas MacArthur* (New York: Henry Holt, 1952), 189.

55. Selwyn Pepper, "An Old Soldier's Stories," *St. Louis Dispatch*, November 23, 1985, found in RG-15, Box 50, Folder 6, MML.

56. Steven Casey, *Selling the Korean War: Propaganda, Politics, and Public Opinion in the United States, 1950–1953* (Oxford: Oxford University Press, 2008), 46 and 45. In Korea, MacArthur would not only reinstate reporters whom his subordinates expelled but ignore calls from veteran reporters for a realist censorship policy. Lee and Henschel, *Douglas MacArthur*, 198.

57. Frank C. Kunz to Lyman H. Hammond Jr., letter, September 3, 1992, found in RG-15, Box 59, Folder 7, MML.

58. Gillison, *Royal Australian Air Force*, 569n3.

59. Gavin Long, *MacArthur as Military Commander* (Princeton, NJ: B. T. Batsford, 1969), 136; Manchester, *American Caesar*, 344–345.

60. Kunz, *Decisions That Counted*, 18, RG-15, Box 59, Folder 7, MML.

61. Long, *MacArthur as Military Commander*, 136; Kunz, *Decisions That Counted*, 18, 21, and 29, RG-15, Box 59, Folder 7, MML; Herman, *Douglas MacArthur*, 555; James, *The Years of MacArthur*, vol. 2, 196; Desmond, *Tides of War*, 246.

62. Beard, *Newsmaker*, 248.

63. Beard, *Newsmaker*, 248; Knightley, *The First Casualty*, 282.

64. Dunn, *Pacific Microphone*, 5.

65. McDonald with Brune, *Valiant for Truth*, 234.

66. Kunz, *Decisions That Counted*, 31, Box 59, RG-15, Folder 7, MML.

67. Rogers, *The Good Years*, 248.

68. Long, *MacArthur as Military Commander*, 136.

69. Pepper, "An Old Soldier's Stories," *St. Louis Dispatch*, November 23, 1985, found in RG-15, Box 50, Folder 6, MML.

70. Rogers, *The Good Years*, 239, 240, and 242.

71. Roger Olaf Egeberg, *The General: MacArthur and the Man He Called "Doc"* (New York: Hippocrene Books, 1983), 33.

72. Herman, *Douglas MacArthur*, 496.

73. Potter, *Bull Halsey*, 220.

74. Manchester, *American Caesar*, 415.

75. Rogers, *The Good Years*, 259.

76. Rogers, 260.

77. Lee and Henschel, *Douglas MacArthur*, 188; Rogers, *The Good Years*, 259–261.

78. James, *The Years of MacArthur*, vol. 2, 165.

79. Lee, *One Last Look Around*, 139.

80. Dunn, *Pacific Microphone*, 161.

81. Robert L. Eichelberger, *Our Jungle Road to Tokyo* (New York: The Viking Press, 1950), 57.

82. Eichelberger, *Dear Miss Em*, 63.

83. Eichelberger to Sutherland, January 7, 1943, letter; Eichelberger to Mac-Arthur, January 18, 1943, letter; Eichelberger to MacArthur, January 21, 1943, letter, RG-41, Box 1, Folder 3, MML; Eichelberger, *Dear Miss Em*, 51 and 52; James, *The Years of MacArthur*, vol. 2, 271 and 274.

84. Kunz, *Decisions That Counted*, 52, RG-15, Box 59, Folder 7, MML.

85. James, *The Years of MacArthur*, vol. 2, 255.

86. Rogers, *The Good Years*, 265.

87. "General Vows To Do His Best," *Chicago Daily Tribune*, March 21, 1942.

88. Kunz, *Decisions That Counted*, 22, RG-15, Box 59, Folder 7, MML.

89. Lee, *One Last Look Around*, 142–143 and 141.

90. George Weller, *Weller's War: A Legendary Foreign Correspondent's Saga of World War II on Five Continents*, ed. Anthony Weller (New York: Crown Publisher, 2009), 357.

91. William J. Dunn, Sydney, Jan. 1, 1943, radio transcript, RG-52, Box 2, Folder 21, MML.

92. Carlos P. Romulo, *I Walked with Heroes* (New York: Holt, Rinehart and Winston, 1961), 224 and 229; Kunz, *Decisions That Counted*, 20, RG-15, Box 59, Folder 7, MML; Carlo P. Romulo, *I Saw the Fall of the Philippines* (New York: Doubleday, Doran, 1942), 206–209.

93. Romulo, *I Walked with Heroes*, 225–228 and 230; Romulo to MacArthur, August 18, 1942, letter, RG-10, Reel 333, MML.

94. Dunn, *Pacific Microphone*, 155; Dunn, Sydney, April 15, 1942, radio transcript, RG-52, Box 1, Folder 12, MML.

95. Diary, May 13, 1942, Reel 7, HLSD.

96. Lee, *One Last Look Around*, 143.

97. Eliot, Diary, March 13, 1942, Box 23, Folder Diary JAN–APR 1942, GFE.

98. Eichelberger, *Dear Miss Em*, 72.

99. James, *The Years of MacArthur*, vol. 2, 215.

100. James, *The Years of MacArthur*, vol. 2, 215; Marshall to MacArthur, August 10, 1942, radio 664, George C. Marshall, *Marshall Papers*, vol. 3, 296–297.

101. James, *The Years of MacArthur*, vol. 2, 215; Marshall to MacArthur, August 10, 1942, radio 664, George C. Marshall, *Marshall Papers*, vol. 3, 296–297 and 297–298n.

102. Manchester, *American Caesar*, 360.

103. Eichelberger, *Dear Miss Em*, 80.

104. T. J. David to MacArthur, January 6, 1944, letter, RG-15, Reel 331, MML.

105. Butcher, Diary, April 8, 1943, Box 166, Folder (January 8, 1943–May 5, 1943) (4), Dwight D. Eisenhower, Papers, PPPF.

106. Butcher, Diary, April 25, 1943, Box 166, Folder (January 8, 1943–May 5, 1943) (5), Dwight D. Eisenhower, Papers, PPPF.

107. Butcher, Diary, July 9, 1943, Box 167, Folder (July 8, 1943–August 17, 1943) (1), Dwight D. Eisenhower, Papers, PPPF.

108. Butcher, Diary, July 9, 1943, Box 167, Folder (July 8, 1943-August 17, 1943) (1), Dwight D. Eisenhower, Papers, PPPF.

109. Butcher, Diary, April 18, 1944, Box 168, Folder (March 3, 1944-May 9, 1944) (3), Dwight D. Eisenhower, Papers, PPPF.

110. Hughes, Diary, September 16, 1944, memorandum page, BoxI 2, ESHP.

111. Chester Hansen, Diary, January 7, 1945, Box 7, Folder 1, CHP.

112. George C. Kenney, *General Kenney Reports: A Personal History of the Pacific War* (New York: Duell, Sloan, and Pearce, 1949), 211.

113. Butcher, Diary, April 8, 1943, Box 166, Folder (January 8, 1943-May 5, 1943) (4), PPPF.

114. Edward S. Miller, *War Plan Orange: The U.S. Strategy to Defeat Japan, 1897–1945* (Annapolis, MD: Naval Institute Press, 1991), 4.

115. Peter J. Dean, *MacArthur's Coalition: US and Australian Operations in the Southwest Pacific Area, 1942–1945* (Lawrence: University Press of Kansas, 2018), 1.

116. Spector, *Eagle against the Sun*, xiii and 560; Hunt, *The Untold Story of Douglas MacArthur*, 285; Peter Calvocoressi and Guy Wint, *Total War: Causes and Courses of the Second World War* (London: Penguin Press, 1972), 772; Dan Van Der Vat, *The Pacific Campaign: World War II the U.S.-Japanese Naval War 1941–1945* (New York: Simon Schuster, 1991), 313; Miller, *War Plan Orange*, 360; Stephen R. Taaffe, *MacArthur's Jungle War: The 1944 New Guinea Campaign* (Lawrence: University Press of Kansas, 1998), 2.

117. MacArthur, *Reminiscences*, 172–173.

118. Manchester, *American Caesar*, 360.

119. George W. Baer, *One Hundred Years of Sea Power: The U.S. Navy, 1890–1990* (Stanford, CA: Stanford University Press, 1993), 241.

120. Walter R. Borneman, *The Admirals: Nimitz, Halsey, Leahy, and King—The Five-Star Admirals Who Won the War at Sea* (New York: Little, Brown, 2012), 261.

121. James, *The Years of MacArthur*, vol. 2, 189–190.

122. Richard B. Frank, *Guadalcanal: The Definitive Account of the Landmark Battle* (New York: Penguin, 1992), 35–36.

123. Symonds, *World War II at Sea*, 310; Frank, *Guadalcanal*, 122 and 124.

124. George C. Kenney, Diary, August 15, 1942, GCK, vol. 1, Box 1, MML.

125. Stimson, Diary, August 10, 1942, Reel 7, HLSD.

126. Marshall to MacArthur, cable, August 13, 1942, 01 Papers of George C. Marshall: Selected World War II Correspondence, 74/49 Folder MacArthur, Douglas, 1942 January–1942 August, George C. Marshall Library, Lexington, Virginia, accessed online through History Vault, ProQuest [hereafter HVP].

127. MacArthur to Marshall, August 15, 1942, cable; MacArthur to Marshall, August 16, 1942; cable, General Headquarters, Southwest Pacific Area, 1941–1945: Chronological Index and Summary of Communications [hereafter Index], HVP.

128. MacArthur to War Department, August 17, 1942, cable, Index, HVP.

129. King to CINCSWPA, August 17, 1942, cable, Index, HVP; James, *The Years of MacArthur*, vol. 2, 228.

130. MacArthur to Marshall, August 17, 1942, cable, Index, HVP.

131. Davies, *Baldwin of the Times*, 136–144; Stimson, Diary, October 30, 1942, Reel 7, HLSD.

132. Stimson, Diary, October 31, 1942, Reel 7, HLSD.

133. Potter, *Bull Halsey*, 155, 168, and 180.

134. Halsey and Bryan, *Admiral Halsey's Story*, xiv.

135. Halsey and Bryan, xv.

136. Potter, *Bull Halsey*, 193.

137. Samuel Eliot Morison, *The Two-Ocean War: A Short History of the United States Navy in the Second World War* (Boston: Little, Brown, 1963), 582.

138. John Wukovits, *Admiral "Bull" Halsey: The Life and Wars of the Navy's Most Controversial Commander* (New York: Palgrave Macmillan, 2010), 124–126; Potter, *Bull Halsey*, 201–202 and 219.

139. Dunn, *Pacific Microphone*, 187.

140. William M. Leary, ed., *We Shall Return! MacArthur's Commanders and the Defeat of Japan 1942–1945* (Lexington: University Press of Kentucky, 1988), ix–x.

141. Rovere and Schlesinger, *General MacArthur and President Truman*, 71–72; Taaffe, *MacArthur's Jungle War*, 5; Eichelberger, *Dear Miss Em*, 20; Shortal, *Forged by Fire*, 65; Perry, *The Most Dangerous Man in America*, 355; Stephen R. Taaffe, *Marshall and His Generals: U.S. Army Commanders in World War II* (Lawrence: University Press of Kansas, 2011), 320–321.

142. Eichelberger, *Our Jungle Road to Tokyo*, 22.

143. Cecil W. Nist to Eichelberger, June 19, 1942, letter, RG-41, Box 1, Folder 2, MML.

144. M.J.C. "I Corps Song," November 11, 1942, memorandum, RG-41, Box 1, Folder 2, MML.

145. Eichelberger, *Dear Miss Em*, 62, 52, and 54.

146. Shortal, *Forged by Fire*, 66–67. Eichelberger never knew MacArthur had come close to relieving him because of slow progress during a campaign that saw a large number of soldiers killed by disease, or that MacArthur had stated he had personal facts about Eichelberger that had led him to turn down the request for the Medal of Honor. Rogers, *The Good Years*, 341; Paul P. Rogers, *The Bitter Years: MacArthur and Sutherland* (New York: Praeger, 1991), 78 and 48.

147. Eichelberger, *Dear Miss Em*, 18 and 65.

148. For two examples see Manchester, *American Caesar*, 370; Michael Schaller, *Douglas MacArthur* (Oxford: Oxford University Press, 1989), 71.

149. Gene Smith, *Until the Last Trumpet Sounds: The Life of General of the Armies John J. Pershing* (New York: John Wiley & Sons, 1998), 166.

150. Search of "Robert Eichelberger" in *New York Times* articles from January 1, 1943, to September 1, 1945, on ProQuest search, accessed 10/18/19.

151. Douglas MacArthur, *Reminiscences*, 157.

152. Kenney, *General Kenney Reports*, 141 and 211.

153. Thomas E. Griffith Jr., *MacArthur's Airman: General George C. Kelley and the War in the South Pacific* (Lawrence: University Press of Kansas, 1998), 111.

154. Kenney, *General Kenney Reports*, 184.

155. MacArthur, *Reminiscences*, 170.

156. Eichelberger, *Dear Miss Em*, 88.

157. Robert M. Whites II to Lyman H. Hammond Jr., April 12, 1982, memorandum, RG-15, Box 13, Folder 17, "While, R," MML.

158. Box 19, Walter Krueger Papers, USMA Library, USMA.

159. Leary, "Walter Krueger: MacArthur's Fighting General," in *We Shell Return!*, 80–81, 86, and 87.

160. Eichelberger, *Dear Miss Em*, 82.

161. Lee, *One Last Look Around*, 144.

162. Alan Rems, *South Pacific Cauldron: World War II's Greatest Forgotten Battlegrounds* (Annapolis, MD: Naval Institute Press, 2014), xiii.

163. James, *The Years of MacArthur*, vol. 2, 280.

164. Spector, *Eagle against the Sun*, 221.

165. Rems, *South Pacific Cauldron*, 24, 31, and 198.

166. Perry, *The Most Dangerous Man in America*, 354.

167. Paul S. Dull, *A Battle History of the Imperial Japanese Navy (1941–1945)* (Annapolis, MD: Naval Institute Press, 1978), 270; Ian W. Toll, *The Conquering Tide: War in the Pacific Islands, 1942–1944* (New York: W. W. Norton, 2015), 225; Griffith, *MacArthur's Airman*, 107; Dean, *MacArthur's Coalition*, 223.

168. Kenney, Diary, March 4, 1943, GCK, vol. 4, Box 1, MML.

169. James, *The Years of MacArthur*, vol. 2, 295–296; Eichelberger, *Dear Miss Em*, 86.

170. Both Griffith and Dean claim Kenney reported only fourteen ships sunk, and MacArthur pushed the number to twenty-two. This number leaves off the six warships that Kenney did include. Griffith, *MacArthur's Airman*, 107; Dean, *MacArthur's Coalition*, 224; Clay Blair Jr., *MacArthur* (New York: Pocket Books, 1977), 124.

171. Kenney, Diary, March 5, 1943, GCK, vol. 4, Box 1, MML; Griffith, *MacArthur's Airman*, 108.

172. James, *The Years of MacArthur*, vol. 2, 296–297.

173. Marshall to MacArthur, September 8, 1943, letter, Index, HVP; Marshall to MacArthur, September 7, 1943, letter, Index, HVP.

174. MacArthur to Marshall, September 7, 1943, letter, Index, HVP.

175. Though MacArthur apparently convinced Marshall, the controversy would continue after the war. See James, *The Years of MacArthur*, vol. 2, 299–301; Charles A. Willoughby and John Chamberlain, *MacArthur 1941–1951* (New York: McGraw-Hill Book Company, 1954), 112 and 111; Lex McAulay, *Battle of the Bismarck Sea* (New York: St. Martin's Press, 1991), 156.

176. Arnold to Kenney, August 10, 1943, letter, GCK, vol. 6, Box 2, MML.

177. James, *The Years of MacArthur*, vol. 2, 301–303.

178. Rogers, *The Bitter Years*, 49.

179. James, *The Years of MacArthur*, vol. 2, 303.

180. Eichelberger, *Dear Miss Em*, 86.

181. Perry, *The Most Dangerous Man in America*, 229.

182. Long, *MacArthur as Military Commander*, 118; James, *The Years of MacArthur*, vol. 2, 303; Griffith, *MacArthur's Airman*, 110.

183. Griffith, *MacArthur's Airman*, 111.

184. Rogers, *The Bitter Years*, 51.

185. Eichelberger, *Dear Miss Em*, 86.

186. Robert La Follette to Philip F. La Follette, May 10, 1943, letter, RG-10, Reel 332, MML; Hamilton Fish to MacArthur, July 20, 1943, letter, RG-10, Reel 331, MML.

187. John Callan O'Laughlin, to MacArthur, October 7, 1943, letter, RG-10, Reel 333, MML.

188. James, *The Years of MacArthur*, vol. 2, 411.

189. Vandenberg, *The Private Papers of Senator Vandenberg*, 79.

190. Robert McCormick to MacArthur, February 7, 1944, letter. RG-10, 333, MML.

191. Julius Klein to MacArthur, August 3, 1943, letter, RG-10, Reel 332, MML.

192. James, *The Years of MacArthur*, vol. 2, 249; Manchester, *American Caesar*, 355–356; Blair, *MacArthur*, 168; Perry, *The Most Dangerous Man in America*, 250; Schaller, *Douglas MacArthur*, 79.

193. Scott Wierenga, "Former Aide Recalls Gen. MacArthur," *Bradenton Herald-Tribune*, September 5, 1978, found in RG-15, Box 50, Folder 6, MML.

194. Lee, *One Last Look Around*, 148.

195. Miller, *Governor Philip F. La Follette*, 174.

196. Rogers, *The Bitter Years*, 23.

197. Arthur H. Vandenberg to C. A. Willoughby, August 17, 1943, letter, RG-10, Reel 334, MML; James, *The Years of MacArthur*, vol. 2, 425.

198. James, *The Years of MacArthur*, 425.

199. Rogers, *The Bitter Years*, 24.

200. Eichelberger, *Dear Miss Em*, 71.

201. Hunt, *The Untold Story of Douglas MacArthur*, 317; James, *The Years of MacArthur*, vol. 2, 423.

202. Eichelberger, *Dear Miss Em*, 91. [Emphasis in original.]

203. James, *The Years of MacArthur*, vol. 2, 248–249.

204. Roy Howard to MacArthur, May 1, 1943, letter, RG-10, Reel 332, MML.

205. Rogers, *The Bitter Years*, 24 and 25.

206. James, *The Years of MacArthur*, vol. 2, 140.

207. Hunt, *The Untold Story of Douglas MacArthur*, 311.

208. James, *The Years of MacArthur*, vol. 2, 251.

209. Perry, *The Most Dangerous Man in America*, 354.

210. Hopkins, *The White House Papers of Harry L. Hopkins*, vol. 2, 867.

211. Rogers, *The Good Years*, 211; Carlos P. Romulo to MacArthur, July 12, 1942, letter, RG-10, Reel 333, MML.

212. James, *The Years of MacArthur*, vol. 2, 413, 414, and 416–417; Eichelberger, *Dear Miss Em*, 90–91.

213. Burns, *Roosevelt*, 501.

214. James, *The Years of MacArthur*, vol. 2, 434–435.

215. Allen Drury, *A Senate Journal 1943–1945* (New York: McGraw-Hill Book, 1963), 139.

216. James, *The Years of MacArthur*, vol. 2, 438.

217. Spector, *Eagle against the Sun*, 259, 266–267, 272–273, 317, and 319; Toll, *The Conquering Tide*, 513; Symonds, *World War II at Sea*, 553.

218. Toland, *The Rising Sun*, 505n and 659; "Army General Relieved in Row over Marine Losses," *San Francisco Examiner*, July 8, 1944; Harry A. Gailey, *Howlin' Mad vs the Army: Conflict in Command, Saipan 1944* (Novato, CA: Presidio Press, 1–6 and 10. For more on this decade's long controversy, including the media's role in it, see Gailey's book.

219. Robert Ross Smith, *The Approach to the Philippines*, The War in the Pacific, *United States Army in World War II* (Washington D.C.: Department of the Army, 1953), 577.

220. King to Clark Lee, April 29, 1946, letter, Box 35, Folder Comments on W.W.II Histories 1946–1950, EJK.

221. James, *The Years of MacArthur*, vol. 2, 522, 524, and 525.

222. Rogers, *The Bitter Years*, 111 and 136.

223. Weldon E. (Dusty) Rhoades, *Flying MacArthur to Victory* (College Station: Texas A&M University Press, 1987), 257.

224. Brower, *Defeating Japan*, 105.

225. Stephen Early to Samuel I. Rosenman, July 25, 1944, memorandum, Box 37, Folder Trip- Pacific, STE.

226. E. B. Potter, *Nimitz* (Annapolis, MD: Naval Institute Press, 1976), 319.

227. Samuel I. Rosenman, *Working with Roosevelt* (New York: Harper & Brothers, 1952), 456–457.

228. William D. Leahy, *I Was There* (New York: McGraw-Hill Book Company, 1950), 250; Rhoades, *Flying MacArthur to Victory*, 258.

229. Leahy, *I Was There*, 251.

230. MacArthur, *Reminiscences*, 197–198.

231. Potter, *Nimitz*, 318.

232. Willoughby with Chamberlain, *MacArthur 1941–1951*, 234; MacArthur, *Reminiscences*, 197–198.

233. Potter, *Nimitz*, 318.

234. Courtney Whitney, *MacArthur: His Rendezvous with History* (New York: Alfred A. Knopf, 1956), 125.

235. Leahy, *I Was There*, 251.

236. Morison, *The Two-Ocean War*, 421–422.

237. Robert Sherwood, *Roosevelt and Hopkins: An Intimate History* (New York: Harper & Brothers, 1948), 809.

238. Press and Radio Conference #962, July 29, 1944, Box 3, Folder Trip- Pacific, STE.

239. Rosenman, *Working with Roosevelt*, 480 and 487.

240. James, *The Years of MacArthur*, vol. 2, 534; Brower, *Defeating Japan*, 105–106; Manchester, *American Caesar*, 429; Lee, *One Last Look Around*, 146. [Emphasis in the original.]

241. James, *The Years of MacArthur*, vol. 2, 536; Larrabee, *Commander in Chief*, 344; Symonds, *World War II at Sea*, 555.

242. Brower, *Defeating Japan*, 108.

243. MacArthur, *Reminiscences*, 198; Whitney, *MacArthur*, 126; Willoughby with Chamberlain, *MacArthur 1941–1951*, 236; Rhoades, *Flying MacArthur to Victory*, 260.

244. Leahy, Diary, July 29, 1944, Reel 3, William D. Leahy Papers [hereafter WDL], LOC.

245. Press and Radio Conference #962, July 29, 1944, Box 37, Folder Trip- Pacific, STE.

246. John W. McCormack to MacArthur, July 20, 1945, letter, RG-10, Reel 333, MML.

247. Kunz, *Decisions That Counted*, page 43, RG-15, Box 59, Folder 7, ibid.

248. Toland, *The Rising Sun*, 540.

249. Lee, *One Last Look Around*, 145.

250. Dunn, *Pacific Microphone*, 6–7.

251. This is a comparison of total US Army, Navy, Marine, and Army Air Force personnel, comparing the total deployed to European, Mediterranean Middle-East, and Atlantic theaters to the total personnel deployed to the Pacific, CBI, and Alaska. Maurice Matloff, *Strategic Planning for Coalition Warfare, 1943–1944*, War Department, *United States Army in World War II* (Washington D.C.: Department of the Army, 1959), 396 and 398. Numerical comparisons are always tricky. For more information see Matloff, *Strategic Planning*, 396–401 and 555; Morison, *Strategy and Compromise*, 78–79; James, *The Years of MacArthur*, vol. 2, 349–353; Herman, *Douglas MacArthur*, 488.

252. Morison, *Strategy and Compromise*, 79.

253. Spector, *Eagle against the Sun*, xi.

254. Baer, *One Hundred Years of Sea Power*, 257.

255. Casey, *The War Beat, Pacific*, 3, 6, and 293.

256. Manchester, *American Caesar*, 450.

257. Dunn, *Pacific Microphone*, 7–9.

Chapter 3. "Pitiless Publicity"

1. Patton, Diary, November 7 and 8, 1942, Box 2, Folder 9, GSPP, LOC; Baer, *One Hundred Years of Sea Power*, 225; Morison, *The Two-Ocean War*, 225.

2. Brian McAllister Linn, *The Echo of Battle: The Army's Way of War* (Cambridge, MA: Harvard University Press, 2007), 5–7.

3. For a selection of authors who highlight Patton's warrior spirit and other aspects of Linn's Heroes see Roger H. Nye, *The Patton Mind: The Professional Development of an Extraordinary Leader* (New York: Avery Publishing Group, 1993), 148; Carlo D'Este, *Patton: A Genius for War* (New York: HarperCollins, 1996), 3; James Kelly Morningstar, *Patton's Way: A Radical Theory of War* (Annapolis, MD: Naval Institute Press, 2017), 3 and 18. Likewise, historians' assessment of Eisenhower fits him into the category of Linn's Managers. Stephen E. Ambrose, *The Supreme Commander: The War Years of General Dwight D. Eisenhower* (Garden City, NY: Doubleday, 1970), 664–665; Carlo D'Este, *Eisenhower: A Soldier's Life* (New York: Henry Holt, 2002), 4–5; Jean Edward Smith, *Eisenhower in War and Peace* (New York: Random House, 2012), xi–xii.

4. George S. Patton, *The Patton Papers, 1940–1945*, vol. 2, ed. Martin Blumenson (Boston: Da Capo Press, 1974), 101.

5. Patton, Diary, November 3, 1942, Box 2, Folder 19, GSPP.

6. Fussell, *Wartime*, 66.

7. "Orientation of Reinforcements," O. N. Bradley, March 7, 1945, Box 1, Folder untitled, ONBC; Stephen E. Ambrose, *Citizen Soldiers: The U.S. Army from the Normandy Beaches to the Bulge to the Surrender of Germany* (New York: Simon & Schuster, 1997), 166; D. A. Lande, *I Was with Patton: First-Person Accounts of WWII in George S. Patton's Command* (St. Paul, MN: MBI Publishing 2002), 6.

8. George S. Patton Jr., "The Secret of Victory," 1926, full unpublished version, reproduced in George S. Patton Jr., *Military Essays and Articles*, ed. Charles M. Province, 305, accessed February 24, 2014, http://www.pattonhq.com/pdffiles/vintagetext.pdf.

9. Patton, "The Secret of Victory," 298, 306, 302, and 307.

10. Patton, *War As I Knew It*, 336.

11. Fussell, *Wartime*, 66–67.

12. Joseph J. Mathews, *Reporting the Wars* (Minneapolis: University of Minnesota Press, 1957), 194.

13. Harry H. Semmes, *Portrait of Patton* (New York: Paperback Library, 1964), 11.

14. Dwight David Eisenhower, *Crusade in Europe*, 82.

15. Morningstar, *Patton's Way*, 42.

16. Fred Ayer Jr., *Before the Colors Fade: Portrait of a Soldier: George S. Patton, Jr.* (Boston: Houghton Mifflin, 1964), 203.

17. Patton, *The Patton Papers, 1940–1945*, 101.

18. Oldfield, *Never A Shot In Anger*, xii.

19. Dwight David Eisenhower, *The Eisenhower Diaries*, 84.

20. "Press Conference, 14 July, 1942," Box 1, Folder, July, 1942, HCB.

21. Dwight David Eisenhower, *Crusade in Europe*, 58.

22. "Public Relations Policies and Procedures," July 20, 1942, Box 1, Folder, July, 1942, HCB.

"Press Conference, 14 July, 1942," Box 1, Folder, July, 1942, HCB.

23. Craig Allen, *Eisenhower and the Mass Media: Peace, Prosperity, and Prime-Time TV* (Chapel Hill: University of North Carolina Press, 1993), 14 and 15.

24. Drew Middleton, *Our Share of Night* (New York: Viking Press, 1946), 306.

25. Virgil Pinkley with James F. Scheer, *Eisenhower Declassified* (Old Tappan, NJ: Fleming H. Revell, 1979), 120–121.

26. Allen, *Eisenhower and the Mass Media*, 11.

27. Allen, 11–13.

28. Fussell, *Wartime*, 160; Butcher, Diary, May 5, 1943, Box 166, Folder (January 8, 1943–May 5, 1943) (5), PPPF; Butcher, Diary, July 8, 1942, Box 165, Folder (July 8–September 15, 1942) (1), PPPF.

29. Hughes, Diary, April 29, 1942, BoxI 1, ESHP.

30. Butcher, Diary, July 13, 1942, Box 165, Folder (July 8–September 15, 1942) (1), PPPF.

31. Butcher, Diary, July 19, 1942, Box 165, Folder (July 8–September 15, 1942) (2), PPPF.

32. Butcher, Diary, September 20, 1942, Box 165, Folder (September 16, 1942–November 2, 1942) (1), PPPF.

33. Butcher, Diary, July 19, 1942, Box 165, Folder (July 8–September 15, 1942) (3), PPPF.

34. Butcher, Diary, September 20, 1942, Box 165, Folder (September 16, 1942–November 2, 1942) (1), PPPF.

35. Butcher, Diary, September 23, 1942, Box 165, Folder (September 16, 1942–November 2, 1942) (1), PPPF.

36. Butcher, Diary, September 26, 1942, Box 165, Folder (September 16, 1942–November 2, 1942) (1), PPPF.

37. Dwight D. Eisenhower, *At Ease: Stories I Tell to Friends* (Garden City, NY: Doubleday, 1967), 195.

38. Dwight David Eisenhower, *Crusade in Europe*, 58.

39. "Press Conference, 14 July, 1942," Box 1, Folder, July, 1942, HCB.

40. "Public Relations Policies and Procedures," July 20, 1942, Box 1, Folder, July, 1942, HCB.

41. "Press Conference, 14 July, 1942," Box 1, Folder, July, 1942, HCB.

42. Butcher, Diary, September 20, 1942, Box 165, Folder (September 16, 1942–November 2, 1942) (1), PPPF.

43. Sweeney, *The Secrets of Victory*, 218.

44. Stoler, *Allies and Adversaries*, 70.

45. Peter S. Kindvatter, *American Soldiers: Ground Combat in the World Wars, Korea, and Vietnam* (Lawrence: University Press of Kansas, 2003), xxiii, 140, 141, and 264.

46. Marshall to Eisenhower, November 8, 1942, radio R-2969, Marshall, *Marshall Papers*, vol. 3, 431n.

47. Clark, *Calculated Risk*, 84.

48. Eisenhower to Marshall, November 9, 1942, radio R-187, 431–432n; Marshall to Eisenhower, November 9, 1942, radio R-2969, 431, in Marshall, *Marshall Papers*, vol. 3.

49. Butcher, Diary, November 11, 1942, Box 165, Folder (November 6, 1942–November 27, 1942) (2), PPPF.

50. Weinberg, *A World at Arms*, 140.

51. Douglas Porch, *The Path to Victory: The Mediterranean Theater in World War II* (New York: Farrar, Straus and Giroux, 2004), 359; Smith, *Eisenhower in War and Peace*, 237.

52. Robert Murphy, *Diplomat among Warriors* (New York: Pyramid Book, 1964), 149.

53. Murphy, 152–154.

54. Clark, *Calculated Risk*, 109, 111, 120, and 122.

55. Eisenhower to Combined Chiefs of Staff, November 14, 1942, cable, Dwight David Eisenhower, *Eisenhower Papers*, vol. 2, 708.

56. Dwight David Eisenhower, *Crusade in Europe*, 108.

57. Edward R. Murrow, *In Search of Light: The Broadcasts of Edward R. Murrow 1938–1961*, ed. Edward Bliss Jr. (New York: Alfred A. Knopf, 1967), 55.

58. Pinkley, *Eisenhower Declassified*, 137.

59. Olson, *Citizens of London*, 193.

60. Dwight David Eisenhower, *Crusade in Europe*, 109.

61. H. L. Nussbaum to T. Tuper, "TFPRO—RADIO," May 22, 1943, Box 2, Folder 000.77–1, RG 331; NARA.

62. Milton S. Eisenhower, *The President Is Calling* (Garden City, NY: Doubleday, 1974), 140 and 141.

63. Winfield, *FDR and the News Media*, 162; Butcher, Diary, December 17, 1942, Box 166, Folder (November 30, 1942–January 7, 1943) (3), PPPF.

64. Casey, *The War Beat, Europe*, 347.

65. Samuel I. Rosenman, *Working with Roosevelt* (New York: Harper & Brothers, 1952), 363–364.

66. Olson, *Citizens of London*, 195–196.

67. Fleming, *The New Dealers' War*, 170.

68. D'Este, *Eisenhower*, 357; Stephen E. Ambrose and Richard H. Immerman, *Milton S. Eisenhower: Educational Statesman* (Baltimore, MD: Johns Hopkins University Press, 1983), 70.

69. John Gunther, *Roosevelt in Retrospect: A Profile in History* (New York: Harper & Brothers, Publishers, 1950), 331.

70. Stimson, Diary, November 4, 1942, and November 16, 1942, Reel 8, HLSD.

71. Morgenthau, Diary, November 17, 1942, Series 1: Morgenthau Diaries, vol. 585, Franklin, accessed June, 3, 2019, http://www.fdrlibrary.marist.edu/archives/collections/franklin/.

72. Stimson, Diary, November 16, 1942, Reel 8, HLSD; November 17, 1942, Series 2: Morgenthau Diaries, Franklin, accessed June, 3, 2019, http://www.fdrlibrary.marist.edu/archives/collections/franklin/.

73. Stimson, Diary, November 16, 1942, Reel 8, HLSD; Wendell Willkie, "Text of Willkie's Address Criticizing Some Allied War Motives," *Daily Boston Globe*, November 17, 1942.

74. Stimson and Bundy, *On Active Service in Peace and War*, 543.

75. Marshall, *Marshall Interviews and Reminiscences*, 487.

76. Jones to Butcher, November 30, 1942, letter, Box 166, Folder (November 30, 1942 –January 7, 1943) (2), PPPF.

77. Marshall to Young, January 6, 1943, memorandum, Marshall, *Marshall Papers*, vol. 3, 507.

78. Sherwood, *Roosevelt and Hopkins*, 653.

79. "Statement on the Temporary Political Arrangements in North and West Africa," November 17, 1942, in Roosevelt, *The Public Papers and Addresses of Franklin D. Roosevelt*, vol. 11, 480.

80. Casey, *Cautious Crusade*, 216.

81. Marshall to Eisenhower, November 20, 1942, radio R-3345, Marshall, *Marshall Papers*, vol. 3, 445.

82. Eisenhower to Clark, November 21, 1942, letter, Dwight D. Eisenhower, *Eisenhower Papers*, vol. 2, 749–750.

83. Eisenhower to Marshall, November 21, 1942, Dwight D. Eisenhower, *Eisenhower Papers*, vol. 2, 748.

84. Eisenhower to Clark, November 21, 1942, letter, Dwight D. Eisenhower, *Eisenhower Papers*, vol. 2, 749.

85. Butcher, Diary, December 12, 1942, Box 166, Folder (November 30, 1942–January 7, 1943) (2), PPPF.

86. Milton Eisenhower, *The President Is Calling*, 139.

87. Butcher, Diary, December 15, 1942, Box 166, Folder (November 30, 1942–January 7, 1943) (3), PPPF.

88. Eisenhower to Surles, December 22, 1942, letter, Dwight D. Eisenhower, *Eisenhower Papers*, vol. 2, 859.

89. Butcher, Diary, December 12, 1942, Box 166, Folder (November 30, 1942–January 7, 1943) (2), PPPF.

90. Butcher, Diary, December 16, 1942, Box 166, Folder (November 30, 1942–January 7, 1943) (3), PPPF; Butcher, Diary, April 25, 1943, Box 166, Folder (January 8, 1943– May 5, 1943) (5), PPPF; Butcher to Surles, letter, May 12, 1943, PPPF; Butcher, Diary, April 17, 1943, Box 166, Folder (January 8, 1943–May 5, 1943) (4), PPPF.

91. Butcher to Krum, February 16, 1943, letter, Box 2, Folder July 1943, HCB.

92. Butcher, Diary, December 16, 1942, Box 166, Folder (November 30, 1942–January 7, 1943) (3), PPPF.

93. Rick Atkinson, *An Army at Dawn: The War in North Africa, 1942–1943* (New York: Henry Holt, 2002), 197.

94. Patton, Diary, January 15, 1943, Box 2, Folder 13, GSPP.

95. "The Organisation of Command Spring 1946," November 18, 1942, letter, in Andrew Cunningham, *The Cunningham Papers*, vol. 2, *The Triumph of Allied Sea Power 1942–1946*, ed. Michael Simpson (Aldershot, England: Ashgate, 2006), 406–407.

96. Clark, *Calculated Risk*, 130.

97. Larrabee, *Commander in Chief*, 425.

98. Casey, *The War Beat*, 45.

99. Butcher, Diary, January 4, 1943, Box 166, Folder (November 30, 1942–January 7, 1943) (4), PPPF.

100. Dwight David Eisenhower, *Crusade in Europe*, 130; Clark, *Calculated Risk*, 132; Murphy, *Diplomat among Warriors*, 165.

101. For those critical of the Darlan Deal see Porch, *The Path to Victory*, 363–364; Olson, *Citizens of London*, 194; Ambrose, *The Supreme Commander*, 126 and 135. For a more favorable view of Eisenhower's actions see D'Este, *Eisenhower*, 358; Geoffrey Perret, *Eisenhower* (New York: Random House, 1999), 181.

102. Casey, *Cautious Crusade*, 121, 124, and 126. Casey is not the only historian to link the Darlan Deal to unconditional surrender. See Gunther, *Roosevelt in Retrospect*, 333; Porch, *The Path to Victory*, 364.

103. Butcher, Diary, January 20, 1943, Box 166, Folder (January 8, 1943–May 5, 1943) (1), PPPF.

104. Helmut Heiber, ed., *Hitler and His Generals: Military Conferences 1942–1945*, trans. Roland Winter, Krista Smith, and Mary Beth Friedrich (New York: Ensigma Books, 2002), 3.

105. Porch, *The Path to Victory*, 371.

106. *The Secret Conferences of Dr. Goebbels: The Nazi Propaganda War 1939–43*, ed. Willi A. Boelcke, trans. Ewald Osers (New York: E. P. Dutton, 1970), 298.

107. Albert Kesselring, *The Memoirs of Field-Marshal Kesselring*, trans. William Kimber (Novato, CA: Presidio Press, 1989), 142.

108. Carlo D'Este, *World War II in the Mediterranean, 1942–1945* (Chapel Hill, NC: Algonquin Books of Chapel Hill, 1990), 7.

109. D'Este, 6, 11, 10 and 15.

110. Patton, *The Patton Papers, 1940–1945*, 164.

111. D'Este, *World War II in the Mediterranean*, 13.

112. Porch, *The Path to Victory*, 382.

113. Eisenhower to Marshall, November 10, 1942, cable #272, Dwight D. Eisenhower, *Eisenhower Papers*, vol. 2, 687.

114. Cronkite, *A Reporter's Life*, 88–90.

115. Marshall to Surles, December 7, 1942, memorandum, Marshall, *Marshall Papers*, vol. 3, 474.

116. Casey, *The War Beat*, 69–70.

117. Butcher, Diary, February 16, 1943, Box 166, Folder (January 8, 1943–May 5, 1943) (3), PPPF.

118. Butcher, Diary, December 17, 1942, Box 165, Folder (November 6, 1942–November 27, 1942) (3), PPPF.

119. Butcher, Diary, January 28, 1943, Box 166, Folder (January 8, 1943–May 5, 1943) (1), PPPF.

120. Brooke, *War Diaries 1939–1945*, 343. [Original in italics].

121. Patton, Diary, January 28, 1943, Box 2, Folder 14, GSPP.

122. Butcher, Diary, February 7, 1943, Box 166, Folder (January 8, 1943–May 5, 1943) (2), PPPF; Porch, *The Path to Victory*, 381.

123. Butcher, Diary, February 16, 1943, Box 166, Folder (January 8, 1943–May 5, 1943) (3), PPPF. Collingwood would receive the George Foster Peabody Award for his work in North Africa. Bob Edwards, *Edward R. Murrow and the Birth of Broadcast Journalism* (Hoboken, NJ: John Wiley, 2004), 63.

124. Butcher to Paley, July 17, 1943, letter, Box 2, Folder August, HBP.

125. Eisenhower to Marshall, February 8, 1943, cable, Dwight D. Eisenhower, *Eisenhower Papers*, vol. 2, 942.

126. Eisenhower to Marshall, April 16, 1943, letter, Dwight D. Eisenhower, *Eisenhower Papers*, vol. 2, 1091.

127. Dennis Showalter, *Patton and Rommel: Men of War in the Twentieth Century* (New York: Berkley Caliber, 2005), 2.

128. Ralf Georg Reuth, *Rommel: The End of a Legend*, trans. Debra S. Marmor and Herbert A. Danner (London: Haus Books, 2005), 121–122.

129. Porch, *The Path to Victory*, 380.

130. Erwin Rommel, *The Rommel Papers*, ed. B. H. Liddell Hart, trans. Paul Findlay (New York: Harcourt, Brace, 1953), 398.

131. Atkinson, *An Army at Dawn*, 389.

132. Patton, *The Patton Papers, 1940–1945*, 181.

133. D'Este, *World War II in the Mediterranean*, 27.

134. Hughes, Diary, February 7, 1943, BoxI 2, ESHP. [Underlined in original].

135. Casey, *The War Beat*, 71–72.

136. Butcher, Diary, March 4, 1943, Box 166, Folder (January 8, 1943–May 5, 1943) (3), PPPF.

137. Eisenhower to Alexander, March 9, 1943, letter, Box 3, Folder Alexander, Harold R. L. (8), PPPF.

138. Bernard Law Montgomery, *Montgomery and the Eighth Army: A Selection from the Diaries, Correspondence and other Papers of Field Marshal The Viscount Montgomery of Alamein, August 1942 to December 1943*, ed. Stephen Brooks (London: Bodley Head, 1991), 367–368n68.

139. Eisenhower to Patton, March 6, 1943, memorandum, Dwight D. Eisenhower, *Eisenhower Papers*, vol. 2, 865.

140. Frank L. Kluckhohn, "'Always Go Forward!'" *New York Times*, March 19, 1943.

141. Patton, *The Patton Papers, 1940–1945*, 178 and 206.

142. "Patton Commands in Mid-Tunisia," *New York Times*, March 19, 1943.

143. "George Does It," *Morning Call*, April 6, 1943.

144. "Rough Rider Patton," *New York Times*, March 19, 1943.

145. "Gen. Patton Is Colorful Leader," *Bismarck Tribune*, March 18, 1943.

146. Casey, *The War Beat*, 75–74.

147. Porch, *The Path to Victory*, 408.

148. "Patton Commands in Mid-Tunisia," *New York Times*, March 19, 1943.

149. Patton, *The Patton Papers, 1940–1945*, 216, 198, 202, and 215.

150. Patton, Diary, April 3, 1943, Box 2, Folder 14, GSPP; Atkinson, *An Army at Dawn*, 470–472 and 477; George F. Howe, *Northwest Africa: Seizing the Initiative in the West*, The Mediterranean Theater of Operations, *United States Army in World War II* (Washington, DC: Department of the Army, 1957), 583.

151. Bradley, "Confidential & Personal," 16, Box 38, ONBC, USMA.

152. Omar N. Bradley and Clay Blair, *A General's Life: An Autobiography* (New York: Simon and Schuster, 1983), 150; Patton, *The Patton Papers, 1940–1945*, 218; Patton to Alexander, April 12, 1943, letter, Box 32, Folder 7, GSPP.

153. Bradley and Blair, *A General's Life*, 150. Historian Stephen Ambrose writes "Pulling . . . the 34th Division, out of the line in Tunisia was the best military policy, but Alexander could not do it because of the alliance." Ambrose, *The Supreme Commander*, 225. As the accounts from Bradley and Patton indicate, it was public opinion as much as the Alliance that persuaded Alexander.

154. William King, "Rommel Escapes Trap," *Boston Globe*, April 13, 1943.

155. "Mixup in Timing Delays Fall of Kairouan A Day," *Chicago Daily Tribune*, April 13, 1943.

156. "How the Yanks Fought," *Time*, April 19, 1943, 31.

157. Marshall to Eisenhower, April 14, 1943, radio R-5940, Marshall, *Marshall Papers*, vol. 3, 643, 644, and 645.

158. Butcher, Diary, April 17, 1943, Box 166, Folder (January 8, 1943–May 5, 1943) (4), PPPF; Omar N. Bradley, *A Soldier's Story* (New York: Henry Holt, 1951), 56–57.

159. Bradley, *A Soldier's Story*, 59.

160. Bradley, "Confidential & Personal," 9, Box 38, ONBC, USMA. [Emphasis in the original].

161. Eisenhower to Alexander, March 23, 1943, letter, Dwight D. Eisenhower, *Eisenhower Papers*, vol. 2, 1056.

162. Bradley, *A Soldier's Story*, 59.

163. Butcher, Diary, April 17, 1943, Box 166, Folder (January 8, 1943–May 5, 1943) (4), PPPF.

164. Patton to Alexander, April 11, letter, 1943, Box 32, Folder 7, GSPP.

165. Bradley, "Confidential & Personal," 9, Box 38, ONBC, USMA.

166. Butcher, Diary, April 17, 1943, Box 166, Folder (January 8, 1943–May 5, 1943) (4), PPPF.

167. Eisenhower to Marshall, April 15, 1943, cable, Dwight D. Eisenhower, *Eisenhower Papers*, vol. 2, 1089.

168. Eisenhower to Marshall, April 16, 1943, letter, Dwight D. Eisenhower, *Eisenhower Papers*, vol. 2, 1091.

169. Atkinson, *An Army at Dawn*, 529.

170. Max Hastings, *All Hell Let Loose: The World at War 1939–45* (London: HarperPress, 2011), 379.

171. Casey, *The War Beat*, 84; Porch also notes that the Tunisia victory "validated Roosevelt's 'European First' strategy." Porch, *The Path to Victory*, 413.

172. James Scott Wheeler, *Jacob L. Devers: A General's Life* (Lexington: University Press of Kentucky, 2015), 1–4. Wheeler offers different reasons why Devers never received much postwar attention.

173. Marshall to Surles, April 1, 1943, memorandum, 625–626; Marshall to Surles, April 4, 1943, memorandum, 631–632, Marshall, *Marshall Papers*, vol. 3.

174. Marshall to Surles, May 8, 1943, memorandum, Marshall, *Marshall Papers*, vol. 3, 686.

175. Reynolds, *By Quentin Reynolds*, 292–294.

176. Butcher, Diary, June 26, 1943, Box 166, Folder (May 8, 1943–July 6, 1943) (4), PPPF.

177. Atkinson, *An Army at Dawn*, 123.

178. Casey, *The War Beat*, 147.

179. Butcher, Diary, June 12, 1943, Box 166, Folder (May 8, 1943–July 6, 1943) (3), PPPF.

180. Butcher, Diary, July 13, 1943, Box 167, Folder (July 8, 1943–August 17, 1943) (1), PPPF.

181. Butcher, Diary, July 9, 1943, Box 167, Folder (July 8, 1943–August 17, 1943) (1), PPPF.

182. Bradley and Blair, *A General's Life*, 193 and 193n. Though the incident was not isolated, in this case it was also understandable. The Canadians were originally

supposed to take Enna, and, according to Patton, they arrived eight minutes after the Americans. Carlo D'Este, *Bitter Victory: The Battle for Sicily, 1943* (New York: E. P. Dutton, 1988), 451; Patton, *The Patton Papers, 1940–1945*, 294.

183. D'Este, *World War II in the Mediterranean*, 61.

184. Stanley P. Hirshson, *General Patton: A Soldier's Life* (New York: Harper-Collins, 2002), 384.

185. Nigel Hamilton, *Monty: Master of the Battlefield 1942–1944* (London: Hamish Hamilton, 1988), 263.

186. Marshall to Eisenhower, May 15, 1943, radio R-232, Marshall, *Marshall Papers*, vol. 3, 694–695.

187. Butcher, Diary, July 11, 1943, Box 167, Folder (July 8, 1943–August 17, 1943) (1), PPPF.

188. Patton, Diary, Appendix 48 "Summery of Events," July 18, 1943, Box 3, Folder 1, GSPP.

189. Albert N. Garland and Howard McGaw Smyth, *Sicily and the Surrender of Italy*, The Mediterranean Theater of Operations, *United States Army in World War II* (Washington, DC: Department of the Army, 1965), 235.

190. Patton, Diary, July 17, Box 3, Folder 1, GSPP.

191. Hirshson, *General Patton*, 380; Hughes, Diary, July 22, 1943, BoxI 2, ESHP.

192. Bernard Law Montgomery, *The Memoirs of Field-Marshal the Viscount Montgomery of Alamein, K.G.* (London: Collins, 1958), 188.

193. Bradley and Blair, *A General's Life*, 191.

194. Hamilton, *Monty*, 320.

195. Kesselring, *The Memoirs of Field-Marshal Kesselring*, 163.

196. D'Este, *World War II in the Mediterranean*, 68; Porch, *The Path to Victory*, 437.

197. Hamilton, *Monty*, 315.

198. Garland and Smyth, *Sicily and the Surrender of Italy*, 235 and 256–257.

199. Gay, Diary, July 25, 1943, Box 2, Folder 1, HRG.

200. D'Este, *World War II in the Mediterranean*, 68.

201. Lucian K. Truscott, *Command Mission* (Novato, CA: Presidio Press, 1954), 222.

202. Hansen, Diary, July 21, 1943, Box 4, Folder 2, CHP.

203. Truscott, *Command Mission*, 224.

204. Rick Atkinson, *The Day of Battle: The War in Sicily and Italy* (New York: Henry Holt, 2007), 134.

205. Don Whitehead, *Combat Reporter: Don Whitehead's World War II Diary and Memoirs*, ed. John B. Romeiser (New York: Fordham University Press, 2006), 178.

206. Robert Capa, *Slightly Out of Focus* (New York: Modern Library, 1999), 71 and 78.

207. Patton, *The Patton Papers, 1940–1945*, 304.

208. Patton, 308, 299 and 300.

209. Porch, *The Path to Victory*, 438.

210. Patton, *The Patton Papers, 1940–1945*, 311.

211. Butcher, Diary, July 17, 1943, Box 167, Folder (July 8, 1943–August 17, 1943) (2), PPPF.

212. Butcher, Diary, August 2, 1943, PPPF.

213. Butcher, Diary, August 4, 1943, and August 6, 1943, Box 167, Folder (July 8, 1943–August 17, 1943) (3), PPPF.

214. Butcher, Diary, August 12, 1943, PPPF.

215. Lucas, Diary, August 7, 1943, Box 14, Folder 1, JPL.

216. Eisenhower to Churchill, August 4, 1943, letter, Box 167, Folder (July 8, 1943–August 17, 1943) (3), PPPF.

217. Eisenhower to Alexander, August 5, 1943, letter, Box 3, Folder Alexander, Harold R. L. (7), PPPF.

218. Butcher, Diary, August 14, 1943, Box 167, Folder (July 8, 1943–August 17, 1943) (3), PPPF.

219. Truscott, *Command Mission*, 229.

220. Patton, Diary, July 25, 1943, Box 3, Folder 2, GSPP.

221. Hamilton, *Monty*, 326–327.

222. D'Este, *Bitter Victory*, 450–451.

223. Atkinson, *The Day of Battle*, 126.

224. Antony Beevor, *D-Day: The Battle for Normandy* (New York: Viking, 2009), 6.

225. Francis de Guingand, *Operation Victory* (New York: Charles Scribner's Sons, 1947), 310.

226. "Some Notes on Morale in an Army," August 1943, in Montgomery, *Montgomery and the Eighth Army*, 268–270.

227. Hamilton, *Monty*, 354.

228. Patton, *The Patton Papers, 1940–1945*, 225.

229. Lucas, Diary, July 5, 1943, Box 14, Folder 1, JPL.

230. Whitehead, *Combat Reporter*, 195.

231. Lucas, Diary, August 1, 1943, Box 14, Folder 1, JPL.

232. Patton, Diary, August 1, 1943, Box 3, Folder 2, GSPP.

233. D'Este, *Bitter Victory*, 449.

234. Hamilton, *Monty*, 301 and 335; D'Este, *Patton*, 523.

235. Montgomery, *Montgomery and the Eighth Army*, 251 and 255; Hamilton, *Monty*, 335.

236. Butcher, Diary, August 3, 1943, Box 167, Folder (July 8, 1943–August 17, 1943) (3), PPPF.

237. De Guingand, *Operation Victory*, 308.

238. Truscott, *Command Mission*, 234.

239. Rupert Prohme, *History of 30th Infantry Regiment World War II* (Washington, DC: Infantry Journal Press, 1947), 65; Patton, Diary, August 10, 1943, Box 3, Fold 2, GSPP; Truscott, *Command Missions*, 235; Garland and Smyth, *Sicily and the Surrender of Italy*, 391.

240. Truscott, *Command Mission*, 234–235; Patton, Diary, August 10, 1943, Box 3, Folder 2, GSPP. Bradley later confirmed Truscott's account, though it is interesting that his first book makes no mention of the incident. Bradley and Blair, *A General's Life*, 196–197. It should also be noted that Bradley's first book makes no mention of the media angle to Patton's thinking. Bradley, *A Soldier's Story*, 159.

241. Garland and Smyth, *Sicily and the Surrender of Italy*, 390.

242. Patton, Diary, August 10, 1943, Box 3, Fold 2, GSPP; Gay, Diary, August 10, 1943, Box 2, Folder 1, HRG.

243. Whitehead, *Combat Reporter*, 199.

244. Operational Report of Third Infantry Division in Sicily July 19–23 July 31–Aug. 17, 1943, Box 5391, RG 407, NARA.

245. Prohme, *History of 30th Infantry Regiment World War II*, 69; Operational Report of Third Infantry Division in Sicily July 19–23 July 31–Aug. 17, 1943, Box 5391, RG 407, NARA.

246. Whitehead, *Combat Reporter*, 206.

247. Operational Report of Second Battalion 30th Infantry While Attached to 3rd Infantry Division, August 26, 1943, Box 5610, 303-INF 1 (7)-0.3.0, Records of the Adjutant General's Office, WWII Operations Reports, 1940–48, 3rd Infantry Division, RG 407, NARA.

248. Bradley and Blair, *A General's Life*, 197; Truscott, *Command Missions*, 240.

249. Patton, Diary, August 11, 1943, and August 12, 1943, Box 3, Folder 2, GSPP.

250. Bradley and Blair, *A General's Life*, 199.

251. Truscott, *Command Missions*, 243.

252. Atkinson, *The Day of Battle*, 170.

253. Gay, Diary, August 17, 1943, Box 2, Folder 1, HRG.

254. Patton, Diary, August 17, 1943, Box 3, Folder 2, GSPP.

255. Patton, Diary, September 2, 1943, Box 3, Folder 3, GSPP.

256. Porch, *The Path to Victory*, 444.

257. Bradley, interview Esther Dora "Kitty" Bradley[wife] by Hanson, December 4, 1974, Box 2, Folder 12, ONBC, USAHEC.

258. Butcher, Diary, August 2, 1943, Box 167, Folder (July 8, 1943–August 17, 1943) (2), PPPF.

259. Patton, *The Patton Papers, 1940–1945*, 306–307.

260. Patton, Diary, August 3, 1943, Box 3, Folder 2, GSPP; Leaver to Arnest, August 4, 1943, "Inspection of 15th Evacuation Hospital by Lieutenant General George S. Patton," Box 91, Folder Patton 4, PPPF.

261. Patton, Diary, August 10, 1943, Box 3, Folder 2, GSPP.

262. Donald E. Currier to Surgeon, II Corps, August 12, 1943, "Visit of Lieutenant General Patton, to the 93rd Evacuation Hospital," Box 91, Folder Patton 4, PPPF; Patton, Diary, August 10, 1943, Box 3, Folder 2, GSPP.

263. Butcher, Diary, August 14, 1943, Box 167, Folder (July 8, 1943–August 17, 1943) (3), PPPF.

264. Butcher, Diary, August 17, 1943, Box 167, PPPF.

265. Farago, *Patton*, 344.

266. Demaree Bess, August 19, 1943, "Report of an Investigation," Box 91, Folder Patton 4, PPPF.

267. Currier to Eisenhower, September 15, 1964, letter, Box 1, DEC; Demaree Bess, August 19, 1943, "Report of an Investigation," Box 91, Folder Patton 4, PPPF.

268. Reynolds, *By Quentin Reynolds*, 296.

269. Demaree Bess, August 19, 1943, "Report of an Investigation," Box 91, Folder Patton 4, PPPF.

270. Butcher, Diary, August 17, 1943, Box 167, Folder (August 18–September 25, 1943) (1), PPPF.

271. Reynolds, *By Quentin Reynolds*, 296.

272. Pinkley, *Eisenhower Declassified*, 160.

273. Reynolds, *By Quentin Reynolds*, 297.

274. Eisenhower to Marshall, November 24, 1943, letter, Box 167, Folder (October 1–December 30, 1943) (2), PPPF.

275. Lucas, Diary, August 3, 1943, Box 14, Folder 1, JPL; "Patton," Box 12, Folder Diary Notes, ESHP.

276. Patton, Diary, September 2, 1943, Box 3, Folder 3, GSPP.

277. "Press and Radio Conference #915," August 31, 1943, in Franklin D. Roosevelt, *Complete Roosevelt Presidential Press Conferences of Franklin D. Roosevelt*, vol. 22 (New York: Da Capo Press, 1972), 80–82; Herman Klurfeld, *Behind the Lines: The World of Drew Pearson* (Englewood Cliffs, NJ: Prentice-Hall, 1968), 70; Oliver Pilat, *Drew Pearson: An Unauthorized Biography* (New York: Harper's Magazine Press, 1973), 175–176.

278. Klurfeld, *Behind the Lines*, 79.

279. Theodore F. Koop, *Weapon of Silence* (Chicago: University of Chicago Press, 1946), 261.

280. Price to James, November 25, 1943, letter, Box 557, Office of Censorship Administrative Division-Service Section Administrative Subject File, RG 216, NARA.

281. Warner to Lockhart, November 21, 1943, memorandum, Box 557, Office of Censorship Administrative Division-Service Section Administrative Subject File, RG 216, NARA.

282. Halpin to Ryan, November 21, 1943, memorandum, Box 557, Office of Censorship Administrative Division-Service Section Administrative Subject File, RG 216, NARA.

283. Pilat, *Drew Pearson*, 176.

284. "Patton's Future," *Washington Post*, November 25, 1943.

285. "Nation's Press Censures Patton, Hits Army for Withholding Facts," *Washington Post*, November 26, 1943, quoting the *San Francisco Chronicle* and the *Herald Tribune*. [Emphasis in the original].

286. Drew Pearson, "Spot One," Box 557, RG 216, NARA.

287. Butcher, Diary, November 23, 1943, Box 167, Folder (October 1– December 30, 1943) (2), PPPF; Dwight David Eisenhower, *Crusade in Europe*, 182.

288. Seymour Korman, "Gen. Patton's Full Story!," *Chicago Daily Tribune*, November 24, 1943; Casey, *The War Beat*, 155.

289. Eisenhower to Surley, December 14, 1943, cable, Box 113, Folder Surles, A.D. (2), PPPF.

290. Herbert Mitgang, *Newsmen in Khaki: Tales of a World War II Soldier Correspondent* (New York: Taylor Trade Publishing, 2004); 71.

291. Hamilton, *Monty*, 374.

292. Virgil Pinkley, with James F. Scheer, *Eisenhower Declassified* (Old Tappan, NJ: Fleming H. Revell, 1979), 161.

293. "A Sorry Job," *Cleveland News*, November 24, 1943, in Box 557, RG 216, NARA.

294. "Nation's Press Censures Patton, Hits Army for Withholding Facts," *Washington Post*, November 26, 1943.

295. "Patton's Slap," *Newsweek*, December 6, 1945, 62 and 64.

296. D. K. R. Crosswell, *Beetle: The Life of General Walter Bedell Smith* (Lexington: University Press of Kentucky, 2010), 535 and 536.

297. Stimson, Diary, November 20, 1943, and November 22, 1943, Reel 8, HLSD.

298. Stimson, Diary, November 25, 1943, Reel 8, HLSD.

299. Mark Perry, *Partners in Command: George C. Marshall and Dwight Eisenhower in War and Peace* (New York: Penguin Press, 2007), 212.

300. "Patton Case," *Washington Post*, November 28, 1943.

301. Stimson to Beatrice Patton, November 26, 1943, letter, Box 78, Folder 10, GSPP.

302. George H. Gallup, *The Gallup Poll Public Opinion 1935–1971*, vol. 1, ed. William P. Hansen and Fred L. Israel (New York: Random House, 1972), 421.

303. Charles R. Codman, *Drive* (Boston: Little, Brown, 1957), 272.

304. "Patton and Truth," *Time*, December 6, 1943.

305. See Box 78, Folder 10, GSPP.

306. D'Este, *Patton*, 550; D'Este, *Eisenhower*, 580; Porch, *The Path to Victory*, 449.

307. Eisenhower to Marshall, August 24, 1943, cable, Dwight D. Eisenhower, *Eisenhower Papers*, vol. 2, 1353.

308. Eisenhower to Marshall, August 27, ibid., 1357.

309. Patton, *The Patton Papers, 1940–1945*, 346.

310. Eisenhower to Herron, June 11, 1943, letter, Dwight David Eisenhower, *Eisenhower Papers*, vol. 2, 1187.

Chapter 4. "War in a Museum"

1. Doolittle and Glines, *I Could Never Be So Lucky Again*, 332.

2. Perret, *Winged Victory*, 210.

3. Doolittle, *I Could Never Be So Lucky Again*, 332.

4. Doolittle, 331.

5. Arnold, *Global Mission*, 514.

6. Butcher, Diary, July 17, 1943, Box 167, Folder (July 8, 1943–August 17, 1943) (2), PPPF.

7. Butcher, Diary, June 19, 1943, Box 166, Folder (May 8, 1943–July 6, 1943) (4), PPPF; Leahy, *I Was There*, 171–172.

8. Doolittle, *I Could Never Be So Lucky Again*, 333.

9. Butcher, Diary, August 6, 1943, Box 167, Folder (July 8, 1943–August 17, 1943) (3), PPPF.

10. Paul Schmidt, *Hitler's Interpreter* (Croydon, England: CPI Group, 2016), 277; Benito Mussolini, *The Fall of Mussolini: His Own Story by Benito Mussolini*, ed.

Max Ascoli, trans. Frances Frenaye (New York: Farrar, Straus and Company, 1948), 51.

11. Moseley, *Mussolini*, 6.

12. Weinberg, *A World at Arms*, 597.

13. Doolittle, *I Could Never Be So Lucky Again*, 333; Mussolini, *The Fall of Mussolini*, 52; Perret, *Winged Victory*, 210; R. J. B. Bosworth, *Mussolini* (Oxford: Oxford University Press, 2002), 400.

14. Atkinson, *The Day of Battle*, 583; James Holland, *Italy's Sorrow: A Year of War, 1944–1945* (New York: St. Martin's Press, 2008), 530; Jon B. Mikolashek, *General Mark Clark: Commander of U.S. Fifth Army and Liberator of Rome* (Philadelphia: Casemate, 2013), 7.

15. Critics include Kennedy, *Freedom from Fear*, 596; Murray and Millett, *A War To Be Won*, 387; Porch, *The Path to Victory*, 461; Lloyd Clark, *Anzio: Italy and the Battle for Rome—1944* (New York: Atlantic Monthly Press, 2006), 323.

16. John Keegan, *The Second World War* (New York: Penguin Books, 1998), 318–319.

17. Smuts to Churchill, September 3, 1943, quoted in Winston S. Churchill, *The Second World War*, vol. 5, *Closing the Ring* (Boston: Houghton Mifflin, 1951), 127 and 130; Jon B. Mikolashek makes a similar point in Mikolashek, *General Mark Clark*, 161.

18. David Hapgood and David Richardson, *Monte Cassino* (New York: Congdon & Weed, 1984), 26; Porch, *The Path to Victory*, 463.

19. Porch, *The Path to Victory*, 460.

20. Porch, 452.

21. Dwight D. Eisenhower, *Crusade in Europe*, 190.

22. Clausewitz, *On War*, 113.

23. Atkinson, *The Day of Battle*, 183 and 377.

24. Eisenhower to Marshall, September 20, 1943, cable, in Dwight D. Eisenhower, *Eisenhower Papers*, vol. 2, 1440.

25. Fussell, *Wartime*, 161; Atkinson, *The Day of Battle*, 184; Porch, *The Path to Victory*, 489; Murray and Millett, *A War To Be Won*, 377; Holland, *Italy's Sorrow*, 529.

26. Capa, *Slightly Out of Focus*, 103.

27. Atkinson, *The Day of Battle*, 184.

28. C. L. Sulzberger, *A Long Row of Candles: Memoirs and Diaries [1934–1954]* (Toronto, Ontario: Macmillan, 1969), 231.

29. Martin Blumenson, *Anzio: The Gamble That Failed* (New York: J. B. Lippincott, 1963), 35.

30. Truscott, *Command Mission*, 247.

31. Eric Sevareid, *Not So Wild a Dream* (New York: Alfred A. Knopf, 1968), 379 and 383.

32. Martin Blumenson, *Mark Clark* (New York: Congdon & Weed, 1984), 198.

33. Sulzberger, *A Long Row of Candles*, 230–231.

34. Blumenson, *Mark Clark*, 200.

35. Bradley and Blair, *A General's Life*, 204.

36. Patton, Diary, January 21, 1943, Box 2, Folder 19, GSPP.

37. Fred L. Walker, *From Texas to Rome: A General's Journal* (Dallas, TX: Taylor Publishing, 1969), 337 and 360.

38. Butcher, Diary, January 28, 1943, Box 166, Folder (January 8, 1943–May 5, 1943) (1), PPPF.

39. Atkinson, *The Day of Battle*, 376.

40. Jay Walz, "Pants for Posterity?," *New York Times*, January 9, 1944.

41. Butcher, Diary, November 23, 1943, Box 167, Folder (October 1–December 30, 1943) (2), PPPF.

42. Eisenhower to Clark, letter, November 22, 1943, Box 23, Folder Clark, Mark W. (4), PPPF.

43. Atkinson, *The Day of Battle*, 376–377 and 184; Clark to C. C. Clark, January 19, 1944, letter, Reel 3, Mark W. Clark Papers, DDEL.

44. Clark to C. C. Clark, March 22, 1944, letter, Reel 3, Mark W. Clark Papers, DDEL.

45. Crosswell, *Beetle*, 396.

46. D'Este, *Patton*, 458.

47. Crosswell, *Beetle*, 454.

48. Ambrose, *The Supreme Commander*, 222.

49. Clark, *Calculated Risk*, 211.

50. Eisenhower to Combined Chiefs of Staff, July 26, 1943, cable, in Dwight D. Eisenhower, *Eisenhower Papers*, vol. 2, 1287.

51. Murphy, *Diplomat among Warriors*, 211; Harold MacMillan, *War Diaries: Politics and War in the Mediterranean January 1943–May 1945* (New York: St. Martin's Press, 1984), 167.

52. Roosevelt to Churchill, July 30, 1943, in *Churchill and Roosevelt: The Complete Correspondence*, vol. 2, *Alliance Forged November 1942–February 1944*, ed. Warren F. Kimball (Princeton, NJ: Princeton University Press, 1984), 366.

53. Churchill to Roosevelt, August 4, 1943, in *Churchill and Roosevelt*, vol. 2, 378.

54. Churchill to Eisenhower, August 16, 1943, Box 23, Folder Churchill, Winston (7), PPPF. This is a copy of an earlier message that was given to Eisenhower on August 3.

55. Roosevelt to Churchill, July 30, 1943, in *Churchill and Roosevelt*, vol. 2, 366.

56. Dwight D. Eisenhower, *Crusade in Europe*, 184.

57. Eisenhower to Marshall, August 4, 1943, cable, in Dwight D. Eisenhower, *Eisenhower Papers*, vol. 2, 1315.

58. Butcher, Diary, August 4, 1943, Box 167, Folder (July 8, 1943–August 17, 1943) (3), PPPF.

59. Churchill to Roosevelt, August 4, 1943, in *Churchill and Roosevelt*, vol. 2, 380.

60. Macmillan, *War Diaries*, 172.

61. Murphy, *Diplomat among Warriors*, 218 and 219.

62. Kesselring, *The Memoirs of Field-Marshal Kesselring*, 170.

63. Weinberg, *A World at Arms*, 598.

64. Murray and Millett, *A War To Be Won*, 377.

65. Dwight D. Eisenhower, *Crusade in Europe*, 186; Atkinson, *The Day of Battle*, 194–195.

66. Eisenhower to Pietro Badoglio, September 8, 1943, cable, in Dwight D. Eisenhower, *The Papers of Dwight David Eisenhower*, vol. 3, *The War Years*, [hereafter *Eisenhower Papers*, vol. 3], ed. Alfred D. Chandler Jr. (Baltimore: Johns Hopkins Press, 1970), 1402.

67. Eisenhower to Combined Chiefs of Staff, September 8, 1943, cable, in *Eisenhower Papers*, vol. 3, 1404.

68. Leahy, *I Was There*, 171.

69. Dwight D. Eisenhower, *Crusade in Europe*, 186.

70. Porch, *The Path to Victory*, 487.

71. Walker, *From Texas to Rome*, 221 and 231.

72. Keegan, *The Second World War*, 352.

73. Blumenson, *Mark Clark*, 119, 199, 121, and 122; Holland, *Italy's Sorrow*, 3.

74. Clark, *Calculated Risk*, 177 and 199–200.

75. Blumenson, *Anzio*, 38.

76. Clark, *Calculated Risk*, 211–210.

77. Blumenson, *Anzio*, 37.

78. Blumenson, 2.

79. Capa, *Slightly Out of Focus*, 111.

80. From Algiers to War [Department], December 14, 1943, cable, Box 46, Folder 14, File MR 000.71 Propaganda, National Archives, accessed January 8, 2018, (National Archives Identifier: 27577827) https://catalog.archives.gov/id/578215.

81. Atkinson, *The Day of Battle*, 329 and 399; Porch, *The Path to Victory*, 511.

82. *Anzio Beachhead 22 January–25 May 1944* (Washington, DC: Center of Military History United States Army, 1990), 3.

83. Clark, *Calculated Risk*, 250 and 284.

84. Carlo D'Este, *Fatal Decision: Anzio and the Battle for Rome* (New York: HarperCollins Publishers, 1991), 401; Mark A. Stoler, *Allies in War: Britain and America against the Axis Powers, 1940–1945* (Hodder Education: London, 2005), 145.

85. Atkinson, *The Day of Battle*, 400, 435, and 436; Fridolin von Senger und Etterlin, *Neither Fear Nor Hope*, trans. George Malcolm, (New York: E. P. Dutton, 1964), 193.

86. Martin Blumenson, *Bloody River: The Real Tragedy of the Rapido* (Boston: Houghton Mifflin Company, 1970), 13.

87. Clark, *Calculated Risk*, 270.

88. Butcher, Diary, January 23, 1944, Box 168, Folder (January 16, 1944–February 29, 1944) (1), PPPF; Butcher, Diary, February 8, 1944, Box 168, Folder (January 16, 1944–February 29, 1944) (3), PPPF; Butcher, Diary, February 11, 1944, PPPF.

89. Sevareid, *Not So Wild a Dream*, 382. [Emphasis in the original].

90. Butcher, Diary, February 17, 1944, Box 168, Folder (January 16, 1944–February 29, 1944) (4), PPPF.

91. Truscott, *Command Mission*, 363 and 314; D'Este, *Fatal Decision*, 169.

92. Justo L. González, *The Story of Christianity*, vol. 1, *The Early Church to the*

Dawn of the Reformation (New York: HarperCollins, 2010), 278, 340, and 375; Arthur Herman, *The Cave and the Light: Plato versus Aristotle, and the Struggle for the Soul of Western Civilization* (New York: Random House, 2013), 230; Hapgood and Richardson, *Monte Cassino*, 4; Atkinson, *The Day of Battle*, 398.

93. Martin Blumenson, *Salerno to Cassino*, United States Army in World War II: The Mediterranean Theater of Operations (Washington, DC: Department of the Army, 1969), 401; Atkinson, *The Day of Battle*, 412 and 433.

94. Hapgood and Richardson, *Monte Cassino* 15 and 6; Atkinson, *The Day of Battle*, 399.

95. Atkinson, *The Day of Battle*, 400, 435, and 436; Senger, *Neither Fear Nor Hope*, 187–188.

96. Lynn Heinzerling, "5th Army Will Open Fire on Hilltop Abbey," *Boston Globe*, February 15, 1944.

97. George Tucker, "Benedictine Monastery Blasted Off Mt. Cassino," *Washington Post*, February 16, 1944.

98. Atkinson, *The Day of Battle*, 433.

99. Hapgood and Richardson, *Monte Cassino*, 163.

100. Atkinson, *The Day of Battle*, 350.

101. Hapgood and Richardson, *Monte Cassino*, 162 and 163.

102. C. L. Sulzberger, "Clark Order Prohibits 5th Army from Attacking Church Property," *New York Times*, January 29, 1944.

103. C. L. Sulzberger, "Stab into Cassino Repulsed by Nazis," *New York Times*, February 4, 1944.

104. Anne O'Hare McCormick, "Abroad: The Symbolic Battle for Monte Cassino," *New York Times*, February 9, 1944.

105. Hapgood and Richardson, *Monte Cassino*, 164 and 165.

106. Atkinson, *The Day of Battle*, 410 and 412; Porch, *The Path to Victory*, 161–162.

107. From Algiers to War [Department], December 14, 1943.

108. Clark, Diary, February 13, 1944, Mark W. Clark Collection, The Citadel Archives and Museum, Charleston, South Carolina; Ernest F. Fisher Jr., *Cassino to the Alps*, Mediterranean Theater of Operations, *United States Army in World War II* (Washington, DC: Department of the Army, 1989), 405; Hapgood and Richardson, *Monte Cassino*, 172.

109. Harold Alexander, *The Alexander Memoirs, 1940–1945*, ed. John North (New York: McGraw-Hill, 1962), 121.

110. Atkinson, *The Day of Battle*, 437.

111. Robert M. Edsel, *Saving Italy: The Race to Rescue a Nation's Treasures from the Nazis* (New York: W. W. Norton, 2013), 84.

112. Atkinson, *The Day of Battle*, 439–440; Alexander, *The Alexander Memoirs*, 119.

113. Blumenson, *Salerno to Cassino*, 401–409.

114. Clark, *Calculated Risk*, 312.

115. Senger, *Neither Fear Nor Hope*, 203.

116. Blumenson, *Salerno to Cassino*, 414–415. According to General Senger's

postwar account, he conducted this interview reluctantly, but was ordered to do it by Berlin. Senger, *Neither Fear Nor Hope*, 203.

117. Blumenson, *Salerno to Cassino*, 414.

118. "1944-Nazi Newsreel Die Deutsche Wochenschau: Defense of Cassino-Monte Cassino Abbey + Russian FR," WWII Public Domain, April 30, 2016, YouTube video, 8:21, https://www.youtube.com/watch?v=CxhEyOjDYa8.

119. "Pope Bitter, Berlin Declares," *New York Times*, February 18, 1944.

120. Senger, *Neither Fear Nor Hope*, 203–204.

121. "Cassino Monastery Bombed," British Pathé, April 13, 2014, Pathe Gazette, YouTube video, 5:16, accessed 12/12/19, https://www.youtube.com/watch?v=u8af-P6GetP8; Atkinson, *The Day of Battle*, 438.

122. Edward T. Folliard, "President Would Force Nazis to Rebuild Historic Shrines," *Washington Post*, February 23, 1944.

123. "Says Nazis in Abbey Cost US Many Lives," *New York Times*, February 20, 1944.

124. "Allied Kill Nazis Fleeing from Abbey," *Los Angeles Times*, February 16, 1944.

125. "Bombing of Monte Cassino Unfortunate Necessity," *Los Angeles Times*, February 16, 1944.

126. Tucker, "Benedictine Monastery Blasted Off Mt. Cassino."

127. Drew Middleton, "Nazis Exploit Our Bombing of Mt. Cassino Monastery," *New York Times*, February 20, 1944.

128. Atkinson, *The Day of Battle*, 441.

129. Clark, *Calculated Risk*, 329.

130. Blumenson, *Mark Clark*, 200.

131. Truscott, *Command Mission*, 369, 374–376; Wilson A. Heefner, *Dogface Soldier: The Life of General Lucian K. Truscott, Jr.* (Columbia: University of Missouri Press, 2010), 172.

132. Blumenson, *Anzio*, 194.

133. D'Este, *Fatal Decision*, 390.

134. Blumenson, *Anzio*, 194.

135. Atkinson, *The Day of Battle*, 548.

136. Mikolashek, *General Mark Clark*, 134.

137. D'Este, *Fatal Decision*, 408.

138. Clark, *Calculated Risk*, 312–313.

139. Alexander, *The Alexander Memoirs*, 128; Atkinson, *The Day of Battle*, 548.

140. Blumenson, *Mark Clark*, 198.

141. Mikolashek, *General Mark Clark*, 123, 125, and 130.

142. Clark, *Calculated Risk*, 352.

143. Mikolashek, *General Mark Clark*, 133.

144. Clark, *Calculated Risk*, 328.

145. Alexander, *The Alexander Memoirs*, 127.

146. Clark's diary quoted in D'Este, *Fatal Decision*, 386.

147. Clark, *Calculated Risk*, 361, 363, and 357; Atkinson, *The Day of Battle*, 554, 565, and 550.

148. Murray and Millett, *A War To Be Won*, 385.

149. Mikolashek, *General Mark Clark*, 132.

150. Alexander, *The Alexander Memoirs*, 127.

151. Atkinson, *The Day of Battle*, 537.

152. Mikolashek, *General Mark Clark*, 128.

153. Atkinson, *The Day of Battle*, 544–545.

154. Mikolashek, *General Mark Clark*, 128.

155. Mikolashek, 165.

156. Atkinson, *The Day of Battle*, 547 and 550.

157. Walker, *From Texas to Rome*, 382.

158. Fisher, *Cassino to the Alps*, 203.

159. D'Este, *Fatal Decision*, 392.

160. Atkinson, *The Day of Battle*, 574–575; Sevareid, *Not So Wild a Dream*, 414.

161. Sevareid, *Not So Wild a Dream*, 364.

162. Clark, *Calculated Risk*, 357.

163. Atkinson, *The Day of Battle*, 575.

164. Sevareid, *Not So Wild a Dream*, 417–418.

165. Thomas R. Brooks, *The War North of Rome: June 1944–May 1945* (Edison, NJ: Castle Books, 1996), 2.

Chapter 5. The Liberation of France

1. Stimson, Diaries, June 5 and 6, 1944, Reel 9, HLSD.

2. Stephen E. Ambrose, *D-Day June 6, 1944, The Climactic Battle of World War II* (New York: Simon & Schuster, 1994), 490, 491, 493, and 496.

3. Dwight D. Eisenhower, *Crusade in Europe*, 300.

4. Bickford Edward Sawyer Jr., "The Normandy Campaign from Military and Press Sources," (MA thesis, University of Missouri, 1957), appears to be the only scholarly piece that focuses directly on the press in Normandy. A number of broader accounts touch on the topic with the best being Casey, *The War Beat*.

5. Butcher, Diary, January 27, 1944, Box 168, Folder (January 16, 1944–February 29, 1944) (2), PPPF.

6. Richard Mead, *The Men behind Monty: The Staff and HQs of Eighth Army and 21st Army Group* (Barnsley, UK: Pen & Sword Books, 2015), 171.

7. Quoted in Olson, *Citizens of London*, 316.

8. Herzstein, *The War That Hitler Won*, 83–84.

9. Nicolaus von Below, *At Hitler's Side: The Memoirs of Hitler's Luftwaffe Adjutant 1937–1945*, trans. Geoffrey Brooks (London: Greenhill Books, 2004), 212.

10. J. B. L. Lawrence, "Accreditation of War Correspondents to U.S. Forces," April 4, 1944, Box 2, Folder 00047–1, RG 331, NARA.

11. Robert Bunnelle to R. Ernest Dupuy, August 16, 1944, letter, Box 9, Folder untitled, RG 331, NARA.

12. "Public Relations," unsigned to C.R. Abraham, April 29, 1943, Box 9, Folder 321.01, RG 331, NARA.

13. Thor Smith to James T. Quirk, August 13, 1943, letter, RG 331, NARA.

14. De Guingand, *Operation Victory*, 380; Casey, *The War Beat*, 222.

15. Oldfield, *Never a Shot in Anger*, 76 and 74.

16. "Final Report on Invasion Reference Library," June 9, 1944, Box 7, Folder 314.7, RG 331, NARA.

17. Olson, *Citizens of London*, 317.

18. D'Este, *Eisenhower*, 461; *Marshall Interviews and Reminiscences*, 402.

19. Butcher, Diary, July 22, 1944, Box 169, (July 17–Aug. 30, 1944) (1), PPPF.

20. Churchill to Roosevelt, December 19, 1944, in *Churchill and Roosevelt*, vol. 2, 624.

21. Butcher, Diary, January 16, 1944, Box 168, Folder (January 16, 1944–February 29, 1944) (1), PPPF.

22. De Guingand, *Operation Victory*, 471. Eisenhower had been offered a similar chance to stay in Italy until Rome was captured. Butcher, Diary, January 23, 1944, Box 168, Folder (January 16, 1944–February 29, 1944) (1), PPPF.

23. Weigley, *Eisenhower's Lieutenants*, 40.

24. Alun Chalfont, *Montgomery of Alamein* (New York: Atheneum, 1976), 223.

25. Eisenhower to Combined Chiefs of Staff, Surles, and Wilson, May 31, 1944, "D Day Guidance for the Press," Box 1, Folder 000.7–1, RG 331, NARA.

26. Michael Howard, *British Intelligence in the Second World War*, vol. 5, *Strategic Deception* (New York: Cambridge University Press, 1990), 114.

27. Butcher, Diary, April 17, 1944, Box 168, Folder (March 3–May 9, 1944) (3), PPPF.

28. Don Whitehead, "A Correspondent's View of D-day," in *D-Day 1944*, ed. Theodore A. Wilson (Lawrence: University Press of Kansas, 1971), 205.

29. Frank T. Mildren, interview by James T. Scott for the Senior Officers Oral History Program, 1980, 55, Box 1, Papers of Frank T. Mildren, USAHEC.

30. "Minutes of Supreme Commander's Conference, Room 105, Norfolk House, 1000 HRS., 24 January, 1944," copied in Butcher, Diary, February 2, 1944, Box 168, Folder (January 16, 1944–February 29, 1944) (2), PPPF.

31. Churchill to Eisenhower, January 28, 1944, and Eisenhower to Churchill, February 6, 1944, Box 22, Folder Churchill, Winston (6), PPPF.

32. Whitehead, "A Correspondent's View of D-day," in *D-Day 1944*, 204.

33. Eisenhower to All Unit Commanders, May 11, 1944, memorandum "Accredited War Correspondents," Box 2, Folder 00047–1, RG 331, NARA.

34. *Know Your War Correspondent: An Informal and Unofficial Discussion for Field Commanders of the S.O.S., ETOUSA*, 13–14, Box 2, Folder Memorabilia, JBL, 1942–87. Though the book is titled for Service of Supply (SOS) Commanders, a note accompanying it implies it was also given to "commanders in the field."

35. Whitehead, "A Correspondent's View of D-day," in *D-Day 1944*, 204.

36. Justus Baldwin Lawrence, unpublished memoir, 129, Box 2, Folder Memoirs World War II (2), JBL.

37. Knightley, *The First Casualty*, 330; Smith, *War and Press Freedom*, vii; Fred Inglis, *People's Witness: The Journalist in Modern Politics* (New Haven, CT: Yale University Press, 2002), xi; Moseley, *Reporting War*, 8.

38. *Know Your War Correspondent*, 7, 14, and 23, Box 2, Folder Memorabilia, JBL.

39. Eisenhower to Combined Chiefs of Staff, Surles, and Wilson, May 31, 1944, "D Day Guidance for the Press," Box 1, Folder 000.7–1, RG 331, NARA.

40. Eisenhower to Combined Chiefs of Staff, Surles, and Wilson, May 31, 1944, "D Day Guidance for the Press."

41. Eisenhower to Combined Chiefs of Staff, Surles, and Wilson, May 31, 1944, "D Day Guidance for the Press."

42. Eisenhower Press Conference, May 22, 1944, Box 5, Folder 000.74 vol. 1 Press Correspondents [201–250], PPPF.

43. De Guingand, *Operation Victory*, 356; Montgomery, *Montgomery Memoirs*, 226.

44. Antony Brett-James, *Conversations with Montgomery* (London: W. Kimber, 1984), 68.

45. Montgomery, *Montgomery Memoirs*, 226–231, 225. [Emphasis in the original.]

46. Butcher, Diary, January 27, 1944, Box 168, Folder (January 16, 1944–February 29, 1944) (2), PPPF.

47. Patton, Diary, February 29 and March 2, 1944, Box 3, Folder 5 Feb.–July 31, 1944 (1 of 2), GSPP.

48. Eisenhower to Marshall, January 18, 1944, cable, Dwight D. Eisenhower, *Eisenhower Papers*, vol. 3, 1665.

49. Howard, *Strategic Deception*, 120–121.

50. Andy Rooney, *My War* (New York: Public Affairs, 2000), 192.

51. F. H. Hinsley and C. A. G. Simkins, *British Intelligence in the Second World War*, vol. 4, *Security and Counter-Intelligence* (New York: Cambridge University Press, 1990), 240.

52. Walter B. Smith to Marshall, April 27, 1944, cable, Box 91, Folder PATTON, George S., Jr. (2), PPPF.

53. Eisenhower, *At Ease*, 224.

54. D'Este, *Patton*, 509–510.

55. Patton, Diary, April 7, 1944, Box 3, Folder 5 Feb.–July 31, 1944 (1 of 2), GSPP.

56. Patton to Hughes, April 26, 1944, letter, Box II 3, ESHP.

57. "Army & Navy—Morale: There He Goes Again," *Time*, May 8, 1944.

58. Marshall to Eisenhower, April 29, 1944, radio WAR-29722, in George C. Marshall, *The Papers of George Catlett Marshall*, vol. 4, *"Aggressive and Determined Leadership" June 1, 1943–December 31, 1944*, ed. Larry I. Bland (Baltimore, MD: Johns Hopkins University Press, 1996), 442.

59. "Patton Trouble," *New York Times*, April 30, 1944.

60. "Congress Members Displeased," *New York Times*, April 26, 1944.

61. "Patton Adds Russia to World's Rulers," *Globe*, April 27, 1944, in Box 1, DEC.

62. Patton, *The Patton Papers, 1940–1945*, 443.

63. Stimson, Diary, May 2, 1944, Reel 9, HLSD.

64. Hughes, Diary, April 28, 1944, Box I 2, ESHP.

65. Eisenhower, *Crusade in Europe*, 224.

66. Eisenhower to Marshall, April 29, 1944, cable, in Dwight D. Eisenhower, *Eisenhower Papers*, vol. 3, 1837.

67. Patton to Hughes, April 26, 1944, letter, Box II 3, ESHP; Patton, Diary,

April 30, 1944, Box 3, Folder 5, GSPP; Eisenhower to Marshall, April 29, 1944, letter, Box 91, Folder PATTON, George S., Jr. (2), PPPF.

68. Marshall to Eisenhower, April 29, 1944, radio WAR-29722, in Marshall, *Marshall Papers*, vol. 4, 443.

69. Eisenhower to Marshall, April 30, 1944, cable, Box 91, Folder PATTON, George S., Jr. (2), PPPF.

70. Marshall to Eisenhower, May 2, 1944, cable W-30586, Box 91, Folder PATTON, George S., Jr. (2), PPPF.

71. Patton, Diary, May 1, 1944, Box 3, Folder 5, GSPP.

72. Eisenhower to Patton, May 3, 1944, Dwight D. Eisenhower, *Eisenhower Papers*, vol. 3, 1846. There are conflicting accounts of how the Knutsford Incident was concluded. In both of his books, Eisenhower claimed he told Patton at the May 1 meeting that he would be kept in command. Eisenhower, *Crusade in Europe*, 225; Eisenhower, *At Ease*, 270. Justus Baldwin Lawrence has Eisenhower telling a similar story after the war, but this account is less reliable since Lawrence jumbles the facts of the Knutsford Incident. Lawrence, Unpublished memoir, 145–147, Box 2, Folder Memoirs-World War II (2), JBL. For the above, I have used Patton's May 3 diary and Eisenhower's cable of the same date since they are contemporary to the event they describe.

73. Butcher, Diary, January 25, 1944, Box 168, (January 16, 1944–February 29, 1944) (2), PPPF; Montgomery, *Montgomery Memoirs*, 224.

74. Robert A. McClure to the Chief of Staff, March 23, 1944, memorandum "Interviews with SHAEF High Commanders," Box 10, Folder 322.011, RG 331, NARA.

75. Bradley, interview by Hanson, February 24, 1975, Box 2, Folder 14, ONBC.

76. Document titled, "The Following story was published in STARS & STRIPES, 8 April 1944," Box 1, Folder untitled, ONBC.

77. Bradley to McClure, April 14, 1944, letter, Box 1, Folder untitled, ONBC.

78. Eisenhower to Marshall, April 29, 1944, letter, Box 91, Folder PATTON, George S., Jr. (2), PPPF.

79. Eisenhower to Senior U.S. Commanders, in Dwight D. Eisenhower, *Eisenhower Papers*, vol. 3, 1865.

80. George Dyer, *XII Corps Spearhead of Patton's Third Army* (The XII Corps History Association, 1947), 96–100. For more on the movie *Patton*'s depiction of the speech see Nicholas Evan Sarantakes, *Making* Patton: *A Classic War Film's Epic Journey to the Silver Screen* (Lawrence: University Press of Kansas, 2012), 1–7.

81. Patton, Diary, June 26, 1944, Box 3, Folder 5, GSPP.

82. "Conversation at Chief of Staff's Meeting," May 12, 1944, Box 1, Folder 00071, RG 331, NARA.

83. Casey, *The War Beat*, 225.

84. Butcher, Diary, May 31, 1944, Box 168, Folder (May 11–May 31, 1944) (2), PPPF.

85. "Copy of Telegram from the Canadian Government to the Dominions Offices," Box 1, Folder 00071, RG 331, NARA.

86. "Governmental Statements in Initial Phases of 'OVERLORD,'" April 12, 1944, Box 1, Folder 00071, RG 331, NARA.

87. Ambrose, *D-Day*, 490.

88. Casey, *The War Beat*, 232.

89. William B. Breuer, *Hoodwinking Hitler: The Normandy Deception* (London: Praeger, 1993), 215.

90. William C. Sylvan and Francis G. Smith Jr., *Normandy to Victory: The War Diary of General Courtney H. Hodges and the First U.S. Army*, ed. John T. Greenwood (Lexington: University of Kentucky, 2008), 9.

91. Oldfield, *Never a Shot in Anger*, 67–69; Butcher, Diary, June 4, 1944, Box 168, Folder (June 1–June 27, 1944) (1), PPPF.

92. Butcher, Diary, June 1, 1944, and June 5, 1944, Box 168, Folder (June 1–June 27, 1944) (1), PPPF.

93. Eisenhower note, in Dwight David Eisenhower, *The Papers of Dwight David Eisenhower*, vol. 4, *The War Years*, ed. Alfred D. Chandler Jr. (Baltimore, MD: Johns Hopkins Press, 1970), 1908.

94. Butcher, Diary, June 6, 1944, Box 168, Folder Butcher (June 1–June 27, 1944) (1), PPPF.

95. Percy E. Schramm, "OKW War Diary: 6 June 1944," in *Fighting the Invasion: The German Army at D-Day*, ed. David C. Isby (Mechanicsburg, PA: Stackpole Books, 2000), 169.

96. Davies, *Baldwin of the Times*, 166.

97. Cronkite, *A Reporter's Life*, 106.

98. Martin Gilbert, *Winston S. Churchill*, vol. 7, *Road to Victory 1941–1945* (Boston: Houghton Mifflin Company, 1986), 808.

99. Butcher, Diary, January 16, 1944, Box 168, Folder (January 16, 1944–February 29, 1944) (1), PPPF; Chester B. Hansen, interview after World War II, Box 1, Folder 2, ONBC.

100. Butcher, Diary, May 19, 1944, Box 168, Folder (May 11–May 13, 1944) (1), PPPF; Below, *At Hitler's Side*, 187.

101. Herzstein, *The War Hitler Won*, 92.

102. Gay, *Assignment to Hell*, 281–182; Ambrose, *D-Day*, 482.

103. Christy Campbell, *Target London: Under Attack from the V-Weapons during WWII* (London: Little, Brown, 2012), 257; Below, *At Hitler's Side*, 204.

104. Herzstein, *The War Hitler Won*, 92.

105. Robert S. Allen, *Forward with Patton: The World War II Diary of Colonel Robert S. Allen*, ed. John Nelson Rickard (Lexington: University Press of Kentucky, 2017), 41.

106. Speer, *Inside the Third Reich*, 356. Hitler's press chief, Otto Dietrich, gives a slightly different account than Speer. "After the first week Hitler was so disappointed by the results that he forbade the weapon's being mentioned in the radio and press, although he himself had previously whipped up a great propaganda campaign for it, replete with exaggerations which went far beyond the alarmist foreign descriptions of the observed effects." Otto Dietrich, *The Hitler I Knew: The Memoir of the Third Reich's Press Chief* (New York: Skyhorse Publishing, 2010), 86. Dietrich does not mention Allied news reports changing Hitler's mind. But neither does he explain why Hitler continued the campaign. Joachim Fest, *Speer:*

The Final Verdict, trans. Ewald Osers and Alexandra Dring (New York: Harcourt, 1999), 221.

107. Heinz Magenheimer, *Hitler's War: Germany's Key Strategic Decisions 1940–1945*, trans. Helmut Bögler (London: Cassell,1988), 253.

108. Richard Havers, *Here Is the News: The BBC and the Second World War* (Gloucestershire: Sutton Publishing, 2007), 269.

109. Gay, *Assignment to Hell*, 281.

110. Winston S. Churchill, *The Second World War*, vol. 6, *Triumph and Tragedy* (Boston: Houghton Mifflin, 1953), 39.

111. Harry Butcher, *My Three Years with Eisenhower* (New York: Simon and Schuster, 1946), 585–586.

112. Hansen, Diary, June 28, 1944, Box 6, Folder 5, CHP. [Date for this entry is unclear.]

113. Drew Middleton, *Our Share of Night* (New York: Viking Press, 1946), 312.

114. Ambrose, *Citizen Soldiers*, 56.

115. Havers, *Here Is the News*, 268 and 269; Ambrose, *The Supreme Commander*, 442.

116. "New Weapon Not a Surprise," *Times*, June 17, 1944; Peter Haining, *The Flying Bomb War: Contemporary Eyewitness Accounts of the German V-1 and V-2 Raids on Britain* (London: Robson Books, 2002), 51, 57, and photos.

117. Ambrose, *The Supreme Commander*, 442.

118. Gilbert, *Road to Victory*, 809.

119. Arthur Tedder, *With Prejudice: The War Memoirs of Marshal of the Royal Air Force Lord Tedder G.C.B.* (Boston: Little, Brown, 1966), 580.

120. Gay, *Assignment to Hell*, 283.

121. Butcher, Diary, June 21, 1944, Box 168, Folder (June 1–June 27, 1944) (3), PPPF; Eisenhower to Tedder, June 18, 1944, memorandum, in Dwight D. Eisenhower, *Eisenhower Papers*, vol. 3, 1933.

122. Ambrose, *D-Day*, 94–95; Tedder, *With Prejudice*, 580–581.

123. Ambrose, *Citizen Soldiers*, 56–57.

124. Stephen Alan Bourque, *Beyond the Beach: The Allied War against France* (Annapolis, MD: Naval Institute Press, 2018), 113.

125. Butcher, Diary, June 17, 1944, Box 168, Folder (June 1–June 27, 1944) (2), PPPF.

126. Hansen, Diary, June 28, 1944, Box 6, Folder 5, CHP.

127. "The New Air Weapon," *Times*, June 20, 1944; "Flying Bomb Lairs Found Near Calais," *Daily Express*, June 21, 1944; "Measures against Flying Bombs," *Times*, June 21, 1944; "Plan for Countering Flying Bombs," *Times*, June 21, 1944; "Attack on Flying Bomb Sites," *Times*, June 22, 1944; "Flying Bomb Bases Hit Again," *Times*, June 24, 1944; "Flying Bomb Sites," *Times*, June 24, 1944.

128. Bourque, *Beyond the Beach*, 257.

129. John Gordon, "The Real Reply to Doodle-Bugs," *Sunday Express*, June 25, 1944; D. R. Davies, "It Is Time for Reprisals!," *Sunday Express*, July 9, 1944.

130. "Flying Bombs Statement by the Home Secretary," *Times*, June 24, 1944.

131. Bernard Donoughue and G. W. Jones, *Herbert Morrison: Portrait of a Politician* (London: Weidenfeld and Nicolson, 1973), 319.

132. Herbert Morrison, *Herbert Morrison: An Autobiography* (London: Odhams Press Limited, 1960), 193.

133. Brooke, *War Diaries 1939–1945*, 563. [Original quote italicized].

134. Gilbert, *Road to Victory*, 838 and 839.

135. Tedder, *With Prejudice*, 581.

136. Gilbert, *Road to Victory*, 849–841.

137. Tedder, *With Prejudice*, 582.

138. Sweeney, *The Military and the Press*, 195.

139. "Use of Flying Bomb against Shipping," *Times*, June 21, 1944; "Plan for Countering Flying Bombs," *Times*, June 21, 1944; "Blast from Flying Bombs," *Times*, June 22, 1944; "Flying Bomb Sites," *Times*, June 24, 1944.

140. Campbell, *Target London*, 310–311.

141. Butcher, Diary, July 10, 1944, Box 168, Folder (June 28–July 14, 1944) (2), PPPF.

142. Hansen, Diary, June 28, 1944, Box 6, Folder 5, CHP.

143. Weigley, *Eisenhower's Lieutenants*, 113.

144. Dwight D. Eisenhower, *Crusade in Europe*, 260.

145. Hansen, Diary, June 29, 1944, Box 6, Folder 5, CHP.

146. Bradley and Blair, *A General's Life*, 268.

147. Hansen, Diary, June 29, 1944, Box 6, Folder 6, CHP.

148. Butcher, *My Three Years with Eisenhower*, 596, 600, and 601.

149. Hansen, Diary, July 1, 1944, Box 6, Folder 6, CHP.

150. Butcher, *My Three Years with Eisenhower*, 602.

151. Bradley and Blair, *A General's Life*, 268.

152. Ambrose, *Citizen Soldiers*, 118.

153. Phillips Payson O'Brien, *How The War Was Won: Air-Sea Power and Allied Victory in World War II* (Cambridge: Cambridge University Press, 2015), 484.

154. Butcher, Diary, June 13, 1944, Box 168, Folder (June 1–June 27, 1944) (2), PPPF.

155. Studs Terkel, *"The Good War": An Oral History of World War Two* (New York: Pantheon Books, 1984), 380–381.

156. Butcher, Diary, June 13, 1944, Box 168, Folder (June 1–June 27, 1944) (2), PPPF.

157. Hansen, Diary, June 11, 1944, Box 6, Folder 4, CHP.

158. Morningstar, *Patton's Way*, 47; Jeffrey D. Lavoie, *The Private Life of General Omar N. Bradley* (Jefferson, NC: McFarland, 2015), 158–160.

159. Middleton, *Our Share of Night*, 301; "Introduction to Bradley by Lee Hills of Miami Herald for the Associated Press Editors Convention," Box 25, ONBC; Steven L. Ossad, *Omar Nelson Bradley: America's GI General 1893–1981* (Columbia: University of Missouri Press, 2017), 8.

160. Hansen, Diary, October 23, 1944, Box 6, Folder 9, CHP.

161. Ernie Pyle, *Ernie's War: The Best of Ernie Pyle's World War II Dispatches*, ed. David Nichols (New York: Random House, 1986), 358. After he returned to the United States Pyle admitted that Bradley was much better known than the reporter had originally feared. Hansen, Diary, November 28, 1944, Box 6, Folder 10, CHP.

162. Fussell, *Wartime*, 161.

163. Bradley, interview by Bradley and Hansen, circa 1969, Box 1, Folder 11, ONBC, USAHEC.

164. Bradley and Blair, *A General's Life*, 257.

165. Bradley, interview by Bradley and Hansen.

166. Bradley and Blair, *A General's Life*, 224.

167. Bradley, *A Soldier's Story*, 147; Bradley, interview by Bradley and Hansen; Bradley and Blair, *A General's Life*, 241.

168. Ossad, *Omar Nelson Bradley*, 11.

169. Bradley, interview by Bradley and Hansen.

170. Marshall to Eisenhower, May 8, radio no. 7586, in Marshall, *Marshall Papers*, vol. 3, 685.

171. Bradley and Blair, *A General's Life*, 159.

172. Butcher, *My Three Years with Eisenhower*, 298. There is no diary entry for May 8, 1943, in Butcher's original diary. It is therefore certain that he added this entry after the war and the date should not be relied on as exact. This is supported by the fact that Pyle did not visit Bradley till Sicily. Bradley, *A Soldier's Story*, 147.

173. Bradley, *A Soldier's Story*, 147–148.

174. D'Este, *Patton*, 467; Porch, *The Path to Victory*, 409; Jerry D. Morelock, *Generals of the Bulge: Leadership in the U.S. Army's Greatest Battle* (Mechanicsburg, PA: Stackpole Books, 2015), 80. For a defense of Bradley's nickname see Alan Axelrod, *Bradley* (New York: Palgrave Macmillan, 2008), 187; Ossad, *Omar Nelson Bradley*, 8–9.

175. Bradley and Blair, *A General's Life*, 241.

176. Hansen, Diary, June 13, 1944, Box 6, Folder 4; Hansen, Diary, June 17, 1944, Box 6, Folder 5, CHP. For a good synopsis of press problems after D-Day see Casey, *The War Beat*, 243–244.

177. Bradley, *A Soldier's Story*, 299.

178. Hansen, Diary, June 24, 1944, Box 6, Folder 5, CHP.

179. Eisenhower, *Crusade in Europe*, 301.

180. Eisenhower to Marshall, June 25, 1944, cable, in Dwight D. Eisenhower, *Eisenhower Papers*, vol. 3, 1950.

181. Marshall to Eisenhower, July 14, 1944, radio WAR-65051, in Marshall, *Marshall Papers*, vol. 4, 522–523.

182. Eisenhower to Bradley, July 15, 1944, cable, in Dwight D. Eisenhower, *Eisenhower Papers*, vol. 3, 2011.

183. Butcher, Diary, July 17, 1944, and July 19, 1944, Box 169 (July 17–Aug. 30, 1944) (1), PPPF.

184. Eisenhower to Montgomery, July 17, 1944, cable, in Dwight D. Eisenhower, *Eisenhower Papers*, vol. 3, 2012–2013.

185. Montgomery, *Montgomery Memoirs*, 262.

186. Hansen, Diary, June 7, 1944, Box 6, Folder 5, CHP; Butcher, Diary, June 27, 1944, Box 168, Folder (June 1–June 27, 1944) (3), PPPF.

187. Ambrose, *Citizen Soldiers*, 50; Carlo D'Este, *Decision in Normandy: The Unwritten Story of Montgomery and the Allied Campaign* (New York: E. P. Dutton, 1983), 73–78.

188. Butcher, Diary, July 7, 1944, Box 168, (June 28–July 14, 1944) (1), PPPF.

189. Montgomery, *Montgomery Memoirs*, 254–256.

190. Dwight D. Eisenhower, interview by Cornelius Ryan, undated, 17–18, Box 43, Folder Eisenhower's Tape, Cornelius J. Ryan Collection, Ohio University, Athens Ohio.

191. The debate was captured in two 1983 histories that came to diametrically opposite conclusions. The first was Nigel Hamilton's second volume of Montgomery's massive official biography. In it, he argued, Eisenhower misunderstood Montgomery's master plan that never envisioned a breakout from Caen. Instead, the city that would serve as a "firm shield behind which Bradley could spread his American net." Hamilton, *Monty*, 645, 650, and 662. Carlo D'Este's study of the Normandy campaign agrees that Montgomery used Caen as a shield but observes that his inability to take the city was a "strategic failure." After the war Montgomery insisted that the master plan had gone according to plan when, D'Este observes, it clearly had not. D'Este adds that "a rapid seizure of the vital Caen-Falaise Plain would not only have eliminated the dreadful battles of attrition during the first six weeks, but might well have shortened the campaign." D'Este, *Decision in Normandy*, 477–478, and 485. By 1994 Montgomery's own son was admitting that his father had diminished his reputation by claiming everything had gone according to plan. Alistair Horne with David Montgomery, *Monty: The Lonely Leader 1944–1945* (New York: HarperCollins, 1994), 251. Later historians have agreed. Mead, *The Men behind Monty*, 179.

192. Montgomery to Eisenhower, July 12, 1944, letter; Eisenhower to Montgomery, July 13, 1944, letter, in Bernard Law Montgomery, *Montgomery and the Battle of Normandy: A Selection from the Diaries, Correspondence and other Papers of Field Marshal The Viscount Montgomery of Alamein, January to August, 1944*, ed. Stephen Brooks (Gloucestershire, England: History Press for the Army Records Society, 2008), 201 and 202. In fact, Montgomery would use the same language as Eisenhower to describe Goodwood in his diary. Montgomery, *Montgomery and the Battle of Normandy*, 204.

193. Montgomery to Brooke, July 18, 1944 letter; Montgomery, Diary notes, July 19–20, 1944, in Montgomery, *Montgomery and the Battle of Normandy*, 218; "Second Army Breaks Through," *Times*, July 19, 1944.

194. Rick Atkinson, *The Guns at Last Light: The War in Western Europe, 1944–1945* (New York: Henry Holt, 2013), 136.

195. "Our Tanks Fanning Out across the Caen Plain," *Daily Express*, July 19, 1944.

196. D'Este, *Decision in Normandy*, 392. Many secondary sources mistakenly put Montgomery's press conference on July 18. Montgomery issued a brief statement to the BBC on that day, but the infamous press conference happened on July 19. See Butcher Diary, July 20, 1944, Box 169, (July 17–Aug. 30, 1944) (1), PPPF; Montgomery to Brooke, July 18, 1944, letter; Diary notes, July 19–20, 1944, Montgomery, *Montgomery and the Battle of Normandy*, 218 and 223.

197. Butcher, Diary, July 20, 1944, Box 169, (July 17–Aug. 30, 1944) (1), PPPF.

198. Montgomery, *Montgomery Memoirs*, 257.

199. Montgomery, *Montgomery Memoirs*; Bradley, *A Soldier's Story*, 325–326; De Guingand, *Operation Victory*, 398.

200. D'Este, *Decision in Normandy*, 393.

201. Bradley and Blair, *A General's Life*, 273.

202. D'Este, *Decision in Normandy*, 392–393.

203. Diary, July 19–20, 1944, Montgomery, *Montgomery and the Battle of Normandy*, 223.

204. De Guingand, *Operation Victory*, 381–382.

205. Nigel Hamilton, *Monty: The Field Marshal 1944–1976* (London: Hamish Hamilton, 1986), 273.

206. Bull to de Guingand, July 13, 1944, letter, Box 1, Folder 6, SHN.

207. Casey, *The War Beat, Europe*, 244.

208. Dupuy to Chief of Staff, "Press Relations," memorandum, July 20, 1944, Box 1, Folder 000.7–1, RG 331, NARA.

209. William B. Breuer, *Death of a Nazi Army: The Falaise Pocket* (New York: Stein and Day, 1985), 11.

210. "Bad Weather at Caen," *Times*, July 22, 1944.

211. De Guingand, *Operation Victory*, 396.

212. Montgomery to Brooke, July 27, 1944, letter, in Montgomery, *Montgomery and the Battle of Normandy*, 246.

213. Grigg to Montgomery, August 1, 1944, letter, in Montgomery, *Montgomery and the Battle of Normandy*, 261.

214. Butcher, Diary, July 7, 1944, Box 168, Folder (June 28–July 14, 1944) (1), PPPF.

215. Eisenhower to Surles, July 30, 1944, cable, in Dwight D. Eisenhower, *Eisenhower Papers*, vol. 4, 2044.

216. Butcher, Diary, July 20, 1944, and July 19, 1944, Box 169, (July 17–Aug. 30, 1944) (1), PPPF.

217. Eisenhower to Montgomery, July 21, 1944, cable, in Dwight D. Eisenhower, *Eisenhower Papers*, vol. 3, 2019.

218. Butcher, Diary, July 22, 1944, Box 169, (July 17–Aug. 30, 1944) (1), PPPF.

219. Montgomery to Eisenhower, in Montgomery, *Montgomery and the Battle of Normandy*, 239.

220. Montgomery, Diary Notes, July 27, 1944, in Montgomery, *Montgomery and the Battle of Normandy*, 252; Brooke, *War Diaries 1939–1945*, 574–575.

221. Brooke to Montgomery, July 28, 1944, letter, in Montgomery, *Montgomery and the Battle of Normandy*, 253–254.

222. Montgomery to Brooke, July 28, 1944, letter, in Montgomery, *Montgomery and the Battle of Normandy*, 255.

223. Montgomery to Brooke, July 26, 1944, letter, in Montgomery, *Montgomery and the Battle of Normandy*, 242.

224. Robert A. Lovett to Carl Spaatz, July 25, 1944, letter, Box 15, Folder July 1944 (Personal), CSP.

225. Montgomery, *Montgomery Memoirs*, 261.

226. Drew Middleton, "Cautious Tactics in Normandy Seen," *New York Times*, July 25, 1944.

227. Everett Hughes to Kate Hughes, July 23, 1944, letter, Folder 4, BoxII 3, ESHP.

228. Hanson W. Baldwin, "Normandy Called a Magnified Anzio," *New York Times*, July 27, 1944.

229. Fletcher Pratt, "War Not as Near End as Many Would Like," *Washington Post*, July 23, 1944.

230. Bradley, interview by Hanson, February 25, 1975, Box 3, Folder 2, ONBC.

231. "G-2 Journal Algiers to the Elbe," 139, Benjamin Abbott Dickson Papers, USMA; "Confidential & Personal" [an early draft of Bradley's memoirs], Box 38, Folder Binder, ONBC.

232. Eisenhower to Bradley, July 20, 1944, letter, Binder titled "Correspondence War Years," ONBC.

233. James Jay Carafano, *After D-Day: Operation Cobra and the Normandy Breakout* (London: Lynne Rienner Publishers, 2000), 1 and 261.

234. Patton, *The Patton Papers, 1940–1945*, 477.

235. Gay, Diary, July 16, 1944, Box 2, Folder May 29, 1944, to August 6, 1944, HRG.

236. Bradley, *A Soldier's Story*, 356.

237. Patton, Diary, July 17, 1944, Box 3, Folder 6, GSPP.

238. Carafano, *After D-Day*, 259.

239. Ambrose, *Citizen Soldiers*, 89.

240. Martin Blumenson, *The Battle of the Generals: The Untold Story of the Falaise Pocket the Campaign That Should Have Won World War II* (New York: Quill, 1993), 162 and 163.

241. Everett Hughes to Kate Hughes, July 3, 1944, letter, Folder 4, BoxII 3, ESHP.

242. Blumenson, *The Battle of the Generals*, 163.

243. D'Este, *Patton*, 632.

244. Bradley, *A Soldier's Story*, 363; Hansen, Diary, August 2, 1944, Box 6, Folder 7, CHP; Patton, Diary, August 2, 1944, Box 3, Folder 7, GSPP.

245. Hansen, Diary, July 1, 1944, Box 6, Folder 6, CHP.

246. Bradley, *A Soldier's Story*, 393 and 357. Patton told General Joe Collins the same thing around the same time. J. Lawton Collins, *Lighting Joe: An Autobiography* (Novato, CA: Presidio Press, 1979), 248.

247. "Army & Navy—Command: Slapper Slapped," *Time*, June 5, 1944.

248. Bradley, *A Soldier's Story*, 357.

249. William Smith White and Don Whitehead, "Bradley Calm As He Sees His Plan Work Out," *Daily News*, August 15, 1944.

250. "Big Battle Won," *Kansas City Star*, August 20, 1944.

251. Casey, *The War Beat, Europe*, 264.

252. Bradley, *A Soldier's Story*, 393.

253. Oldfield, *Never a Shot in Anger*, 106–107.

254. Hansen, Diary, August 12, 1944, Box 6, Folder 7, CHP.

255. Bradley, *A Soldier's Story*, 393.

256. Ambrose, *Citizen Soldiers*, 98.

257. Eisenhower to Marshall and the Combined Chiefs of Staff, August 8, 1944, FWD 12907, Box 6, Folder 12, SHN.

258. Bradley, *A Soldier's Story*, 376–377.

259. Patton, Diary, August 13, 1944, Box 3, Folder 7, GSPP.

260. Atkinson, *The Guns at Last Light*, 160.

261. Bradley, *A Soldier's Story*, 376–377; Horne with Montgomery, *Monty*, 247.

262. Hansen, Diary, August 21, 1944, Box 6, Folder 7, CHP.

263. Omar N. Bradley, early draft of book manuscript, Box 38, Folder "Personal & Confidential," ONBC.

264. Martin Blumenson, *Breakout and Pursuit*, The European Theater of Operations, *United States Army during World War II* (Washington, DC: Department of the Army, 1961), 506–507.

265. Blumenson, *Breakout and Pursuit*, 509.

266. Blumenson, *The Battle of the Generals*, 261 and 273.

267. D'Este, *Patton*, 643; see also D'Este, *Eisenhower*, 580.

268. Hansen, Diary, August 12, 1944, Box 6, Folder 7, CHP.

269. Hansen, Diary, August 13, 1944, Box 6, Folder 7, CHP.

270. Hansen, Diary, August 14, 1944, Box 6, Folder 7, CHP.

271. Hamilton dismisses Hansen's comments as "jingoistic rumours." Hamilton, *Monty*, 787. D'Este agrees, arguing that it "was evidently written *after* the conclusion of the Falaise battles, as it would have been impossible for him to have known any Germans would escape on that date. More probably, it reflected the opinion of officers in Bradley's operations staff." D'Este, *Decision in Normandy*, 450 and 452 [emphasis in the original]. Yet Hansen's opinion appears to reflect Bradley's thoughts. On August 12, Bradley noted in his memoirs: "Nineteen German divisions were now stampeding to escape the trap." Two days later, Bradley observed, "It is believed that many of the German divisions which were in the pocket have now escaped." According to Atkinson, this came from faulty Ultra intelligence. Bradley, *A Soldier's Story*, 336–337; Atkinson, *The Guns at Last Light*, 161–163. Montgomery wrote in his diary on August 12 that the Germans were escaping. Diary August 12, 1944, in Montgomery, *Montgomery and the Battle of Normandy*, 293. Therefore, there is nothing to suggest that Hansen did not write his diary on August 13 or early on August 14.

272. Hansen, Diary, August 14, 1944, Box 6, Folder 7, CHP.

273. See *Daily Herald* from July 28 and August 14, 1944.

274. Butcher, Diary, July 31, 1944, Box 169, (July 17–Aug. 30, 1944) (2), PPPF.

275. Butcher, Diary, August 8, 1944, Box 169, (July 17–Aug. 30, 1944) (2), PPPF.

276. Dupuy to Smith August 13, 1944, letter, Box 9, no folder, RG 331, NARA.

277. Oldfield, *Never A Shot In Anger*, 102.

278. Weigley, *Eisenhower's Lieutenants*, 247; Butcher, Diary, September 12, 1944, Box 169, (Aug. 31–Oct. 15, 1944, 1944) (2), PPPF.

279. Hansen, Diary, August 14, 1944, Box 6, Folder 7, CHP.

280. Patton, Diary, August 16, 1944, Box 3, Folder 7, GSPP.

281. Richard Rohmer, *Patton's Gap: An Account of the Battle of Normandy 1944* (New York: Beaufort Books, 1981), 225.

282. D'Este, *Decision in Normandy*, 454–455.

283. Atkinson, *The Guns at Last Light*, 168, 169, and 170.

284. Dwight D. Eisenhower, *Crusade in Europe*, 279.

285. Ambrose, *Citizen Soldiers*, 106.

286. Joachim Ludewig, *Rückzug: The German Retreat from France, 1944*, trans. David T. Zabecki (Lexington: University Press of Kentucky, 2012), 100.

287. Max Hastings, *Overlord: D-Day and the Battle for Normandy* (New York: Simon & Schuster, 1984), 314; Blumenson, *The Battle of the Generals*, 263; Robert M. Citino, *The Wehrmacht's Last Stand: The German Campaigns of 1944–1945* (Lawrence: University Press of Kansas, 2017), 267–268.

288. Breuer, *Death of a Nazi Army*, 295.

289. Hansen, Diary, August 20, 1944, Box 6, Folder 7, CHP.

290. Hansen, Diary, August 22, 1944, Box 6, Folder 7, CHP.

291. Bradley, *A Soldier's Story*, 392.

292. "Minutes of Public Relations Council Conference held at Widewing on 21 June 1944," Box 1, Folder 6, SHN.

293. Butcher, Diary, August 28, 1944, Box 169, (July 17–Aug. 30, 1944) (4), PPPF.

294. Dwight D. Eisenhower, *Crusade in Europe*, 297–298.

Chapter 6. The Press of Prestige

1. Bradley, interview by Bradley and Hansen, circa 1969, Box 1, Folder 12, ONBC, USAHEC.

2. Bradley, interview by Hanson, February 25, 1975, Box 3, Folder 2, ONBC, USAHEC.

3. Hansen, Diary, August 6, 1944, Box 6, Folder 7, CHP; Hansen, Diary, August 11, 1944, Box 6, Folder 8, CHP.

4. Sylvan and Smith, *Normandy to Victory*, 159; Patton, *War As I Knew It*, 113.

5. Richard Kasischke, "'Legendary,' 'Superman' Patton Hailed as Hero in British Press," *St. Louis Post-Dispatch*, August 19, 1944.

6. Sylvan and Smith, *Normandy to Victory*, 122.

7. Smith to Butcher, September 6, 1944, letter, Box 10, Folder 322 1st Army Group, SHAEF, RG 331, NARA.

8. Smith to SHAEF Main Personal for Dupuy, September 6, 1944, letter, Box 10, Folder 322 1st Army Group, SHAEF, RG 331, NARA.

9. Sylvan and Smith, *Normandy to Victory*, 92 and 96.

10. Butcher to PRD First Army for Andrews, September 7, 1944, in 21st Army Group Records, WO 229–55, TNA.[Emphasis in original.]

11. Sylvan and Smith, *Normandy to Victory*, 134.

12. Hansen, Diary, October 23, 1944, Box 6, Folder 9, CHP.

13. Justus Lawrence, unpublished memoir, 195–196, Box 2, Folder Memoirs-World War II (2), JBL.

14. Dwight D. Eisenhower, *Crusade in Europe*, 301.

15. Oldfield, *Never a Shot in Anger*, 93.

16. Ossad, *Omar Nelson Bradley*, 301.

17. Dupuy to Smith, August 18, 1944, memorandum, Box 5, Folder 000.73/5, PPPF.

18. Associated Press, "Bradley Directs All U.S. Forces in France, Including New 3rd Army," August 15, 1944, *New York Times*.

19. Brooke, *War Diaries 1939–1945*, 586.

20. Ambrose, *The Supreme Commander*, 505.

21. Butcher, Diary, August 19, 1944, Box 169, Folder (July 17–Aug. 30, 1944) (4), PPPF.

22. Dupuy to Smith, August 18, 1944, memorandum, Box 5, Folder 000.73/5, PPPF.

23. Hanson W. Baldwin, "Separate Commands," August 17, 1944, *New York Times*; "British Control of Allied Staff Shown in Press," *Chicago Daily Tribune*, August 18, 1944.

24. Bradley, *A Soldier's Story*, 354.

25. Montgomery, Diary, August 18–20, 1944, in Montgomery, *Montgomery and the Battle of Normandy*, 308–309.

26. Churchill to Eisenhower, August 31, 1944, letter, Box 22, Folder Churchill, Winston (5), PPPF.

27. Eisenhower to Churchill, September 1, 1944, letter, PPPF.

28. Marshall to Eisenhower, August 17, 1944, radio WAR-82265, in Marshall, *Marshall Papers*, vol. 4, 550–551.

29. Marshall to Eisenhower, August 17, 1944, 550–551.

30. Quotation included in Surles to Davis, August 18, 1944, cable, Box 10, Folder 322.011, RG 331, NARA.

31. Eisenhower to Marshall, August 19, 1944, cable, in Dwight D. Eisenhower, *Eisenhower Papers*, vol. 4, 2074–2076.

32. Hansen, Diary, August 18, 1944, Box 6, Folder 7, CHP.

33. Dupuy to Smith, August 18, 1944, memorandum, Box 5, Folder 000.73/5, PPPF.

34. Hughes, Diary, August 19, 1944, BoxI 2, ESHP.

35. Harry Butcher to Ruth and Bev. Butcher, August 25, 1944, letter, Box 3, Folder Correspondence File: August, 1944, HCB. Historians have given different explanations of Butcher's role in this incident. David Eisenhower contended that Gallagher got his story from Butcher, who was exiled to London as punishment. David Eisenhower, *Eisenhower: At War 1943–1945* (New York: Random House, 1986), 413–414. Hughes would later speculate that Eisenhower simply wanted Butcher out of the house. Hughes, Diary, September 4, 1944, BoxI 2, ESHP. Steven Casey states, however, that Gallagher's information came from the Third Army, which is supported by the subsequent investigation. Casey, *The War Beat*, 271–272.

36. Hughes, Diary, September 4, 1944, BoxI 2, ESHP.

37. Montgomery to Brooke, August 18, 1944, in Montgomery, *Montgomery and the Battle of Normandy*, 307; Montgomery, *Montgomery Memoirs*, 266. Montgomery wrote after the war that Bradley had "agreed entirely" with his plans but changed his mind on the 23rd. Montgomery, *Montgomery Memoirs*, 267 and 268. Hansen's diary does not support this observation.

38. Hansen, Diary, August 19, and 20, 1944, Box 6, Folder 7, CHP.

39. Montgomery, *Montgomery Memoirs*, 268; D'Este, *Eisenhower*, 599.

40. D'Este, *Eisenhower*, 594, 589, 598, and 603.

41. Ambrose, *The Supreme Commander*, 513; Chester Wilmot, *The Struggle for Europe* (New York: Harper & Brothers, 1952), 733.

42. Hansen, Diary, August 19, 1944, and August 20, 1944, Box 6, Folder 7, CHP; Bradley, *A Soldier's Story*, 399.

43. Bradley Press Conference, August 21, 1944, Box 2, Folder Press Conference Lt. Gen. Omar N. Bradley 21, August 1944, Thomas R. Goethals Papers, USMA.

44. Hansen, Diary, August 22, and 23, 1944, Box 6, Folder 7, CHP.

45. Butcher, Diary, September 9, 1944, Box 169, Folder (Aug. 31-Oct 15, 1944) (1), PPPF.

46. Eisenhower to Combined Chiefs of Staff, September 9, 1944, cable, in Dwight D. Eisenhower, *Eisenhower Papers*, 2125.

47. Montgomery, *Montgomery Memoirs*, 269.

48. Oldfield, *Never a Shot in Anger*, 98.

49. Hansen, Diary, August 25, 1944, Box 6, Folder 7, CHP; Sylvan and Smith, *Normandy to Victory*, 108.

50. Hughes, Diary, September 4, 1944, BoxI 2, ESHP.

51. Brooke, *War Diaries 1939–1945*, 586.

52. Montgomery, *Montgomery Memoirs*, 271–273.

53. Atkinson, *The Guns at Last Light*, 245.

54. Montgomery, *Montgomery Memoirs*, 274–276; D'Este, *Eisenhower*, 606.

55. Eisenhower to Bradley, September 15, 1944, cable, in Dwight D. Eisenhower, *Eisenhower Papers*, 2146–2147.

56. Lewis H. Brereton, *The Brereton Diaries: The War in the Air in the Pacific, Middle East and Europe* (New York: William Morrow, 1946), 336.

57. Hansen, Diary, September 15, 1944, Box 6, Folder 8, CHP.

58. Ossad, *Omar Nelson Bradley*, 262.

59. Cornelius Ryan, *A Bridge Too Far* (New York: Simon and Schuster, 1974), 11. [Original in italics.]

60. Murray and Millett, *A War To Be Won*, 442.

61. Antony Beevor, *The Battle of Arnhem: The Deadliest Airborne Operation of World War II* (New York: Viking, 2018), 365.

62. D'Este, *Eisenhower*, 624.

63. Beevor, *The Battle of Arnhem*, 370.

64. Hansen, Diary, December 4, 1944, Box 6, Folder 11, CHP.

65. Montgomery, *Montgomery Memoirs*, 283–284; D'Este, *Eisenhower*, 623–624.

66. McDonald with Brune, *Valiant for Truth*, 395.

67. Butcher, *My Three Years with Eisenhower*, 717.

68. Butcher, 671 and 672.

69. SHAEF to 21st Army Group, cable, FWD 12748, August 10, 1944, 21st Army Group Records, WO 229-55, TNA.

70. Hansen, Diary, August 14, 1944, Box 6, Folder 7, CHP.

71. SHAEF to 12th Army Group, 1st Allied Airbourn [*sic*] Army, cable, September 11, 1944, 21st Army Group Records, WO 229-55, TNA.

72. Butcher, Diary, September 14, 1944, Box 169, Folder (Aug. 31–Oct 15, 1944) (2), PPPF.

73. Bradley, *A Soldier's Story*, 363.

74. Hansen, Diary, August 6, 1944, Box 6, Folder 7, CHP.

75. Patton, Diary, September 9, 1944, Box 3, Folder 7, GSPP. Many years later Bradley denied this account, stating he did not remember the conversation with Patton and explaining that with the capture of Antwerp Brest was not needed, and "all we did then was to try to contain Brest." Bradley, interview by Hanson. In his second autobiography, published after his death, however, Bradley's coauthor had the general explain, "We might have been well advised at this point to give up the good fight and let Brest remain in German hands. . . . But by then, Brest had taken on a symbolic value far exceeding its utilitarian value and, perhaps imprudently, I was stubbornly determined to capture it." Bradley and Blair, *A General's Life*, 305.

76. Atkinson, *The Guns at Last Light*, 152.

77. John Nelson Rickard, *Patton at Bay: The Lorraine Campaign, 1944* (Washington, DC: Brassey's, 2004), 118, 120, and 124.

78. Atkinson, *The Guns at Last Light*, 343.

79. Gay, Diary, October 4, 1944, Box 2, Folder September 1, 1944, to October 6, 1944, HRG.

80. Atkinson, *The Guns at Last Light*, 345.

81. Collins, *Lighting Joe*, 269 and 271.

82. Ambrose, *Citizen Soldiers*, 146–147.

83. Weigley, *Eisenhower's Lieutenants*, 364; Robert Sterling Rush, *Hell in Hürtgen Forest: The Ordeal and Triumph of an American Infantry Regiment* (Lawrence: University Press of Kansas, 2001), 123.

84. Hansen, Diary, October 24, 1944, Box 6, Folder 9, CHP; Bradley to Eisenhower October 24, 1944, copied in Box 6, Folder 9, CHP.

85. Butcher, *My Three Years with Eisenhower*, 690.

86. Eisenhower to Ramsay, Montgomery, Bradley, Leigh-Mallory, Brereton, Spaatz, Harris, September 4, 1944, cable, in Dwight D. Eisenhower, *Eisenhower Papers*, 2115.

87. Butcher, *My Three Years with Eisenhower*, 656–657.

88. Surles to Eisenhower, October 4, 1944, letter, Box 113, Folder Surles, A. D., (2), PPPF.

89. Bissell (signed Marshall) to Eisenhower (for Betts), October 12, 1944, in 21st Army Group Records, WO 229–55, TNA.

90. Eisenhower to Aksel Nielsen, October 20, 1944, cable, in Dwight D. Eisenhower, *Eisenhower Papers*, 2235.

91. Hansen, Diary, December 5, 1944, Box 6, Folder 11, CHP.

92. Omar Bradley, "Minutes of Press Conference," December 15, 1944, found in Hansen's Diary, December 13, 1944, Box 6, Folder 11, CHP.

93. Roeder, *The Censored War*, 1. For more on this subject see McCallum, *U.S. Censorship, Violence, and Moral Judgement in a Wartime Democracy*, 544; Maury Klein, *A Call To Arms: Mobilizing America for World War II* (New York: Bloomsbury Press, 2013), 743–766.

94. L.F. Heald, Directive no. 1, Box 7, Folder 314.7, RG 331, NARA.

95. Knightley, *The First Casualty*, 324; Moseley, *Reporting War*, 8 and 351–352.

96. Patton, *War As I Knew It*, 139.

97. Blumenson, *The Patton Papers, 1940–1945*, 566.

98. "Conference between General Patton and Third Army Correspondents," November 6, 1944, Box 53, Folder 7, GSPP.

99. Patton to John A. Bockhorst, December 4, 1944, letter, Box 53, Folder 7, GSPP.

100. "Transcript of Conference," September 7, 1944, Box 53, Folder 7, GSPP.

101. Lawrence, unpublished memoir, 219.

102. Tom Curley and John Maxwell Hamilton, introduction to *Ed Kennedy's War: V-E Day, Censorship, and The Associated Press*, ed. Julia Kennedy Cochran (Baton Rouge: Louisiana State University Press, 2012), xi.

103. Lawrence, unpublished memoir, 219.

104. Lawrence, unpublished memoir, 219.

105. Mathews, *Reporting the Wars*, 194.

106. Thomas Alexander Hughes, *Over Lord: General Pete Quesada and the Triumph of Tactical Air Power in World War II* (New York: Free Press, 1995), 14; Mark Clodfelter, *Beneficial Bombing: The Progressive Foundations of American Air Power, 1917–1945* (Lincoln: University of Nebraska Press, 2010), 100.

107. Hansen, Diary, December 13, 1944, Box 6, Folder 11, CHP.

108. Patton, Diary, December 9, 1944, Box 3, Folder 9, GSPP.

109. "Conference between General Patton, General Weyland and Third Army Correspondents," December 9, 1944, Box 53, Folder 7, GSPP.

110. Omar Bradley, "Minutes of Press Conference," December 15, 1944, found in Hansen's Diary, December 13, 1944, Box 6, Folder 11, CHP. Bradley would continue advocating for tactical air support after the war ended. Tami Davis Biddle, *Rhetoric and Reality in Air Warfare: The Evolution of British and American Ideas about Strategic Bombing, 1914–1945* (Princeton, NJ: Princeton University Press, 2002), 277.

111. "Conference between General Patton and Third Army Correspondents," November 6, 1944, Box 53, Folder 7, GSPP.

112. Gay, Diary, November 6, 1944, Box 2, Folder October 7, 1944, to November 20, 1944, HRG.

113. Rickard, *Patton at Bay*, 175.

114. Eisenhower to Surles, October 6, 1944, letter, Box 113, Folder Surles, A. D., (2), PPPF.

115. Weinberg, *A World at War*, 765–766; Simms, *Hitler*, 522.

116. Heiber, *Hitler and His Generals*, 539–540.

117. Murray and Millett, *A War To Be Won*, 465.

118. Murray and Millett, 469; Allen, *Forward with Patton*, 127.

119. "General Bradley Personal & Confidential," Box 38, Folder "General Bradley Personal & Confidential," ONBC, USMA.

120. Morelock, *Generals of the Bulge*, 234.

121. Hughes, Diary, December 26, 1944, BoxI 2, ESHP; Everett Hughes to Kate Hughes, December 26, 1944, letter, BoxII 3, ESHP.

122. Hughes, Diary, January 7, 1945, BoxI 2, ESHP.

123. Hansen, Diary, December 17, 1944, Box 6, Folder 11, CHP.

124. Bradley, *A Soldier's Story*, 477.

125. Wesley K. Clark, forward to Axelrod, *Bradley*, ix; Axelrod, *Bradley*, 161; Allen, *Forward with Patton*, 138. Patton's posthumously published memoirs somewhat insensitively stated that Bradley had received "practically a demotion." Patton, *War As I Knew It*, 186.

126. "Personal & Confidential," [an early draft of Bradley's memoirs], Box 38, Folder Personal & Confidential, ONBC, USMA.

127. Allen, *Forward with Patton*, 130 and 135–136.

128. Memorandum for the Army Commander, December 26, 1944, quoted in Patton, *War As I Knew It*, 194.

129. Casey, *The War Beat*, 302–304.

130. Oldfield, *Never a Shot in Anger*, 175–176.

131. Casey, *The War Beat*, 302–304. This was untrue. Eisenhower had ordered a news "blackout" in the names of liberated French towns in the summer of 1944 when the war was going extremely well for the Allies. Butcher would even claim that the blackout during the Bulge was for the same reason. Butcher, *My Three Years with Eisenhower*, 658 and 729.

132. Gay, Diary, December 21, 1944, Box 2, Folder Nov. 21, 1944–December 31, 1944, HRG.

133. Hansen, Diary, November 5, 1944, Box 6, Folder 10, CHP; Bradley, interview by Bradley and Hansen.

134. Brooke quoted in Hamilton, *The Field Marshal*, 219.

135. D'Este, *Eisenhower*, 655.

136. Allen, *Forward with Patton*, 135.

137. Montgomery to Eisenhower December 29, 1944, letter, in Montgomery, *Montgomery Memoirs*, 318.

138. D'Este, *Eisenhower*, 656.

139. "Allied Generals May Be Moved," *Daily Express*, December 30, 1944. [Original headline in all capitals.]

140. Marshall to Eisenhower, December 30, 1944, radio W-84337, in Marshall, *Marshall Papers*, 720–721.

141. Eisenhower to Marshall, January 1, 1945, cable, in Dwight D. Eisenhower, *Eisenhower Papers*, 2390.

142. De Guingand, *Generals at War*, 108–109; Hamilton, *Monty*, 274. Hamilton claims certain details about de Guingand's account are mistaken. In his earlier book, titled *Operation Victory*, de Guingand gives a slightly different version of events. However, his account given in *Generals At War* more accurately fits other evidence.

143. De Guingand, *Generals at War*, 110–112, and 115; Hamilton, *Monty*, 279; Hansen, Diary, December 25, 1944, Box 6, Folder 11, CHP.

144. De Guingand, *Generals at War*, 113–114.

145. Hamilton, *Monty*, 297.

146. Churchill to Roosevelt, January 7, 1945, in Winston S. Churchill and Franklin D. Roosevelt, *Churchill and Roosevelt: The Complete Correspondence*, vol. 3, *Alliance*

Declining February 1944–April 1945, ed. Warren F. Kimball (Princeton, NJ: Princeton University Press, 1984), 498.

147. Hamilton, *Monty*, 298 and 299.

148. Brigadier Sir Edgar Williams, interview of 20.12.79 quoted in Hamilton, *Monty*, 304.

149. Montgomery, *Montgomery Memoirs*, 311–314.

150. Hamilton, *Monty*, 303.

151. Oldfield, *Never a Shot in Anger*, 180n.

152. Ralph Ingersoll, *Top Secret* (New York: Harcourt, Brace, and Company, 1946), 279n.

153. Wilmot, *The Struggle for Europe*, 611n. Montgomery, *Montgomery Memoirs*, 314. It should be noted that Montgomery never claimed that German black propaganda alone caused the uproar, and he regretted giving the press conference.

154. "Person & Confidential," Box 38, Folder Personal and Confidential, ONBC, USMA.

155. Eisenhower to Surles, January 5, 1945, cable, Box 1, Folder 000.73, RG 331, NARA.

156. Chester Wilmot, "5 January 1954," in Desmond Hawkins and Donald Boyd, eds., *War Report: A Record of Dispatches Broadcast by the BBC's War Correspondents with the Allied Expeditionary Force 6 June 1944–5 May 1945*, ed. by the BBC (London: Oxford University Press, 1946), 309–311.

157. Hansen, Diary, January 6, 1945, Box 7, Folder 1, CHP.

158. Hansen, Diary, January 6, 1945.

159. Casey, *The War Beat*, 310.

160. Kay, Diary, January 8 and 9, 1945, Box 140, Folder Diary: Summersby, PPPF; Hansen, Diary, January 8, 1945, Box 7, Folder 1, CHP.

161. Hansen, Diary, January 9, 1945, Box 7, Folder 1, CHP.

162. Charles B. MacDonald, *A Time for Trumpets: The Untold Story of the Battle of the Bulge* (New York: Bantam Books, 1985), 614.

163. "Command Setup," January 23, 1945, Untitled Correspondent Album, ONBC, USMA.

164. Hansen, Diary, January 9, 1945, Box 7, Folder 1, CHP.

165. Ninth Army Diary, January 19, 1945, Box 7, Folder 7, William Simpson Papers, USAHEC.

166. Hansen, Diary, January 6, 1945, Box 7, Folder 1, CHP; Allen, *Forward with Patton*, 127.

167. Dwight D. Eisenhower, *Crusade in Europe*, 356.

168. Dupuy, "Press Release on German Ardennes Counter-Offensive," February 6, 1945, WO-229-55, TNA.

169. "Command Setup," January 23, 1945, Untitled Correspondent Album, ONBC, USMA.

170. Eisenhower to Marshall, February 9, 1945, letter, in Dwight D. Eisenhower, *Eisenhower Papers*, 2473. [Emphasis in the original.]

171. Brooke, *War Diaries 1939–1945*, 642–643.

172. Macmillan, *War Diaries*, 707.

173. Leahy, Diary, February 2, 1944, Reel 4, WDL; Brooke, *War Diaries 1939–1945*, 655; Marshall, *Marshall Interviews and Reminiscences*, 345.

174. Montgomery, *Montgomery Memoirs*, 324–326.

175. Eisenhower to Brooke, February 16, 1945, letter, Box 3, Folder Alanbrooke, (Lord) (2), PPPF.

176. Eisenhower to Marshall, February 20, 1945, letter, in Dwight D. Eisenhower, *Eisenhower Papers*, vol. 4, 2490–2491.

177. Churchill to Eisenhower, February 22, 1945, letter, and Eisenhower to Churchill, February 25, 1945, letter, Box 22, Folder Churchill, Winston (4), PPPF.

178. Tedder, *With Prejudice*, 664.

179. Dwight D. Eisenhower, *Crusade in Europe*, 353.

180. Atkinson, *The Guns at Last Light*, 474.

181. Wheeler, *Jacob L. Devers*, 387.

182. Dwight D. Eisenhower, *Crusade in Europe*, 352.

183. Kay, Diary, January 3, 1945, Box 140, Folder Diary: Summersby, PPPF.

184. William K. Wyant, *Sandy Patch: A Biography of Lt. Gen. Alexander M. Patch* (New York: Praeger, 1991), 164; Wheeler, *Jacob L. Devers*, 387.

185. John A. Adams, *General Jacob Devers: World War II's Forgotten Four Star* (Bloomington: Indiana University Press, 2015), 296.

186. Charles de Gaulle, *The War Memoirs of Charles de Gaulle: Salvation 1944–1946*, trans. Richard Howard, (New York: Simon and Schuster, 1960), 159–160; Adams, *General Jacob Devers*, 300.

187. De Gaulle, *The War Memoirs of Charles de Gaulle*, 163.

188. Devers, Diary, December 29, 1944, Box 1, JLDP.

189. Wheeler, *Jacob L. Devers*, 388 and 391. Devers denied he was delaying and cited problems in repositioning his forces. "Summary of Directions," January 3, 1944, memorandum, Box 1, Folder Office of the Chief of Military History, JLDP.

190. De Gaulle, *The War Memoirs of Charles de Gaulle*, 166.

191. "For General Jenkins," January 2, 1945, memorandum, Box 1, Folder Office of the Chief of Military History, JLDP.

192. De Gaulle to Eisenhower, January 3, 1944, letter, Box 169, Folder Butcher's Diary-Jan. 1–Jan. 28, 1945, (1), PPPF.

193. De Gaulle to Eisenhower, January 3, 1945, letter, General Jacob Devers Collection, York County History Center, York, Pennsylvania.

194. De Gaulle wrote after the war that Eisenhower was still determined to reposition the forces of the Sixth Army Group. De Gaulle, *The War Memoirs of Charles de Gaulle*, 169. Historian James Scott Wheeler likewise claims that Eisenhower was disingenuous when he wrote Marshall a few days later that a change of plans was already being put in place when de Gaulle arrived. Wheeler, *Jacob L. Devers*, 394. Historian Rick Atkinson believes Eisenhower changed his mind before seeing de Gaulle. Atkinson, *The Guns at Last Light*, 479. This position is supported by Alan Brooke, who wrote in his diary that "Ike had already decided to alter his dispositions so as to leave the divisions practically where they are." Brooke, *War Diaries 1939–1945*, 642. This is confirmed by Smith's phoning Devers before de Gaulle arrived and saying

that "it looks now as if you will have to hold Strasbourg." "Summary of Directions," and "Notes on decisions . . . ," January 3, 1944, memorandum, Box 1, Folder Office of the Chief of Military History, JLDP.

195. Kay, Diary, January 3, 1945, Box 140, Folder Diary: Summersby, PPPF.

196. Brooke, *War Diaries 1939–1945*, 642. Brooke implies this conversation took place before they met de Gaulle.

197. Churchill, *Triumph and Tragedy*, 281.

198. Eisenhower to Marshall, January 6, 1945, cable, in Dwight D. Eisenhower, *Eisenhower Papers*, vol. 4, 2400–2401.

199. De Gaulle, *The War Memoirs of Charles de Gaulle*, 169–170; Eisenhower to Marshall, January 6, 1945, cable, in Dwight D. Eisenhower, *Eisenhower Papers*, vol. 4, 2400–2401. Dwight D. Eisenhower, *Crusade in Europe*, 363. At least one historian of the campaign has taken de Gaulle's threats seriously. See David P. Colley, *Decision at Strasbourg: Ike's Strategic Mistake To Halt the Sixth Army Group at the Rhine in 1944* (Annapolis, MD: Naval Institute Press, 2008), 185.

200. Wheeler, *Jacob L. Devers*, 393; De Gaulle, *The War Memoirs of Charles de Gaulle*, 171; Eisenhower to Marshall, January 6, 1945, cable, in Dwight D. *Eisenhower Papers*, vol. 4, 2400–2401. In his memoirs, Eisenhower repeats this story. Dwight D. Eisenhower, *Crusade in Europe*, 363.

201. Gay, Diary, January 24, 1945, Box 3, Folder January 1945, HRG; Patton, Diary, January 24, 1945, Box 3, Folder 9, GSPP; Crosswell, *Beetle*, 852–853. Gay and Patton's diaries give different accounts of who from SHAEF was on the phone. Gay said he did not know but wrote in that it was Bedell Smith. Patton said Whiteley. Since Patton seemed more certain I have gone with Whiteley.

202. Allen, *Forward with Patton*, 160–161, 166, 167, and 179. [Emphasis in the original].

203. Hansen, Diary, January 10, 1945, Box 7, Folder 1, CHP.

204. Hansen, Diary, February 4, 1945, Box 7, Folder 2, CHP; Hansen, Diary, March 27, 1945, Box 7, Folder 3, CHP.

205. Patton, Diary, January 13, 1945, Box 3, Folder 9, GSPP.

206. Butcher, *My Three Years with Eisenhower*, 774.

207. Bill Mauldin, *The Brass Ring: A Sort of a Memoir* (New York: W. W. Norton, 1971), 254–255.

208. Gay, Diary, February 27, 1945, Box 3, Folder February 1945, HRG.

209. Mauldin, *The Brass Ring*, 259, 261, and 264.

210. Butcher, *My Three Years with Eisenhower*, 796.

211. "Soldier Opinion of 'The Stars and Stripes,'" March 1945, Box 111, Folder Stars and Stripes, PPPF.

212. Keith Winston, *V-Mail: Letters of a World War II Combat Medic*, ed. Sarah Winston (Chapel Hill: Algonquin Books, 1985), 212.

213. For example see Todd DePastino, *Bill Mauldin: A Life Up Front* (New York: W. W. Norton, 2008), 302; Rooney, *My War*, 196; Pinkley with Scheer, *Eisenhower Declassified*, 208.

214. Butcher, *My Three Years with Eisenhower*, 774.

215. Manchester, *American Caesar*, 20.

216. Mauldin quoted in D'Este, *Patton*, 694.

217. Eisenhower to Oscar Nathaniel Solbert, March 11, 1945, letter, in Dwight D. Eisenhower, *Eisenhower Papers*, vol. 4, 2519.

218. Eisenhower to Ben Lear, April 2, 1945, letter, in Dwight D. Eisenhower, *Eisenhower Papers*, vol. 4, 2578.

219. Pinkley with Scheer, *Eisenhower Declassified*, 208.

220. Truscott, *Command Mission*, 333; Keyes to Mauldin, May 13, 1945, letter, Box 4, Folder Keyes, Geoffrey, the Papers of William H. Mauldin, LOC; Clark to Mauldin, May 17, 1945, Box 2, Folder Clark, Mark W., the Papers of William H. Mauldin, LOC.

221. "Digest of Conferences between Generals Morgan and Whiteley and Colonel Dupuy," February 3, 1945, Box 1, Folder 00071, RG 331, NARA.

222. Hansen, Diary, February 22, 1945, Box 7, Folder 2, CHP.

223. SHAEF Main from Allen signed Eisenhower to Allied Army Groups, February 7, 1945, Box 1, Folder 00071, RG 331, NARA.

224. Dupuy to Chief of Staff, "Unbalanced Publicity for Commanders," March 9, 1945, WO 229–55, TNA.

225. Hansen, Diary, March 6, 1945, Box 7, Folder 3, CHP.

226. Eisenhower to Allen, March 10, 1945, memorandum, in Dwight D. Eisenhower, *Eisenhower Papers*, vol. 4, 2517.

227. Eisenhower to Marshall, March 12, 1945, letter, in Dwight D. Eisenhower, *Eisenhower Papers*, vol. 4, 2521.

228. Eisenhower to Bradley and Devers, March 12, 1945, letter, in Dwight D. Eisenhower, *Eisenhower Papers*, vol. 4, 2523–2524.

229. Patton, Diary, March 17, 1945, Box 3, Folder 10, GSPP.

230. Patton, Diary, March 17, 1945, Box 3, Folder 10, GSPP. That same day Eisenhower wrote Marshall saying he wanted to highlight the accomplishments of some of his commanders in the press. Eisenhower to Marshall, March 17, 1945, cable, in Dwight D. Eisenhower, *Eisenhower Papers*, vol. 4, 2531; Allen, *Forward with Patton*, 189.

231. Eisenhower to Marshall, February 26, 1945, letter, in Dwight D. Eisenhower, *Eisenhower Papers*, vol. 4, 2498.

232. Bradley and Blair, *A General's Life*, 404–406; Oldfield, *Never a Shot in Anger*, 212; Derek S. Zumbro, *Battle for the Ruhr: The German Army's Final Defeat in the West* (Lawrence: University Press of Kansas, 2006), 126.

233. Sylvan and Smith, *Normandy to Victory*, 324; Hansen, Diary, March 8, 1945, Box 7, Folder 3, CHP.

234. Bradley and Blair, *A General's Life*, 412; Casey, *The War Beat*, 323; Marshall to Eisenhower forwarded to Bradley, cable, Binder titled "Correspondence War Years," ONBC.

235. Casey, *The War Beat*, 325.

236. Bradley, interview by Hanson.

237. Gay, Diary, March 23, 1945, Box 3, Folder March 1945, HRG. This account of Bradley's comments is taken from what Gay wrote in his diary.

238. Allen, *Forward with Patton*, 200.

239. Butcher, *My Three Years with Eisenhower*, 776.

240. Casey, *The War Beat*, 327.

241. Hughes, Diary, March 24, 1945, BoxI 2, ESHP.

242. Dwight D. Eisenhower, *Crusade in Europe*, 396. See also Eisenhower to Montgomery, April 8, 1945, in Dwight D. Eisenhower, *Eisenhower Papers*, vol. 4, 2594.

243. Ambrose, *Citizen Soldiers*, 453.

244. Casey, *The War Beat*, 331; Oldfield, *Never a Shot in Anger*, 230.

245. Bradley, *A Soldier's Story*, 535.

246. Ambrose, *Citizen Soldiers*, 457.

247. Walter Bedell Smith, "Conference," April 21, 1945, Box 6, Folder "Press Conference," TMSP.

248. Allen to Smith, "Copy Filed as result of Press Conference," April 23, 1944, Box 37, Folder Chief of Staff's Press Conference April 21, 1945, Walter Bedell Smith: Collection of World War II Documents, 1941–1945, DDEL.

249. Casey, *The War Beat*, 333.

250. Ambrose, *Citizen Soldiers*, 457.

251. Smith, "Conference," April 21, 1945, Box 6, Folder "Press Conference," TMSP.

252. Eisenhower to Marshall, March 31, 1945, cable, in Dwight D. Eisenhower, *Eisenhower Papers*, vol. 4, 2566.

253. Dupuy to Allen, "Final Announcement," March 30, 1945, memorandum, Box 1, Folder 00071, PRD, RG 331, NARA.

254. Butcher, *My Three Years with Eisenhower*, 828–829; Kennedy, *Ed Kennedy's War*, 153.

255. Oldfield, *Never a Shot in Anger*, 242.

256. Kennedy, *Ed Kennedy's War*, 156–157.

257. D'Este, *Eisenhower*, 702 and 703.

258. Kennedy, *Ed Kennedy's War*, 159–161, 163, 165–167, and 172.

259. Ambrose, *Citizen Soldiers*, 166; MacDonald, *A Time for Trumpets*, 614; Kindsvatter, *American Soldiers*, 236.

Conclusion

1. Chappell, *Before the Bomb*, 3. For an excellent look at press coverage of the battle for Okinawa and its effects on strategy see Sarantakes, "Warriors of Word and Sword," 334–367.

2. Borneman, *The Admirals*, 447.

3. Vladislav M. Zubok, *A Failed Empire: The Soviet Union in the Cold War from Stalin to Gorbachev* (Chapel Hill: University of North Carolina Press, 2007), 30.

4. Spector, *Eagle against the Sun*, 546 and 554; Casey, *Cautious Crusade*, 220. Historian Tsuyoshi Hasegawa, however, finds congressional and editorial opinion more divided. But as one recent study highlights, Truman noted public opinion but also intercepted messages from Japan showing the Japanese were willing to fight to avoid unconditional surrender. Japan wanted peace, not surrender. See Tsuyoshi Hasegawa, *Racing the Enemy: Stalin, Truman, and the Surrender of Japan* (Cambridge, MA: Harvard University Press, 2005), 222–224. Marc Gallicchio, *Unconditional:*

The Japanese Surrender in World War II (Oxford: Oxford University Press, 2020), 210 and 211.

5. Sadao Asada, "The Shock of the Atomic Bomb and Japan's Decision to Surrender," in *Hiroshima in History: The Myths of Revisionism*, ed. Robert James Maddox (Columbia: University of Missouri Press, 2007), 50.

6. Spector, *Eagle against the Sun*, 556.

7. Richard B. Frank, *Downfall: The End of the Imperial Japanese Empire* (New York: Random House, 1999), 313–314.

8. Toland, *The Rising Sun*, 851; Frank, *Downfall*, 319.

9. Miller, *War Plan Orange*, 358.

10. Sevareid, *Not So Wild a Dream*, 380.

11. Sweeney, *Secrets of Victory*, 204–205.

12. Casey, *The War Beat*, 3, 347, and 352.

13. Jordan, *FDR, Dewey, and the Election of 1944*, 321.

14. McCallum, *U.S. Censorship, Violence, and Moral Judgement in a Wartime Democracy*, 543.

15. Fletcher Pratt, "War Not as Near End as Many Would Like," *Washington Post*, July 23, 1944.

16. Hansen, Diary, October 24, 1944, Box 6, Folder 9, CHP; Bradley to Eisenhower October 24, 1944, copied in Box 6, Folder 9, CHP.

17. De Guingand, *Generals At War*, 114.

18. Walker, *From Texas to Rome*, 440.

19. Bradley, interview by Bradley and Hansen, circa 1969, Box 1, Folder 11, ONBC, USAHEC.

20. Eisenhower to Pyle, December 15, 1944, in Dwight D. Eisenhower, *Eisenhower Papers*, vol. 4, 2349.

21. Ernie Pyle, *Brave Men* (New York: Henry Holt, 1944), 319.

22. Knightley, *The First Casualty*.

23. Gay, Diary, Telephone Conversation, December 21, 1944, Box 2, Folder Nov. 21, 1944–Dec. 31, 1944, HRG; Butcher, Diary, November 23, 1943, Box 167, Folder (October 1–December 30, 1943) (2), PPPF.

24. Gay, Diary, January 1, 1945, Box 3, Folder January 1945, HRG.

25. Hansen, Diary, March 6, 1945, Box 7, Folder 3, CHP.

26. Sweeney, *The Military and the Press*, 108; Thomas B. Buell, *Master of Sea Power: A Biography of Fleet Admiral Ernest J. King* (Annapolis, MD: Naval Institute Press, 1980), 502–505.

27. Bradley, *A Soldier's Story*, xiii–xx; Bradley and Blair, *A General's Life*, 9.

28. Michael J. Yavenditti, "John Hersey and the American Conscience: The Reception of 'Hiroshima,'" *Pacific Historical Review* 43, no. 1 (February 1974): 26.

29. Robert P. Newman, "Hiroshima and the Trashing of Henry Stimson," *New England Quarterly* 71, no. 1 (March 1998): 30; Yavenditti, "John Hersey and the American Conscience," 31, 32, and 43–44; James G. Hershberg, *James B. Conant: Harvard to Hiroshima and the Making of the Nuclear Age* (Stanford, CA: Stanford University Press, 1995), 291–297.

30. Yavenditti, "John Hersey and the American Conscience," 49.

31. This is an extremely brief summary of the historiography surrounding the dropping of the atomic bomb. For a more detailed explanation see Rosemary B. Mariner and G. Kurt Piehler, *The Atomic Bomb and American Society* (Knoxville: University of Tennessee Press, 2009).

32. Hansen, Diary, September 18, 1944, Box 6, Folder 8, CHP.

33. Hansen, Diary, January 8, 1945, Box 7, Folder 1, CHP.

34. Ingersoll, *Top Secret*, 56, 75, and 280. Many of Ingersoll arguments were echoed by Roosevelt's son Elliott. Elliott Roosevelt, *As He Saw It* (New York: Duell, Sloan and Pearce, 1946).

35. D'Este, *Decision in Normandy*, 488n4.

36. Butcher, *My Three Years with Eisenhower*, 75.

37. Butcher, Diary, August 26, 1942, Folder July 8—September 15, 1942, (4), PPPF.

38. Butcher, *My Three Years with Eisenhower*, 644.

39. David Reynolds, *In Command of History: Churchill Fighting and Writing the Second World War* (New York: Random House, 2005), 40–41.

40. Reynolds, *In Command of History*, 40 and 42.

41. Eisenhower to Brooke, March 4, 1946, letter, Box 3, Folder Alanbrooke, (Lord) (1), PPPF.

42. Dwight D. Eisenhower, *Crusade in Europe*, 4.

43. Reynolds, *In Command of History*, 42 and xx.

44. For a few significant examples see, Wedemeyer, *Wedemeyer Reports!*; Christopher Thorne, *Allies of a Kind: The United States, Britain and the War against Japan, 1941–1945* (Oxford: Oxford University Press, 1978); David Irving, *The War between the Generals: Inside the Allied High Command* (London: Allen Lane, 1981); Stoler, *Allies and Adversaries.*

45. McDonald with Brune, *Valiant for Truth*, 450 and 445.

46. B. H. Liddell Hart, *The German Generals Talk* (New York: Quill, 1948), x and 300.

47. McDonald with Brune, *Valiant for Truth*, 449 and 450.

48. Wilmot, *The Struggle for Europe*, 12–14, 716, 714, 715, 713, 13, and 12.

49. B. H. Liddell Hart, *History of the Second World War* (London: Cassell, 1970), 701 and 712–713; Montgomery, *Montgomery Memoirs.*

50. Casey, *Cautious Crusade*, 18–19 and 129.

51. S. L. A. Marshall, *Men against Fire: The Problem of Battle Command in Future War* (Gloucester, MA: Peter Smith, 1978), 50; Peter R. Mansoor, *The GI Offensive in Europe: The Triumph of American Infantry Divisions, 1941–1945* (Lawrence: University Press of Kansas, 1999), 6 and 260.

52. Klein, *A Call to Arms*, 1; O'Brien, *How the War Was Won*, 6. Mansoor links this view to the German generals' argument. Mansoor, *The GI Offensive in Europe*, 2.

53. Weigley, *Eisenhower's Lieutenants*, 729; Martin van Creveld, *Fighting Power: German and U.S. Army Performance, 1939–1945* (Westport, CT: Greenwood Press, 1982).

54. Symonds, *World War II at Sea*, 641.

55. O'Brien, *How the War Was Won*, 16.

56. Stephen Ambrose, *The Victors, Eisenhower and His Boys: The Men of World War II* (New York: Simon & Schuster, 1998), 141.

57. Holland, *Italy's Sorrow*, 530.

58. Mansoor, *The GI Offensive in Europe*, 5. See also Porch, *The Path to Victory*, 346.

59. Ambrose, *Citizen Soldiers*, 14, 473, and 22.

60. John Sloan Brown, *Draftee Division: The 88th Infantry Division in World War II* (Lexington: University Press of Kentucky, 1986); Michael D. Doubler, *Closing with the Enemy: How GIs Fought the War in Europe, 1944–1945* (Lawrence: University Press of Kansas, 1994); Mansoor, *The GI Offensive in Europe*; John C. McManus, *The Deadly Brotherhood: The American Combat Soldier in World War II* (Novato, CA: Presidio Press, 1998); Rush, *Hell in Hürtgen Forest*; Michael E. Weaver, *Guard Wars: The 28th Infantry Division in World War II* (Bloomington: Indiana University Press, 2010).

61. Marshall, *Marshall Interviews and Reminiscences*, 147.

62. Hastings, *All Hell Let Loose*, xv.

63. D'Este, *Patton*, 765.

64. Manchester, *American Caesar*, 763–764.

65. Allen, *Eisenhower and the Mass Media*, 12.

66. John S. D. Eisenhower, *General Ike: A Personal Reminiscence* (New York: Free Press, 2003), 138.

67. De Guingand, *Operation Victory*, 466.

68. Dwight D. Eisenhower, *At Ease*, 320.

69. "The War in the Pacific," 6, Kenney Diary, vol. 1, Box 1, RG-54, GCK; Baer, *One Hundred Years of Sea Power*, 298–300.

70. Wedemeyer, *Wedemeyer Reports!*, 82.

71. To the Chief of Staff, "Report of Board of Officers on Reorganization of the War Department," memorandum, Box 6, Folder unnumbered, Alexander Patch Papers, USMA.

72. Koop, *Weapon of Silence*, 271.

73. George Kennan, *Measures Short of War: The George F. Kennan Lectures at the National War College 1946–47*, ed. Giles D. Harlow and George C. Maerz (Washington, DC: National Defense University Press, 1991), 9.

74. Gregory M. Tomlin, *Murrow's Cold War: Public Diplomacy for the Kennedy Administration* (Lincoln, NE: Potomac Books, 2016), xx–xxi.

75. Bradley, interview by Hanson, October 9, 1975, Box 3, Folder 14, ONBC, USAHEC.

76. Tomlin, *Murrow's Cold War*, xix.

77. Carew, *The Power to Persuade*, 201; Fussell, *Wartime*, 153.

78. Gay, *Assignment to Hell*, 448 and 450.

79. Cloud and Olson, *The Murrow Boys*, 364–365.

80. Tomlin, *Murrow's Cold War*, 255.

81. Casey, *Selling the Korean War*, 360–361.

82. Casey, 8–9.

83. Sweeney, *The Military and the Press*, 131 and 132–133.

84. Casey, *Selling the Korean War*, 9, 361, and 360.

85. Sweeney, *The Military and the Press*, 135.

86. Casey, *Selling the Korean War*, 5 and 8.

87. Douglas Kinnard, *The War Managers* (Hanover, NH: University of New England, 1977), 126.

88. Hammond, *Public Affairs*, 7–8.

89. David F. Schmitz, *The Tet Offensive: Politics, War, and Public Opinion* (New York: Rowman & Littlefield, 2005), xiv and 160–161; Sweeney, *The Military and the Press*, 146.

90. Sweeney, *The Military and the Press*, 146; Edwin E. Moïse, *The Myths of Tet: The Most Misunderstood Event of the Vietnam War* (Lawrence: University Press of Kansas, 2017), 5 and 185; Hammond, *Public Affairs*, 9. It should be added that at least one study has claimed that the media coverage of Tet was not negative (Moïse, *The Myths of Tet*, 178). However, enough participants certainly remembered it that way. Likewise, Moïse's chapter on the media during Tet ignores or fails to analyze several important issues, including the most famous image of the battle: a South Vietnamese general summarily executing a Vietcong sniper.

91. Hammond, *Public Affairs*, 9.

92. Schmitz, *The Tet Offensive*, 163.

93. Lyndon Baines Johnson, *The Vantage Point: Perspectives of the Presidency 1963–1969* (New York: Holt, Rinehart and Winston, 1971), 418.

94. Hammond, *Public Affairs*, 4.

95. Knightley, *The First Casualty*, 315–316.

96. Bradley, interview by Hanson, December 4, 1974, 22–23, Box 2, Folder 12, ONBC, USAHEC.

97. Daniel C. Hallin, *The "Uncensored War": The Media and Vietnam* (Oxford: Oxford University Press, 1986), 6.

98. Kinnard, *The War Manager*, 132–133.

99. Kinnard, 124.

100. Kindsvatter, *American Soldiers*, 147.

101. Bradley, interview by Hanson, February 27, 1975, Box 3, Folder 6, ONBC, USAHEC.

102. Gay, *Assignment to Hell*, 453 and 456.

103. W. A. Swanberg, *Luce and His Empire* (New York: Charles Scribner's Sons, 1972), 3.

104. Paul Johnson, *A History of the American People* (New York: Harper Perennial, 1997), 846–847.

105. Jeffrey Toobin, *American Heiress: The Wild Saga of the Kidnapping, Crimes and Trial of Patty Hearst* (New York: Doubleday, 2016), 11, 14, 35, 134, 148, and 159.

106. Pete Williams, "The Press and the Persian Gulf War," *Parameters* 21, no. 1 (Autumn 1991): 5 and 7; Sweeney, *The Military and the Press*, 158 and 168.

107. H. Norman Schwarzkopf with Peter Petre, *It Doesn't Take A Hero* (New York: Bantam Books, 1992), 468.

108. See the introduction for scholarship on the "CNN Effect."

109. Ben R. Rich and Leo Janos, *Skunk Works: A Personal Memoir of My Years at Lockheed* (New York: Little, Brown, 1994), 340.

110. Emile Simpson, *War from the Ground Up: Twenty-First-Century Combat As Politics* (Oxford: Oxford University Press, 2013), 228.

111. Simpson, 232.

112. Sweeney, *The Military and the Press*, 206.

Bibliography

Archives

Air Force Historical Research Agency, Archives Branch, Maxwell AFB, Alabama
Henry Harley "Hap" Arnold Papers, 1905–1953 (microfilm)
The Citadel, Archives and Museum, Charleston, South Carolina
Mark W. Clark Collection, https://citadeldigitalarchives.omeka.net/items/browse
?advanced%5B0%5D%5Belemen_id%5D=49&advanced%5B0%5D%5B
type%5D=is+exactly&advanced%5B0%5D%5Bterms%5D=Clark%2C
+Mark+W.+%28Mark+Wayne%29%2C+1896-1984
Eisenhower Presidential Library, Abilene, Kansas
Harry C. Butcher Papers
Mark W. Clark Papers (microfilm)
Eisenhower Pre-Presidential Papers, Principal File
Courtney H. Hodges Papers
C. D. Jackson Papers
Justus Baldwin Lawrence Papers
Thor M. Smith Papers
Walter Bedell Smith: Collection of World War II Documents, 1941–1945
Franklin D. Roosevelt Presidential Library, Hyde Park, New York
Stephen T. Early Papers
Harry L. Hopkins Papers
Henry Morgenthau Diaries, http://www.fdrlibrary.marist.edu/archives/collections
/franklin/index.php?p=collections/findingaid&id=535
Franklin D. Roosevelt Papers as President
FDR Map Room Papers, 1941-1945, http://www.fdrlibrary.marist.edu/archives
/collections/franklin/?p=collections/findingaid&id=511
The President's Secretary's File, http://www.fdrlibrary.marist.edu/archives
/collections/franklin/?p=collections/findingaid&id=502
George C. Marshall Foundation, Lexington, Virginia
George C. Marshall Papers, https://www.marshallfoundation.org/library/?fwp
_format=6
General Headquarters, Southwest Pacific Area, 1941–1945: Chronological Index and
Summary of Communications
Papers of George C. Marshall: Selected World War II Correspondence
Library of Congress, Manuscript Division, Washington, DC
Henry Harley Arnold Papers
Hanson W. Baldwin Papers

James H. Doolittle Papers
George Fielding Eliot Papers
William F. Halsey Papers
Everett Strait Hughes Papers
Frederick Joseph Horne Papers
Ernest J. King Papers
William D. Leahy Papers
Curtis E. LeMay
Archibald Macleish Papers
William H. Mauldin Papers
John L. McCrea Papers
George S. Patton Jr. Papers
Carl Spaatz Papers
MacArthur Memorial Library and Archive, Norfolk, Virginia
    RG-2: Records of Headquarters, US Army Forces in the Far East (USAFFE),
        1941–1942
    RG-3: Records of Headquarters, Southwest Pacific Area (SWPA), 1942–1945
    RG-4: Records of Headquarters, US Army Forces Pacific (USAFPAC), 1942–1947
    RG-10: General Douglas MacArthur's Private Correspondence, 1848–1964
    RG-15: Materials Donated by the General Public
    RG-41: Selected Papers of Lieutenant General Robert L. Eichelberger, USA
    RG-52: Papers of William J. Dunn
    RG-54: Diaries of General George C. Kenney, USAAC, 1941–1945
National Archives, UK, Kew Gardens, London
    Records of the War Office (WO), https://discovery.nationalarchives.gov.uk/de
        tails/r/C259
Ohio University, Archives and Special Collections, Athens, Ohio
    Cornelius J. Ryan Collection
ProQuest History Vault, https://about.proquest.com/en/products-services/history
    vault/
US Army Heritage and Education Center, Carlisle, Pennsylvania
    Clay and Joan Blair Papers
    Omar Nelson Bradley Papers
    Donald E. Currier Papers
    Jacob L. Devers Papers
    James M. Gaven Papers
    Hobart R. Gay Papers
    Chester Hansen Papers
    Paul Harkins Papers
    John P. Lucas Papers
    Robert A. McClure Papers
    Frank T. Mildren Papers
    Raymond G. Moses Papers
    Sidney H. Negrotto Papers
    Arthur S. Nevins Papers

William Simpson Papers
John Waters Papers
Albert Wedemeyer Papers
Proceedings of the American-British Joint Chiefs of Staff Conferences Held in Washington, DC, on Twelve Occasions between December 24, 1941 and January 14, 1942
US Military Academy, Archives and Special Collections, West Point, New York
Omar Nelson Bradley Papers
John Wesley Castles Jr. Papers
Benjamin Abbott Dickson Papers
Thomas R. Goethals Papers
Walter Krueger Papers
Will Lang Papers
Alexander Patch Papers
US National Archives, College Park, Maryland
RG 216: Records of the Office of Censorship
RG 331: SHAEF, Special Staff, Public Relations Division, Executive Branch, Decimal File 1943–45
RG 407: Records of the Adjutant General's Office, 1917-[AGO]
Yale University, Sterling Library, New Haven, Connecticut
Henry Lewis Stimson Diary, Yale University Library (microfilm)
York County History Center, York, Pennsylvania
General Jacob Devers Collection

Books

Aandahl, Fredrick, William M. Franklin, and William Slany, eds. *Foreign Relations of the United States: The Conferences at Washington, 1941–1942, and Casablanca, 1943.* Washington, DC: US Government Print Office, 1968.

Adams, John A. *General Jacob Devers: World War II's Forgotten Four Star.* Bloomington: Indiana University Press, 2015.

Alexander, Harold. *The Alexander Memoirs, 1940–1945.* Edited by John North. New York: McGraw-Hill Book Company, 1961.

Allen, Craig. *Eisenhower and the Mass Media: Peace, Prosperity, and Prime-Time TV.* Chapel Hill: University of North Carolina Press, 1993.

Allen, Robert S. *Forward with Patton: The World War II Diary of Colonel Robert S. Allen.* Edited by John Nelson Rickard. Lexington: University Press of Kentucky, 2017.

Alwood, Edward. *Dark Days in the Newsroom: McCarthyism Aimed at the Press.* Philadelphia: Temple University Press, 2007.

Ambrose, Stephen E. *Americans at War.* Jackson: University Press of Mississippi, 1997.

———. *Citizen Soldiers: The U.S. Army from the Normandy Beaches to the Bulge to the Surrender of Germany.* New York: Simon & Schuster, 1997.

———. *D-Day June 6, 1944, The Climatic Battle of World War II.* New York: Simon & Schuster, 1994.

————. *Eisenhower.* Vol. 1, *Soldier General of the Army President-Elect 1890–1952.* New York: Simon and Schuster, 1983.

————. *The Supreme Commander: The War Years of General Dwight D. Eisenhower.* Garden City, NY: Doubleday, 1970.

————. *The Victors, Eisenhower and His Boys: The Men of World War II.* New York: Simon & Schuster, 1998.

Ambrose, Stephen E., and Richard H. Immerman. *Milton S. Eisenhower: Educational Statesman.* Baltimore, MD: Johns Hopkins University Press, 1983.

Andrews, J. Cutler. *The North Reports the Civil War.* Pittsburgh: University of Pittsburgh Press, 1955.

Anzio Beachhead 22 January–25 May 1944. Washington, DC: Center of Military History United States Army, 1990.

Arnold, H. H. *Global Mission.* New York: Harper, 1949.

Atkinson, Rick. *An Army at Dawn: The War in North Africa, 1942–1943.* New York: Henry Holt, 2002.

————. *The Day of Battle: The War in Sicily and Italy.* New York: Henry Holt, 2007.

————. *The Guns at Last Light: The War in Western Europe, 1944–1945.* New York: Henry Holt, 2013.

Asasa, Sadao. "The Shock of the Atomic Bomb and Japan's Decision to Surrender." In *Hiroshima in History: The Myths of Revisionism,* edited by Robert James Maddox, 24–58. Columbia Press: University of Missouri, 2007.

Axelrod, Alan. *Bradley.* New York: Palgrave Macmillan, 2008.

Ayer, Fred Jr. *Before the Colors Fade: Portrait of A Soldier George S. Patton Jr.* Boston: Houghton Mifflin, 1964.

Baer, George W. *One Hundred Years of Sea Power: The U.S. Navy, 1890–1990.* Stanford, CA: Stanford University Press, 1993.

Baldoli, Claudia, and Andrew Knapp. *Forgotten Blitzes: France and Italy under Allied Air Attack, 1940–1945.* London: Continuum International Publishing Group, 2012.

Barker, Anthony J., and Lisa Jackson. *Fleeting Attraction: A Social History of American Servicemen in Western Australia during the Second World War.* Nedlands: University of Western Australia Press, 1996.

Beard, Patricia. *Newsmaker: Roy W. Howard: The Mastermind behind the Scripps-Howard News Empire from the Gilded Age to the Atomic Age.* Guilford, CT: Rowman & Littlefield, 2016.

Beevor, Antony. *The Battle of Arnhem: The Deadliest Airborne Operation of World War II.* New York: Viking, 2018.

————. *D-Day: The Battle for Normandy.* New York: Viking, 2009.

Bell, David. *The First Total War: Napoleon's European and the Birth of Warfare as We Know It.* Boston: Houghton Mifflin Harcourt, 2007.

Below, Nicolaus von. *At Hitler's Side: The Memoirs of Hitler's Luftwaffe Adjutant 1937–1945.* Translated by Geoffrey Brooks. London: Greenhill Books, 2004.

Berinsky, Adam J. *In Time of War: Understanding American Public Opinion from World War II to Iraq.* Chicago: University of Chicago Press, 2009.

Biddle, Tami Davis. *Rhetoric and Reality in Air Warfare: The Evolution of British and American Ideas about Strategic Bombing, 1914–1945.* Princeton, NJ: Princeton University Press, 2002.

Black, Jeremy. *The Age of Total War, 1860–1945.* Westport, CT: Praeger Security International, 2006.

Blair, Clay Jr. *MacArthur.* New York: Pocket Books, 1977.

Blumenson, Martin. *Anzio: The Gamble That Failed.* New York: J. B. Lippincott, 1963.

———. *The Battle of the Generals: The Untold Story of the Falaise Pocket—The Campaign that Should Have Won World War II.* New York: Quill, 1993.

———. *Bloody River: The Real Tragedy of the Rapido.* Boston: Houghton Mifflin, 1970.

———. *Breakout and Pursuit.* European Theater of Operations. *United States Army during World War II.* Washington, DC: Department of the Army, 1961.

———. *Mark Clark.* New York: Congdon & Weed, 1984.

———. *Patton: The Man Behind the Legend 1885–1945.* New York: Quill, 1985.

———. *Salerno to Cassino.* United States Army in World War II: The Mediterranean Theater of Operations. Washington, DC: Department of the Army, 1969.

Blumenson, Martin, and James L. Stokesburg, *Masters of the Art of Command.* Boston: Houghton Mifflin, 1975.

Borneman, Walter R. *The Admirals: Nimitz, Halsey, Leahy, and King—The Five-Star Admirals Who Won the War at Sea.* New York: Little, Brown, 2012.

Bosworth, R. J. B. *Mussolini.* New York: Oxford University Press, 2002.

Bourque, Stephen Alan. *Beyond the Beach: The Allied War against France.* Annapolis, MD: Naval Institute Press, 2018.

Bradley, Omar. *A Soldier's Story.* New York: Henry Holt, 1951.

Bradley, Omar, and Clay Blair. *A General's Life: An Autobiography.* New York: Simon and Schuster, 1983.

Brereton, Lewis H. *The Brereton Diaries: The War in the Air in the Pacific, Middle East and Europe.* New York: William Morrow, 1946.

Brett-James, Antony. *Conversations with Montgomery.* London: W. Kimber, 1984.

Breuer, William B. *Death of a Nazi Army: The Falaise Pocket.* New York: Stein and Day, 1985.

———. *Hoodwinking Hitler: The Normandy Deception.* London: Praeger, 1993.

Brewer, Susan A. *To Win the Peace: British Propaganda in the United States During World War II.* Ithaca, NY: Cornell University Press, 1997.

Brinkley, Alan. *The Publisher: Henry Luce and His American Century.* New York: Alfred A. Knopf, 2010.

Brooke, Alan. *War Diaries 1939–1945: Field Marshal Lord Alanbrooke.* Edited by Alex Danchev and Daniel Todman. London: Weidenfeld & Nicolson, 2001.

Brooks, Thomas R. *The War North of Rome: June 1944–May 1945.* Edison, NJ: Castle Books, 1996.

Brower, Charles F. *Defeating Japan: The Joint Chiefs of Staff and Strategy in the Pacific War, 1943–1945.* New York: Palgrave Macmillan, 2012.

Brown, John Sloan. *Draftee Division: The 88th Infantry Division in World War II.* Lexington: University Press of Kentucky, 1986.

Buell, Thomas B. *Master of Sea Power: A Biography of Fleet Admiral Ernest J. King.* Annapolis, MD: Naval Institute Press, 1980.

Burns, James MacGregor. *Roosevelt: The Soldier of Freedom.* New York: Smithmark, 1970.

Butcher, Harry. *My Three Years with Eisenhower.* New York: Simon and Schuster, 1946.

Butler, Christopher. *Postmodernism: A Very Short Introduction.* Oxford: Oxford University Press, 2002.

Calvocoressi, Peter, and Guy Wint. *Total War: Causes and Courses of the Second World War.* London: Penguin Press, 1972.

Campbell, Christy. *Target London: Under Attack from the V-Weapons during WWII.* London: Little, Brown, 2012.

Capa, Robert. *Slightly Out of Focus.* New York: Modern Library, 1999.

Capozzola, Christopher. *Uncle Sam Wants You: World War I and the Making of the Modern American Citizen.* Oxford: Oxford University Press, 2008.

Carafano, James Jay. *After D-Day: Operation Cobra and the Normandy Breakout.* London: Lynne Rienner Publishers, 2000.

Carew, Michael G. *The Power to Persuade: FDR, the Newsmagazines, and Going to War, 1939–1941.* New York: University Press of America, 2005.

Carlson, Elliot. *Stanley Johnston's Blunder: The Reporter Who Spilled the Secret behind the U.S. Navy's Victory at Midway.* Annapolis, MD: Naval Institute Press, 2017.

Carruthers, Susan L. *The Media at War.* New York: Palgrave Macmillan, 2000.

Casey, Steven. *Cautious Crusade: Franklin D. Roosevelt, American Public Opinion, and the War against Nazi Germany.* Oxford: Oxford University Press, 2001.

———. *Selling the Korean War: Propaganda, Politics, and Public Opinion in the United States, 1950–1953.* Oxford: Oxford University Press, 2008.

———. *The War Beat, Europe: The American Media at War Against Nazi Germany.* Oxford: Oxford University Press, 2017.

———. *The War Beat, Pacific: The American Media at War Against Japan.* Oxford: Oxford University Press, 2021.

———. *When Soldiers Fall: How Americans Have Confronted Combat Losses from World War I to Afghanistan.* Oxford: Oxford University Press, 2014.

Chalfont, Alun. *Montgomery of Alamein.* New York: Atheneum, 1976.

Chappell, John D. *Before the Bomb: How America Approached the End of the Pacific War.* Lexington: University Press of Kentucky, 1997.

Chennault, Claire Lee. *Way of the Fighter: The Memoir of Claire Lee Chennault.* Edited by Robert Holt. New York: G. P. Putnam's Sons, 1949.

Churchill, Winston S. *The Second World War.* Vol. 3, *The Grand Alliance.* Boston: Houghton Mifflin, 1950.

———. *The Second World War.* Vol. 4, *The Hinge of Fate.* Boston: Houghton Mifflin, 1950.

———. *The Second World War.* Vol. 5, *Closing the Ring.* Boston: Houghton Mifflin, 1951.

———. *The Second World War.* Vol. 6, *Triumph and Tragedy.* Boston Houghton Mifflin, 1953.

Churchill, Winston S., and Franklin D. Roosevelt. *Churchill and Roosevelt: The Complete Correspondence.* Vol. 1, *Alliance Emerging October 1933–November 1942.* Edited by Warren F. Kimball. Princeton, NJ: Princeton University Press, 1984.

————. *Churchill and Roosevelt: The Complete Correspondence.* Vol. 2, *Alliance Forged November 1942–February 1944.* Edited by Warren F. Kimball. Princeton, NJ: Princeton University Press, 1984.

————. *Churchill and Roosevelt: The Complete Correspondence.* Vol. 3, *Alliance Declining February 1944–April 1945.* Edited by Warren F. Kimball. Princeton, NJ: Princeton University Press, 1984.

Chuev, Felix. *Molotov Remembers: Inside Kremlin Politics.* Edited by Albert Resis. Chicago: Ivan R. Dee, 1993.

Citino, Robert M. *The Wehrmacht's Last Stand: The German Campaigns of 1944–1945.* Lawrence: University Press of Kansas, 2017.

Clark, Lloyd. *Anzio: Italy and the Battle for Rome—1944.* New York: Atlantic Monthly Press, 2006.

Clark, Mark. *Calculated Risk.* New York: Harper & Brothers, 1950.

Clausewitz, Carl von. *On War.* Translated by Michael Howard and Peter Paret. New York: Alfred A. Knopf, 1993.

Clayton, James. *The Years of MacArthur.* Vol. 2, *1941–1945.* Boston: Houghton Mifflin, 1975.

Clodfelter, Mark. *Beneficial Bombing: The Progressive Foundations of American Air Power, 1917–1945.* Lincoln: University of Nebraska Press, 2010.

Cloud, Stanley, and Lynne Olson. *The Murrow Boys: Pioneers on the Front Lines of Broadcast Journalism.* Boston: Houghton Mifflin, 1996.

Codman, Charles R. *Drive.* Boston: Little, Brown, 1957.

Cohen, Eliot A. *Supreme Command: Soldiers, Statesmen, and Leadership in Wartime.* New York: Free Press, 2002.

Colley, David P. *Decision At Strasbourg: Ike's Strategic Mistake to Halt the Sixth Army Group at the Rhine in 1944.* Annapolis, MD: Naval Institute Press, 2008.

Collier, Richard. *The Warcos: The War Correspondents of World War Two.* London: Weidenfeld and Nicolson, 1989.

Collins, J. Lawton. *Lighting Joe: An Autobiography.* Novato, CA: Presidio Press, 1979.

Craven, Wesley Frank, and James Lea Cate, eds. *The Army Air Forces in World War II.* Vol. 1, *Plans and Early Operations, January 1939 to August 1942.* Chicago: University of Chicago Press, 1948.

Cronkite, Walter. *A Reporter's Life.* New York: Alfred A. Knopf, 1996.

Crosswell, D. K. R. *Beetle: The Life of General Walter Bedell Smith.* Lexington: University Press of Kentucky, 2010.

Cunningham, Andrew. *The Cunningham Papers.* Vol. 2, *The Triumph of Allied Sea Power.* Edited by Michael Simpson. Aldershot, England: Ashgate, 2006.

Danchev, Alex. *Establishing the Anglo-American Alliance: The Second World War Diaries of Brigadier Vivian Dykes.* London: Brassey's, 1990.

Davidson, Edward, and Dale Manning. *Chronology of World War Two.* London: Cassell, 1999.

Davies, Robert B. *Baldwin of the Times: Hanson W. Baldwin, A Military Journalist's Life, 1903–1991*. Annapolis, MD: Naval Institute Press, 2011.

Davis, Kenneth S. *FDR: The War President 1940–1943*. New York: Random House, 2000.

Dean, Peter J. *MacArthur's Coalition: US and Australian Operations in the Southwest Pacific Area, 1942–1945*. Lawrence: University Press of Kansas, 2018.

De Gaulle, Charles. *The War Memoirs of Charles de Gaulle: Salvation 1944–1946*. Translated by Richard Howard. New York: Simon and Schuster, 1960.

De Guingand, Francis. *General at War*. London: Hodder and Stoughton, 1964.

———. *Operation Victory*. New York: Charles Scribner's Sons, 1947.

DePastino, Todd. *Bill Mauldin: A Life Up Front*. New York: W. W. Norton, 2008.

Desmond, Robert W. *Tides of War: World News Reporting 1931–1945*. Iowa City: University of Iowa Press, 1982.

D'Este, Carlo. *Bitter Victory: The Battle for Sicily, 1943*. New York: E. P. Dutton, 1988.

———. *Decision in Normandy: The Unwritten Story of Montgomery and the Allied Campaign*. New York: Penguin Books, 1983.

———. *Eisenhower: A Soldier's Life*. New York: Henry Holt, 2002.

———. *Fatal Decision: Anzio and the Battle for Rome*. New York: HarperCollins, 1991.

———. *Patton: A Genius for War*. New York: HarperCollins, 1996.

———. *World War II in the Mediterranean, 1942–1945*. Chapel Hill, NC: Algonquin Books of Chapel Hill, 1990.

Dietrich, Otto. *The Hitler I Knew: The Memoir of the Third Reich's Press Chief*. New York: Skyhorse Publishing, 2010.

Donoughue, Bernard, and G. W. Jones. *Herbert Morrison: Portrait of a Politician*. London: Weidenfeld and Nicolson, 1973.

Doolittle, James H. "Jimmy", and Carroll V. Glines. *I Could Never Be So Lucky Again: An Autobiography*. New York: Bantam Books, 1991.

Doubler, Michael D. *Closing with the Enemy: How GIs Fought the War in Europe, 1944–1945*. Lawrence: University Press of Kansas, 1994.

Douhet, Giulio. *The Command of the Air*. Translated by Dino Ferrari. Washington, DC: Office of Air Force History, 1942.

Dower, John W. *War without Mercy: Race and Power in the Pacific War*. New York: Pantheon Books, 1986.

Drury, Allen. *A Senate Journal 1943–1945*. New York: McGraw-Hill Book, 1963.

Dull, Paul S. *A Battle History of the Imperial Japanese Navy (1941–1945)*. Annapolis, MD: Naval Institute Press, 1978.

Dunn, William J. *Pacific Microphone*. College Station: Texas A&M University Press, 1988.

Dyer, George. *XII Corps: Spearhead of Patton's Third Army*. N.p.: XII Corps History Association, 1947.

Edsel, Robert. *Saving Italy: The Race to Rescue a Nation's Treasures from the Nazis*. New York: W. W. Norton, 2013.

Edwards, Bob. *Edward R. Murrow and the Birth of Broadcast Journalism.* Hoboken, NJ: John Wiley & Sons, 2004.

Edwards, Julia. *Women of the World: The Great Foreign Correspondents.* New York: Ivy Books, 1989.

Egeberg, Roger Olaf. *The General: MacArthur and the Man He Called "Doc".* New York: Hippocrene Books, 1983.

Eichelberger, Robert L. *Dear Miss Em: General Eichelberger's War in the Pacific, 1942–1945.* Edited by Jay Luvaas. Westport, CT: Greenwood Press, 1972.

———. *Our Jungle Road to Tokyo.* New York: Viking Press, 1950.

Eisenhower, David. *Eisenhower: At War 1943–1945.* New York: Random House, 1986.

Eisenhower, Dwight D. *At Ease: Stories I Tell to Friends.* Garden City, NY: Doubleday, 1967.

———. *Crusade in Europe.* Garden City, NY: Doubleday, 1949.

———. *The Eisenhower Diaries.* Edited by Robert H. Ferrell. New York: W. W. Norton, 1981.

———. *The Papers of Dwight David Eisenhower.* Vol. 1, *The War Years.* Edited by Alfred D. Chandler Jr. Baltimore: Johns Hopkins Press, 1970.

———. *The Papers of Dwight David Eisenhower.* Vol. 2, *The War Years.* Edited by Alfred D. Chandler Jr. Baltimore: Johns Hopkins Press, 1970.

———. *The Papers of Dwight David Eisenhower.* Vol. 3, *The War Years.* Edited by Alfred D. Chandler Jr. Baltimore: Johns Hopkins Press, 1970.

———. *The Papers of Dwight David Eisenhower.* Vol. 4, *The War Years.* Edited by Alfred D. Chandler Jr. Baltimore: Johns Hopkins Press, 1970.

Eisenhower, John S. D. *General Ike: A Personal Reminiscence.* New York: Free Press, 2003.

Eisenhower, Milton S. *The President Is Calling.* Garden City, NY: Doubleday, 1974.

Falk, Stanley L. "Douglas MacArthur and the War against Japan." In *We Shall Return! MacArthur's Commanders and the Defeat of Japan 1942–1945.* Edited by William M. Leary. Lexington: University Press of Kentucky, 1988.

Farago, Ladislas. *Patton: Ordeal and Triumph.* New Dell edition. New York: Dell Publishing, 1964.

Farndale, Nigel. *Haw-Haw: The Tragedy of William and Margaret Joyce.* London: Macmillan, 2005.

Fest, Joachim. *Speer: The Final Verdict.* Translated by Ewald Osers and Alexandra Dring. New York: Harcourt, 1999.

Fisher, Ernest F. Jr. *Cassino to the Alps.* Mediterranean Theater of Operations. *United States Army in World War II.* Washington, DC: Department of the Army, 1989.

Fleming, Thomas. *The New Dealers' War: Franklin D. Roosevelt and the War within World War II.* New York: Basic Books, 2001.

Franco, Chiara De. *Media Power and the Transformation of War.* New York: Palgrave Macmillan, 2012.

Frank, Richard B. *Downfall: The End of the Imperial Japanese Empire.* New York: Random House, 1999.

———. *Guadalcanal: The Definitive Account of the Landmark Battle.* New York: Penguin, 1992.

Fuchida, Mitsuo, and Masatake Okumiya. *Midway: The Battle That Doomed Japan.* Edited by Clarke H. Kawakami and Roger Pineau. New York: Ballantine Book, 1955.

Fussell, Paul. *Wartime: Understanding and Behavior in the Second World War.* Oxford: Oxford University Press, 1989.

Fyne, Robert. *The Hollywood Propaganda of World War II.* London: Scarecrow Press, 1994.

Gailey, Harry A. *Howlin' Mad vs The Army: Conflict in Command, Saipan 1944.* Novato, CA: Presidio Press, 1986.

Gallicchio, Marc. *Unconditional: The Japanese Surrender in World War II.* Oxford: Oxford University Press, 2020.

Garland, Albert N., and Howard McGaw Smyth. *Sicily and the Surrender of Italy.* Mediterranean Theater of Operations. *United States Army in World War II.* Washington, DC: Department of the Army, 1965.

Gay, Timothy M. *Assignment to Hell: The War against Nazi Germany with Correspondents Walter Cronkite, Andy Rooney, A. J. Liebling, Homer Bigart, and Hal Boyle.* New York: Penguin, 2012.

Gilbert, Martin. *Winston S. Churchill.* Vol. 7, *Road to Victory 1941–1945.* Boston: Houghton Mifflin, 1986.

Gillison, Douglas. *Royal Australian Air Force 1939–1942.* Adelaide: Griffin Press, 1962.

Gilmore, Allison B. *You Can't Fight Tanks With Bayonets: Psychological Warfare against the Japanese Army in the Southwest Pacific.* Lincoln: University of Nebraska Press, 1998.

Glines, Carroll V. *Doolittle's Tokyo Raiders.* Princeton, NJ: Van Nostrand, 1964.

———. *Jimmy Doolittle: Daredevil Aviator and Scientist.* New York: Macmillan, 1972.

Goebbels, Joseph. *The Goebbels Diaries, 1942–1943.* Translated and edited by Louis P. Lochner. Garden City, NY: Doubleday, 1948.

———. *The Secret Conference of Dr. Goebbels: The Nazi Propaganda War 1939–43.* Edited by Willi A. Boelcke. Translated by Ewald Oser. New York: E. P. Dutton, 1970.

González, Justo L. *The Story of Christianity.* Vol. 1, *The Early Church to the Dawn of the Reformation.* New York: HarperCollins, 2010.

Goodwin, Doris Kearns. *No Ordinary Time: Franklin and Eleanor Roosevelt: The Home Front in World War II.* New York: Simon & Schuster, 1994.

Gordon, Matthew. *News Is a Weapon.* New York: Alfred A. Knopf, 1942.

Greenfield, Kent Robert. *Command Decisions.* Washington, DC: Office of the Chief of Military History, 1959.

Griffith, Thomas E. Jr. *MacArthur's Airman: General George C. Kelley and the War in the South Pacific.* Lawrence: University Press of Kansas, 1998.

Guillain, Robert. *I Saw Tokyo Burning: An Eyewitness Narrative from Pearl Harbor to Hiroshima.* Translated by William Byron. Garden City, NY: Doubleday, 1981.

Gunther, John. *Roosevelt in Retrospect: A Profile in History.* New York: Harper & Brothers, 1950.

Haining, Peter. *The Flying Bomb War: Contemporary Eyewitness Accounts of the German V-1 and V-2 Raids on Britain.* London: Robson Books, 2002.

Hallin, Daniel C. "The 'Living-Room War': Media and Public Opinion in a Limited War." In *Rolling Thunder in a Gentle Land,* edited by Andrew Wiest, 276–291. Oxford: Osprey Publishing, 2006.

———. "The Media and War." In *International Media Research,* edited by John Corner, Philip Schlesinger, and Roger Silverstone, 206–232. New York: Routledge, 1997.

———. *The "Uncensored War": The Media and Vietnam.* Oxford: Oxford University Press, 1986.

Halsey, William F., and J. Bryan III. *Admiral Halsey's Story.* New York: Whittlesey House, 1947.

Hamilton, Nigel. *The Mantle of Command: FDR at War 1941–1942.* New York: Houghton Mifflin Harcourt, 2014.

———. *Monty: The Field Marshal 1944–1976.* London: Hamish Hamilton, 1986.

———. *Monty: Master of the Battlefield 1942–1944.* London: Hamish Hamilton, 1988.

Hammond, William H. *Public Affairs: The Military and the Media, 1962–1968.* Vol. 1, *The U.S. Army in Vietnam.* Washington, DC: Center of Military History, 1988.

———. *Public Affairs: The Military and the Media, 1968–1973.* Vol. 2, *The U.S. Army in Vietnam.* Washington, DC: Center of Military History United States Army, 1996.

Hankinson, Alan. *Man of Wars: William Howard Russell of The* Times. London: Heinemann, 1982.

Hapgood, David, and David Richardson. *Monte Cassino.* New York: Congdon & Weed, 1984.

Hasegawa, Tsuyoshi. *Racing the Enemy: Stalin, Truman, and the Surrender of Japan.* Cambridge, MA: Harvard University Press, 2005.

Hastings, Max. *All Hell Let Loose: The World At War 1939–45.* London: HarperPress, 2011.

———. *Overlord: D-Day and the Battle for Normandy.* New York: Simon & Schuster, 1984.

Havers, Richard. *Here Is the News: The BCC and the Second World War.* Gloucestershire, England: Sutton Publishing, 2007.

Haverstock, Nathan A. *Fifty Years at the Front: The Life of War Correspondent Frederick Palmer.* Washington, DC: Brassey's, 1996.

Hawkins, Desmond, and Donald Boyd, eds. *War Report: A Record of Dispatches Broadcast by the BBC's War Correspondents with the Allied Expeditionary Force 6 June 1944–5 May 1945.* Edited by the BBC. New York: Oxford University Press, 1946.

Heefner, Wilson A. *Dogface Soldier: The Life of General Lucian K. Truscott, Jr.* Columbia: University of Missouri Press, 2010.

Heiber, Helmut, ed. *Hitler and His Generals: Military Conferences 1942–1945.*

Translated by Roland Winter, Krista Smith, and Mary Beth Friedrich. New York: Ensigma Books, 2002.

Hellbeck, Jochen. "Battles for Morale: An Entangled History of Total War in Europe, 1939–1945." In *The Cambridge History of The Second World War*, vol. 3, *Total War: Economy, Society and Culture*, edited by Michael Geyer and Adam Tooze, 329–362. Cambridge: Cambridge University Press, 2015.

Herman, Arthur. *The Cave and the Light: Plato Versus Aristotle, and the Struggle for the Soul of Western Civilization*. New York: Random House, 2013.

Herman, Douglas. *Douglas MacArthur: American Warrior*. New York: Random House, 2016.

Hershberg, James G. *James B. Conant: Harvard to Hiroshima and the Making of the Nuclear Age*. Stanford: Stanford University Press, 1995.

Herzstein, Robert Edwin. *The War That Hitler Won: The Most Infamous Propaganda Campaign in History*. New York: G. P. Putnam's Sons, 1978.

Hinsley, F. H., and C. A. G. Simkins. *British Intelligence in the Second World War*. Vol. 4, *Security and Counter-Intelligence*. New York: Cambridge University Press, 1990.

Hirshson, Stanley P. *General Patton: A Soldier's Life*. New York: HarperCollins, 2002.

Hitler, Adolf. *Mein Kampf*. Translated by Ralph Mannheim. Boston: Houghton Mifflin, 1925.

Hohenberg, John. *Foreign Correspondence: The Great Reporters and Their Times*. Syracuse, NY: Syracuse University Press, 1995.

Höhne, Heinz. *The Order of the Death's Head: The Story of Hitler's SS*. New York: Penguin Books, 1969.

Holland, James. *Italy's Sorrow: A Year of War, 1944–1945*. New York: St. Martin's Press, 2008.

Holzimmer, Kevin C. *General Walter Krueger: Unsung Hero of the Pacific War*. Lawrence: University Press of Kansas, 2007.

Honig, Jan Willem. "The Idea of Total War: From Clausewitz to Ludendorff." In *The Pacific War as Total War*. International Forum on War History, Tokyo National Institute for Defense Studies, 2011, 29–41. Accessed December 8, 2018. http://www.nids.mod.go.jp/english/event/forum/e2011.html.

Hooper, Alan. *The Military and the Media*. Hant, England: Gower Publishing, 1982.

Hopkins, Harry E. *The White House Papers of Harry L. Hopkins*, vol. 2. Edited by Robert E. Sherwood. London: Eyre & Spottiswoode, 1949.

Horne, Alistair, with David Montgomery. *Monty: The Lonely Leader 1944–1945*. New York: HarperCollins, 1994.

Howard, Michael. *British Intelligence in the Second World War*. Vol. 5, *Strategic Deception*. New York: Cambridge University Press, 1990.

———. *Clausewitz*. Oxford: Oxford University Press, 1983.

Howe, George F. *Northwest Africa: Seizing the Initiative in the West*. Mediterranean Theater of Operations. *United States Army in World War II*. Washington, DC: Department of the Army, 1957.

Hughes, Thomas Alexander. *Over Lord: General Pete Quesada and the Triumph of Tactical Air Power in World War II.* New York: Free Press, 1995.

Hunt, Frazier. *The Untold Story of Douglas MacArthur.* New York: Devin-Adair, 1954.

Ingersoll, Ralph. *Top Secret.* New York: Harcourt, Brace, 1946.

Inglis, Fred. *People's Witness: The Journalist in Modern Politics.* New Haven: Yale University Press, 2002.

Irving, David. *The War between the Generals: Inside the Allied High Command.* London: Allen Lane, 1981.

Isby, David C., ed. *Fighting the Invasion: The German Army at D-Day.* Mechanicsburg, PA: Stackpole Books, 2000.

Ismay, K. G. *The Memoirs of General Lord Ismay.* New York: Viking Press, 1960.

James, D. Clayton. *The Years of MacArthur.* Vol. 2, *1941–1945.* Boston: Houghton Mifflin, 1975.

Johnson, Lyndon Baines. *The Vantage Point: Perspectives of the Presidency 1963–1969.* New York: Holt, Rinehart and Winston, 1971.

Johnson, Paul. *A History of the American People.* New York: Harper Perennial, 1997.

Jordan, David M. *FDR, Dewey, and the Election of 1944.* Bloomington: Indiana University Press, 2011.

Joswick, Jerry J., and Lawrence A. Keating. *Combat Camera Man.* New York: Pyramid Book, 1961.

Keegan, John. *The Second World War.* New York: Penguin Books, 1998.

Kennan, George. *Measures Short of War: The George F. Kennan Lectures at the National War College 1946–47.* Edited by Giles D. Harlow and George C. Maerz. Washington, DC: National Defense University Press, 1991.

Kennedy, David M. *Freedom from Fear: The American People in Depression and War, 1929–1945.* Oxford: Oxford University Press, 1999.

Kennedy, Ed. *Ed Kennedy's War: V-E Day, Censorship, and The Associated Press.* Edited by Julia Kennedy Cochran. Baton Rouge: Louisiana State University Press, 2012.

Kenney, George C. *General Kenney Reports: A Personal History of the Pacific War.* New York: Duell, Sloan, and Pearce, 1949.

Kesselring, Albert. *The Memoir of Field Marshal Kesselring.* Translated by William Kimber. Novato, CA: Presidio Press, 1989.

Kindsvatter, Peter S. *American Soldiers: Ground Combat in the World Wars, Korea, and Vietnam.* Lawrence: University Press of Kansas, 2003.

King, Ernest J., and Walter Muir Whitehill. *Fleet Admiral King: A Naval Record.* New York: W. W. Norton, 1952.

Kinnard, Douglas. *The War Managers.* Hanover, NH: University Press of New England, 1977.

Klein, Maury. *A Call To Arms: Mobilizing America for World War II.* New York: Bloomsbury Press, 2013.

Klurfeld, Herman. *Behind the Lines: The World of Drew Pearson.* Englewood Cliffs, NJ: Prentice-Hall, 1968.

Knightley, Phillip. *The First Casualty: From the Crimea to Vietnam: The War*

Correspondent as Hero, Propagandist, and Myth Maker. New York: Harcourt Brace Jovanovich, 1975.

Koop, Theodore F. *Weapon of Silence.* Chicago: University of Chicago Press, 1946.

Krasilshchik, S., ed. *World War II: Dispatches from the Soviet Front.* Translated by Nina Bouis. New York: Sphinx Press, 1985.

Lambert, Andrew, and Stephen Badsey. *The War Correspondents: The Crimean War.* Gloucestershire, England: Alan Sutton Publishing, 1994.

Lande, D. A. *I Was with Patton: First-Person Accounts of WWII in George S. Patton's Command.* St. Paul, MN: MBI Publishing, 2002.

Larrabee, Eric. *Commander in Chief: Franklin Delano Roosevelt, His Lieutenants, and Their War.* New York: Harper & Row, 1987.

Lavoie, Jeffrey D. *The Private Life of General Omar N. Bradley.* Jefferson, NC: McFarland, 2015.

Leahy, William D. *I Was There.* New York: McGraw-Hill Book Company, 1950.

Leary, William M., ed. *We Shall Return! MacArthur's Commanders and the Defeat of Japan 1942–1945.* Lexington: University Press of Kentucky, 1988.

Lee, Clark. *One Last Look Around.* New York: Duell, Sloan and Pearce, 1947.

Lee, Clark, and Richard Henschel. *Douglas MacArthur.* New York: Henry Holt, 1952.

Liang, Chin-tung. *General Stilwell in China 1942–1944: The Full Story.* New York: St. John's University, 1972.

Liddell Hart, B. H. *The German Generals Talk.* New York: Quill, 1948.

———. *History of the Second World War.* London: Cassell, 1970.

Linn, Brian McAllister. *The Echo of Battle: The Army's Way of War.* Cambridge, MA: Harvard University Press, 2007.

Lisio, Donald J. *The President and Protest: Hoover, MacArthur, and the Bonus Riot.* New York: Fordham University Press, 1994.

Livingston, Steven. "Beyond the 'CNN Effect': The Media-Foreign Policy Dynamic." In *Politics and the Press: The News Media and Their Influences,* edited by Pippa Norris, 291–317. London: Lynne Rienner Publishers, 1997.

Lockhart, R. H. Bruce. *Comes the Reckoning.* New York: Arno Press, 1972.

Long, Gavin. *MacArthur as Military Commander.* Princeton, NJ: B. T. Batsford, 1969.

Lord, Walter. *Day of Infamy.* New York: Holt, Rinehart and Winston, 1957.

Ludendorff, Erich. *The Nation at War.* Translated by A. S. Rappoport. London: Hutchinson, 1936.

Ludewig, Joachim. *Rückzug: The German Retreat from France, 1944.* Translated by David T. Zabecki. Lexington: University Press of Kentucky, 2012.

MacArthur, Douglas. *Reminiscences.* New York: McGraw-Hill Book Company, 1964.

———. *A Soldier Speaks: Public Papers and Speeches of General of the Army Douglas MacArthur.* New York: Frederick A. Praeger, 1965.

MacDonald, Charles B. *A Time for Trumpets: The Untold Story of the Battle of the Bulge.* New York: Bantam Books, 1985.

MacMillan, Harold. *War Diary: Politics and War in the Mediterranean January 1943–May 1945.* New York: St. Martin's Press, 1984.

Magenheimer, Heinz. *Hitler's War: Germany's Key Strategic Decisions 1940–1945.* Translated by Helmut Bögler. London: Cassell, 1988.

Manchester, William. *American Caesar: Douglas MacArthur, 1880–1964.* New York: Dell Publishing, 1978.

Mansoor, Peter R. *The GI Offensive in Europe: The Triumph of American Infantry Divisions, 1941–1945.* Lawrence: University Press of Kansas, 1999.

Mariner, Rosemary B., and G. Kurt Piehler. *The Atomic Bomb and American Society.* Knoxville: University of Tennessee Press, 2009.

Marshall, George C. *George C. Marshall Interviews and Reminiscences for Forrest C. Pogue.* Edited by Larry I. Bland and Joellen K. Bland. Lexington, VA: George C. Marshall Research Foundation, 1991.

———. *The Papers of George Catlett Marshall.* Vol. 3, *"The Right Man for the Job": December 7, 1941–May 31, 1943.* Edited by Larry I. Bland. Baltimore: Johns Hopkins University Press, 1991.

———. *The Papers of George Catlett Marshall.* Vol. 4, *"Aggressive and Determined Leadership": June 1, 1943–December 31, 1944.* Edited by Larry I. Bland. Baltimore: Johns Hopkins University Press, 1996.

———. *The Papers of George Catlett Marshall.* Vol. 5, *"The Finest Soldier": January 1, 1945–January 7, 1947.* Edited by Larry I. Bland. Baltimore: Johns Hopkins University Press, 2003.

Marshall, M. L. A. *Men against Fire: The Problem of Battle Command in Future War.* Gloucester, MA: Peter Smith, 1978.

Marszalek, John F. *Sherman's Other War: The General and the Civil War Press.* Memphis, TN: Memphis State University Press, 1981.

Mathews, Joseph J. *Reporting the Wars.* Minneapolis: University of Minnesota Press, 1957.

Matloff, Maurice. "Allied Strategy in Europe, 1939–1945." In *Makers of Modern Strategy from Machiavelli to the Nuclear Age,* edited by Peter Paret, 677–702. Princeton, NJ: Princeton University Press, 1986.

———. *Strategic Planning for Coalition Warfare, 1943–1944.* War Department. *United States Army in World War II.* Washington, DC: Department of the Army, 1959.

Mauldin, Bill. *The Brass Ring: A Sort of a Memoir.* New York: W. W. Norton, 1971.

McAulay, Lex. *Battle of the Bismarck Sea.* New York: St. Martin's Press, 1991.

McCrea, John L. *Captain McCrea's War: The World War II Memoir of Franklin D. Roosevelt's Naval Aide and USS Iowa's First Commanding Officer.* Edited by Julia C. Tobey. New York: Shyhorse Publishing, 2016.

McDonald, Neil, with Peter Brune. *Valiant for Truth: The Life of Chester Wilmot, War Correspondent.* Sydney, Australia: NewSouth Publishing, 2016.

McManus, John C. *The Deadly Brotherhood: The American Combat Soldier in World War II.* Novato, CA: Presidio Press, 1998.

McPherson, James M. *Crossroads of Freedom - Antietam: The Battle That Changed the Course of the Civil War.* Oxford: Oxford University Press, 2002.

Mead, Richard. *The Men behind Monty: The Staff and HQs of Eighth Army and 21st Army Group.* Barnsley, UK: Pen & Sword Books, 2015.

Meade, George Gordon. *The Life and Letters of George Gordon Meade*, vol. 1. Edited by George Gordon Meade. New York: Charles Scribner's Sons, 1913.

Meo, L. D. *Japan's Radio War on Australia 1941–1945*. London: Melbourne University Press, 1968.

Metaxas, Eric. *Bonhoeffer: Pastor, Martyr, Prophet, Spy*. Nashville, TN: Thomas Nelson, 2010.

Middleton, Drew. *Our Share of Night*. New York: Viking Press, 1946.

Mikolashek, Jon B. *General Mark Clark: Commander of America's Fifth Army in World War II and Liberator of Rome*. Philadelphia: Casemate, 2013.

Miller, Edward S. *War Plan Orange: The U.S. Strategy to Defeat Japan, 1897–1945*. Annapolis, MD: Naval Institute Press, 1991.

Miller, John E. *Governor Philip F. La Follette: The Wisconsin Progressives, and the New Deal*. Columbia: University of Missouri Press, 1982.

Mitgang, Herbert. *Newsmen in Khaki: Tales of a World War II Soldier Correspondent*. New York: Taylor Trade Publishing, 2004.

Mitter, Rana. *Forgotten Ally: China's World War II, 1937–1945*. New York: Houghton Mifflin Harcourt, 2013.

Moïse, Edwin E. *The Myths of Tet: The Most Misunderstood Event of the Vietnam War*. Lawrence: University Press of Kansas, 2017.

Montgomery, Bernard Law. *The Memoirs of Field-Marshal the Viscount Montgomery of Alamein, K. G.* London: Collins, 1958.

———. *Montgomery and the Battle of Normandy: A Selection from the Diaries, Correspondence and Other Papers of Field Marshal the Viscount Montgomery of Alamein, January to August, 1944*. Edited by Stephen Brooks. Gloucestershire, England: History Press for the Army Records Society, 2008.

———. *Montgomery and the Eighth Army: A Selection from the Diaries, Correspondence and other Papers of Field Marshal The Viscount Montgomery of Alamein, August 1942 to December 1943*. Edited by Stephen Brooks. London: Bodley Head, 1991.

Morelock, Jerry D. *Generals of the Bulge: Leadership in the U.S. Army's Greatest Battle*. Mechanicsburg, PA: Stackpole Books, 2015.

Morison, Samuel Eliot. *History of United States Naval Operations in World War II*. Vol. 3, *The Rising Sun in the Pacific 1931–April 1942*. Boston: Little, Brown, 1965.

———. *Strategy and Compromise*. Boston: Little, Brown, 1958.

———. *The Two-Ocean War: A Short History of the United States Navy in the Second World War*. Boston: Little Brown, 1963.

Morningstar, James Kelly. *Patton's Way: A Radical Theory of War*. Annapolis, MD: Naval Institute Press, 2017.

Morrison, Herbert. *Herbert Morrison: An Autobiography*. London: Odhams Press, 1960.

Morton, Louis. "Germany First: The Basic Concept of Allied Strategy in World War II." In *Command Decisions*, edited by Kent Roberts Greenfield, 11–47. Washington, DC: Office of the Chief of Military History, United States Army, 1959.

Moseley, Ray. *Mussolini: The Last 600 Days of Il Duce*. New York: Taylor Trade Publishing, 2004.

————. *Reporting War: How Foreign Correspondents Risked Capture, Torture and Death to Cover World War II*. New Haven, CT: Yale University Press, 2017.

Murphy, Robert. *Diplomat among Warriors*. New York: Pyramid Books, 1964.

Murray, Williamson, and Allan R. Millett. *A War To Be Won: Fighting the Second World War*. Cambridge, MA: Belknap Press of Harvard University Press, 2000.

Murrow, Edward R. *In Search of Light: The Broadcasts of Edward R. Murrow 1938–1961*. Edited by Edward Bliss Jr. New York: Alfred A. Knopf, 1967.

Mussolini, Benito. *The Fall of Mussolini: His Own Story by Benito Mussolini*. Edited by Max Ascoli and translated by Frances Frenaye. New York: Farrar, Straus, 1948.

National Education Association. "News." In *Building America: Illustrated Studies on Modern Problems*, vol. 3. New York: Americana Corporation, 1942.

Nelson, Craig. *The First Heroes: The Extraordinary Story of the Doolittle Raid—America's First World War II Victory*. New York: Viking, 2002.

Nye, Roger H. *The Patton Mind: The Professional Development of an Extraordinary Leader*. New York: Avery Publishing Group, 1993.

O'Brien, Phillips Payson. *How The War Was Won: Air-Sea Power and Allied Victory in World War II*. Cambridge: Cambridge University Press, 2015.

O'Connell, Aaron B. *Underdogs: The Making of the Modern Marine Corps*. Cambridge, MA: Harvard University Press, 2012.

The Officer's Guide. Harrisburg, PA: Military Service Publishing, 1943.

Oldfield, Barney. *Never a Shot in Anger*. New York: Duell, Sloan and Pearce, 1956.

Olson, Lynne. *Citizens of London: The Americans Who Stood with Britain in Its Darkest, Finest Hour*. New York: Random House 2010.

————. *Those Angry Days: Roosevelt, Lindbergh, and America's Fight over World War II*. New York: Random House, 2013.

Ossad, Steven L. *Omar Nelson Bradley: America's GI General 1893–1981*. Columbia: University of Missouri Press, 2017.

Pach, Chester J. Jr. "The War on Television: TV News, the Johnson Administration, and Vietnam." In *A Companion to the Vietnam War*, edited by Marilyn B. Young and Robert Buzzanco, 450–469. Oxford: Blackwell Publishing, 2002.

Patton, George S. Jr. *The Patton Papers, 1940–1945*, vol. 2. Edited by Martin Blumenson. Boston: Da Capo Press, 1974.

————. *War As I Knew It*. New York: Bantam Books, 1947.

Perret, Geoffrey. *Eisenhower*. New York: Random House, 1999.

————. *Winged Victory: The Army Air Forces in World War II*. New York: Random House, 1993.

Perry, James M. *A Bohemian Brigade: The Civil War Correspondents—Mostly Rough, Sometimes Ready*. New York: John Wiley & Sons, 2000.

Perry, Mark. *The Most Dangerous Man in America: The Making of Douglas MacArthur*. New York: Basic Books, 2014.

————. *Partners in Command: George C. Marshall and Dwight Eisenhower in War and Peace*. New York: Penguin Press, 2007.

Persico, Joseph E. *Roosevelt's Centurions: FDR and the Commanders He Led to Victory in World War II*. New York: Random House, 2013.

Pike, Francis. *Hirohito's War: The Pacific War, 1941–1945.* New York: Bloomsbury, 2015.

Pilat, Oliver. *Pearson: An Unauthorized Biography.* New York: Harper's Magazine Press, 1973.

Pinkley, Virgil, with James F. Scheer. *Eisenhower Declassified.* Old Tappan, NJ: Fleming H. Revell, 1979.

Porch, Douglas. *The Path to Victory: The Mediterranean Theater in World War II.* New York: Farrar, Straus and Giroux, 2004.

Potter, E. B. *Bull Halsey.* Annapolis, MD: Naval Institute Press, 1985.

———. *Nimitz.* Annapolis, MD: Naval Institute Press, 1976.

Prange, Gordon W. *At Dawn We Slept.* New York: Viking, 1981.

Prange, Gordon W., with Donald M. Goldstein and Katherine V. Dillion. *Miracle at Midway.* New York: Penguin, 1982.

Pratt, Fletcher. *America and Total War.* New York: Smith & Durrell, 1941.

Procter, Ben. *William Randolph Hearst: Final Edition, 1911–1951.* Oxford: Oxford University Press, 2007.

Prohme, Rupert. *History of 30th Infantry Regiment World War II.* Washington, DC: Infantry Journal Press, 1947.

Pyle, Ernie. *Brave Men.* New York: Henry Holt, 1944.

———. *Ernie's War: The Best of Ernie Pyle's World War II Dispatches.* Edited by David Nichols. New York: Random House, 1986.

Rems, Alan. *South Pacific Cauldron: World War II's Greatest Forgotten Battlegrounds.* Annapolis, MD: Naval Institute Press, 2014.

Reuth, Ralf Georg. *Rommel: The End of a Legend.* Translated by Debra S. Marmor and Herbert A. Danner. London: Haus Books, 2005.

Reynolds, David. *In Command of History: Churchill Fighting and Writing the Second World War.* New York: Random House, 2005.

Reynolds, Quentin. *The Amazing Mr. Doolittle: A Biography of Lieutenant General James H. Doolittle.* New York: Appleton-Century-Crofts, 1953.

———. *By Quentin Reynolds.* New York: McGraw-Hill Book Company, 1963.

Rhoades, Weldon E. (Dusty). *Flying MacArthur to Victory.* College Station: Texas A&M University Press, 1987.

Rich, Ben R., and Leo Janos. *Skunk Work: A Personal Memoir of My Years at Lockheed.* New York: Little, Brown, 1994.

Rickard, John Nelson. *Patton at Bay: The Lorraine Campaign, 1944.* Washington, DC: Brassey's, 2004.

Roberts, Andrew. *Napoleon: A Life.* New York: Viking, 2014.

Robinson, Piers. *The CNN Effect: The Myth of News, Foreign Policy and Intervention.* New York: Routledge, 2002.

Roeder, George H. Jr. *The Censored War: American Visual Experience during World War Two.* New Haven, CT: Yale University Press, 1993.

Rogers, Paul P. *The Bitter Years: MacArthur and Sutherland.* New York: Praeger, 1991.

———. *The Good Years: MacArthur and Sutherland.* New York: Praeger, 1990.

Rohmer, Richard. *Patton's Gap: An Account of the Battle of Normandy 1944.* New York: Beaufort Books, 1981.

Rommel, Erwin. *The Rommel Papers.* Edited by B. H. Liddell Hart. Translated by Paul Findlay. New York: Harcourt, Brace, 1953.

Romulo, Carlos P. *I Saw the Fall of the Philippines.* New York: Doubleday, Doran, 1942.

—————. *I Walked with Heroes.* New York: Holt, Rinehart and Winston, 1961.

Rooney, Andy. *My War.* New York: Public Affairs, 2000.

Roosevelt, Elliott. *As He Saw It.* New York: Duell, Sloan and Pearce, 1946.

Roosevelt, Franklin D. *Complete Presidential Press Conferences of Franklin D. Roosevelt.* Vols. 19–20, *1942.* New York: Da Capo Press, 1972.

—————. *Complete Presidential Press Conferences of Franklin D. Roosevelt.* Vol. 22, *1943.* New York: Da Capo Press, 1972.

—————. *F.D.R. His Personal Letters 1928–1945.* Vol. 2. Edited by Elliott Roosevelt. New York: Duell, Sloan and Pearce, 1950.

—————. *The Public Papers and Addresses of Franklin D. Roosevelt.* Vol. 10, *The Call to Battle Stations.* Edited by Samuel I. Rosenman. New York: Harper & Brothers Publishers, 1950.

—————. *The Public Papers and Addresses of Franklin D. Roosevelt.* Vol. 11, *Humanity on the Defensive.* Edited by Samuel I. Rosenman. New York: Harper & Brothers Publishers, 1950.

Rosenman, Samuel I. *Working with Roosevelt.* New York: Harper & Brothers, 1952.

Rovere, Richard H., and Arthur Schlesinger Jr. *General MacArthur and President Truman: The Struggle for Control of American Foreign Policy.* London: Transaction Publishers, 1951.

Rush, Robert Sterling. *Hell in Hürtgen Forest: The Ordeal and Triumph of an American Infantry Regiment.* Lawrence: University Press of Kansas, 2001.

Ryan, Cornelius. *A Bridge Too Far.* New York: Simon and Schuster, 1974.

Sakai, Saburo, with Martin Caidin and Fred Saito, *Samurai!* New York: E. P. Dutton, 1957.

Sarantakes, Nicholas Evan. *Making* Patton: *A Classic War Film's Epic Journey to the Silver Screen.* Lawrence: University Press of Kansas, 2012.

Sawyer, Bickford Edward Jr. "The Normandy Campaign from Military and Press Sources." MA thesis, University of Missouri, 1957.

Schaller, Michael. *Douglas MacArthur: The Far Eastern General.* Oxford: Oxford University Press, 1989.

Schmidt, Paul. *Hitler's Interpreter.* Croydon, England: CPI Group, 2016.

Schmitz, David F. *The Tet Offensive: Politics, War, And Public Opinion.* New York: Rowman & Littlefield Publishers, 2005.

Schramm, Percy E. "OKW War Diary: 6 June 1944." In *Fighting the Invasion: The German Army at D-Day.* Edited by David C. Isby. Mechanicsburg, PA: Stackpole Books, 2000.

Schwarzkopf, H. Norman, with Peter Petre. *It Doesn't Take A Hero.* New York: Bantam Book, 1992.

Scott, James M. *Target Tokyo: Jimmy Doolittle and the Raid That Avenged Pearl Harbor.* New York: W. W. Norton, 2015.

Seib, Philip. *Broadcasts from the Blitz: How Edward R. Murrow Helped Lead America into War.* Washington, DC: Potomac Books, 2006.

Semmes, Harry H. *Portrait of Patton.* New York: Paperback Library. 1964.

Senger und Etterlin, Frido von. *Neither Fear Nor Hope.* Translated by George Malcolm. New York: E. P. Dutton, 1964.

Sevareid, Eric. *Not So Wild a Dream.* New York: Alfred A. Knopf, 1968.

Sherwood, Robert E. *Roosevelt and Hopkins: An Intimate History.* Rev. ed. New York: Harper & Brothers, 1950.

Shirer, William L. *The Rise and Fall of Nazi Germany: A History of Nazi Germany.* New York: Simon and Schuster, 1960.

Shortal, John F. *Forged by Fire: General Robert L. Eichelberger and the Pacific War.* Columbia: University of South Carolina, 1987.

Showalter, Dennis. *Patton and Rommel: Men of War in the Twentieth Century.* New York: Berkley Caliber, 2005.

Shulman, Holly Cowan. *The Voice of America: Propaganda and Democracy, 1941–1945.* Madison: University of Wisconsin Press, 1990.

Simms, Brendan. *Hitler: A Global Biography.* New York: Basic Books, 2019.

Simpson, Emile. *War from the Ground Up: Twenty-First-Century Combat as Politics.* Oxford: Oxford University Press, 2013.

Smith, Gene. *Until the Last Trumpet Sounds: The Life of General of the Armies John J. Pershing.* New York: John Wiley & Sons, 1998.

Smith, Jean Edward. *Eisenhower in War and Peace.* New York: Random House, 2012.

Smith, Jeffery A. *War and Press Freedom: The Problem of Prerogative Power.* Oxford: Oxford University Press, 1999.

Smith, Robert Ross. *The Approach to the Philippines.* War in the Pacific. *United States Army in World War II.* Washington DC: Department of the Army, 1953.

Sorel, Nancy Caldwell. *The Women Who Wrote the War: The Riveting Saga of World War II's Daredevil Women Correspondents.* New York: Arcade Publishing, 1991.

Sparrow, James T. *The Warfare State: World War II Americans and the Age of Big Government.* Oxford: Oxford University Press, 2011.

Spector, Ronald H. *Eagle against the Sun: The American War with Japan.* New York: Free Press, 1985.

Speer, Albert. *Inside the Third Reich.* Translated by Richard and Clara Winston. New York: Macmillan, 1969.

Steele, Cherie, and Arthur A. Stein. "Communications Revolutions and International Relations." In *Technology, Development, and Democracy: International Conflict and Cooperation in the Information Age,* edited by Juliann Emmons Allison, 25–54. Albany: State University of New York Press, 2002.

Steele, Richard W. *The First Offensive 1942: Roosevelt, Marshall and the Making of American Strategy.* Bloomington: Indiana University Press, 1973.

Stimson, Henry L., and McGeorge Bundy. *On Active Service in Peace and War.* New York: Harper & Brothers, 1947.

Stoler, Mark A. *Allies and Adversaries: The Joint Chiefs of Staff, The Grand Alliance, and U.S. Strategy in World War II*. Chapel Hill: University of North Carolina Press, 2000.

———. *Allies in War: Britain and America against the Axis Powers, 1940–1945*. London: Hodder Education, 2005.

Strobel, Warren P. *Late-Breaking Foreign Policy: The News Media's Influence on Peace Operations*. Washington, DC: United States Institute of Peace Press, 1997.

Sulzberger, C. L. *A Long Row of Candles: Memoirs and Diaries [1934–1954]*. Toronto, Ontario: Macmillan, 1969.

Swanberg, W. A. *Luce and His Empire*. New York: Charles Scribner's Sons, 1972.

Sweeney, Michael S. *The Military and the Press: An Uneasy Truce*. Evanston, IL: Northwestern University Press, 2006.

———. *Secrets of Victory: The Office of Censorship and the American Press and Radio in World War II*. Chapel Hill: University of North Carolina Press, 2001.

Sweeney, Michael S., and Natascha Toft Roelsgaard. *Journalism and the Russo-Japanese War: The End of the Golden Age of Combat Correspondence*. Lanham, MD: Lexington Books, 2020.

Sylvan, William C., and Francis G. Smith Jr. *Normandy to Victory: The War Diary of General Courtney H. Hodges and the First U.S. Army*. Edited by John T. Greenwood. Lexington: University Press of Kentucky, 2008.

Symonds, Craig L. *World War II at Sea: A Global History*. Oxford: Oxford University Press, 2018.

Taaffe, Stephen R. *MacArthur's Jungle War: The 1944 New Guinea Campaign*. Lawrence: University Press of Kansas, 1998.

———. *Marshall and His Generals: U.S. Army Commanders in World War II*. Lawrence: University Press of Kansas, 2011.

Tedder, Arthur. *With Prejudice: The War Memoirs of Marshal of the Royal Air Force Lord Tedder G.C.B.* Boston: Little, Brown, 1966.

Terkel, Studs. *"The Good War": An Oral History of World War Two*. New York: Pantheon Books, 1984.

Thomas, Even. *Sea of Thunder: Four Commanders and the Last Great Naval Campaign 1941–1945*. New York: Simon & Schuster, 2006.

Thorne, Christopher. *Allies of a Kind: The United States, Britain and the War against Japan, 1941–1945*. Oxford: Oxford University Press, 1978.

Toland, John. *The Rising Sun: An Uneasy Truce*. Evanston, IL: Northwestern University Press, 2006.

Toll, Ian W. *The Conquering Tide: War in the Pacific Islands, 1942–1944*. New York: W. W. Norton, 2015.

Tomlin, Gregory M. *Murrow's Cold War: Public Diplomacy for the Kennedy Administration*. Lincoln: University of Nebraska Press, 2016.

Toobin, Jeffrey. *American Heiress: The Wild Saga of the Kidnapping, Crimes and Trial of Patty Hearst*. New York: Doubleday, 2016.

Tooze, Adam. *The Wages of Destruction: The Making and Breaking of the Nazi Economy*. New York: Viking, 2006.

Truscott, Lucian K. *Command Mission*. Novato, CA: Presidio Press, 1954.

Tugwell, Rexford G. *The Democratic Roosevelt: A Biography of Franklin D. Roosevelt.* Garden City, NY: Doubleday, 1957.

Ugaki, Matome. *Fading Victory: The Diary of Admiral Matome Ugaki 1941–1945.* Edited by Donald M. Goldstein and Katherine V. Dillon. Translated by Masataka Chihaya. Annapolis, MD: Naval Institute Press, 1991.

US Department of State. *Foreign Relations of the United States: The Conferences at Washington, 1941–1942, and Casablanca, 1943.* Edited by Fredrick Aandahl, William M. Franklin, and William Slany. Washington, DC: Government Printing Office, 1968.

Van Creveld, Martin. *Fighting Power: German and U.S. Army Performance, 1939–1945.* Westport, CT: Greenwood Press, 1982.

Vandenberg, Arthur. *The Private Papers of Senator Vandenberg.* Edited by Arthur H. Vandenberg Jr., with Joe Alex Morris. Westport, CT: Greenwood Press, 1952.

Van Der Vat, Dan. *The Pacific Campaign: World War II the U.S.—Japanese Naval War 1941–1945.* New York: Simon Schuster, 1991.

Vaughn, Stephen. *Holding Fast the Inner Lines: Democracy, Nationalism, and the Committee of Public Information.* Chapel Hill: University of North Carolina Press, 1980.

Voss, Frederick S. *Reporting the War: The Journalistic Coverage of World War II.* Washington, DC: Smithsonian Institution Press for the National Portrait Gallery, 1994.

Wagner, Lilya. *Women War Correspondents of World War II.* New York: Greenwood Press, 1989.

Walker, Fred L. *From Texas to Rome: A General's Journal.* Dallas, TX: Taylor Publishing, 1969.

Watson, Alexander. *Ring of Steel: Germany and Austria-Hungary in World War I.* New York: Basic Books, 2014.

Weaver, Michael E. *Guard Wars: The 28th Infantry Division in World War II.* Bloomington: Indiana University Press, 2010.

Weber, Thomas. *Becoming Hitler: The Making of a Nazi.* New York: Basic Books, 2017.

———. *Hitler's First War: Adolf Hitler, The Men of the List Regiment, and the First World War.* Oxford: Oxford University Press, 2010.

Wedemeyer, Albert. *Wedemeyer Reports!* New York: Henry Holt, 1958.

Weigley, Russell F. *The American Way of War.* Bloomington: Indiana University Press, 1973.

———. *Eisenhower's Lieutenants: The Campaign of France and Germany 1944–1945.* Bloomington: Indiana University Press, 1981.

Weinberg, Gerhard L. *A World at Arms: A Global History of World War II.* Cambridge: Cambridge University Press, 1994.

Weller, George. *Weller's War: A Legendary Foreign Correspondent's Saga of World War II on Five Continents.* Edited by Anthony Weller. New York: Crown Publisher, 2009.

Werth, Alexander. *Russia at War 1941–1945.* New York: E. P. Dutton, 1964.

Wheeler, James Scott. *Jacob L. Devers: A General's Life.* Lexington: University Press of Kentucky, 2015.

Whitehead, Don. *Combat Reporter: Don Whitehead's World War II Diary and Memoirs.* Edited by John B. Romeiser. New York: Fordham University Press, 2006.

————. "A Correspondent's View of D-day." In *D-Day 1944*, edited by Theodore A. Wilson, 203–212. Lawrence: University Press of Kansas, 1971.

Whitney, Courtney. *MacArthur: His Rendezvous with History.* New York: Alfred A. Knopf, 1956.

Williams, Kevin. "Something More Important than Truth: Ethical Issues in War Reporting." In *Ethical Issues in Journalism and the Media,* edited by Andrew Belsey and Ruth Chadwick, 154–169. New York: Routledge, 1992.

Willmott, H. P. *Empires in the Balance: Japanese and Allied Pacific Strategies to April 1942.* Annapolis, MD: Naval Institute Press, 1982.

Willoughby, Charles A., and John Chamberlain. *MacArthur 1941–1951.* New York: McGraw-Hill Book Company, 1954.

Wilmot, Chester. *The Struggle for Europe.* New York: Harper & Brothers Publishers, 1952.

Wilson, Normand J. *History In Crisis? Recent Directions in Historiography.* 2nd ed. Upper Saddle River, NJ: Pearson, 2005.

Winfield, Betty Houchin. *FDR and the News Media.* Urbana: University of Illinois Press, 1990.

Winston, Keith. *V-Mail: Letters of a World War II Combat Medic.* Edited Sarah Winston. Chapter Hill: Algonquin Books, 1985.

Wukovits, John. *Admiral "Bull" Halsey: The Life and Wars of the Navy's Most Controversial Commander.* New York: Palgrave Macmillan, 2010.

Wyant, William K. *Sandy Patch: A Biography of Lt. Gen. Alexander M. Patch.* New York: Praeger, 1991.

Zubok, Vladislav M. *A Failed Empire: The Soviet Union in the Cold War from Stalin to Gorbachev.* Chapel Hill: University of North Carolina Press, 2007.

Zumbro, Derek S. *Battle for the Ruhr: The German Army's Final Defeat in the West.* Lawrence: University Press of Kansas, 2006.

Periodicals

JOURNALS

Bell, P. M. H. "War, Foreign Policy and Public Opinion: Britain and the Darlan Affair, November–December 1942." *Journal of Strategic Studies* 5 no. 3 (1982): 393–415. Reproduced in *The Second World War,* vol. 7, *Alliance Politics and Grand Strategy,* edited by Jeremy Black, 63–83. Hampshire, UK: Ashgate Publishing, 2007.

Black, Jeremy. "Midway and the Indian Ocean." *Naval War College Review* 62, no. 4 (2009): 131–140.

Broers, Michael. "The Concept of 'Total War' in the Revolutionary—Napoleonic Period." *War in History* 15, no. 3 (2008): 247–268.

Citino, Robert M. "Military Histories Old and New: A Reintroduction." *American Historical Review* 112, no. 4 (October 2007): 1070–1090.

Fine, Richard A. "Edward Kennedy's Long Road to Reims: The Media and the Military in World War II." *American Journalism* 33, no. 3 (2016): 317–339.

———. "'Snakes in Our Midst': The Media, the Military and American Policy toward Vichy North Africa." *American Journalism* 27, no. 4 (2010): 59–82.

Fitzsimmons, Daniel. "Media Power and American Military Strategy: Examining the Impact of Negative Media Coverage on US Strategy in Somalia and the Iraq War." *Innovations: A Journal of Politics* 6 (2006): 53–73.

Gilboa, Eytan. "The CNN Effect: The Search for a Communication Theory of International Relations." *Political Communications* 22 (2005): 27–44.

McCallum, John. "U.S. Censorship, Violence, and Moral Judgement in a Wartime Democracy, 1941–1945." *Diplomatic History*, 41, no. 3 (2017): 543–566.

Newman, Robert P. "Hiroshima and the Trashing of Henry Stimson." *New England Quarterly*, 71, no. 1 (March 1998): 5–32.

Pach, Chester J. Jr. "'Our Worst Enemy Seems To Be the Press': TV News, the Nixon Administration, and U.S. Troop Withdrawal from Vietnam, 1969–1973." *Diplomatic History* 34, no. 3 (June 2010): 555–565.

Sarantakes, Nicholas Evan. "Warriors of Word and Sword: The Battle of Okinawa, Media Coverage, and Truman's Reevaluation of Strategy in the Pacific." *Journal of American–East Asian Relations* 23, no. 4 (2016): 334–367.

Steele, Richard W. "The Great Debate: Roosevelt, the Media, and the Coming of the War, 1940–1941." *Journal of American History* 71, no. 1 (1984): 69–92.

Sweeney, Michael S., and Patrick S. Washburn. "The *Chicago Tribune*'s Battle of Midway Story and the Government's Attempt at an Espionage Act Indictment in 1942." *Journalism and Communication Monographs* 16, no. 1 (March 2014): 7–97.

———. "It Ain't Over 'Til It's Over: Ending (?) the Narrative about the *Chicago Tribune* and the Battle of Midway." *American Journalism* 35, no. 3 (2018): 357–369.

Williams, Pete. "The Press and the Persian Gulf War." *Parameters* 21, no. 1 (Autumn 1991): 1–9.

Yavenditti, Michael J. "John Hersey and the American Conscience: The Reception of 'Hiroshima.'" *Pacific Historical Review* 43, no. 1 (February 1974): 24–49.

POPULAR MAGAZINES
Life
Newsweek
Time

NEWSPAPERS
The Baltimore Sun
The Bismarck Tribune
Chicago Daily Tribune
Cleveland News
Daily Boston Globe
Daily Express (London)
Daily Herald (London)
Daily News (New York City)

The Kansas City Star
Los Angeles Times
Miami Daily News
The Morning Call (Allentown, PA)
New York Times
Philadelphia Inquirer
The San Francisco Examiner
The Salt Lake Tribune
St. Louis Post-Dispatch
Sunday Express (London)
The Tampa Tribune
The Times (London)
Washington News
Washington Post
Washington Star

Other Sources

Adamson, William G. "The Effects of Real-Time News Coverage on Military Decision-Making." Research paper presented to the Research Department, Air Command and Staff College, March 1997.

Bates, Richard W. "The Battle of the Coral Sea: Strategical and Tactical Analysis." Bureau of Naval Personnel, Naval War College, Newport, RI, 1947.

"Cassino Monastery Bombed." British Pathé, April 13, 2014. YouTube video, 5:16. Accessed 12/12/19. https://www.youtube.com/watch?v=u8afP6GetP8.

Gallup, George H. *The Gallup Poll Public Opinion 1935–1971*, vol. 1. Edited by William P. Hansen and Fred L. Israel. New York: Random House, 1972.

"1944-Nazi Newsreel Die Deutsche Wochenschau: Defense of Cassino–Monte Cassino Abbey + Russian FR." WWIIPublic Domain, April 30, 2016. YouTube video, 8:21. https://www.youtube.com/watch?v=CxhEyOjDYa8.

Patton, George S. Jr. "The Secret of Victory." In *Military Essays and Articles*. Accessed February 24, 2014. http://www.pattonhq.com/pdffiles/vintagetext.pdf.

US Army. "Maj. Gen. Alexander Day Surles." US Army Public Affairs Hall of Fame Inductees. Accessed 1/25/20. https://www.army.mil/publicAffairs/halloffame/?from=pa_ad.

Willard, Dallas. "Truth: Can We Do without It?" Dallas Willard. Accessed April 2, 2020. http://www.dwillard.org/articles/individual/truth-can-we-do-without-it.

Wolfe, Hugh J., and William D. Sabin. *Our Miracle Man*. Binghamton, New York: Hugh J. Wolfe, 1942.

Index

Aachen, Battle for, 195, 219
Afghanistan
    Soviet occupation of, 228
Alexander, Harold
    attack on church property and, 142
    at Battle of Anzio, 139, 147
    Clark and, 134, 147–148
    commander of the Eighteenth Army
        Group, 107
    Eisenhower and, 106, 107, 109, 111, 207
    Montgomery and, 134
    photograph of, 134
    political career of, 230
    reporters and, 139
    reputation of, 134
    Tunisian campaign, 110, 275n153
Allen, Craig, 95
Allen, Frank, 190, 217, 218
Allen, Robert, 200, 206, 216, 222
Allied forces
    division of, 103–104
    intelligence, 46
    logistics, 190
    morale boost, 197–198
    operational command, 104–105
    resources, 228–229
    strategic planning, 190
    tensions within, 109, 110, 113, 116, 188–
        189, 221, 226
Ambrose, Stephen E., 151, 165, 178, 229,
    275n153
American, British, Dutch, Australian
    Command (ABDACOM), 33, 35
American Expeditionary Forces (AEF), 16
Anderson, Kenneth, 104
Andrews, J. Cutler, 13
Anzio, Battle of, 138–139
Arcadia Conference, 48, 53
Ardennes Offensive. See Bulge, Battle of
Arnett, Peter, 235

Arnold, Henry "Hap"
    on bombing of Rome, 129
    concern of publicity, 80
    Doolittle and, 40, 41
    evacuation of MacArthur and, 32, 33
    landing in Normandy, 169
    military strategy, 257n193
    on strike on Japan, 39, 254n123
Atkinson, Rick, 109, 112, 144, 146, 180,
    298n271, 306n194
Australia
    censorship, 61, 62, 66
    MacArthur in, 36, 38, 57, 59, 61, 65,
        67–69, 261n33
    as theater of war, 69–70
    threat of Japanese invasion, 79
Axis powers
    invasion of Tunisia, 104
    propaganda campaigns, 6, 104

Badoglio, Pietro, 130, 135
Baldwin, Hanson, 43, 73, 74, 107, 162, 176
Bataan Death March, 6, 62
battlefield decisions
    military-media relationship and, 3, 153,
        219, 221
    public opinion and, 1, 221
Beard, Patricia, 64
"Beat Japan First" slogan, 70
Beattie, Ed, 163
Bell, David, 10
Bell, P. M. H., 3
Benton, William, 231
Berlin
    Allied race to, 216–217
    fall of, 217
Bess, Demaree, 112, 122, 123, 125
Bethmann Hollweg, Theobald von, 15
Bigart, Homer, 235
Bismarck Sea, Battle of, 71, 77, 79–80

Blumenson, Martin, 132, 137, 138, 146, 178, 180–181
Bonaparte, Napoleon, 10, 11
Bourque, Stephen Alan, 165
Boyle, Hal, 232, 235
Bradley, Omar
  on Anglo-American relations, 205–206
  Battle of the Bulge, 1, 199, 200
  capture of Brest and, 219, 302n75
  capture of Enna and, 113
  censorship of, 211
  as commanding officer, 189, 204, 210
  concern over prestige, 110, 199–200, 221, 298n271
  Eisenhower and, 204–205
  at Falaise, action of, 180–181
  ghostwriter for, 224
  liberation of Paris and, 183–184
  media policies, 169, 171, 194, 195, 198, 204, 211, 213, 223, 230, 232
  on military-media relationship, 234, 235
  Montgomery and, 171, 182–183, 191, 225, 300n37
  Normandy campaign, 172
  Operation Cobra, 177
  Patton and, 178–179, 194
  personality of, 169–170, 196, 210
  postwar career of, 230
  press image of, 170, 179, 181, 187, 293n161
  public relations skills, 160, 216
  race to Messina, 120
  radio address on Rhine crossing, 215–216
  Sicilian campaign, 115–116, 120–121
  Soldier's Story, A, 224
  Stars and Stripes opinion, 204
  strategic planning, 7, 107, 167, 168, 191
  Tunisian campaign, 110, 111, 170, 275n153
Brest
  liberation of, 194, 302n75
Brett, George H., 37
Breuer, William B., 183
British First Army, 104, 106, 107
British Political Warfare Executive (PWE), 135
Brittain, Vera, 93
Brokaw, Tom
  Greatest Generation, The, 229

Brooke, Alan, 51, 52, 106, 154, 175–176, 188, 201, 226
Brooks, Thomas R., 150
Brower, Charles F., 3
Brown, John Sloan, 229
Bulge, Battle of
  Allied actions, 199, 206
  beginning of, 193
  infantry problem, 223
  media war and, 206, 207, 221, 225, 226
  news "blackout" during, 200, 304n131
  supply shortages, 71
Bull, Harold, 191
Buna, Battle of, 78
Bunnelle, Robert, 152
Burns, James MacGregor, 83
Butcher, Harry
  on American public, 70
  on bias of the press, 107, 175
  bombing of Rome and, 129
  on censorship, 304n131
  Darlan deal and, 99, 106
  D-Day preparations and, 161–162
  diary of, 224, 292n172
  Eisenhower and, 95, 97, 102
  on FDR, 71
  Gallagher story and, 300n35
  military career of, 95
  My Three Years with Eisenhower, 225–226
  on Patton, 122
  press relations, 95–96, 195, 222
  on robot bombs, 167
  on Smith, 223
  Stars and Stripes cartoon and, 211
  on victory in North Africa, 103

Canadian troops, 161, 276n182
Capa, Robert, 116
Carruthers, Susan, 13
Casablanca Conference, 78, 103
Casey, Steven
  on Allied strategy during the war, 227–228
  Cautious Crusade, 2
  on censorship, 16, 108
  on FDR, 53, 101, 103, 248n4
  on military-media relationship, 6, 89, 99, 161, 179, 216, 222

on Pacific theater of war, 111
War Beat, Europe, The, 3, 5
censorship
of casualty figures, 6
Eisenhower's policy of, 125, 304n131
in Korean War, 63, 232–233, 262n56
limits of, 222
MacArthur's policy of, 34, 60–63, 65–66,
73, 77, 79, 262n56
morale and, 223
of news from the Philippines, 31
in Russo-Japanese War, 14
self-, 233
in Southwest Pacific Area, 60–61, 63
in Vietnam War, 234
Central Intelligence Agency (CIA), 232
Chambers, Whittaker, 235
Chennault, Claire Lee, 45
Chiang Kai-shek, 45
Chicago Daily Tribune, 22, 30, 33, 34, 110
Chicago Sunday Tribune, 47
Chicago Tribune, 21, 27, 58, 61, 188
China-Burma-India Theater, 228
Churchill, Winston
on bombing of German towns, 166
on capture of Rome, 131, 146
diplomatic relations, 49
Eisenhower and, 117, 207–208
FDR and, 51
Grand Alliance, The, 226
Italian campaign and, 134–135
media relations, 154, 181–182
on Operation Sledgehammer, 52
personality of, 225
on vengeance weapons, 164, 165
war correspondent career, 19
on war histories, 225–226
Clapper, Raymond, 27, 81, 100
Clark, Mark
actions near Rome, 132
advance toward Rome, 146, 148
Alexander and, 147–148
Anglophobia of, 136, 147
on attack on church property, 141–142
Darlan Deal and, 98
disobedience of, 147
education of, 131
Mauldin and, 213
media policy, 132, 148

meeting with anti-Vichy leaders, 133
military career of, 131
mission to North Africa, 97–98, 101
negative portrayal of, 101
Operation Buffalo and, 145, 146
personality of, 131, 132
postwar career of, 230
pursuit of publicity, 4, 133–134, 146, 147,
148, 149, 150, 221
wife of, 133
Clark, Maurine Doran "Renie," 133
Clarkson, Herbert S., 123
Clausewitz, Carl von
war theory of, 11–12, 131, 152
CNN Effect, 2
Cohen, Eliot, 12
Cold War, 216
Collingwood, Charles, 99, 106
Collins, J. Lawton, 171, 195
Committee on Public Information (CPI), 16
communications revolution, 13
Conner, Fox, 96
Coral Sea, Battle of, 24, 46, 47, 61–62
Crimean War, 13
Crocker, John, 109, 110
Cronkite, Walter, 105, 163, 232, 235
Crosswell, D. K. R., 134
Cuneo, Ernest, 123–124
Cunningham, Andrew, 103
Curley, Tom, 197
Currier, Donald E., 122
Curtin, John, 61, 67, 89, 252n71, 261n33

Daily Boston Globe, 26, 30, 140
Daily Express, 173, 201
Daily Mirror, 188, 189
Daly, John, 122
Daniell, Ray, 96
Daniels, Josephus, 55
Darlan, Jean François, 98, 103
Darlan Deal
backlash of, 101
FDR and, 101, 102
historiography of, 103
Milton Eisenhower's investigation of, 102
negotiations of, 98–99, 100, 103
public opinion on, 3, 222–223, 228
Davies, D. R., 166
Davis, Elmer, 19

Davis, Kenneth S., 33
Davis, Richard Harding, 14
Davis, T. J., 70, 181
D-Day. *See* Normandy campaign
Dean, Peter J., 266n170
de Gaulle, Charles, 98, 99, 184, 208–210, 219, 306n194
Dempsey, Miles, 182
Desmond, Robert W., 61
D'Este, Carlo, 113, 115, 118, 119, 138, 145, 149, 170, 182, 190, 225, 295n191, 298n271
Devers, Jacob, 111, 190, 208, 306n189, 306n194
Dewey, Thomas, 87
Diamare, Gregorio, 140, 143, 144
Dietrich, Otto, 291n106
Dill, John, 48
Diller, LeGrande A., 62, 63, 79, 81
Dönitz, Karl, 217
Donovan, William, 50
Doolittle, James H.
    Arnold and, 40, 41, 255n127
    education of, 40
    media portrayal of, 56
    mission of, 40–41, 45, 129, 130
    promotion of, 43–44
    publicity of, 43
Doolittle Raid
    FDR and, 24
    goal of, 45
    Japanese reaction to, 44, 55
    origins of, 1, 39, 43, 254n124
    press coverage of, 41–42, 43, 44–45, 47–48
    psychological effect of, 42, 43, 44
    public opinion on, 43
    strategic consequences of, 45–46
Drew, John, 167
Drury, Allen, 83
Duncan, Donald B. "Wu," 40
Dunn, William J., 9, 62, 64, 66, 67
Dupuy, R. Ernest, 174

Early, Steve, 25, 55
Edsel, Robert M., 143
Egeberg, Roger Olaf, 65
Eichelberger, Robert, 6, 66, 76–77, 81, 265n146
Eisenhower, David, 300n35

Eisenhower, Dwight D.
    Alexander and, 111, 139
    Allied command crisis and, 96, 105, 109, 110, 116, 117, 187, 188–189, 207
    armistice negotiations with Italy, 136
    Battle of the Bulge, 199
    Butcher's book on, 225, 226
    censorship policy, 125, 304n131
    Clark and, 133, 139
    as commanding officer, 38, 153, 154, 188, 215, 216–217, 306n194
    communication skills of, 95
    concern of effect of flying bombs, 168
    control of strategic bombers, 165
    criticism of, 100, 106, 125, 222–223, 224
    Crusade in Europe, 226
    Darlan Deal and, 100, 103, 105
    D-Day preparations, 161–162
    de Gaulle and, 209
    Echo of Battle, The, 91
    French problem, 208–209
    friends of, 95
    Italian campaign and, 134–135, 136, 139, 150
    Knutsford Incident and, 290n72
    MacArthur and, 35, 71
    Malta headquarters, 113
    managerial style of, 97
    media policy, 94, 101–102, 127–128, 150–151, 155–157, 161, 162, 171–172, 182, 184, 186, 230, 232, 308n230
    military career of, 32, 106
    Montgomery and, 1, 175–176, 181, 191–192, 201, 202, 295n191
    news consumption, 7
    nickname of, 95
    Normandy campaign, 169, 183, 184
    Operation Market Garden, 193
    Operation Torch and, 97–98
    Patton and, 127, 159–160, 184–185, 186
    pets of, 152
    philosophy of war, 103, 190
    photographs of, 152
    political pressure on, 103, 192
    post-war career of, 230
    public image of, 91, 94–95, 102, 103, 154, 187
    public opinion considerations, 96–97, 127, 221

public relations, 152, 190, 213–214, 215, 231
  Pyle and, 223
  reporters and, 94, 95–96, 113, 122–123, 128, 155–156
  reputation of, 111, 112
  on second front, 51
  slapping incidents and, 122–123, 125–127
  Stars and Stripes cartoon scandal and, 213
  strategic planning, 190, 191, 192
  Tunisian campaign, 109, 110–111
  Vichy regime and, 5, 98–99
  on war operations, 48
Eisenhower, Milton, 102
Eliot, George Fielding, 69
Estoff, Bill, 211
European Theater of Operations, 229
Evatt, H. V., 58

FDR. *See* Roosevelt, Franklin D.
Fenton, Roger, 13
Fiji Islands, 46
First United States Army Group (FUSAG), 157
Fleming, Thomas, 99
Fondouk, Battle of, 109, 110
Formosa operation, 85, 86–87
Frankfurter, Felix, 69, 100
Fraser, Peter, 74
Fredendall, Lloyd, 104, 107, 112
French Army, 208–209
Freyberg, Bernard C., 141, 142
Fuchida, Mitsuo, 45
Fussell, Paul, 15, 92, 93, 169–170

Gallagher, Wes, 188, 189, 204, 217, 300n35
Gallup, George, 19
Gannett, Frank, 81
Gay, Hobart, 198, 223, 307n201
Germany First strategy
  FDR and, 24, 55
  formation of, 7
  media and, 25–26, 27–28, 221
  opposition to, 28, 29, 57, 70, 71
  public opinion and, 26
  supporters of, 25, 88
  US commitment to, 49, 50
Gervasi, Frank, 140, 144

Gilbert and Marshall Islands campaign, 84
Giraud, Henri, 98
GIs. *See* US troops
Godkin, Edwin, 13
Goebbels, Joseph
  call for total war, 20, 152
  on democracy, 5, 51
  propaganda campaigns, 6, 19, 104, 105, 183
  on vengeance weapons, 163
Gordon, John, 166
Gordon, Matthew, 19
Grand Alliance, 225, 226
"Greatest Generation" argument, 229
Griffith, Thomas E., Jr., 266n170
Grigg, James, 174
Guadalcanal campaign, 72, 73, 74, 78
Guam, Battle of, 84
Guingand, Francis de, 118, 154, 173–174, 201, 202, 223, 231
  Operation Victory, 304n142
Gulf War
  media coverage of, 236
Gunther, John, 100

Hadden, Briton, 18
Halberstam, David, 235
Hallin, Daniel C., 2, 234
Halsey, William "Bull," 41, 65, 74–75
Hamilton, John Maxwell, 197
Hamilton, Nigel, 53, 114, 295n191, 298n271, 304n142
Hammond, William M., 16, 233
Hansen, Chester B.
  on Anglo-American relations, 206
  on Bradley, 167
  diary of, 115, 224, 298n271
  as ghostwriter, 224
  on Montgomery, 167
  on Patton, 186
  public relations, 170, 171, 182–183, 211, 222
  on V-1 launching site, 165, 168, 191
Hapgood, David, 140
Harmon, Millard F., Jr., 41
Harris, Arthur, 165
Hasegawa, Tsuyoshi, 309n4
Hastings, Max, 178, 230
Havers, Richard, 164

Hearst, Patricia, 236
Hearst, William Randolph, 21, 84, 235
Heinzerling, Lynn, 140, 141
Hellbeck, Jochen, 18
Herman, Arthur, 32, 65
Hermann Göring Division, 140
Hersey, John, 224
Herzstein, Robert Edwin, 17, 19, 163
Hindenburg, Paul von, 15
Hirohito (Emperor of Japan), 221
Hitler, Adolf
    Ardennes Offensive, 199
    Battle for Aachen, 195
    death of, 217
    declaration of Rome as an open city,
        148–149
    interest in press and propaganda, 17, 18,
        19
    invasion of the Soviet Union, 227
    Mein Kampf, 17, 246n50
    response to Operation Torch, 104
    vengeance weapons of, 153, 291n106
    war on America, 25
Hodges, Courtney, 179, 186–187, 195, 204,
    210
Honolulu Conference, 88
Honshu islands, 220
Hopkins, Harry, 23, 26, 100
Howard, Michael, 12, 157
Howard, Roy, 21, 64, 82
Huebner, Clarence R., 195
Hughes, Everett S., 71, 95, 117, 123, 159,
    176, 189–190
Hull, Cordell, 99, 123
Hunt, Frazier, 71
Huss, Pierre J., 26
Hussein, Saddam, 236

Ingersoll, Ralph, 205, 206, 211, 222, 224–
    225, 227
Italian campaign
    Anzio stalemate, 138–139, 140, 147
    armistice negotiations, 135–136beginning
        of, 136–137
    Gustav Line, 137–138, 140
    media war, 143–144
    Monte Cassino Abbey, battle for, 139–144
    offensive toward Rome, 145–149
    Operation Buffalo, 145

Operation Turtle, 145
propaganda campaigns, 139, 150
public opinion and, 149–150
resource allocation, 228
Valmontone, battle at, 145–146
See also Rome

James, D. Clayton, 66, 69, 80, 87
Japan
    atomic bombing of, 220, 222, 224
    capitulation of, 220–221, 309n4
    defense perimeter, 46
    Doolittle Raid, 39–40, 42, 44
    Germany and, 25, 26
    Imperial House, 220
    invasion of Burma, 33
    invasion of China, 45–46
    media campaign against, 25–26
    Midway operation, 46
    Pearl Harbor operation, 20, 30
    propaganda campaigns, 6, 42
Jodl, Alfred, 218
Johnson, Lyndon B., 233–234, 235
Johnston, George H., 64
Johnston, Stanley, 257n187
Jones, Alexander F., 100

Kasserine Pass, Battle of, 107
Kelly, Colin P., Jr., 31
Kennan, George, 231
Kennedy, Edward, 218
Kenney, George, 63, 72, 77, 79, 266n170
Kesselring, Albrecht, 104, 135, 140
Keyes, Geoffrey, 115, 120, 213
Kindsvatter, Peter S., 235
King, Ernest
    demand for resources, 78, 89
    Doolittle Raid and, 40, 254n124
    leadership of, 85
    MacArthur and, 72
    Normandy campaign, 169
    relations with the press, 47–48, 74, 224
    on second front, 48
Klein, Julius, 81
Kluckhohn, Frank, 106, 107, 108
Knightley, Phillip, 5, 7, 20, 58, 60, 234
Know Your War Correspondent (pamphlet),
    155, 156
Knox, Frank, 27, 28, 74, 78, 79

Knutsford Incident, 290n72
Koop, Theodore F., 231
Korean War
  censorship, 63, 262n56
  military-media relationship, 232–233
  public opinion and, 230, 232
Krueger, Walter, 77–78
Kunz, Frank C., 64
Kuroshima, Kameto, 46
Kyushu islands, 220

La Follette, Philip, 59
La Guardia, Fiorello, 45
Lambert, Gerald B., 36
Lang, Will, 211
Lattre de Tassigny, Jean de, 208
Laurence, William, 222
Lawrence, David, 27
Lawrence, Justus, 187, 290n72
Leahy, William, 34, 85, 86
Leary, William M., 76, 78
Lee, Clark, 62, 63, 66, 67, 69, 78
Lee, John C. H., 211
Lee, Robert E., 14
Lehrbas, Lloyd, 81, 222
Leyte Gulf, Battle of, 75, 87, 89
Liddell Hart, B. H., 226–227, 228
Liebling, A. J., 224
Life magazine, 18, 77, 84, 119, 137, 225
Lindley, Ernest, 27, 100
Linn, Brian, 91, 230
Lippmann, Walter, 25, 100, 101
Litvinov, Maxim, 50
Lockheed Advanced Development Projects,
  236
London, Jack, 14
Long, Gavin, 64
Los Angeles Times, 21, 26, 27, 30, 144
Lovett, Robert A., 176
Low, Francis S., 40
Lucas, John P., 119, 123
Luce, Henry, 18, 21, 58, 235
Ludendorff, Erich, 15, 16, 18–19
Ludendorff Bridge
  capture of, 215
Ludewig, Joachim, 183

MacArthur, Douglas
  antiauthoritarianism of, 213

in Australia, 36, 38, 57, 59, 61, 65, 67,
  68–69, 261n33
battle with the Navy, 78, 80
censorship policy, 34, 60–63, 65–66, 73,
  77, 79, 262n56
criticism of, 83
defeats of, 33, 85
demand for resources, 70, 82, 88–89, 228,
  229
Diller and, 63
Eichelberger and, 265n146
evacuation from the Philippines, 24, 29,
  33, 34, 35, 36, 55, 57, 252n71
family of, 36
FDR and, 36–37, 85–87, 88
on Formosa operation, 86–87
Germany First strategy and, 57
Halsey and, 78
Korean War and, 63, 232, 262n56
Marshall and, 29–30, 35, 37, 38, 69–70,
  71, 72, 73
media policy, 3, 6–7, 27, 59, 60, 63–64,
  67, 69–70, 72, 75–76, 89–90, 132, 221,
  232
military career of, 29, 37, 70
New Dealers and, 82–83
Pearl Harbor attack and, 29–30
personality of, 65
political ambitions of, 69, 81–84, 230
popularity of, 30–31, 32, 34, 35, 36, 37,
  58, 212–213
promotion of, 32, 33
public image of, 34–36, 37, 56, 58, 61, 83
public relations, 58–59, 62, 67–68, 71
relations with reporters, 63–64, 65,
  67–69, 233
reputation of, 29
scholarship about, 58–59
secret cables of, 31–32
subordinates of, 76–78
surrender of Japan and, 220
theater of operations, 1, 72
White House communication with,
  31–32, 63, 69–70
MacArthur's communiqués
  on Battle of the Coral Sea, 61
  casualties figures in, 65–66
  censorship of, 31
  criticism of, 67

MacArthur's communiqués, *continued*
  on enemy losses, 79
  mistakes and exaggerations in, 66–67,
    79–80, 90
  purpose of, 66, 89–90
MacDonald, Charles B., 205
MacLeish, Archibald, 8, 19, 100
Macmillan, Harold, 135, 207
Makin, Battle of, 84
Manchester, William, 59, 72, 212–213
Mansoor, Peter, 229
Marshall, George C.
  on Bradley, 170
  British manipulation of, 225
  Clark and, 133
  criticism of, 227
  on democracy and war, 5
  Eisenhower and, 201
  idea of second front and, 49
  Italian campaign and, 114, 146
  Knutsford scandal and, 159
  landing in Normandy, 169
  London mission of, 50
  MacArthur and, 29–30, 35, 37, 38, 69–70,
    71, 72, 73
  media policy, 74, 97, 101, 105, 171, 231–232
  news consumption, 7
  on operation in North Africa, 28
  Patton and, 127
  on politicians, 52–53
  position on censorship, 62
  on power of the press, 229–230
  on total war, 22
  Tunisian campaign, 111–112
  at Western front, 197
Marshall, S. L. A., 228
Marshall Islands, 46
Mathews, Joseph J., 93
Mauldin, Bill, 211, 212, 213, 232
Mauldin-Patton episode, 211–212
McAuliffe, Tony, 203
McCarten, John, 83
McChrystal, Frank, 124, 125
McChrystal, Stanley, 237
McClure, Robert, 160
McCormack, John W., 34, 88
McCormick, Anne O'Hare, 141
McCormick, Bertie, 81, 82
McCormick, Robert R., 21, 81, 105

McDonald, Neil, 193
McManus, John C., 229
McPherson, James, 229
media
  Anglo-American alliance and, 105, 152,
    218–219
  impact on morale, 229
  as instrument of war, 19, 218, 231
  military decisions and, 9
  overoptimism in, 198–199
  power of, 1, 4, 6, 229–230, 237
  propaganda and, 231–232
  publication of obituaries, 167
  real-time broadcasting, 236, 237
  reputation and, 231
  technology and, 13
media revolution, 18
Middleton, Drew, 94, 107, 144, 164, 176, 234
Midway, Battle of, 46–47, 55, 257n186,
    257n187, 257n191
Mikolashek, Jon B., 146, 148
military-media relationship
  battlefield decisions and, 3, 153, 219, 221
  evolution of, 4, 230, 232–233, 236, 237
  Korean War and, 232–233
  negative portrayal of, 223
  popular memories of, 4–5
  psychological factors and, 231
  senior commanders and, 223, 234–235
  television and, 236
  tensions in, 96, 222–223
  in total war, 10, 224
military technology
  revolution in, 13
Miller, Edward, 221
Millett, Allan, 130
Moïse, Edwin E., 313n90
Moltke, Helmuth von, 15
Monk, Noel, 64
Monte Cassino Abbey
  battle for, 139–143
  destruction of, 143, 149, 150
  German occupation of, 143
  war propaganda and, 143–144
Montgomery, Bernard Law
  Allied command crisis and, 188, 204–
    205, 206–207
  American attitude toward, 206
  background of, 118

Battle of the Bulge and, 199, 200, 201, 225
Bradley and, 171, 182–183, 191, 300n37
British press on, 201–202
as commanding officer, 74, 104, 167–168
criticism of, 227
demand for supplies, 194
on destruction of robot bomb launch sites, 168
Eisenhower and, 175–176, 181, 191–192, 202, 295n191
insubordination of, 201
Italian campaign, 112, 136, 137
media relations, 160, 173, 174–175, 202–203, 221
military doctrine of, 172
Normandy campaign, 1, 154, 172–173, 295n191, 298n271
Operation Goodwood, 173–174, 175
Operation Market Garden, 193, 194
Patton and, 117–118, 182
personality of, 157, 202
philosophy of warfare, 157, 190
postwar career, 230
promotion to field marshal, 188–189
publicity, 106, 113, 114
reputation of, 118, 181
Rhine crossing, 216
Sicilian campaign, 114, 116–117, 119
strategic planning, 190, 192, 215
Moody, Blair, 132
Moorehead, Alan, 183, 203
Morelock, Jerry D., 199
Morgan, Frederick, 181
Morison, Samuel Eliot, 52, 75, 91
Morningstar, James Kelly, 93
Morrison, Herbert, 164, 166
Mountbatten, Louis, 51
Mueller, Merrill, 122, 123, 124–125
Murphy, Robert, 97
Murray, Williamson, 130
Murrow, Edward R., 98, 99, 153, 232, 235
Mussolini, Benito, 129, 134, 135
My Three Years with Eisenhower (Butcher), 225–226

Nazi Germany
Pearl Harbor attack and, 25–26, 55
propaganda machine, 19–20

rise of fascism, 17
surrender of, 217–218
Netherlands
liberation of, 192–193, 221
New Guinea
war in, 77, 78
Newman, Al, 122
news reporting
Allied tensions and, 105, 106, 113
anti-British feelings in, 107
delaying of, 6
historiography of, 6–7
influence of, 1
lack of regular highlights, 7
of liberated towns, 194
processing of, 105
telegraph and, 13–14
truth and, 5–6, 7
New York Daily News, 21, 179, 203
New York Times, 26, 27, 43, 45, 58, 73, 77, 81, 105–106, 107–108, 133, 141, 144, 159, 163, 222
Nimitz, Chester, 38, 61, 71, 86, 88, 220, 228
Normandy campaign
American public and, 153
beginning of, 221
Caen, battle for, 172–173, 295n191
Canadian troops, 161
Cherbourg, battle for, 172, 175
deception strategy, 154–155, 161
difficulties of, 183
Eisenhower-Montgomery-Patton relationship and, 180–181
Falaise battles, 180–181, 182, 298n271
filming of, 153
human losses, 173–174, 183
media coverage of, 150, 151, 169, 173–174, 176–177, 184–185
Operation Cobra, 177–178
Paris, liberation of, 183–184
preparations for, 154–155, 158–160
press relations during, 4, 153, 156, 162–163
public announcement of, 161, 162
slow progress of, 176
strategy for, 168
North African campaign, 24, 28, 48, 52, 91, 97, 98, 119, 127

O'Brien, Phillips Payson, 168, 228
O'Connell, Aaron, 9
Office of War Information (OWI), 16
Officer's Guide, 60
Okinawa, Battle for, 220
Okumiya, Masatake, 45
O'Laughlin, John, 81
Oldfield, Barney, 2, 13, 182
Olson, Lynne, 153
Onishi, Takijiro, 20
Operation Avalanche, 130
Operation Bolero, 48, 49, 52, 54, 55
Operation Cartwheel, 78, 81, 85
Operation Crossbow, 163, 165, 168–169
Operation Fortitude, 154, 157–158, 177
Operation Goodwood, 173–174, 175
Operation Gymnast, 28, 48, 51, 52
Operation Husky
    advance to Palermo, 112, 114–116
    Allied tensions during, 113, 116
    amphibious landing at Brolo, 120
    German losses, 120
    media coverage of, 112, 113, 114, 117, 121
    military decisions, 114
    planning of, 118
    public opinion considerations, 127
    race to Messina, 112, 118, 119–120
    US Seventh Army's role in, 114, 121
Operation Iraqi Freedom, 237
Operation Magnet, 28
Operation Market Garden, 192–193, 194, 196
Operation Overlord, 151, 225
    See also Normandy campaign
Operation Sledgehammer, 49, 52, 54, 55
Operation Torch, 54, 97–98, 103, 104
    See also North African campaign
Operation Victory (De Guingand), 304n142
Osmeña, Sergio, 88

Pacific War
    Allied forces in, 33
    battles of, 78, 79
    command arrangement, 38
    development of, 89
    Japanese advancement, 33
    lobby of, 55
    news reports about, 28, 66
    public opinion on, 111, 220

resource allocation, 78, 228
Soviet entry into, 220
Palermo
    Allied advance to, 112, 114–116
    strategic value of, 115
Palmer, Frederick, 14, 16
Papuan campaign, 66
Paris
    American parade in, 184
    controversy over destruction of, 183
    liberation of, 183–184
Patterson, Eleanor "Cissy," 21
Patterson, Joseph, 21
Patton, Beatrice, 126–127
Patton, George S., Jr.
    Alexander and, 115
    background of, 118
    battlefield decisions, 108, 109, 113
    Bradley and, 178–179, 194, 210
    capture of Metz and, 219
    career of, 93
    cinematic depiction of, 160
    concern over prestige, 194–195
    correspondence of, 94, 108
    criticism of, 5, 121, 124, 158–159
    Eisenhower and, 127, 184–185, 186
    influence of the troops, 158
    investigation of, 123, 124
    Knutsford scandal, 158–160
    media relations, 1, 4, 94, 124, 127–128,
        177–178, 186, 197, 198, 218, 221, 230,
        235
    on military leadership, 92–93
    Montgomery and, 117–118, 181, 182
    Normandy campaign, 177–178, 179–180,
        194
    North African campaign, 91
    occupation of Fort Driant, 194–195
    Operation Fortitude and, 157–158
    personality of, 108–109, 179
    philosophy of warfare, 92, 93–94, 108,
        118–119
    praise of soldiers, 160, 197
    publicity of, 91, 94, 108, 112, 116, 125,
        179, 186, 214
    public relations skills, 216
    reputation of, 70, 126, 213, 230
    Sicilian campaign, 112, 114–115,
        119–121

slapping incidents, 121–122, 124, 125–
126, 127, 128
Stars and Stripes cartoon scandal and,
211–212
supply shortage, 194
"Secret of Victory, The," 92
Tunisian campaign, 107, 275n153
Pearl Harbor attacks
effect of, 21, 42
Japan's preparation for, 20
media and, 23, 24, 25, 222
Nazi Germany and, 25, 26, 55
US Supreme Court investigation of,
254n123
Pearson, Drew, 21, 73, 123–124, 200
Pegler, Westbrook, 25
Perry, Mark, 79, 82, 252n71
Pershing, John J., 16, 77
Philippines
Allied invasion of, 88
declaration of independence, 29
liberation of, 67, 87–88, 90
MacArthur's evacuation from, 24, 29, 34,
35, 36, 55, 252n71
news reports on, 31
request for self-government, 32–33
strategic importance of, 85
Phillips, Joe, 106
Pinchot, Gifford, 42
Pinkley, Virgil, 95, 99, 125
Pogue, Forest, 53
Polish propaganda campaign, 20
Porch, Douglas, 104, 106, 130
Potsdam Declaration, 220
Potter, E. B., 31
Pratt, Fletcher, 177
America and Total War, 19
propaganda, 2, 6, 17, 18–19, 231–232, 247n75
public information officers (PIOs), 232, 233
public opinion
battlefield decisions and, 1, 221
democracy and, 5, 51
on the destruction of church property,
144
limitations of, 3, 7–8
manipulation of, 28
military and, 1
polling of, 8, 19
power of, 55, 96–97

on a second front, 68
on strategic direction of war, 26–27, 39,
50
public relations, 230–231, 237
Public Relations Division (PRD) of SHAEF,
60, 151, 152, 170–171, 189, 222, 231
public relations officers (PROs), 1, 60
Pyle, Ernie, 152, 169, 170, 223, 293n161,
294n172

Quebec Conference, 130
Quezon, Manuel, 32–33

Rabaul, Battle of, 78–79
radio networks, 21, 99
Republican Convention of 1944, 83–84
Reynolds, David, 225, 226
Reynolds, Quentin, 112, 122, 123
Reynolds, Robert R., 126
Rhoades, Weldon E. "Dusty," 85
Richardson, David, 140
Ridgway, Matthew, 233
Roberts Commission, 254n123
Roberts Report, 40
Robinson, Henry Crabb, 11
robot bombs, 163, 164, 165, 166, 167, 168
Roeder, George H., Jr., 6, 196
Roelsgaard, Natascha Toft, 14
Rogers, Paul P., 59, 65, 80, 82
Rohmer, Richard, 182
Rome
bombing of, 129, 130, 135
cultural significance of, 129, 150
liberation of, 138, 148–149
as open city, declaration of, 134
Rommel, Erwin, 94, 104, 106–107
Romulo, Carlos P., 67–68, 83, 222
Rooney, Andy, 232
Roosevelt, Eleanor, 77
Roosevelt, Franklin D. (FDR)
1944 presidential bid, 5
bombing of Japan and, 39, 40
bombing of Rome and, 129
on censorship, 62
choice of supreme commander, 153–154
Churchill and, 51
criticism of, 101, 222, 227
Darlan Deal statement, 101
on destruction of Monte Cassino, 144

Roosevelt, Franklin D. (FDR), *continued*
MacArthur and, 32, 33–34, 36–37, 38,
83, 85–87, 88
media relations, 4, 19, 24, 47, 153, 221
Murrow's broadcast and, 99–100
national address, 23, 26
news consumption, 8
Operation Gymnast and, 51, 52–53
Operation Torch and, 54
political pressure on, 21, 39–40, 42–43
publicity, 132
public opinion and, 28, 53–54, 55, 248n4
second front and, 49, 52, 53
visit to North Africa, 132
war strategy, 2–3, 23–24, 25, 39
Roper, Elmo, 19
Rosenman, Samuel, 86, 99
Russell, Howard, 13
Russo-Japanese War, 14
Ryan, Cornelius, 193

Saipan, Battle of, 84
Sarantakes, Nicholas Evan, 3
Savo Island, Battle of, 72
Schlesinger, Arthur, Jr., 20
Schmitz, David F., 233
Schuck, Hugh, 203
Schulman, Sammy, 112
Schwarzkopf, H. Norman, 236
second front, 48, 50–51, 54, 68, 130
Semmes, Harry H., 93
Senger und Etterlin, Fridolin von, 140, 143,
285n116
Sevareid, Eric, 139, 149, 150, 222, 232
SHAEF (Supreme Headquarters Allied
Expeditionary Force), 151
SHAEF PRD, 60, 151, 152, 170–171, 189,
222, 231. *See also* Public Relations
Division (PRD) of SHAEF
Sheehan, Neil, 235
Sherman, William Tecumseh, 14
Sherwood, Robert, 31, 82, 87
Shirer, William, 18
Sicily
Allied invasion of (*see* Operation Husky)
terrain, 119
Sidi Bouzid, Battle of, 107
Simpson, Emile, 237
Simpson, Kirke L., 27

Simpson, William, 206
Smith, Holland M. "Howlin' Mad," 84
Smith, Jeffery, 60
Smith, Ralph, 84
Smith, Walter Bedell "Beetle," 125, 186,
202, 217, 223, 232, 306n194, 307n201
Smuts, Marshal J. C., 130
Southwest Pacific Area (SWPA), 35, 58,
60–61, 63, 71, 82
Soviet Union, 50–51, 130, 220, 228
Spaatz, Carl, 165
Sparrow, James, 19
Spector, Ronald, 71, 72, 89
Speer, Albert, 18, 163, 291n106
Stalin, Joseph, 220, 227
Stalingrad, Battle of, 104
Stars and Stripes (newspaper), 223
cartoon scandal, 204, 211–212
Steele, Richard W., 50
First Offensive 1942, The, 2
Steward, Tom, 45
Stimson, Henry
Allied command crisis and, 38, 61,
261n33
on atomic bombing, 224
bombing of Rome and, 129
on campaign in the Philippines, 32
Churchill's meeting with FDR and,
51–52
on Germany First strategy, 25
idea of second front and, 48–49
public relations, 54, 74, 100, 101, 126
reflection on the war, 151
visit to Algeria, 117
Stokesbury, James L., 11
Stoler, Mark, 24, 52
Strand, William, 34
Strasbourg
controversy over evacuation from, 208–
210, 219, 221
Struggle for Europe, The (Wilmot), 226,
227
Sudetenland, 217
Sulzberger, C. L., 131, 132, 141
Summer, Jesse, 159
Supreme Headquarters Allied
Expeditionary Force (SHAEF), 151
See also Public Relations Division (PRD)
of SHAEF

Surles, Alexander D.
  assessment of public opinion, 196
  public relations, 91, 189–190, 191–192,
    198–199, 231
  reporters and, 54, 69
Sutherland, Richard, 8, 78
Sweeney, Michael S., 14, 61
Symbionese Liberation Army (SLA), 236
Symonds, Craig L., 72, 228

Tarawa, Battle of, 84
Tedder, Arthur, 175, 207
television, 230, 234, 235, 236
Tet Offensive, 233–234, 235, 313n90
Thomas, Evan, 41
Thompson, Dorothy, 26
Thomson, George, 167
Time magazine, 18, 21, 34, 74, 78, 84, 110,
    116, 158, 170, 204
Tinian, Battle of, 84
Tojo, Hideki, 41
total war, 10, 15, 16, 20, 22, 23, 221–222
Trohan, Walter, 33, 34
Truman, Harry, 220, 309n4
Truscott, Lucian, 114, 120, 121, 132, 145
truth
  news reporting and, 5–6, 7
  in postmodernism, 14
Tucker, George, 140, 144
Tunisian campaign, 103–112
  American role in, 109, 110, 111, 127
  Axis prisoners, 111
  Bizerte crisis, 111
  German invasion, 104
  ublic attention to, 111–112, 127

Ugaki, Matome, 6, 41, 42
United States
  anti-British feelings, 106
  Civil War, 13–14
  declaration of war on Japan, 22
  isolationist movement, 21
  Second War Loan Drive in, 45
  World War II and, 20, 21–22, 38, 228, 229
unmanned weapons systems, 236
US Air Force, 8–9
US Second Armored Division, 115, 116
US First Army, 154, 171, 186–187, 195, 200,
    203, 206

US Third Army, 154, 160, 177–178, 180,
    184, 186, 188, 195, 198, 199, 200, 201,
    204, 210, 214
US Seventh Army, 112, 113–115, 116, 117,
    119, 121
US Eighth Army, 136–137
US Ninth Army, 206, 215, 216
US Sixth Army Group, 208, 209
US Twelfth Army Group, 8, 154, 179, 188,
    191, 199, 201, 204, 206, 210, 213
US Twenty-First Army Group, 173, 174,
    175, 180, 188, 192, 193, 201, 202
US Thirty-Fourth Division, 109–110
US Information and Education Exchange
    Act, 232
US Marine Corps, 8–9, 84, 214
US Navy, 71–72, 73
USS *Augusta*, 91
USS *Baltimore*, 86
USS *Brooklyn*, 91
USS *Hornet*, 40, 41
USS *Saratoga*, 33
US troops
  egalitarianism of, 59
  morale boost, 211–212, 215
  motivation of, 229
  national prestige of, 110, 205, 219
  publicity of, 113–114, 117, 197–198, 204
  quality of, 107–108, 109, 112

V-1 and V-2 pilotless aircrafts. *See*
    vengeance weapons
Vandenberg, Arthur, 21, 81
Vaughn, Stephen, 16
vengeance weapons
  attacks of, 163–164, 168, 185, 192
  British propaganda and, 166–167
  casualties caused by, 164, 165, 166, 167
  damage due to, 165
  launching sites of, 165, 166, 168, 191
  media attention to, 164, 165–167
  psychological effect of, 164, 166, 167, 192,
    221
  technical characteristics of, 192
Vichy France, 98
Victor Emmanuel III, King of Italy, 129,
    135
Vietnam War, 228
  censorship during, 234

Vietnam War, *continued*
  media coverage of, 233–234, 235–236,
    313n90
  public opinion and, 1–2, 230

Walker, Fred L., 132, 136, 148, 223
Walt, Lewis W., 235
war
  democracy and, 5
  information and, 1, 17
  public morale and, 12
  technology and, 17
  theory of, 11–12
  totalitarian, 16, 17
  truth as casualty of, 5
  See also total war
war correspondents
  accreditation of, 4, 59–60
  during Civil War, 14
  contribution to WWII history, 224–225
  emergence of, 11
  espionage and, 257n187
  as part of the military, 4
  postwar careers of, 232
War Department's Bureau of Public
    Relations, 231
War on Terror, 237
War Plan Orange, 71
Washington Post, 25, 30, 39, 43, 45, 69,
    126
Washington Times-Herald, 21, 37, 47
Watson, Alexander, 14–15
Wavell, Archibald, 33
Weber, Thomas, 246n50
Wedemeyer, Albert C., 17, 114, 231
Weigley, Russell F., 8, 228
Weinberg, Gerhard L., 135
Weller, George, 67
Western Front (World War II)
  Ardennes Offensive, 199
  attack on Metz, 218
  Colmar Pocket, 208, 210
  German surrender, 217–218
  media coverage of, 195, 213
  National Redoubt myth, 217

overoptimism about war on, 195–197
  progress on, 195
  Rhine crossing, 215–216
  strategic planning, 190–192
Westmoreland, William, 233
Weyland, Otto Paul, 198
Wheeler, James Scott, 210, 306n194
Wherry, Kenneth S., 159
White, Robert M., 77–78
White, Theodore, 235
Whitehead, Don, 119, 120, 155
Whiteley, John, 210, 307n201
Williams, Al, 39
Williams, Edgar, 203
Willkie, Wendell, 34
Willoughby, Charles A., 69, 80, 81
Wilmot, Chester, 64, 203, 204, 227
  Struggle for Europe, The, 226
Winchell, Walter, 21, 124
Wood, John Shirley, 178
World War I
  military-media relationship, 14–15, 16
  public opinion and, 15
  as total war, 15, 16
World War II
  Allied strategy in, 227–228
  American contribution to, 20, 21–22, 38,
    59, 228, 229
  beginning of, 20
  end of, 217–218
  fatalities, 84–85, 230
  historiography of, 2–3, 224–225, 226–
    227, 228, 229
  mass armies, 92
  as media war, 1
  mistakes of, 227
  public relations during, 16, 230–231
  resource allocation, 228–229
  theaters of, 7, 24, 70, 89, 228–229
  transportation and communication
    during, 8

Yalta Agreement, 216
Yamamoto, Isoroku, 20, 46
Yavenditti, Michael J., 224